The
Book
of the
Nine Judges

Translated & Edited by
Benjamin N. Dykes, PhD

The Cazimi Press
Minneapolis, Minnesota
2011

Published and printed in the United States of America
by the Cazimi Press
621 5th Avenue SE #25, Minneapolis, MN 55414

© 2011 by Benjamin N. Dykes, Ph.D.

All rights reserved. No part of this publication may be reproduced, stored in or introduced into a retrieval system, or transmitted, in any form or by any means (electronic, mechanical, photocopying, recording or otherwise), without the prior written permission of both the copyright owner and the above publisher of this book.

The scanning, uploading, and distribution of this book via the Internet or via any other means without the permission of the publisher is illegal and punishable by law. Please purchase only authorized editions and do not participate in or encourage electronic piracy of copyrighted materials. Your support of the author's rights is appreciated.

ISBN-13: 978-1-934586-20-4

Acknowledgements

I would like to thank the following friends and colleagues, in alphabetical order: Charles Burnett, Deb Houlding, and David Juste.

Also available at www.bendykes.com:

Designed for curious modern astrology students, *Traditional Astrology for Today* explains basic ideas in history, philosophy and counseling, dignities, chart interpretation, and predictive techniques. Non-technical and friendly for modern beginners.

Two classic introductions to astrology, by Abū Ma'shar and al-Qabīsī, are translated with commentary in this volume. *Introductions to Traditional Astrology* is an essential reference work for traditional students.

The classic medieval text by Guido Bonatti, the *Book of Astronomy* is now available in paperback reprints. This famous work is a complete guide to basic principles, horary, elections, mundane, and natal astrology.

The Search of the Heart is the first in a new horary series, and focuses on the use of victors (special significators or *almutens*) and the practice of thought-interpretation: divining thoughts and predicting outcomes before the client speaks.

The Forty Chapters is a famous and influential horary work by al-Kindī, and is the second volume of the horary series. Beginning with a general introduction to astrology, al-Kindī covers many horary topics such as war, wealth, travel, pregnancy, marriage, and more.

 The first volume of the *Persian Nativities* series contains *The Book of Aristotle*, an advanced work on natal astrology and prediction by Māshā'allāh, and a beginner-level work by his student Abū 'Alī, *On the Judgments of Nativities*.

 The second volume of *Persian Nativities* features a shorter, beginner's level work on nativities and prediction by 'Umar al-Tabarī, and a much longer book on nativities by his younger follower, Abū Bakr.

 The third volume of *Persian Nativities* is a translation of Abū Ma'shar's work on solar revolutions, devoted solely to the Persian annual predictive system. Learn about profections, distributions, *firdāriyyāt*, transits, and more!

 This compilation of sixteen works by Sahl bin Bishr and Māshā'allāh covers all areas of traditional astrology, from basic concepts to horary, elections, natal interpretation, and mundane astrology. It is also available as two separate paperbacks.

 Expand your knowledge of astrology and esoteric thought with the Logos & Light audio series: downloadable, college-level lectures and courses on CD at a fraction of the university cost! It is ideal for people with some knowledge of traditional thought but who want to enrich their understanding.

TABLE OF CONTENTS

Translator's Introduction...1
  §1: The structure and background of *Judges*........................2
  §2: The Latin prefaces to *Three Judges* and *Nine Judges*........16
  §3: An introduction to questions...20
§A: INTRODUCTORY MATTERS
  §A.127: On the method and manner of inquiring—Māshā'allāh.....43
  §A.128: On those things which are necessary for both the judge and the querent—'Umar 45
  §A.129: On choosing the significator of the querent and the question—'Umar...46
  §A.130: Another chapter on the same thing—'Umar...................49
  §A.131: More on producing and denying an effect—'Umar...........53
  §A.132: Receiving management, reflection, transfer, collection—Māshā'allāh...55
  §A.133: [A few notes on timing]—al-Kindī..............................57
  §A.134: Summary—Unknown...58
§1: FIRST HOUSE
Sahl's Method for Questions 59
  §1.1: On those things which pertain to the first house—Sahl..........59
Life..69
  §1.2: On the quantity of life—al-Khayyāt...............................69
  §1.3: On life already gone by, and the portion of it left—Dorotheus 70
  §1.4: On the life of the querent that has gone by, and the portion of it left—Jirjis..73
  §1.5: On the life of the querent—Jirjis....................................73
  §1.6: On the life of the querent—Aristotle..............................74
§2: SECOND HOUSE
  §2.1: On those things which pertain to the second house—Sahl....75
  §2.2: On acquiring money—'Umar..76
  §2.3: On acquiring money—al-Kindī......................................76
  §2.4: On acquiring money—al-Khayyāt..................................80
  §2.5: On acquiring money—Dorotheus...................................81
  §2.6: What is the source and kind of the acquiring—Sahl............82
  §2.7: What is the origin and kind of acquiring—'Umar................82
  §2.8: Whence he would have it—al-Kindī...............................83
  §2.9: Whence he would have it, and what is the kind of [thing] acquired—al-Khayyāt...84
  §2.10: Whence he would have it—Dorotheus.........................85
  §2.11: On the quantity and number of money acquired—al-Khayyāt 85

§2.12: On the quantity and number of the money acquired—Dorotheus 87
§2.13: On the hour of acquiring money—'Umar 87
§2.14: On debts—al-Khayyāt 88
§2.15: On the fortune of worldly things, and their greatness in terms of worthiness—al-Kindī 88
§2.16: On a thing lent, or deposited with someone for safekeeping—Aristotle 94

§3: THIRD HOUSE
§3.1: On those things which pertain to the third house—Sahl 96
§3.2: On the status of the brothers—al-Khayyāt 97
§3.3: On the status of the brothers—Dorotheus 98
§3.4: Whether he is absent or not—Dorotheus 98

§4: FOURTH HOUSE
Real Estate **100**
§4.1: On those things which pertain to the fourth house—Sahl 100
§4.2: On the condition of lands, fields, and the like—al-Kindī 100
§4.3: Whether someone would get a house or real estate—al-Khayyāt 104
§4.4: On acquiring houses or inheritances—Dorotheus 104
§4.5: On the purchase of fields—Sahl 104
§4.6: On selling real estate or houses—'Umar 106
§4.7: On the quantity of the price—'Umar 108
§4.8: On the cultivators of fields—al-Khayyāt 110
§4.9: On the status of fields—Dorotheus 111
§4.10: On foremen and subordinates of this kind—Dorotheus 112
§4.11: For leasing fields—Sahl 113
§4.12: On leasing fields—al-Khayyāt 113
§4.13: On the building of the houses of cities—al-Kindī 114
§4.14: On digging riverbeds and those things which pertain to irrigating arable land—al-Kindī 115

Buried Treasure **118**
§4.15: On treasures and concealed things—'Umar 118
§4.16: Whether it could be found—'Umar 120
§4.17: On treasure and any hidden thing—al-Kindī 122
§4.18: On treasure or some hidden thing—Jirjis 125

Outcomes **129**
§4.19: On a suspicion or matter, whether it would come to be for certain or not—'Umar 129
§4.20: On some matter, whether it has been done or will be—'Umar 130
§4.21: On the hour of the outcome—'Umar 130
§4.22: When the effecting of matters would follow—Jirjis 133

§5: FIFTH HOUSE
Pregnancy & Birth **134**
§5.1: On those things which pertain to the fifth house—Sahl 134
§5.2: On having children—Dorotheus 136
§5.3: Whether someone is going to have children—Dorotheus 136
§5.4: Whether someone is going to have children—Aristotle 137
§5.5: When someone is going to have children—Aristotle 137
§5.6: Whether a woman is pregnant and will give birth—Sahl 138
§5.7: On pregnant women—'Umar 139
§5.8: On pregnant women and the number of children—al-Kindī
.... 139
§5.9: Whether a woman is pregnant—al-Khayyāt 140
§5.10: Whether a woman is pregnant—Dorotheus 140
§5.11: Whether she (whom someone has married), would
  conceive—Jirjis 141
§5.12: On pregnant women—Aristotle 141
§5.13: When someone ought to be impregnated—Aristotle 141
§5.14: On the time of the conception—'Umar 141
§5.15: On the time of the conception—al-Kindī 142
§5.16: Whether she would have a miscarriage—'Umar 142
§5.17: Whether she would have a miscarriage—al-Kindī 143
§5.18: Whether she would have a miscarriage—al-Khayyāt 143
§5.19: Whether she would have a miscarriage—Dorotheus 144
§5.20: Whether she would have a miscarriage—Aristotle 145
§5.21: Whether some woman has already given birth—Aristotle .. 145
§5.22: On the hour of birth—'Umar 145
§5.23: On the hour of birth—al-Kindī 145
§5.24: When she would give birth—Aristotle 146
§5.25: Whether she would give birth by night or day—'Umar 146
§5.26: On the status of a pregnant woman—al-Kindī 147
§5.27: Whether she would give birth to twins—Sahl 147
§5.28: Whether they are one or more—'Umar 148
§5.29: Whether they are one or more—al-Kindī 148
§5.30: Whether they are one or many—al-Khayyāt 148
§5.31: Whether there would be twins—Aristotle 148
§5.32: Whether it is male or female—Sahl 149
§5.33: Whether it is male or female—'Umar 150
§5.34: Whether it is male or female—al-Kindī 150
§5.35: Whether it is male or female—al-Khayyāt 150
§5.36: Whether it is male or female—Jirjis 151
§5.37: On the sex—Aristotle 151
§5.38: On the number of siblings and [their] sex—Aristotle 151

News, Rumors, & Legates 153
    §5.39: On someone, whether he has the father whom public belief is reporting—Aristotle 153
    §5.40: On the truth of rumors—'Umar 153
    §5.41: On legates—'Umar 154
    §5.42: On rumors and their end—al-Kindī 154
    §5.43: On the truth of rumors—al-Khayyāt 155
    §5.44: On the truth of rumors—Dorotheus 156
    §5.45: When something that news announces, will come to be—Jirjis 157
    §5.46: For rumors—Jirjis 157
    §5.47: On rumors—Aristotle 158
    §5.48: On messengers—al-Kindī 159
    §5.49: On someone, whether he is absent from his own home—Jirjis 159
    §5.50: On the messenger's adversity—'Umar 159
    §5.51: On the return of the messenger—al-Kindī 160
    §5.52: On the hour of turning back—al-Kindī 160
    §5.53: On the hour of turning back—[Unknown] 161
    §5.54: On the return of a messenger—Aristotle 161
    §5.55: On a legate, whether he would bring the money sought—'Umar 161
    §5.56: Whether someone would reach the destined place—Dorotheus 162
    §5.57: Whether he would find the one whom he sought—al-Kindī 162
    §5.58: Whether he bears much money—Aristotle 162
    §5.59: Whether he bears much money—[Unknown] 163
Letters 164
    §5.60: On a paper or letter—'Umar 164
    §5.61: On messengers and a legation of letters—al-Khayyāt ... 165
    §5.62: On a paper or letter—Dorotheus 166
    §5.63: Whether a letter was sent out from the king—Sahl 166
    §5.64: Concerning a letter, whether it would reach the king—'Umar 166
    §5.65: Whether a letter would reach the king—Dorotheus 167
    §5.66: On a paper, what it contains of the true and the false—'Umar 167
    §5.67: What good or evil the paper contains—al-Khayyāt 168
    §5.68: [Whether rumors are true or false]—Sahl 168
    §5.69: On a letter, whether it is marked with a seal—'Umar ... 169
    §5.70: On a paper's or letter's seal—Jirjis 169
    §5.71: On the response to the writing or letter—[Unknown] ... 170
    §5.72: Whether some messenger would arrive—Jirjis 170

§5.73: On accepting a paper or letter—Jirjis 171

§6: SIXTH HOUSE
Illness 173
  §6.1: On those things which pertain to the sixth house—Sahl 173
  §6.2: On the status of one growing sick, and the doctor—'Umar.176
  §6.3: On the hour of health and death—'Umar................................178
  §6.4: On those growing sick, what would happen to them—al-Kindī
 178
  §6.5: On those growing infirm—al-Khayyāt 179
  §6.6: On those growing ill—Dorotheus..183
  §6.7: Whether he would escape—Jirjis 186
  §6.8: On an infirm person—Aristotle...186
  §6.9: On the nature of the disease—'Umar 188
  §6.10: On the nature and cause of the disease—al-Kindī 190
  §6.11: On the disease and its cause—Jirjis..190
  §6.12: In what limb he would suffer—'Umar 190
  §6.13: In what limb he suffers—al-Kindī..191
  §6.14: In what part of the body he would suffer—Jirjis.................192
  §6.15: Whether he would be cured by a doctor who is brought in—
  al-Kindī..192
  §6.16: Whether he would be healed by the doctor that is
  introduced—al-Khayyāt..194
  §6.17: Whether he would be healed by the doctor—Dorotheus ...194
  §6.18: Whether the doctor would be useful to the infirm person—
  Aristotle 195
  §6.19: On critical days—Sahl 195
  §6.20: On critical days—'Umar..196
  §6.21: On critical days—al-Kindī 197
  §6.22: On critical days—al-Khayyāt..198
  §6.23: On critical days—Dorotheus...198
  §6.24: About anyone, whether he is infirm—Sahl..........................199
  §6.25: About anyone, whether he is infirm—al-Khayyāt...............199
  §6.26: Whether someone is growing infirm—Dorotheus...............199
  §6.27: On bloodletting and cupping—al-Kindī 199
  §6.28: On surgery—al-Kindī 201
  §6.29: On taking potions—al-Kindī...201
Slaves & Captives..203
  §6.30: On a captive: whether he could be freed—Sahl....................203
  §6.31: On a captive: whether he could be freed—'Umar................203
  §6.32: On captives or the liberation of a slave, and their status—
  'Umar 204
  §6.33: On the liberation of a captive—'Umar..................................205
  §6.34: On captives—al-Kindī..205
  §6.35: Whether he would be held long—al-Kindī 206

§6.36: What would happen to him after leaving—al-Kindī............206
§6.37: Whether he would become a freedman—al-Khayyāṭ..........207
§6.38: On imprisoned people—Dorotheus.......................................207
§6.39: Whether an exit is being prepared for a captive—Dorotheus 208
§6.40: On the hour of liberation—ʿUmar..208
§6.41: When he would be freed—al-Kindī......................................209
§6.42: Whether he is destined to grow infirm in prison—ʿUmar...209
§6.43: Whether he would die in prison—ʿUmar.............................210
§6.44: Whether he would die in prison—al-Kindī..........................210
§6.45: Whether he would be afflicted by blows or torments or tortured in some manner—ʿUmar..210
§6.46: Whether he would be afflicted by tortures in prison—al-Kindī..211
§6.47: Whether a tortured man would come to death—ʿUmar......212
§6.48: Whether he would be hung—ʿUmar....................................212
§6.49: Whether a captive or slave would be sold—Sahl.................213
§6.50: On the number of masters [and his sale price]—ʿUmar......213
§6.51: On the hour of the sale—ʿUmar...216
§6.52: Whether he would be sold—al-Khayyāṭ..............................216
§6.53: Whether a slave would be sold—Dorotheus........................217
§6.54: If a slave ought to be sold—Dorotheus................................217
§6.55: Whether or not it would be better for a female captive to be sold—Dorotheus 217
§6.56: Whether it is better to sell or keep a captive—Sahl.............218
§6.57: Whether it is better for a captive or slave to be sold—al-Khayyāṭ..218
§6.58: Whether it would be better for a captive to be sold or kept—Dorotheus 219
§6.59: On buying slaves—Sahl...220
§6.60: On buying slaves—al-Khayyāṭ..220
§6.61: For buying a female captive—Sahl.......................................220
§6.62: For buying a female captive—al-Khayyāṭ............................221
§6.63: Whether profit would follow from a captive—Sahl.............221
§6.64: Whether he could have the captive whom he hopes for—Sahl 221
§6.65: On a murderer or anyone frightening—ʿUmar....................222
§6.66: On the prison where he is held, whether he could escape—ʿUmar 223
§6.67: On someone, whether at some time he ought to be captured—Aristotle...223
§6.68: Whether he would be held a long time, or even if the captivity would be hard—Aristotle..224

§7: SEVENTH HOUSE
Marriage & Relationships **226**
§7.1: On those things which pertain to the seventh house—Sahl.226
§7.2: On a marriage-union—'Umar 227
§7.3: On establishing a marriage-union—al-Kindī 228
§7.4: On marriage—al-Khayyāt 229
§7.5: On marriage—Dorotheus 230
§7.6: Concerning a marriage-union, slaughter, war, controversy, partnership, and a fugitive—Jirjis 231
§7.7: When someone ought to take a wife—Aristotle 231
§7.8: What the cause of the impediment is—Sahl 232
§7.9: Whether an impediment would occur—al-Khayyāt 233
§7.10: On the cause of the impediment—Dorotheus 234
§7.11: Whether he would marry the wife whom he hoped for—Dorotheus 235
§7.12: Whether someone marries the wife he was hoping for—Jirjis 235
§7.13: Whether the marriage-union is lawful—'Umar 235
§7.14: On the wife's sexual impurity—Sahl 236
§7.15: Whether she is good looking—al-Kindī 237
§7.16: Whether she is rich or from a poor home—al-Kindī 238
§7.17: Which one is more noble—Aristotle 239
§7.18: Whether a suspicion of sexual impurity is true—'Umar ..239
§7.19: On the chastity or sexual impurity of the wife—al-Kindī ...240
§7.20: On chastity or sexual impurity —Jirjis 241
§7.21: On the shape of her with whom someone is having an affair—Aristotle 241
§7.22: Which suspected man a woman has had sex with—'Umar 242
§7.23: How many men a woman is going to have—Jirjis 243
§7.24: On the future status of the marriage-union—Sahl 243
§7.25: Whether they love each other or not—al-Kindī 244
§7.26: On the future status of the marriage-union—al-Khayyāt....245
§7.27: On the future status of the marriage-union—Dorotheus ...246
§7.28: Whether the man or wife would die first—Jirjis 246
§7.29: Which one would die first, the husband or wife—Aristotle 246
§7.30: On a lost wife: whether or not she would return—Sahl 247
§7.31: On a fugitive or dismissed wife—'Umar 247
§7.32: On a wife who has fled or been sent away—al-Khayyāt 248
§7.33: On a missing wife—Dorotheus 248
§7.34: Whether she is a virgin—Sahl 252
§7.35: Whether she has already given birth—Sahl 252
§7.36: Whether a pregnant woman conceived lawfully—Sahl 253

Controversies & Lawsuits 254
    §7.37: On a controversy or legal case—Sahl 254
    §7.38: On legal cases or controversies—'Umar 254
    §7.39: On those things which happen between two people—al-Kindī 255
    §7.40: On controversies—al-Khayyāt 256
    §7.41: On a trial or controversy—Dorotheus 257
    §7.42: On the same thing, which of them would get the victory—Sahl 259
    §7.43: Which if them will win—'Umar 259
    §7.44: Who would give in, in the situation—al-Kindī 260
    §7.45: From whom the beginning of peace is taken up—al-Khayyāt 260
    §7.46: Who would yield in the trial—Dorotheus 261
    §7.47: Who will obtain the victory—Aristotle 263
    §7.48: On the king or judge: which of them he favors—Sahl 264
    §7.49: On the king or the judge, which one of them he favors—'Umar 265
    §7.50: On the judge's faithfulness—al-Kindī 266
    §7.51: Whom the king favors—al-Khayyāt 267
    §7.52: Whether there will be peace between them—'Umar 268
    §7.53: Why there is a controversy—'Umar 268
    §7.54: With whom the lawsuit must be carried out—'Umar 269
    §7.55: On the end of the lawsuit, and the hour—'Umar 269

Trades & Sales 270
    §7.56: On business deals and commerce—Sahl 270
    §7.57: On business deals and trades—'Umar 271
    §7.58: On commerce—al-Khayyāt 271
    §7.59: On trade—Dorotheus 273

Commodities & Prices 274
    §7.60: On things for sale, and their status—'Umar 275
    §7.61: When they are going to be more burdensome or easier—'Umar 279
    §7.62: (More on the same topic)—'Umar 282
    §7.63: [Another example, from the following month]—'Umar 283
    §7.64: On the price of things for sale—'Umar 285
    §7.65: On the procuring of things for sale—'Umar 286
    §7.66: On things for sale—al-Kindī 291
    §7.67: On the signification of the lights with respect to the status of things for sale, through the individual months—Dorotheus 292
    §7.68: On the price of things for sale—Jirjis 293
    §7.69: On the same thing, through individual months—Jirjis 294
    §7.70: On the price of things for sale—Jirjis 295
    §7.71: On the price or status of things for sale—Aristotle 295

Fugitives **297**
   §7.72: On a missing captive or any thing gone missing—Sahl 297
   §7.73: On a fugitive and lost thing—ʿUmar 301
   §7.74: On a fugitive, whether he would be found—ʿUmar 301
   §7.75: On the hour of discovery—ʿUmar 302
   §7.76: On missing things and those who slip away due to escaping—
      al-Kindī 303
   §7.77: On a fugitive and a lost thing—al-Khayyāt 304
   §7.78: On a lost thing or a fugitive—Dorotheus 306
   §7.79: In what place the fugitive or missing thing is being held—
      Sahl 308
   §7.80: To what place he is fleeing—ʿUmar 308
   §7.81: In what place the lost things would be found—al-Kindī 309
   §7.82: In what place the missing things would be held—al-Kindī 311
   §7.83: On the same thing—al-Kindī 312
   §7.84: In what place the fugitive is being held—al-Khayyāt 312
   §7.85: In what place the fugitive or lost thing is being held—
      Dorotheus 313
   §7.86: What was the reason for losing it—al-Kindī 313
   §7.87: Whether he escaped on his own or through the advice of
      another—al-Kindī 315
   §7.88: Whether he is noble—al-Kindī 320

Theft **321**
   §7.89: On something stolen, whether it could be recovered—Sahl
   321
   §7.90: On recovering lost things—Sahl 324
   §7.91: On theft—ʿUmar 325
   §7.92: Whether it could be found—ʿUmar 326
   §7.93: On theft—al-Kindī 326
   §7.94: Whether it could be recovered—al-Kindī 327
   §7.95: On discovering what was stolen—al-Kindī 328
   §7.96: Whether the stolen goods could be recovered—al-Khayyāt
   329
   §7.97: Whether the stolen goods would be recovered quickly or
      not—al-Khayyāt 331
   §7.98: Whether it could be recovered—Dorotheus 331
   §7.99: On the same thing, but in another way—Dorotheus 332
   §7.100: On theft—Aristotle 334
   §7.101: Whether a thing taken by theft could be recovered—
      Aristotle 334
   §7.102: How much should be recovered, [and how he entered the
      home]—ʿUmar 335
   §7.103: How much should be recovered—al-Kindī 336
   §7.104: When it would be returned—al-Kindī 336

§7.105: Whether he is an outsider or someone familiar—Sahl 338
§7.106: Whether he is a stranger or familiar—ʿUmar 339
§7.107: Whether he is a stranger or familiar—Aristotle 339
§7.108: Of what age or sex he is—Sahl...340
§7.109: Whether it is a male or female—ʿUmar.................................340
§7.110: Of what age he is—ʿUmar..341
§7.111: Whether it is one or many—al-Kindī....................................341
§7.112: Whether they are one or more—al-Kindī.............................342
§7.113: The form of the robber—ʿUmar..342
§7.114: The form of the robber—al-Kindī...343
§7.115: On the form of the robber—al-Kindī....................................347
§7.116: On the robber's form—Jirjis..348
§7.117: Whether the thief would be found—Jirjis............................349
§7.118: On the form of the robber—Aristotle...................................349
§7.119: Whether the thief could be found—al-Kindī.......................350
§7.120: Whether he would be able to escape—al-Kindī...................351
§7.121: Whether he would have run away—al-Kindī.......................352
§7.122: In what direction he tends—al-Kindī...................................354
§7.123: In what direction he would head—Aristotle.......................354
§7.124: On the thief, if he carried something away with him—Aristotle 355
§7.125: In what place the stolen thing is being held—Sahl............357
§7.126: On the stolen goods, where they are—ʿUmar.....................357
§7.127: In what place it is concealed—al-Kindī...............................358
§7.128: Whether the stolen goods are yet being held in the same place—Aristotle...360
§7.129: In what part of a house—Sahl 360
§7.130: To whom he hands it, or with whom he deposits it for safekeeping—ʿUmar..361
§7.131: What indications would be had in that house—al-Kindī ..361
§7.132: On the quantity and number of what was taken by theft—Sahl...363
§7.133: On the number of things taken by theft—ʿUmar...............363
§7.134: What it is that was taken by theft—Sahl 364
§7.135: Concerning the thing taken by theft: of what kind [it is]—ʿUmar..366
§7.136: On the kind of stolen thing—al-Kindī.................................366
§7.137: What it is that was stolen by theft—Jirjis...........................371
§7.138: Of what type the stolen thing is—Aristotle.......................373
§7.139: On recognizing the name of the robber—ʿUmar...............373
§7.140: On the number of letters—ʿUmar..377
§7.141: On the letters of the planets—ʿUmar..................................378
§7.142: On the order of letters in names—ʿUmar...........................384
§7.143: Of what law or nation he is—ʿUmar....................................385

§7.144: On the etymology of the name—'Umar 385
§7.145: On the composition of the name and the joining of the letters—'Umar 387
§7.146: On finding the number and name of a concealed thing—Jirjis 389

Partnerships 393
§7.147: On the status of a partnership—Sahl 393
§7.148: On the association or hatred or love of two people—'Umar 394
§7.149: On the status of the association—al-Khayyāt 395
§7.150: On a partnership or association—Dorotheus 396
§7.151: On any association—Aristotle 396
§7.152: On the stability of the association—Aristotle 397
§7.153: On the success or harm of an association—'Umar 397
§7.154: On the usefulness of the association—Jirjis 398
§7.155: On the result and reward of the association—Aristotle 398
§7.156: On the hour of attaining the advantage or disadvantage (or rather, the harm)—'Umar 398

Journeys to Find Someone 400
§7.157: On a journey established by someone—Sahl 400
§7.158: On a journey established [to meet] someone—al-Khayyāt 400
§7.159: On a journey established [to meet] someone—Dorotheus 400

War 401
§7.160: On war—Sahl 401
§7.161: On war—'Umar 404
§7.162: On war—al-Kindī 404
§7.163: On war and its outcome—al-Khayyāt 408
§7.164: On entering into war—Dorotheus 410
§7.165: On war and a marriage-union, and the rest of what is like that—Jirjis 410
§7.166: On a future war between two cities or peoples—Aristotle 411
§7.167: On the quality and manner of the war—Sahl 412
§7.168: On the misfortune and success of wars—'Umar 414
§7.169: On the vigor or laziness of those fighting—'Umar 415
§7.170: On those who have left the king and become rebels against him—'Umar 416
§7.171: Again on war—al-Kindī 416
§7.172: Whether the combatant would meet death—al-Kindī 418
§7.173: On peace and concord—Sahl 419
§7.174: On the end of the war—'Umar 420
§7.175: On the end of the war—al-Kindī 420

§7.176: Who, and of what type, is the mediator—al-Kindī 422
§7.177: On the origin of the war and which side is more just—Sahl
....425
§7.178: To whom victory would be given—al-Kindī......................427
§7.179: Whom would the people of note would favor—al-Kindī.427
§7.180: At what hour the combatant or adversary would begin to
fight, or when they ought to flee—al-Kindī..................................428
§7.181: About someone going to war—Aristotle............................433
§7.182: In what limb he is struck—Aristotle..................................434
§7.183: On partners and those whom they prevail upon, and on
sending generals to war—'Umar...434
§7.184: On riders sent to plunder—al-Khayyāt.............................439
§7.185: On those whom we reckon to be rebels, wanting to turn
against their masters—al-Kindī..440
§7.186: On someone, whether he would strike against the king—
Dorotheus..447
§7.187: On those having left the king—Dorotheus......................447
§7.188: On the status of a besieged city—'Umar..........................448
§7.189: Whether he would be overcome by surrender or war—
'Umar...448
§7.190: On the besieging of cities—al-Kindī.................................449
§7.191: What is the condition of peace—al-Kindī........................450
§7.192: When [the city] would be stormed—al-Kindī..................451
§7.193: From where one should have fear—al-Kindī...................452
§7.194: On the citizens' courage—al-Kindī..................................452
§7.195: What was the reason for surrender—al-Kindī.................453
§7.196: For whom are there more allies—al-Kindī......................454
§7.197: Whose cause is more just—al-Kindī................................454
§7.198: On storming fortresses—Dorotheus.................................455

Hunting & Fishing..**456**
§7.199: On the hunt—Sahl...456
§7.200: On the multitude or scarcity of the catch—Sahl.............457
§7.201: On hunts—'Umar..457
§7.202: On fishing—Sahl..459
§7.203: On fishing—'Umar..460

§8: EIGHTH HOUSE
Death **462**
§8.1: On those things which pertain to the eighth house—Sahl....462
§8.2: On the life or death of an absent person—al-Khayyāt.........463
§8.3: On someone, whether he is living or dead—Dorotheus.......464
§8.4: What is the cause of death—Dorotheus................................465
§8.5: What kind of death ought to end his life—Aristotle............466

Fear..**467**
§8.6: On fear—'Umar..467

§8.7: On security or worry—Dorotheus 468

§9: NINTH HOUSE

Travel 469
  §9.1: On those things which pertain to the ninth house—Sahl 469
  §9.2: On travel, whether it would happen or not—'Umar 471
  §9.3: On travel—al-Kindī 472
  §9.4: On travel—al-Khayyāt 473
  §9.5: On travel, whether it would happen or not—Dorotheus 475
  §9.6: On travel and any change [of place]—Jirjis 477
  §9.7: On travel, a marriage-union, or kingdom—Jirjis 478
  §9.8: On travel—Aristotle 478
  §9.9: What the journey is, in days—Aristotle 480
  §9.10: Whether a premeditated journey would be brought to its
    end—Aristotle 481
  §9.11: To what men he heads, and what would happen to him on
    the journey—Sahl 481
  §9.12: On the return of the one traveling, even what would happen
    to him (and how) while he goes—Sahl 482
  §9.13: On changing [one's] place—Sahl 484
  §9.14: On something proposed—Sahl 484
  §9.15: What would happen to him on a journey, and how—al-Kindī
    484
  §9.16: What would happen to him, and how, while he was there—
    al-Khayyāt 493

Imprisonment 495
  §9.17: On imprisoned people and their liberation—Sahl 495
  §9.18: On incarcerated people, whether they are about to escape—
    al-Khayyāt 497
  §9.19: On imprisoned people and their liberation—Dorotheus 499

Absent People 501
  §9.20: On the return of an absent person—Sahl 501
  §9.21: On the return of an absent person—'Umar 502
  §9.22: On the status of an absent person—al-Kindī 503
  §9.23: On the return of an absent person—al-Kindī 504
  §9.24: On the return of an absent person—al-Khayyāt 504
  §9.25: On the return of an absent person—Dorotheus 505
  §9.26: On anyone's status—Jirjis 506
  §9.27: When an absent person would return—Jirjis 506
  §9.28: When someone would return to his own nation—Aristotle
    506
  §9.29: On the return of an absent person—Aristotle 507
  §9.30: On the hour of turning back—'Umar 507
  §9.31: Whether he is healthy or infirm—'Umar 508
  §9.32: Whether he is living or dead—'Umar 508

§9.33: Whether he is living or dead—al-Kindī..................508
§9.34: Whether he would head eagerly for diverse journeys—'Umar 509
§9.35: Whether he would undertake to turn back by day or night—'Umar 510
Dreams **511**
§9.36: On dreams—'Umar..................511
§9.37: On the nature of dreams—Dorotheus 512
Alchemy & Other Knowledge **513**
§9.38: On alchemy—Sahl..................513
§9.39: On alchemy—'Umar..................513
§9.40: On the knowledge of something—'Umar..................514
Ships..................**515**
§9.41: On a ship or the status of those sailing—'Umar..................515
§9.42: On constructing ships—al-Kindī..................517
§9.43: On ships, what good or bad should happen to them—al-Kindī..................518

§10: TENTH HOUSE
Honors **527**
§10.1: On those things which pertain to the tenth house—Sahl ...527
§10.2: When he would attain the honor—Sahl..................528
§10.3: Over which region he would be in charge—Sahl..................529
§10.4: On anyone, whether he would be able to get a kingdom or dignity—'Umar..................532
§10.5: Whether he would obtain an honor sought from the king—'Umar..................534
§10.6: On the attainment of an honor—al-Kindī..................536
§10.7: On acquiring kingdoms and dignities—al-Khayyāt..................539
§10.8: On kingdoms and dignities, whether they could be obtained—Dorotheus 542
§10.9: On attaining an honor—Jirjis..................543
§10.10: On the acquisition of an honor—Aristotle..................543
Kingdoms & Rulerships **544**
§10.11: How it will go with him, or if he would be deposed—Sahl 544
§10.12: On the steadiness of the reign, or if he would be deposed—Sahl..................547
§10.13: For how long he is going to reign—'Umar..................549
§10.14: For how long he would possess the honor attained, or when he would be driven out—'Umar..................550
§10.15: For how long he is going to reign, or if perhaps he would be deposed—al-Khayyāt..................552
§10.16: On the kingdom's prosperity or troubles—al-Kindī..................554
§10.17: On underofficials—al-Kindī..................556

§10.18: On his predecessor—al-Kindī..................556
§10.19: On his successor—al-Kindī....................557
§10.20: On kingdoms and dignities—Jirjis 558
§10.21: If he would shed the dignity given, and if perhaps he would happen to come back—Dorotheus 559
§10.22: How long he is going to reign—Dorotheus 559
§10.23: About a king who has left his place or reign, or an absent king: whether he would return—Sahl..................561
§10.24: On an absent king, or anyone in exile, whether he would return to his original dignity—al-Khayyāt 563
§10.25: On those who are parting from the king or their family, slaves, friends, partners, or the region, or a wife from her man—ʿUmar 565
§10.26: On recovering lost patrimony, or if it is good to withdraw from friends or the fatherland—al-Khayyāt 567
§10.27: On inquiring into the life of kings through interrogations—ʿUmar 569
§10.28: On discerning the life of kings from the cycle of mundane years—ʿUmar..................571
§10.29: Likewise on obtaining the life and dignity of the king—ʿUmar 572
§10.30: Likewise on obtaining the life and dignity of the king—ʿUmar 573
§10.31: On inquiring into the hour of the king's death—ʿUmar ...575
§10.32: On the death of the king, through interrogations—ʿUmar 576
§10.33: On anyone advanced to an honor, from the cycle of mundane years—ʿUmar..................577
§10.34: On estate managers and supervisors, and their authority, acts, and life—ʿUmar..................579
§10.35: If someone in power would please the people—ʿUmar 581
§10.36: On the household intimates of kings, whether they would obtain something good from them—ʿUmar..................581
§10.37: Whether they would be his household intimates for a long time—ʿUmar..................583
§10.38: Whether it is useful to keep close to the king—Dorotheus 584

Trades & Professions 585
§10.39: On trades—ʿUmar..................585

§11: ELEVENTH HOUSE
Things Hoped For..................586
§11.1: On those things which pertain to the eleventh house—Sahl 586

§11.2: On those things which someone holds back in his mind, nor does he want to name it—Sahl 587
§11.3: On hope—ʿUmar 587
§11.4: On the hope of a promised honor—al-Khayyāt 587
§11.5: On the hope of a promised gift—Dorotheus 588
Friendships **589**
§11.6: If a friendship is true, or even should someone come together with a friend—Sahl 589
§11.7: On love and hate—ʿUmar 589
§11.8: Concerning anyone, whether he would come together with a friend—al-Khayyāt 590
§11.9: On friends, brothers, and relatives: whether they would come together—Dorotheus 590
§11.10: On the concord or love of two people—al-Khayyāt 591
§11.11: On the concord of two people—Dorotheus 591
§11.12: Concerning someone, whether it is a friend or flatterer—Jirjis 591

§12: TWELFTH HOUSE
Horse Racing **592**
§12.1: On those things which pertain to the twelfth house—Sahl 592
§12.2: On the racing of horses, and their victory—al-Kindī 594
§12.3: On the racing of horses—al-Khayyāt 594
Revenge & Enemies **597**
§12.4A: On enemies—Sahl 597
§12.4B: On revenge—Sahl 597
§12.5: On enemies—al-Khayyāt 598
§12.6: On enemies—Dorotheus 599

§Z: WEATHER & DISASTERS
§Z.1: On the corruption and detriment of things—ʿUmar 600
§Z.2: On the quality of the air and the seasons—ʿUmar 603
§Z.3: On rain and lightning and thunder and wind—ʿUmar 607
§Z.4: On the hour of rain and winds, heat and cold—ʿUmar 608
§Z.5: On the places of the foundations—ʿUmar 609
§Z.6: On the hour of rain—ʿUmar 610
§Z.7: On pestilence, war, submersions, conflagration, and earthquake—ʿUmar 611
§Z.8: On the quality of the air through individual years—al-Kindī 613
§Z.9: On years of pestilence and good health—al-Kindī 616
§Z.10: On heavy rains—Dorotheus 618
§Z.11: On rains throughout the quarters of the year—Dorotheus 620
§Z.12: On the knowledge of heavy rains through individual months—Dorotheus 620

§Z.13: On daily heavy rains—Dorotheus 621
§Z.14: On rains—Jirjis 623
GLOSSARY 625
APPENDIX A: SAHL'S *THE FIFTY JUDGMENTS* 644
APPENDIX B: EXCERPT FROM BONATTI'S *THE BOOK OF ASTRONOMY* TR. 6: ON QUESTIONS 659
APPENDIX C: SELECTING SIGNIFICATORS, FROM MĀSHĀ'ALLĀH'S *OR* CH. 2 684
APPENDIX D: APHORISMS ON QUESTIONS FROM AL-RIJĀL I.5.1 688
APPENDIX E: TABLE OF QUESTIONS BY HOUSE 692
APPENDIX F: TABLE OF 'UMAR PASSAGES 696
APPENDIX G: ALTERNATIVE WAYS OF EXTRACTING NAMES 699
APPENDIX H: LOTS IN *JUDGES* 701
APPENDIX I: *THE ESSENTIAL MEDIEVAL ASTROLOGY* CYCLE 703
BIBLIOGRAPHY 705
INDEX OF NAMES 708

Book Abbreviations

BA	Māshā'allāh	*The Book of Aristotle* (in *PN*)
BOA	Bonatti, Guido	*The Book of Astronomy*
CA	Lilly, William	*Christian Astrology*
Carmen	Dorotheus of Sidon	*Carmen Astrologicum*
Chap. Rains	Māshā'allāh	*Chapter on Rains in the Year* (in *WSM*)
Forty Chapters	Al-Kindī	*The Forty Chapters*
ITA	Abu Ma'shar et al.	*Introductions to Traditional Astrology: Abū Ma'shar & al-Qabīsī*
OHT	Māshā'allāh	*On Hidden Things* (in *WSM*)
On Elect.	Sahl bin Bishr	*On Elections* (in *WSM*)
On Quest.	Sahl bin Bishr	*On Questions* (in *WSM*)
OR	Māshā'allāh	*On Reception* (in *WSM*)
PN 1-3	Various	*Persian Nativities I-III*
Search	Hermann of Carinthia	*The Search of the Heart*
Skilled	Al-Rijāl	*The Book of the Skilled in the Judgments of the Stars*
TAFT	Dykes, Benjamin	*Traditional Astrology for Today: An Introduction*
Tet.	Claudius Ptolemy	*Tetrabiblos*
Twelve Dom.	Māshā'allāh/Jirjis	*What the Planets Signify in the Twelve Domiciles of the Circle*
WSM	Sahl bin Bishr & Māshā'allāh	*Works of Sahl & Māshā'allāh*

TABLE OF FIGURES

Figure 1: Mercury reflecting light by transfer (*ITA* III.13.2) 29
Figure 2: Jupiter reflecting light by collection (*ITA* III.13.1) 29
Figure 3: Table of prevented connections (from *ITA* Appendix B) 31
Figure 4: Size of planetary bodies/orbs, in front and behind 34
Figure 5: Should I move in with my stepsister? 37
Figure 6: Table of introductory sections in *Judges*, and their equivalents 42
Figure 7: Questions of the first house 59
Figure 8: Sahl's chart according to Hugo 66
Figure 9: Sahl's chart according to John 66
Figure 10: Likely chart for Sahl's example 67
Figure 11: Table of planetary years 70
Figure 12: Quarters of heaven: directions, ages, and parts of the day 72
Figure 13: Questions of the second house 75
Figure 14: Questions of the third house 96
Figure 15: Questions of the fourth house 100
Figure 16: Angles for buying lands (al-Kindī §4.2) 102
Figure 17: Al-Rijāl's electional version 102
Figure 18: Angles for what is on the land 105
Figure 19: Angles for making the sale ('Umar §4.6) 106
Figure 20: Al-Kindī's example of finding treasure 123
Figure 21: Finding a hidden object (Jirjis) 127
Figure 22: Questions of the fifth house 134
Figure 23: Questions of the sixth house 173
Figure 24: The angles in illness 174
Figure 25: Significations in illness ('Umar §6.2) 177
Figure 26: Angular significations in illness (al-Kindī §§6.4 and 6.15) ... 179
Figure 27: Typical degrees of critical days in illness 196
Figure 28: Will a captive/slave be freed 203
Figure 29: Freeing one's own captive ('Umar §6.33) 205
Figure 30: Subsequent masters 214
Figure 31: Subsequent masters 215
Figure 32: Questions of the seventh house 226
Figure 33: Angular significations for sales (*Carmen* V.9) 272
Figure 34: 'Umar's chart for §7.61, based on the 1509 diagram 280
Figure 35: Likely chart for 'Umar's §7.61 (in whole signs) 280
Figure 36: 'Umar's chart for §7.63, based on the Vienna diagram 284
Figure 37: Likely chart for 'Umar's §7.63 (in whole signs) 285
Figure 38: Angular significations for fugitives 299
Figure 39: Angular significations for fugitives (Sahl §7.72) 300
Figure 40: Angular significations for fugitives (al-Kindī §7.76, §7.82) .. 300
Figure 41: Example of theft #1 (al-Kindī) 316
Figure 42: Example of theft #2 (al-Kindī) 317

Figure 43: Example of theft #3 (al-Kindī) 318
Figure 44: Likely chart for al-Kindī's example #3 319
Figure 45: Angular significations for theft (Sahl §7.89, ʿUmar §7.91) 323
Figure 46: Angular significations for theft (al-Kindī §7.93) 323
Figure 47: Angular significations for theft: 324
Figure 48: Signs and directions in space, according to "Aristotle" 355
Figure 49: Chart suggested by ʿUmar for determining names (§7.141) 379
Figure 50: Letters of the Arabic planetary names 380
Figure 51: Arabic names of the signs 380
Figure 52: Apparent order of 24 Arabic letters in Vienna manuscript 390
Figure 53: Distribution of 22 letters through the triplicities 390
Figure 54: Example distribution of Hebrew letters 390
Figure 55: Angular significations for partnerships 394
Figure 56: Al-Kindī's directions for fighting 429
Figure 57: Al-Rijāl's proposed correction to al-Kindī 429
Figure 58: Time-based scorched period, ...431
Figure 59: Al-Kindī's scheme of angles for rebellion 440
Figure 60: Questions of the eighth house 462
Figure 61: Questions of the ninth house 469
Figure 62: Angular significators for travel (Sahl §9.1, al-Kindī §9.15) 471
Figure 63: Parts of ship attributed to signs (ʿUmar §9.41) 516
Figure 64: Angles of the chart & ship: 519
Figure 65: Al-Kindī's ship-house associations (Robert & Hugo) 519
Figure 66: Al-Kindī's ship-house associations (Latin al-Rijāl III.14) 520
Figure 67: Proposed correction to al-Rijāl (Dykes) 520
Figure 68: Proposed correct attributions (Dykes) 523
Figure 69: Questions of the tenth house 527
Figure 70: A few eminence configurations (ʿUmar §10.4) 533
Figure 71: Angular significations for attaining a dignity (ʿUmar §10.34) 579
Figure 72: Questions of the eleventh house 586
Figure 73: Questions of the twelfth house 592
Figure 74: Mundane questions on weather and disasters 600
Figure 75: Weather prediction in ʿUmar and al-Kindī 603
Figure 76: Weather prediction in Māshāʾallāh and Dorotheus 603
Figure 77: The twelve "posts" (al-Kindī §Z.8) 610
Figure 78: Perfection by a direct connection 662
Figure 79: Perfection by a transfer of light 663
Figure 80: Perfection by a collection of light 665
Figure 81: Ranking of effective connections (Bonatti) 669
Figure 82: A question about marriage 680

Translator's Introduction

The Book of the Nine Judges (hereafter, *Judges*) is the third and final installment of the horary[1] portion of my *Essential Medieval Astrology* series.[2] For the typical traditional student who already knows the basics of chart reading and the meanings of houses and planets, these three books should form a pretty complete picture of how to answer questions in a traditional way. For those who are new to traditional astrology generally, I recommend that you first read my *Traditional Astrology for Today*, on traditional philosophy, concepts, and interpretation basics. Then, you should have my *Introductions to Traditional Astrology* (hereafter, *ITA*) at hand, since that material is used in every branch of traditional astrology, and I make frequent reference to it throughout this version of *Judges*.

Following are some of the features of each of the three volumes in the horary series:

- *The Search of the Heart* (hereafter, *Search*) describes the use of thought-interpretation and victors in consultation charts or the charts of questions. Thought-interpretation identifies a special planet or point in the chart, which indicates the client's core intention or thought or problem. Since a chart contains many possible competing candidates for this role, the one which wins this role is called a "victor." Thought-interpretation seems to have been used alongside more straightforward horary procedures (at least until the 9th Century AD), making it both historically and procedurally prior to answering formal questions.
- *The Forty Chapters* of al-Kindī is a famous, self-contained book on numerous questions, with a great deal of basic introductory material. As such, it is a good beginning point for learning how to answer questions. Most of *Forty Chapters* is also contained in *Judges*.
- *The Book of the Nine Judges* is the most compendious in terms of questions. It was originally written by its author-compilers as a complete introduction to astrology and questions, but most manuscripts and printed editions omitted the lengthy introductory portions. In the present translation, I have supplemented the standard, truncated version

---

[1] "Horary" is a more recent name for "questions," the branch of astrology that casts charts at the time of a question presented to an astrologer.
[2] See Appendix I for a complete listing as of 2011.

of *Judges* with a table of equivalent source material, my own introductory comments, and other helpful passages from Sahl and Bonatti in the Appendices. For most of the astrological authorities in this book, this is their first English translation.

So, each of these has its own value as a course text and for learning how to approach thoughts and questions. *Search* is the best guide to thoughts and victors, and presents some basic ways of approaching a chart. *Forty Chapters* is the best for those wanting a smaller and more manageable introduction to questions and astrological principles. And *Judges* is the best for serious students who know all the basics but want many source texts plus handy guides to horary interpretation.

§1: The structure and background of *Judges*[3]

Judges is famous (and occasionally legendary) compilation of material on questions, from the first half of the 12th Century AD. It is composed of works by numerous Perso-Arabic astrologers and astrological writers, probably all of which were active between the 8th and 9th Centuries AD (the most important and creative period of Perso-Arabic astrology). The distinguishing feature of *Judges* is its careful collating of sources. Rather than present consecutive translations of each author, its chief compiler (Hugo of Santalla) translated the works separately and then put all of the matching material together. For example, all of the passages on finding buried or hidden treasure are put together (§§4.15-18), as are the opinions on missing or runaway wives (§§7.30-33).[4] But it was not Hugo's first attempt at such a project. It is actually the expansion of an earlier compilation by him (and possibly also Hermann of Carinthia), *The Book of the Three Judges*.[5] Burnett (1977) believes that *Three Judges* can be dated to before 1151, and says that some of the chapters in it are closer to the Arabic sources than they become in *Judges*: probably

---

[3] My historical description of *Judges* is based on Burnett 1977, 2001, and 2006. Above all others, Charles Burnett has done the most to explain the history and interest of *Judges*, and I am grateful to him and David Juste for their help and advice.

[4] Since not every author had arranged his paragraphs in the same way, the order of sections is not always precise for every possible topic: in Appendix E I have listed all of the main topics and questions, and the sections corresponding to them.

[5] According to Burnett, the material from Sahl in *Three Judges* bears a style more like Hermann's than Hugo's.

Hugo reworked the Latin for its final form. To my mind, both versions of *Judges* probably belong to the 1130s-1140s, as that was a particularly active time for both Hugo and Hermann (see my introductions to *The Book of Aristotle* and *Search*).

By the 14th Century, a legend reported in one of the manuscripts says that the book originated as a gift from the Sultan of Baghdad to Holy Roman Emperor Frederick II (13th Century). This certainly captures the idea that *Judges* is a great gift of Arabic astrology to the West, but given Hugo's authorship of the compilation, it is of course false. Nevertheless, it was a highly esteemed enough to undergo numerous manuscript copies and printed editions. But its value was not always appreciated. In his preface *To the Reader* in *Christian Astrology*, William Lilly disdains its Latin translator as someone who does not understand astrology. Lilly also includes the translator of al-Kindī's *Forty Chapters*, which was undoubtedly Robert of Ketton, suggesting that what he objected to was not the rendition of the astrology, but the writing—or rather, that the Latin was so unusual that it made it difficult to learn the astrology described. Lilly was already drawing on alternative translations of material from the Latin al-Rijāl as well as translations by John of Seville, whose clear and straightforward Latin lacks Hugo's curlicues and artifice. But Lilly was wrong to think that one cannot learn astrology from these texts. Hermann and Hugo may never have cast a chart, but as I believe the reader of *Forty Chapters* and *Judges* will see, only a little mental adjustment is needed to get valuable astrology from both texts. The trick is really to slow down. A typical sentence from John's Latin might read, "If the lord of the first house and the Moon are applying to lord of the tenth, then the querent will get the honor he hopes for." This is a friendly, if-then statement. But the equivalent sentence in Hugo might read, "The lord of the east, and no less the Moon, rendering counsel to [the lord] of the house of kings, really obtains the hoped-for position." Once we know that "rendering counsel" is Hugo's translation of the Arabic "pushing management" or simply "applying," we know exactly what the sentence means. I have included Hugo's special vocabulary in the Glossary, and frequently alert readers to the relevant chapters of my *Introductions to Traditional Astrology* (*ITA*) for these technical terms.

It seems to me that *Judges* should be understood as being divided into the following two parts, although the official section numbering I have adopted from Charles Burnett does not match it precisely:

1. §A-§1.1: *Introduction.* The lengthy introduction, which can be understood as having three parts. This translation of *Judges* has only the last part.
    a. §§A.1-125: *Introduction to astrology.* An introduction to astrology, covering everything from the natures of the signs and planets, to planetary configurations such as aspects and transfers of light, to cookbook interpretations of planets in the houses, and aphorisms on interpreting charts. This introduction is virtually equivalent to all of the material in *ITA* I-V, and includes a translation of Sahl's *Fifty Judgments* and much of al-Kindī's own introduction to *Forty Chapters*. Since so much of this is already translated by me in *ITA*, *Forty Chapters*, and *WSM*, I have elected to omit it. Below, I provide a table of these sections with their English equivalents, for those who wish to review the material.
    b. §A.126: *The "hidden" preface.* A short preface by Hugo of Santalla (the primary translator and compiler), which acts as a transition between the material on astrology basics, and general instructions on questions. In it, Hugo describes some of his views on magic, talismans, and astrology. Burnett (2006) translated this preface, and I summarize its main points below.
    c. §A.127-134, and §1.1: *Introduction to questions and victors.* This part primarily contains the views of Māshā'allāh, 'Umar, and Sahl on determining significators and the basic types of planetary configurations which provide positive answers to questions. The material from Sahl, which is taken from the opening of his *On Questions*, also contains a valuable chart example from 824 AD. To this we might also add §Z.1, which is really a list of problematic configurations which prevent a matter from coming about.
2. §1.2-Z.14: *House-based questions, and weather/disasters.* The bulk of *Judges* is organized according to house topic (such as wealth in §2 and attaining positions of honor in §10), with §Z covering mundane questions on weather and disasters.

In his preface to *Three Judges*,⁶ Hugo described how he worked. He wanted to make a convenient handbook for people not otherwise well introduced to this branch of astrology, and so took excerpts from three different authors: 'Umar al-Tabarī, Sahl bin Bishr, and al-Kindī. After putting their introductory material first, he then organized the excerpts on questions both by individual question and by house topic ("the order of signs") for easy comprehension. Hugo probably felt compelled to emphasize this point about house order, because neither al-Kindī nor 'Umar followed any discernible order of questions in their books.⁷ Readers of my translation of *Forty Chapters* will see that al-Kindī ranges from controversies and wars to theft and fugitives, then travel, honors, sieges, more on war, and so on. In Appendix F below, one may see that 'Umar wanders from topics such as children and absent people, to marriage and the sciences. On the other hand, Sahl's *On Quest.* generally follows a logical order of topics following the houses. So Hugo must have thought that his compendium might set a new and better standard for learning questions, since it improved on the style of two of its three sources. As it happened, such a hope would have been disappointed: despite its numerous manuscript copies and printed editions, *Judges* was never as popular as other works on questions, including those which used the same house-based organization: John of Seville's Sahl was more popular for its size and easier Latin, and al-Rijāl's huge and likewise easy-to-read *Book of the Skilled* (known in Latin as *On the Judgments of the Stars*) organized its material by house topics for nativities and elections as well, and not just for questions.

The transformation of *Three Judges* into *Nine Judges* was roughly as follows. First, Hugo (and possibly Hermann, even with the cooperation of Robert of Ketton) translated and collated the material from the following works, to create *Three Judges*:

---

⁶ *Three Judges* seems also to have been dedicated to Hugo's employer, Bishop Michael of Tarazona. This is the same Michael who got Hugo to translate the so-called *Book of Aristotle*, a Hellenistic work by Māshā'allāh on nativities, and available in my *Persian Nativities I*.
⁷ Recall that the natal topics in Ptolemy's *Tet.* did not follow a house order, either, but were broadly based on the typical order of events in life.

1. Al-Kindī (ca. 801 – 870 AD), from *The Forty Chapters*.
2. 'Umar al-Tabarī (d. ca. 815 AD), from his *Book of Questions in the Judgments of the Stars*,[8] a 138-chapter book on judgments.[9]
3. Sahl bin Bishr (fl. first half of 9th Cent.), from his *On Questions*.

The question might be raised as to whether Hugo arranged the Arabic material first and then translated it, or translated his Arabic sources first. Based on my own work here, I believe he translated each work separately. For one thing, I find the Latin of Hugo's 'Umar much more turgid and frustrating than his rendition of the other authors. Likewise, in the "Dorotheus" passages for *Nine Judges*, Hugo uses the verb *expostulo* four or five times, but not at all for any other author. Since Dorotheus has close (and sometimes word-for-word) parallels with both Sahl and al-Khayyāt, it is more likely that this difference in vocabulary is due to Hugo translating it separately and on its own, rather than at the same time as the others.

Be that as it may, when expanding *Three Judges*, Hugo added the following authors to both the introductory portions and the body of the work:

4. Abu 'Ali al-Khayyāt (ca. 770 – ca. 835 AD), from his book on questions called the *Book of the Secret of Hope*,[10] which (like Sahl's *On Questions*) was itself largely taken from Māshā'allāh but in several places borrows from 'Umar.
5. "Dorotheus," an unknown person or text which drew on Māshā'allāh, and perhaps mistook Māshā'allāh's own Arabic translation of Dorotheus's *Carmen* (now largely lost) to be by Dorotheus himself. (It must be noted that much of *Carmen* V can be found in *Judges* or in Sahl's *On Elect*.). From this point on, I will refer to this unknown person or text as Dorotheus, and when referring to the historical Dorotheus represented by the Arabic *Carmen*, I will refer to *Carmen*.
6. "Aristotle," another unknown person or text, whose methods often differ from everyone else's. According to Burnett, this material is

---

[8] *Kitab al-Masa'il fi-Akhkam al-Nujum*. See Sezgin p. 112, #2.
[9] Portions of this translation are found (with the chapters somewhat in order) as the medieval *De Iudiciis Astrorum*: see Carmody, p. 39. Since there is no complete English translation of 'Umar, I have listed the correspondences between 'Umar's Arabic and *Judges* in Appendix F, using the unpublished table of contents provided to me by Burnett.
[10] See Sezgin p. 121.

found medievally in works attributed to Ptolemy, Aristotle, and Raymond of Marseilles. But I note that in his *Great Introduction*, Abū Ma'shar refers to an 'Istrātu or 'Istrātuā, whose name John of Seville transliterates as Asthoathoal, Arsthotho, Asthotho, and so on. The similarity of the Arabic name to Aristotle is close enough to make him a candidate for being the "Aristotle" of *Judges*. From this point on, I will refer to this unknown person as Aristotle, and when referring to the philosopher Aristotle, I will make that distinction clear.

7. Jirjis, whose name is transliterated in various texts as Egregius, Zymus, and others. Burnett suggests this might be an Arabic rendition of the Greek name *Georgios*, which would make this person a Byzantine Greek, perhaps of the 9th Century. In *WSM*, I translated a work on the planets in the houses attributed to both Māshā'allāh and Jirjis, and this very work was included by Hugo in the introductory portion of *Judges* under the name Jirjis.

Finally, to these seven authors, Hugo added the following two, solely for the introductory portion:

8. Māshā'allāh (ca. 740 – ca. 815 AD). According to Burnett,[11] the sections attributed to Māshā'allāh are not taken directly from his own *Book of Questions*, but from some intermediary source which is related to al-Khayyāt and Dorotheus. Nonetheless, if it forms a single continuous text, then it contains the significations of the planets, a list of 14 planetary configurations (which in turn underlies the lists in Sahl and 'Umar), information on the Sun and Moon, and finally the instructions for questions which appear in this version of *Judges* (§§A.127 and 132).

9. Abu Ma'shar (787 – 886 AD). This consists primarily of abbreviated lists of significations of the planets, from his *Great Introduction* VII.

And so, the original three judges became nine. But as I mentioned above, since I have omitted most of the introductory portions (using only the standard, truncated form of *Judges*), nothing of Abū Ma'shar appears here. The

---

[11] Burnett 2011, "A complete list of the chapters of the *Liber novem iudicum*," privately circulated.

reader will therefore only find eight judges in the text. Let me now describe some of the sources used for this translation and for Burnett's itemized table of contents, the order of individual astrologers or judges in the text, and their interpretive groupings.

Sources. This translation is based on two manuscripts and one printed edition: Vienna 2428 (12th Century), Madrid 10,009 (13th Century), and Peter Liechtenstein 1509. Of these, Vienna is the most complete and I usually favored it when deciding on particular word choices. Madrid is in very fine shape but not as complete, missing 21 sections from the main body of *Judges*. Liechtenstein was obviously the easiest to read, but is riddled with spelling errors and lacks the same sections as Madrid. At late stages of editing I had access to the full introduction of Vat. Lat. 6766 (13th-14th Century), itself a complete version of *Judges*. In addition, I consulted both the 1485 and 1551 Latin editions of al-Rijāl's *Skilled*, since numerous passages of these authors also appear there: al-Rijāl often supplies more information and better readings for difficult passages in Hugo's translation.

I am also grateful to Charles Burnett and David Juste for providing me with a copy of Burnett's table of contents for the complete *Judges*. For the most part I have numbered the sections following Burnett, such that §A indicates introductory sections, numbered sections cover house topics, and §Z covers mundane questions (and one short paragraph on difficult planetary configurations). In his table of contents, Burnett also identifies the individual judges for almost every section, supplies all of the incipits, and also sources for several of the authors. For the correspondence between ʿUmar's own Arabic and *Judges*, see Appendix F. For al-Khayyāṭ, Māshāʾallāh, and Dorotheus, Burnett relied on two manuscripts containing works of al-Khayyāṭ: EKh (Escorial 938) and BKh (Berlin 5876). I will have more to say about this group of astrologers below.

Order of judges and interpretive groups. In *Three Judges*, Hugo preferred to give the opinion of Sahl first, as he was following Sahl's organization of material by house. In *Nine Judges*, Hugo prefers the following order, starting with the members of *Three Judges*: Sahl, ʿUmar, al-Kindī, al-Khayyāṭ, Dorotheus, and then (in no order of preference) Jirjis and Aristotle. Actually, there is something of a method in this approach, because when the texts are compared we can see four interpretation styles for questions. Of the primary judges, the first group is (1) the "Māshāʾallāh" group, led by Sahl and followed by al-Khayyāṭ and Dorotheus as alternative readings; then comes (2) ʿUmar, then

(3) al-Kindī. Finally, bringing up the rear are (4) Jirjis and Aristotle. In terms of Western treatments of questions,[12] we can say generally that (1) the Māshā'allāh group has been the most popular, with (3) al-Kindī appearing quietly through certain material in Lilly, but still largely unrecognized. (2) 'Umar is basically unknown. (4) Aristotle and Jirjis are totally unknown.

I will describe each briefly below, but it is important to recognize this: each interpretive style is more or less consistent within itself and with basic astrological principles, but differs from the rest. Currently, I am not sure if we can reliably define what the "core" of each approach is. But it is good to remember that the same astrological principles can give rise to rival interpretive styles and variety, even if they do not produce serious incompatibility or radical difference.

(1) The Māshā'allāh group: Sahl, al-Khayyāt, Dorotheus

The first and historically most important interpretive stream is the "Māshā'allāh group," which includes Sahl, al-Khayyāt, and Dorotheus. I call it the Māshā'allāh group, because it is evident from the text that a work by Māshā'allāh lies in the background. In his comments on his own table of contents for *Judges*, Burnett argues that the passages attributed to al-Khayyāt and Dorotheus are really two different versions of the same underlying text. I believe the situation is a bit more complicated, and my current view is this: the texts from all three of these writers derive from a work of Māshā'allāh, which would have included both the introductory material on questions (appearing here as §§A.127 and A.132), and a treatment of individual questions based on his own translation of *Carmen* V. The fact that Māshā'allāh both translated *Carmen* and wrote material on questions helps explain why certain sections in *Judges* are attributed to Dorotheus, since Māshā'allāh probably noted that he was drawing on *Carmen* in his work.

If true, this is important for two reasons. First, it means that much of the popular received tradition on questions is really due to a transmission by Māshā'allāh, who now must stand as a towering figure in this branch of as-

---

[12] This is a bit tricky, since it is one thing to make it into a Western language, another for its correct author to be recognized, and yet another for it to be used widely. For example, al-Rijāl includes the vast majority of the 'Umar passages in his own book, but almost never gives his source: so although al-Rijāl's name and book were well known, people using it would not have recognized that they were really drawing on 'Umar. And yet, the majority of the popular books on questions such as *CA* draw on Sahl and his group.

trology. Second, it means that Māshā'allāh's translation of *Carmen* has not really been largely lost (as has been supposed). Large portions of *Carmen's* natal material are reflected in Māshā'allāh's *Book of Aristotle*, and the material on elections and/or questions in *Carmen* V survive as questions in this group in *Judges*.[13] The Arabic versions of these three authors would help us know the exact style and wording of the underlying Māshā'allāh text. In fact, to my mind, a more likely explanation for all of this is that Mash'allah never made a stand-alone translation of *Carmen*. That is, Māshā'allāh's translation of *Carmen* was never lost because it never existed in the first place: rather, Māshā'allāh translated *Carmen* directly into the organization of natal material and horary questions found in *BA* and what underlies the texts of *Judges*.

These considerations lead further to a strange fact: while most of Māshā'allāh's translation or reworking of *Carmen* no longer exists but seems to survive in *BA* or *Judges*, 'Umar's own independent translation of *Carmen* does survive, but *is hardly represented in his own material here*. It is easy to find parallels between individual sentences in *Carmen* V and the Māshā'allāh group, but very difficult to find them between 'Umar's own *Carmen* and his passages here. Why did 'Umar not use his own version of *Carmen* V in a recognizable form here? We do not know, nor do we really know why his book on nativities (*TBN*, in my *PN2*) cannot often be traced to *Carmen*.

Of the parallel passages in this group, Sahl is often the longest and contains extra material not found in al-Khayyāt or Dorotheus. Dorotheus is usually the shortest, and sometimes uses only a sentence or two to explain something that appears in a longer form in Sahl and al-Khayyāt. Al-Khayyāt himself is usually somewhere in the middle in terms of length, and although he is obviously drawing on the same material as the others, he does also draw on 'Umar: for example, al-Khayyāt's §10.26 is cribbed from 'Umar's §10.25, and his §2.9 repeats material from 'Umar's §2.2. It is possible that 'Umar was drawing from al-Khayyāt, since elsewhere 'Umar does explicitly quote Māshā'allāh (see below); but my sense is that if this shared 'Umar-al-Khayyāt material really derived from al-Khayyāt (and ultimately Māshā'allāh), we would also see it in Sahl and Dorotheus.

Following are a few reasons we can feel confident that there is a common Māshā'allāh-*Carmen* text underlying the authors in this group:

---

[13] Actually, there is a lot of electional material from *Carmen* in Sahl's *On Elect.* as well, but perhaps even that work of Sahl's derives from Māshā'allāh.

- First, there is a known pattern of copying from Māshā'allāh by Sahl and al-Khayyāt. For example, Sahl's own book on nativities in Arabic is almost identical, sentence-by-sentence, to the *BA*. If there were a common Māshā'allāh-*Carmen* text behind this group, it would explain why parallel material in *Judges* was attributed to Dorotheus by whoever wrote that text.
- Second, there is an evident but inexact correlation between the Arabic *Carmen* (by 'Umar) and the individual members of this group, so that some version of *Carmen* is common to them.
- Third, the individual passages in this group often match each other sentence-by-sentence and paragraph-by-paragraph.
- Finally, these authors occasionally state that their material comes from Māshā'allāh.[14] In the case of the weather material, §§Z.10-13 (attributed there to Dorotheus) are virtually identical sentence-by-sentence with the Arabic *Chapter on Rains in the Year* by Māshā'allāh, which was translated into English for my *WSM*.[15]

In light of these facts, I proceeded as follows. After translating the sections in this group author-by-author, I edited the translation by putting their questions in parallel to one another. It is easy to see that their individual sentences and even paragraph structures line up very neatly together, and I have tried to make the paragraph breaks identical in each, for easier cross-comparison. One will see in the footnotes how I have occasionally used one text to clarify another, or noted differences in their material. For the student, this means that Sahl, al-Khayyāt, and Dorotheus should be studied together and not separately.

(2) 'Umar al-Tabarī

Although 'Umar's approaches to questions are less well known in the West, his reputation with respect to them must have been great, as most of his book on questions not only appears here, but in al-Rijāl as well. That is to say, Hugo did not simply include him by accident because his text happened

---

[14] See Sahl §1.1, al-Khayyāt §§3.2 and 9.18, and Dorotheus §§5.62, 7.67, and 10.22. §10.22 is parallel to Sahl's *On Times* §12, which Sahl explicitly attributes to Māshā'allāh.
[15] I do note that in §Z.10, the text refers to al-Khayyāt in the third person, but this only means that al-Khayyāt himself must have copied this material from Māshā'allāh. It could mean, however, that the Dorotheus material was in part gotten from al-Khayyāt.

to be readily available, since even an Arabic compiler like al-Rijāl saw fit to include most of his material as well.

As I mentioned above, 'Umar's rules differ from those of the other authors in *Judges*, but we can also see other peculiar characteristics here.

- 'Umar's angular significators frequently differ from the other sources. For example, in the treatment of illness, everyone in the Māshā'allāh group gives the Ascendant to the doctor and the seventh to the disease (see the figure in §6.1); but 'Umar gives the Ascendant to the patient and the seventh to the cause of death (see the figure in §6.2). In some cases it could be that different authors are conceiving of the question in a slightly different way, but it is not always easy to discern that.
- He is also dependent on Māshā'allāh as an authoritative writer. For example, his §§A.128 and A.130 have close parallels with Māshā'allāh, and he explicitly cites Māshā'allāh in §§5.64 and 7.183. In his material on prices, 'Umar first cites Māshā'allāh (§7.64), and in his own version of the following section ('Umar's §7.65), al-Rijāl says that that material is from Māshā'allāh. So, much of the material in *Judges* on prices and weather seems to derive from Māshā'allāh, whether under the name of Dorotheus (see above), or 'Umar. In addition, 'Umar §5.64 uses material later attributed to Dorotheus (§5.65), and 'Umar §5.69 is very close to Sahl's *On Quest.* §13.6-7: again, such material is implicitly based on Māshā'allāh.
- 'Umar is the only author in the book to cite Valens (§§7.161, 10.13-14, and 10.30). This is probably not the historical Valens who wrote the *Anthology*, but may reflect methods by Persian writers on Valens, such as Buzurjmihr (6th Century), who had produced a well-known Pahlavi version of Valens, with commentary.
- It is now well known that traditional authors (especially up through the Perso-Arabic period) relied on the use of whole-sign angles from houses and Lots for delineating various topics, and even in profections and transits. In *Judges*, 'Umar also frequently includes the whole-sign angles from the lord of a place. A key text is §9.30, which in Hugo's translation is as follows: "And so, one must note that the types of pivots are two: for some pivots are of the signs, others are [pivots] of the stars. Whenever therefore any star would occupy the pivot of another star, it urges the effecting of the affair."

Although 'Umar's view is clearly inspired by traditional sources, I do not recall other authors taking this into account, at least not on a regular basis.
- One unusual feature of the 'Umar passages is his inclusion of the assembly, along with the square and opposition, as being difficult. I believe this is largely a mistake by Hugo, perhaps inspired by a combination of the use of whole-sign angles (see immediately above) and common statements by traditional astrologers about the malefics. Normally, there are two types of statements along these lines in traditional texts: namely, that (1) the square and opposition are difficult aspects in general, and that (2) the *assembly and* the square and opposition *of the malefics* are especially difficult. There is evidence in al-Rijāl that 'Umar himself did not include the assembly itself as bad, since his own versions of 'Umar do not usually mention it.[16] And so, Hugo might have creatively combined these ideas and changed the text, to yield the idea that assemblies themselves (regardless of the planet involved) were bad, just as the square and opposition are. The fact that this view only appears in the 'Umar material suggests to me that the reader should ignore this statement about the assembly being bad, where it occurs in Hugo's translation.
- Another strange feature of 'Umar's text is his use of Lots. For one thing, his Lots are often calculated differently than the same Lots in other authors: indeed, it is often impossible to find parallels elsewhere. I cannot explain this departure from other sources, although it is possible that 'Umar was drawing on other, unknown texts. In addition, the calculations are sometimes nonsensical or incomplete (see Appendix H). Although Hugo's translations are frequently substandard when it comes to instructions about Lots (among other things), the problem does not seem to lie with him: in at least one instance (§4.7), al-Rijāl's 'Umar gives the same unusual calculation. These considerations suggest that 'Umar's Lots really were highly divergent from the tradition, and should not be trusted or considered authoritative.
- Finally, a short passage in §7.73 draws a distinction between two common words, although I cannot be sure that this distinction is being made by Hugo or is in the 'Umar original: unfortunately, al-

---

[16] An exception would be al-Rijāl I.35, which corresponds to the end of §4.7 below.

Rijāl does not include it as something that can be cross-checked. The first word is *cadens*, which means "falling," and which we translate as "cadent." It refers to the twelfth, ninth, sixth, and third houses, because as the heavens turn clockwise these places are where planets "fall away" from the angle or pivot. For example, planets rise up and culminate in the tenth house, but then fall downwards as the heavens move them into the ninth house. The second word is *remotus*, which means "remote, removed." Hugo uses it for every author in the book, and it can also be found in authors such as Bonatti. Now, in §7.73, Hugo's 'Umar makes the following parenthetical statement: "but they are 'remote' [when] nearby before the pivot, 'cadent' after the pivot." I take this to mean that cadent planets are just those which I mentioned above: their position has moved beyond the angle, and is now "after" the angle, in a cadent house.[17] But "remote" planets are those which may still be in the angle (or perhaps even a succeedent house), but are remote or far away from it. 'Umar may mean the following: suppose the Midheaven is in the tenth sign, at 1° Cancer. In that case, a cadent planet would be in the ninth house, somewhere in Gemini, having already passed beyond or "after" the angle. But a remote planet might still be in Cancer, "before" or "in front of" the Midheaven, but far away from it, such as in 29° Cancer. Unfortunately, there are two problems with this distinction. In the first place, throughout the rest of the book Hugo uses "remote" to indicate what everyone else means by "cadent," so that this distinction is not observed (and so is not helpful) in the rest of the authors: we know this, because our other Latin translations of these authors show they are speaking simply of cadent places. In the second place, the distinction does not really tell us what the range of remoteness is. It is true that the farther away from an angle a planet is, the less "powerful" it is considered to be: but how far is too far? Does it include succeedent places? Does it go beyond that? For instance, suppose again that the Midheaven is at 1° Cancer, while the Ascendant is at 1° Libra. A planet in Virgo and the twelfth house would be very remote indeed from the Midheaven—but then it would also be cadent from the Ascendant,

---

[17] This might possibly include situations where the planet is still in the angular sign (or the same sign as the degree of the Midheaven), but has moved beyond the degree itself.

making the planet remote from the Midheaven degree but cadent from the Ascendant degree. Since both remoteness and cadency typically make a planet less powerful or stimulated, it is hard to see in every case what interpretive difference this could make. In questions involving the tenth house, it could make a difference that a remote planet is moving towards the Midheaven while a cadent one is already past it; but this cannot apply to every situation or as a general astrological principle. There may be value in it, but the reader should proceed with caution. It is probably best simply to think of both remote planets and cadent planets as simply being "cadent."

(3) Al-Kindī

The al-Kindī material in *Judges* is basically the majority of Hugo's translation of *The Forty Chapters* (which I published separately in English in 2011),[18] with only a few differences in words here and there. I have pasted my translation into the text with only minor changes, and have kept the paragraph numbering intact, so readers may be easily led to the appropriate places in *Forty Chapters*.

Readers who want a more in-depth introduction to al-Kindī should consult my own introduction to *Forty Chapters*, but here are a few key points. Al-Kindī was primarily a philosopher who worked with a circle of translators to expose the Arabic-speaking public to Greek and Persian thought. He wrote a number of works on astrology from an Aristotelian background (thus preferring naturalistic explanations for astrology), of which the best known is *Forty Chapters*. After a lengthy introduction to astrological principles and how to judge questions, al-Kindī focuses primarily on questions that involve the angles as significators (especially the seventh): partnerships, marriage, theft, fugitives, travel, war, land and buried treasure, and so on. He also includes mundane questions about weather and commodities. Al-Kindī seems to use Regiomontanus houses, and emphasizes the importance of a planet aspecting its own domicile, which sometimes sits uneasily with his house system: by whole signs, no planet besides the luminaries is ever totally in aversion from its domiciles, and al-Kindī repeatedly talks about using that one of a planet's domiciles which it aspects, or aspects best. But in a quadrant-derived house

---

[18] My translation of *Forty Chapters* is based on Hugo's Latin version, with reference to Robert of Ketton's translation and the parallel sections in al-Rijāl.

system like Regiomontanus, where a house is identified with the house cusp, a planet might not aspect any of its domiciles with a degree-based aspect. And so, in al-Kindī we see a tension between whole-sign concepts like being in aversion, and the use of quadrant-based houses.

(4) Jirjis and Aristotle

This final and minority group is the hardest to characterize. For one thing, their sections are not as numerous as the others (not to mention that their true names and complete works are currently unknown). For another, their sections are very short and only give us a taste of their thought. In some cases, their instructions seem to be more akin to short notes based on other works. It is uncommon to find any clear parallels between them and the authors above.

§2: The Latin prefaces to *Three Judges* and *Nine Judges*

It is well known that Hermann of Carinthia wrote an original philosophical work outlining a Neoplatonic and astrological worldview, his *On Essences*. But it is less well known that Hugo wrote a short outline justifying astrology using a similar Neoplatonic approach, both for *Three Judges* and *Nine Judges*. For one thing, *Three Judges* was a more obscure work; for another, manuscripts and printed editions of *Nine Judges* rarely included the lengthy introduction to astrology at all, much less Hugo's brief preface. In recent years, both prefaces have been translated by Charles Burnett (1977 and 2006, respectively), and I will summarize their contents here. They are very similar to attitudes found in Bonatti's *BOA* Tr. 1 and the first treatises of Abū Ma'shar's *Great Introduction*.

In the preface to *Three Judges*, Hugo reminds us that astronomy[19] is the highest of the disciplines in the traditional curriculum of the *quadrivium* (arithmetic, geometry, music, astronomy): by combining time, number, and shapes together, it is the most sophisticated of the disciplines. Moreover, it deals with the most elevated sensible objects (the planets and stars), which enjoy a more everlasting and constant existence than what exists on our earth. For traditionally, things which do not suffer change to their fundamen-

---

[19] For the most part, we should understand "astrology" here.

tal being (as do other things, such as when humans die, or one elemental object is transformed into something else) are more divine and knowable, because they have more consistent being. So astronomy (and astrological judgments drawn from it) deals with more divine objects and is a more sophisticated kind of knowledge.

However, Hugo points out that some people object to astronomy for flimsy and inconsistent reasons. For example, some say astronomy (by which they probably mean astrology) is incomprehensible. But then, why would Plato and Aristotle (whom these critics probably admire) think it was so important? Other people object to what they see as astrology's rejection of free will,[20] assuming that a "certain force of necessity" (that is, compulsion) or "restraint" or "control" is being substituted to explain human life instead. This is a common complaint even today, and I discuss it to some extent in several places in my *Traditional Astrology for Today* (2011).

But Hugo has two interesting responses. First, he points out that even such critics tend to believe in Divine Providence, which of course involves certain necessary and unalterable decrees. But these decrees do not simply manifest as external forces: they manifest in and through many of the choices and actions which we normally suppose belong only to us. In fact, this view is with us even today. People do not usually speak of "Providence" with any seriousness anymore, but will often speak with hand on heart about some form of historical spiritual "evolution," sometimes complete with various developmental schemata and philosophical categories to explain just how we will advance unalterably to some state of enlightenment—and nowadays, that enlightenment is assumed to be just around the corner. Or, people simply speak of the modern age itself as a proxy for Providence, and assume that because something happens later in time ("what is wrong with so-and-so, it's 2011 already!"), it must be better, more enlightened and advanced, and so on. These are just updated (though temporally more linear) versions of Providence, a divine plan which works in some necessary way through our actions and choices.

Second, Hugo draws on Plato's *Timaeus*, the Psalms, and other ideas, to propose a compromise solution between free-will extremism and absolute determinism.[21] (This kind of solution was common in the Middle Ages.) Alt-

---

[20] *Liberum arbitrium*. *Liberum* here means free (i.e., not externally coerced), while *arbitrium* has to do with individual caprice, whims, and desires.
[21] Hugo also enlists the help of other authorities, such as Apuleius, Jeremiah, Solomon, Job, David, Abraham, and Hippocrates.

hough it is true, Hugo says, that God has deputized the planets and stars to determine much of what happens in the world, He has reserved some things for Himself and others to other particular, created beings (by which Hugo must mean at least humans). And so, humans are indeed responsible for certain things not directly indicated or causally controlled by the stars—although it is unclear from this whether Hugo does believe in indeterminate free will, and to what extent.

Finally, Hugo cautions us about the scope of astrology and its relation to other occult practices. We should not associate astrology with lower magic of any kind, such as sorcery, haruspexy, casting lots, and various types of crude divination.[22] Rather, we must remember that astrology is a higher science which was used even by the prophets for determining Divine intent. On the other hand, we should not assume that we can know *everything* by astrology. For we have only fallible human intellects, which, even if highly trained in astrology, cannot grasp the fullness and completeness of the Divine Reason.[23]

Hugo expands a bit on these ideas in the "hidden" preface[24] to *Nine Judges*, and makes a connection to magic and talismans. The hidden preface relies on a number of authorities to lend support to its ideas (including Hermes,[25] Abidemon, Ptolemy, Trismegistus,[26] and Plato. (According to Burnett, the preface is Hugoan in style, but has similarities to Hermann's translation of Abū Ma'shar's *Great Introduction*, Hermann's own *On Essences*, and Hermann's preface to Ptolemy's *Planisphere*.) Hugo follows certain traditional views of the planets as being ensouled or animate, and distinguishes how their powers or forces affect mundane things. Although animate beings like humans do feel their effects, inanimate things are affected more swiftly (in accordance with things' ability to receive effects, and the kind of matter they have). The reason seems to be that inanimate things, being more passive, have less internal resistance to the formal effects of the stars: I imagine that Hugo would

---

[22] I am not sure how Hugo would explain the divinational aspects of horary.
[23] I have addressed this issue and made my own suggestions about a "determinism of types" in *Traditional Astrology for Today*.
[24] Equivalent to §A.126 in the complete version of *Judges*, omitted in the present edition. Burnett designated it as a "hidden" preface because it is wedged inconspicuously between the lengthy introduction to astrology, and Māshā'allāh's opening material on answering questions.
[25] Hugo relates Hermes to Persia and India.
[26] Hermann of Carinthia associated Trismegistus with the author of the Hermetic *Asclepius*.

explain astrological weather prediction and the consecration of properly-prepared talismans along these lines. But animate beings are driven in part by their own internal souls, which makes planetary effects unfold more over time and in more subtle ways.

It would be nice to know more about Hugo's views on talismans, because these views (as stated) do not make a lot of sense to me, particularly in the context of horary. For one thing, Hugo seems to take a causal view of astrology: this might be all right for certain approaches to nativities or weather prediction, but horary astrology is much more divinatory. Charts for questions certainly *describe* the situation, but it is hard to see exactly how they *cause* the situation to be as it is. For example, in questions about finding buried treasure (see §§4.15-18), a benefic planet in the seventh indicates that something is hidden in the place in question, but the benefic did not cause it to be there. So there is something missing about how a causal view of astrology fits in with the practice of questions. Secondly, since Hugo holds the well-pedigreed view that humans are microcosms of the macrocosmic structure, we would expect him rather to say both that humans are affected more deeply by planetary influences than inanimate things are, and that we feel them more immediately and in greater detail. Indeed, horary questions are supposed to describe situations in great detail, and often with respect to many events happening right now—but Hugo's stated views on the differences between inanimate and animate beings does not seem to reflect that. Of course, part of the problem here is that many of the traditional philosophers who opined about astrology, did not necessarily have horary astrology in mind: horary has a way of throwing a monkey wrench into simple (and especially causal) views of astrology.

§3: An introduction to questions

In this section I will provide an introduction to questions, which is often called "horary" astrology. The word horary simply means "pertaining to the hour," indicating that a client's questions derive from current problems of the moment.[27] There are a number of good introductions to questions available in English, most notably Treatises 5 and 6 of Bonatti's *BOA*, as well as William Lilly's *CA*. There are also several contemporary courses one may take. Here, I will draw on my own translations and my study under Deb Houlding and Sue Ward, to paint a picture of how to approach questions—particularly from the Perso-Arabic perspective of *Search* and *Judges*. Although I believe my summary is relatively complete, at least for beginners, the student should also read thoroughly and understand the following texts from the traditional astrologers:

- The introduction to *Search*, on victors and thought-interpretation.
- All of *Judges* §A.
- Sahl's own introduction and chart example, in *Judges* §1.1.
- Māshā'allāh's significator selection rules from *OR*, in Appendix C.
- *ITA* III, on planetary configurations.
- Sahl's *Fifty Judgments*, in Appendix A.
- Bonatti's opening material on questions, in Appendix B.
- Al-Rijāl's aphorisms on questions, in Appendix D.
- *Judges* §Z.1, on problematic configurations.
- If possible, Bonatti's *146 Considerations* (*BOA* Tr. 5).

(1) The thought and initial consultation

As I argued in my introduction to *Search*, the astrologer's first step in a live consultation was to cast a chart for that consultation, and find the significator of thought. In most cases this involved finding a victor of some sort, but *Search* describes other methods as well. I have found the twelfth-part method

---

[27] Sometimes there is overlap between questions that can be answered through a nativity or solar revolution (or other natal techniques), such as questions about life as a whole, or what the coming year will be like, or even what certain areas of life will be like in the next year. But here we will assume the formal horary questions such as are found in *Judges*, like the location of stolen goods, or whether a house will sell, how long a king will reign, and so on.

attributed to the Indians in *Search* I.9.3 to be helpful. The purpose of the significator of thought was to identify the core issue at hand, or even to guide the astrologer's attention to one area of the chart for the subsequent interpretation. In al-Rijāl I.24 for example, the significator of thought first identified a house, and through a discussion with the client, a specific question was decided upon. (I believe 'Umar's methods for finding this significator can be found in *Judges* §A.129.) Over time, the use of these significators as a separate step was omitted altogether. Or, since the lord of the Ascendant and other planets are supposed to describe the situation accurately anyway, astrologers relied on the lord of the Ascendant and other key planets to play this role instead. I include it here because it was part of the original Perso-Arabic approach to questions.

(2) The question

This is a complicated matter, and I have tried to put the material in some kind of reasonable order, but it really boils down to a few points: identify a problem, commit to the solution, understand the procedures, and interpret the chart.

Identify the problem. Many texts on questions (traditional and modern) warn the astrologer of two kinds of questions: superficial questions, and those posed by tricksters and skeptics. To my mind, Deb Houlding distills this nicely by saying that the question has got to involve an actual *problem* requiring counsel. So, idle questions about possible future love, or a lost object that one does not really miss, or situations whose outcome is virtually known and accepted, tend to be ruled out. This also will tend to rule out skeptics, provided that we remember two things: first, that a trickster or skeptic will not often know how to pose an actual problem because there is none there to begin with;[28] second, that the chart must accurately describe the situation.[29] Without a real problem, the chart is more likely to be indeterminate and should be avoided.

This emphasis on problems also touches on another warning: that the astrologer should not ask his or her own question, but rather consult someone

---

[28] See §A.127, and *OHT* §2 (in *Search* Appendix C).
[29] For example, the separations and applications of the planets (and especially the Moon), and the placements of the planets generally, should describe the situation.

else.[30] To my mind there are two sides to this issue. On the one hand, there is the issue of subjectivity and the astrologer's own emotions perverting the judgment. On the other hand, an astrologer may be especially tempted to cast a chart for small and superficial matters simply because he or she can do it quickly and easily. I believe astrologers can ask their own questions, provided that they do three things: slow down and consider whether they actually have a problem that needs counsel; mentally rehearse how they would actually answer the question astrologically; and become emotionally prepared for the answer they *don't* want. For some questions these steps are not that important (such as the location of a lost object), but for others they are. In the end, the astrologer might decide it is best to ask someone not emotionally involved.

These warnings also hold good for another common problem, especially for beginners: the tendency to be too eager to answer questions—especially, soliciting questions from friends and family, either out of excitement or a desire to prove oneself. I can confirm from experience a statement made by Deb Houlding: that beginners often have very ambiguous charts, including the presence of many "considerations before judgment," factors that alert the astrologer to difficulties in the chart. For example, if the degree of the Ascendant is in the first few degrees of its sign, it can indicate that the question or situation is premature, or that the client is not prepared for the answer, or hasn't thought it out. An Ascendant in the last few degrees can indicate a situation which cannot be changed, or a result that is already known but not accepted yet. It is better to decline a question or put it off, than to commit too hastily to a question that is not really a problem needing counsel, or to interpret a chart that is wholly vague.

Commit to the question and cast the chart. If the question presents a problem which you actually want to answer, then commit to the question and cast the chart for the time you make that commitment. Cast the chart for the location of the astrologer. I have found this advice about commitment helpful, because most texts say to cast the chart at the time of the question—but what counts as that time? This can cause a lot of anxiety for the astrologer, especially in the age of the internet: should it be for the time the client wrote the question and sent it to you by e-mail, even if it was yesterday? Or when you decide to open it? What if you accidentally open an e-mail and glance at the

---

[30] *OR* Ch. 2 (in Appendix C below), echoed by Bonatti in Tr. 6 Part 2, Ch. 4 (Appendix B below).

question, but were not planning on taking questions that day—should it be for that accidental time? To my mind it makes more sense to cast it for the time when you commit to the question and sit down to answer it.

As part of this commitment, one must also review the rules that are involved in answering a specific question. In part this means reviewing the particular sections devoted to that question, and I have inserted tables at the beginning of each major house section listing the sections that address each type of question. Remember that the authors do not order their paragraphs in the same way, so one must read everything thoroughly and not simply pick out a paragraph based on its section title, and then immediately look at the chart. Understand what the author's approach is, and *why* he is telling you to look at something.

In addition, keep in mind that traditional texts describe ideal and often extreme conditions.[31] Normally, a traditional text will describe the best and strongest types of "perfection" (that is, conditions which complete and bring about a positive and easy result), the worst situations, and then something in the middle. Sometimes a chart will exhibit, almost point-by-point, the conditions set out by the rules. But at other times, you must use your knowledge of astrological principles and your own ingenuity to figure out the answer. An unusual chart might describe unusual circumstances, but that is where communication with the client and your own experience and knowledge come into play.

Assign significators. The next step is to assign and analyze the significators, and there are two general terms for these. The first is "querent," which in Latin (*quaerens*) means "the one who is seeking." This refers to the client or the person on whose behalf the questioner is asking. The second is "quaesited," which in Latin (*quaesitus*) means "the thing that is sought." Normally, the Ascendant is given to the client/querent, because he or she is initiating the matter at hand (but in some questions the querent or person under consideration is given a different house). This person is sometimes called "the owner of the question." But the quaesited, or the quaesited matter, is meant more broadly, and its house is considered the "house of the question." For example, if one is seeking a lost object, then the house desig-

---

[31] Here I should insert one hint about Hugo's style: oftentimes, when Hugo lists various planets to look at, he introduces the last one with the term "or rather" (*potius*): for example, "if the lord of the Ascendant or rather the Moon...". This does not actually express a preference for the Moon, but is simply his idiosyncratic way of introducing the last choice in a list of options.

nating the object (such as the second, for possessions) is the same as the thing sought. But in other matters, the quaesited is a house indicating another person involved. For example, in sales and purchases of land, what we ultimately seek is the land, the fourth house. But the question more immediately concerns the business deal itself and the person we are doing business with: thus the seventh (other people, a partner in some affair) would count as the house of the quaesited. Different questions will identify different houses and significators. (One must also note planets in the key houses, as they will help characterize the situation and may help in perfecting matters.)

Now, it is clear from both from §§A.129-30 and *OR* (see Appendix C) that choosing the significator of the querent (and sometimes the quaesited) was not always a straightforward matter. In later horary practice, the lord of the Ascendant was always the significator. But in earlier practice, one had to note whether the lord of the Ascendant actually aspected the rising sign with a whole-sign aspect. If it did not—that is, if it was in aversion to the rising sign—one had to see whether it applied to a planet which *did* aspect the rising sign: this is a version of "reflecting" light (see below). If all else failed, one then had to consider the Moon. I myself am undecided about this approach. The motivation here was to find the planet (either the lord of the Ascendant or the Moon) that had more obvious, direct control over the Ascendant. And this is in accordance with normal astrological principles: a planet in aversion to its own sign will often be more unreliable and intermittent in its management of that sign. But such a planet is also making a statement all by itself: namely, it says something about the person represented by the Ascendant, and his or her role in the situation. So this attempt to find the "better" planet may circumvent other important information that affects the interpretation. On the other hand, one might look at it like this: if the lord of the Ascendant is in aversion to the rising sign, and no other planet reflects light to the rising sign, it means that (a) there is something uncertain about the querent's control, and (b) that the Moon should be examined as a next-best alternative to effecting the matter. In other words, we can take the information about aversion into account while still hoping to find "perfection" by other means using the "better" planet (see below).

This brings us to the Moon. The Moon acts as a general significator of the question, its nature and its flow of events, because she is a general communicator of influences and significations for all of the planets. When the house of the querent and that of the quaesited are ruled by the same planet, she can also be of special help in indicating the course of things. Generally speaking, her separations show things which have happened, and her applications show things which are about to happen.[32] The reader will notice that in the introductory material by Sahl and others, she is combined with the other significators in a way that makes her seem integral to perfection: for example, an author might say that both the Moon and the lord of the Ascendant must apply to the lord of the quaesited. This is not strictly speaking true: in accordance with how traditional texts are written, this is an idealized, best-case scenario. Finally, I would also note that in some of the texts of *Judges*, instructions sometimes refer to "the significator, that is, the Moon." In such cases we are not talking about the significator of thought or the victor of the chart, but the Moon. This does not seem to be a mistake by Hugo, as it sometimes appears in al-Rijāl.

When assigning house significations, avoid "turning" the chart or using derived houses too much. For example, it is true that the eleventh is the second from the tenth, and so shows an authority figure's money or allies. But traditional texts are clear that the normal house meanings are still primary and should not be overcomplicated by obsessive chart turning. The eighth from the tenth may show the death of a king, but the eighth house itself also indicates death. If the querent asks about the lost dog of the aunt of a friend, do not look at the sixth from the third from the fourth from the eleventh (that is, the dog of the sister of the parent of the friend): just look at the sixth itself. In fact, if the lost dog is not the querent's problem anyway and she is asking without the aunt's knowledge, it might be best not to take the question. Keep things as simple and direct as possible, remembering your astrological principles and definitions, and do not get involved in every possible question.

Examine other notable planets. After selecting the significators, we should also identify notable planets in the chart. First among these are angular planets, especially those within a few degrees of the axes (the Ascendant-Descendant, and the Midheaven-IC). In accordance with general astrological principles, angular planets show something immediately present and vivid which must be looked at, while cadent planets show things less available or vivid, less lasting, and so on. Therefore, angular planets show known and present influences on the situation, and the particular angle involved may also show *why* that planet is important. But as the introductory sections point out, cadent

---

[32] See Judgments 7 and 8 in Appendix A.

planets are sometimes very relevant if the question involves something like escape or travel—a particular signification of cadent places.

Another indication which may be helpful is a planet or cusp which is very close to something in the querent's nativity. This can help the astrologer see that the question is well rooted in the client's life and concerns, and may also identify what natal area of life is being brought into play by the questions. Topics indicated by other notable planets in the chart of the question, may connect the situation of the question to something else that is not obvious but still relevant.

Tell the story. Next, an examination of the planets and the conversation with the client should allow us to tell a little story about what is going on. The chart must accurately and clearly describe the situation, the known flow of events, and the people involved: if it does not, or if key planets contradict the situation as it is currently known, something is wrong with the conception of the question and one's initial view of the chart. Likewise, if the chart does not already reflect the situation, avoid the temptation to hunt down every obscure technique in an attempt to shed light on it. I can speak from experience here: many years ago, when I either saw an answer I didn't want, or was asking a redundant question I pretty much already knew the answer to, or saw a very ambiguous chart, I would start calculating all sorts of Lots (some of my own invention), look at antiscia and contrantiscia, and so on, in order to solve the problem. What was really wrong was my question or the approach to it.

Look for perfection. The next step is to look for what is called "perfection," and that is the immediate goal of most of the rules you will find in this book. In Latin, to "perfect" (*perficio*) means to do or carry something out thoroughly; it is very close in meaning to "completing" or "fulfilling" something (*compleo*). Much of horary practice comes down to the basic question of who or what is getting planets' light, and so in practice, perfection refers to aspects which planets complete by exact degree. If they are able to perfect their assembly or aspect, then what they indicate (and what the client wants) will come to be. There are four basic ways by which planets perfect their signification:

- *Direct connection* (*ITA* III.7). This is an application by assembly or aspect, in which two significant planets connect by degree without anything hindering them. For example, if Mercury is at 10° Leo, and applies by trine to Mars at 20° Leo, with nothing like retrogradation or another planet hindering them before they complete the aspect by degree.

- *Transfer of light* (*ITA* III.11). In this case, the two planets are configured by whole sign, but not in a position to perfect their aspect directly; however, a third planet is separating from the early one and applying to the later one, transferring the light of one to the other through its own body.[33] For example, suppose Mercury applied to Mars by a trine, and for some reason could not perfect the aspect: if the Moon were separating from an assembly or aspect with Mercury, and could herself complete an assembly or aspect with Mars, she would perfect their trine through a transfer of their light. Symbolically, this shows a third party or factor which helps the matter come to be.
- *Collection of light* (*ITA* III.12). Here, two planets configured by sign but unable to complete their assembly or aspect, both apply to some slower planet. This planet "collects" their light and again acts as some third party or factor assisting them. For example, if the Sun applies to Jupiter, but before they perfect their aspect, each applies to Saturn.
- *Location.* This is a next-best scenario. 'Umar (§A.130) describes it as a significator applying to a planet in the house of the question, provided that the planet also has an important connection to the house: this probably means that it has a rulership there, or has a natural signification there (such as Jupiter in the second house). Bonatti describes it in much the same way, and also allows the lord of the quaesited to be in or aspecting the house of the querent or subject of the question: for example, if the question were about a sister's money, and the lord of her derived house of money (the fourth house) were in the third.[34]

---

[33] But in some cases, the middle planet is slower than the fastest planet: see the example in *ITA* III.11.

[34] Bonatti also allows another possibility: if a well-disposed and strong benefic (or a malefic with reception) has some rulership in the Ascendant, and is joined either to the Moon or to the significator of the querent, with reception. To my mind this sounds more like a "general good luck" indication which helps bring things about.

Now, I have presented these four according to the later medieval understanding of them, especially that of the 9th Century astrologer Abū Ma'shar. If you read §A, you will encounter variations which can be a little confusing because there was a change in vocabulary and understanding. What Māshā'allāh and 'Umar call a transfer and collection, is something which Abū Ma'shar calls:

- *Reflection of light* (*ITA* III.13). In this case, the two key planets cannot perfect an assembly or aspect because they *are not* configured by sign at all: that is, they are in aversion to each other and so have no explicit relationship. However, some planet which aspects each of them by sign, transfers or collects their light and perfects the aspect by degree. In other words, Abū Ma'shar's "reflection" is really just a transfer or collection of light *from aversion*, and the reflecting planet and its sign act as a mirror, so that each key planet indirectly "sees" or aspects the other through that reflecting planet. For example, suppose that the Moon is at 23° Gemini, but Mars is at 29° Capricorn: Gemini and Capricorn are in aversion to each other, and so the Moon and Mars are in no position to perfect any aspect. But suppose that Mercury is at 26° Virgo, being applied to by the Moon and applying to a trine with Mars: Mercury "reflects" the light from the Moon and bounces it towards Mars. This is essentially a transfer of light from aversion. A reflection that involves a collection of light is very similar, but contains adds an extra detail: the collecting planet then bounces their light to the other signs which it aspects. In this case, the implication seems to be that the success of the reflection depends on the collecting planet being able to aspect either the rising sign (the querent) or the sign of the question (the quaesited), as Māshā'allāh suggests in §A.132. Reflection seems to be a next-best version of perfection, perhaps with uncertain results. Or, the fact that the key planets are in aversion, suggests that the parties involved have little contact, or have some basic disconnection in their interests, but the situation can still be salvaged with work and with the help of other influences.

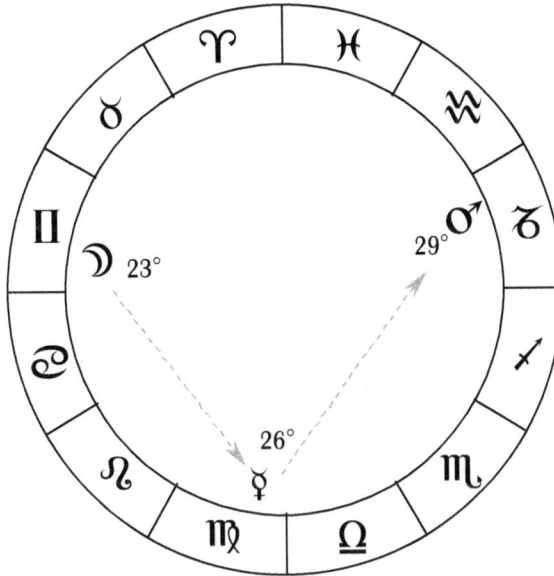

Figure 1: Mercury reflecting light by transfer (*ITA* III.13.2)

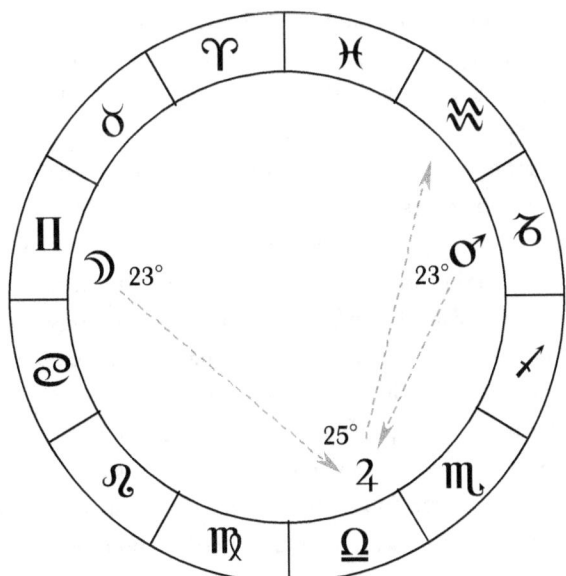

Figure 2: Jupiter reflecting light by collection (*ITA* III.13.1)

If we remember our basic astrological principles, then even if there is perfection of some sort, the kind of aspect involved (as well as the kind of signs involved) will also provide other information. Bonatti (Appendix B) is especially good at describing the differences between, say, perfection by trine versus perfection by opposition. Many of the source texts in *Judges* also rehearse these differences in the context of particular questions.

In all of these cases, the texts emphasize that the planet which finally gets or receives the light, is the one with the responsibility for the matter, because it is as though everything is "pushed" into its hands. That is to say, the applying planet "pushes" its influence towards, and confers it upon, the planet being applied to, which then "receives" or "gathers" that influence unto itself. In a sense, this receiving planet has the upper hand or is more momentous. For example, if the question is about a love interest and the querent's planet is the lighter, pushing planet, then the querent is more eager and making advances, while the receiving or gathering planet (representing the love interest) has the upper hand because it is waiting for the querent's planet to come to it. (Obviously, this is a common situation in romantic contexts.) In that case, it is also important to note what kind of condition the planets are in, and even what kind of signs are involved. For example, if the receiving or gathering planet is in its detriment, then perhaps a situation which seems at first to go well, then begins to fail and fall apart. Or if the applying, pushing planet is in the fall of the receiving, gathering planet, then the receiving, gathering planet might not be as willing to accept this influence from the sign which represents its downfall. For example, Cancer is the fall of Mars: if, then, Mercury in Cancer applies to Mars, the person represented by Mars might be reluctant or unwilling or fearful to accept this advance from Mercury. Sahl[35] calls this kind of situation "not-reception," because it is as though Mars does not want to receive or gather influence from anything coming out of Cancer. Al-Kindī[36] describes similar variations.

Above I mentioned that perfection takes place when nothing hinders the key planets from perfecting their connection. Because the planets change direction, move into different signs, or encounter other planets along the way, there are a number of ways in which a connection may be hindered. In *ITA* III, Abū Ma'shar and al-Qabīsī describe all variations on these, each

---

[35] *Introduct.* §5.9.
[36] *Forty Chapters* Ch. 2.1.8.

with its own meaningful and picturesque name. Below is a table from Appendix B of *ITA*, which organizes all of these together:

	Blocking/failure	*Direct/retrograde*	*Same/next sign*
Barring:	Blocking	Direct	Same
Obstruction:	Blocking	Retrograde	Same
Cutting #1:	Blocking	Retrograde	Next
Escape:	Failure	Direct	Next
Revoking:	Failure	Retrograde	Same
Cutting #2	Failure	Direct	Same

Figure 3: Table of prevented connections (from *ITA* Appendix B)

All of these should be studied in *ITA* individually. But let's take obstruction as an example, which has the following features: blocking from another planet, through retrogradation, in the same sign. Suppose that Mercury is assembled with Mars in the same sign, and is applying to Mars. But Venus, who is later in the sign, turns retrograde, connects with Mars first, and then continues on, while retrograde, to connect with Mercury. In that case, Venus represents some sudden obstruction which interferes and prevents the desired assembly between Mercury and Mars.

Give counsel. Finally, an examination of the chart, and a conversation with the client, should produce *counsel*. Remember that the client or querent is a *quaerens*, "one who is seeking," and we rarely seek just a flat, yes-or-no answer to our questions. We want context and advice, and the planets can help provide that. In fact, Hugo himself suggests this in his translation: instead of simply saying, "look at the lord of the Ascendant and the Moon," he frequently says something like "the lord of the east and the Moon *give counsel* for a question about *x*." In practice, this involves describing opportunities and pitfalls for a situation, which can help the client figure out what he or she is willing to undertake or avoid. Again, I emphasize that this should take place in the context of a dialogue between the astrologer and client: sometimes, describing the situation will bring other possibilities and details to light. For example, I once had a client who was trying to decide whether or not to move out of state, due to some problems where he was living at the time. The focus of the reading was on the current problems to see how bad they really were, but I noticed that the lord of the Ascendant was also applying to the lord of the third, not a planet which seemed to fit into the story. When we talked about the third as indicating siblings or people who were like siblings (that is, very close friends),[37] the client remembered that some of his closest friends lived in the city he was considering moving to. The idea of forming a closer connection with them had been an attractive benefit to moving, but he had not thought to mention it when posing the question. This planetary indication helped him evaluate the benefits of such a connection, and helped him make a decision.

(3) Special considerations

Following are some special features of question charts which can be very valuable in evaluating them:

- *Changing signs.* It is useful to see whether a key planet, or even the Ascendant or Midheaven, is about to change signs. This is especially relevant in cases such as the Moon being in an empty or void course (*ITA* III.9) or in certain hindrances such as "escape" (*ITA* III.22). Moving into a new sign suggests new or changing circumstances—either circumstances which happen on their own, or a change in life circumstances which the client may make. This can be even more important if there is a notable change in dignity in the next sign: for example, a planet moving into the sign of its fall.
- *Dignities.* Planetary dignities are always important, and in both *ITA* I.8 and *TAFT* Ch. 8 I provide guidelines on what different dignities (or a lack of dignity) mean. Planetary dignity in questions and nativities seem to differ in the following way: in questions, they are more concretely vivid and literal, whereas in nativities they are more functional and general. The reason for the difference seems to be this. In nativities, the planets indicate broad classes of material which are relevant across the whole life, although they may only be relevant at certain times or undergo annual modifications (through profections, solar revolutions, and so on). But in questions, we are often dealing with the most concrete situations and known individuals, so the indications are going to be more literal and immediate. For example,

---

[37] Traditionally, the third does also indicate friends, and al-Kindī (*Forty Chapters*) in particular talks about houses indicating people who are "like" that house. For example, the fourth is not only fathers and parents, but people who play those roles in the client's life.

in a nativity, Mars in detriment may indicate a person from time to time, but will more often characterize periods of life or general qualities of an area of life. In a question about a theft however, Mars in detriment may be said to indicate "a criminal" or other wicked person, with very specific types of behavior and traits. Even so, remember that a planet in dignity or in a counter-dignity like detriment does not always imply a moral quality, but often denotes confidence and skills (or a lack thereof). This can be combined with angularity to describe a situation or person further. For example, a planet in a dignity but in a cadent place, suggests a person of worth or confidence, who has little opportunity to exercise those skills; a planet in a counter-dignity but in an angular place, might show someone without skill or confidence, but who is prominent and successful anyway.

- *Orbs and moieties.* Traditional texts do sometimes talk about the "orbs" of aspects: that is, when the aspect "officially" becomes active.[38] And they agree that an aspect that is closer by degree is more intense and engaged than merely an aspect by sign. But my own view is that for the most part, orbs of aspect should not be paid attention to, certainly not in any obsessive way. It is better to treat aspects by degree as simply showing levels of intensity and engagement. For one thing, the importance of telling the story, and watching for perfection or hindrances, basically makes orbs less relevant: if two planets are "within orbs" of each other, but some other planet bars or obstructs or otherwise hinders them (see above), then their being within orbs does not really help us in the end. I would recommend the following three principles, based on Sahl and 'Umar and others: (a) do not use out-of-sign aspects, since the concept of aversion rules these out; (b) possibly consider out-of-sign bodily conjunctions, but even then they are subject to principles of perfection and hindrance; and (c) being under the Sun's rays or being scorched (combust) takes place at the usual degree-intervals,[39] *without regard* to sign boundaries. This is because these re-

---

[38] See *ITA* III.5 for the general "orb" of an assembly in the same sign; the standard, Persian-derived planetary orbs for assemblies and aspects are listed below.

[39] Normally, being under the rays takes place at an interval of 15° and less from the Sun, and being scorched (combust) at 7.5° and less. I say "normally," because different planets have different levels of brightness: at some geographical or ecliptical latitudes, a planet

lations to the Sun are a matter of visibility, not aspects. Thus, being within 15° of the Sun but in an adjacent sign, still counts as being under the rays.

♄	9°
♃	9°
♂	8°
☉	15°
♀	7°
☿	7°
☽	12°

Figure 4: Size of planetary bodies/orbs, in front and behind

- *Considerations before judgment*. In later traditional astrology and especially in contemporary handbooks on questions, one sometimes comes across "considerations before judgment," which unfortunately are occasionally rendered as "strictures *against* judgment." These represent special warnings or alerts to the astrologer about the chart or situation. Now, famous astrologers like William Lilly listed various considerations (such as Saturn in the seventh, the Moon in the scorched path or *via combusta*), but then seemed to ignore them in practice: this has led some contemporary writers to believe that the considerations basically provided astrologers easy excuses to decline a consultation. It is true that some considerations might make one hesitate to get involved, but I cannot agree that they were excuses or tricks. Bonatti, for example, is too serious about his theological understanding of questions,[40] to take that route. The considerations are meant to help tell the story and impel the astrologer to dig deeper into the matter, not simply to prevent an answer. To my mind, the considerations may be understood in two ways.
    - (a) First, as a warning about the client's motives, and whether the chart is properly "rooted" in a clear or meaningful intention. Māshā'allāh and 'Umar (§§A.127-28) suggest that since the chart reflects the situation, and a

---

might actually become invisible or visible at greater or lesser distance than at other latitudes. But astrologers tend to stick to these standardized distances of 15° and 7.5°.
[40] See Bonatti's *146 Considerations* (*BOA* Tr. 5), Considerations 1-2.

mere trickster or skeptic "would not even know how to form a question," the chart may reveal that deception. In Appendix B, Bonatti provides some examples which purport to show whether the client asks from a solid and true intention. If one wanted to be strict about using the considerations for this purpose, one should use Bonatti's suggestions, as well as looking for connections between the chart of the question and the nativity of the querent or even the astrologer. Perhaps the use of the significator of thought would be helpful here, too: if the significator of thought sheds no light on the question, perhaps there is something wrong.

o (b) Second, alerts about special objective features of the question, including the client's (or perhaps the astrologer's) epistemological situation. This would include the early and late Ascendants mentioned above.

- *Reception*, especially "pushing nature" and mutual reception. Above, I mentioned a very general use of the term "reception," to mean the gathering, getting, or receiving of an aspect from an applying planet that is pushing it. A more narrow and important sense of reception is known as "pushing nature" (*ITA* III.15), although there are a few rarer senses as well (*ITA* III.25).

    o In pushing nature, the applying planet is in the domicile, exaltation, or perhaps even two of the lesser dignities of the other planet to which it applies: for example, the Moon in Aries, applying to Mars. Already, the Moon and Mars are actively engaged by the aspect, which is what we want; but pushing nature adds the special element of the guest-host relationship that is involved in rulership. The Moon in Aries is in the house or domicile of Mars, and so he is actively engaged (aspect) as her host and provider (rulership). Because a general sense of "rules of hospitality" is involved, pushing nature or classical reception typically implies a greater willingness to cooperate, along with a sense of safety and moderation in the events and their effect. In this example, Mars is getting light pushed to him from a house which he rules and is congenial with, and so he is more disposed to accept it with open arms. (But this is not always the case: in questions of illness and death, Māshā'allāh [in *OR*] warns that if the lord of the Ascendant receives the lord of the eighth house, this increases the likelihood of fatality. The idea seems to be that guests get much leeway to do what they want, and so when the lord of death is your guest, he will create trouble.) Reception can also make more difficult aspects easier to work with, as Bonatti explains in Appendix B.

- o One version of classical reception or pushing nature, is mutual reception: when each of the planets involved in the application are in the domicile or exaltation of the other. This is normally understood as intensifying the sense of cooperation and congeniality. But Deb Houlding warns that this is not universally the case: if Mars and Venus mutually receive each other, then while Mars is obliged to be more congenial to Venus's interests, she in turn must be more congenial to his. That is, the sense of obligation tends to even out, and a planet like Mars might still create some problems.
- *Timing.* Finally, there are some relatively standardized approaches to timing in texts on questions. Key sections in *Judges* include §§A.133, 1.2-3, and 4.22. One should also consult my introduction to *WSM* for methods used by Sahl and Māshā'allāh in particular. These can be divided into two groups:
    - o *Symbolic times.* Here, the distance in degrees between two planets' exact assembly or aspect is converted into units of time. Depending on what is actually possible given the type of question, fixed signs show the longest units of time before something comes to be (such as years), movable signs are the quickest (such as days), and common signs in the middle (such as weeks or months). Likewise, because the angles or pivots tend to indicate things present or ready-to-hand, they tend to indicate the fastest times; cadent places are slowest, and succeedent places in the middle. If we combine these with the planet's actual motion relative to its average, this should help us identify the time units more

accurately: for example, a fast-moving planet in an angle and a movable sign, will tend to favor very short time units. A slow-moving planet in a fixed sign and cadent place may indicate the longest ones.

o *Real-time motions.* In these cases, we watch for the actual transits of key planets as they connect with each other or transit important cusps (such as the real-time perfection of an aspect, or the Moon's transit to the Ascendant of the question), or even make their phases and stations (such as turning direct, or emerging from the Sun's rays). Many of these are described in Sahl's *On Times*, found in *WSM* and *Search* II.5.

Example chart:

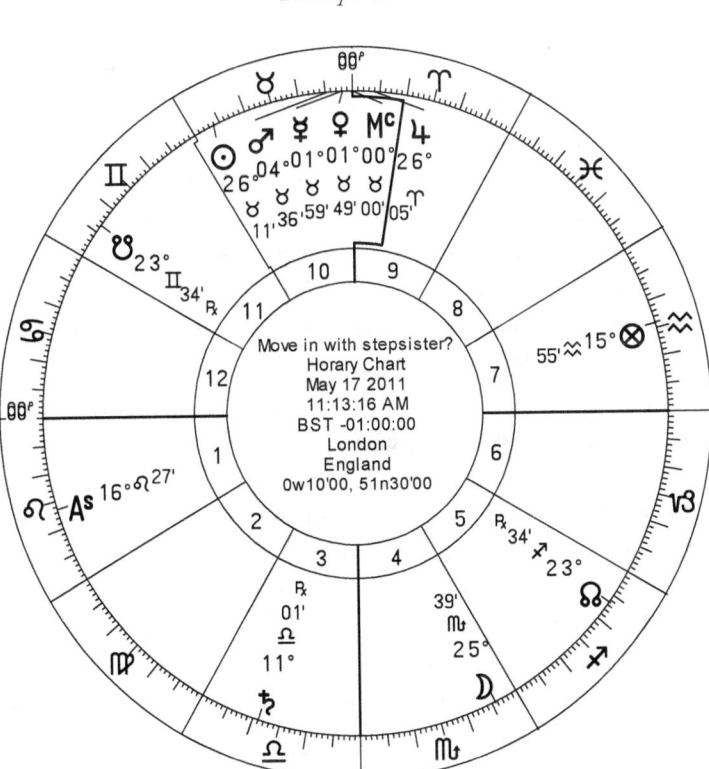

Figure 5: Should I move in with my stepsister?

In this example, the astrologer asked his own question, but only after careful consideration and rehearsing the kinds of problems and opportunities that the answer might provide. He wanted to know whether it was a good idea to move in with his stepsister. At the time, she was estranged from her husband, and their three boys were about to move into a new house with her. The husband did not want to separate, but for the moment had agreed to move into an apartment. Since the querent was self-employed and wanted to spend more time with his nephews anyway, she suggested that he could live rent-free in the basement, in exchange for performing child-care duties. This would have in turn relieved her of the many hassles and costs involved with babysitters. Already, the querent could think of reasons why this could be a bad idea, but he was attracted by the idea of not having to pay rent as well as being more involved in the children's lives.

The chart is cast in whole-sign houses, since that is what the astrologer uses in practice. The Ascendant of the chart represents the querent, and is only a couple of degrees from his natal Midheaven. The third and its lord Venus represent the stepsister, because for all intents and purposes she is a sister and kin, and he thinks of her as such. An exalted Saturn is in her house, and because Saturn was the astrologer's profected lord of the year, this also suggested that the question was well-rooted and the intention was clear.

In fact, this Saturn was the astrologer's first warning sign, because in his own natal profection and solar revolution for that year, Saturn indicated family disruptions and isolation. He was already worried that this new location in a distant suburb would make him feel isolated from his usual routine and friends, since he would have to rely on difficult public transportation. Exalted planets can show great confidence, but also pride and heavy authority: since Saturn characterizes the sister, it suggested another point: that the querent would be basically powerless. Without a formal rental agreement, he would have little to stand on if the situation changed.

Looking at the angles, we see that the Midheaven of the chart has Venus on it, and she rules the stepsister: so she is an especially notable planet. She is in her own domicile, which symbolizes the sister being strong in her own house. But the Sun is also in Taurus: as the lord of the Ascendant, it shows the querent in her house, just as in the hypothetical situation being asked about.

The Moon is also notable not only in her own right, but because she is in an angle of the chart that is also important: namely, the fourth, the actual domestic and living situation. She is in her fall in Scorpio, a wet sign that signifies putrefaction. The querent had not seen the house yet, but had been told it was a single dark room with almost no natural light, and it had a moisture (and possibly odor) problem. This Moon in fall well signifies a damp, obscure, and unpleasant room.

Now let's look at the primary significators themselves. The Sun and Venus are assembled in the same house. Venus is dignified, while the Sun is peregrine, and is also about to change signs within a few degrees: this suggests a change in situation, which is most likely the querent moving out of the house shortly after moving in. We want to see a harmonious connection between the two significators, but they cannot complete their assembly by degree. In fact, the next planet Venus connects to is Mars: what is he doing in the chart? Well, in the first place he is in detriment, which is not a good indicator for a pleasant, harmonious situation. In questions we want to be as concrete as possible, so does he indicate any particular person? He already rules the fourth house, and this is not very promising: the Moon is in fall in the fourth, and he is in detriment. This looks like either a family disruption or emphasizes the quality of the living situation, as I mentioned above. Mars also rules Aries, which in this chart is the seventh from the third: the stepsister's husband. The querent already knew that the husband was reluctant to separate, and he did not relish being put into the position of helping to raise the children of another, reluctant man. So the Mars in detriment also indicates the unhappy husband, to which Venus connects while the Sun leaves the sign.

Is there any redeeming feature of this chart? The Moon applies to the Sun and receives him by exaltation. But this does not really help. It suggests being received into a situation which he does not really want. The Moon and Mars have a mixed reception by sign (though not by application), but neither one on its own provides good indications. Together, they suggest an unhappy husband cooperating in a situation with unpleasant surroundings.

Although the question did not ask about a timeline, the querent knew that the stepsister wanted an answer within a few weeks, around the time she actually moved into the house. The Sun is leaving his sign within about 4°, and about four weeks later the querent saw the house and knew right away he was going to decline the offer. As it happened, the stepsister and her husband reconciled temporarily, he moved in, and then she kicked him out again. A few months after that, there was a family controversy that led to the stepsister being completely estranged from the querent's parents. The querent felt he had dodged a bullet, because he could only imagine the difficulty of living in the basement of a relative who was not speaking to his parents. He knew that the situation might have been intolerable, and that he might have had to move out only months after moving in.

I hope you can see that this judgment includes many of the helpful conceptual tools I have reviewed in this introduction to questions. Not every chart will be this notable and striking, but if we stick to our principles, we can draw out a lot of detail even in more ambiguous charts.

§A: INTRODUCTORY MATTERS

Comment by Dykes. As I pointed out in my introduction, the first portion of *Judges* was originally a lengthy introduction to astrology generally and especially to questions. Most manuscripts and printed editions (including this one) begin with §A.127, the introduction to questions. In the table below, I group all of the initial sections from §A as it was originally written, with equivalent readings from other translations of mine (where possible). After the table, the introduction to questions begins.

§A	Subject	Equivalent
1	Great circles	*Forty Chapters* §1
2-4	Classifications of the signs	*Forty Chapters* §§2-12; *Introduct.* §1; *ITA* I.9.1-I.10.
5-8	Faces and bounds	*Forty Chapters* §§24-28, 42-43; *ITA* I.5, VII.4.
9-10	Planetary hours	*Forty Chapters* §§29-31; *ITA* V.13.
11	Quarters of the circle	*Forty Chapters* §32; *ITA* I.11.
12	Masculine & feminine hours	*Forty Chapters* §35; *ITA* V.14.
13	Bodily description by sign	Similar to *Forty Chapters* §§177-88; *Judges* 7.114.
14	Hot/cold, straight/crooked signs	*Forty Chapters* §§21-22; *ITA* I.9.1-I.10.2.
15-28	Meanings of the houses	*Forty Chapters* §§73-76; *Introduct.* §§2-3; *ITA* I.13.
29-33	Angularity of houses	*Forty Chapters* §§37-39; *Introduct.* §4; *ITA* I.14; cf. also *Judges* §2.15.
34-40	Dignities & relations of domiciles	*Forty Chapters* §§14-18; *ITA* III.6
41	Transition to planets	(Unnecessary)
42-47	Saturn	*Forty Chapters* §§44-45; *ITA* V.1.
48-53	Jupiter	*Forty Chapters* §§46-47; *ITA* V.2.
54-59	Mars	*Forty Chapters* §48; *ITA* V.3.

60-65	Sun	*Forty Chapters* §49; *ITA* V.4.
66-71	Venus	*Forty Chapters* §50; *ITA* V.5.
72-77	Mercury	*Forty Chapters* §§51-54; *ITA* V.6.
78-83	Moon	*Forty Chapters* §§55-62; *ITA* V.7.
84-102	Planetary configurations	*Forty Chapters* §§82-96; *ITA* III.
103-05	Planetary strengths and weaknesses	*Forty Chapters* §§97-109; *ITA* IV.1-5.
106-15	Special roles of Sun *&* Moon	(No translation available)
116-22	Planets in the houses	= *Twelve Dom.*; *JN* Ch. 48.
123	Sahl's *Fifty Judgments*	= Appendix A; *BOA* Tr. 5.
124-124a	Natural significations of planets; general indications of planetary conditions and signs	*Forty Chapters* §§77-80, 104-12
125	Planetary joys	*Forty Chapters* §§111-12; *ITA* I.10.7, I.16.
126	Hugo's preface to *Judges*	See introduction above.

Figure 6: Table of introductory sections in *Judges*, and their equivalents

§A.127: On the method and manner of inquiring—Māshā'allāh

Of all the things which have being under the Lunar circle and enjoy life, once creation was had, the Creator God (rounding off [the time of creation] with a six-fold ranking), distinguished certain and common things of their worldly mass, with an equal number.[1]

Of all of which, He wanted the origin and beginning of a nation and of the generation of nations to come first. In second place come families of individual homes. Thirdly, the affairs of kings and powerful people are established. Then come the nativities of individuals. In the fifth place follow the beginnings of works.[2] Finally, with respect to those things which someone bears in his mind or undertakes to address in his heart,[3] He established interrogations in last place.

The most ancient of the philosophers professed varied and manifold opinions about all of these things. If a question would be proposed about the six things which we related above (namely [nations], the generation of a [nation], of a family, the affairs of kings and princes, nativities, the undertakings of works, and inquiries), they insist on both seeking and explaining the solution to [each of these] individually—both [the seeking] but especially the manner [of solving it].[4] And from there they leave the explaining of the effects to us, concerning all of these things which are naturally arranged in the circle, so far as that pertains to questions: wherefore, we have decided to act with respect to these principally.[5]

The sequence of the present discussion [now] makes its start. For it was pleasing to assign a proper method throughout the individual affairs (and the places whence they are taken), to individual [affairs].

---

[1] That is, human social entities and concerns are divided into categories that reflect the six days of creation. "Hexameral" ("six-day") thought constituted a special genre of literature in the medieval West.
[2] That is, elections.
[3] Or, "feelings, mind" (*animo*).
[4] This is my best rendition of *singula inquam ex his tam quaerendi quam enodandae solutionis alium prorsus et alium expostulant modum.*
[5] Māshā'allāh seems to mean that while the ancient astrologers explained how to look at many issues, they were not fully complete in their treatment of questions—but Māshā'allāh is taking it upon himself to fill that gap.

The[6] manner [of asking] is that there be a question appearing simple and absolute, [so that] something *not* asked is in no way mixed in with things *already* asked. So if [there were] someone asking about marriage, he should submit a new question once more about a matter he had contrived at the very last [moment], just after a little interval of time, [before he] expects a response.[7]

Nevertheless, before a certain and firm intention is had about any affair, one taken with respect to diverse affairs should be led back properly to a corresponding status, if individual [affairs] would be sought from the specific places of the zodiac and through the twelve signs.[8]

But I believe that a question should not even be proposed about two matters whose manner is approximately the same. Nor should one respond except to earnest and definite questions, or for someone who, with the greatest care and concern for himself (or for another with whom he concerns himself very much, he being a concerned inquirer), approaches [the astrologer] himself or through another messenger. But if anyone made a question in order to test [the astrologer] or in order to scoff, the effect and end of the affair in no way leaves the proper intention untouched[9]—but he would not even know how to form any question, or how to assert what he is retaining in his mind, and how to reduce anything [to a particular topic], with care.[10]

Therefore, in all of these things, the chief thing for forming a question is that someone would ask through himself or through his own messenger, or at least [that it would be] someone equally worried about that very matter.

Finally, let anyone eager to pursue the truth of judgments, and attain the gift of truth, and drawn to gaining praise for his great effort, hasten to note

---

[6] From here through the end of this section, the sense of the text reads almost identically to Sahl in §1.1 below, and may be read with it. Sahl was undoubtedly copying from this passage of Māshā'allāh's. See also §A.128 below.

[7] Reading a little freely for *sub modico expectandae responsionis intervallo*. Māshā'allāh means that additional questions thought of at the last moment, should not be asked until the querent thinks about it for a while. In his *On the Interpretation of Thought/Cognition* (in *WSM*), Māshā'allāh makes this a 24-hour period.

[8] Māshā'allāh either means that if someone asks about multiple matters, each one must be assigned to its own house and considered separately (to its "corresponding" house and situation), or that if the client has a jumble of questions, each one must be made certain and firm by itself, corresponding to what we'd expect for *one* question.

[9] *Effectus finisque negotii intentionem nullatenus relinquunt propriam*. That is, the chart will display signs that the person is insincere. Māshā'allāh must be referring to the considerations before judgment which indicate insincerity. See my Introduction.

[10] *Et cura unum aliquid redigere novit*. That is, while an earnest person will have a clear idea of what he wants, the insincere person will not even know what he is looking for.

with a vigilant mind, and commend to [his] persistent memory, not just what has already been set out, but even the precepts which are written below.

§A.128: On those things which are necessary for both the judge and the querent—'Umar

The satisfaction of all astronomy turns chiefly on discerning the outcomes of matters before they come to be. What category of judgment is at hand,[11] moreover the truth of judgment, opens up the whole question.

Lest[12] the cloud of someone's error (from whatever source) be able to throw the methodical arrangement of each[13] into confusion, a certain foresight must be applied to an inquiry into matters, namely so that the question is simple and absolute—namely to the extent that he should take care to add nothing which was devised afterwards,[14] to the proposed interrogation.

In fact,[15] the job of the judge in the understanding of a question demands no little caution, so that he should attend studiously (but with the appraisal of foresight) to the question as a whole, and [pay attention to] the hour of the question (namely, whether it is before midday or after the descent of the Sun [from the meridian], and so on), overlooking nothing of what is necessary, discovering with a wise consideration, making note with an ever-watchful mind, and resting in the folds of memory.[16] So that finally, being thus instructed in manifold deliberation, let him try to explain (with some effort, I say) in particular what and how much of the client's affair is being principally presented to his ears by [the querent's] speech.[17]

---

[11] Lit., "obtains the turn/role."
[12] Cf. the parallel paragraph in §A.127 above.
[13] *Ordinem*. I believe 'Umar means the way in which one determines and applies the category (*genus*) and truth (*veritas*) of judgment mentioned above.
[14] That is, something proposed as an afterthought, something which was not his original concern.
[15] The rest of this section is very similar to the main points in *OHT* §1: namely, that the astrologer must understand the question correctly, calculate the chart correctly, and beware of charts in which the testimonies of the benefics and malefics are roughly equal.
[16] That is, relying confidently on his memory of the necessary rules (and probably similar cases, *etc.*).
[17] That is, part of the astrologer's skill is in understanding what are the salient points of the question, and how they can be understood in light of the chart. 'Umar is also suggesting that clients do not always reveal everything, and that the chart will more reliably show the facts. But 'Umar might be hinting at what Sahl suggests in §1.1 below, that you must be clear on whether as client is asking about life as a whole, or something about a specific time period.

For[18] the Divine power of the celestial circle, and the property of effectiveness at the hour of his question, seem to be related by a certain likeness to the intelligence and mind of those asking. [That is], I say that the motion of the circle compels the querent to ask [the question], for the human condition does not cease to imitate duly the order and progressions of the heavenly dispositions, both of the stars and the circles, as though by the chains of someone's love.[19]

Next, I think one should pay attention to this, once a question is proposed: if the testimonies of the benevolents were equal to those of the infortunes. So long as a certain equality of characteristics is in all of them, it is impossible for error to be entirely avoided. Whence, the expert astuteness of the judge remembers that the question must be repeated at another time, and the judgment must be deferred. For a confusion in matters of this kind frequently involves the proposed question in much ambiguity.[20]

§A.129: On choosing the significator of the querent and the question—'Umar[21]

Therefore, with these things having been managed by such a method, we should deal with the appropriate choosing of the useful and very necessary "leader" (or rather, "significator").

And so, the star specially embracing the signification of the quaesited matter is deservedly allotted the name of "leader" and "minister." And it is the

---

[18] Cf. the parallel statement in *On Quest.* §1.1 and *OHT* §2.

[19] *Dilectionis*. This is an intriguing phrase, since in Aristotle's metaphysics and theology, all living beings are motivated by the good, and the celestial circles turn out of desire for the Aristotelian God, who is the ultimate source of rationality and goodness.

[20] If we pair this statement with the previous paragraph, it suggests that a confusion in the planetary condition reflects a confusion in the querent's mind and condition: so that while the stars have impelled the querent to consult the astrologer, the situation itself (and the querent's mind) might not be of sufficient clarity to allow a firm answer.

[21] Cf. al-Rijāl I.9.2. I believe this section is for determining the significator of thought: the independent significator over the whole chart and matter, as I describe in *Search* and my introduction above. At first it does seem as though 'Umar begins by looking at the victor over the house of the quaesited, and then that of the querent. But there are two reasons to think something else is going on here. First, the wide variety of options for the latter go way beyond what we'd expect for a victor over the Ascendant, and are more typical for the kinds of things found for a victor of the chart in *Search*. Second, §A.130 below describes how to find the significators over the first and another house, in the direct way we are familiar with in horary (as in Māshā'allāh's *OR* Ch. 2 (in Appendix C) and Sahl §1.1 below.

one which obtains the most dignity in the place of the question, or whom the most testimonies support, from wherever.[22]

We enjoin [you] to pursue the establishment of this matter in such a way: namely that once the beginning is taken up from the lord of the house,[23] 5 points are devoted to it: being stronger and more worthy, [and] engaged in the manifold gift of dignity, it is put before all the rest. From that one, the minister of the high command or sovereignty holds second place, with 4 being taken. But the lord of the bound exceeds by 3. But the one who is in charge of the triplicity possesses twin dignities. On the other hand, the [planet] which is influential over the decan or face deserves to be enriched by only 1, because the signification of its leadership is weaker than of the others. Some astrologers even, wanting to ascribe a certain portion of dignity to the lord of the hour,[24] seem to have strayed far from the opinion of certain others.[25]

Then,[26] once this consideration is had, take note especially of the eastern lord (because this one signifies the querent), [since] a certain excellence and strength is ascribed to it. If it obtained the principal position of sovereignty or bound, triplicity or even decan (apart from its own proper dignity which it collects from the Ascendant),[27] it will merit being enriched with the more excellent benefit of the signification, wholly denying the partnerships of the rest.

However, if this same [lord of the Ascendant] is traversing in a pivot (especially in the tenth), without, I say, any [other] dignity,[28] it[29] will be single in the leadership of the east, [and] fully claims the signification of the whole question (to the extent that it pertains to the querent), without the fellowship of [another] partner—unless (I say) any [other] star is blessed with the rul-

---

[22] This seems to mean, "no matter what house the supporting aspects come out of."
[23] Al-Rijāl omits any consideration of weighted points here.
[24] Al-Rijāl says "one dignity."
[25] For example, ibn Ezra (*Search*, App. F) and al-Kindī (*Forty Chapters* Ch. 3.1).
[26] In the next few paragraphs, 'Umar examines the lord of the Ascendant and other planets. Hugo's reading does not match al-Rijāl's reading, so there are two ways to look at the criteria. See below.
[27] This seems to mean, "if it also happened to be in one of its dignities where it currently is, in addition to being the lord of the Ascendant." But al-Rijāl reads this as meaning, "if it has more than one rulership over the degree of the Ascendant."
[28] Again, Hugo's 'Umar means, "if it is in a pivot but *not* also in a dignity where it is." But al-Rijāl reads this as though the lord of the Ascendant has *only* domicile rulership over the degree of the Ascendant.
[29] Reading for "that partner," for the sake of clarity.

ership of the sovereignty and bound (but even of the triplicity), likewise appearing in a pivot. Which if [that] sometimes happens, [such a star] seems not to be foreign from a partnership with the eastern lord, provided that the lord of the east possesses the beginning of the sign up to 15°.[30] For if the significator of the triple power is in the tenth, and placed in that same degree,[31] [then] it takes possession of the signification, as the one individually stronger.

On the other hand, with the lord of the east being deprived of every dignity, and being cadent,[32] the minister of a three-fold power merits a stronger signification, [if it is] at the beginning of [its] sign. Which if it held onto the end, reckon the stronger one to be one which is blessed by a twin dignity,[33] if it were in fully in control of the bound and the sovereignty or, at least, the triplicity. For [a planet] which is in charge of the decan is weaker than all the rest, unless it manages the power and ownership of the house which the Sun is holding onto by day (and the Moon by night), or at least that of the hour.

Moreover, the pivots strengthen their own lords in the power of signification; but [if the lords are] cadent, a not-moderate humbleness is noted.

Moreover, [if] the lords of the Solar house in a diurnal question (even the Lunar one in a nocturnal [question]), but even of its hour, are co-equal in power of this kind, they bequeath this gift of superiority to the one which is in control of the Solar rulership by day (of the Lunar one by night), or rather[34] that of the hour.

Therefore, one must use discernment about this leader and significator, until you discover the power of one star or two, or even many. Which if the strength of two partners were equal, you will note to which of them the Moon will be applying, or at least [if] the Moon would possess her own house in the east,[35] or preferably if it[36] would be the minister of the Solar dignity[37] by day or the Lunar one by night (for I advise the stronger significa-

---

[30] Al-Rijāl reads as though the lord of the Ascendant cannot be more than 3° beyond the angle of the axis, not that it must be in the first half of its sign.
[31] That is, while the domicile lord is further away from the angle.
[32] Al-Rijāl has the lord simply non-angular, which would still allow it to be succeedent.
[33] That is, two dignities.
[34] Hugo is not expressing a preference by saying "rather": it is a way he tends to introduce the last member of a list of choices.
[35] I take this to mean that even if the Moon rules the Ascendant (and even if she rules it and is in it), we should still look at the planet to which she is applying.
[36] I take this to be one of the candidate planets just mentioned.
[37] Al-Rijāl has "the bound of" the Sun and Moon.

tion of this belongs especially to the one which obtains the shift);[38] I say the stronger one will be the one to which the Moon applies from the east.

And so that I might tie all of this up briefly: any star blessed with the support of many witnesses [and] the Lunar application (and after observing these things which were said), is preferable in the principal rulership.

Even the Lot of Fortune always exhibits a stronger signification in the night.[39]

§A.130: Another chapter on the same thing—'Umar[40]

[Primary significators]

Now that things have been attended to in an order of this kind, in every affair it is suitable to investigate the nature of that significator which is called the "victor" among the Arabs, and the one which is in charge of the question.[41]

And so,[42] the lord of the east principally claims this dignity, if it itself regarded the east. But with it being cadent [from the Ascendant], the Moon principally acquires the signification of the querent, if she blesses the east with *her* own regard. One must even note whether it[43] is applying or withdrawing. For although it may be deprived of the gift of the proper quality of each, in no way will it lose the signification which it holds onto.

---

[38] That is, the sect light. Arabic writers use "shift" (*nawbah*) to describe the alternating command over charts taken by the luminaries, as the charts are diurnal or nocturnal. Al-Rijāl adds that it would be good if it were also the lord of the Lot of Fortune, and especially if it were in its own domain (*ITA* III.2).

[39] Omitting "for nocturnal affairs," following al-Rijāl.

[40] Cf. al-Rijāl I.9.1. This section forms the second of three parts in Ch. 2 of 'Umar's own Arabic work. The first one only appears in the *Three Judges*, while the last part is below, in §A.131.

[41] Al-Rijāl speaks of this indifferently as the victor over the querent, the quaesited matter, and the situation between the querent and someone else.

[42] The instructions in this part are virtually identical to Māshā'allāh's *OR* Ch. 2 (in Appendix C).

[43] This must refer to the Moon. 'Umar seems to mean that if the Moon is the significator of the querent, her separations and applications will be very important. He then goes on to say that even if she is not separating or applying (i.e., she is void in course), she will still be the significator. Māshā'allāh (Appendix C) says that in such a case she should be moved into the next sign to find her next application. .

And the lord of the seventh,[44] [if it is] regarding [the seventh], will be in charge of the question; or [if it does not regard it, take] rather the lord of the Lunar lodging-place.

Which if the Moon did not regard[45] the east (as was just stated), [then] provided that she has an application and withdrawal, the star from which she is being separated belongs to the querent; but the one to which she applies merits the signification of the question.

On the other hand, once the eastern lord is discovered to be cadent [from the Ascendant], [and] the Moon cadent from the east, while she neither applies to nor withdraws from [a planet], it will be permitted to establish her as belonging to the querent, and the lord of her lodging-place as the significator of the question. Moreover, the Moon lingering in her own sovereignty (and being foreign to any application and recession), will still belong to the querent, and the lord of her triplicity will have to be put over the question.

Which if some star would be transferring light or collecting it between the lords of the east and the seventh (or at least between the Moon and another star), that star will belong to the [topic of the] question, but the Moon will be allotted the command of the querent.

[Secondary significators]

But generally, if a [peregrine] star were in the east (and the seventh), [or] even[46] the lord of the east and the seventh, they present testimonies to the querent and the question, even if [the lords of these houses] are deprived of a mutual aspect [to their house].[47] But the victor of the business is said to be the star that is stronger in the place of the matter, even one established in that same place.[48]

It seems that everywhere, the Moon must be brought to bear upon all of these.

---

[44] 'Umar seems to be using the seventh as an example of another house, just as he earlier framed this as being a situation between the querent and someone else (the seventh).
[45] Reading with al-Rijāl.
[46] Omitting "if it is," to clarify with al-Rijāl.
[47] Adding and reading with al-Rijāl. That is, a planet in the Ascendant (or the seventh) will be an important significator, even if the lord of the Ascendant does not aspect the Ascendant (based on the al-Rijāl).
[48] I feel rather confident about this somewhat awkward sentence in Hugo, which is not mirrored in al-Rijāl.

[Direct connections between significators][49]

On the other hand, an observation of this kind must be made about the status of the significator[50] and its properties: namely, to whom it would be applying in the sign in which it is, or which one [would be applying] to it. It is good for the manner of this application to be considered according to the greatness of the stars' rays.[51] For the rays of the infortunes spoil the effects of affairs; those of the benevolents on the contrary, hasten [them]. But I figure that it was [already] stated [well enough] above, by how many degrees the rays of the planets are stretched out in each direction, in front and behind.[52]

And so, the application of the eastern significator (appearing in a pivot or after a pivot) with the lord of the quaesited matter, promises the effect of the question—if, I say, [something] would be sought with respect to the business of kings or powerful men or suchlike.[53] For that same [planet] being cadent from a pivot and from those which follow the pivots (or, being "remote"), removes the effect, unless the question proceeds with respect to travel or some change of place, and things which are of this kind: for, an application being made from cadency of this kind, brings [the matter] to a conclusion.[54]

[Transfers, collections, and perfection by location][55]

Which if any star would be found [1] transferring the light of one to some other, namely, through a certain guiding [activity] (especially [separating] from the lord of the question [and] applying to the eastern significator), and no less too [2] a collection of light, even [3] with that significator occupying the place of the question, they portend the effecting of matters. And the

---

[49] Cf. *ITA* III.5-7. From here to §A.133, 'Umar and Māshā'allāh now turn to methods of perfection. See my introduction, as well as Sahl in §1.1 below and Bonatti in Appendix B.
[50] From here on, we seem to be dealing only with the significators of the querent and the quaesited, not the independent significator of thought or chart.
[51] Omitting "or their," which only appears (misspelled) in Madrid and 1509. The "greatness" or "quantity" of an aspect refers to how big it is: a square (90°), a trine (120°), etc. See my Introduction to *WSM*.
[52] 'Umar must subscribe to the unequal medieval orbs also endorsed by Sahl (*Introduct.* §5.3). See the table in my introduction above, from *ITA* III.6.
[53] That is, if it is about gaining something concrete and lasting.
[54] See *Forty Chapters* §39 for a similar statement about the cadent places, as well as the material on travel in §9 below. This view is echoed by Māshā'allāh in §A.132 below.
[55] Cf. *ITA* III.11-12.

minister of the quaesited matter being in the east, free of fall and scorching, applying to the eastern leader, signifies the same thing.

Even an application of the significator to some [star] in the place of the question does not disagree with this—while, I say, it would acquire something of the proper quality in that place.

On the other hand, the lord of the question[56] applying to any [star] in the east, so that [it would be in] its own domicile, sovereignty, even bound), portends the same.

[The effect of benefic and malefic planets][57]

Which if they were infortunes (while, however, they obtained the signification), they introduce delay and bar the effect. No less, too, does the application of [malefic] significators with each other (from the pivots of the signs or [the pivots] of malevolents) generate corruption: whence, the one whom the lord of the question is looking after,[58] incurs difficulty and hindrance. For difficulty and delay proceeds from Saturn, [but] the signification of Mars in particular furnishes lies and defrauding in affairs. But with a minister or significator [of this kind], should some type of application of friendship or co-partnership[59] conjoin it and Venus, it commends the effect of those things which are of a proper Venusian quality (such as sexual immorality, and procuring,[60] and what is of this type).[61]

Also, the fortunate ones accelerate their benefit and efficacy whenever they undergo an assembly of the significators or are applying to them in the pivots. No less does the application of the significators with those lucky [planets] from a strong place [indicate the same], according to the nature and proper quality of the question. The benignness of the Sun especially, and Jupiter, [indicate the same] in discerning the affairs of kings and kingdoms, whenever the significators (being established in the Midheaven) apply to them from a strong place. Settling [all of this] really bestows upon these

---

[56] That is, the lord of the quaesited, according to Sahl in §1.1.
[57] Cf. *ITA* V.9.
[58] That is, "the person indicated by the significator of the quaesited."
[59] *Consortii*, a word sometimes used by Hugo to mean assembly in the same sign (*ITA* III.5).
[60] *Impetratio*. I take this to mean prostitution, but *impetro* itself simply means to obtain or procure something.
[61] In this sentence, 'Umar is describing the addition of Venus to a *malefic* signification, hence the negative Venusian qualities.

[matters] what belongs to [the planets], [in terms of their] signification and nature.[62]

But if the ministers[63] would be allotted something of power and dignity, they advance lofty affairs belonging to kings and prominent people, and even kingdoms, particularly from the sign of the Midheaven.

And in this way, provided that they manage what belongs to the question in some place of the circle—with, I say, an application of the significators with them being indicated in advance—one will have to judge how much pertains to them in terms of loftiness, success, and hastening. For in fact Venus administers affairs with respect to women and what belongs to women, and that kind [of thing], but a corresponding judgment about the remaining stars depends on the proper qualities of [their] nature.

§A.131: More on producing and denying an effect[64]—'Umar[65]

Moreover, it must be noted that the Tail of the Dragon stains both fortunate [stars] with its perversity. No less is Mercury [affected], should either one (the Head or the Tail) possess the same degree [as he does]. For with the power of the signification being taken up thusly, it perverts the question, [and] worse so with [the Tail] occupying the degree of the east. It will be permitted or all right to judge no otherwise with respect to the Sun. For whenever he would be distant from the Head or Tail by 4° (but the Moon from each Node by 12°), it generates corruption.

[Perfection by direct connection]

Here though, if an application is focused towards the rays of the stars,[66] it will remove [any] delay in judgment: for provided that no star perverting the judgment with its light or rays is in between,[67] this is a sign of the fulfilling of one's wishes.

---

[62] Tentatively translating *His quae eius sunt significationis et naturae arbitrium profecto largitur.*
[63] That is, the significators and the other planets related to them.
[64] This is a better description than the original title, "On the Tail of the Dragon."
[65] Cf. *ITA* V.8.
[66] That is, if the significators have a straightforward connection by degree.
[67] I.e., by barring or cutting the light: see *ITA* III.14 and III.23.

[Assembly in the same sign][68]

Moreover, with two stars being established in the same sign, if the earlier one which is approaching the later one attains it within that same sign (provided that the aspect of another [planet] does not interrupt [them]),[69] it announces the outcome of the matters.

[Escape, and avoiding escape][70]

Which if it is impossible for it to reach [it] in the same [sign], as long as it crosses over into the next sign [and] the light of another [planet] is removed until it reaches it, it does not disagree with the previous judgment.

[Out-of-sign conjunctions][71]

Also, it is not otherwise [for] a star traversing in any sign, while it touches the degree of another star appearing in the second [sign] from it, with a ray of its own light. For if such a contact were missing, it would wholly remove the effect.

[More on malefic planets]

On the other hand, with the infortunes arranged in the bound of the east, or at least being associated[72] to its degree, the matter is deprived of the effect. But in the rest of the pivots in this way, provided that they [are] in the opposite from the degree and bound of the pivot, but they are traversing in more degrees.[73] It is very bad whenever a question proceeds with respect to

---

[68] Cf. *ITA* III.14, and III.21-22.

[69] This would be a case of barring (*ITA* III.14) or the cutting of light #3 (*ITA* III.23.3).

[70] Escape (*ITA* III.22) is when two planets are in a sign, and the later one crosses over into the next sign—but before the earlier one can catch up to it in the next sign, it encounters the ray of a third planet instead. Here, 'Umar says that perfection is still possible, and "escape" is avoided, if no third planet intervenes. Ibn Ezra likewise describes this situation in *ITA* III.22. In fact, it is possible that the definition of escape was derived from this positive situation in 'Umar.

[71] Sahl likewise allows out-of-sign conjunctions in *Introduct.* §5.3.

[72] Reading *affinibus* for *affinius*. I am not sure if this means they rule the bound, or aspect it. Certainly, aspecting would be worse.

[73] Perhaps because they are not only aspecting closely by zodiacal degrees, but moving toward the angle by the rotation of the heavens as well.

money and sovereignty or authority or friendship ([and] finally, about every [type of] success): for it threatens detriment and hatred towards the querent.

[The corruption of the Moon and the Ascendant][74]

A corrupted Moon in an interrogation does not deny the effect, whenever the significators hold onto the places of the question (namely, those from which the judgment emanates), but it affects the querent with much trouble, and often stirs up the greatest anguish, according to the manner of corruption.

In addition, even the corruption of the east induces ruin and death.

§A.132: Receiving management, reflection, transfer, collection—Māshā'allāh[75]

[Perfection by a direct connection][76]

Finally, in every affair the receiver of counsel[77] should principally be noted, and what place from the east it maintains or holds onto.[78] In fact, being free of the infortunes, nor scorched nor cadent, it takes care of the things asked about. (But for a journey and withdrawing, and changing places—as was stated above—and for leaving prison and things like these, being cadent sometimes helps.)[79]

---

[74] For a list of different corruptions of the Moon which is probably 'Umar's, see *Search* Ch. I.5; for Sahl's longer list, see *Introduct.* §5.16 and *Search* Ch. II.4.3; for Abū Ma'shar's list, see *ITA* IV.5.
[75] This was originally titled "On the Tail of the Dragon," which is clearly not pertinent to the topic, and may have been a mislabeling carried down from §A.131 above.
[76] Cf. *ITA* III.7.
[77] That is, the receiver of management (*ITA* III.18) or planet to which the key significators are applying (preferably, this planet will be the lord of the Ascendant or of the quaesited matter).
[78] *Retineat vel obtineat.* I take this to refer to both the house it rules as well as the one it currently occupies.
[79] See also *Forty Chapters* §39. Note the similarity in this paragraph with *On Quest.* §§1.2-3.

[Perfection by transferring from aversion (reflection of light)][80]

But if the testimonies proceed from a reflection of light,[81] the star to whom the reflector of light[82] applies, should be noted. In fact, with these being cleansed of the infortunes (as was said above with respect to the receiver of counsel), and even with the Moon attesting, it promises the effect. But if the planet claiming the rulership of the east or of the question ([that is], the one to which the reflecting one is applying) is unlucky or corrupted, it introduces corruption. With it being safe, it [still] speaks against [a successful] business, provided that the Moon is being corrupted.[83] In fact, a transfer of light or even a collection, is a middling testimony. If therefore the Moon does not aid, no effect will follow, since they do not have full testimony.

But if the one reflecting the light with its body receives it from the lord of the east or of the question, it would not be able to bar[84] [the connection], as though cutting it off (though the tetragon and opposition spoil[85] [things], and they instill something other than hope). For barring takes place with the body alone, as the opinion of the ancients and Māshā'allāh has it. But Māshā'allāh's assertion [should be noted]:[86] that if the one reflecting [the light] takes it from the body [of one planet] and confers it to the rays [of the other], it strengthens the beginning [of the matter], but makes the end weak. But if, taking it from the light [of one by aspect and], it sent it to the body [of the other], [after] weakening the beginning, it strengthens the end.

---

[80] Cf. *ITA* III.11 and III.13.
[81] *Redditione.* For an explanation of reflection, see my introduction.
[82] The middle planet in the configuration.
[83] Compare this statement with that of 'Umar in the previous section. 'Umar says that the corruption of the Moon will not prevent the outcome, provided that the key significators occupy the key houses. So, why does Māshā'allāh think a transfer by reflection will not save the outcome? It could be that reflection is an uncertain or unreliable form of perfection (as I argued in *ITA* III.13), so that we need a good Moon to assist it: the importance of the Moon (in addition to the other significators) is certainly emphasized in a similar passage in *On Quest.* §1.8. Note also the next sentence, where even a normal transfer or collection is not as sure as a straightforward connection between significators or their being located in the key houses.
[84] Sometimes called "prohibition": see *ITA* III.14. The point is that if a planet is reflecting or transferring light, it is helping the significators and not hindering them.
[85] Reading *pervertunt* for *praevertunt*.
[86] See Sahl's *On Quest.* §5.7, the "third way."

[Perfection by collecting from aversion (reflection of light)]

But the one which equally collects the light of the lord of the east and of the question, if it would assume the signification and it would be lingering in the Midheaven or in the east, it is good to notice the Moon: for, her applying to the lord of the east or of the question, perfects the things asked about.[87] But if she would apply to neither, but she is nevertheless cleansed of the infortunes, the matter reaches its effect with many things coming in between.

Moreover, a star collecting the light in the place of the question (or at least supporting [the place] with its aspect), nor being cadent, supplies much comfort with respect to the effect. But with a regard [to that place] being denied, it bars the things asked about from coming into being.

§A.133: [A few notes on timing]—al-Kindī[88]

§134. But the degrees of application will indicate the end-point of this effect, to which we sometimes grant days, months, or years, just as the nature or time of the matter itself demands. For there are certain things whose time cannot be ended in anything other than days, [and] others whose time indicates only months (such as those who are enclosed in the uterus of the mother before birth). But certain ones get years, like if someone posed a question about when a palm tree which he planted would bear fruit. In all of these, the nature of the quaesited matter must be considered.

§135. Now, however, we will have to write down which matters' time would be ended in days, months, and years. And so, the degrees of the application frequently take days if their signs were convertible, particularly if [such signs] arise in less than two hours,[89] or in [exactly] two full [hours]. Also, the double-bodied signs take months, especially if their arising had less than two. But a signification of years comes to be if they were fixed signs, especially if their ascension demands more than two hours.

---

[87] As stated before, transfers or collections of light (particularly by reflection) need support by the Moon in order to be effective.

[88] Cf. also §§1.2-3 and 4.22 below.

[89] That is, the crooked signs (here) and the straight ones (below): see *ITA* I.9.1. The crooked signs run from the beginning of Capricorn to the end of Gemini, while the straight signs run from the beginning of Cancer to the end of Sagittarius.

§A.134: Summary—Unknown[90]

Once a question is supplied, it seems one's not-moderate judgment must be applied to these aforestated things. From the beginning of this last treatise we have diligently described the method and search[91] for the managing star (or rather, the significator), and we have warned that it must be chosen by so many different and places and individual[92] [criteria]. From this it seems not unwarranted to relate that a keen observation of all [of this should be had], since that generally resolves every question in full, but especially the ambiguity which is concerned with doubts about the outcomes of things (namely whether or not they would come to be).

Nor does a consideration of [only] one significator suffice.

And so, a diligent observation of the kinds of questions and types of interrogations (according to the twelve lodging-places of the zodiac and their signification, just as the ancient astrologers teach) could obtain greater evidence of all of these things, [namely] as to what the individual domiciles hold onto in the matters of the celestial places, or what is subject to the course of the mortal quality of the stars (though, with Divine law confirming them). We will describe the rest of the things which remain in addition to what was written above, in a corresponding order.

But we have presented these things and what is like them *prior to* the establishment of the houses,[93] for this reason:[94] since they are equally relevant to all the secrets of judgments, and there would be more work than honor in writing them down again in [other] individual places, [then since] they are laid out once in this place, the reasoning can be carried over in common [throughout the book].

---

[90] According to Burnett, this is based on the BKh manuscript. It may be a continuation of Māshā'allāh above. It seems to pertain to the significator of the whole chart.
[91] Reading *indagationem* for *indaginem*.
[92] Reading *singulis* with Madrid for *signis*.
[93] That is, before all of the individual questions and rules for the twelve houses, which follows.
[94] I have translated the rest of this sentence somewhat loosely.

§1: FIRST HOUSE

1st House	
How to interpret charts	§1.1
Longevity	§§1.2-6
Success & failure in life	§2.15

Figure 7: Questions of the first house

SAHL'S METHOD FOR QUESTIONS

§1.1: On those things which pertain to the first house—Sahl[1]

Before all else, the first thing (as we said before) is the east, which chiefly presents itself sooner,[2] once the interrogation is made and understood prudently. Therefore (as the order demands), from that beginning which is taken up, one must investigate into which domicile (or rather house) the question falls, having accurately observed the method of the above-written [chapters].[3]

Finally, once this has been known beforehand with a full intention, you must beware, lest after this you add something contrived,[4] it being confused with the quaesited matter. But it can happen that many questions come to be together under one and the same east, which the sequence of matters promises (and reason demands) to establish in their own places.[5] Nor however can it come about that a double question be established in the same place.[6]

[Then], on every occasion one must respond immediately as to how [the answer] is contained in what has been set forth, and after carelessness has been removed: [for] I would wish that you not make an observation for [just] anybody. Nor should one give counsel unless it is by means of the sequence [of steps] and necessary inquiries, as Māshā'allāh teaches.[7] For (as 'Umar

---

[1] Cf. *On Quest.* §§1.1-1.8.
[2] Hugo seems to mean that the first house is the first one in order, and also that (because it signifies the querent), it is the first one we must examine.
[3] Sahl or Hugo is referring to the methodological sections above, in which one finds the victors and significators (§§A129-30).
[4] That is, something which the client has not actually asked about.
[5] That is, you may take multiple questions in the same chart, provided that you carefully assign the significators to their proper houses.
[6] For example, do not ask two completely different seventh-house questions in the same chart, because the significators will give a similar answer for each one.
[7] See above, §A127.

claims), the mind of the querent imitates the state and manner of the circle.[8] A question about the life [of the querent himself] and the status of [his] life is even usually judged to be more firm and certain.[9]

Also, one must especially pay attention to the intention of this interrogation itself: for often it happens that a general question arises (such as for all the days and manner of his life), but sometimes a particular [time period][10] is presented in the same way. I reckon that all of these things must be discerned—as to how and in what way they arise—with the greatest effort.

But nor does anyone in a question of this kind come [to you] unless he follows the manner of the circle (as was already stated above),[11] namely so that the manner of the circle itself may be understood equally as being virtually the nature and state of the man.

Therefore, he whom the lord of the east and equally the Moon would bless with a prosperous aspect, the method of the judgment will profess him to be blessed with happiness; and the regard of a perverse figure portends the contrary. For the benevolents and the unlucky ones it is the same, so that if you knew them to be safe and cleansed, judge him lucky; if corrupted, he is less fortunate.

[General appraisal, and perfection][12]

Therefore, whenever a question would be presented about those things which are going to happen in life, [see] what agreement there is between the lords of the east and of the question: if they apply to each other, which one applies to the other, and even what reception there is. But after that, whether they are cleansed (that is, "free") of, or corrupted by, the infortunes.

But when it is asked about whatever he hopes for or fears (such as about escape or travel and what is like these),[13] what come after the pivots (namely

---

[8] See above, §A128.
[9] Sahl means that questions are judged more firmly if the question is about the querent himself, as opposed to being about other people; but Hugo has not really brought out this point well.
[10] For example, "Will I ever have much money?" as opposed to "Will I have much money this month?"
[11] In §A.128.
[12] Cf. *On Quest.* §§1.2-1.4.
[13] What Sahl means is that the cadent places are used for severing connections, movement, change, travel, escape from difficulties, etc. This is in contrast to the previous paragraph, which concerns making connections that have stable results (and would there-

those which are remote from and falling from the pivots) will have to be handled.

And so that I might tie up the rest in a few words: in whatever sign you determine that the question falls (such as if it is asked about life or money, or even brothers or parents), you will have to establish it in that one, I say, for its nature and status. Once these and the like have been gotten, let the east itself, and its lord, and the Moon, be established as significators of the person of the querent himself. But let the domicile where [the question] falls, and equally the lord of its lodging-place, assume the signification and rank of the question.

And finally, [see] which one (the lord of the east or the Moon) is stronger than the other, namely even which one occupies a pivot and occurs in the regard of the east.[14] And so, let this one (which you chose as the stronger one) be engaged with the lord of the question. For if it should apply to [the lord of the question], you would know that the matter is going to happen through the querent's effort and labor; but in the reverse order, the lord of the question applying to the eastern [lord] announces it is going to happen without his labor.

On the other hand, should the lord of the east[15] traverse in the place of the question, or at least should the significator of the question do so in the east, it leaves nothing ambiguous about the effect, unless perhaps it would be scorched in that place, or would have [its] fall in that same place. Moreover, if it should happen that either the lord of the east or the Moon applies to a star appearing in the place of the question (and it having some dignity in that same place), or at least in the reverse order—should the significator itself (that is, the lord of the question) apply to one appearing in the east, so that [the star in the place] is a partner of something in that same place[16]—it declares the certain effecting of the quaesited matter.

Which if it happened not to be found so, a transfer of light will have to be noted. For should the Moon or any star of the light ones, being separated from the lord of the east, apply to the lord [of the question], or rather should it apply from the lord [of the question] to the eastern lord, it announces or

---

by probably also focus on the pivots and the succeedents). John's Sahl is much clearer on this point, and 'Umar §A.130 and Māshā'allāh §A.132 also make this same point.

[14] I have used *On Quest.* to clarify this sentence. Note the insistence on regarding the east, as in §A.130 and Appendix C.

[15] John's Sahl also allows the Moon.

[16] Namely, that it has some dignity there.

demonstrates that the matter is going to come to pass through intermediaries.

On the other hand, with a transfer of this kind being omitted and denied, it is right to investigate the collection of light. And so, should the lords of the east and of the question equally apply to some heavier [planet] at the same time, and it collects the light of both, it regarding the east or the place of the question,[17] or should it linger in the east or at least in the tenth, they affirm the matter without a doubt; but you should recognize that the end of the whole business will be resolved through the hands of magnates and powerful people.

[Summary of the three principal types of perfection][18]

Finally, the subject reminds [us] to recount the four principal ways by which every fixed question is ascertained.[19]

Therefore, the first is that the Moon (not without the lord of the east) and the significator of the question should respond to each other with some agreement of bearing.[20]

The second is that there be a conferring of light[21] between them.

Third, that there be a collection of light between them.

Fourthly, and what must then be considered, is which one (between the lord of the east and the significator, that is, the minister of the question) dispatches the light and counsel, or which of them collects the light.[22] And so this one, provided that it happens to be free and in a pivot or after a pivot (not retrograde nor scorched) affirms the matter without delay. But if it is corrupted by the infortunes, he will procure the matter but afterwards he will lose it through the staining corruption. Moreover, its retrogradation denies and wholly speaks against [success].

---

[17] John's Sahl has it only aspecting the place of the question, as in Māshā'allāh §A.132 above.
[18] Cf. *On Quest.* §1.4.
[19] Reading *invenitur* for *invertitur* (1509) and *invititur* (Madrid).
[20] That is, by assembly or aspect.
[21] That is, a transfer of light.
[22] Or rather, "receives" or "gathers." That is, which planet is applied to, and so ends up with the light.

[Whether it will happen easily or with difficulty][23]

Moreover, if the manner [of the perfection] should come into question, as to whether the effecting of the matter would follow easily or with difficulty, one must look for what figure of application there is between the lords of the east and of the question. A regard of application from a trigon or hexagon eases the business, [while] the tetragon and opposition introduce difficulty and trouble.[24]

[Who will perfect the matter]

If a transfer of light is observed, one must pay attention to that one of them from which the transferring [planet] is being separated, so that it applies to the other: for the movement and counsel of the whole business proceeds from that one (from whom the separation happens). [If from a collection of light, a person represented by the collecting planet will bring the matter to a conclusion.][25]

[Spoiling the matter]

But this comes to be noticed: an application of the Moon or of the eastern lord being made to the significator of the question, [while they are] lingering in [that planet's] own fall, speaks against what is asked about, and resists it. [An example] of this type is if it would apply to Mars from Cancer, or to Jupiter from Capricorn.[26]

No less do they spoil the querent's business if they should apply to a significator appearing in [the *applying* planet's] own fall, so that the one to which the application happens in no way receives them: such as if the Moon, I say,

---

[23] Cf. *On Quest.* §§1.5-1.6.
[24] Hugo here omits two short paragraphs which describe whether or not the matter will require much effort on the querent's part. Basically, if the lord of the Ascendant or the Moon are making the application or are in the place of the question, the querent will have to put in some effort; but if the significator of the question is making the application or is in the Ascendant, the other person will make the effort and the querent will not have to do much. However, Hugo did say something similar above.
[25] Paraphrasing an omitted sentence from *On Quest.* §1.6.
[26] This is called "not-reception," described in Sahl's *Introduct.* §5.9; cf. also *Forty Chapters* Ch. 2.1.8.

would be applying to some [planet] in 3° of Scorpio, or should Mars himself, being the lord of the Ascendant, apply to the same [while it is in Cancer].[27]

[An application] by a hostile figure makes a bad and the worst judgment. However, an application made from a prosperous figure does not threaten so dangerously.

[When one planet rules both places][28]

Moreover, whenever some one star[29] would happen to have rulership over the east and the question together at the same time, it seems one must pay attention to it with the greatest effort: it being established in a familiar and friendly way, and in a safe place (namely so that it is cleansed of the infortunes, free, and, applying to some [planet], being received), it will have such power [that] it shows the affair is found to be firm and steady. No less, too, if the Moon (being free and safe) should apply to the same, even should she apply to no other.[30]

[Testimonies of the signs][31]

But consequently, the testimonies of the signs will have to be discovered. For I reckon it is useful and necessary that the east be a firm [sign], or at least one of the double-bodied ones, and that the pivots be upright.[32] But we call a pivot "upright" whenever any pivot by itself exists in its own place, namely so that the tenth does not fall into the ninth [sign], nor the fourth in the third [sign].[33]

---

[27] Adding with John's Sahl, as Hugo runs this together with the next paragraph.
[28] Cf. *On Quest.* §1.6.
[29] Reading *una aliqua stella* for *uni alicui stellae*, following John's meaning.
[30] John's Sahl omits this last bit about the Moon applying to no other.
[31] Cf. *On Quest.* §1.7.
[32] *Recti*, which can also mean "direct, straight, correct."
[33] That is, that the MC-IC axis falls into the proper whole signs: the tenth and fourth signs. But I imagine that a second-best option would be for it to fall into the succeedent signs (the eleventh and fifth). Sahl is definitely trying to avoid putting the MC-IC axis into the cadent signs.

[Testimonies of the planets][34]

But the testimonies of the stars consist principally in three [of them], and these really make a judgment firm. But these are believed to emanate especially from the eastern lord, even from the Moon, and from the significator of the question itself.[35] And so, whenever one of the number of those three is safe, should [its] application to the lord of the question be observed, they make one-third of the affair firm. The freedom and safe testimonies of two, make two-thirds [firm]; but with three being observed, so that all are equally safe and received, they perfect and greatly increase what had been asked about.

[A question presented about a kingdom][36]

Therefore, so that the performance of the whole business may be brought to greater vividness, I have appended an example of this kind for the good of all.

Therefore, with a question presented about a kingdom, the east was Gemini in the twentieth degree; Pisces in the first.[37] And this was the position of the stars:[38] the Sun was staying in the twelfth of Cancer, with the Moon traversing in the seventeenth of Virgo, but Mercury was traversing in the twenty-seventh of Gemini, with Mars going through the eighth of Cancer, Venus in the third of the same, Jupiter in the twentieth of Pisces and in his first station, Saturn retrograde in the seventh of the same,[39] the Tail was staying with Jupiter. With all of them established thus, the order [of interpretation] demands [as follows]:

---

[34] Cf. *On Quest.* §1.8.
[35] This seems to be the significator of thought, the victor over the question or chart. See my introduction.
[36] Cf. *On Quest.* §1.8.
[37] Reading with Vienna and John's Sahl. The positions of the Ascendant and Midheaven are somewhat unclear if we compare the different versions. Madrid has the Ascendant in the twentieth degree of Gemini, and Pisces in the tenth. 1509 is rather garbled but seems to mean that the Ascendant is in 16 Gemini or its sixteenth degree, while Pisces is in the tenth. Using John's and Vienna's values, the chart was cast for about 34° N.
[38] I have followed Vienna, but the positions in John's Sahl are more accurate: see the likely chart below.
[39] Saturn could not be retrograde in this position.

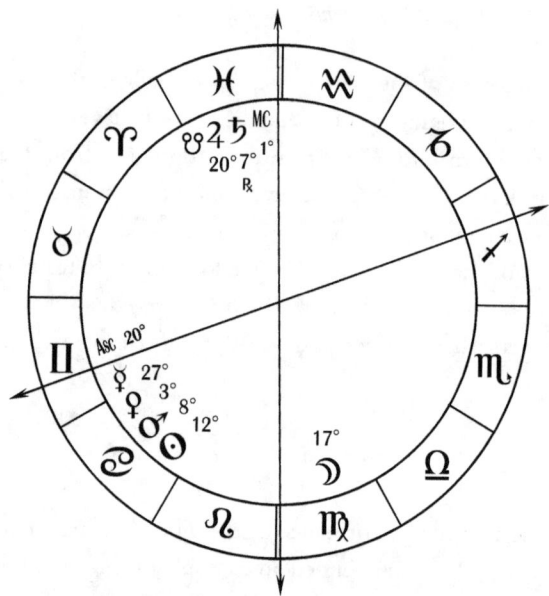

Figure 8: Sahl's chart according to Hugo

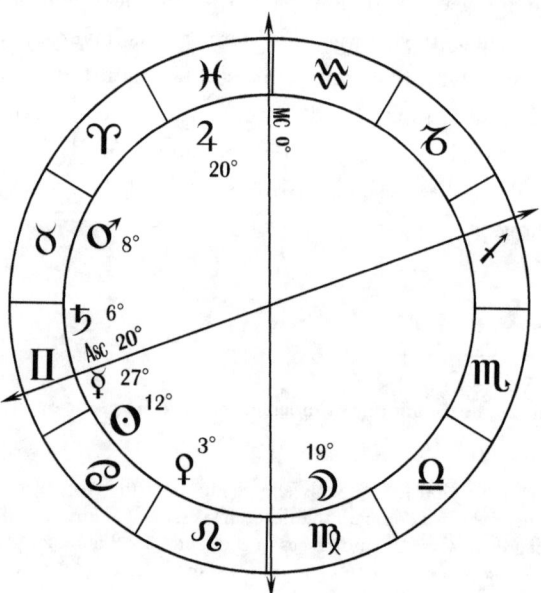

Figure 9: Sahl's chart according to John

§1.1: SAHL'S METHOD FOR QUESTIONS

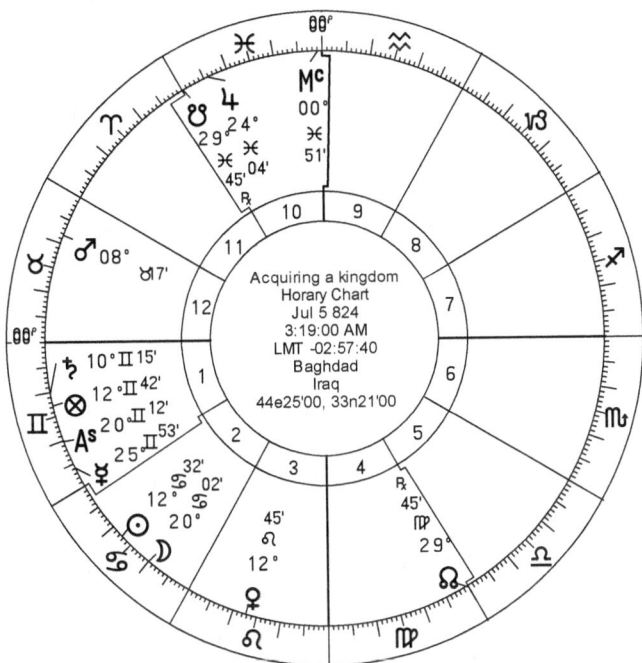

Figure 10: Likely chart for Sahl's example

The first observation is of the east and its lord, and of the Moon. Also, secondly we are invited [to look] at the pivot of the tenth and its lord.[40] Therefore Mercury (with his rulership of the east being assumed) was holding onto the last part [of Gemini]. Likewise Jupiter, assuming the signification of the question, was in the house of the question itself, but Mercury [was] already separated from him. And so, with this being abandoned and put aside,[41] I crossed over to the Moon, who, being in the pivot of the earth but who was applying to Jupiter from the opposite, earned the signification of the querent. Therefore, the application being made from the opposition demonstrated that the outcome of the quaesited matter would be troublesome.[42]

---

[40] The first and its lord and the Moon signify the querent; the tenth and its lord represent the kingdom or rulership.
[41] That is, their separation does not support perfection, so Sahl goes to the Moon as a next-best option.
[42] Note that in my recalculated chart, she is actually applying by trine from Cancer, which should make things easier.

But because Jupiter, gathering and taking up her counsel, was standing toward retrogradation, it is a sign that, although it had been obtained, it ought to be quickly cut short by the one giving [the kingdom]. For Jupiter himself was in 20°, so he was not obtaining a prosperous-enough rulership over the gift.[43] But if on the other hand the lord of the east was collecting the already-stated counsel (namely from the lord of the tenth), and [the lord of the east] had been unsound and less powerful, we would have suggested that the blame would emanate from the one taking it.[44] Again, the lord of the Ascendant was wanting to cross over from the east into the second, which we consider a sign of his hastened change toward [seeking] livelihood. However, he would not be successful, and in no way be received: because, traversing in Cancer, Mars in no way receives the applying one.[45] Moreover, because Mars claimed the sixth [house], he formed it so that harm would come to him because of slaves or troubles from his own body.

But because I found the Tail with Jupiter, under the rulership or signification of Jupiter, I acknowledge that it would throw [the affair] into not a little confusion. Moreover, the Mercurial separation from Jupiter portends that he formerly came into hopes of [having the kingdom], and he has already withdrawn, almost desolate. But the Moon (as was already said) seemed to draw [us] back [to this conclusion].

And so, the method of judgments encourages and warns us that everything else is to be scrutinized in this way.

---

[43] Hugo himself seems to have added the degree, even though it is not really relevant. The point is simply that since Jupiter signifies the current ruler, and is separating by retrogradation from Mercury in an earlier degree, the current ruler will renege on the promise.

[44] Translating somewhat freely from Hugo's compressed Latin, following John. So, if Jupiter had been applying to Mercury but Mercury had been weak and corrupted, then the querent would be largely responsible for the problems. Recall above, where the planet being applied to has the final management power.

[45] After changing signs, Mercury will apply to a sextile with Mars, but from the sign of Mars's fall: a case of "not-reception" (see above).

LIFE

§1.2: On the quantity of life—al-Khayyāt

The first house (namely the east) signifies life. Whenever therefore a question about the quantity of life would be presented by the one asking, a first and principal observation of the lord of the east and of the Moon should be had. For the Lunar separation judges about life that is passed, but [her] application suggests the remaining part. The eastern lord already being under the rays and entering into scorching, while certain infortunes would be lingering in the east or in the seventh, it really suggests death.

The hour and term of death could be discovered from the lord of the east. For, how many degrees it is distant from scorching should be especially noted, and those degrees of distance determine the final hour: from a firm sign, they testify he will survive [that many] years; from a double-bodied one, months; from a convertible one, days. And more distinctly and firmly so, if a malevolent traversing in the east (or which regards it) would rule over the lodging-place of the fourth or eighth.[1] But if benevolents would bear testimony to the east, while equally the Moon and the lord of the east would be saved (they being cleansed of the infortunes), they suggest long-lasting state of life.

In addition, it seems one must note [this]: once the degrees from the Moon to the malevolent by which she is corrupted, and from the lord of the east to the scorching, are discovered, the number of degrees of the Moon to the malevolent prefigures life's losses and impediments, [but] from the lord of the east to scorching, the quantity of life.

Moreover, the traversing of the eastern lord or of the Moon with the lord of the house of death, or of each (or one) in the house of death [itself], or their burning, or application to one of the malevolents from the tetragon or opposition, or the lord of the eighth in the east, is fatal in the same way; but conversely, their freedom promises escape. For the period and quantity [of life], imitate the opinion stated above.

The traversal of the benevolents in the east, or at least should the lord of the east or the Moon apply to fortunate ones, does not throw in so much hasty fear. Nevertheless, while they bear themselves thusly, a living status is

---

[1] Reading with Vienna for 1509's "sixth or eighth" and Madrid's "fourth and seventh." See Dorotheus's alternative account below.

promised according to the years of that benevolent: for, that lucky one being in a pivot promises or bestows the greater years; after the pivot, the middle ones; from the remote [places], the lesser ones.

	Lesser	Middle	Greater	Greatest
♄	30	43 ½	57	265
♃	12	45 ½	79	427
♂	15	40 ½	66	284
☉	19	69 ½	120	1,461
♀	8	45	82	1,151
☿	20	48	76	480
☽	25	66 ½	108	520

Figure 11: Table of planetary years

§1.3: On life already gone by, and the portion of it left—Dorotheus[2]

If someone made a question about life, the lord of the east and the Moon should be consulted. For the Lunar[3] separation shows the portion of life passed by, but the application settles what is left. The health and freedom of the lord of the east, preserves the length of the remaining part; being burned up and unlucky, reveals its shortness. If therefore the testimonies of the fortunate ones show favor to the east, while the Moon and the lord of the east are being cleansed of the infortunes or stars harmful to them (which are the lord of the eighth and sixth and twelfth, even [the primary lord] of the triplicity of the fourth—namely the one which possesses the shift[4]—[and] moreover the lord of the fourth), it watches over the increase of life and the health of the body. Likewise, the lord of the east entering into scorching, and the Moon being cadent from the east and corrupted, or if the degree of the infortunes would hold onto the east or the seventh, it takes away from the querent's life. However, the degrees of the eastern lord (those which make the distance between it and scorching), undoubtedly lay bare the hour of this trouble. Traversing in a convertible [sign] turns the degrees of distance into

---

[2] According to Burnett, the second part of this section is not in the Arabic of BKh.
[3] Reading *lunaris* for *luminis*.
[4] *Nobam*, a transliteration for the Ar. *nawbah*. The "shift" refers to the shifting of sects between night and day, and the role played by the planets of each sect in that shift. So, Dorotheus is telling us to use the primary triplicity lord of the fourth, which changes by night and day. *Carmen* refers to this triplicity lord as indicating death in several places, such as *Carmen* IV.1.81.

days; in a double-bodied one, months; in a firm one too, it changes the degrees placed in between into years. It is difficult and the worst with the infortunes being established in the east, or if they would regard it from the opposition or tetragon, or at least some portion of the harmful [stars would do so].

Then also, the distance which is between the Moon and an infortune and the harmful stars, must be noted. For whenever the number of degrees is given up,[5] it determines harm and troubles up until the end of life.

Likewise, it is appropriate to note the lords of the triplicity of the east, and their benevolence and corruption, because they signify the health of life and its troubles.

Again, the lord of the fourth portends the end of life to be safe or the contrary for him, while it surpasses the eastern lord in power, and over the east in signification.

Now, the lord of the east declares the end of [the querent's] own person, but the lord of the Lunar lodging-place [indicates] what troubles there are.

☋   ☊   ☋

[Quarters of life]

With[6] a question being presented as to what quarter of life is going to be preferable, the first [quarter] is conceded to the east, the second to the south, the third to the west, the fourth to the north. Where, therefore, the benevolent stars and the Lot of Fortune, but even the Moon (they being cleansed of the infortunes and scorching) would happen to be found, you will remember to judge that quarter [of life] as being preferable.[7]

[Geographical areas]

Also in this manner: should one seek a part of the whole earth which should be chosen for you to turn to on a journey, I say that the one which the fortunate ones possess ([provided that it is] in the regard of the east, I say) should be judged as being more useful than the rest.

---

[5] I believe Dorotheus means "once the years indicated by the distance have expired."
[6] For the rest of this section, cf. Lilly's version in *CA* pp. 137-38.
[7] Omitting *si*.

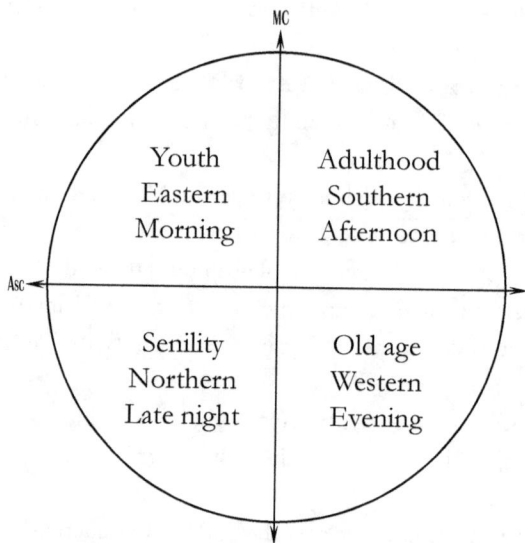

Figure 12: Quarters of heaven: directions, ages, and parts of the day

[Times of day]

If however a matching[8] question will be given about the quarters of the day—namely, should you more familiarly choose each of them as being as propitious for carrying out one's affairs—the east itself and the pivots should be consulted. From the east to the Midheaven, claims the east; from the degree of the Midheaven to the seventh is left to the south; but from the seventh to the pivot of the earth possesses the west; moreover the north takes it from the pivot of the earth to the east. Therefore, with fortunate ones being placed in the eastern part, one will have to accomplish business in the first part of the day; but being established in the southern [part] invites us to the second [part of the day]; in the western one they commend the third [part]; but possessing the north, they suggest the fourth [part] is more advantageous.

Also, the method of Hermes: with the eastern part being possessed by fortunate ones, it commits [the part] from the middle of the day to the arising of the Sun to doing business; but from the middle of the day to the setting of the Sun [it is committed] to those holding the south; now, if they

---

[8] Reading *consimilis* for what looks like *consina*.

should traverse in the western [direction], it claims that from the setting to the middle of the night is better; also, in the northern [direction], [it means] the quarter from the middle of the night to the rising of the Sun [is better]. If the infortunes would occupy any quarters, it encourages you to wholly avoid them.

§1.4: On the life of the querent that has gone by, and the portion of it left—Jirjis

It is good to note how many degrees the lord of the eastern face has crossed through in its own sign, but even how many [degrees] of the east there were. Once these [degrees] which it has crossed through, have been multiplied[9] the eastern degrees, if they went over the sum of 100, then once 100 have really been thrown away, what is left over suggests the years of life already gone by. But if how many degrees were left to that star in its own sign, would be multiplied by the remaining [degrees] of the east, if that went beyond the sum of 100, [then] with 100 being thrown away in the same manner, it undoubtedly shows the years of future life left.

§1.5: On the life of the querent—Jirjis

But it is good that the degrees which the lord of the eastern triplicity has crossed through in the face of its sign, be multiplied by the degrees of the eastern bound that have passed by. But if it went beyond the sum of 100, [then] with [100] being thrown away, it will be permitted to recognize the life passed by, through what is left over. But, multiplying the remaining [degrees] of the eastern bound by those which are left over to its lord in its own face, if it went beyond the sum of 100, you will throw away 100. Therefore, how many were left suggests the years of the querent's future life.

---

[9] Since we are dealing with decans and a maximum of 100, I believe Jirjis means to multiply the number of degrees each has passed through *within its current decan*. So for example, if the lord of the eastern face has passed through 5° of its current face (wherever that is within the sign as a whole), while the Ascendant has passed through 7° of whatever face it is in, that yields 35 years. But I do wonder whether we are supposed to use the lord of the face, or the lord of the Ascendant.

§1.6: On the life of the querent—Aristotle

If however you desire to know whether someone should live long, it will be good to consult the eastern lord. For, the eastern lord traversing in a pivot, testifies he is going to live longer; if after the pivots, it promises it is more diminished; in the remote [places], it suggests a shorter life.

§2: SECOND HOUSE

2nd House	
Acquiring money	§§2.1-5
Source of money	§§2.6-10
Quantity of money	§§2.11-12
When acquired	§2.13
Collecting debts	§§2.13-14, 2.16

Figure 13: Questions of the second house

§2.1: On those things which pertain to the second house—Sahl[1]

Whenever inquiries of the second after the east are brought forth (of which kind is that for livelihood, profit, and expected acquisition—or even what is going to come unexpectedly), first of all it is good to observe the significators of the querent himself: namely, the lord of the east and the Moon. But after that, the second and the lord of the second must be consulted. But everywhere we even apply the partner, Jupiter, because he portends wealth and resources.[2]

And so, the Moon or the lord of the east applying to the significator (that is, the minister of the question),[3] or the significator [applying to] the eastern [lord], or at least if there is a transfer of light between them, it promises livelihood and makes a certain judgment of acquisition. Venus and Jupiter being found in the domicile of resources even conveys the same thing.

Likewise, with these things (which were stated above) being in no way found, wealth and the acquisition of livelihood is denied. But if the malevolents traverse in the second (which is the domicile of profit), they do not only destroy livelihoods, but prepare and introduce losses. But if the Moon happened to be found treading in a solitary way, this misfortune will be long-lasting and unwavering.[4]

---

[1] Cf. *On Quest.* §2.1. This should be read with §§2.4 and 2.5.
[2] This sentence is not in John's Sahl, and may have been inserted by Hugo in accordance with al-Khayyāt in §2.4 below.
[3] That is, the lord of the second, according to al-Khayyāt.
[4] I take this to mean that the Moon must be void in course *in addition to* the other indicators of misfortune.

§2.2: On acquiring money—'Umar

And so, a question about obtaining money usually comes to be in a manifold way. For most often, someone about to seek it falls into doubt as to whether he should demand it from the king or approach someone else completely.[5]

Moreover, with respect to acquiring wealth, sometimes an indefinite question is brought up.[6] If therefore someone asking about getting resources asked in an indefinite way, it seems appropriate to attend to whether or not the lord of the east and the Moon (or either of these) would regard the east,[7] [and] even the star which collected the light of each, or which rendered light between each, or [the light] of one of them to the east: because that one deserves to have control over the duty of the significator. Therefore, this [significator] applying to fortunate ones and being received, really lavishes money from that party[8] which it regards. And if it were variously demanded from the tetragon or opposition or assembly, it will bring profit after labor. From a trigon or hexagon, it introduces it easily.

Moreover, if he would try to obtain something from the king, while [the significator] would apply to the lord of the Midheaven (not without its reception), even being regarded by the lord of the eleventh, he will wrest the favor from the king. However, a tetragonal or oppositional regard or application, or from an assembly, is difficult; from the trigon or hexagon, it wholly confers it without labor.[9]

§2.3: On acquiring money—al-Kindī[10]

§453. Anyone worried about accumulating money, [who] burns avidly [with a desire] to increase his possessions, [but is] uncertain by what means or from whom or where and whence he would be able to acquire it, should consult the lord of the Ascendant. For an application of it with the lord of

---

[5] *Absolute.*
[6] That is, without a specific person involved, and perhaps without a specific timeline: see §1.1 above.
[7] 'Umar is telling us to decide which planet will be the querent's primary significator, just as he has in §A.130, and as Māshā'allāh does in OR Ch. 2 (Appendix C below).
[8] *Parte.* I take 'Umar to mean that the nature and rulerships of the fortunate planet will indicate the kind of person who supplies the money.
[9] This question is continued in §2.7 below.
[10] Cf. al-Rijāl I.24-25.

money,[11] and being received by it, it even being in the regard of the Sun and Moon (particularly if the lord of money would regard the Ascendant itself or][12] the lord of the Ascendant), greatly increases the hope of acquiring it.[13]

§454. On the other hand, an application of the lord of the Ascendant[14] with the lord of the Lot of Fortune, and [the lord of the Lot's] status (or rather its manner of bearing itself) with the Sun and Moon being no other than with the lord of the second, especially with the Moon regarding the Lot of Fortune, it indicates the same.

But if an application of the lord of the Ascendant with the [lord of the][15] Lot of Fortune is removed, but an application of the same [is] transferred to the lord of [the Lot of][16] money, while the lords of the Ascendant and of the Lot of money bear themselves with the Sun and Moon as was stated before, they mitigate the hope of acquiring it.[17]

[Jupiter]

§455. Jupiter seems to confirm the same thing [when] regarding the Ascendant [or] its lord [or the significator of assets],[18] whichever of these three significators of money it was. Also, Jupiter is asserted to be stronger in the signification or leadership of money when he appears in the second with the lord of the Ascendant and the significator of money, or in the Ascendant,[19] or in the eleventh or in the tenth or in the rest of the pivots, or even after the pivots.[20]

☽   ☽   ☾

---

[11] The lord of the second.
[12] Adding with al-Rijāl.
[13] Robert reads: "The lord of the east joined to the lord of assets, and received by it, and seen by the lights (especially if the lights would be aspecting the lord of assets)."
[14] Al-Rijāl reads this as the lord of the second.
[15] Adding with al-Rijāl.
[16] Adding with al-Rijāl. But one might expect this also to work with the lord of the second, as Hugo has it.
[17] That is, they relieve the querent's sense of urgency precisely because his hopes will be fulfilled.
[18] Probably the lord of the second (adding with al-Rijāl), but see §460 below, which suggests the significator of money is the victor over the matter as described in *Forty Chapters* Ch. 3.1. Al-Qabīsī, drawing on al-Kindī, describes his own victor of money in *ITA* I.18.
[19] Al-Rijāl reads as though Jupiter is in the second with the lord of the Ascendant, while the significator of assets is in the Ascendant, eleventh, etc.
[20] For four more paragraphs on Jupiter by al-Kindī, see §2.8 below.

§460. Again, the lords of the Ascendant and of money, even Jupiter and the significators written above, appearing with the significator of money,[21] in the pivots, show manifold and steady money, and of a stronger nature.

§461. But among these, the Ascendant is established as being best, after this the tenth, then the seventh, lastly the fourth. But of those which follow the pivots, we choose the eleventh in first place, then the second, after that the fifth,[22] finally the eighth.

§462. Moreover, the significator of money or Jupiter being eastern and direct, in some place of its authority, and being received (as was said above), describes much and the best money. Likewise, the significator being received and regarding Venus and being cleansed of the infortunes, hastens the same thing. Likewise, Mercury in the [significator's] regard and receiving[23] it, he being fortunate and strengthened in his own light, indicates the success and enjoyment of money. Which if they would bear themselves otherwise, they bring a different judgment.

[The time of wealth]

§463. The degrees of application declare the hour at which acquiring money should undoubtedly be expected, by alternating days or months or years according to the nature of the signs.

[Yet more indicators of success]

§464. Which if there would be an application of the lord of the Ascendant ([and] no less, even any of the significators of money)[24] to the fortunate ones in a pivot, it promises long-lasting and useful supplies.

§465. Moreover, the significator of money applying to the lord of the Ascendant: he acquires it easily. But the application of the lord of the Ascendant [to the significator of money] does not bring it without labor and

---

[21] Again, this is probably the victor of the topic from *Forty Chapters* Ch. 3.1.
[22] Al-Rijāl has the fifth before the second. This list is probably the source for ibn Ezra's house strengths in his victor calculation (*Search*, App. F). This particular assignment, which seems to be based on the Nechepso version of advantageous houses (see *ITA* III.2-3) is not used in the methods drawing on "Māshā'allāh" and Dorotheus in *Search* I.3.4 and III.1.1.
[23] Reading *recipiens* for *respiciens*, with Robert.
[24] Reading *cuiuslibet ducum pecuniae* (following Robert) for Hugo's *cuiuslibet eorum assignant* and *Judges' cuiuslibet eorum qui assignati*. Al-Rijāl has the lord of assets.

training.[25] Which if this application happened from retrogradation, he amasses riches from something unexpected. The retrogradation of all of the significators (once their signification would already incite the hope of inquiring about money), puts dangers and impediments in front of it.[26] Their unluckiness attacks and perverts the same thing according to the nature of the infortune itself and its own house (namely the one it looks at with a familiar aspect).[27]

§466. If however a question of this kind happened with respect to a [specific][28] man or some land, the Ascendant designates the one seeking it, but the seventh bears the signification of that man from whom he greatly desires to obtain it, or of the region about which he set forth the question.

§467.[29] Wherefore, [1] an application of the lord of the Ascendant with the lord of the money of the seventh;[30] or if [2] the lord of the Lot of Fortune of the seventh or the Lot of money of the seventh would apply to the lord of the Ascendant or of the second; or [3] the lord of the Ascendant [would apply] to the lord of the Lot of money of the seventh or to the lord of its Lot of Fortune—if the witnesses which we said before were present—they confirm the hope of acquiring money.

[Robert]: And if there were a conjunction of: [1] the ruler of the east with the lord of the assets of the seventh, or conversely; or [2] of the lord of the assets of the seventh with the lord of the assets of the east;[31] or [3] of the lord of the Lot of Fortune (or [the lord] of the Lot

---

[25] *Exercitio.* One might have preferred *nisu* or *studio*, "effort."
[26] That is, their connection shows he will get the money, but he must overcome obstacles first.
[27] Al-Rijāl reads, "and of the house in which the infortune was, and according to the aspect which it had with the significators." Robert seems to agree with al-Rijāl.
[28] Adding on the basis of al-Rijāl. That is, if the querent is not asking just about wealth in general but about getting money from a specific man, or through a journey to a particular place. See also *Forty Chapters* Ch. 22.
[29] This paragraph must have been particularly vexing in the Arabic, as none of the Latin authors agrees on all of the conditions. What makes it complicated is that it requires separate calculations of the Lots of Fortune and assets/money, for both the Ascendant and the querent. So for example, the Lot of assets or money of the seventh would require counting forward from the lord of the eighth to the eighth, and projecting that distance from the degree of the Descendant; in the same way, the Lot of Fortune of the seventh would project the usual Sun-Moon distance from the Descendant instead of from the Ascendant.
[30] That is, the lord of the Ascendant with the lord of the eighth.
[31] That is, the lord of the eighth with the lord of the second.

of money) of the seventh with the corresponding Lots of the east or [with] the lord of the second; or [4] even of the lord of the east with the aforesaid Lots of the seventh—and the testimonies of discovering [money] stated above, were in agreement—the attainment or conveying of the matter will invariably follow.

[al-Rijāl I.25]:[32] And if the lord of the house of assets applied to the Ascendant or with the lord of the Ascendant, or the lord of the Ascendant with the lord of the second, or the Lot of Fortune [were] in the seventh house, or the Lot of assets of the seventh [were] with the lord of the Ascendant or with the lord of the second, or the lord of the Ascendant and the lord of the Lot of assets of the seventh [were] with the Lot of Fortune, and the fortunes [were] testifying, he will have the assets just as we stated in the chapter before.

§468. But their different causes and their mutual status and manner (just as has often been said), render a different opinion.

§2.4: On acquiring money—al-Khayyāt

The lord of the east and the Moon give counsel for a question about money (namely whether someone would obtain what he hopes for, or not). For, with the application of each with the lord of the second being discovered, or provided that the Moon would apply to the eastern lord from the lord of the second,[33] it consoles the hope of obtaining money.

Moreover, with a lucky one being placed in the house of resources, or at least should the Moon or the lord of the east apply to a benevolent, it is the same. But if that lucky one is ascending,[34] while however it regarded the east, it promises honors and dignities, not without much convenience. Likewise, with it being cadent and corrupt, he will perhaps acquire his daily sustenance for individual days, [but] he will never have hope concerning the honor.[35]

---

[32] Reading this paragraph with the 1485 edition of al-Rijāl, as it contains a phrase missing in 1551.
[33] That is, a transfer of light.
[34] Reading *ascendens* with Vienna for *conscendens*. But a planet in the second cannot aspect the Ascendant. See §2.5, where Dorotheus allows an aspect to a planet which itself regards the east. Al-Khayyāt probably means "*or* while it regarded…".
[35] Or rather, he will never have the honor hoped for.

But should the Moon or the lord of the east apply to a malevolent, or with infortunes being placed in the second, they wholly speak against and deter the querent. Finally, with the Moon wandering alone, it suggests the querent will have that steady and invariable status up until the last moment of life. The preferable benevolent in the second is Jupiter, for he greatly bestows resources and countless coins.

Moreover, for money and dignities, as to whether someone would be able to get them, the lord of the east and the Moon and the Lot of Fortune should be consulted. But the Lot of Fortune, being lucky, applying with the lord of the east and the Moon, strengthens hope and blesses with manifold dignity. With the eastern lord then being corrupted, it detracts in many ways from the hope that was had. With the Lot being corrupted, if the Moon (being equally unlucky) would regard [the Lot], it wholly speaks against what was sought—or, if he got a moderate amount, it has no usefulness. The luckiness of the Moon and the corruption of the Lot lavishes a moderate amount, and then uses it up.

§2.5: On acquiring money—Dorotheus

When inquiries of the second occur, as to what kind or in what manner of acquiring the expected money it is, the lord of the east and the Moon should be consulted. For their application with the lord of money testifies that he is going to obtain it.

If however the benevolents apply to some [planet which is] regarding the east, [it indicates] the greatest and steady and lasting profit, and they convey manifold resources. Which if this fortunate [planet] is Jupiter, it is the best. Moreover, this benevolent being cadent or scorched, and if it manages the resources, it introduces them, but [they are] inconstant, and in the succession of days [it will be] with shame and difficulty.

Moreover, an application of the Moon and the eastern lord being had with an infortune appearing in the twelfth, threatens detriment and particularly the loss of the resource.

§2.6: What is the source and kind of the acquiring—Sahl[36]

Finally, once the certainty of profit has been discovered, next is the source and kind of acquisition: and among the significators, the one which gathers the counsel of the other [indicates it].[37] For, it traversing in the east or second, prepares riches and promises resources through his own business and labor. But if it should linger in the third, he grows rich with the help of brothers and sisters. Concerning the fourth, it introduces it because of parents and paternal relatives. If in the fifth, he would obtain gifts and children. In the sixth, it was on the occasion of infirmities, captives, and the rabble. Established in the seventh, he even contracts this from women and a controversy. In the eighth, because of inheritance and old things. Traversing in the ninth, he will be made rich through travels, teachings, laws, and that sort. In the tenth, through the resources and counsel of kings and magnates. But concerning the eleventh, he will possess resources because of friends and commerce. If you find it in the twelfth, he will claim the aforestated livelihood from enemies—which if it were a four-footed [sign], he will rejoice in the acquired resources of four-footed beasts; if of a human form, prison and captives.

And so, this nature or proper quality of the signs, and this status and progress through the individual houses, manages the path and order of judgments, both of trouble and reward (just as the places of the lucky ones and the malevolents demand), through a most certain method.

§2.7: What is the origin and kind of acquiring—'Umar

Which if he would approach someone else in particular rather than the king,[38] it will be good to discern the affair from its own category, namely whether he would expect something from a child or brother, and that sort of thing, according to the proper quality of the question. For if the significator itself[39] would apply with the lord of that house, or there would be a transfer between them, or one which would transfer light to the lord of the east, resources and favors are designated from that category; but without that, not at

---

[36] Cf. *On Quest.* §2.2. It should be read with §§2.9 and 2.10.
[37] That is, the planet which is applied to indicates the source and kind.
[38] See §2.2 above, where 'Umar considers both getting wealth in general and from the king.
[39] Either the lord of the Ascendant or the Moon, according to his procedure in §2.2.

all. However, from the tetragon or opposition and the assembly, let no other judgment be given than the one above;[40] but from the trigon or hexagon, the opinion remains the same as what is above.

§2.8: Whence he would have it—al-Kindī

It even seems that this must be appended:

§456. That if either Jupiter or one of the significators[41] were established in the Ascendant, it multiplies the acquired resources through his own labor. Also, with him appearing in the second as we said before, he gets rich through the actions of those serving and attending him, and through the profit of money. Appearing in the tenth, he is made rich because of the king or a royal affair. Again, in the eleventh, from the underofficials and friends of the king, and even hope, and [his] storehouses will overflow with due ease.

§457. Which if [Jupiter were] in the seventh, he incurs riches from women and trade, controversy and quarrels. The same [planet] even in the eighth introduces inheritances, things deposited for safekeeping, [and] goods acquired through someone's death, into his possession. Moreover in the fourth, because of some ancient thing or land or agriculture. Which if he would dwell in the fifth, [his] possession is increased through children and gifts and promises.

§458. On the other hand,[42] Jupiter being situated with the lord of the Ascendant[43] and the significator of money in the twelfth, although [he will suffer] badly from enemies, resources are often gathered together because of charity[44] and the benefits of the dead, and prisons. But with him appearing in the ninth, journeys and certain low-quality and less fitting affairs, even things found on a journey, will show the increase of riches.

§459. In the sixth, slaves and people of this kind, and humble things (and so on), someone's disease, animals, a short captivity, render him rich. But if

---

[40] That is, in §2.2. Squares and oppositions make difficulties, sextiles and trines make easy acquisition.
[41] In *Forty Chapters*, these paragraphs only deal with Jupiter. Hugo seems to have added "or one of the significators" on his own, for his purposes here.
[42] This paragraph refers to Jupiter in the cadent places, but note that he requires the help of the lord of the Ascendant and the significator of money.
[43] Al-Rijāl reads as though Jupiter *is* the lord of the Ascendant.
[44] Reading *elemosinis* as a transliteration of the Ar. ʾinsāniyyah, "charity, humanity." This also appears in Sahl's *On Quest.* §10.3.

in the third, brothers, journeys and his own friends, [and] the father's friends, adorn him most abundantly with riches.

§2.9: Whence he would have it, and what is the kind of [thing] acquired—al-Khayyāt

But whence and on what occasion he would have the aforesaid resources, could be discovered thusly. For the star which promises wealth of this kind being placed in the east, he will possess the already-stated wealth through his own labor or office. In the second, the same; in the third, from brothers and a short journey; in the fourth, from parents and relatives; and in this manner through the rest of the domiciles. A malevolent being just as we stated, it will be spoiled and deny [the acquisition]; the occasion of the corruption will be according to the nature of its own place where it is staying.

But if he would like to obtain the money from the king, let the east be put in charge of the querent, the tenth the king, the eleventh the royal resources. Therefore, an application of the eastern lord or his significator (namely, the Moon)[45] with the lord of the eleventh (as was stated about the rest above), they console the hope of acquiring [it].

But if someone made a question about the money and what is left over by [someone] dead, the eighth lodging-place should be noted. The eastern lord or the significator[46] applying to [the lord of][47] it, or it to it, commends the things that are sought. Moreover, for acquiring wealth through the business of commerce, the application of the lord of the eighth with the lord of the east or second, has a judgment of the same thing.

But with respect to all of these, another opinion is given according to the ancients: for if the querent anticipates money hoped for from the king especially, or certain nobles, the matter encourages us to attend to the Solar place[48] and that of Jupiter[49] ([although] they are considered secondary compared with the east and its lord). For, each one occupying a pivot with the Lot of money or its lord, or being placed in the house of money (with Mars

---

[45] This is in 1509, and handwritten above the line in Vienna. Since it seems to be taken from 'Umar in §2.2 (which also uses the lord of the Ascendant and the Moon), I have retained it.
[46] Again, probably the Moon, if she fulfills 'Umar's rules.
[47] Added by Dykes.
[48] For the king.
[49] For nobles.

being cadent from them, and adverse), they easily obtain the wealth that is sought. But Mars being stronger than Jupiter and traversing in [Jupiter's] pivot,[50] while he regards the lord of the second or the Lot of Fortune, there will be labor and difficulty from the owner of those resources, and much scattering of them. However, with Saturn occupying the place of Mars, there will be slowness in it, and delay through the king or powerful person. In fact, the traversal of Saturn from the place of Jupiter,[51] even though it takes away very little, still today [it grants] very little, [but] tomorrow a moderate amount in return.

§2.10: Whence he would have it—Dorotheus

But the star designating money especially responds to the question as to whence and from whom he would reach resources of this kind. It being placed in the east, teaches money acquired through his own nature; likewise in the second; but in the third, he will be enriched from the direction of brothers; in the fourth, from the parents and wife; and one will have to report it in this manner through the rest of the domiciles, according to the manner of their signification and [their] prosperity. After that, with the Moon being unlucky, corruption of this kind proceeds from the place[52] with she claims in the circle.

§2.11: On the quantity and number of money acquired—al-Khayyāt

If someone would ask about the quantity and number of the money acquired, the solution should be sought from [the lord of][53] the second house and the Lot of resources and Mercury. For the stronger of these, and the stronger minister of its own place, and propped up by many testimonies, really takes on the role of the signification.

Therefore Mercury (with the signification being taken [by him]), appearing in his own fall or placed perversely, conveys 20 *denarii* (or *solidi*).[54] Which if he would linger in his own triplicity, he lavishes 200. From his own domicile,

---

[50] That is, being in Jupiter's sign or in a whole-sign square or opposition to him.
[51] That is, being in the whole-sign angles from Jupiter.
[52] Reading *loco* for *loci*.
[53] Adding based on Dorotheus in §2.12 below.
[54] Types of ancient coinage.

2,000. Being in his own sovereignty, 20,000.[55] In this way too, the generality of the stars acquits[56] the things promised, according to their lesser years and their number, if (I say) they would traverse in their own fall or would walk to that very place. But if they would linger in their own triplicity, for the lesser number of years they change it by a multiple of 10.[57] From [their own] houses, it is that much by 100. From [their] supremacies, an equal amount by 1,000.

But with a star going retrograde, one-half of the aforesaid is subtracted. Which if it were burned up, one will have to subtract according to the manner of scorching and its distance from the Sun by 12°. For whenever it was distant by 6°,[58] one-half of its signification will be bestowed. But if it would be overcome by [the Sun] by only 4°, it will allot a one-third portion. Which if the distance of each is the greatest one, one will have to report it according to the quantity of the number. But when traversing with the Sun, it conveys nothing at all.

The regard of a malevolent[59] diminishes the amount of things, in terms of its strength and power where it traverses (such as was said about the house, sovereignty, triplicity and even fall).

In fact, Jupiter regarding the significator from his own sovereignty, will apply 12,000;[60] from the house, 1,200; from the triplicity he will add 120. But whenever from the fall or [something] of this kind, he will show an increase of 12. In scorching, he takes a moderate amount away according to his distance from the Sun. Therefore, in order that I might conclude briefly, both

---

[55] I have corrected the numbers in this sentence (which vary between manuscripts) in accordance with the rules given here and in 'Umar's §4.7 and §6.50 below. 'Umar is not absolutely precise about all of the conditions, but if the planet is in any dignity between its fall and its triplicity, it will indicate as many units as its lesser years (for a table, see §1.2). In its triplicity, it will indicate those units or at most the lesser years multiplied by 10. In its own domicile, the years multiplied by 100; in its exaltation, multiplied by 1,000. In §6.50 below, 'Umar wants these same planets to be angular as well, which suggests that the worse the condition is, the less the amount. See further in §6.50, where 'Umar outlines some further conditions.

[56] *Exsolvunt*.

[57] That is, the lesser years are multiplied by ten.

[58] Reading with Madrid and Vienna for 1509's *v*.

[59] In this paragraph and the next, al-Khayyāt is applying rules similar to the addition or subtraction of other years from the *kadukhudhāh* in longevity calculations. See *TBN* I.4 (in my *PN2*), and *JN* Ch. 3 (in my *PN1*).

[60] In this paragraph, I have assigned the numbers according to the rules described above, but the manuscripts vary wildly. For the exaltation, they give 12 or 12,000; for the domicile, 11 or 2 or 2,000 or 200; for the triplicity, 250.

the fortunate ones and the infortunes add or subtract according to the manner of this example.

Whenever therefore the significator that points out the number and which indicates the increase would be staying in a double-bodied sign, let there be a duplication of the number.

Nevertheless it can even happen that the infortunes have a signification of this kind, but what belongs to their signification is equally lavished.[61]

§2.12: On the quantity and number of the money acquired—Dorotheus

The lord of the [second] lodging-place and the Lot of its money explain the quantity of the money acquired. For the stronger of them, and the one whom more testimonies favor, will be ascribed the signification of the wealth.

And so, Mercury appearing in his own fall and a wicked place, bestows the gifts of 20 *denarii*. In the triplicity he conveys 200 *denarii*; in [his] sovereignty, he introduces 20,000 coins.[62] The remaining stars of the houses [are treated] in this likeness, according to the quantity of the lesser years: if they would hold onto [their] fall or an unlucky place, they bless with the promised gifts. Likewise, traversing in the triplicity they bestow multiples of ten for the number of the triplicity. Also, in [their own] house they increase its number by [multiplies of] 100. But in [their] sovereignty, he will rejoice in an increase to that number [by multiples of 1,000]. Which if the star were retrograde, it goes back to one-fourth [of the number].[63]

We recommend that you never fall away from this kind of [step-by-step] increase.

§2.13: On the hour of acquiring money—'Umar

However, through this method one will plainly discover the time or hour, namely at which the divine virtue of the stars, which is always conferring favors (even though diverse ones) upon certain animated things, would favor the querent with the expected resources. For whenever the significators

---

[61] That is, even though an infortune may signify the amount, if its condition is good enough, it will not take away from, but actually give, all of its amount.
[62] Again, I have made this number conform to the rules in al-Khayyāt above.
[63] Note that al-Khayyāt takes away only one-half of the number for a retrograde planet.

would apply to the querent's chief star, in some dignity (in a pivot of the signs, I say, or of the stars), while however there is reception between them, he will accept the desired favor.

§2.14: On debts—al-Khayyāt[64]

But if a question about debts came out into the open, the east is conceded to the querent (be he the debtor or creditor). But the seventh suggests him about whom it is asked. The money will be handed over to Mercury and the Moon. For if they should regard it[65] by a trigon or hexagon, all things will be called back to peace and concord; with an aspect being denied, the presence of each is denied to both.[66]

But the Moon (or any other [planet]) transferring the light [means that] he restores it unexpectedly through a mediator or messenger. The luckiness of the Moon [means] he receives it well and honorably.

But with Mercury being corrupted by the malice of Saturn, the creditor seeks the accepted money all over again, and in demanding it again, he will bring lying witnesses to bear. Being corrupted by Mars, he mixes in discord, sows quarrels, and prepares a controversy.

Finally, with the Moon being scorched (as was shown about her above),[67] it will not be unuseful to pursue the signification of the Sun; and the application of each with the benevolents or the hostile [planets] should be noted.

§2.15: On the fortune of worldly things, and their greatness in terms of worthiness—al-Kindī[68]

§114. The pivots and those stars which are staying in the pivots, untie the knot of this question, for they designate noted, famous, and public things. But those which are remote from the pivots (or those which are called "cadent") are to the contrary. In fact the ninth and third [indicate] what is

---

[64] Cf. *Carmen* V.20.
[65] I am not sure who is meant here.
[66] *Utrique utriusque negatur praesentia.* I take this simply to mean that there will be no communication between them, or at least no real engagement.
[67] I am not sure which earlier passage al-Khayyāt is referring to.
[68] This was originally part of al-Kindī's introduction to astrology in *Forty Chapters*, but Hugo seems to be using it for purposes of wealth here.

obscure and unknown.[69] Also, recognition of the abject, low-class and hidden things, even misfortune and the whole affair of being sunken down[70] depends on the twelfth and the sixth.

[Lords of the angles in the angles and the eleventh]

§115. Moreover, the pivots and their lords (provided that they were in pivots) magnify prosperity, greatly increase luckiness, [and] put off ruin. But those same [lords] in the remote and cadent [places] take away from fortune, and threaten abjectness and blunders. But if [they were] after the pivots (and first of all after the tenth), if they bore themselves in the manner stated above,[71] they mean a state of middling fortune, they fulfill hope and a favorable opinion, [and] bring friends to bear.

[Lords of the angles in the fifth, second, and eighth]

§116. But those which will be placed after the fourth watch over the steadiness of middling fortune, and they introduce gifts with every [type of] exultation, but because of children. But those which follow the Ascendant bestow the steadiness of the aforewritten luckiness, by means of money and family that is not absent.[72] Also, after the seventh, because of inheritance and ancient things. All of these advance according to their own rank [in the houses].

[The lord of the Ascendant in the angles]

§117. Finally, the highest and greatest prosperity of all is that which the lord of the Ascendant signifies. Which if it were in the Ascendant, it indicates things will be acquired through his own labor and vigor. But if it were in the Midheaven, he will possess it because of some king and grand duties. Which if it dwelled in the seventh, because of borrowing[73] and adversaries and a

---

[69] This should also be taken in the spiritual sense (since these are places of religion): namely, dealing with the unseen, what is mental, conceptual, non-sensible.

[70] *Demissionis negotii*, which could include morale in addition to objective states of affairs.

[71] Probably, being in one of their dignities, regarded by a fortunate planet, *etc.*

[72] That is, immediate family that is nearby and ready to hand (as opposed to long-lost relatives or those on long journeys).

[73] *Mutuationis*. Or rather, business partnerships generally.

betrothal. In the fourth, they especially make the reason for luckiness to be lands, fathers, waterways and the tilling of lands, and the building of cities,[74] even things which are ancient and original.[75]

[The lord of the tenth in the angles]

§118. Moreover, if the lord of the Midheaven would indicate this [good fortune] and it [were] in the Midheaven, it confers a command, [such that] some king and the highest duties seem to present the reason for it. Also, the same [planet] in the seventh will give a command and make him calm because of adversaries and a betrothal. But if in the fourth, he is raised to being a king since he abounds in taxation, occupies lands, constructs cities, breaks up riverbeds, guards cities, and excels in this kind of ancient thing. If this [planet] would possess the Ascendant, he is enriched with the benefit of a command through his own effort, and closeness to the king, and the assent of the common people.

[The lord of the seventh in the angles]

§119. But the lord of the seventh, being in the seventh: he whom it signifies will benefit in wares and borrowing because of taxes, women, adversaries. But with it appearing in the fourth, it blesses with borrowing, women and wares, with the assisting cause of fathers and lands and agriculture. Meanwhile, it being placed in the Ascendant, physics and astronomy and those things which are jobs of his own training and effort, and that type [of thing], greatly bestow the rulership of borrowing and commerce. But if it occupied the tenth, he will redound in commerce, be blessed with a wife, satisfying the king and [his] duties.[76]

[The lord of the fourth in the angles]

§120. Which if the lord of the fourth [were] in the fourth, it grants the gift of the aforewritten luckiness and presents the highest borrowing of commerce, is replete with fruits, multiplies agriculture, but it happens [because

---

[74] Reading the parts about tilling and building more with al-Qabīsī's Arabic (see *ITA* I.15 and al-Qabīsī I.73), for Hugo's "and the tilling of their leasing."
[75] Or, "deep-rooted" (*ITA* I.15).
[76] *Regis et officiorum gratia faciente* (Robert reads, "from actions and ruling").

of] fathers and a gift of some antiquity. But if it were in the Ascendant, he will shine with fruits and agriculture through his own effort, and no moderate deliberation. And in the tenth, he will rejoice in the fertility of fields [and] the resources of fruits, with the king or his own profession conferring it. Which if it would promise it from the seventh, he will redound in the resources of fruits and agriculture, but women and adversaries [and] even commerce will be credited with its cause.

[The lords of pivots in pivots, applying to other planets]

§121. On the other hand, whenever the lords of the pivots, appearing in the pivots, apply to other stars also in the pivots, they promise the form of the aforewritten luckiness, and the greatness of its rank, and watch over its steadiness in that same category—[and] in any [matter] they promise that no ruin or harm will come to be for the whole life of its possessor.

Moreover, provided that the lords of the pivots appear in the pivots, if their application should come to be with some stars in what follows the pivots, they transform that height of prosperity into what is lesser.

§122-24. But the same [lords of the pivots] being in pivots, [and] applying to stars cadent from the pivots, threaten that the ruin of the height of luckiness will happen, just as the nature of the one to which the application happens, will teach it.

If therefore they applied to Saturn, we believe men of lower rank, fathers, ancient things, and what is like these will enter into the cause.

Which if their application would come to be with Jupiter, it conveys ruin because of some judge, the law, children, money, and fairness, and what is like these.

But if to Mars, brothers, murder or some army, a general and prince of wars, even discords or thieves, drive him away from honor.

But if their application is made with the Sun, a king and those aristocrats who are in charge of ruling under him, sometimes divination or medicine, fathers, hunting and the more promoted people from among the commoners, and an immoderate reputation for excessive consumption and expenses, and the consumption of money, will strip him of luckiness.

Also, applying to Venus, women or being prone to and [having] an irrevocable appetite for games and illicit sex, lack of self-control, immodest love, and that sort of thing, drive him away from honor.

But if to Mercury, they deprive him of luckiness because of the corruption[77] of knowledge, writing, and speech.

Moreover an application of these [lords of the pivots in the pivots] being made to the Moon, they create the loss of downfall because of a royal slave-girl, or messengers, and some change of place or foreign business.

§125-26. But often the same thing tends to happen according to the nature of that house which that [planet] (to which the application happens) is holding onto. If it would make its stay in the Ascendant, he undergoes that harm for the guilt of his own crime. Which if in the second, money shows the reason for ruin. And if in the third, [good fortune] is expelled by the offenses of brothers. Which if [it is] in the fourth, he tumbles down because of the father, lands and some ancient thing. In the fifth, children. In the sixth, disease or animals. In the seventh, he will slip by means of the deeds of women and adversaries. Which if it dwelled in the eighth, inheritances enter into the cause. But in the ninth, law or some journey. Likewise in the tenth, duties. In the eleventh, friends and money and the search for money. In the twelfth, he merits being deposed because of enemies [and] captivity.

§127a. Moreover, the sum and principal beginning of the outcomes of this whole occasion [for trouble], is believed to flow from out of the house of the one to which the application of the rest comes to be: namely the nature of [the house] which it supports by its own aspect, just in that way it was said before about the house in which it is [actually] situated.

---

[77] Reading *corruptionis* for *correptionis*.

[Lords of the pivots in the succeedent places and applying to other planets]

§127b-128. Moreover, if the lords of the pivots would appear after the pivots, and their application would happen to [stars] appearing in the same places,[78] the moderate favor of the prosperity which is had, does not forsake [him] for the whole space of life. Which if they, appearing in that same place, would apply to another [star] in a pivot, the present luckiness is converted into something greater. But the arising and cause of this blessedness demands to be noted in the way which was stated above with respect to the cadents.[79]

[Lords of the pivots in the cadent places and applying to other planets]

§129. Again, if the lords of the pivots would be tumbling down from the pivots, they will present no favor of good fortune for the whole life of a man, but rather they will make it flow from something bad to something worse. But those same [lords of the pivots] being cadent, while they apply to those placed after the pivots, [after] the anxiety and the absence of prosperity (by which he will be sad in the beginning of life), he will [later] rejoice in middling luckiness. Likewise, if the lords of the pivots (being cadent) applied to others in the pivots, [after being] free of the prior starvation he will attain the highest honor; and once the cloud of prior difficulty is dissolved, he will have this [good fortune] for longer.

[The planet in charge][80]

§130. No less too, does the minister which the Arabs call the "the one in charge"[81] mean the highest fortune, if it crossed the Sun and would appear

---

[78] That is, in the succeedents.

[79] In other words, according to the meaning of (1) the planet to which they apply, (2) the house it occupies, and (3) the house of its own which it regards most strongly or best.

[80] This subsection seems to give criteria for judging the favorability of the victors to be determined in *Forty Chapters* Ch. 3—it does not identify a wholly separate victor or ruler. If so, then it should be considered *in addition to* the determinations of strength by dignity (Chs. 3.1-2), just as Ptolemy (*Tet.* III.3 and III.5), and Dorotheus (*Carmen* III.1.1-6) and ibn Ezra (*Nativities* p. 14) stress the importance of solar phase in their versions of victors and chief significators. See especially *ITA* II.10, and *Search*.

[81] Or, "ruler, administrator": Ar. *al-mustawli* (Lat. *almuzeth, almustaul*), from *waliya* (Forms I and V), "to be in charge, manage, assume responsibility for." Thanks to Charles Burnett for pointing this out.

eastern, so that it would be separated from the Sun by 12° or a little more, and would appear in the east in the morning. Which if it would be arising distant from the Sun by double the number of degrees of the first [distance], it is a sign of middling luckiness. But if it is remote from him by the tripled prior distance, it introduces lesser fortune.

§131. Also, with that same [distance] being quadrupled and it being foreign to[82] the Sun, it signifies a lesser punishment. But fivefold, it designates middling anguish. After that, it harms with greater misfortune until it undergoes scorching.

§2.16: On a thing lent, or deposited with someone for safekeeping—Aristotle

If someone made a question about recovering something owed, or something deposited for safekeeping, it will be good to consult the lords of the east and the second equally. For, with the lord of the second being corrupted, namely so that it would be cadent or burned up, or retrograde, part is restored and part is lost.

Moreover, with malevolents being discovered in the second or with its lord, the one to whom [the things] had been committed neglects to return [them]. With him fighting against it, while Mars would hold onto the rulership of the second, [and] possessing the other of his houses, it would not be able to be recovered without war or some force.

Moreover, with benevolents in the second, if they would have command over the second, he lets go of what [the querent] was seeking, on his own and from benevolence. But if they in no way rule [the second], while however they traverse in it, they bring aid in recovering the thing. Mercury in the second, and he being the lord of the second, restores the whole thing because he overcomes [the other person] by persuasion.[83]

In addition, with the lord of the second bearing itself well, [and] even the malevolents being both in aversion to it and from the second itself, you will note the status of the [planet] which possesses [the second], and its lord. For,

---

[82] I believe this means that it is in a trine from the Sun by sign, so it is "cadent" from the whole-sign angles of the Sun. This would place the planet near the beginning of its retrogradation. But it might also mean that it is in aversion to the Sun (i.e., in the eighth sign from the Sun).

[83] Reading somewhat loosely for *quare ad causam invitando superat*. *Invito* can mean to request, court, ask, allure; so, in the context of Mercury, I have opted for "persuade."

it being cleansed of the unfortunate ones (they being remote from it and from the second), restores it all in a benign way. On the other hand, with it being corrupted, or if malevolents would be lingering in the second or with its lord, while[84] the lord of the second appeared free, he would not be able to compelled to return it unless forced to, and finally he restores it reluctantly.

---

[84] Omitting what seems to be *cui*.

§3: THIRD HOUSE

3rd House	
Status of siblings	§§3.1-3
An absent sibling	§3.4

Figure 14: Questions of the third house

§3.1: On those things which pertain to the third house—Sahl[1]

Likewise, once a question of the third has been proposed (such as for the status of brothers and what is of this kind), we enjoin you to look principally at the third and its lord: namely, how they bear themselves with the regard of the benevolents and the harmful [planets], and what good or evil they convey.

If therefore the lord of the third would apply to the lord of the sixth, or it would traverse in the sixth, or even should the lord of the sixth happen to be found in the third, it is a sign of fraternal illness. Moreover, if you find the lord of the third (namely the significator of brothers) in the fifth or eleventh,[2] you should not doubt but that he has changed locations.

Finally, any corruption of the significator of the brother portends adversity: and so, [the significator in the twelfth indicates the brother will have infirmity and sorrow];[3] the significator being scorched and unlucky [as well], imposes no end to infirmities and misery. Nor is it otherwise according to the nature and manner and even accidents of the other [domiciles].

We[4] should approach the path of the rest of the judgments in this way: it is right to observe inquiries about the fourth as being for parents, about the fifth as for children, about the sixth for the topic of slaves and sick people, about the seventh for spouses and controversy. And the same method through the rest of the domiciles wholly responds according to each signification.

---

[1] Cf. *On Quest.* §3.
[2] That is, the third house and ninth house of the brother, respectively.
[3] Adding with John's Sahl.
[4] For this paragraph, cf. al-Rijāl I.28 (last half).

§3.2: On the status of the brothers—al-Khayyāt[5]

With a question being given about the status of the brothers, the third and its lord should be consulted, [and] even whether the benevolents or infortunes regard it.[6]

Therefore, the lord of the third in the sixth or applying to its lord, portends that the brother about whom it is asked is growing infirm; on the other hand, though, the lord of the sixth in the third [indicates the same]. [The lord of the third] in the fifth or in the eleventh, declares that the brother is absent.

Moreover, with the lord of the third being corrupted or lingering in the twelfth, he is vexed by the anxiety of some trouble or disease. But if the lord of the third and Mars[7] are equally undergoing scorching, he will not escape, for they being scorched threatens certain destruction. The nature of the disease or trouble can be discovered from the specific places or houses of the circle.

Furthermore, the aspect of the fortunes or malevolents into the place of the question, or if they would regard its lord, or they would be lingering there, reveals the same thing. From the nature of the benevolents emanates joys, conveniences, and all prosperity; [but] anxiety and disease depend on the infortunes.

In addition, so that a more definite discernment may be had in all of this, it seems the proper quality of the circles with their houses must be linked. For example, the linking of the Sun and Moon pertains to parents[8] (if an interrogation would be about them). Venus has the affairs of women and children. Mars even participates in brothers. Mercury pertains to slaves and captives. The proper quality of Saturn is referred to old men and older people. Jupiter watches over judges and parents. And this is the opinion of both Māshā'allāh and the ancients.

---

[5] Cf. al-Rijāl I.28.
[6] *Ipsum*. This could refer either to the third itself, or its lord.
[7] Mars is a general significator of brothers.
[8] Literally, "fathers" (*patres*).

§3.3: On the status of the brothers—Dorotheus

When inquiries of the third happen, such as for brothers and their status, it will be good to attend to the third and its lord, and their places (of the fortunate ones, I say, and the infortunes), in terms of regard.

[The third and its lord] being free of the infortunes and scorching and stars hostile to them, preserves the brother's health up to the end. Moreover, the lord of the third in the sixth or applying to the lord of the sixth, claims he is sick; it is not otherwise too, [if] the lord of the third is established with the lord of the eighth or twelfth: for it asserts he is extinguished. Likewise, corrupted (or rather, unlucky) lords of the third or the twelfth, teach that he is oppressed by enemies or men seeking him through fraud. Which if the lord of the sixth would linger in the third, it signifies a disease. That same lord of the sixth traversing in the third with Mars, while each would be starting to undergo scorching, is fatal to one growing sick. Being scorched too, they portend nothing else, unless some fortunate one would be staying in the third or would regard its lord. Likewise, the benevolents being cadent from[9] the third and its lord, and at the entrance of scorching, threatens death to the brother; they even warn of the worst status for the rest.[10]

§3.4: Whether he is absent or not—Dorotheus

Moreover, at the suggestion of the sage,[11] one must enter into the counsel of the one who rules over the third. For, it occupying the ninth, fifth, seventh, and twelfth, testifies that he is absent; but without that, it is otherwise.

Concerning the joint or mutual status of each brother, the eastern lord and that of the third equally respond to the one inquiring. They being remote from each other and possessing an optimal place in the regard of the east, or with one occupying the place of the other while it aspects [the other] with a friendly regard, or should it be in the sovereignty of the other, designates the healthful and friendly status of each, and [their] joint benevolence; but without that, it is otherwise.

---

[9] That is, "in aversion to."
[10] *Reliquis.* I am not sure what Dorotheus means here, unless this is a general statement about all questions (as with Sahl and al-Khayyāt in §3.1 and §3.2).
[11] *Sapientis.* I am not sure who this is, unless this is Hugo's own way of referring to Dorotheus.

Moreover, for the same question, it is appropriate to attend to the lord of that place,[12] and the position of its lord in that same place. But there will be oppression and disease in it according to the nature of the infortunes. Moreover, the proper quality of the fortunate ones lays bare the kind[13] of liveliness and manner of prosperity.

It even seems that the nature of the circle of each in the places of the houses, must be linked. The Sun and the Moon [indicate parents][14] if the question would pertain to their nature. And so, the common company of Venus is referred to women and children and their affairs. The partnership of Mars, to brothers. But that of Mercury looks to captives or slaves.

---

[12] The third, as in §3.2.
[13] Reading *genus* for *genere*.
[14] Adding based on al-Khayyāt in §3.2 above.

§4: FOURTH HOUSE

4th House	
Buying & selling real estate	§§4.1, 4.3-10
Condition of real estate	§4.2
Leasing real estate	§§4.11-12
Building houses & cities	§4.13
Digging	§4.14
Buried treasure	§4.15-18
Outcomes	§§4.19-22

Figure 15: Questions of the fourth house

REAL ESTATE

§4.1: On those things which pertain to the fourth house—Sahl[1]

When inquiries of the fourth occur (such as for the acquisition of any fields, houses, or lands), before all else (as usually happens) I ascribe the signification of the querent to the lord of the east and to the Moon. But the fourth and its lord declare the quaesited matter.

Which if they applied to each other in common (namely so that an application of the Moon or the eastern lord with the significator is discovered), or should they at least traverse in the fourth (or even in the converse order, with the significator being with either of them, or with it being placed in the east), it prefigures that he is able to have and obtain it.

§4.2: On the condition of lands, fields, and the like—al-Kindī

§469. The distribution of lands is in two parts: for one is given to buildings and the habitation of men, the other to agriculture. The Ascendant and its lord, moreover the Lunar lord and the Moon herself, even the pivots and their lords, [and] in the same way fortunate ones, placed in the pivots and having some dignity in them (particularly in the Ascendant and the fourth), preserve that [part] which farmers are allotted. Moreover, let the infortunes be established as remote from the pivots. Likewise, let the Sun and the Moon

---

[1] Cf. *On Quest.* §4.1.

be regarding the fourth in a friendly way, and be themselves strong. But of those which rule the pivots, none [should be] retrograde, nor should any retrograde star hold onto the pivots.

§470. For the prosperity of the fourth watches over the health of the land and the increase of [its] fruits. But the Midheaven signifies [trees and][2] cliffs and rocks, and—if they are in them—mountains. The Ascendant looks at the possessor of the land and his buildings. Also, the seventh claims the farmers and inhabitants and partners dwelling [there].[3]

§471. Let even the Lot of Fortune and the lord of the twelfth from the Moon,[4] moreover the lord of the second, be supported by an aspect of fortunate ones, [and] let their lords be strong and appear in the pivots. Likewise, let the Lot of Fortune rejoice in the friendly view of the Sun and Moon and lucky ones.

§472. Wherefore it seems one must beware with the utmost effort lest some infortune appear in the ninth or eleventh or fifth: for it introduces harm and loss from the farmers.

§473. Moreover, we warn you to avoid there being a fiery sign in the fourth, or some fiery [planet] in it, and one estranged from the fortunes. For it corrupts the fruits with fire or heat and thirst if Mars would regard it, but more expressly if the regard would proceed from a pivot. Moreover, Saturn regarding the fourth and it being a watery [sign], does not free it from heavy rains and the damage of waters. The hostile regard of each, I say (namely of Saturn and Mars), and they being raised up above the ether,[5] increases the same.

---

[2] Adding with Robert.
[3] But al-Rijāl's version (VII.22) allots these differently: the Ascendant for the buyer and the success of the venture (since it is an election), the Midheaven for things above the earth (such as trees), the fourth for the lands and inhabitants and servants (he also mentions that some assign it to the vegetation), and the seventh for its fertility and sowing.
[4] This probably means the twelfth-part of the Moon (*ITA* IV.6). But it may also indicate the lord of the Moon's sign itself.
[5] Robert reads, "ascending in the circle," apparently referring to ascending in the circle of their apogee (see *ITA* II.1).

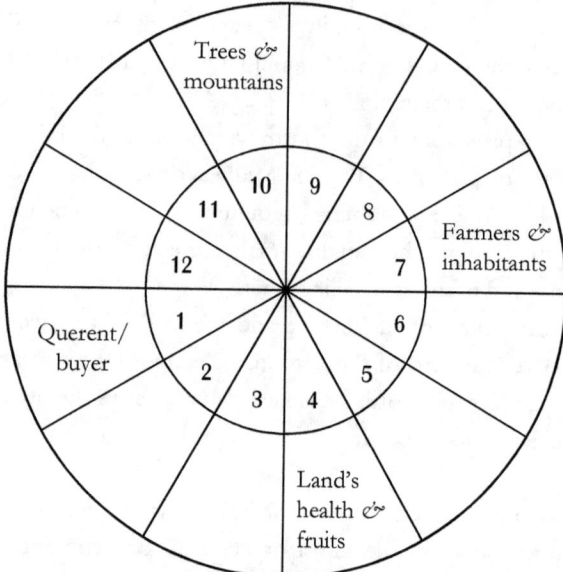

Figure 16: Angles for buying lands (al-Kindī §4.2)

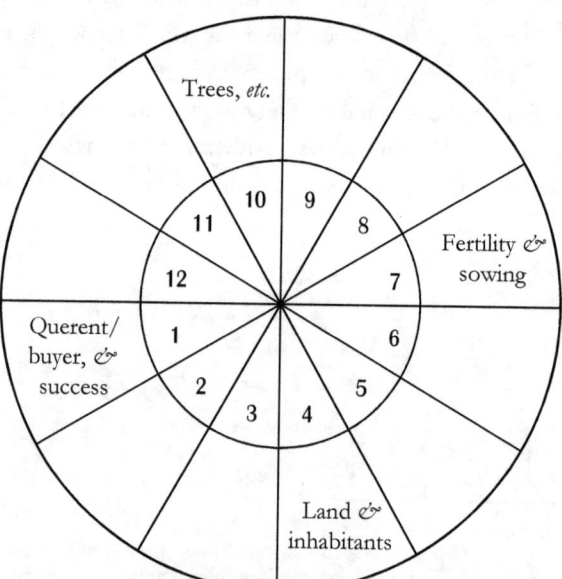

Figure 17: Al-Rijāl's electional version of al-Kindī's angles (al-Rijāl VII.22)

§474. On the other hand, one must beware lest they corrupt the Midheaven, with it being an earthy sign. The perversity of Mars in it scorches the fruits, [and] afflicts with heat and dryness. But Saturn spoils with thirst and a lack of water. Moreover, should Mars corrupt it (it being a watery sign) [while] also descending,[6] it consumes the harvests with rot. The descent of Saturn in the ether, and corrupting [the Midheaven if it is a] watery sign, weakens the fruits, being deprived of maturity.

[A question on buildings]

§475. Furthermore, whenever a question about land destined for buildings were made known, let a firm sign be arranged in the fourth place (likewise the rest of the pivots), with the fortunate ones bearing themselves as was stated above; moreover, the lords of the pivots eastern and adding in course and being raised up in the north:[7] they portend the steadiness and firmness of the buildings, and the respectability and appropriateness of those affairs which pertain to that; finally, that all things are suitable and wholesome.

§476. One will even have to beware of the aforesaid status of the infortunes. For Mars bearing himself as was now said above, and corrupting, does not remove thieves and scorching. He being in a human sign admits thieves, enemies, plunderers, often even the violence and hand of the king. In a sign of another form, he threatens fire. But if Saturn would take up the role of Mars in that same status, it testifies to the ruin of a collapse, and hastened dissolution.[8] Which if Mercury will be associated with Saturn, being invested with the virtue of Saturn himself,[9] and being estranged from the fortunes, and corrupting the fourth, it indicates the family's diseases, death, and scarcity.

---

[6] Probably descending in the circle of the apogee.
[7] In northern ecliptical latitude.
[8] This "dissolution" refers to decay.
[9] This probably means that because Mercury is a very flexible planet, he takes on the nature of Saturn by mixing with him.

§4.3: Whether someone would get a house or real estate—al-Khayyāt[10]

The method placed below will give counsel for land or a house or real estate, when it should come into question as to whether someone would be able to get it.

For if the lord of the east and the Moon would apply to the lord of the fourth (or it to [the lord of the east or the Moon]), or while both or at least the lord of the fourth[11] would be in the fourth, it testifies that he is able[12] to get it. The Moon transferring from one to another [indicates] the same, but through middle men and messengers.

§4.4: On acquiring houses or inheritances—Dorotheus

But with a question of the fourth happening, such as for acquiring a home or real estate, it will be good to look to the lord of the east and the Moon.

For if each would apply to the lord of the fourth (or it to the eastern [lord]), or should [the lord of the east] be in the fourth, or the lord of the fourth in the east, it claims that what is sought would be gotten. Also, the Moon transferring light from one to the other teaches that it is acquired through his own hands.[13] But with any of these significators being received by a trigon or a hexagon, it is a sign of acquiring it.

§4.5: On the purchase of fields—Sahl[14]

Now, if anyone made a question about buying fields or houses (and what is of this kind)—namely what kind it is or what it contains—the east itself takes the inhabitants of the fields and their signification; moreover from the fourth is found the status and quality of the fields; but the seventh contains the produce and what is contained there (except for trees); but we find the trees themselves from the tenth.

---

[10] This section originally lacked an author, but it must be al-Khayyāt due to its placement and matching Sahl and Dorotheus.
[11] This should probably read, "east," as with Dorotheus in §4.4.
[12] Reading *posse* with Vienna for *post se*.
[13] This should be through middle men, as in §4.3.
[14] Cf. *On Quest.* §4.2.

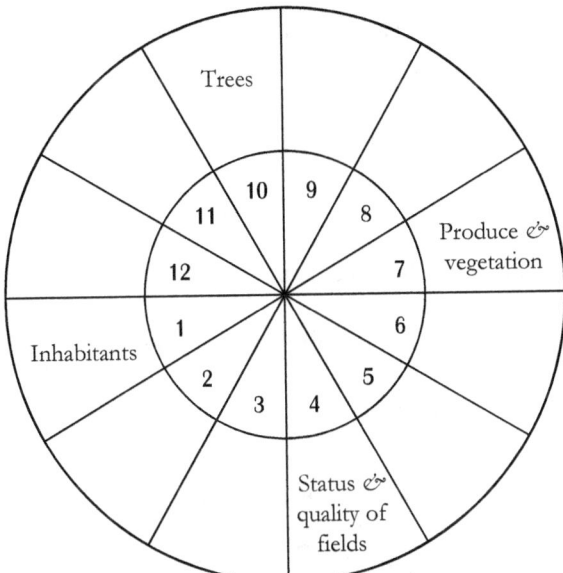

**Figure 18: Angles for what is on the land
(Sahl §4.5, al-Khayyāt §4.8, Dorotheus §4.9)**

Therefore, with any of the malevolents placed in the east, it shows the inhabitants are fraudulent, and their worthlessness. But its course being direct, holds them back; retrogradation makes them abandon the care of the fields. But if a benevolent would be lingering in the east, it commends their purpose. The retrogradation or direct course of it makes a judgment similar to the above.

Moreover, any lucky one (and direct) occupying the tenth, [means] it has many healthy and fruitful trees; but retrograde, it supports useless and infertile ones. Likewise a malevolent in the tenth (and direct), although it bears fewer, still they should be preserved; moreover retrograde, the worthy ones fail and are discarded. With none occupying the tenth, its lord should be consulted: this one regarding [the tenth] testifies there are trees there. Which if it were contrary [to it], with [its] regard being denied, it denies what was stated above. Again, the lord of the tenth appearing eastern, means young ones; western, old and ancient ones. Direct, it signifies ones which will endure; retrograde, they will perish quickly.

We will look at the seventh for the produce in this way as well, as we have laid out the natures and paths with the rest.

Lastly, the nature and quality of the land is found from the fourth domicile. So, the fourth being fiery, indicates hard, mountainous, even rough land. But earthy demonstrates level ground. Airy, it is shown as being partly mountains, partly level ground. Finally watery, designates it is abundant[15] or watery or near waters.

§4.6: On selling real estate or houses—'Umar[16]

And so, with any question proposed about buying a house or country home or real estate, the querent himself claims the east and its lord, the seller (or the one about whom it is asked) [claims] the seventh and its lord, but the fourth (with the Moon) is allotted the signification of the thing to be sold. We hand over the price to the lord of the Midheaven.[17]

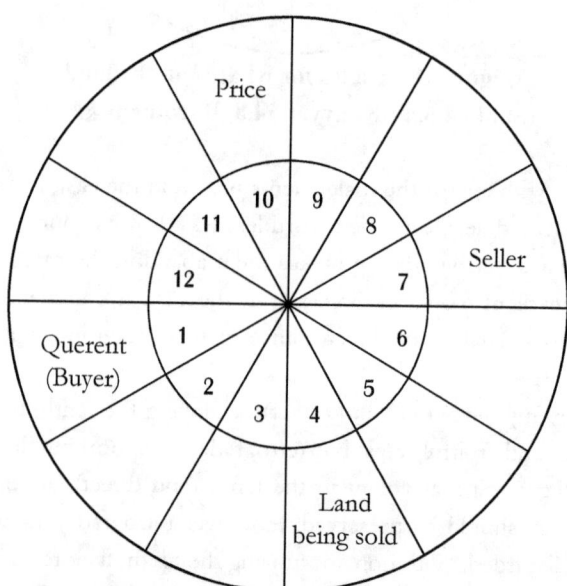

Figure 19: Angles for making the sale ('Umar §4.6)

---

[15] Or perhaps, "flooded" (*influam*).
[16] Cf. al-Rijāl, I.32 (first part), and *Carmen* V.9. This question is also about buying land, but really in terms of the business deal itself.
[17] Al-Rijāl adds that the separation of the Moon indicates the buyer, her application the seller, and a planet in the fourth also indicates what is sold. Deb Houlding argues that the tenth and its lord are not really the "price" as such, but the profit or result for what is being bought: if the querent is the buyer, a good tenth house shows a good deal for the price; if the querent is the seller, it shows a good profit for what is sold.

If therefore the eastern [lord] would regard the lord of the seventh, or would apply to it, it means the querent looks for[18] the things for sale. But an application of the lord of the seventh with the eastern [lord], denotes that the seller is inclined [to the sale]. With an application being denied, while there is no transfer or collection of light, they speak against the sale, and deny that they can come together amongst themselves.

Moreover, an application of the eastern lord with that of the seventh[19] (or of [the latter] to [the former]) from a tetragon or opposition or assembly,[20] promises that it comes about, [but] not without labor and trouble coming afterwards. Which if reception is present, the impediment is judged as being less, and the end easier. Moreover, an application discovered from the trigon or hexagon bestows the effect without the whole trouble[21] of labor. Finally, with reception being had, it commends the benevolence of the buyer.

Furthermore, with the infortunes possessing the fourth, and being made firm in them, but being peregrine, the forsakenness or corruption of the things for sale is designated. [The lord of the fourth house signifies the same, if it were retrograde or unfortunate, or is in its fall from its own house or exaltation.][22] Now, if the fortunate ones would be in that same place, be they alien or closely related,[23] they inhabit and wholly save what is sold.

Next too,[24] the lord of the fourth and the Moon applying to the eastern lord with reception, undoubtedly buys the things for sale, especially if the Moon and the lord of the fourth would possess any dignity of the eastern lord. Which if it would happen otherwise than what we said before, namely

---

[18] *Postulare.* That is, the querent is more eager than the seller.
[19] Reading *septimi* for *septimo* ("the seventh").
[20] This reference to the assembly must be something added by Hugo, as al-Rijāl omits it (nor does it make sense).
[21] Reading *toto laboris incommodo* for *totius laboris incommodo.*
[22] Adding with al-Rijāl.
[23] This must mean "be they peregrine or having a dignity there."
[24] Al-Rijāl is a bit more lengthy here, and reads more like Sahl's *On Quest.* §4.1: "Afterwards, look to see if the lord of the Ascendant or the Moon would apply itself to the lord of the fourth, or if the lord of the fourth or the Moon would apply itself to the lord of the Ascendant: and if the lord of the fourth house alone applied itself to the lord of the Ascendant, and it receives it (or both of them if both applied to it), or if the lord of the Ascendant and the Moon [were] in the fourth house, and the lord of the fourth in the Ascendant, it signifies that the real estate will be bought, and that he will obtain it. But this were not so, and the Moon conveys the light of one of them to the other, it denotes that the matter will come to be, but through mediators and the hands of legates. But if no application came between [them], nor a transfer of light, nor a planet which would conjoin [i.e., collect] their lights, it portends that there will be no sale of the estate."

so that there would be no application of each of the aforesaid, nor of either one, with the eastern lord, while there is no transfer nor one who would collect their lights, it fully speaks against the purchase.

§4.7: On the quantity of the price—'Umar[25]

Moreover, the quantity of the price could be scrutinized in such an order. For the lord of the Midheaven, or that star which is placed firmly in it (the one of them, I say, which is stronger), is deservedly allotted the role of the signification (but to be the stronger one is to be eastern or direct, traversing in [its own] house or sovereignty or triplicity). And thus the individual units [of currency] will have to be bestowed according to the lesser years of that star. For, being in its own house, it indicates thousands or hundreds; but in the trigon, [multiples] of ten or single units.

Also, with the lord of the Midheaven being estranged from every dignity of its own, while however it is retrograde or scorched or descending,[26] or affected by any kind of corruption, observe diligently [to see] if a strong star placed in the tenth would be staying [there] more firmly: for that one will elicit the quantity and manner of the price. Which if no star would possess the Midheaven, [take the] lord of the tenth, [even] with it being cadent from it [and] even with its regard being denied, [even] if it would be unlucky (namely retrograde or scorched): it lavishes units [of currency] according to its lesser years, or [multiples] of ten.[27]

[A Lot of real estate]

It will be permitted to claim all things from the Lot of real estate: namely that you should begin from the degree of the lord of the fourth, taking it to the degree and point of Saturn, [and] draw it down it from the fourth: for where the number will be ended, it is necessary that this Lot be found.[28]

---

[25] Cf. al-Rijāl I.32 (middle), and I.33-35. I have made certain corrections based on al-Rijāl.
[26] That is, in its own fall.
[27] Al-Rijāl does not list the multiples of ten, and he is probably right.
[28] 'Umar's calculation seems to be this: by day, from the lord of the fourth to Saturn, and projected from the IC; but if Saturn rules the fourth, go from the IC to Saturn, and project from the fourth (which does not make sense, because by definition Saturn would be the location of the Lot). To me it makes more sense to project from the Ascendant. Al-Rijāl himself (I.32) cites the Lot of real estate according to Hermes, found in *ITA* VI.2.10: by day or night from Saturn to the Moon, and projected from the Ascendant.

Moreover, with Saturn claiming the rulership of the fourth, [start by] taking it up from the degree of the fourth to the degree of the Saturn; [and] with the degrees of that fourth being added, and the beginning of the drawing-down being taken from the fourth, you will really find the Lot at the ending of the number. By[29] night on the other hand, taking it from the degree of Saturn to the degree of the fourth, you will thus make the beginning of the reduction from it; where the number left off indicates this Lot.

And so, an application of [the Lot's] lord with a lord of the seventh that is receiving it, claims a sale. (In like manner, one of the lord of the east and [the lord of the Lot] will make good on it; even one of this lord and of the lord of the seventh, pursues the action: for a joint regard of these finally confirms the sale.)[30] [But if the degree of the Lot and the degree of its lord were unfortunate, it signifies the pillaging and devastation of the estate. If the Lot and its lord were fortunate, it signifies the perpetuation and success of the estate.][31]

[The profit and difficulty of the purchase]

In addition, the joint application of the lord of the seventh and of the Moon, but equally that of the Lot and its lord and the eastern lord, more clearly responds to a question as to whether any usefulness will follow from a purchase that has been made. An application of them (or of the majority) from a trigon or hexagon with reception, designates the effected and useful possession of the thing.

The lord of the fifth, taking on a signification of this kind, principally introduces the testimonies of the matter:[32] for, it applying to the lord of the east by a trigon or hexagon, and likewise being fortunate and lucky, testifies there is pleasantness[33] in it. Which if it happened otherwise, namely from either a tetragon or opposition or assembly, [then] should an application of all or at least a major portion [of them] be found with the eastern lord, it

---

[29] This sentence originally appeared below, but I have brought it up here for clarity's sake.
[30] I have put this comment in parentheses because it does not appear in al-Rijāl, and so may be a later addition.
[31] Adding with al-Rijāl, in place of Hugo's rather lame "And so, the degree of the Lot being corrupted along with its own lord, shows the real estate is uncultivated; but the luckiness of each promises it is inhabited."
[32] That is, of its profit and success (al-Rijāl).
[33] This should be profit or success (*profectum*, al-Rijāl), since the fifth is the second (wealth) from the fourth.

lavishes no profit without anxiety. But reception being present, mitigates the hour of the sale a little bit.[34]

With a tetragonal or opposite application from the eastern lord with the lord of the seventh (or from the assembly),[35] if, I say, reception is present, and if they apply in degrees, they prefer to introduce the hour of the purchase after the troubles of labor and difficulty.[36]

§4.8: On the cultivators of fields—al-Khayyāt

With a question made about its cultivators or farmers, and their status and steadfastness, but even about what is contained on the land, the east comprehends the farmers and cultivators, the fourth house the status of the land, the seventh the germinating things of the land, the Midheaven the produce and trees.

Therefore, a malevolent traversing in the east denotes fraudulent and the worst farmers. A benevolent in the same place portends the contrary. The direct course of a benevolent testifies that they stay, retrogradation drives them away. Moreover, a direct malevolent suggests [their] steadfastness,[37] retrogradation their flight.

Any lucky one in the Midheaven, and direct, indicates many and strong trees. But retrograde, [it means] many but weak ones, whence the one who buys [the land] will be afflicted by regret. A malevolent in the same place means a scarcity of trees. Its retrogradation destroys what is left. But if [the situation] in the Midheaven were established so that the lord of the Midheaven would regard the Midheaven itself, it promises they are there. Being eastern, it means recent [trees], [and] the distance of the star[38] from the Solar circle really indicates the age. Western shows they are old. Being direct, it denotes the steadfastness of the trees, being retrograde likewise [indicates] to

---

[34] That is, "it will come about with less labor" (al-Rijāl).
[35] In this case, al-Rijāl does include the assembly.
[36] Al-Rijāl then continues with a sentence that may be 'Umar's own: "Moreover, if you wished to know when the estate would be given to you, look at the application of the lord of the Ascendant with the lord of the fourth house, and carefully examine the time from this aspect, just as we have stated, and you will find it, God granting."
[37] That is, the bad farmers will stay as long as possible.
[38] That is, the lord of the Midheaven.

the contrary. But if the lord of the Midheaven does not regard the tenth,[39] it indicates [the land] is empty of trees.

Moreover, the status of the harvests and germinating things especially emanates, and is distinguished from, the seventh—as was stated above with respect to the lord of the Midheaven.

But the fourth reveals the nature of the land. Therefore, Aries or any [sign] of its triplicity being in the fourth indicates mountainous land, hard and rough, even full of stones. Taurus or its triplicity denotes that it is level. The triplicity of Gemini, partly flat, partly mountainous. Cancer or its triplicity: [it is] near waters, having lakes and swamps. But if the fourth were double-bodied, an inequality is demonstrated: namely so that it has flat land here, mountains there.

§4.9: On the status of fields—Dorotheus[40]

Which if it was sought with respect to the status of the land and its living things, and what things are on it, note that the east portends the cultivators and inhabitants and what is handed in it. But the fourth determines whatever status of the land there is. The seventh means what things are in it[41] that are smaller than trees. Moreover, from the Midheaven are designated the produce and trees.

And so, infortunes established in the east testifies that the inhabitants are fraudulent, untrustworthy, and thieves. But fortunate ones in that same place shows just and pious and faithful ones; [their] retrogradation means their withdrawal. Moreover, infortunes being firmly in the east denotes lasting difficulties; retrogradation, the contrary.

Also, [benevolents] in the Midheaven, and being direct, indicate the toughness and strength of the trees. But being retrograde they portend fragile ones, and for that matter they devastate [them], so that one after another they will lay them out for sale. Malevolents in that same place mean few [trees]; being direct, they preserve the trees, [but] with them being retrograde, they will be destroyed by the possessor. Which if no [star] is holding onto the Midheaven, but its lord is regarding its own place, it indicates it is planted with trees. With it being eastern, the planting is recent. The long distance of

---

[39] And there is no star in the tenth?
[40] Cf. al-Rijāl I.32 (last part).
[41] Reading *insunt* for *innuunt*.

the star from the Sun shows its steadiness. Its direct course watches over the trees, [but] on the contrary retrogradation lays waste [to them]. On the other hand, the lord of the Midheaven diverting the aspect from its own place,[42] removes the trees.

Also, the recognition of growing things (comprised of what is below trees) depends on the seventh.

Again, the fourth sign from the east lays bare the nature of the land and its quality. Which if it were Aries or one of its triplicity, it claims it is packed full of steep mountains and the roughness of cliffs. Taurus or any of its triplicity denotes flatness. Even Gemini and its triplicity professes that it is not wholly flat, nor everywhere mountainous. Neighboring on water is designated by Cancer or its triplicity. The fourth even being double-bodied, affirms it is uneven.[43]

§4.10: On foremen and subordinates of this kind—Dorotheus[44]

With a question being given about foreman and officials, and if [people] are of this kind, we judge them from the east, but the affairs that are assumed and which pertain to them, from the Midheaven. But the fourth resolves the end of the whole matter.

Therefore, fortunate ones holding onto the east commend the benevolence of the subordinates assuming [their role]. But infortunes [indicate] the contrary, for they either abandon the office they have assumed, or they hold onto it fraudulently and with a crooked intention.

Likewise, malevolents in the seventh testify that the subordinate will be regretful because of himself, and they ascribe fraud to him. Fortunate ones in that place, everywhere commend the end.

Moreover, the infortunes in the tenth (or if they would regard it in a wicked way) show unjust officials.

Likewise, the fourth being possessed by infortunes (or at least regarded [by them]), declare a wicked end for the subordinates; but fortunate ones placed thus, the contrary.

---

[42] And without a planet being in the tenth?
[43] That is, it is a mixture of terrains and not simply one type.
[44] This section is out of order and should be paired with §§4.11-12.

§4.11: For leasing fields—Sahl[45]

Once these things have been carried out in such a way, if anyone made a question about renting out or contracting for fields, we discover the status and manner of contracting for [the fields] from the east, while the seventh designates the one renting them out;[46] finally, we observe the produce and price from the tenth, [and] the end of the whole business from the fourth.

Whence, a benevolent being in the east: he acquires benefit, not without joy; but a malevolent: he abandons it uselessly.

Nor is an infortune found in the seventh otherwise: it shows the one who rents it out demands what is his with a quarrel. A benevolent assures things with usefulness.

Moreover, a perverse one traversing in the tenth (or regarding [the tenth] in a bad way): he loses the value without all of the produce and livelihood.

Finally, it is good to observe everything which exists in the fourth through the proper qualities of the fortunate ones and the infortunes, and the location [of the fields] in no other order.

§4.12: On leasing fields—al-Khayyāt[47]

This method will even be given for those who rent out and contract for fields. Therefore, the one who contracts for it is distinguished by the east, but the one who rents it out from the seventh. The manner and understanding of its usefulness, depends on the Midheaven. But the fourth resolves the end of the whole affair.

Therefore, a lucky one in the east, [means] he actually contracts for it.[48] A malevolent in that same place, he regrets it or perhaps, being about to deceive or having the hope of fraud, it does not lead to the goal.

Which if these things were borne out in the seventh (as they were stated about the east), [the owner] will not rent out what he had promised—which if it did happen, he really incurs loss and trouble, nor would he be able to reach his goal.[49] A benevolent in the west: he rents out[50] the fields.

---

[45] Cf. *On Quest.* §4.2. This question assumes that the querent wants to work someone else's land for profit, paying a portion of the income to the owner (the seventh house).
[46] John's Sahl assigns the Ascendant to the "seller," and the seventh to the "buyer."
[47] Cf. al-Rijāl I.36 (first half).
[48] And it is a successful arrangement, as Sahl says in §4.11.
[49] Or generally, to conclude the business properly.

A malevolent traversing in the Midheaven, or should it regard it by a hostile figure, denotes that the unfaithful, false, and unconcerned farmers give up.

Moreover, the traversal of a malevolent in the fourth, or regarding it, warns of a most difficult end; but a lucky one commends the same.

§4.13: On the building of the houses of cities—al-Kindī[51]

§477. The solution of this question engages the Lunar counsel. For, the Moon made fortunate by lucky and eastern [planets], and set up in a place of her own authority, moreover her reception and that of the fortunate ones, approves [the construction]; or if the Moon would be set up in a pivot and ascending into the north, quick in course, in a fixed and straight sign,[52] even regarded even by her own lord; moreover the Lot of Fortune in some pivot and made fortunate (as was already said); also, let the pivots be set up as being firm and immovable, nor drawn back.[53] Moreover, the lords of the fourth and of the Ascendant [should be] in a place of their own power, and eastern, and all that we said before [should be] cleansed of the infortunes, even the pivots free of the infortunes.

§478. But [let] the lord of death[54] be estranged from [and] absent from the lord of the Ascendant and the Moon and the pivots. Also, the Tail in the twelfth, moreover let the lord of the sixth be entrusted to be estranged from the Ascendant and the Moon. Let the lord of the degree of the assembly or opposition be in a place of its own proper quality,[55] free of the infortunes, appearing in a pivot or after the pivots. Which if it were possible, Venus or Jupiter should be arranged in the pivot of the fourth or the tenth.

§479. In fact, such a disposition of these [planets] introduces no [merely] moderate money: [that is], the highest joy; but a special heap of gladness is

---

[50] Reading *occidente* for *oriente* ("east"), and *locat* with al-Rijāl for *conducit*.
[51] Cf. *Carmen* V.6.
[52] That is, a sign of straight or direct ascensions.
[53] Reading *nec* ("nor") for *vel* ("or"), since "drawn back" is normally used by Hugo to mean "cadent," which is not at all what one wants for a firm and upright building. So, I take this instruction to mean that the degree of the Midheaven should not be in the ninth sign (which is a cadent sign). See Bonatti's discussion of this idea (with reference to al-Rijāl) in *BOA* Tr. 7 Ch. 11 (pp. 673-74), but also Sahl in §1.1 for the importance of this generally.
[54] The lord of the eighth.
[55] Robert: "dignity."

amassed [with] Venus dwelling in the fourth, especially while she would favor the lord of the second and the Lot of Fortune and the Lot of money.

§480. Again, one must beware with the utmost effort lest Saturn or Mars hold onto the pivots: for Saturn devastates, expels the inhabitants, portends the unsteadiness of fragility, slows profit, blocks joys, and tries to put off better outcomes. Moreover Mars declares plunder, burning, the constant attacks of enemies, (and as though eager to devour), the harming of the citizens, and wars breaking out.

§481. Moreover, in building cities it is good that Mars (as was stated above) be held back in [his] corruption from those who assist the lord of the Ascendant and the fourth and the Moon, [but] to favor [an aspect of] peace and health, [and] for them to be complected to part of them by some kind of reception.[56] Moreover, Venus being established in a trigon or tetragon introduces no moderate triumph from plowing.

§4.14: On digging riverbeds and those things which pertain to irrigating arable land—al-Kindī

§482. In digging out canals, let the Moon be in the first tetragon of the Sun, made fortunate, and received in a pivot; let even the pivots be disposed firm and straight,[57] also the lord of the Ascendant should be eastern and in some place of its own dignity, in a pivot or after a pivot; let even the ascending sign be watery and favored by a thriving fortune. Let the pivot of the fourth be strong, not deprived of the blessing of the lucky ones.

§483. But let the Lunar lord be in a place of its own authority, received, blessed. Moreover let the Lot of Fortune be supported by the regard of the Sun and Moon. Let the degree of the assembly[58] be favored by the regard of fortunate ones. But let the application of the Moon (after her first withdrawal from the assembly or opposition of the Sun) come to be with a strong fortune in a pivot or after a pivot. Moreover, the lord of the assembly or opposition should bear itself in the same way. But let the infortunes be ca-

---

[56] I take this to mean that these other significators will have receptions amongst themselves. But Robert plausibly reads, "but if [Mars] would be applied to them in any way, let him receive [them]."

[57] Again, signs of straight or direct ascension.

[58] *Alestima*, a transliteration of the Ar. *al-ijtimāʿ*, "assembly." That is, the lunation prior to the election (I would include the opposition, since the next sentence includes that).

dent from the pivots and from the Sun and Moon and Lot of Fortune, [and] the Lunar lord.

§484. Which if it would be possible [for this] to happen as we have determined, it repels [any] hindrance from the digging out of the canal, it multiplies the waters and makes it support not-moderate profit [from them],[59] and keeps them harmless, and guards those sailing and the ships unharmed, and renders them unfailing.

[On the instruments for wells]

§485. Moreover, in [constructing] certain irrigation instruments for wells (which tend to be used among some peoples for drawing forth the depths of waters, which are even called by the common name of "storks" on account of the likeness of their form),[60] let the Ascendant and pivots be established as firm and immovable, nor drawn back,[61] even straight [in ascensions]; also, the Ascendant [should be] an earthy sign. The pivot of the earth and the rest [of the pivots should be treated] in this manner.

§486. Let the pivots be cleansed of the infortunes and defended, being made fortunate by the lucky ones. Venus in the Ascendant or in the fourth, namely in an earthy sign, produces a more powerful effect; also, the Moon in an earthy sign and dominant in the north or the south,[62] and in a place of her own authority, received by an eastern fortune, [indicates] the same.

[Constructing dams]

§487. Likewise the construction of dams follows the art of the aforesaid wells. For wells are dams.[63]

---

[59] Reading with guidance from the Arabic.
[60] According to Burnett (1993 p. 113), Hugo is describing a *shādūf* (Ar.), a long pole resting on a fulcrum, with a bucket dangling down into the water of a well. By pulling down on the free end, the pole lifts up the bucket full of water.
[61] This seems to mean that al-Kindī does not want the axis of the MC-IC to fall into a cadent sign. See §477 above.
[62] Reading with Burnett's translation from the Arabic (1993, p. 113). It probably means, "ruling the fourth or tenth."
[63] Reading with Burnett again. Again, Hugo seems to have latched onto the irrigation mechanism rather than the earthworks and digging itself: thus in his own version he thinks al-Kindī means the construction of waterwheels, saying "waters are extracted with the benefit of each instrument in the irrigation of fields."

[Cultivating lands][64]

§488. But the Moon being received by fortunate ones consults for the cultivation of lands, [and] let the one by whom she is received be pivotal or after the pivots (but more powerful is [if] it or at least the Moon [is] in a pivot). Moreover, let the status of the lord of the Ascendant be corresponding to the status of the lord of the Moon.[65] Moreover, let the pivots be strengthened, cleansed of the infortunes [and] defended by the lucky ones, particularly while one of the fortunate ones would be set up as the lord of the house of money or of the Lot of Fortune or of the Lot of money. Moreover, let the [degree of the] assembly or the opposition fall into a pivot.[66]

§489. Then, the Moon's application by assembly or opposition of the Sun[67] should be directed towards some fortune in a pivot or after a pivot. But let the lord of the assembly be lucky, moreover the Lunar lord and [the lord] of the fourth acquire the benefit of happiness.

---

[64] Reading with Burnett on this topic for Hugo's "inhabiting lands." As Burnett (1993, p. 117) points out, Hugo and Robert thought this section was about clearing land for the first time rather than simply cultivating it. But one can see why they might have thought so: cultivating land can be done every year, and has to be done on a schedule—unlike the special act of clearing it for the first time, which is more suitable for an election.

[65] Al-Rijāl (VII.23) clarifies that their condition should be *good*.

[66] Al-Rijāl's list of conditions differs somewhat, such as having a benefic *in* the second house rather than simply being its ruler.

[67] That is, the degree of the conjunction or prevention of the luminaries which most recently preceded the horary question or election. But I am not sure what is being timed here.

BURIED TREASURE

§4.15: On treasures and concealed things—'Umar[1]

In this kind of business, one must principally discern the querent's intention: namely, whether he is asking about money which he himself hid away (and as frequently happens, the memory does not retain the place), or rather [whether it is] within the home or atrium, [or] buried by another and he does not know the place; or [whether the question is] about ancient treasures, of which sort are the reserves of the brothers or parents, and if they are of this kind; or if he is bringing forth an indeterminate question with respect to any resources buried in the ground.

Therefore, after having an understanding of this manifold intention, we put the east in charge of the querent. But if the question proceeds with respect to a thing of his own which he himself has hidden away, we should pursue the lord of the second. For, this [lord] being arranged in the pivots of the signs or in [the pivots] of the lord of the east,[2] portends it is hidden away in his own [house; if it were in the Ascendant or in the sign of the lord of the Ascendant, say the thing is in the] palace [where he is staying];[3] but being in the seventh, in a house of women; in the Midheaven, the office of someone's trade profession; but in the fourth, it prefigures the rooms of a parent or grandparent or the father's relatives (which if he did not have parents,[4] in the middle of his own home).

Also, in this manner the lord of the second being in the assembly of the eastern lord testifies that it is buried in his own hearth.[5] But in the seventh, it is concealed [in a place] of women (as was said above); in the fourth, it signals the paternal hearth or that of the grandparents, or the middle of his own home. Which if they lacked a mutual aspect, nor was there a transfer or collection of light between them, the work will be useless.

---

[1] This section should be read along with Hermann's version in *Search* II.2.2. Cf. also al-Rijāl I.39.1. I have used al-Rijāl to make certain corrections and clarifications.

[2] That is, in the normal pivots of the chart, or in the whole-sign angles of the lord of the east. The version in *Search* has two different options: (1) the lord of the second being in the east itself, or (2) the lord of the east being in the pivots of the chart or in its own house.

[3] Adding bracketed material with al-Rijāl.

[4] That is, older relatives.

[5] Or, "household" (*lares*).

Also, in no other way will it be permitted to investigate the resources and reserves of the parents from their house of money.[6] If however [the question were] about the money of brothers, we will [likewise] follow this method. At last, we proceed through the rest of the signs according to their own proper significations.

☊ ☊ ☋

Which if it would be an indeterminate question about treasures (as was stated above),[7] first it seems one must pay attention to whether anything is contained in a specific place or not. If therefore fortunate ones occupied the seventh, they testify that something is in there. But if it is possessed by the infortunes, they indicate there had been something there, but it has already been taken out.[8]

Moreover, if there is no remaining uncertainty about a treasure,[9] [look at the planet in the seventh which signified that it was there, and see if it is the victor of the seventh house. If it were the victor, you should know of what nature that planet is; but if it is not the victor, associate it with the lord of the seventh house, and see if there were some partnership between them, and take the combined nature of both. But if something did not happen between them, the lord of the seventh house is the significator, and its nature shows what is buried].[10] If therefore the Sun were in that same place,[11] in Aries or Leo, it indicates gold or a precious asset (but of a red color). But whenever the Moon possessed a place of coldness (particularly in Cancer or Taurus), [it indicates] silver, crystal, and precious things of this kind. Also, Mars occupying the place of the Sun[12] (in whatever house of his), [indicates] lead or iron

---

[6] The fifth, in which case we would use the lord of the fourth for the parents, and the lord of the fifth for their money.
[7] Referring to the beginning of this section (but recall his similar discussion in §2.2). So far we have asked about known amounts of money with known owners. Now we are identifying a possible location of treasure, and asking whether or not something is in there.
[8] See a similar but different view of al-Kindī's in §4.17 below.
[9] That is, if one knows that a treasure is indeed in a specified place.
[10] I have read the material in brackets with al-Rijāl for the following, which is my best reading of Hugo and Hermann in *Search*: "...its quality and nature can be determined thusly: for the star which is possessing the seventh, and its partner (and if it is fortunate), shows that the nature of what is buried [is in accordance with] the lord of the seventh. Which if [the star that] would be staying in the seventh, [is] devoid of all dignity, it would share with the lord of the seventh."
[11] That is, assuming that he is the significator.
[12] That is, being in the seventh, as the Sun was just said to be.

or a stone like a magnet, and what is of this kind. Which if Jupiter would possess the place of the Sun, placed in any of [his] houses, [it indicates] pearls, coral, and such things which the sea produces, and the rest of this type of thing. Moreover, with Mercury occupying the place of the Sun and in either of [his] houses, coins, quicksilver, books, leather, little pitchers, and what is like these, are designated.

But[13] if these planets were not in their own houses, mix the one which was the significator with the planet to which it applies, or which applies to it, and express the prophecy thus. [And if there were a commixture of Saturn with Mercury in this matter, or that he would be in his house, and he in that of this one, and either of them were the significator of the thing dug up, say that it is something of black magic, or what is like that. The same thing will happen to you if there were a conjunction of Mercury with the Tail.]

§4.16: Whether it could be found—'Umar[14]

[1] If however it came into question whether he could get what is sought, the star designating the concealed thing (namely the one found in the seventh, [which] possesses something there),[15] or the lord of the seventh itself, should be principally noted. Which if they applied to the lord of the east, or it to [one of them], or there is a transfer between them, or one who collects their lights, they testify that it will be gotten. Which if it were from the tetragon or opposition or assembly,[16] it confers [it] after labor and difficulties.[17]

[2] Furthermore, once you discover the extent of any place within which the money written about before would be contained, it is necessary that the sign and which part of the circle the significator[18] holds onto, be scrutinized. [2a] For, in western ones, it means the western part of the room or house;

---

[13] I have read this paragraph with al-Rijāl (and added the material in brackets from him), in place of Hugo's "But if the stars which we stated before would be walking outside of their own houses, along with those which do not give up their own lodging-places, but which are applying to them, it is necessary to make them submit [to each other] or unite them in some manner."

[14] Cf. al-Rijāl I.39.2 (first part), and I.39.3. For the sake of clarity, I have numbered 'Umar's five steps in answering this question.

[15] See the previous section.

[16] Al-Rijāl omits this, probably correctly.

[17] *Search* says: "And if it is from the trigon or hexagon, quickly and easily; and from the tetragon or opposition, the opposite. An assembly between each shows success, provided that it is with reception."

[18] *Search* indicates the lord of the seventh here.

but in eastern ones, toward the eastern [part].[19] [2b] However, the nature of the sign which the significator possesses, indicates in what and how large a part of that place the hidden thing is being held (namely, whether it is under the earth or in a wall, or the ceiling): for a firm [sign] hides it underground, but a double-bodied one in the wall, [and] a convertible one in the ceiling of that quarter (I mean the eastern or western one).

[3] Furthermore, if it should come into question as to in what place of that quarter it is being held, one must next divide the home (or however big the space of the area[20] is) into two parts: namely into an eastern and western part, and see which of them the significator occupies. [Then] one will have to measure the exterior wall or inner wall or wall or ceiling by the kind of measurement one is able to (namely by cubits or rods or feet).

[4] Now, once the amount of the measurement is determined, it will be appropriate to know equally [4a] how many degrees of its own sign the significator of the concealed thing has passed through, [and] even [4b] in what decan it is lingering (namely in the first face, or the second or third), or in how many degrees of it [it is]. Moreover, with the quantity of that [part of the room or house][21] being divided into three, if the significator occupies the first decan, it designates [that the object] is contained in the first one-third; but if the second, in the second [one-third]; which if [it is] the third, in the third [one-third] (I mean of the eastern or western [side]).

[5] Then too, once it is known in which part of the quadrant it is being contained, one should take up another division. With the quantity of this part [of the room or house] being determined, one will have to divide according to the already-crossed degrees of that decan [itself] which the significator comprises. The individual portions of it suffice for presenting the measure, as to [whether it is] in the earth or in the wall or ceiling.

---

[19] This must identify the "part" of the circle the planet is in. It probably means either the western or eastern hemisphere, or else the eastern and western quarters. The eastern quarters are from the Ascendant to the MC, and from the Descendant to the IC; the other two are western.

[20] *Atrii.* Technically this means a hall or atrium, but Hermann also allows any fenced-in space.

[21] Reading with *Search* for "face."

§4.17: On treasure and any hidden thing—al-Kindī[22]

§639. With a question being proposed about treasure and any hidden thing, namely as to whether or not a place (which has already been considered) contains it, before all else the Ascendant and the pivots should be established. Therefore, any lucky star in the Ascendant [or any of the pivots],[23] affirms it is in the allotted place. Wherefore, one will be able to decide the status of the concealed thing, and the proper quality of [its] nature, and the price, according to the manner and nature, strength and weakness of the fortunate and lucky [star].

§640. In fact, that lucky [star] being corrupted by a powerful infortune, spoils the hidden things, as it portends that the whole (or the majority of) it has [already] been carried off.[24] Which if it is blessed by the luckiness of other [planets], it preserves what he was seeking in that same place.

§641. But the lord of the Ascendant and the Moon respond to the question as to whether it could be found. For their common application with the significator of the concealed thing, [with reception],[25] affirms its discovery. But if it happened differently, let the opinion of the judgment be changed.

§642. Therefore, once one has faith about its discovery, let such a description of the place where it is shut up lead right to it.[26] And so, let a division of its place (which [one's] masterful assessment has indicated) be drawn from its center to every outermost limit, in twelve directions, bounded in right angles.[27] Moreover, let the line of the sign which the star is holding onto (dividing a triangular place according to the quantity of its course),[28] be drawn out from the center of that same door:[29] so that if [the planet] is crossing one-third or one-fourth of the sign, the line will either cut off or enclose one-third or one-fourth of the triangle.

---

[22] See also Hermann's version in *Search* II.2.3, and al-Rijāl I.39.3 (second half).
[23] Adding with Burnett 1997, based on the Arabic.
[24] See a similar but different view of ʿUmar's in §4.15 above.
[25] Adding with Burnett 1997, based on the Arabic.
[26] In his example, al-Kindī may be drawing on a source very close to *Carmen*. A Greek text attributed to Erasistratos (Schmidt 1995, p. 41) says that the Ascendant signifies the door of the place, and the Moon the location of the object.
[27] Probably because al-Kindī supposes the house or property is roughly square-shaped; but he also seems to mean that the lines should be evenly spaced and form right angles just as the lines dividing the signs of a quadruplicity do. See diagram.
[28] What Hugo means is that one should divide the significator's sign into three (or four, see immediately below) parts so as to estimate where in that direction the treasure is, proportionate to the significator's position in the sign.
[29] Or rather, that portion of the house.

§§4.15-18: BURIED TREASURE

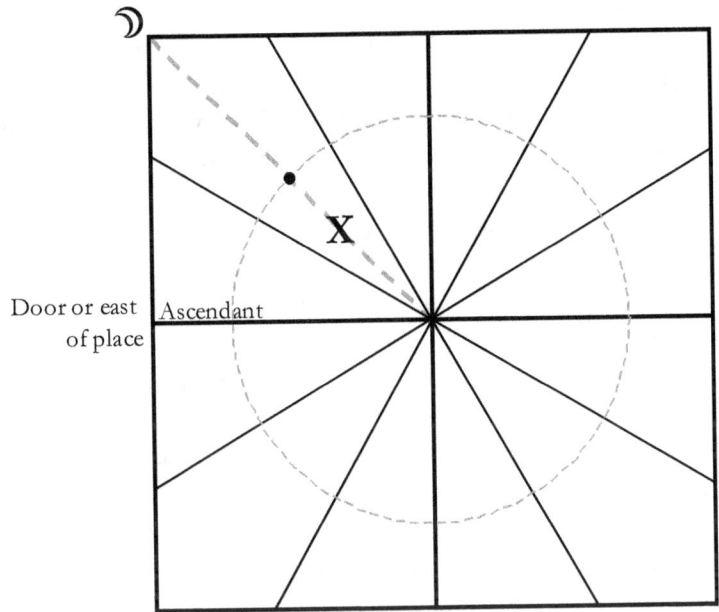

Figure 20: Al-Kindī's example of finding treasure[30]

§643. The[31] line produced from the center separates the whole space [within] the outermost [limits] of the sign, [according to] how[ever] many

---

[30] In this example from al-Kindī's *Letter* (Burnett 1997, pp. 70-71), the treasure is in a house, and the Ascendant represents the door. The square house is divided into twelve equal parts representing the signs (§642). The Moon happens to be the significator of the treasure, and is 45° to the south of the Ascendant, with 2° northern latitude. Hugo's version has us estimate which third of the sign the planet is in (§643), but al-Kindī's *Letter* recommends using the exact degree. We draw a dotted gray line from the center of the house towards the southeast, at an angle of 45° from the Ascendant (§642-43). Then, divide this line in half with a mark (§644), and use a compass to draw a circle representing the ecliptic (the circle is actually unnecessary, what matters is dividing the line). Then, determine what the maximum latitude of the planet is, and what its latitude actually is at the time (§644-45): in this case, the Moon's maximum latitude is 5°, but she is actually at 2° N. Northern latitudes will be between the mark and the center of the house, southern latitudes between it and the circumference of the figure (§645). Since she is 2/5 of the way towards her northernmost latitude, the treasure will be at a distance 2/5 of the way from the mark to the center of the house, marked by the X. Her distance towards or away from her apogee (or perhaps, her elevation in the sky) will determine how high up or low the treasure is (§647).

[31] Reading this and the next sentence with the Arabic as a guide, since Hugo seems to have misunderstood what was being divided or determined.

degrees of the sign the significator of the hidden thing has passed through. So that if it is now leaving one-third [of the sign], the line will cut off, by [its] angle, one-third of the sign which the significator is holding onto. To make this matter obvious, the point of the Ascendant designates the degree of the east in that same place or home. Therefore, by how great the distance the significator[32] was from the Ascendant, you will note that much distance of the concealed thing from the east.

§644. Again, if you wanted to determine whether it is closer to the center or to the end-point of the line in which it is discovered to be, cut that same line in half. The mark of its division [in half] also represents the circle of signs[33] which we call the zodiac. Then the latitude of the star from the ecliptic (namely its departure towards the south or towards the north) should be noted. For a northern [latitude] invites us towards the north [and the center][34] from the point fixed before, but a southern [latitude] towards the south [and the circumference].[35]

§645. Moreover, it will be good to divide the distance [between] the mark[36] and the center [of the room] according to the degrees of its latitude. For example, if the [maximum] latitude of the star from the ecliptic were proven to be 5°, the aforesaid distance [between] the point and the center shares in [those] five equal degrees. If therefore the star departed somewhat from the ecliptic, what is sought is asserted to be distant from the mark [in the center of the line] by that same amount. Like if it completed one-fifth of [its] latitude from the ecliptical point, it means one-fifth of the line extended from the center to the mark. But if one-third, [then one-third of the line], in this manner. So, if it departs towards the south, the matter warns [us] to measure that portion in such a manner [toward the circumference]; likewise toward the north [and the center of the home].

§646. Which if the [planet][37] came to be discovered in the middle of the signs,[38] with the southern and northern part being left behind, search for what you intended in that sign, [in the place] where the line is divided.

---

[32] Reading with the Ar. and the logic of the paragraph, for Hugo's "of the lord of the significator."
[33] Omitting the transliteration *deirataburoig* (Ar. *dāʿirah al-burūj*, "circle of signs").
[34] Adding with Burnett 1997, based on the Arabic.
[35] Adding with Burnett 1997, based on the Arabic.
[36] That is, the mark indicating the center of the line.
[37] Reading *planetam* for *notam*.
[38] That is, right on the ecliptic.

§647. Moreover, the depression of the star, or [its] loftiness above the ethers,[39] should be noted. For, a consideration of this matter shows how far below the earth it is being held. Its middle loftiness means [it is] between the surface of the earth and the impenetrable bedrock or water.[40] But its uppermost status suggests a place of height, in the way it was said about the status of a home, above.[41]

[Election: When to dig it up]

§648. Moreover, in choosing the hour for digging it up, an application of the Moon with the fortunate significator should be noted, [and] in the same way an application of the lord of the Ascendant at that hour to [that same significator]—indeed an assembly[42] of each with it is more powerful. In the hour of extracting it, you will no less take care to make the infortunes be absent from the pivots.

§4.18: On treasure or some hidden thing—Jirjis[43]

For treasure or any hidden thing, you will note the seventh from the east. For, any fortunate one appearing in that same place portends that the treasure or some hidden thing is in there. Moreover, any of the benevolents traversing in a pivot [indicates] the same thing.

Whenever therefore the Sun and the east would support the east with their own aspect, the hidden thing is being held in the house. Likewise, if the lord of the hour would be lingering in the east, it hides the thing at the gate of the house; its position in the Midheaven, [means] in the middle of the

---

[39] This appears to mean whether the planet is ascending or descending in its apogee (*ITA* II.1). Burnett believes it is the star's altitude above or below the horizon (1997, p. 60), but that does not seem right to me. The translator of the version in *OHT* §7 (in *WSM*) explicitly names the apogee.
[40] Reading with Burnett's Arabic (1997, p. 75) for Hugo's "intact earth which the Arabs call *gibel almuntaneah*."
[41] This appears to be a reference to finding the home of a thief: see *Forty Chapters* Chs. 6-9 and that topic below, but I do not find a similar statement there.
[42] Reading with Burnett's Ar. for "with reception." An assembly is a conjunction within the same sign: see Ch. 2.1.1 above, and *ITA* III.5.
[43] See also Hermann's version in *Search* II.2.1. I have added bracketed numbers to clearly identify the steps in Jirjis's method. Note that Hugo's version here (unlike *Search* but like *OHT* §5) also mentions the Lot of Fortune after his example below.

house; in the seventh, toward the west; in the pivot of the earth, it invites us toward the northern[44] part. Moreover, it being eastern indicates a new thing;[45] western, an old thing.

Mercury in the east portends [it is] buried underground; the position of Venus in the same [place], toward a couch;[46] Jupiter, in the wall; which if Saturn were here, in an obscure place or in a collapsed building; but the Sun, [in a middle place of the house; the Moon],[47] in the places of women or a storage area; also Mars: in a pathway[48] or kitchen, or where fire tends to be ignited. The Head of the Dragon, in a lofty and high place; the Tail makes an indication for an obscure place.

The traversal of the Sun and Moon in the east, or if they should regard [the east], demonstrates that it can be found quickly. Moreover, any star traversing in the seventh reveals whatever hidden thing is being held. But with no [planet] traversing in that place, the lord of the seventh assumes the signification of the thing.

[1] But the home must be divided into four parts: namely (I say) an eastern and western, southern and northern [part]. Then, it will be good to multiply how much the lord of the hour has traveled through its own sign, by 12: the sum is collected together, [and] you should bestow it to [individual] signs by [increments of] 30 [degrees] to the individual [signs].[49] At the termination of the number it indicates the concealed thing is being held [in a place corresponding to] the sign: either eastern or western, northern or southern.

[2] But even attend diligently to see how many degrees the lord of the sign (where the ending of the [first] number is) has traveled in its own sign. After attributing 7.5° [of that longitude] to each sign[50] [from the position of that planet], you will understand again [by means of] the sign where the number is ended, whether the sign is eastern or western, northern or southern. For there is no ambiguity but that what is hidden is being held in that direction.

[3] Moreover, with the [most recent] place being divided into four directions, look to see where the lord of the sign (where the number had been ended), would be staying: [see] how many degrees the lord of *that* lodging-

---

[44] Reading *septentrionem* with *OHT* and *Search* for *australem* ("southern").
[45] Or possibly, "recent" (as with *Search: recens*), that is, recently buried.
[46] Or, "bed" (*lectum*).
[47] Adding with *Search*.
[48] *Via*. Or perhaps a duct, such as in or near a heating duct. *Search* adds the places of foreign tenants, which would indeed be a Martial signification.
[49] Or simply project the sum from the degree of the Ascendant.
[50] That is, in 30° increments. See the example below.

place, has passed through in *its* own sign. If you attributed 7.5° to each sign, the sign where the number was ended portends the hidden thing is being held in that direction.

[4] Nor should one deviate from the order of this method,[51] until you arrive by a certain calculation to a quantity of one cubit [from the object's position].[52]

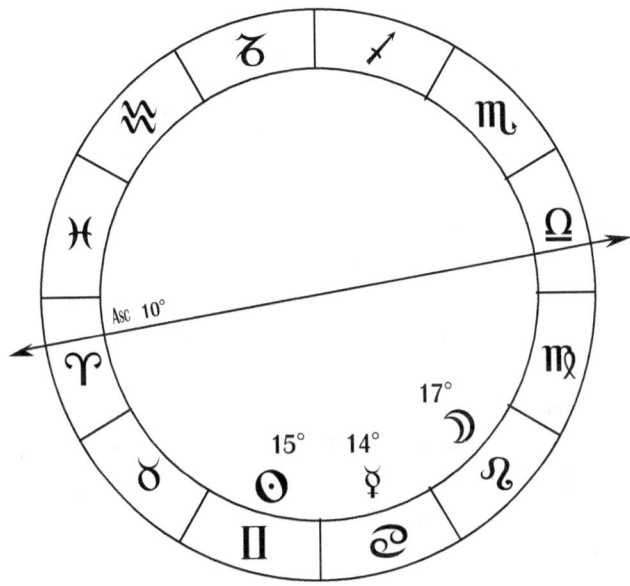

Figure 21: Finding a hidden object (Jirjis)

For example, the east was Aries, in its tenth degree. Mercury, the lord of the hour, was holding onto the fourteenth degree of Cancer.

[1] Therefore, this heap [of degrees], drawn out by 12, made 168. Therefore, with the beginning being taken up from the east, granting 30° to each sign, the numbering reached Virgo (which is a southern sign).[53]

---

[51] From now on, always taking the domicile lord of the previous planet, and projecting its longitude out in increments of 7.5° for every 30° of longitude. See example below.
[52] Note that in this method, one finally uses 7.5° increments for everything. If each sign is granted 7.5°, that means 90° for the whole circle, precisely the size of a quarter of the circle, which is the very manner of finding the object (i.e., by dividing a place or home into quarters). Because the longitude of a planet is projected onto the succession of triplicities (fire, earth, air, water), it means that the object's location is implicitly found in a clockwise fashion, as though forming a set of spirals throughout the home or place.

[2] And so, we divided the southern quarter [of the home] into four further parts. And, having recourse to the place of Mercury (possessing the fourteenth [degree] of Cancer), beginning from that same [place], with 7.5° being attributed to every sign, we recognized that the number ended in Virgo (namely, a southern one).[54] Whence we could affirm that [the object] was manifestly in the southern quarter [of the home].[55]

[3] Again, with that quarter being divided into four [further] parts, since Mercury was staying in the lodging-place of the Moon, and she happened to be found in the seventeenth degree of Leo, [then] with these being attributed at 7.5° to each sign, the number reached Libra (namely, a western sign): therefore we reported that it was hidden in the western direction.[56]

[4] Moreover, since the Moon was holding onto the domicile of the Sun, [and] likewise the Sun was traversing in 15° Gemini, [then] with 7.5° being attributed to each sign (as usual), the number arrives from the place of the Sun to Cancer. And so, with the numbering from the Sun's place leaving off at the sign where it had arrived, it is good to note which direction that is.[57]

With this partitioning [of the home] being made, continue until it guides the querent to the quantity of a cubit or less [from the object's location.

[5] But even the assistance of the Lot of Fortune should be taken: [namely] wherever it fell.[58]

---

[53] At 28° Virgo. This would have indicated that the object is in the southern part of the home.
[54] Mercury is at a position of 14° Cancer. The first 7.5° of that is given to the 30° increment from his own position, up to 14° Cancer. Then the remainder of his 14° (i.e., 6° 30') is given proportionally to the next increment, which makes the end of his numbering end in Virgo.
[55] Or more precisely, in the southern part of the southern part of the home.
[56] Reading *parte* for *signo*.
[57] Namely, the north (Cancer is a watery sign). So far, the object is in the [4] northern part of the [3] western part of the [2] southern part of the [1] southern part of the home.
[58] In *OHT*, the previous parts of this section were attributed to Dorotheus, and only this part is attributed to Jirjis. *OHT* clarifies that the signs in which the Lot and its lord fall, show the direction (fiery signs mean in the east, and so on). *OHT* also adds a few comments about the fourth, its lord, the lord of the Ascendant, and the Moon.

Outcomes

§4.19: On a suspicion or matter, whether it would come to be for certain or not—'Umar

The solution of this question proceeds from the tenth and its lord. For, [the lord] being in a pivot, not scorched, announces the effect. Which if it possessed a pivot of the east, or the tenth [itself], a manifest effect will follow on that same day or in that same hour. Moreover, with the lord of the tenth being cadent from the Midheaven, it is a sign of an effect that has already passed. But being in the third or sixth or twelfth, it removes the effect altogether.

However, the supports of the Lot written below must be applied.[1] Wherefore, it is taken up from the lord of the hour to the lord of the east, [and the projection] will begin from the Midheaven. It is reasonable that the sign and bound in which it leaves off, be scrutinized. Now, if the lord of that same bound regarded the east, there will be no ambiguity as to the effect; but if it is otherwise, it happens to the contrary.

Furthermore, if it pleased you to investigate the precise hour of the outcome, [1] once the degrees from the lord of the east to the east itself are taken up, you will always ascribe[2] one month to [each increment of] 2.5°, so that once these have finally been carried out in such a way, [any] delay in the effect is absent.[3] [2] According to the claim of others, it is possible for [the timing] to be found in another way: namely from the lord of the hour to the Midheaven. On the other hand, with the lord of the Midheaven being cadent,[4] you will take the degrees interposed from it[5] up to the lord of the hour. Thus in the end it is reasonable to declare individual days or months or hours for the individual degrees.

An understanding of this matter especially depends on each light, and the east, and the Lot of Fortune, and their lords. For, a regard of these lords to them shows there is an efficacy to the business. If two of them regarded, but

---

[1] This is the Lot attributed to Dorotheus in *Search* I.3.2 (though *Search* says that the distance from the lord of the hour to the lord of the east may also be projected from the Sun). In *Search*, it is used to find a significator of thought.
[2] Reading *ascribes* for *ascribens*.
[3] To put Hugo's tiresome phrasing differently, the effect will manifest once those months expire.
[4] That is, if the lord of the Midheaven is in aversion to it.
[5] I am not sure if this is the Midheaven or the lord of the Ascendant.

[the other] two did not, [then] once the stronger aspect is noted, the integrity of the end (or the trouble of [its] corruption) could be discovered from it. Moreover, with all of these being deprived of an aspect, turn the eyes of your mind toward each of the lights and the lord of the Ascendant: for, being in the pivots or after the pivots, they are consoled about the effect; but those which are cadent wholly pervert it.

§4.20: On some matter, whether it has been done or will be—'Umar[6]

And so, the Moon being found in the second, holding onto the tetragon of the fortunate ones and a double-bodied sign, really signifies the affair is done or will be done. But she being in the east, likewise [indicates] it will be. In the second,[7] too, the same, but it brings it about with delay. And these are the testimonies of the Moon with respect to the effecting of matters.

Furthermore, the lord of the east regarding it, even the lord of the lights (and the lights themselves) being in the regard of one to the other, likewise the Moon [regarding] the bound of the twelfth-part,[8] and [the lord] of the Lot of Fortune the Lot, [and] especially regarding the place of the quaesited matter, wholly convey certain and firm testimonies.

§4.21: On the hour of the outcome—'Umar[9]

The significator of any affair, and the victor over the east,[10] principally determine the hour of the matter's effect. For once a question is given, if the joint aspect of each is discovered (and the promise of their effect), then it is suitable to describe [its] nature. Which if they would be deprived of this benefit and solace, these things must be passed over.

---

[6] Cf. *Forty Chapters* Ch. 2.5. I have had to translate this section rather freely, as the sentence structure is rather confused.

[7] I have a feeling 'Umar means a place "following" (*secundo*) a pivot: in other words, in any succeedent place. But if *secundo* is right, he might mean "in the following pivot," namely, in the fourth.

[8] *Terminum duodenae*. I am not sure what this means, though it is certainly in error.

[9] The following section is quite difficult and many parts are confusing, This topic must have been somewhat vexed among many authors, because both versions of Sahl's *On Times* (in *WSM* and in *Search*) likewise have very uncertain instructions. Hugo's own desire to compress the material also makes it frustrating.

[10] See §A129 for 'Umar's ideas about finding this victor. *Search* also has many other approaches.

Therefore, it is necessary to attend (not without hard work) to the status of each significator, and [the] pivot in their own places,[11] [and their] position by regard.

And the rest of the manifold properties, I say, [are] easternness and westernness, the first and second stay,[12] [and] retrogradation. A signification will even have to be ascribed to those stars which are namely diurnal or nocturnal, as well as the testimonies of their light (or rather brilliance),[13] whether they are fortunate ones or the contrary. Moreover, eastern ones mean a quick effect (no less, too, in the pivots). But even their testimonies and rulership and their brilliance [means the same thing]. Those especially of the one to which the shift is ascribed,[14] establish the same thing. Any of the diurnal ones (in a diurnal inquiry) or any of the nocturnal ones (it being a nocturnal question) is not otherwise.

In this way too, with the testimony or support of its own lord being had, or with any fortunate one accompanying [it], [and] should the support of the fortunate ones not be absent from the pivots (namely the east and the Midheaven), even should an application from neighboring degrees be present (preferably from its own bound and from the assembly in the house of the affair itself—while they bear themselves thusly, they introduce the hour or day (and that sort) of the effect more quickly. But in the rest of the pivots (namely, the one under the earth, and the seventh), a delay up to a month or [something] of this kind is reaffirmed. Likewise, in the fifth and eighth it suggests up to many months. With it moreover withdrawing from the pivots, a delay is generated [corresponding to] the amount which the proper quality of the stars promises.

Wherefore, the hour itself when the significator itself attains full and complete power, or changes its figure over to that, and [to] the strength of the nature of the east, [or] even when the significator itself will be able to reach a star applying to it, or the place of the affair [reaches] the place of the significator[15] (with, I say, the regard of the east), [it will be] according to the

---

[11] *Et in propriis locis cardinem.* That is, their whole-sign angles.
[12] That is, "station."
[13] 'Umar may be distinguishing between their rays or aspects ("light") and the glow they have around their own bodies ("brilliance"), which would pertain to their assemblies.
[14] That is, the luminary of the sect (the Sun in diurnal charts, the Moon in nocturnal ones). Hugo then adds the following odd parenthetical comment: "which is a configuration and form."
[15] This is probably by a transit of the significator to the cusp or sign, or by the symbolic degrees already described in §4.19 and in the last paragraph below (or even §4.22 below).

number of degrees. Or rather, were the Sun able to arrive from the east to a fortunate one, and to the eastern degrees, or at least should he be made equal to the pivots and to the circle of the lesser significator.

Not otherwise is it possible to elicit the hour for initiating affairs, if a question is presented. With the degrees (however many there were) being taken up from the degree of the east to the bound of the one which has control over the rulership of the significator,[16] if they are less than 180, they are taken away from their own degrees. But if they went over 180, they will have to be reduced from the opposite degrees.[17] Where therefore the number left off, it is suitable to attend to the lord of that bound and its place from the east of the question or the undertaking.[18] For from this depends the recognition of the hour and of its quickness, in the way that was stated above. If however the east and its lord would fall in the bound of that star (namely, the significator), that matter or beginning really will not be deprived of an effect on that day. But proceeding from a tetragon, it means the quickest change on that same day. However, should they bear themselves just as was stated [but] from a trigon, it prolongs the same thing.

Moreover, the conjunction of each from the east or the seventh determines the hour, if, I say, the signification of the question looks to [matters of the seventh].[19] Which if their signification would pertain to children, the conjunction of each will be in the fifth; but with respect to captives, in the sixth; concerning kings, too, in the tenth. Therefore, their assembly in that place really describes the hour.

The opposition or assembly of each in a pivot of the east will even profess the same thing.

Which if this signification would be ascribed to that star to which the Moon applies, or from which she withdraws, it is appropriate to note with the greatest effort when it meets (by approaching it) that sign which the Moon possesses at the hour of the question, or by a tetragon, or rather should it be opposed [to that sign]: for from this proceeds a recognition of the hour.

Finally, in all of this, it is more certain and without all ambiguity if you understand diligently in how many days what was stated above (about the

---

[16] I believe this means, to the bound of the significator itself.
[17] I believe Hugo's 'Umar is simply saying to take the shortest distance between the east and the significator.
[18] That is, the election.
[19] Reading [res] septimi or simply septimum for Saturnum.

tetragon and the opposition) would happen: for it will undoubtedly be permitted to describe days or months or even years for the effect and its kind, according to the number of degrees and the progressing of the star.

§4.22: When the effecting of matters would follow—Jirjis[20]

First therefore, it is good to note the Moon and the one to which she applies, and by how many degrees they are distant from each other. For if the sign of the star to which the Moon applies, were a firm one, grant one year to each of the degrees put between [them]. But if it would linger in a double-bodied one and after a pivot, it will be permitted to grant that same amount of months. In a double-bodied one but remote, have a month for [every] degree-and-a-half.[21] But in a turning one, and remote, it will prolong that same amount of days. Moreover, with the Moon lingering in a turning one, you will take a month for [every] two-and-a-half [degrees]. Moreover, she bearing herself thusly but after a pivot, [every] 30° promise a full day. She being remote, you would attribute an hour for [every] 12°. For then the effecting of the quaesited matter will follow.

The Moon even applying to benevolents, promises nothing other than a certain good.[22]

---

[20] 1509 attributes this to ʿUmar, but according to Burnett it is properly Jirjis.
[21] This should probably be "two-and-a-half degrees."
[22] This sentence seems misplaced here.

§5: FIFTH HOUSE

5th House	
Whether one will have a child	§§5.1-5
Whether a woman is pregnant	§§5.6-12
Time of conception	§§5.13-15
Miscarriage	§§5.16-20
Already given birth?	§§5.21, 7.35
Time of birth	§§5.22-25
Experience of labor	§5.26
Number of children	§§5.27-31, 5.37
Sex of child	§§5.32-38
Rumors: true or false?	§§5.39-40, 5.42-44, 5.47, 5.66, 5.68
Content of rumors/legations	§§5.41, 5.46
Outcomes of rumors	§5.45
Messengers & their return	§§5.48-59, 5.72
Letters, papers, & their arrival	§§5.60-73

Figure 22: Questions of the fifth house

PREGNANCY & BIRTH

§5.1: On those things which pertain to the fifth house—Sahl[1]

[Having a child with a specific person or woman]

If at some time an inquiry of the fifth should occur, about having children by [the woman] whom he has, the method written below will give counsel. For, the lord of the east or the Moon applying to the lord of the fifth or traversing in the fifth, or even in the reverse order (should the lord of the fifth apply to the eastern one or to the Moon, or rather should it linger in the east), it generates the sweetest affection of offspring. Moreover, a transfer of light[2] does the same thing, but more slowly.

But should either one gather the counsel of the other, [see] whether it is even cleansed of the infortunes or rather is corrupted. For, being free, neither retrograde nor scorched,[3] brings about the sure hope of children. Moreover, with any of these being discovered (as, namely, scorching or ret-

---

[1] Cf. *On Quest.* §5.1.
[2] But John's Sahl implies that this is a reflection of light (*ITA* III.13).
[3] John's Sahl includes being in aversion to the Ascendant or cadent from the angles.

rogradation, or should any other corruption of this type be able to be discovered), it conveys children but in no way surviving for long.

If Jupiter, being placed well, should regard the east itself well, being free of scorching and corruption, it claims the same thing. But if Venus would be conjoined to the infortunes, or should the Moon apply to the malevolents, they take away the hope of children and wholly deny it.

Again, a benevolent traversing in the fifth suggests she is already pregnant. But an infortune found in that same place, or at least regarding the fifth, speaks against it.

[Having a child in the future][4]

But should there arise an interrogation about someone else of either sex, it seems such an observation must be had. Therefore, a fortunate one being found in the east, or if the lord of the east would be lingering in the east or tenth or even the fifth or seventh,[5] as likewise should you find Jupiter placed well, it speeds up the conception. But if a malevolent should either traverse in the east or regard it in a bad way, or even should the lord of the east be staying in a perverse place, and Jupiter be found adverse (retrograde or scorched), or finally in the eighth, it is a sign of few offspring, nor will they remain long.

Moreover, I reckon in all of this the fifth should in no way be overlooked. Should a benevolent possess it, it makes a judgment of an accelerated conception; on the other hand, an infortune both delays it and finally takes it away.

Again, Jupiter being eastern and in a pivot, accelerates the conception; but if he would be western and lingering in a pivot—as equally should you find the lord of the east well placed—the conception will be with a delay.

---

[4] Cf. *On Quest.* §5.2. The previous question was on having a child with a specific person; this question is more general, and specifically suggests the querent may be of either sex.
[5] I read John's Sahl as listing the "eleventh or fifth," not the "fifth or seventh." Dorotheus seems to use the tenth or seventh in §5.3 below.

§5.2: On having children—Dorotheus[6]

If perhaps an ambiguity of the fifth would come into question (such as about children: would he often have them), the eastern lord and the Moon respond. For, their application with the lord of the house of children in the east, or would either of them linger in the lodging-place of children, it multiplies offspring. Moreover, the lord of the domicile of children being after the pivots and received, regarding its own house, produces the sweet affections of children. Which if there would be a transfer [of light] from one to the other, it promises the same but with delay.

Next, the receiver of the counsel of each, being cleansed of the infortunes [and] free of scorching, retrogradation and fall, resembles what was said before. If[7] the planet from which the Moon is being separated, is even the lord of the fifth sign from the place of the planet to which the Moon applies, and both planets aspected each other, it signifies that he will have a child. But with a regard being denied, while the one to which the Moon applies is in a pivot and received, the same thing is indicated.

§5.3: Whether someone is going to have children—Dorotheus[8]

As the claim of the ancients teaches, for a question about any man or woman as to whether he would ever be consoled by the generation of offspring,[9] an observation of the east enters in. For if the fortunate ones would regard it, while the eastern lord would possess it or the tenth or the seventh,[10] and thus Jupiter [would be] in a prosperous place, with the lords of his[11] triplicity accompanying [him], but he being free of scorching, it indicates he is fertile and it indicates offspring. Likewise,[12] Jupiter being in a

---

[6] This is very similar to al-Rijāl I.40 (last part).
[7] Reading with al-Rijāl I.40, for Hugo's "It is not otherwise [for] the star from which the Moon is separating, [if it] holds onto a face in the fifth sign. But likewise the one to which she applies, if (I say) it would regard the two stars."
[8] Cf. al-Rijāl I.41.
[9] Slightly changing Hugo's redundant styling, "the offspring of children" (*filiorum prole*).
[10] Reading *vii* with Sahl above for Vienna's *xii*. Al-Rijāl I.41 reads, "tenth or eleventh or fifth."
[11] Al-Rijāl identifies this with the Ascendant, but Hugo's text might be correct, given the copious use of Jupiter's triplicity lords in *Carmen*.
[12] In the following two sentences, al-Rijāl has Jupiter in the eastern or western angles, not simply being in an angle and being either eastern or western from the Sun. My sense is that Hugo is correct here.

pivot and eastern, accelerates it. But being western, possessing a pivot, with the eastern lord being arranged in an optimal way, introduces a delay.

§5.4: Whether someone is going to have children—Aristotle

With a question of this kind being proposed, if the nativity would be unknown,[13] you will seek the whole affair from the east and the fifth. If however the eastern lord would be lingering in the fifth or with the lord of that fifth, or on the other hand if [the lord of the fifth] would do so in the east or with the lord of the east, [and] even were one of the benevolents (such as is the Head of the Dragon) found in the fifth or with the lord of the fifth, he will rejoice in the sweet affection of children.

However, malevolents in the fifth or with its lord, the lucky ones being wholly unfavorable and remote from there, are inconsistent with procreating offspring and wholly deny it.

But the traversal of the lucky ones with the malevolents, either promises that the children will in no way survive, or, if they do survive, it attacks their bodies with a long-lasting difficulty.

In addition, while signs of much offspring (of which kind are Cancer, Scorpio, and Pisces) are holding onto the place of the east or the fifth, they multiply offspring. They being removed from thence, one will have to judge according to the nature of the other [signs][14] and according to what was said about the position of the stars.

§5.5: When someone is going to have children—Aristotle

It could even be identified when he would rejoice in the gift of the children promised, in such a way: the lord of the fifth traversing in the second from the fifth (that is, in the sixth), greatly bestows the promised offspring in the following year. Which if it would traverse in the third [from the fifth], you will expect it for the third year; in the fourth [from the fifth], for the fourth; in the fifth [from the fifth], the fifth; and it promises thus with respect to the rest.

---

[13] This is an important point, suggesting that sometimes using the nativity is preferable to a question.
[14] Typically, the watery signs are the most fertile signs, while Gemini, Virgo, and Leo are sterile; the rest of the signs are somewhere in the middle. See for example *ITA* I.10.6.

But another opinion on this affair is given according to others' school of thought. For if (as they say) the lord of the fifth would possess the fourth place from the east, he will rejoice in children[15] in the following year. But if it would be lingering in the third, he will expect the third year; if in the second from the first, the fourth [year]; if in the east itself, the fifth [year]; but in the twelfth, it prefigures the seventh [year]; and this with the rest.

Moreover, the lord of the fifth being placed in the fifth itself, [indicates] he procreates children in that same year.

In addition, with the east being Virgo, Leo, or Gemini, however the lord of the fifth may possess any of these, it is a certain affirmation that he will remain sterile.

§5.6: Whether a woman is pregnant and will give birth—Sahl[16]

And if you were asked about some woman, whether she is pregnant or not, and whether she will give birth or not, or it would be perfected for her or not, look at the lord of the Ascendant and the Moon (which are the significators of the children). If you found the lord of the Ascendant and the Moon in the house of children, and the lord of the house of children were in the Ascendant, free from the malefics, say that she is pregnant. And if the lord of the Ascendant and the Moon pushed (that is, if they committed) their own disposition [to a planet in an angle], there will be a pregnancy; and better than that if it were received. And if they were joined to a planet cadent from the Ascendant, it signifies detriment and that the pregnancy will be in vain—and more strongly than that if the Ascendant were a movable sign, or there were a malefic in an angle, or if the Moon were joined to a malefic: because all of these things signify detriment. But the receiver of the disposition (that is, the heavier planet who receives all the disposition from the lord of the Ascendant or the Moon[17]), if it were free from the malefics (that is, if it was not joined to them nor were they joined to it), and it were in a good place, the pregnancy will be perfected.

And if he asked about a pregnancy, whether it would be true or false (that is, whether it would come to effect or be in vain), look at the lord of the As-

---

[15] Omitting Hugo's odd redundancy, *filiorum...sobole*.
[16] Cf. al-Rijāl I.42, and *On Quest.* §§5.3-4. I have used the text from *On Quest.*, as the last half of Hugo's text is hopelessly mixed up in his attempt to condense the material.
[17] Reading *luna* for *lunae*.

cendant. Which if it were joined to a planet cadent from the Ascendant, nor to one receiving [it], it signifies detriment. Likewise if [the lord of the Ascendant] were joined to a retrograde planet—unless[18] the Moon were received, or the lord of the Ascendant were in a good place from the Ascendant: because then it signifies pregnancy.

§5.7: On pregnant women—'Umar[19]

With a question proposed about pregnant women, the fifth and its lord, but even the Moon and the Lunar lord, should be consulted. For, with the lord of the fifth being in the east or the tenth, nor falling away [from its own house or sovereignty],[20] there is no ambiguity about the conception. Which if the lord of the Lunar lodging-place would assent to that,[21] [especially][22] with it being placed in the east or the rest of the pivots, it portends [the same]. Thus even the lord of the hour being in any pivot, it seems to claim the same thing.

§5.8: On pregnant women and the number of children—al-Kindī

§537. For a question as to whether or not a woman is pregnant, the lord of the Ascendant and of the fifth, and the Moon, should be consulted. If therefore some type of application would be noted between the lord of the fifth and that of the Ascendant (or the Moon), particularly if the Ascendant and the Moon would possess double-bodied signs, [and] in the same way the significators [would be] in the pivots or after the pivots, while a lucky star would be in the Ascendant or the second, they affirm she is pregnant. But if not, should they bear themselves [in] neither an application nor the pivots as we have said above, they deny[23] she is pregnant.

§538. Which if some star[24] would be arranged with the Moon and be received by her, or at least be with the lord of the Ascendant,[25] it claims she is

---

[18] Reading *nisi* with the *BN* manuscript.
[19] Cf. al-Rijāl I.42 (middle).
[20] Adding with al-Rijāl. That is, being in its fall or descension. See also §5.16 below.
[21] Al-Rijāl says, "testifies to that."
[22] Adding with al-Rijāl.
[23] *Inficiantur.*
[24] I imagine al-Kindī means a fortunate star.

fertile.[26] Moreover, some star with the Sun (namely in his degree[27] or under his rays), particularly a fortunate one, especially exhibits the signification of her being pregnant.

§5.9: Whether a woman is pregnant—al-Khayyāt

However, when a question about someone is given, as to whether she is pregnant or if she is going to bring about a conception, the lord of the east or the Moon being in the fifth, or the lord of the fifth[28] being in the east, free of the infortunes, means she is pregnant. Which if the lord of the east or the significator would render counsel to any [star] appearing in a pivot, [it is made] firm, and it is preferable with reception.

But if they would confer it to some cadent and hostile [star], they corrupt or deny it. And one must fear it more if the east were a turning [sign], or a malevolent would be lingering in a pivot. If that same significator would render the counsel of application to a malevolent not having testimony [where it is], it corrupts.

§5.10: Whether a woman is pregnant—Dorotheus[29]

With a question presented about any woman (whether she is pregnant or not), or concerning a pregnant woman, whether she would reach the time of giving birth, one will have to engage the counsel of the eastern lord and the Moon. For, they being established in the domicile of children, or if the lord of that same lodging-place would linger in the east, free of the infortunes, it claims she is pregnant. Moreover, the eastern lord or the significator[30] rendering counsel to that star appearing in a pivot, resembles the aforesaid, especially [if] received.[31]

---

[25] Al-Rijāl I.48 says: "If perhaps there were a direct planet with the Moon, applying to the lord of the Ascendant." But probably the Latin of al-Rijāl is wrong, and mistakenly reads *directus* for the more accurate *receptus* ("received").
[26] That is, she has been fertilized and is pregnant.
[27] Reading with al-Rijāl and Robert for Hugo's *affinitate*.
[28] The Vienna scribe adds, "and the Moon" below the line, but this does not match the other readings (such as in §5.6 above).
[29] Cf. al-Rijāl I.42 (first part), where this is attributed to Māshā'allāh.
[30] According to al-Rijāl I.42, this is the lord of the fifth.
[31] *Receptus*, indicating either the lord of the east or the lord of the fifth.

§5.11: Whether she (whom someone has married), would conceive—Jirjis

The east being female and its lord female, absolutely refuses conceptions. But if both were male, she will not ever conceive (for thus, either the man is sterile or [his] genitals are corrupted).[32]

§5.12: On pregnant women—Aristotle

With a question as to whether a woman would be pregnant (it being proposed by her own man), one must seek the advice from the lord of the east and of the fifth equally. For, the eastern lord in the fifth or with its lord, or at least the contrary (namely so that the lord of the fifth would be lingering in the east or with the lord of the east), means she is pregnant. The Moon in the fifth demonstrates the same thing. Moreover, the lord of the fifth traversing in the fifth itself, if it would look at the lord of the east by any aspect, does not convey anything else, but it testifies she is pregnant. Which if they would bear themselves otherwise, they corrupt a pregnant woman and deny it.

§5.13: When someone ought to be impregnated—Aristotle

If you desire to know when someone ought to be pregnant, but with no question being put forth, the method submitted [here] will give the judgment. Therefore, once the east is discovered, it is good to note both the lord of it and of the fifth. For if the eastern lord would happen to be found in the fifth or with its lord (or conversely, the lord of the fifth in the east or with its lord), then finally she could be made pregnant. But if not, then it will happen no further.

§5.14: On the time of the conception—'Umar[33]

Then, as to whether she has conceived very recently or is pregnant for a long time, the lords of the house of children and of the hour, but even the Moon, principally respond. If a withdrawal with more affinity should loom

---

[32] Jirjis is implying that conception will only be possible if the Ascendant and its lord are of opposite genders.
[33] Cf. al-Rijāl I.45.

over one of them,³⁴ that one will possess the signification—with the rest of the significators still being noticed. And so, if the majority of them would withdraw from a trigon, it is a conception of three or five months; but from a hexagon, it has been there for two³⁵ or six months. But from a tetragon, four; from the opposition, seven months; and in the assembly this is proved to be the first month. Finally,³⁶ that one whom many testimonies follow, really resolves the end of the judgment.

§5.15: On the time of the conception—al-Kindī

§540. With him asking you about the hour of conception, you will note how many ninth-parts of the Ascendant have passed by to completion: for, by taking months for individual ninth-parts, it asserts that that much [time] has passed by from the hour of the conception up to the time of the question. But how much of the Ascendant is left, designates the remaining time [until] the birth, as a month is granted to each ninth-part.

§5.16: Whether she would have a miscarriage³⁷—'Umar³⁸

And so, with faith about a conception already had, the lord of the fifth lays bare as to whether it would advance to the time of being born, or for some reason it would be corrupted before emerging. For, it being neither retrograde nor scorched, nor descending,³⁹ nor unlucky,⁴⁰ received from a tetragon or opposition or assembly, even by a trigon or hexagon, it preserves the birth unharmed. [If] it is deprived of reception, to the contrary, while it is unlucky, nor is scorching or retrogradation or depression⁴¹ absent, it threatens detriment.

---

³⁴ According to al-Rijāl, this means the one which is nearer to a separation from some planet; nor does al-Rijāl say that we should still examine the rest.
³⁵ Reading with al-Rijāl for Hugo's "three."
³⁶ This is not in al-Rijāl.
³⁷ Or, "abortion" (*abortivum*). Here and below I will assume that Hugo and the Arabic authors mean a miscarriage.
³⁸ Cf. al-Rijāl I.43 (first part).
³⁹ That is, being in in its fall or descension.
⁴⁰ That is, being *made* unlucky by an aspect with the infortunes (al-Rijāl).
⁴¹ Again, being in its fall or descension.

Finally, one must observe the testimonies of the lord of the Moon and the eastern [lord],[42] but even that of the hour, while you notice good health or fear corruption. But the lord of the filial lodging-place and of the Moon being corrupted, with however the lord of the hour being safe, they introduce danger. Two of them being safe while the third is corrupted, generate good health.

§5.17: Whether she would have a miscarriage—al-Kindī

§539. If however the infortunes would fill the role of the fortunate ones in every signification of theirs, [she is not pregnant or][43] they promise a miscarriage. Which if a wicked Mars would appear in that same place, she is corrupted with a flowing of blood. But if Saturn, [the fetus] is dissolved through an excess of waters and winds.

§5.18: Whether she would have a miscarriage—al-Khayyāt

In addition, an application [of the Moon][44] being made with a cadent star, nor one receiving [it], or even to a retrograde one, is a sign of corruption and miscarriage, unless she is received or the lord of the east is placed well and well-fortified by certain and firm testimonies. The one who received [her] being in the fifth, [means] the same thing. But the Moon being corrupted, corrupts [the matter].

Now, according to the most ancient of the philosophers,[45] a Full Moon being in the assembly of Mars (or applying to him) threatens a miscarriage and is fatal to the mother. Moreover, Venus regarding Mars, and she being in Scorpio, is a sign of miscarriage. Likewise, a malevolent occupying the tenth from Venus[46] corrupts the conception.

---

[42] Al-Rijāl omits the eastern lord, and is probably correct.
[43] Adding with al-Rijāl.
[44] Note that Sahl above has the lord of the Ascendant.
[45] Cf. *Carmen* V.18.
[46] That is, being in a superior square or "overcoming" her.

§5.19: Whether she would have a miscarriage—Dorotheus[47]

Which if the lord of the east or the significator itself[48] rendered to a cadent star, it is a sign of corruption and a lie. But it is more severe if the east is a convertible [sign], or with a malevolent holding onto a pivot, or should the significator itself render counsel to any infortune which has no testimonies, or to a retrograde [star]: for thus they promise a miscarriage. Moreover, the receiver of counsel being free of the infortunes testifies that she has already conceived; but an application of it with a cadent star corrupts it. Likewise, it applying to some star that is drawn back,[49] ruins it, unless perhaps the Moon is received and the eastern lord is arranged optimally (and not without testimonies): for thus there is no ambiguity with respect to observing the conception. The receiver of counsel traversing in the fifth, free of the infortunes, being powerful in testimonies, and received, [indicates] no other [judgment].

I even think one should pay attention to this: because the Moon being at the Full Moon and in the assembly of Mars (or regarding him), renders a miscarriage and threatens death to the woman. Moreover, with Venus corrupted and in Scorpio, it does not deny a miscarriage. The malevolents possessing the tenth place from Venus[50] are hostile to a conception, and corrupt it.

Likewise,[51] the lord of the east being in the fourth or seventh, while a question is presented about generating children, and Jupiter being arranged in an optimal way, introduces offspring but slowly. Moreover, the east being corrupted by the infortunes, and its lord being established in an adverse place, with Jupiter (I say) cadent or scorched, or possessing the house of death,[52] procreates few children, nor ones surviving long. The Moon being corrupted in the same way perverts a conception.

Among all of these things, it is necessary to observe the sign of children diligently. For, it being possessed by the fortunate ones or being in their regard, accelerates what was stated about a conception. The infortunes [indicate] to the contrary.

---

[47] Cf. al-Rijāl I.42 (first part).
[48] Based on al-Rijāl's version of §5.10, this is the lord of the fifth.
[49] *Reductae.* I am not sure what distinction 'Umar or Hugo is drawing between a cadent star earlier in the sentence, and one that is drawn back.
[50] That is, "overcoming" her (see Glossary).
[51] Cf. al-Rijāl I.41 (middle).
[52] Reading *mortis* with al-Rijāl, for *Martis* ("of Mars").

§5.20: Whether she would have a miscarriage—Aristotle

If however it is asked whether she would have a miscarriage, it seems such an observation must be had. For, the east being a firm [sign] (of which kind are Taurus, Leo, Scorpio and Aquarius), she in no way has a miscarriage. Which if it were of the number of the turning [signs] (which are Aries, Cancer, Libra, Capricorn), she will mourn the misfortune of a miscarriage.

§5.21: Whether some woman has already given birth—Aristotle[53]

Therefore, with someone asking about his own wife, as to whether she has already given birth, one must consult the lord of the seventh. For if that same lord of the seventh has already gone past the lord of the fifth from the seventh, just as withdrawing from it, or if the lord of the fifth [from] the seventh from [that of] the seventh, or even has the Moon passed beyond the Sun, it is clear that she has already given birth. Which if there were nothing of these, you should respond that she has not yet given birth.

§5.22: On the hour of birth—'Umar[54]

Moreover, the destined hour of birth could be discovered by such a method. For, the assembly of Mars or preferably the Sun, but even the lord of the domicile of children, no less too the Moon and the lord of the hour (or at least of the majority [of them]), really suggest the hour.

§5.23: On the hour of birth—al-Kindī

§541. But sometimes, the degrees by which the applying star and the one with which the application is, are distant [from one another], determine the hour of giving birth, by representing months in this judgment—if, I say, the degrees appeared to be fewer than the time [left in] the pregnancy. But[55] if not (namely if the degrees would indicate more months than is possible), the number of degrees explain the same thing in terms of days.

---

[53] Cf. §5.24 below.
[54] Cf. al-Rijāl I.47 (first part).
[55] Translating somewhat freely from Hugo's very cramped style, along with al-Rijāl.

§5.24: When she would give birth—Aristotle[56]

If however you want to know when she should give birth, one will have to deviate in no way from the method written below. For, the lord of the seventh and of the fifth from the seventh, when they reach the same degree, and were together in it, she about whom it is asked, will then finally give birth. Moreover, if you would state an hour close to the birth, or [if] there would be much delay, attend thusly: therefore, the lord of the seventh traversing in the fifth from the seventh, or the lord of the fifth from the seventh [traversing] in the seventh itself, it suggests the impeding birth will come to be.

Likewise, you will note the eleventh if the question would be about a friend; but if about a female slave, the sixth; if about the mother, the tenth; and about the rest through the rest of the domiciles. If the woman asked about herself,[57] the east will be given to her.

§5.25: Whether she would give birth by night or day—'Umar[58]

The recognition of this question must be taken up from the Ascendant and its lord, and also from the star which possesses the east, likewise from the fifth and its lord. For if all of these signs happened to be masculine, or at least a majority [were] in male signs, the birth really claims a diurnal time. But they being female signs for the most part, they leave it for the night.

Furthermore, in discerning the affairs of pregnant women, there come to be the supports of the Lot written below. This Lot is taken up from the degree of the house of children to the degree and point of its lord, [and] you will take the beginning from the east.[59] Which if this Lot and its lord would possess a diurnal sign, a diurnal birth would be judged; but if nocturnal, it comes to be by night.

Lastly, the discernment of the sex undergoes the same judgment. Let the intention of the one judging be led back to the lord of the filial lodging-place and the Moon, even the lord of the hour and the Lot and its lord (as was already stated above). Of which, if the testimonies would favor a masculine

---

[56] Cf. §5.21 above.
[57] Reading more naturally and with §5.31 for *de ipsa muliere quaesierit*.
[58] Cf. al-Rijāl I.48 (first part).
[59] In other words, count from the degree of the fifth to the lord of the fifth, and project that distance from the degree of the Ascendant.

[and][60] womanly sign equally, they promise that the one who is born will have no [sex] or a shared one (such as an androgyne and hermaphrodite).[61] In fact, they ascribe the hour of birth to be the border of night and day (namely, twilight).

§5.26: On the status of a pregnant woman—al-Kindī[62]

§544. Moreover, you will diagnose how she would be doing while she was pregnant, from the second and its status.[63] Likewise, the twelfth place makes clear how she is going to be after the birth. For the presence of the fortunes in it portends good, [but] the infortunes the contrary, just as their nature demands.

§545. Which if Mars does not corrupt the significators of birth[64] but [would be receiving them][65] and would be supported by a friendly aspect[66] (particularly from a hot sign), it beings about a birth without labor. But Saturn (Mars's role being taken [by him]) indicates an anxious and difficult one.

But the most recent application of the Moon upon exiting [her] sign,[67] and the manner and nature of her application, and the place which it is allotted (in the arrangement of the square of signs), will declare the mother's status after the birth.

§5.27: Whether she would give birth to twins—Sahl[68]

With a question presented about twins, we will observe the east and the fifth. For if [either] were of the two-parted signs, or if two safe and cleansed stars possessed either of them, it is manifest that she is pregnant with twins—especially with the Moon and Sun being found in a sign of two bodies. But if neither the fifth nor the east happened to be two-parted, [and] with

---

[60] Reading *et* for *aut* ("or").
[61] But see §5.37, where Aristotle says to defer the question.
[62] Cf. al-Rijāl I.43 (middle), where al-Rijāl attributes this view to "other sages."
[63] The idea is that she is represented by the Ascendant, her time so far in the pregnancy by the second, and the events after pregnancy by the twelfth.
[64] Reading *partus* with Robert for *aut eorum partem*.
[65] Adding with al-Rijāl.
[66] Al-Rijāl says, "and that a fortune would aspect Mars."
[67] That is, the last aspect she will make before leaving (al-Rijāl).
[68] Cf. *On Quest.* §5.5 and al-Rijāl I.44 (first part).

the rest of the things we stated being wholly removed, it portends she has only one in her uterus.

§5.28: Whether they are one or more—'Umar[69]

But if it is asked about one [child] or twins, you will note what kind of signs the house of children [is] and its lord is traversing in; no less must the lord of the hour and the Moon be consulted. Which if their testimonies particularly favored common signs (namely Gemini, Virgo, Sagittarius and Pisces), they bring forth twins. But in the rest, though, they generate one.

§5.29: Whether they are one or more—al-Kindī

§543. Likewise, the plurality of the significators [occupying] signs of much offspring and number, reveals that she bears many in her womb.

§5.30: Whether they are one or many—al-Khayyāt

In addition, if one [child] or twins should come into question, the east and the fifth will have to be looked at (as it is with the opinion of the ancients). For if this one or that were two-parted, or two safe stars were in either one, she is pregnant with twins—especially if the lights happened to be found in two-parted [signs] and those of two bodies. But if neither the east nor fifth [were] two-parted, nor could two stars happen to be found in them, nor the two lights in two-parted [signs], we will judge that there will only be one [child].

§5.31: Whether there would be twins—Aristotle

Knowledge of twins can be discovered in such a way: and so, the east being a double-bodied [sign], testifies that she has twins in the womb. Benevolents traversing in an east of this kind, and with the unlucky ones being removed, affirm that both are viable. Moreover, Saturn and Mars in that place, warn of death for each. One of the malevolents, kills one. An equality

---

[69] Cf. al-Rijāl I.44 (first part).

of benevolents and unlucky ones preserves one, with the other being killed. But if more were propitious ones, both are saved. But if more were malevolent, it will destroy each. Moreover, two wicked ones, if none of the lucky ones stood [there], kills both. But only one of the malevolents alone, will kill one.

Mars in the east (because the east in this affair agrees with mothers) suffocates the woman giving birth. Saturn in the same place, is fatal not to the mother, but to the boy in the belly or at least the one already born. But the Tail [there], even though it often leaves the mother unharmed, still in no way permits the child to escape.

But we have said this, if the woman had made the inquiry about herself.

But if another asked about her, such as a brother about a sister, you will attribute the east to the brother inquiring, the third to the sister, so that once the third has been observed (which belongs to the woman), you will note the fifth and its lord.[70] And you will pursue the judgment stated above, and in this way through the rest of the domiciles of the signs.

§5.32: Whether it is male or female—Sahl[71]

But if someone brought a question about [the child's] sex, the summary judgment of this matter flows from the east and the fifth and their lords. For if the eastern lord and that of the fifth were equally and both found to be in male signs, they will judge the sex to be masculine; in feminine ones, we will judge it is female. Which if one would walk through a feminine sign but the other one a male one, it is right to investigate the Moon. For she, being in a male sign or applying to a male star, fulfills a judgment of the masculine sex; likewise, if she would appear in a feminine one or apply to a female one, it attests that it is female. Nor should this be erased by the inconvenience of forgetfulness: while Mercury appeared eastern, he is masculine; while western, feminine.

---

[70] The fifth still indicates children, even if it is not the fifth derived from the third (or from whatever other house indicates the woman).

[71] Cf. *On Quest.* §5.6 and al-Rijāl I.46.

§5.33: Whether it is male or female—'Umar[72]

Whenever an inquiry about the sex would happen, the domicile of children and of the lord of the hour, but even the Moon, should be consulted. Should all of them (or at least the majority) hold onto male or female signs, it undoubtedly resolves the judgment.

§5.34: Whether it is male or female—al-Kindī

§542. Moreover, male significators (or at least being in male signs) will indicate the male sex; but bearing themselves otherwise, they testify to a female.

§5.35: Whether it is male or female—al-Khayyāt[73]

Likewise, with a question being made about the sex, the lord of the east and of the fifth both being equally in masculine signs, bear a masculine [child]; but if in female ones, they generate a female. But if you should find one in a male one, the other in a female one, you will have to have recourse to the Moon's testimonies and the one of them to which she bears testimonies: [this] will lay out the whole indication. For, she being in a male sign, or applying to a male star, gives birth to a male; in a female one, a female. The star receiving the Moon's counsel should even be applied as a partner [in this matter].

Moreover, antiquity says: the east and the fifth and their lords both, and also the lights, and those who are in charge of their houses as lords,[74] [and the lord of the hour],[75] are noted with the greatest diligence. Therefore, those who enjoy greater testimony in male or female signs,[76] one must especially favor these. But this must come to be noted: Mercury, being eastern, [is] male; western, female.

---

[72] Cf. al-Rijāl I.46 (first part).
[73] Cf. al-Rijāl I.46 (first part).
[74] That is, the domicile lords of the signs the luminaries are in.
[75] Adding with al-Rijāl.
[76] This simply means that more of the planets are in signs of one gender, over another.

§5.36: Whether it is male or female—Jirjis

The lord of the east and equally that of the face being female, indicate a female; [if] male, a male. But even the east and the fifth should be noted, so that should [a star] of the males or of the other sex be lingering there, it would be distinguished more certainly. But those which are in charge[77] over the others, suggest their own sex.

§5.37: On the sex—Aristotle

Whenever you wanted to know what a pregnant woman would have in the womb, and about its sex, among all things you will note the east. For it being male, and its lord in a male sign, moreover with respect to the fifth and its lord, but even with respect to the Moon and the lord of the hour, and in what signs they traverse—a method had in this way, they testify to a male. They being female, and their lords being female and in female signs, indicate a female.

Then, one must discover if more happened to travel through male signs: they prefigure the male sex; if more are female, a female.

Finally, if just as many masculine ones are lingering in male ones, as there are female ones in feminine ones, [then] should there happen to be more signs of one[78] kind, they will reveal a certain judgment of the proper sex. Which if there would occur an equality of sex in both signs and planets, the question should be deferred to another time.

§5.38: On the number of siblings and [their] sex—Aristotle

If however someone asks about the number of siblings and [their] sex, the intention of the mind should be drawn back to the third sign. For however many stars of each kind there are (lucky ones, I say, or wicked ones), by whatever figure they regarded the third ([but] not its lord), they promise that many in the number of brothers and sisters.

---

[77] This suggests the lord of the fifth, but perhaps even a victor over several places.
[78] Reading *utrius* ("one of two") for *utriusque* ("each"), otherwise the logic of the sentence and paragraph would not make sense.

And finally, we suggest this method for their sex. Of those which regard the third, how many traverse in male signs, portend that many males; how many do so in female signs, so many of that sex.

NEWS, RUMORS, & LEGATES

§5.39: On someone, whether he has the father whom public belief is reporting—Aristotle

With anyone asking about a son, as to whether he is his father, you should consult the east and the fifth. For, the lord of the east traversing in the fifth, or at least being with the lord of the fifth, or contrariwise (namely the lord of the fifth being in the east or with the eastern lord), suggests he is his son. With none even being found in the east or fifth, the same judgment should be held. Moreover any benevolent, while it would linger in the fifth or in the east or at least with their lords, you should not change the consideration of the already-stated opinion.

On the other hand, whenever Mars or Saturn or even the Tail of the Dragon will possess the east or fifth, or should linger with the lord of each, they certainly stand in the way of the already-stated approach, and they testify he was the offspring of another.

§5.40: On the truth of rumors—'Umar[1]

The east and the Moon and their lords principally respond to a question as to whether or not what a messenger announces is true or false, good or bad. If therefore what the querent demands from you were pleasing and well-known,[2] [and] the lord of the east and the Moon and their lords happened to be in the pivots or in those which follow the pivots, being invested by the fortunate ones and cleansed of the infortunes and those which could be such (as are the lord of the sixth and the twelfth), they portend that what is announced is true and respectable. Which if they were less than that, you will judge it to be more loose,[3] and you will avoid part of it as being to the contrary.[4]

---

[1] Cf. al-Rijāl I.30.1 (middle), and also §5.43 below.
[2] That is, a popular rumor that may be too good to be true.
[3] *Remissius.* That is, unserious.
[4] In other words, not all of it is true.

§5.41: On legates—'Umar[5]

Moreover, you will have it thusly with respect to legates and legations. And so, the lord of the fifth from the east, [and] the Moon as a partner, will possess the signification. However, the signification of the legation will have to be derived especially from the star to which the lord of the fifth applies, [and] even from the one to which the Moon [applies]. Now, the application of each or either one with the fortunate ones from a tetragon or assembly or opposition, not without reception, or should there be a transfer between them, or should there be one who collects their lights, while the [star getting or transferring or collecting the light][6] would rule over the Midheaven, the legation will pertain to the duties of laws or princes or persons of note. Likewise, from a trigon or hexagon it designates no other thing. Next, too, it will be permitted to extend [this indication] in the eleventh and in the rest of the houses, according to their signification. However, an application with the infortunes, nor being received, tends to declare evil. Which if reception is present, it is somewhat more modest.

§5.42: On rumors and their end—al-Kindī

§600. The firmness of the pivots, and the Moon being received in a firm sign, likewise the luckiness of the Ascendant and of the Moon, attest to the truth of the rumors. If [the rumors] announce good things but the pivots are turning [signs], [and] if even the Moon and the lord of the Ascendant would hold onto turning [signs], and they are made wicked,[7] they falsify rumors of the aforesaid kind. Moreover, if [the news were bad but] the pivots were firm, and should the Moon be dwelling in a firm [sign] and likewise the lord of the Ascendant, received, and if a significator or some assistant would be unfortunate, they do not recede from what is true. But if the pivots bore themselves thusly, and if infortunes would be regarding the Moon and the lord of the Ascendant, the truth of the rumors is [also] affirmed.

---

[5] Cf. al-Rijāl I.50.1.
[6] Reading with al-Rijāl for "lord of that same star."
[7] That is, "unfortunate" (Robert).

[The cause of the rumors]

§601. Furthermore, in discerning the cause of rumors, you will note what sign the lord of the Ascendant and the Moon would be holding onto: for the judgment proceeds from these same places. Also, the lords of their signs, and their nature, make the causes clear.

[The outcome of the rumors]

§602. If therefore certainty is had over the truth of the rumors, the Lunar lord and the lord of the Ascendant suggest the end. For the indication of the end depends on their nature and their places which they claim in the circle, likewise from [the places of] their lords and the dignity[8] they hold onto in the circle. For fortunate ones portend good according to the nature of the one making [them] fortunate, [but] unfortunate ones the contrary, according to the manner of the one corrupting.

[How public the rumors are]

§603. Moreover, the lord of the Ascendant being scorched or under the rays, hides it from the majority of the whole public. Being eastern or in the aspect of the Sun (especially while [the Sun is][9] regarded by the Moon, or should each consider[10] the Ascendant), they announce it in public (whether it is true or false).

§5.43: On the truth of rumors—al-Khayyāt[11]

Moreover, for rumors—are they true or false, with respect to hope or fear—one will have to observe the lord of the east and the Moon. And the beginning will come to be from the one which is staying in a pivot, or which manages more in the east.

---

[8] Al-Rijāl reads, "power" (*potentia*).
[9] Adding with al-Rijāl.
[10] That is, "aspect."
[11] Cf. *On Quest.* §13.9, and §5.68 below. If we compare Bonatti, al-Khayyāt, and Sahl, the general rules for the truth of rumors (and the manifestation of their content) are these: if the planet which gets the light is angular, or a benefic, or a malefic with reception (or in a good condition), it suggests truth and their manifestation; but if it is a malefic without reception, or a cadent benefic without reception, it suggests falsity and non-manifestation.

Therefore, the one which is holding onto a pivot being free of the infortunes, nor applying to a remote star, [but] so that it is already being received, [indicates] that the rumors are well known, but it denies that [what they say] would come into being.[12]

With the lord of the east lingering outside a pivot, while however it would apply to one holding onto a pivot, if [that other planet] were a lucky one or receives it, it denotes [the rumor] is true and is made public. But if it would apply to a malevolent, nor being received, it will be an indication of falsity.

Moreover, the lord of the east being in a pivot, applying to a remote star, reports a lie, unless it[13] is received. The same [lord of the east] applying to an infortune not receiving it, corrupts what the report was suggesting, through the fault of the querent. Moreover, with a malevolent applying to the lord of the east, the corruption will be from elsewhere.

An application of the lights with the lord of the east (it being in a pivot, cleansed of the infortunes), confirms the whole affair. [The lord of the east] being corrupted finally corrupts the matter when it is [already] thought to be certain. With the lord of the east being cadent, and the lights in the pivots, they establish the affair. The lord of the east applying to a star in its fall, heaps on corruption; but from its own fall (so that there is neither reception from here or there),[14] it is the same.

§5.44: On the truth of rumors—Dorotheus

The east being a firm [sign], nor a slanting one,[15] and the Moon in a firm sign, declares it is true and certain. But if in a turning [sign], it is false, just as if the east is a turning or slanting [sign] and the Moon were in like [signs].

Moreover,[16] taking up the degrees interposed from the lord of the hour to the lord of the east, you will begin [projecting them] from the Sun: where the number will be ended, the one who is in charge of that bound will assume

---

[12] Sahl reads that an application to a cadent star (evidently with reception) makes the rumors true, but that without reception they will not manifest.
[13] This probably means the lord of the east.
[14] This might be some variation of not-reception.
[15] *Obliquum.* That is, a "crooked" sign (from the beginning of Capricorn to the end of Gemini).
[16] This is a Lot calculation. In *Search* I.3.2 it is attributed to Dorotheus, and indicates the thought of the querent. But in I.11.2 (and calculated from the lord of the east to the lord of the hour, projected from the Sun) it shows whether a matter would be useful or effective.

the signification. Therefore, that significator[17] traversing in the house and bound of a benevolent, declares it is true and has an effect; in the house and bounds of malevolents, it denies the effect and means it is false.

§5.45: When something that news announces, will come to be—Jirjis

The lord of the east in the east signifies three days, or this signification will be according to the hours of the day [already] passed, and their number. Moreover, in the Midheaven it portends hours; in the west, months; in the pivot of the earth, years.

§5.46: For rumors—Jirjis

For rumors, the separation of the Moon must be noted. For the nature of the star from which the Moon is separated, lays bare the proper quality of the rumors.

But even whether they would come in writing or a messenger himself would report [them] with his tongue, is discovered from Mercury and the Moon. For the Moon, regarding Mercury and applying to him, while however she withdraws from the lord of the seventh, the rumors are announced in writing. Likewise, withdrawing from Mercury or his lord, if she would apply to the degree of the east, the messenger reports them with his own mouth (not in writing).

The separation of Mercury (not his place nor application) discovers whether what is announced (in [writing] or [orally]) is good or bad. For it is necessary that it be reported according to the nature and proper quality of his place, be it the sign or the star from which he is being separated. Therefore, he withdrawing from a benevolent or a fortunate sign, whatever the writing or messenger would report is popular and praiseworthy. But if he would be separating from a malevolent, there is evil and sudden confusion.

However, in order that you may recognize in how many lines a letter is written, it could be discovered thusly. For, how many arisings[18] belong to the sign which Mercury holds onto, it is necessary that the lines be that many.

---

[17] I would have expected that the house and bound of the *Lot* would declare the nature of the rumors, but Dorotheus seems to want to look at where the bound lord is, instead.
[18] That is, the ascensions (*orientia*). A table of ascensions for each sign at different degrees of latitude may be found at www.bendykes.com.

Or, in another way: with the rays of Mercury being discovered at the beginning of a sign[19] (or wherever they were), you will take the horizon of the arisings where the Mercurial rays fall.[20] In addition to the number of the arisings of the sign, reckon the number of lines to be how many are interposed, or the quantity of the arisings of the sign where the star (with whom the application of Mercury is happening) is.[21]

§5.47: On rumors—Aristotle

For learning the truth of rumors, one must look at the east. Saturn, and even Mars or the Tail being in that same place, stain all that is reported with lies. But the traversal of Venus or Jupiter, even the Sun or the [Head] of the Dragon in it, show a judgment of truth. But Venus demands a feminine place, Jupiter and the Sun a masculine one; the [Head of the] Dragon, however, [can be in either] this or that. But if stars of each kind would be lingering there, one will have to reckon it partly true, partly false.

Moreover, if Mercury or the Moon would walk through the aforesaid place with the malevolents, it is a sign of falsity;[22] if with the lucky ones, it will be permitted to affirm the contrary. The Moon being alone in that place and in a female sign, portends the rumors are true. Which if Mercury alone [were there], you should not presume to affirm either this or that, because of his unsteadiness.

With none appearing there, you will revert to the fifth, [and] profess no other judgment about that. Moreover, with it being deprived of all of these and being empty, if the rumors come from remote parts, an observation that is had of the ninth ([but] if from nearby ones, the third) demands that a judgment come to be just like (and not other than) what was stated about the first above.

Finally, if none would possess the first, ninth, third or fifth, it wholly prohibits you from responding with anything.

---

[19] I am not sure exactly which sign Jirjis is recommending here; probably the rising sign.
[20] For example, if the ray of Mercury fell onto 10° of a sign, see how many ascensions are contained up through those 10°.
[21] In other words, we can look at the degrees between Mercury and the star he applies to (perhaps in terms of ascensions), or the ascensions of the sign in which that other star is.
[22] Reading *falsitatis* for *veritatis* ("truth").

§5.48: On messengers—al-Kindī[23]

§604. The lord of the Ascendant and the Moon give counsel as to whether a messenger would reach the desired place.[24] For, each (or either) of them in the seventh, or an application of them with the lord of the seventh already being made, suggests he is already persisting in the desired region. But a withdrawal from fortunate ones conveys health and opportunity on the journey; withdrawing from infortunes, the contrary. Therefore, it seems one must report [this matter] according to the nature of the fortunate or unfortunate ones, and their dignity in the circle, [and] strength and weakness. Moreover, an application of [a significator] made with fortunate ones, renders everything prosperous in that place; with the infortunes, the contrary. The nature and place and dignity of the fortunate and unlucky ones in the circle ([and] even their weakness and virtue) will show what must be said about the matter.

§5.49: On someone, whether he is absent from his own home—Jirjis

Therefore, with the east being established, if the lord of the east would be lingering in the east, it detains him about whom it was asked, at home. Outside the pivots, it means he is absent. Being in the Midheaven but scorched, it preserves him in his own home. But if not, not. Moreover, the east being less than the middle [of the sign], he is held in his own home; but being beyond the middle, he is spending time outside it.

§5.50: On the messenger's adversity—'Umar

Moreover, the significator of the one who is in charge of the legation applying to the infortunes from a tetragon or opposition or assembly, before it is separated from the lord of the seventh, is harmful to his return and introduces danger on the road. Which if this application with the infortunes preceded its application with the lord of the seventh, it threatens [danger] on the journey in the same way—namely before he reaches where he is headed

---

[23] Cf. al-Rijāl I.50.2.
[24] As al-Rijāl explains in his version, the Ascendant and the Moon represent the one who has sent the messenger, while the seventh and its lord signify the person to whom he is sent.

to. However, if the infortunes would occupy the ninth, he incurs the threat of ambushes.

§5.51: On the return of the messenger—al-Kindī[25]

§606. A question coming out into the open about the return of the messenger: each significator (or either one) being drawn back from[26] the seventh or from the pivots, and withdrawing from the lord of the seventh, means his return. Which if it would apply with its own lord while it is being drawn back from the pivots, the same.[27] Also, an admixture of the infortunes seems to speak against [his return]: which will seem to consist of the nature and status and place of the infortune, and what dignity it would claim in the circle. But the fortunate ones also [speak in favor of his return] in this manner.

§5.52: On the hour of turning back—al-Kindī[28]

§607. For if it would be asked about the hour of his return, an application of them with the lord of the Ascendant or with its own [lord], the degrees, I say, of the application sometimes put hours or days or months or years in between,[29] according to the nature of the convertible or fixed or double-bodied [signs], or even according to the quickness or slowness of the significator, also especially if[30] the [number of the] degrees of the aforesaid application would be equal to that of the Moon [in her application] with the degree of the Ascendant [by body] or with her own [lord], or [her application with] that of the lord of the Ascendant. Also, the exit of a star from scorching, or the application[31] [of a star into][32] the degree of a dignity which it possesses in the heavens, explains the same thing. No less, moreover, does the retrogradation of the significator indicate [his return], at the point where it goes direct: for, how many degrees are left until going direct, we bid you to compute that many hours or days or months or years.

---

[25] Cf. al-Rijāl I.50.2.
[26] That is, being cadent.
[27] Robert (but not al-Rijāl) adds: "and likewise [if] retrograde."
[28] Cf. al-Rijāl I.50.2.
[29] That is, between the time of the question and the messenger's return.
[30] For the rest of this sentence, adding material in brackets from al-Rijāl.
[31] Reading with Robert (*inire*) and al-Rijāl (*applicatio*), for Hugo's *status*.
[32] Adding with al-Rijāl.

§5.53: On the hour of turning back—[Unknown][33]

And so, the Moon in the east or the Midheaven, consoles with respect to a return. Likewise in the fourth and seventh. Moreover, the lord of the fifth in the ninth, being prepared to enter the Midheaven, indicates nothing different than what the status of the Moon does.

§5.54: On the return of a messenger—Aristotle

Whenever a question of this kind is brought into the open, if the lord of the fifth would be traversing in the east or at least with the lord of the east, it announces he is returning. However, while it bears itself this way, being scorched or retrograde or in its own fall portends his return, afflicted by some illness. But retrogradation will not be fatal, though fall or scorching should be feared more—not always with respect to death, but one must judge according to the greatness of the misfortune.

Moreover, its application to the lord of the east is a sign of present preparation and a close return. In addition, with it bearing itself thusly, if retrogradation is present, he is arranging to make a present return, [but] some disease will hinder him, and he will return when [the planet] goes direct.

Which if it bore itself otherwise, you will not affirm that he is going to return. Moreover, with it[34] lingering in the fall of the lord of the fifth, it must be feared lest he has already incurred death. Retrogradation afflicts him with a disease, nor does he care to return.

§5.55: On a legate, whether he would bring the money sought—'Umar[35]

The east and its lord are in charge of the one sending[36] the legation, the seventh and its lord [over the one] to whom he is going. But likewise even the Moon [for the legation itself] and the lord of the fifth [for the messenger].[37] Now should the Moon or the lord of the fifth (one of them) occupy a pivot, it will have control of the role of the signification. If therefore it would

---

[33] This is an abbreviated version of a passage in al-Rijāl I.56.
[34] I believes this means the lord of the east.
[35] Cf. al-Rijāl I.50.2 (first part).
[36] Reading *mittenti* for *mittendi*.
[37] Adding material in brackets based on al-Rijāl.

withdraw from the lord of the seventh and apply to the lord of the east, the legate has accomplished what had been enjoined, while he would return to the lord of the east (who had sent him). Which if, in addition to this withdrawal, it withdrew from the lord of the house of money (whether the lord of the east is lucky or rather corrupted), he brings the money with him. For the rest of the signs, another judgment should not be given.[38]

§5.56: Whether someone would reach the destined place—Dorotheus

With someone uncertain as to whether someone would be able to reach the destined place, the significator itself[39] is consulted. Its retrogradation promises a return.[40] Being direct, it bars a return and he finishes the business.

§5.57: Whether he would find the one whom he sought—al-Kindī[41]

§605. If therefore certainty would be had about reaching the place, for a question as to whether he has come to the person he was heading for, an application of either (or each) of the aforesaid significators with the lord of the seventh, or at least one [of them] applying with the lord of its own place, testifies he has found him. Otherwise they mean a contrary judgment. But [if the applying one were] received by the one with which it applies itself, it makes him be taken in diligently and in a friendly way. But with it made from the opposition, [it means] the opposite; from the tetragon [it means] the same, but makes it less slyly.

§5.58: Whether he bears much money—Aristotle

In addition, whether the messenger is bearing much money could be discovered in such a way: with the lord of the sixth[42] bearing itself well, he will bring back manifold resources. Likewise, the lord of the sixth being cadent or scorched testifies that he bears absolutely nothing. It being retrograde, or at

---

[38] That is, the planet from which the lord of the fifth separates, indicates something of what has just happened.
[39] Probably the lord of the fifth.
[40] That is, before he reaches his destination.
[41] Cf. al-Rijāl I.50.2.
[42] The sixth is the second (money) from the fifth (legates).

least the presence of the malevolents in the sixth, he brings nothing or very little.

§5.59: Whether he bears much money—[Unknown][43]

Moreover, the Moon and the lord of the fifth,[44] and their withdrawal[45] (after reception) from a star having the likeness of the affair, while there is an application to the degree of the east or to its lord, brings the quaesited matter with him; but without that, not at all.

---

[43] This also seems to be a version of the unattributed text in al-Rijāl I.56.
[44] Reading with al-Rijāl (if I have identified the correct parallel text) for Hugo's "sixth."
[45] Reading *recessus* for *recedens*.

LETTERS

§5.60: On a paper or letter—'Umar

Moreover, for a letter, we choose to imitate the counsel of the Moon and Mercury. For Mercury indicates the paper itself, and its letters, and whatever is depicted in it. However, the Moon [indicates] whatever good and bad is contained in it. Therefore, she applying to unfortunate ones, portends that evil is announced. Which if she would apply to none, while however she is being separated from some [star], attribute the role of the signification to the star from which she withdraws. Now, if she is deprived of each (namely, of an application and a withdrawal), the letter itself does not contain anything good or evil. Furthermore, the Moon herself being cadent and applying to an infortune, judges evil; but her fall and application with the fortunate ones, [judges] to the contrary.

I even think one must pay attention to the one to which the Moon or the lord of the east applies. Which if there would be a transfer to the lord of the Midheaven, or [there would be] one which collects the lights (between [the lord of the east] and the lord of the tenth), while this application is fortunate, it declares that some dignity or gift of authority and a kind of profit is lawfully conveyed from the king or princes or because of their trade or profession. But if the application from the lord of the east were perverse, and[1] the Moon is received, it signifies that what was stated (and how) is conferred by the king unjustly, or rather is earned unlawfully.

Again,[2] if the lord of the east or the Moon would apply to the lord of the eleventh,[3] what is conferred is directed to the proper quality of the brothers or sisters. In no other way, too, will the rest of the houses everywhere propose what is appropriate to their nature.

And if the aforesaid application were from the tetragon or opposition or assembly, a steady and true mandate is contained in what is written; but with reception, much more expressly so. Which if reception is absent, they will be less than this, but the paper itself describes something troublesome. Now,

---

[1] Reading *aut* for *vel* ("or"). This sentence might also read, "But if the application were perverse, but received by the lord of the east or the Moon...", but I am not sure what that would mean.
[2] Reading as *iterum*.
[3] Unless this is a mistake, it could mean that the eleventh is the third (siblings) from the ninth (news, travel, rumors).

with an application from a trigon or hexagon being discovered, really what is announced is something humorous, pleasing, and respectable, and what is of this kind (with reception, I say, and without it).

§5.61: On messengers and a legation of letters—al-Khayyāt[4]

Concerning messengers and a legation of letters, one must pursue it [in this manner]:[5] we hand him who is writing or commissioning [the messenger] over to the lord of the east and to the star from which the Moon is being separated; but the lord of the seventh and the one to whom the Moon is applying, suggests the one to whom it is written. However, the place of the Moon and Mercury really determines the hope or fear of each, and what is contained in the paper (even hatred or concord).

Moreover, the seventh and its lord, [and the east and its lord],[6] and the status and disposition of both (namely, insofar as they are regarded by the benevolents or the infortunes), really decide what each one is thinking about.[7] Therefore, should one of the significators occur in a pivot or in a place where it is received, or [in a place] whence it regards its own place,[8] it suggests that the [person] it is handed over to, is of greater dignity.

Moreover, the star from which the Moon is being separated being a lucky[9] one, or traversing in its own sovereignty, conveys something written or sends the messenger from a magnate or prince or one of royal dignity. It appearing in the sovereignty but remote from a pivot, shows him to be stripped of the dignity of rule.[10] In [its own] house but traversing in a pivot, claims he is of the stock of nobles. Concerning the triplicity,[11] he is designated as [being someone] lesser. After that is the bound, [and] the face follows the bound.[12]

---

[4] Cf. al-Rijāl I.52.
[5] Vienna has *hic* + written above the line, and the abbreviation *qm*.
[6] Added by Dykes, otherwise the sentence would not make sense.
[7] Al-Rijāl adds, "and those things which will happen because of the paper."
[8] That is, it regards its own sign. Al-Rijāl omits this.
[9] Reading *felix* for *infelix*, with Dorotheus below.
[10] That is, the exaltation shows dignity, but being cadent shows him falling from that dignity.
[11] Reading *ternario* for *termino*.
[12] That is, they indicate someone even lesser in rank. For other analogies of the dignities, see *ITA* I.8.

§5.62: On a paper or letter—Dorotheus[13]

With a question presented about a paper or letter, and the status of a messenger, Māshā'allāh put the eastern lord, even the star from which the Moon is being separated, in charge of the one sending it. But the seventh and the one to which the Moon applies, determines him to whom it is sent. Even the Lunar place, and that of Mercury, contains the secret things which are written. Moreover, the entire recognition of the status of each (namely, of the one writing and the one to whom it is written) depends equally on the lord of the east and of the seventh, and their places.

And so, the regard of the fortunate ones and the infortunes into their own proper places, with reception, signifies a not-humble home. Then, the star from whom the Moon is being separated being lucky and holding onto its own sovereignty, testifies that he who is writing is of the rank of kings or princes. However, being in the sovereignty but being drawn back from a pivot, portends he is already stripped of that dignity. Likewise, traversing in [its own] house but in a pivot, it specifies some magnate, and with a good name, from a royal family.

§5.63: Whether a letter was sent out from the king—Sahl[14]

But with an inquiry of this kind, Mercury determines it: for, withdrawing from the Sun or from the lord of the tenth, with the withdrawal being strong and nearby,[15] it does not deny it was sent out [from the king]; if not, not.

§5.64: Concerning a letter, whether it would reach the king—'Umar

The eastern lord and the Moon must be consulted as to whether a letter would reach the royal majesty. For, should the regard of either one[16] proceed to the east, it acquires the signification of this business. Which if would happen to each, one must note which one regarded the other, and that one

---

[13] Cf. al-Rijāl I.52, and Sahl's *On Quest.* §13.1. Sahl's version is longer and contains more detailed instructions on different dignity combinations.
[14] Cf. *On Quest.* §13.7.
[15] Omitting a redundant *determinat*.
[16] Reading *utrius* with Madrid and Vienna for *utriusque*.

merits the signification.[17] No less successful, too, is an observed Mercurial application with the significator or the lord of the Midheaven, or to the star of any signification about which you (being worried) are inquiring. For thus, whatever pertains to the paper and at what hour it would be given, could be discovered. And moreover, the star which transfers or collects the light between the significators and the lord of the Midheaven, should not slip from memory: for if they bear themselves thusly, they teach that the letter will reach where it was sent to.

In this place,[18] it seems that Māshā'allāh's opinion must be appended. For the east is responsible for the one sending [it], the Midheaven for the king, but Mercury as the significator of the letter, as the astrologer claims. Mercury withdrawing from the lord of the east, applying to the lord of the Midheaven, commends the effect of the legation. The withdrawal of any star from the eastern lord or the degree of the east itself, while it would apply to Mercury and the lord of the Midheaven, testifies that it will reach the entrance [of the king].

§5.65: Whether a letter would reach the king—Dorotheus

Now, while it is asked whether a note or letter would reach the king's presence, we entrust the querent to the east, the paper to Mercury, the king to the Midheaven. Therefore, the Moon withdrawing from the eastern lord, applying to Mercury or the lord of the Midheaven, testifies that it can arrive [there]; but without that, not at all.

§5.66: On a paper, what it contains of the true and the false—'Umar

However, for a question as to what truth or lies a paper would contain, one must apply the counsel of the Moon. In fact, a Lunar application with the fortunate ones declares it is true; with the same being had with the infortunes, it portends the contrary.

---

[17] But between the lord of the east and the Moon, the Moon will always be the applying one, so what does 'Umar mean here?

[18] Cf. §5.65 below, attributed to Dorotheus.

§5.67: What good or evil the paper contains—al-Khayyāt[19]

But the star from which Mercury or the Moon is being separated, answers what good or evil the writing contains. The command itself is sought from Mercury,[20] but the lord of the third and [the lord] of the eleventh[21] should be taken as partners in a moderate way.[22] If therefore they would withdraw from fortunate ones, they note that good is contained in it; separated from malevolents, the contrary.

§5.68: [Whether rumors are true or false]—Sahl[23]

The eastern lord and the Moon[24] being in a pivot [and] cleansed of the malevolents, provided that there is an application of none of them with a cadent star, [indicates the rumors are true]. [But if they were in a pivot and applying with a cadent star without reception], it partly corrupts the message,[25] partly indicates it is true.

Moreover, the eastern lord being outside a pivot but [applying to a] lucky [star in a pivot], introduces a friendly message [that will manifest; but if to an infortune that does not receive it, the rumors are false]. But it being outside a pivot [and] applying to a cadent star, [the message] is misleading unless reception is present.

[But] if [the lord of the east] would apply to [an infortune] without reception, it corrupts with falseness [and the querent will prove it false]. But [an unfortunate] star regarding the eastern lord, [indicates the message is false and it is proven false by someone else].

---

[19] Cf. al-Rijāl I.58.
[20] Al-Rijāl reads, "because the papers and commands belong to Mercury and the Moon."
[21] Al-Rijāl reads, "ninth," and is probably right.
[22] *In modico*.
[23] Cf. *On Quest.* §13.9 and al-Khayyāt's version in §5.43 above. John's Sahl is a much longer chapter and explains the subject better. I have liberally supplied missing information in brackets.
[24] John's Sahl says to take whichever one is in a pivot. Both of them being placed thusly would be helpful, though.
[25] *Mandata*, lit. "commands, instructions," but John's Sahl refers to rumors, so I have compromised by using "message." What Sahl means is that although the rumor has some basis in fact, it will not manifest (or at least, not fully).

§5.69: On a letter, whether it is marked with a seal—'Umar[26]

Moreover, it seems that an observation of the significator[27] seems necessary as to whether a letter or paper would be marked with a seal. For, it applying to Mercury imposes a seal.[28] [Judge] in this manner as well, if the Moon would be joined to him. Now, if she would go before him, being joined to him by at least one degree or two or three, or wholly until (I say) she enters the next bound, it sends a letter stamped[29] with a seal.

It is not otherwise, too, [if there is] an application of the significator with the lord of the Midheaven or with the Sun; but even Mercury applying to the Sun or being placed with him in a pivot is not hostile to the prior judgment, for it indicates it was or will be stamped. Moreover, an application already made, or he being established as having transited within the bound, indicates [a letter] impressed with a mark.

Which if the Moon would not apply to Mercury, nor Mercury to the Sun, it denies the aforesaid.

In an observation of this business, even the testimonies of the east come forth. For, Mercury being conjoined in the assembly of the Sun or applying to him, while they each regard the east, wholly removes the impression of the seal.[30]

§5.70: On a paper's or letter's seal—Jirjis[31]

For an affair of this [kind], Mercury and the Moon should be consulted. For, the Moon applying to Mercury, [means] it is [not yet][32] stamped with a seal. But if she would be separated from Mercury according to the quantity of a star's bound,[33] it favors a seal and impression. For thus Mercury claims the letter, the Moon the seal.

---

[26] Cf. *On Quest.* §§13.6-7.
[27] Sahl's version only has the Moon; if Hugo's translation of 'Umar is accurate, then some kind of victor is meant.
[28] Or perhaps (as with Jirjis/al-Rijāl), it *will* be sealed, but is not yet sealed.
[29] *Firmatam.*
[30] This is contrary to the parallel statement in *On Quest.* §13.6: if they are conjoined and aspecting the east, there should be a seal.
[31] Cf. al-Rijāl I.55, and compare also with 'Umar/Sahl in §5.69 above.
[32] Omitting *inficiatur et negat*, and simply reading *non iam*.
[33] For example, if she were separating bodily from him, and had already moved out of the bound he is in.

§5.71: On the response to the writing or letter—[Unknown]

For one worried[34] about the response to a writing, it will be permitted to consult Mercury as the significator of the letter. For he, as the partner of the east or the significator in anything, indicates[35] the one sending the response. The hour of the matter is determined whenever he reaches the degree of the east or crosses [it], traversing fully in it [by body] or in one just like it [by aspect]. Which if he would possess neither a dignity nor a regard in the east, it conveys no response in that hour. Moreover, he withdrawing from the lord of the seventh, applying to the eastern [lord], testifies that it[36] has already gotten [there].

Moreover, the Mercurial withdrawal from any star decrees what the paper contains: withdrawing from the infortunes [indicates] evil; from the benevolents, the contrary. The star from which the withdrawal of the Moon and Mercury is, and their places from the east, suggest the same thing.

§5.72: Whether some messenger would arrive—Jirjis

At the hour of the question, with the east being established, one must observe the Moon and Mercury to see in what places they are traversing. For the one which traverses with more affinity to the east[37] justly deserves the signification of this matter. It being received [and being anywhere] from the Midheaven to the east, denotes he is coming. Moreover, you will note the distance in degrees which is between the tenth and Mercury or the Moon: it really indicates days or months, years or hours, according to the number of these degrees.

---

[34] Reading *sollicito* for *sollicitum*.
[35] Reading for Hugo's *visitat* ("visits"), which is confusing. This whole question seems to relate to a written invitation, and the sender (the querent) is worried about whether it will be answered or when the invited guest will arrive.
[36] Or perhaps, "he," indicating the invited guest?
[37] *Orienti...affinior.* I think this simply means "closer by degree."

§5.73: On accepting a paper or letter—Jirjis[38]

Mercury being the one to assume the signification of this matter, [if you found him having dignity in the Ascendant or in the significator of the question (which is the victor), say that the letter is sent.

Then consider][39] whenever he will have crossed the east by an equal number of degrees (from the left or the right),[40] then finally it testifies that the paper will come, especially if the application to it would be from a pivot.

Mercury and even the Moon[41] being deprived of a dignity in the east [or in] the significator, and [Mercury] does not regard the east [nor the significator], it speaks against the paper arriving.

But with [Mercury] not regarding [the east, but] having a portion [of dignity], while however he would regard and apply to the significator, it is a sign of the arriving letter, [at the time when Mercury applies to the significator by an exact degree].

Moreover, if Mercury would regard the east, while the Moon would be separated from Mercury, it brings the paper or letter at the hour of the application [of the Moon to the degree of the east].

Likewise, Mercury withdrawing from the lord of the seventh, [and] applying to the eastern lord or the degree of the east, declares the writing is going to come at the hour he will apply either to the lord of the east[42] or to the eastern degree.

But if that same Mercury would be wholly devoid [of a dignity in] the significator and the east, and even [in] the Moon, [nor an aspect with any of them], it blocks the aforesaid things—unless, I say, he would be lingering in the twelfth and would hasten to enter the eastern degree. For once he[43] has attained [that degree], it conveys the paper.

---

[38] Cf. al-Rijāl I.53. I have used al-Rijāl to flesh out and correct Hugo's compressed version.
[39] Adding with al-Rijāl.
[40] That is, once he has transited the degree exactly, no matter from what side or aspect.
[41] Al-Rijāl has Mercury being deprived of any dignity in the place of the Moon, not that the Moon herself does not have any dignity.
[42] Al-Rijāl says, "to the significator which is the victor."
[43] Preferring Hugo here for al-Rijāl's "Moon."

Moreover, Mercury withdrawing from the degree of the second, [and] applying to the degree of the east or its lord, will bring the paper in question, [with assets and usefulness].[44]

Now, if [Mercury] would be separated from the lord of the fifth,[45] it bestows the effect to the aforesaid things, and [with] gifts if the lord of the fifth is fortunate and lucky, and Mercury is received. (The nature and proper quality of the fifth determines the gifts.) However, one will have to pursue it no otherwise with respect to Mercury's withdrawal from the lords of the rest of the houses and his application with the degree of the east or its lord.

---

[44] Reading with al-Rijāl for "if perhaps a benevolent would accompany the lord of the second."
[45] Reading with al-Rijāl for "seventh."

§6: SIXTH HOUSE

6th House	
Illness: outcome	§§6.1-8, 6.15-18
Nature of disease, where affected	§§6.9-14
Critical days	§§6.19-23
Whether he is infirm	§§6.24-26
Specific medical procedures	§§6.27-29
Would a captive be freed	§§6.30-34, 6.37-39, 6.66
How long the captivity is	§6.35
What happens afterwards	§6.36
When he will be freed	§§6.40-41
Die or suffer in captivity?	§§6.42-48, 6.68
Buying & selling captives & slaves	§§6.49-64
Whether he will be captured	§§6.65, 6.67
Prisoners & their freedom	§§9.17-19

Figure 23: Questions of the sixth house

ILLNESS

§6.1: On those things which pertain to the sixth house—Sahl[1]

If perhaps it came into question how it is for an infirm person (whether he would be able to be freed), the ambiguity of the sixth [is solved in this way]: we observe the doctor from the east, the infirm person from the tenth, the disease from the seventh, the medicines and the end from the fourth. Therefore, whenever a malevolent possesses the east, it portends that the doctor labors in vain; a lucky one has the contrary judgment. Moreover, the traversal of a malevolent in the tenth ascribes the occasion for the disease to the infirm person himself.[2] But if it is a fortunate one, a judgment of health emanates from him himself. But while a perverse one would be staying in the seventh, it even varies the infirmity, and leads [him] from disease to disease. A fortunate one in that same place introduces health without any wealth of medicines. With a malevolent possessing the fourth, it greatly increases the pain by means of the medicine; a lucky one in the same place shows the contrary.

---

[1] Cf. *On Quest.* §6.1.
[2] John's Sahl adds that the patient will be unlikely to obey the doctor's instructions.

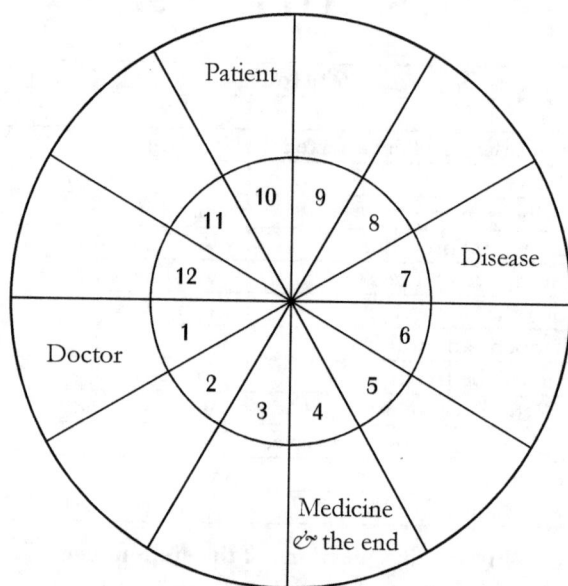

Figure 24: The angles in illness
(Sahl §6.1, al-Khayyāt §6.16, Dorotheus §6.17)

And so, between the lord of the east and the Moon, should either one be in a pivot or regard the Ascendant, I believe one should pay attention to it (that is, the one which is [so placed]). For if it[3] is safe, nor scorched (so that you understand the lord of the eighth to be turned away from the east),[4] it will be a judgment of escape; nor does the application of either of them with the benevolents make another [judgment]. Moreover, the retrogradation of this fortunate one prolongs the disease, but does not destroy the hope of health.

Again, the Moon being under the earth (from the second up to the sixth), applying to some [star] appearing above the earth in the upper hemisphere, announces health (unless perhaps the star which gathers the Lunar counsel happens to be scorched). Moreover in the reverse order, the Lunar application from the upper hemisphere to a perverse [star] appearing below, is fatal.

---

[3] Sahl, al-Khayyāt, and Dorotheus all assume we are speaking of the lord of the Ascendant here, even though the rule which was just stated allows the Moon to be considered, too.
[4] John's Sahl (like al-Khayyāt and Dorotheus) has the lord of the eighth in aversion to the Moon/lord of the Ascendant.

But meanwhile, if the Moon (increasing both in light and computation) should apply to the eastern lord (even though it is staying under the earth), it announces that health is near.

A Lunar application to a star placed in the eighth, is fatal. Moreover, the lord of the east applying to the lord of the eighth (if the Moon is equally corrupted) has a judgment of death. With even the Moon transferring the light from the lord of the east to the lord of the eighth, one must be afraid; but the Moon's reception[5] prolongs the illness. Now, should the lord of the east, being in a pivot, apply to the lord of the eighth, it designates the same according to the space of his life, [up to] where the lord of the eighth reaches the eastern degree.[6]

But if there would be a transfer of light from the lord of the east to the lord of the eighth, while however the eastern lord was cadent [and] the hostile one[7] would occupy an angle, it is fatal. The lord of the eighth in the east even portends the same, provided that the eastern lord and the Moon happened to be corrupted. It is no less while any malevolent (and the Moon being corrupted) would regard the lord of the east [while the lord of the east] is in the eighth, or if the lord of the east would apply to the lord of the eighth without the corruption of the Moon. Moreover, should the star which gathers the counsel of the Moon be a malevolent, it repeats the disease.[8]

With the lord of the eighth going through a pivot, one must have fear. Likewise, whenever the lord of the eighth possessed a pivot, one must have fear.[9]

Now, with the eastern lord appearing below the earth (provided that it applies to a lord of the eighth which is appearing in the fourth or eighth), it brings forth a judgment of death. [And if the lord of the eighth did not aspect the lord of the east, but another planet reflected their light, and the lord

---

[5] I take this to mean that the Moon is received by the lord of the eighth.
[6] Undoubtedly by transit.
[7] That is, the lord of the eighth.
[8] That is, the disease will reappear after it seems to be healed, such as when cancer returns.
[9] John's Sahl does not have this sentence; Hugo may simply be saying that it is dangerous no matter whether it is somewhere inside the angular house, or right on the axial degree. (On the other hand, maybe this sentence is simply redundant and an error.) But Hugo does not use the word *possideo* to mean "rule," so he is not referring to its rulership of any angle.

of the east were cadent and the lord of the eighth in an angle, it signifies death.]¹⁰

But whenever the lord of the east happened to be within 12° of the Sun, going to be scorched, nor however received,¹¹ it is fatal. Moreover, with the eastern lord being of the heavier stars, nor being scorched, namely [so that] it in no way applies to another, while the Moon is equally safe, it is a promise of health.

But the sixth sign being of the convertible [signs],¹² alternates the disease. Two-parted, it carries him over or changes him [from one] disease to another. A firm [sign] preserves him in the same condition. (Through all things, it is necessary to answer in this way according to its proper nature.)¹³

Finally, the Lunar separation from a western star is a sign of a disease that has been had for a long time; if she would be separating from an eastern one, it portends he is made worse by a new disease.

§6.2: On the status of one growing sick, and the doctor—'Umar

Also, the east and its lord determine the status of one growing infirm, while the sixth and the one which is in charge of it [indicate] the disease; the eighth and its lord reveal death, but the fourth and its lord decide the end; the ninth and its lord explain the doctor and the prudence of the medicating. The testimonies of the Lot of Fortune resemble all of these. Now, it will be permitted to observe the status of the medicating from the Midheaven and its lord, but the causes of death from the seventh and its lord.

Therefore, the lord of the sixth (which is the house of infirmity) principally comes to be noticed. But it being placed in the east or the tenth prefigures an evident disease, while in the fourth or seventh, a hidden one.

---

¹⁰ Adding from John's Sahl.
¹¹ This is a nice reminder that reception by the Sun (i.e., while he is in Leo or Aries) can save a planet from scorching.
¹² That is, in the movable signs. John's Sahl says that he will be "relieved at one time and made worse at another time." But at least it means being cured for the present.
¹³ I believe what Hugo means is that this view of the quadruplicities carries over to many different topics, not just illness.

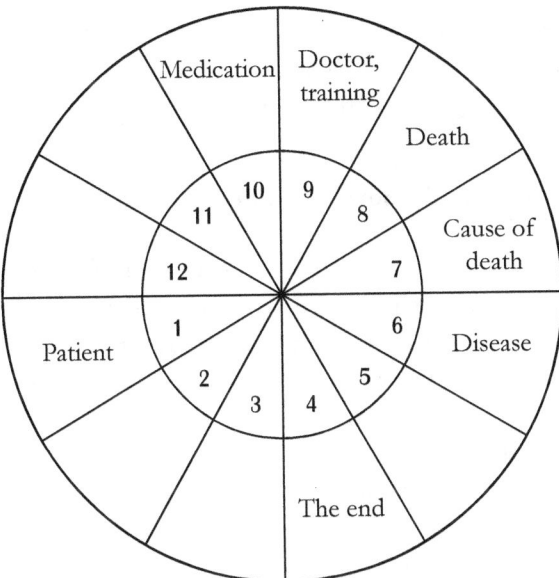

Figure 25: Significations in illness ('Umar §6.2)

Moreover,[14] the Moon being corrupted along with the east, but the lord of the east and [the lord] of the Moon (along with the Sun)[15] being lucky, promises that the body grows ill but not the soul. Contrariwise, too, the Lunar lord and that of the east equally (along with the Sun) being corrupted, while the east and the Moon are saved, suggests a disease of the soul, not the body. Likewise, with the significators of each (of the body, I say, and the soul) being corrupted, namely the east and the Moon equally, and the lord of the Moon (along with the Sun), it is a sign of the infirmity of each.

Which if the ninth would be corrupted, it confirms the ignorance of the doctor, nor does it promise that [the patient] can be healed by him.

I even think one should pay attention to this: because the lord of the house of death being in a pivot (especially in the tenth) really threatens death, if, I say, it would regard the lord of the east, or [the lord of the east] would apply to the lord of the house of death. Which if they would be deprived of a mutual aspect, while the lord of the house of death at least regarded the lord of the Lunar lodging-place or the Sun [himself], it does not take away the

---

[14] For this paragraph, cf. al-Rijāl II.2.3 (first part).
[15] Al-Rijāl omits the Sun, here and in the rest of the paragraph.

hope[16] of death from the one who is made infirm. Moreover, that same lord of the house of death being in the fourth or seventh, if it does not suggest a difficult disease, still [it indicates] a hidden one.

§6.3: On the hour of health and death—'Umar

Death is especially designated whenever the lord of the east and of the house of death equally are conjoined, or are in a tetragon or opposition: for then he could in no way avoid death. Moreover, for health the lord of the east should be consulted, namely [to see] when it will arrive at a strong place (namely [its own] house or sovereignty), or when it will walk faster or in a direct course, with the lord of the house of death being cadent from it:[17] for it introduces health at that hour.

§6.4: On those growing sick, what would happen to them—al-Kindī[18]

§612a. The Moon and the Sun and the lord of the Ascendant, being cleansed of the infortunes (especially from the lord of the house of death), promise the health of the one who has grown ill. But if two bore themselves thusly, no matter if the third one would apply with the lord of the house of death, they convey health. Also, with the third one bearing itself [safely] but the remaining two being cleansed of an application with the lord of the house of death or with an adverse infortune (particularly one who appears as a partner of the fourth or of the second[19] in something), as long as they were cleansed, they liberate.

---

[16] Or rather, "threat." This is an example of Hugo's irony, which occasionally surfaces.
[17] That is, in aversion to it.
[18] Cf. al-Rijāl II.2.5.
[19] Al-Rijāl: "ruling over the fourth or eighth or second."

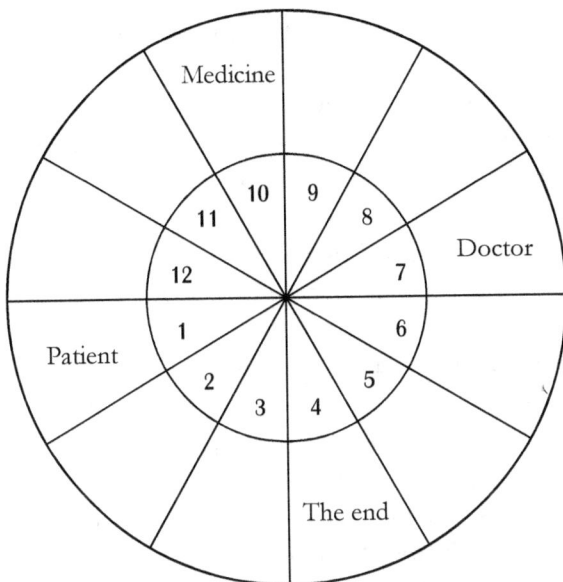

Figure 26: Angular significations in illness (al-Kindī §§6.4 and 6.15)

§6.5: On those growing infirm—al-Khayyāt

If perhaps questions of the sixth would come out into the open (such as for an infirm person, whether he would escape or not), the lord of the east and the Moon should be principally consulted. For the beginning will be from that one which is staying in a pivot or regards the east.[20] Therefore, it[21] being cleansed of scorching and the infortunes, and free of the lord of the eighth, promises escape; it is no less if the fortunate ones are applying.

Moreover, the significator[22] being corrupted from a tetragon or an assembly, is fatal, if the lord of the east is equally being corrupted. Now, these infortunes are two, [but] even the Sun is an infortune from the assembly, [namely] for a star to which he is conjoined by scorching.

Likewise, the Moon increasing in light and computation, rendering the counsel of an application to the eastern lord—even though it may be staying

---

[20] Al-Khayyāt used this same formula in his long question on the truth of rumors (§5.43), but instead of it aspecting the east, he had it having more management in the east.

[21] Sahl, al-Khayyāt, and Dorotheus all assume we are speaking of the lord of the Ascendant here, even though the rule which was just stated allows the Moon to be considered, too.

[22] This is apparently the Moon, based on scribal notes and parenthetical remarks.

under the earth—still accelerates good health and restores the integrity of the body.

Which if [the lord of the east] were received, it is wholly healthful. Moreover, with reception denied, while it is scorched or corrupted by an enemy star (the lord of the eighth, I say, or one of this kind), one must wholly have fear, especially if that same eastern lord would be corrupted in a pivot.

Moreover, should the significator render counsel to a star in the seventh (and one already wanting to be in its fall),[23] it seems to be mortal, because it is as though entering into scorching.

But[24] if [the Moon] should render counsel to the lord of the eighth, with the Moon being in a pivot and the lord of the east being [both] corrupted, it is mortal. Whenever the lord of the east, being in a pivot, applying to the lord of the eighth from a trigon, renders counsel [to the lord of the eighth], it promises or ordains that space of life up to where the lord of the eighth reaches the degree of the east. But [do it] in this way with the rest of the pivots, namely whenever a malevolent which rules over the eighth, would touch [the pivots].[25]

A transfer of light that is made from the lord of the east to the lord of the eighth, while namely the lord of the east is cadent, [and the lord] of the eighth would equally be lingering in a pivot, it is fatal. (But if its corruption would happen from a trigon, while the one which corrupts would be lingering outside those places, it is a sign of a long-lasting illness.)[26] Whenever the lord of the east would traverse in the sixth (or preferably the lord of the sixth in the east), it prolongs the disease until the star would go out of that sign. But it being a turning [sign], makes the infirmity change;[27] a double-bodied one prepares another disease; but a firm one preserves it through the year.

Moreover, the lord of the east applying to the lord of the sixth makes the disease worse, and he [has chronic suffering],[28] or it suggests he has labored with that disease repeatedly, and it means it is customary [with him].

The application of the eastern lord with the lord of the second is a sign of being freed, [but] not unless it is with difficulty and expenses. The lord of the

---

[23] Reading with Dorotheus in §6.6 for *cadens* (normally, "cadent").
[24] For this paragraph, cf. Dorotheus in §6.6, which is significantly different in certain respects. Cf. also Sahl above.
[25] That is, by transit.
[26] That is, instead of death.
[27] This seems to mean that he will be cured quickly.
[28] Reading with Dorotheus for Hugo's *apparente* [?] *contrahit*.

fourth applying to it, brings in paternal destruction; and in this manner with the rest of the houses.

The lord of the eighth in the east, with the eastern lord and the significator[29] being corrupted, brings in death as though without a cause. It is no less, should the lord of the east happen to be found in the eighth, under the regard of a malevolent, or with the significator being corrupted. But it is worse if some star would transfer their light to the east.

In addition it must be noted that the significator being corrupted or in no way received, while the lord of the east would render counsel to the lord of the eighth, is mortal (especially the lord of the eighth being in a pivot).

One must even note that with the benevolents being received, scorching is not harmful.

The lord of the east being above the earth, applying to the lord of the eighth (it appearing in the fourth or in the eighth), really threatens death.

Moreover, with the eastern lord undergoing scorching, nor being received, while it is less than 12° distant from the Sun, it is fatal. It is no less, too, with the Moon being in front of scorching [and] in no way received. But if the eastern lord is a heavy [planet], so that it does not render counsel (of which type is Saturn or Jupiter),[30] while it underwent scorching, it is fatal; but being free [of the rays] and with the Moon safe, it is a promise of good health.

With the lord of the east lingering in the sixth, eighth, or twelfth, it is good to diligently note the status of the significator,[31] because the whole judgment depends on it. If therefore it will be wandering alone, let it be changed over to the following sign: for it is fatal, however much there may be a delay (certain people are sometimes cured, but after that they die, having relapsed).[32]

Moreover, the lord of the east being in the eleventh or the fifth, is stronger in any illness than in the ninth and third:[33] for these two repeat, [but] the

---

[29] This is apparently the Moon, based on scribes' notes and parenthetical remarks, here and below.
[30] Jupiter and Saturn are the slowest planets, so it is unusual for them to apply to another planet (unless perhaps by retrogradation).
[31] Again, this seems to be the Moon.
[32] I believe what al-Khayyāt means is this: if the significator is void in course, then it suggests possible death or at least a prolonging of the illness; but since entering into a new sign provides new opportunities, if the planet is in a better situation in the next sign, it can show escape and healing. Dorotheus in §6.6 is simpler and clearer.
[33] If I am understanding Dorotheus correctly, Hugo's al-Khayyāt has this somewhat backwards. The idea seems to be that cadent places like the third and ninth are somewhat better for the patient than the succeedent places like the eleventh and fifth, because ca-

two prior ones make it firm. The malevolents even in those same places, are stronger than in the third and ninth.

Thereafter,[34] one must note that the lord of the east is corrupted by a lord of the second that is an infortune, just as it is by the lord of the eighth. But if the lord of the east would render counsel to it, it is the worst. Moreover, the lord of the twelfth is similar to the lord of the eighth. However, the lord of the sixth wears down and dries out the body, and propels it as though into failure.

But the Sun appearing as the lord of the east, if he would render counsel to a Jupiter which is not regarding [Pisces],[35] [even if] should the rendering come to be from the assembly or opposition, it is not harmful. But if, [while] regarding that place, the Sun would receive counsel,[36] and with the significator being corrupted, it is the most severe thing.

With these bearing themselves so, Jupiter traversing in the eighth and the pivot of the Sun, or even in its other pivots,[37] is thoroughly fatal. It is nothing else with the Sun in the eighth, [and] Jupiter holding onto a pivot, while the Moon would transfer the Solar light to Jupiter.

But the Moon transferring the light of a benevolent to the lord of the east, is healthful.

In addition, the turning signs make an easy disease, and they hasten death or health; but the double-bodied ones observe [something] in the middle; the firm ones wholly make it worse.

---

dent places show change—that is, it shows the illness changing quickly rather than persisting. Of course, Dorotheus and al-Khayyāt have cleverly isolated these four houses in particular, because the two other succeedents (second, eighth) and the two other cadents (sixth, twelfth) have problematic indications in illness.

[34] Compare with Dorotheus in §6.6. It seems to me that this paragraph is really comparing (1) a malefic lord of the second, with the lord of the eighth, and (2) the lords of the sixth and twelfth. (This makes sense especially since these were the four non-angular houses omitted in the previous set of statements.) But both al-Khayyāt and Dorotheus seem to have confused what was being compared.

[35] I have added Pisces with Dorotheus, since the object of the verb was missing in al-Khayyāt. At first I believed that Dorotheus/al-Khayyāt should be speaking of Jupiter regarding the east: that is, we want the planet which is receiving the light to aspect the Ascendant (as Māshā'allāh insists in *OR* Ch. 2 (see Appendix C). But Pisces is also the eighth from Leo, so the idea seems to be that if Leo is rising and Jupiter is therefore the lord of the eighth, he will not cause that much trouble (since he is a great benefic), even though he does not aspect his own domicile.

[36] Dorotheus still has this the other way around, with Jupiter receiving counsel from the Sun.

[37] I am not sure what distinction in pivots al-Khayyāt is trying to draw. Dorotheus omits these details.

But the best is the lord of the east (if it would enjoy the aspect of the benevolents), being strong in its own place, and even free of the infortunes; but there is detriment [when] under the aspect of the infortunes and traversing in a pivot.

§6.6: On those growing ill—Dorotheus

When inquiries of the sixth occur, such as for a sick person (as to whether or not he would escape), the eastern lord and the Moon, and which of them possesses a pivot or regards the east, claims the starting-point of this ambiguity. For, it[38] being cleansed of the infortunes and free of the lord of the house of death, being outside of scorching and [its own] fall, promises health. The Moon applying to fortunate ones signifies the same thing.

However, the significator[39] being corrupted from a tetragon, assembly or opposition, really threatens death. A regard of the infortunes from a strong place, stains the eastern lord. The Sun corrupts in the same way, when he burns it[40] up in his own assembly.

Moreover, this comes to be noted: because if the Moon would render her own proper counsel to the lord of the east, she being both increasing in light and adding in computation, it declares a quick escape and renders his body sound.

With the eastern lord and the Moon being placed under the earth, while she rendered counsel to a star likewise under the earth, one must notice whether it[41] is received. For reception liberates; [but] with it being denied, the lord of the east should be consulted: for, it being scorched and corrupted by a star inimical to it, is mortal (but more expressly so while [the lord of the east] is corrupted in a pivot).

Which if the significator itself would render its own counsel to a star in the opposite of the east, while [that star] would hasten to [its own] fall, it is fatal—as would be the case if the star wants to enter into scorching.

Moreover, the significator being in a pivot, rendering counsel to the lord of the eighth, if the lord of the east itself would be occupying a pivot [and]

---

[38] Sahl, al-Khayyāt, and Dorotheus all assume we are speaking of the lord of the Ascendant here, even though the rule which was just stated allows the Moon to be considered, too.
[39] The al-Khayyāt text in §6.5 suggests the Moon.
[40] This probably refers to the eastern lord, the Moon, or the significator indifferently.
[41] I am not sure if this is the Moon herself, or the planet to which she applies.

equally be rendering counsel to the lord of the eighth, each one (namely the lord of the eighth and of the east) must be noted: for, both [of them] being corrupted, really threatens death. Which if this rendering would come to be from a trigon, with the lord of the eighth being in a pivot of the east, while the lord of [the east] (as was said) would render counsel to the lord of the eighth, [then] whenever, I say, it[42] would reach the eastern degree, it is wholly dangerous. One must likewise have fear if that infortune which rules over the eighth, would attain a pivot of the east.

Furthermore, if there is a transfer of light from the eastern [lord] to the lord of the eighth (with the eastern lord, I say, being cadent, while the lord of the eighth occupies a pivot), it is mortal. Also, the lord of the east being placed in the sixth, and cadent, warns that it is not otherwise to be feared, until that star leaves the sign behind. Then, too, the east[43] being convertible declares an easy disease, but a double-bodied one vexes in a middling way (for it threatens that it is now more serious, now more easy). But a firm one presses on.

Moreover, an application of the eastern lord with the lord of the sixth prolongs the illness[44] and vexes with a chronic suffering, while it relates that he has undergone a disease of this kind many times.

Likewise, the lord of the eighth in the east, also with the eastern [lord] and the significator and the Moon[45] being corrupted by it, warns of a sudden death. Also, if the eastern lord would be in the seventh,[46] regarded by an infortune, or with the significator being corrupted, it is dangerous; however it is more serious if it were a transfer of light [to the east].[47]

Moreover, with the significator not being received, and the eastern lord rendering counsel to the lord of the eighth, it is mortal (but worst if the lord of the eighth [were] in a pivot).

Finally,[48] [applying?] to any received star, even though it would be a fortunate one, they harm and [their] rays are hostile.

Moreover, the eastern lord being above the earth, applying to the lord of the eighth [which is] under the earth in the fourth, [or in the] eighth, is mor-

---

[42] This must be the lord of the eighth.
[43] This should probably be "sixth," with Sahl and al-Khayyāt.
[44] Reading with al-Khayyāt for "health."
[45] Since the significator seems to be the Moon anyway, this statement is redundant.
[46] Al-Khayyāt says "eighth," but I can see why the seventh would work as well.
[47] Adding based on al-Khayyāt.
[48] This sentence makes no sense. Much better (and very different) is al-Khayyāt: "One must even note that with the benevolents being received, scorching is not harmful."

tal. If a regard is absent, but a transfer of light is not absent,[49] it is likewise fatal. Which if there is reception by a trigon, but the corruptor is remote from these two places, it is a sign of prolonging [the disease].[50]

On the other hand, the lord of the east entering into scorching, while the distance between it and the Sun were less than 12°, it is mortal. The Moon in the same way too, unless she is received by someone before the scorching.

Which if the lord of the east would possess the sixth or eighth or twelfth, all good health and fitness of the affair will have to be referred to the indication of the significator.[51] And so, with the significator roaming alone,[52] remember to bring it down to the following sign, for thus it introduces death and delay (but very frequently certain people have escaped).[53]

Moreover, the lord of the east in the eleventh and fifth[54] [is] strong, but stronger in the ninth and third: for these places signify remoteness and unsteadiness, but the pivots give birth to steadiness. The infortunes are even strengthened in them, but they do not have as much power in effectiveness in the third and in the ninth.

Furthermore,[55] the lord of the eighth corrupts the eastern lord, if it were one of the malevolents. But the lord of the twelfth is comparable to the lord of the sixth. Nevertheless, [the lord of the sixth] corrupts bodies by infecting [them], whence it conveys what the lord of the twelfth does not bestow.

With the Sun claiming the rulership of the east, while he rendered counsel to Jupiter, and Jupiter did not regard the sign of Pisces, even though this rendering may be from the opposition or the assembly, nothing could be harmful. If however he did regard his own place, [and] was taking up counsel from the Sun, and with the significator being corrupted, it threatens something difficult for this question.

---

[49] This would be a case of "reflecting light," where the two planets are in aversion but a third planet transfers light between them. See *ITA* III.13.

[50] In other words, if the corruptor (the lord of the eighth) is in a place that already signifies death, then it is fatal; but if it is not in these places and there is also reception, it is still difficult but the situation is only prolonged, not made fatal.

[51] Again, this seems to be the Moon.

[52] That is, being void in course (or at least, being alone in its sign).

[53] See my interpretation of this in al-Khayyāt above.

[54] Reading with al-Khayyāt for "fourth."

[55] Compare with al-Khayyāt. It seems to me that this paragraph is really comparing (1) a malefic lord of the second, with the lord of the eighth, and (2) the lords of the sixth and twelfth. (This makes sense especially since these were the four non-angular houses omitted in the previous set of statements.) But both al-Khayyāt and Dorotheus seem to have confused what was being compared.

But if the rest of the things which were said agreed with [the situation involving] Jupiter, it is mortal.[56]

Furthermore, a star transferring light to the lord of the east[57] is a sign of good health.

Also, convertible signs warn of an acute disease, for they put off good health and threaten disease. But double-bodied ones [do so] in a middling way. Fixed ones afflict with a steady and long-lasting disease.

But[58] among all of this especially, if the eastern lord would enjoy the aspect of the benevolents, it being established in a strong place and free of the infortunes, it at least accelerates good health; to the contrary too, [there] is detriment whenever unfortunate[59] ones would regard it [while it is] lingering in a pivot, for thus it introduces death more quickly.

§6.7: Whether he would escape—Jirjis

As to whether an infirm person would escape or not, you will have it thus: the lord of the east and the Moon traversing with malevolents, really have a judgment of death, namely on the day they reach the infortune. Their traversal with fortunate ones portends health on the day the significator reaches the benevolent. Nor should someone presume to judge about death unless (I say) the corruption of the eastern lord and the Moon is equally discovered. Therefore, with this method the occasion for death and the nature and place of the illness could be discovered most certainly.

§6.8: On an infirm person—Aristotle

With someone growing ill, if a question would be proposed about his health. Let the east be sought for the infirm person—if, I say, a stranger asked about him: for if he himself sent a closely-related person, the status of the one growing ill should be sought in its own proper place, but again, the

---

[56] See al-Khayyāt for a list of possibilities here.
[57] Al-Khayyāt reads this as the Moon transferring the light of a benevolent to the lord of the east, which makes more sense.
[58] I have broken up and rearranged a couple of clauses in this long sentence.
[59] Reading *infortunatae* for *fortunatae* ("fortunate ones").

east belongs to the infirm person.[60] Therefore, with [both][61] the malevolents or the Tail being placed in the east, while the lord of the east bears itself badly, without a doubt it is fatal. Furthermore, with the perverse ones being placed in the east (as was already stated), even though its lord would bear itself well and promise good health, it will be a judgment of death. With one of the malevolents in the east, while its lord would traverse in a prosperous way, it is a sign of escape. But if that same [lord] would linger in a perverse way while one of the unlucky ones would occupy the east, it is mortal. With the benevolents even being placed in the east or with its lord, one should not have fear, however much the unlucky ones would possess the east.

In addition, the Moon and the lord of the east being in the fourth warn of death. Moreover, with both of them being in the other pivots or in the fifth or eleventh (while each malevolent would possess their pivots),[62] it is fatal. Moreover, the Moon or the lord of the east in the aforesaid places, while any of the malevolents could linger in its fourth or tenth or seventh,[63] likewise kills.

The wickedness of Saturn being placed in the east, is milder than the Martial [wickedness], but it prolongs the infirmity. If however the malevolents would be lingering in the east or in the eighth or with its lords, one should equally fear death. Moreover, with them holding the pivots from the place of the infirm person, it is the worst. Likewise, if the benevolents would walk through the places of the unlucky ones already stated, they are healthful.

Which if the lord of the eighth happened to be in the east, the eastern one in the eighth, it is bad. In addition even, should the lord of the eighth traverse with the eastern [lord]—with, I say, the lucky ones being remote from it or at least from the eighth or from the pivots—he will in no way escape.

Moreover, the lord of the one growing ill traversing within 5° of the Sun, if it should head towards conflagration, it really threatens death.

---

[60] Aristotle seems to mean that if the querent is a stranger to the sick person, we should use the Ascendant; but if the querent were (say) a brother, then the sick person is especially indicated by the third, but also by the Ascendant.
[61] Adding based on the logic of the following sentences.
[62] For example, if the Moon and the lord of the east were in the eleventh, and the malevolents were in their whole-sign angles (in the second, fifth, and eighth, or in the eleventh itself).
[63] Preferring "seventh" (1509) to "second" (Vienna, Madrid), because the seventh is a whole-sign angle from it. But I can also see the rationale for the second from it, since the second sign can indicate "what happens next."

Finally, should the good ones and the unlucky ones be made equal in number and in power, one must note to which ones the lord of the east is advancing. For, advancing thus toward the worse half (which bears itself badly), it is mortal; but if [to the half which bears itself] well, not.

Likewise, with the lord of the east being placed in an optimal way, even though the testimonies of the bad ones are more and stronger, he will escape. Which if the situation bore itself in the contrary way, it is fatal in like manner.

Nor will you change this judgment, even if the status of the one growing ill is found somewhere else than in the east.

§6.9: On the nature of the disease—'Umar

The lord of the eighth[64] and its proper quality opens up the nature of the disease. For, it being a cold and dry star, [and] in the same way the sixth sign being cold and dry, generates a disease from black bile,[65] whose type Saturn portends everywhere: such as paralysis and scrofula[66] and stinking breath, arthritis, gout, and lice.

Which if the nature of that star (which is in charge of the sixth) is hot and moist, and likewise too the sign of infirmity, it predicts that the disease is of that nature, to whose proper quality the signification of Jupiter universally responds: as are scrofula and abscesses, and what is of this kind.

Moreover, the Sun having control over the rulership of it, while the sign is hot and dry, ascribes it to that property (namely, red choler), and whatever represents the Solar nature is especially referred to it: as are an acute and tertian fever.[67]

---

[64] This should probably read, "sixth." It seems to me one should also examine any planet in the sixth.

[65] *Melancolia.* One might also add melancholy as the psychological manifestation of black bile.

[66] Scrofula is associated with tuberculosis and the inflammation of the lymph nodes in the neck. It appears as a non-warm, non-painful mass with a dark color. The darkness and lack of warmth are probably why it is associated with Saturn: heat and redness would suggest Mars.

[67] Classically, fevers were categorized according to the cycle of their spiking and ebbing. A quotidian ("every day") fever spikes about once every day; a tertian ("on the third") fever, such as can happen with malaria, spikes every 48 hours; a quartan ("on the fourth") spikes every 72 hours. Normally we think of 48 hours as being two days, but if a fever spikes on Monday, and then 48 hours later on Wednesday, then it has spiked on the third day from Monday (counting Monday as the first day).

Moreover, it being cold and moist, but the sign cold and moist, asserts that the causes of phlegm are harmful: such as apoplexy,[68] leprosy, and whatever exhibits the nature of phlegm.

On the other hand, if the nature of the star and the sign differ from one another, the judgment should imitate the effectiveness of the larger and greater nature:[69] all of these could be discovered by such a method.

Now, the nature of the star possessing the east, and that of the sign which it holds onto, come to be noted first. And, if it is possible, establish it as being eastern of the Sun. So that if (for example) Saturn came into view,[70] since he is cold and dry, should he be arranged in Aries, since the nature of the sign which he possesses is really more effective than his own,[71] a judgment of hot and dry should be related. And it is permitted to observe it in this manner with respect to both the stars and the signs.

Moreover, it is good that one consider a star[72] that is western of the Sun and in the circle[73] (but Saturn is neither eastern nor western from the Sun, or in the circle), as to whether any testimonies of the signs in which they are, would give support (namely, that of [its] house or sovereignty or triplicity or bound). For it is necessary to produce a judgment from their nature.

Furthermore, the east being convertible and the Moon in a convertible one, introduce health or death more quickly.[74] But the firmness of the east threatens the harshness of death after a long-lasting illness. Likewise, the east being double-bodied and the Moon in a double-bodied one, diverts it to health (if, I say, she were fortunate: for being corrupted, it warns of a hastened death).

---

[68] Apoplexy often referred to any sudden and serious loss of consciousness, such as a stroke.
[69] I take this to mean (for example) that if the planet is hot and dry, while the sign is cold and dry, dryness prevails.
[70] *In commune procedat.*
[71] I am not sure what 'Umar means here.
[72] 'Umar seems to want to include all western stars, since he uses the plural in the rest of the instructions.
[73] I take this to mean rising before the Sun, and in an eastern quadrant (from the Ascendant to the Midheaven, and from the Descendant to the IC). However, I do not understand the next comment about Saturn. If Saturn were actually rising before the Sun in the east, then he would indeed not be western, but 'Umar's parenthetical comment says that Saturn is not even eastern.
[74] That is, depending on what the condition of the planets actually is.

§6.10: On the nature and cause of the disease—al-Kindī

§612b. The proper quality of the [planet] by which the significator is corrupted will demonstrate the nature of the disease. Also, the place of the corruptor (in the arrangement of the signs), suggests the causes of the infirmity.[75]

§6.11: On the disease and its cause—Jirjis

Therefore, with a question about a sick person and the occasion for the disease being presented, the lord of the east and the Moon are especially to be noted. For, the one which traverses in a closer way to the malevolents, that one assumes the signification of the whole question.

Therefore, Saturn being in possession of the signification and place of this kind, suggests a cold and dry disease. Traversing even in a fiery sign, it afflicts with a horrible fever. Concerning an earthy one, he is vexed by black choler.[76] Under an airy one, winds.[77] Under a watery one, it is a sign of dysentery and windiness. But if Mars appeared as [the indicator of the sickness], walking through a fiery sign, it generates an acute fever, and makes him frenzied.[78] In an earthy one, it threatens exhaustion and he grows weaker. In a watery one, dropsy. In an airy one, [it makes him] leprous. But the Tail being in possession of this role, makes ulcers and impetigo. Moreover, when Saturn and Mars would come together for equal reasons in a signification of this kind they bring about water[79] from the one growing ill, [but] not without poison, especially from an earthy sign.

§6.12: In what limb he would suffer—ʿUmar

If therefore the lord of the sixth would hold onto the sign of Aries, it testifies that he suffers in the head; in Taurus, the neck; it is permitted to judge in this manner, too, with the rest of the limbs.

---

[75] *Judges* mistakenly put al-Kindī's §619 after this one, but I have put it in its proper place, in §6.15 below.
[76] This likely means constipation, but one might also consider depression (i.e., melancholy).
[77] Winds and windiness seem to indicate gas pains.
[78] *Maniacum*.
[79] This must refer to urine.

Even the testimonies of the death-bearing Lot[80] will have to be applied in this place. Once [the distance] is taken up from the degree and point of the lord of the house of death to the degree and point of the eastern lord, the degrees of the house of death must be applied. Finally, what was collected being thrown down from the beginning of the sign designating death, where the number will be ended, it testifies that the Lot of death falls in that same place. By day one will have to do no differently. And so, the degree [of the Lot] or at least the lord of the house of the Lot being in the east or with the Moon, or being established with the Lunar lord, or should they be staying in the tetragon or opposition or assembly of the Lunar lord, they really declare death. But if those degrees (namely of the Lot and [its] lord), or either one, would be cadent from the degree of the east or the assembly or tetragon of the eastern lord or of the Moon, it is a sign of health.

§6.13: In what limb he suffers—al-Kindī[81]

§616. You will even explain in what part of the body (namely the upper part or middle or lower), or finally in what limb he suffers, in this order, [according to the place of the corrupted significator.][82] For, the Ascendant designates the head; by the second is denoted the neck; the hands and shoulders are designated by the third; but the fourth indicates the[83] chest and lungs; the fifth portends the stomach and liver and what are the receptacles of foods.

§617. But the sixth [indicates] the sides and rear parts.[84] The seventh, the kidneys and vital organs. The eighth portrays the virile parts, the bladder, testicles, kidneys.[85] The ninth declares the buttocks and colon (which in Latin

---

[80] In this paragraph, 'Umar's Lot seems to be taken from the lord of the eighth to the lord of the Ascendant, and projected from the eighth. Perhaps this is a Lot of his own invention, but it is also possible that 'Umar has mixed up two other Lots. The Lot of death (*ITA* VI.2.27) is taken by day and night from the Moon to the eighth sign (or the eighth house), and projected from Saturn (though Rhetorius Ch. 77 projects from the Ascendant). The Lot of the killing planet (*ITA* VI.2.28) is taken from the lord of the Ascendant to the Moon, and projected from the Ascendant. See also my footnote to §8.3 below.
[81] Cf. al-Rijāl I.2.4.
[82] Adding with Robert.
[83] Omitting *tenus* with *Judges*.
[84] *Terga*. That is, the back parts above the waist or hips.
[85] Robert omits the kidneys.

we call the anus). The[86] tenth, the haunches and knees; the eleventh, the shins; but the twelfth, the feet.

§618. Moreover, such a judgment is given for what part of the body he is vexed in. Now, the significator being corrupted above the earth [indicates] the right [side]; but under the earth, it afflicts the left with pain. If the infortune would be set up in a sign of many ascensions,[87] it indicates the disease will be in a larger portion[88] of the body; but in others, the contrary.

§6.14: In what part of the body he would suffer—Jirjis

However, in order that you may discover definitely in what part of the body he would suffer, observe diligently the malevolent significator of the illness. For if it would be staying at the beginning of a sign, it will afflict the upper parts of the body. In the middle, the middle ones. But at the end, it wears out the lower ones.

That malevolent traversing with the Sun, really weakens the right side. But if it would be staying with the Moon, the left one plainly gets sick. Moreover, with the significator lingering in a diurnal sign, he will be vexed in the front [parts]; in a nocturnal one, it condemns the back ones with pain.

Finally, in what limb of the body he would suffer, could be discovered in such a way. For there is no ambiguity [but that] the limb dedicated to that sign will be weakened.

§6.15: Whether he would be cured by a doctor who is brought in—al-Kindī

§619.[89] If therefore the truth of the question would promise health, [then] if one is asked about a doctor, one will have to relate this according to the nature of the fortune which liberates [him]. Even the house of the fortune itself (namely the one which it looks at with a more loving aspect)[90] lays it out clearly.

---

[86] Adding this sentence with *Judges*.
[87] That is, those of straight ascension (Cancer through Sagittarius).
[88] Following al-Rijāl for Hugo's "enlargement."
[89] *Judges* mistakenly puts this paragraph at the end of §6.10 above, but I have put it in its proper place here.
[90] That is, see which of its own domiciles the fortunate planet aspects, by a better or stronger aspect. This is common practice in al-Kindī and other traditionalists. Here, al-

§620. But the lord of the seventh will indicate whether it is possible to be healed by the doctor who is brought in. For if it would make the lord of the Ascendant fortunate, or if it would aid it in something, it testifies that the doctor will be useful for the sick person. But if not, [then] not at all. Which if it would corrupt [the lord of the Ascendant], it promises he is harmful. But if it would be the lord of the house of death or of the second (along with this corruption), it signifies he will be killed by him.[91]

§621. Again, the lord of the seventh receiving the lord of the Ascendant, means a merciful, pious doctor, and one dealing diligently with health. Moreover, the lord of the Ascendant receiving the lord of the seventh, makes the diligence of the one who has grown sick, be suitable to the healer.[92] But the mutual reception of these indicates mutual courtesy.

§622. Moreover, the lord of the seventh being eastern, in its own light, received, and fortunate, confirms the prudence of the healer and the effect of [his] remedies. Moreover, the same thing amplifies the wisdom and grace and courtesy of the healer.

§623. Furthermore, the shape of the seventh, and its lord, will indicate the form of the healer.

§624. Moreover, you will note whether the one about to take the remedies, would approach [it] willingly. The lord of the Ascendant being received by the lord of the Midheaven, will indicate the effectiveness and appropriateness of the remedies that are taken. Which if they would bear themselves otherwise, they pervert the judgment. No less do the lord of the seventh and the Moon and the lord of the Midheaven come to be considered in this matter.

§625. Also, the final conclusion for the sick person depends on the lord of the Ascendant and the Lunar [lord] and [the lord] of the fourth, according to their luckiness or corruption. But the lord of the significator in particular decrees the same thing.

Kindī must mean that the topic of that house helps explain why and how he gets better. See the next paragraph.
[91] Reading *perimi ducetur* with *Judges* for Burnett's *primi dicetur*.
[92] That is, the patient will do what the doctor instructs.

§6.16: Whether he would be healed by the doctor that is introduced—al-Khayyāt

Of the pivots however, the east is given to the doctor, the tenth to the infirm person, the seventh to the infirmity, the fourth is left to the medicines. Therefore, a malevolent traversing in the east testifies that the doctor will be of no use, but rather is harmful. If a fortunate one, it suggests he will be useful.

But if a malevolent would occupy the tenth, the infirm person, while he does not look after himself, nor would he be obedient to the doctor, greatly increases his own disease. If a fortunate one, he looks after himself.[93]

An infortune traversing in the seventh threatens that disease will follow disease; but a fortunate one notes he is going to escape without medicines.

But whenever an infortune traverses in the fourth, there will be an increase of pain through the medicine; but a benevolent, to the contrary.

§6.17: Whether he would be healed by the doctor—Dorotheus

And so, it must be known that we put the east in charge of the doctor, the tenth over the infirm person, the seventh over the disease, the fourth over the medicines. Therefore, the east being possessed by the infortunes shows that the doctor will be unuseful, but more importantly: harmful. But the fortunate ones in that same place, testify he is helpful.

Moreover, the malevolents in the Midheaven claim that [the patient] himself had been the cause of the disease for himself. Also, with the fortunate ones being placed in that same place, he will be prudent [and] careful about himself.

Likewise, the infortunes in the seventh change him from disease to disease; but the fortunate ones free him without a remedy.

Again, the malevolents occupying the fourth testify that the remedy was harmful. But the fortunate ones in that same place portend it is useful, and so on.

---

[93] *Sibi consulit.*

§6.18: Whether the doctor would be useful to the infirm person—Aristotle

For an affair of this kind, the east should be consulted. For, the Moon with any of the malevolents (or with the Tail) in the east, or anywhere, allows the doctor to be of good in nothing. Even the Moon traversing with the Sun (wherever you please), the same. Any of the malevolents being placed in the east will be no more helpful.

The Moon with the benevolents presents the greatest help from the doctor, no less so if she regarded the Sun well. In the same way, if you find the lucky ones with the Sun, moreover the [Head of the] Dragon or any of the benevolents established in the seventh, it notes that the medicine will be useful, even if it were given by someone less experienced. But with any of the malevolents traversing in the same place, [the medicine][94] is proven to be not only unuseful, but harmful.

Finally, the benevolents in the pivots make the doctor and the medicine useful; the unlucky ones, to the contrary.

§6.19: On critical days—Sahl[95]

On the other hand, for the recognition of critical days, it is good to note the four principal places of the Moon, discovered from the day of going to bed or even from the day of the question. But these are the seventh and fourteenth [days], then the twenty-first and twenty-eighth—which they tend to call "critical" for the determination made under them, of an illness.

Under any of these days, the Moon applying to malevolents or to the lord of the sixth (on that day itself, I say), makes the illness especially worse. But if on that day she would apply to fortunate ones, or she were regarded by them, [he will get better]:[96] we call that same [day] "critical," or "declarative."[97]

---

[94] Reading more simply with the parallel passages in the other authors, for Aristotle's *quae congrua est et optima*. What he may mean is "[the medicine] which is [normally] appropriate and the best, is proven…".
[95] Cf. *On Quest.* §6.2. Al-Rijāl has a general treatment in II.2.9.
[96] Adding from John's Sahl.
[97] This should more properly be something like "susceptible to judgment," as the concept and term "critical" has to do with making a declarative judgment based on evidence.

Moreover, once days of this kind have been most definitely discovered, they tend to count 90° from the place of the Moon at the hour of going to bed itself (or [at the hour] of the question): for where the number will be ended, this is called the seventh day. With the same amount being counted from that place, you will have the fourteenth; and from thence with so many being brought in [again], reckon the twenty-first; moreover, the twenty-eighth occurs with so many being counted from that. Also, we should do it thus until finally it returns to the same point of the hour of going to bed or the question that is made.

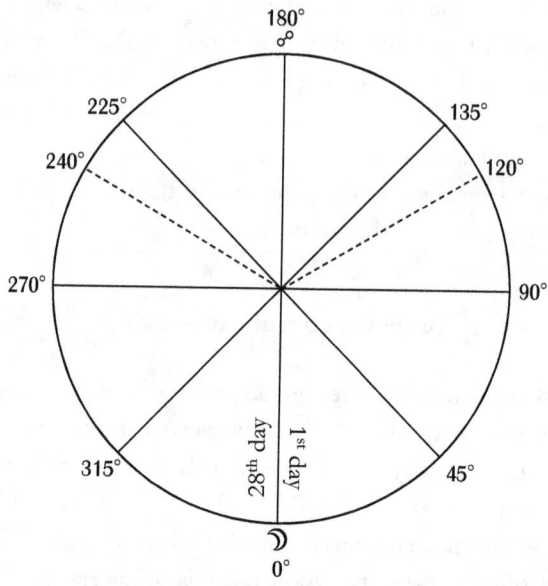

Figure 27: Typical degrees of critical days in illness[98]

§6.20: On critical days—'Umar

Moreover, the Moon principally determines the critical days: namely, the seventh from the one on which the infirm person went to bed, or the ques-

---

[98] This diagram is based on the views handed down by many traditional authorities, and elaborated from the accounts given here. It does not show the 10° or 40° divisions suggested in *Carmen* V.41.20 and mentioned here by 'Umar, al-Khayyāt, and Dorotheus. Also, I have added dotted lines for the trines from the Moon's original position, which is what *Carmen* uses instead of the squares. Please note that while traditional texts frequently identify the day on which the Moon will reach some degree, it is not always so. Therefore I have supplied the degrees themselves instead of giving each approximate day.

tion about him went forth. For if on that day the Moon would hold onto (or preferably reach) the right tetragon (the tenth [sign],[99] I say, from the original one), [then], in order that finally the truth of the judgment will be free of all error, attend diligently to the place of that Moon (namely where she is after the tenth[100] from the first [day] of going to bed or the degree of the question).

It is no less good, too, to consider her progressing through 40°,[101] until she crosses them. Now, if 47°[102] were reached, it designates a place to be feared. For while she touches that, she being corrupted from whatever place suggests the long-lastingness of the disease. However, being made fortunate from any place (and from a strong place), it brings peace to the disease.

§6.21: On critical days—al-Kindī

§613. The degrees of application by which the stronger significator approached the fortunate ones, judge the days between the question and the hour of health, especially if it were the lord of the Ascendant or the Moon, and if the Moon claimed the shift (no less too does the Sun [do so] as the lord of the shift).[103] The application of the stronger significator especially with the lord of the house of death does not expel death, but rather introduces death according to the degrees of application.

Therefore, the application of any significator to the infortunes increases the diseases, up to where it withdraws from it. Also, [its application] with the fortunate ones soothes and mitigates [the illness] until [its] withdrawal. And so, it will be right to diagnose the days of the whole infirmity in this manner. Which if the infortune would be likened to the nature of the illness, it enlarges it; but a dissimilar infortune mitigates it.[104]

---

[99] This is wrong: it should be the fourth. But when the Moon is in the fourth sign from the original position, the original position will be in the tenth from where the Moon then is.
[100] 'Umar probably means "10,", as with al-Khayyāt and Dorotheus below.
[101] Intervals of 40° divide the circle by nine, and traditional religions all over the world had many sacred periods which lasted for nine days or which had a sacred day every nine days.
[102] This should probably read, "45°," indicating the semi-quarters of the circle.
[103] That is, the sect light of the chart of the decumbiture or the question (the "decumbiture" is the time at which the patient was so sick as to have to "lie down" in bed).
[104] Which must mean that if the disease is cold and dry, then the involvement of Mars should mitigate it, since Mars signifies heat and dryness.

§6.22: On critical days—al-Khayyāt

But in order that you may discover the critical days in a precise way, it seems that the places of the Moon on the fourth, seventh, eleventh, and fourteenth day must be noted.[105] Therefore, if the Moon were corrupted on any of these, it makes the disease more serious on that day, unless (I say) she would traverse with fortunate ones or would stay in their aspect: for the association[106] or regard of a lucky one breaks the malice of the infortune which is hostile to the Moon. Moreover, the Moon being fortunate and lucky on any of those days, contributes a remedy to the illness.

And there is another knowledge of the critical days, namely one which has very specific days and hours, which could be discovered thusly. From the hour of going to bed (or of the question), 10 or 40 degrees[107] will have to be computed from the degree of the Moon. Should the Moon, reaching those certain degrees, then be applying to fortunate ones, that critical day will be one of health; but an application made with the malevolents increases the pain.

§6.23: On critical days—Dorotheus

For critical days, the place of the Moon comes to be noted, namely on the seventh and fourteenth and twenty-first [day]. She being adverse or unlucky on any of these days threatens it will be difficult for the sick person, unless perhaps some one of the benevolents appeared as a partner[108] for her, or would regard her: for thus it relieves the sick person and takes away from the disease.

Moreover, the Lunar progression from her own place by 10° and even 40° must be noted. For an application with fortunate ones being made in that same place, mitigates; also, with the infortunes, he grows worse.

---

[105] This takes us through the first half of the critical days, with the 45° marks indicated.
[106] *Consortium.* That is, assembly by sign.
[107] Every 10° is equivalent in longitude to a face or decan (important in Egyptian astrology and magic), and the Egyptian decan gods were closely related to personal health/illness and good luck/disasters.
[108] *Consors.* That is, an assembly by sign.

§6.24: About anyone, whether he is infirm—Sahl[109]

With a question being raised about someone, as to whether or not he is infirm, we consult the lord of the east and the Moon. For if the stronger one (namely, the one which is in a pivot) applies to the lord of the sixth, or (as often happens) should it linger in the sixth, in fall[110] or scorched, it portends that the one about whom it is asked will be made worse by the disease; but if not, one should not have fear.

§6.25: About anyone, whether he is infirm—al-Khayyāt

If perhaps it is asked about someone whether he is infirm or healthy, the lord of the east and the Moon respond. For the one among them which is found to be stronger, being in the sixth or applying to the lord of the sixth, or traversing in its own fall, or scorched, or corrupted in whatever other way, makes an indication of one growing ill. But if it were otherwise, not at all.

§6.26: Whether someone is growing infirm—Dorotheus

Then, for a question as to whether or not someone is growing infirm, the eastern lord and the Moon give counsel. The stronger of them claims the signification. Placed in the sixth or applying to its lord, even being cadent[111] or scorched, there is no ambiguity about the disease; but without that, not at all.

§6.27: On bloodletting and cupping—al-Kindī[112]

§626. The letting of blood maintains this in common with cupping, that blood is drawn off in both cases; but in what characteristic they differ, will be stated separately in its own place. For, the cutting of veins which they call "phlebotomy" always seems to differ from cupping in this, that the use of cupping glasses comes to be more suitable after the opposition of the Sun and Moon (namely in the latter half of the [Lunar] month). Also, phlebotomy

---

[109] Cf. *On Quest.* §6.3.
[110] Reading with John's Sahl for *cadens*.
[111] Again, according to al-Khayyāt and Sahl, this is being in its fall.
[112] Cf. *Carmen* V.39.

claims the prior half of the [Lunar] month as being more useful, while the fortunes bear themselves as was stated above.

§627. But as for what [these practices] are partners in, it is good to establish the lord of the Ascendant and the Moon in an airy or fiery sign, made fortunate in a pivot or after the pivots, in its own light,[113] but no less [should you make] their lords fortunate.

§628. If someone desired to purge the defects of the sanguine [humor], let the Moon or the lord of the Ascendant be arranged more suitably in earthy[114] signs. But [to purge] choler, it seems that watery [signs] are more powerful than fiery or airy ones. Which if [it is] black bile, they will hold onto airy ones better so than fiery ones. But a purgation of phlegm seems more appropriately to demand fiery ones.[115]

§629. In all of these, we warn you to beware lest that limb which belongs to the sign the Moon or the lord of the Ascendant is holding onto, should ever by hurt by iron.[116] To make this matter evident, we entrust the limbs of the body to the individual signs by such a distribution: and so, Aries looks to the head, Taurus the neck, Gemini the shoulders and hands, Cancer the chest and what belongs to the chest, but Leo the stomach and vital organs and what is next to these, Virgo takes the loins and back and sides.

§630. Moreover, Libra claims the *findas*[117] and what is adjacent to these, Scorpio the cock, bladder, buttocks,[118] Sagittarius the testicles, colon and *hiran*,[119] Capricorn the thighs and knees, Aquarius the shins. To Pisces are granted the feet. Therefore, someone instructed in this distribution will never presume to cut (with iron) the limb belonging to the sign which the Moon or the lord of the Ascendant possesses.

§631. Moreover, let the lord of the eighth be deprived of the companionship of the Moon and the lord of the Ascendant, [and] in the same way be estranged from their lords and from a pivot; also, [it is] best if the lord of the Midheaven [is] lucky, regards the Moon and the lord of the Ascendant, [and] moreover that the Moon or the lord of the Ascendant in no way should possess the fourth.

---

[113] This generally means that it is out of the Sun's rays.
[114] Reading with al-Rijāl for Hugo's "airy."
[115] Thus the sign indicates the opposite of the type of humor being purged.
[116] That is, for such a surgical intervention.
[117] Unknown, but Libra generally has the area around the hips. Hugo reads "calves" (*suras*), which does not make sense.
[118] Reading Hugo's euphemism *renes* for *rinones/rignones* (kidneys).
[119] Or *huan* (Vienna). Unknown.

§6.28: On surgery—al-Kindī

§632. The use of surgery demands the same care as the cutting of veins, namely that the limb designated by the sign which the Moon or the lord of the Ascendant is holding onto, should not incur any wound by iron, nor should someone presume to risk it.

§633. Moreover, one must take care with a vigilant soul, lest the lord of the Ascendant or the Moon be falling down from the pivots, nor should they be set up as scorched or retrograde: their preferable position is in a pivot. Furthermore, the lord of the Ascendant should be put in the Ascendant or the Midheaven, [and] likewise the Moon in the Midheaven or the seventh. Also, let the infortunes lack the regard of the Ascendant and its lord (moreover that of the Moon and of the Lunar lord), but remember to place them in the falling of the pivots.[120]

§634. The establishment of all of these will finally be perfect if the strength of the lord of the Ascendant and of the Moon would be present, and the lord of the sixth would be set up as being unsound (more often however, it profits no moderate amount to support [the lord of the sixth], wherever it happened [to be]). The end of the matter should be observed in the way it was stated above with respect to phlebotomy. Moreover, the light of the fortunate ones will increase the advantageousness of the pivots.

§6.29: On taking potions—al-Kindī[121]

§635. The Moon in the last half of Libra or in the first [half] of Scorpio[122] supports the taking of potions. Let her lord[123] be fortunate, strong, eastern and in a pivot, but the one by whom it is blessed should be pivotal and eastern (also, let the lord of the Ascendant be likewise). Likewise let the infortunes be cadent from the Moon and from the pivots, with the Moon received by fortunate ones. Which if the lord of the Moon were unlucky, let him still regard her from a trigon [or hexagon].[124]

Therefore, whoever will have to apply a cure to a limb, let one of the fortunate ones be set up strongly in the sign to which [the limb] is reckoned [to

---

[120] That is, the infortunes should be cadent.
[121] Cf. al-Rijāl VII.47.
[122] The so-called "burnt path" or *via combusta*.
[123] If we followed the previous instruction, this would have to be Venus or Mars.
[124] Adding with al-Rijāl.

belong], [and] moreover let the lord of the Ascendant[125] and of the fourth be situated in the same way the Lunar [lord] is.

§636. One should even avoid placing some significator in a sign which presents the form of [animals] chewing the cud, nor the Ascendant being one of this type: for then, he will vomit forth the remedies he has taken, [and they will be] ineffective.[126] Which if the purging is arranged to take place in the upper parts [of the body], let them be in these [signs] which were [just] prohibited [for laxatives], with the above-written prosperity of the signs and significators.

§637. Whenever it was good to chill or heat the body, to moisten or dry it out,[127] let the Moon and the lord of the Ascendant (or either of them) hold onto signs of a corresponding nature; apart from that, [follow] what was written above about [their] prosperity.

§638. However, the cadency[128] and unluckiness of the significators should be avoided, with the virtue of the infortunes being removed[129]—for these convey no little harm. Let the lord of the house of death be dwelling in none of the pivots, nor should it enjoy partnership or any companionship with the significators. Therefore, a diligent observation of all of these things furnishes the rest as you wish.

---

[125] Al-Rijāl uses only the lord of the fourth, not the lord of the Ascendant. Hugo may have repeated this because it appears above.
[126] This is for laxatives.
[127] That is, if the potion is supposed to provide these medicinal effects.
[128] Reading with al-Rijāl and Robert for Hugo's "fall."
[129] Al-Rijāl has this as "nor should an infortune be firm," suggesting that it is in a fixed sign.

Slaves & Captives

§6.30: On a captive: whether he could be freed—Sahl[1]

Here, should it be asked about a slave or captive (as to whether he would happen to be freed), one must engage the counsel of the eastern lord and the Moon. The separation of the stronger of the two being made from the lord of the Midheaven or from the Sun, or from infortunes (provided that it applies to none of these), carries a judgment of freedom; but if not, not.

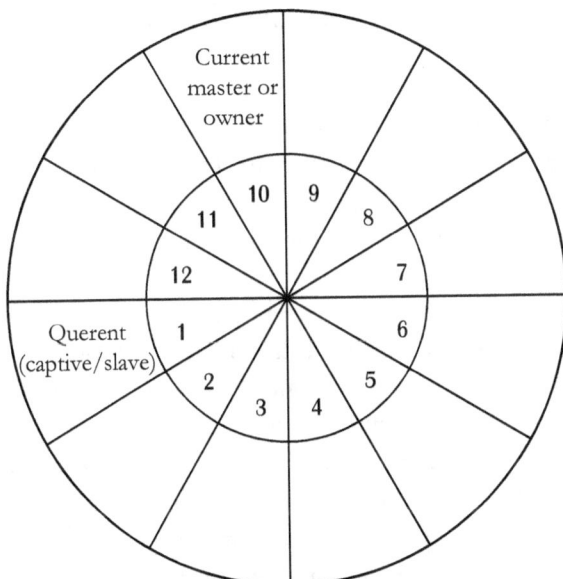

Figure 28: Will a captive/slave be freed
(Sahl §6.30, 'Umar §6.32, al-Khayyāt §6.37, Dorotheus §6.38)

§6.31: On a captive: whether he could be freed—'Umar

With a question proposed about captives and those detained in prison, the east and the Moon and the lords of each respond. For, the lord of the east and equally that of the Moon, with the Moon herself (or the majority of them) being in a firm sign, defers his departure, especially with them being established in a pivot. Moreover, the lord of the east and the Moon being in

---

[1] Cf. *On Quest.* §6.4, and al-Rijāl II.4 (first part).

the east itself, [but] the lord of the Lunar lodging-place and the Moon being in a convertible one (being drawn back, I say, or cadent), accelerates the departure. Which if the aforewritten significators (or the majority of them) would be holding onto double-bodied signs, the judgment will be the same. It is not otherwise in pivots of this kind:[2] they introduce a change of prison, or some alternation with respect to the affairs of the captive himself, or they determine a middling span of captivity.

§6.32: On captives or the liberation of a slave, and their status—'Umar[3]

The east and its lord will indicate the captive or slave, if he gave the question on his own behalf; but we commit the one who possesses the slave to the Moon and the Midheaven and its lord. Therefore, with an application of the eastern lord and the Moon (or either one) with the [lord] of the Midheaven, or [the lord of the Midheaven's application] with one of them, [or] while any star would transfer or collect the light of each, and the application (as was stated) is from the tetragon or opposition or assembly, without reception, it introduces harsh torments to the captive, and without any kindness, and it wholly denies freedom, nor does it attest that he would escape the hands of the one possessing him, nor shake off the yoke of slavery, while he survives. [But] with reception being had, after the torments inflicted upon the captive, the kindness of the master is revealed. But he will always possess him, nor free him, nor permit him to depart from his authority, especially if the significators would be holding onto firm signs.[4]

Moreover, if a joint aspect of the lord of the Midheaven and equally the eastern [lord] would be noted, [and] even that of the Moon, or there is an application of one to the other from a trigon or hexagon, or rather that between them is a collecting star or one that would transfer their lights, he leaves, free, for a price, with respectable assent on both sides. But reception being present, restores everything to the better.

---

[2] Namely, being in common (double-bodied) signs in the pivots.
[3] Cf. al-Rijāl II.4 (second part).
[4] Al-Rijāl adds, "or the application is from an angle."

§6.33: On the liberation of a captive—'Umar[5]

However, if the master himself made the question about collecting the revenue of a captive,[6] establish the east for the master, and the sixth and the Moon for the captive. With them being distinguished thus, one will have to claim not otherwise than as it was stated above[7] about the lord of the east and of the Midheaven equally, and the Moon, with respect to an application and collection or transfer of light, likewise with respect to the regard of a tetragon and the opposite and conjunction, or even from a trigon or hexagon. For the same method of judging appears here and there.

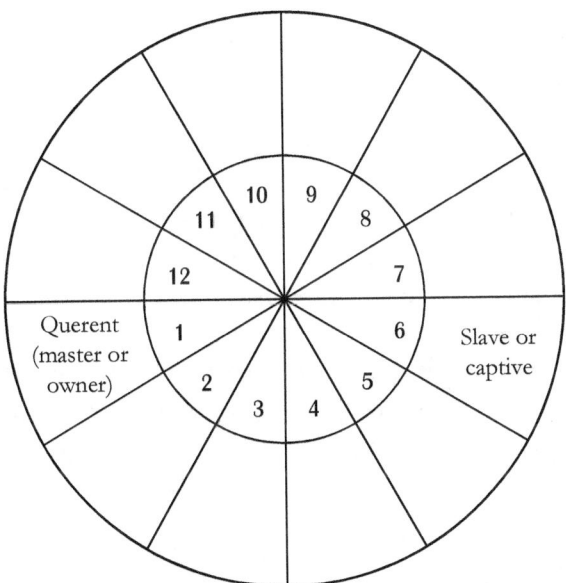

Figure 29: Freeing one's own captive ('Umar §6.33)

§6.34: On captives—al-Kindī

§553. A question having been proposed about the liberation of some captive, an understanding of the hour at which he was led into captivity resolves no little part of the doubt, through its own signification. It being unknown,

---

[5] Cf. al-Rijāl II.5.
[6] Hugo's version here makes this a question of finances, but that is not expressed by al-Rijāl.
[7] In §6.32.

let the question proceed in general terms: the lord of the Ascendant and the Moon, or the one which is asserted to be stronger in the Ascendant and question,[8] withdrawing from an infortune [which is] the lord of the twelfth or seventh or eighth, and applying to fortunate ones, means freedom and safety. The significators being drawn back from the pivots even bring about this same thing.

§6.35: Whether he would be held long—al-Kindī

§561. Furthermore, the firmness of the signs which the significators and their lords are holding onto, suggests openly enough the long-lastingness of the captivity: for they designate the period of the captivity. The significators being in convertible signs and drawn back from the pivots, promise a quick exit. The signs being in the pivots or after the pivots, [indicate] a slower exit.

§562. Furthermore, the departure of the lord of the Ascendant from scorching at the hour of the question, [and] in the same way the liberation of the Moon or of the Lunar lord or of a star in some authority of theirs (namely of one appearing in its house or sovereignty, from under the rays), permits freedom from prison.

§563. Furthermore, the lord of the assembly or opposition which preceded the captivity (or at least, the question) withdrawing from being scorched, or being drawn back from a pivot, being fortunate and cleansed of the infortunes, indicates [his] exit can in no way be impeded.

§6.36: What would happen to him after leaving—al-Kindī

§564. Moreover, with that freedom already being indicated through the benefit of the stars, the Lunar lord and [the lord] of the Ascendant [indicate] the status of the captive and what should happen to him after the captivity. Being made fortunate and lucky, they testify to respectable events and an appropriate end. Which if the lord of the Midheaven would be the one favorable to them, it promotes him to [a position of] authority and to a dignity. But if [it were] the lord of the second, they introduce prosperity. And so, in

---

[8] Robert: "the lord of the question or the victor."

this manner of consideration it will be permitted to judge with respect to individual houses and their lords.

§565. But this is the analogy which we state:[9] insofar as the Sun himself would be the lord of the Midheaven, it raises him into royal service. But if Jupiter, he is made a judge. Saturn too, arranges him into the rank of senior people, but more often it establishes him as a guard of revenues and personal property, and an inhabitant of agricultural areas, and a minister of buildings. Mercury makes him a writer or merchant. Venus claims he is a teacher of (or devoted to) cheerfulness, jokes, and women. Also, the Moon commends him as a minister of legations and servitude and leadership. Finally, Mars calls forth a minister of wars [or] a soldier.

§566. And I say that the aforesaid distribution or association of the stars' [signification] should be made through the individual houses by this analogy. [With this exception, that the significator returning by retrogradation into the sign which it had held onto at the hour of flight, or being in combustion, signals [his] return.][10]

§6.37: Whether he would become a freedman—al-Khayyāt

For a question about a slave or captive, whether he would become a freedman, the lord of the east and the Moon equally give counsel. For, if the stronger of these would be separated from the lord of the Midheaven or [from] the Sun, finally applying to none, without a doubt it makes him a freedman; but if otherwise, not at all.

§6.38: On imprisoned people—Dorotheus

Moreover, with a question given about a captive, as to whether he would be made free or not, the eastern lord and the significator itself[11] will have to be consulted. In fact, the stronger of them withdrawing from the lord of the Midheaven or from the Sun, but applying to none, promises freedom; but bearing themselves otherwise, they in no way release him.

---

[9] That is: when looking at the planet which is making the aforesaid planets fortunate, the house it rules will show the area of life providing the benefit (§564), but the planetary nature modifies that area (§565). See §566.
[10] Adding with Robert.
[11] I.e., the Moon.

§6.39: Whether an exit is being prepared for a captive—Dorotheus

Next, if it came into question whether he would happen to leave the hands of his possessor some day, the eastern lord being in a pivot [and] rendering counsel to none of the stars, nor even to some [star that is] drawn back [from a pivot],[12] impedes his departure. Moreover, with it referring counsel to the lord of the third or ninth, it is a sign of leaving. Also, the lord of the east being corrupted by an assembly or opposition or from a tetragon, or entering into scorching, really threatens death.[13] Moreover, that same [lord of the east] rendering counsel to a star in the third or in the ninth, testifies that he is able to leave.

§6.40: On the hour of liberation—'Umar

However, it seems that the hour of liberation or departure from fetters (which the benignness of the stars establishes), could be discovered thus. For, the significators written above[14] being found outside the pivots, while the lord of the east and the Moon would possess a quarter which belongs to travel (but the quarters which designate travel are the feminine ones), the one who had been captured is released from fetters. But if that same lord of the east and the star would apply to any stars in the remaining, masculine quarters, they indicate he will be held longer.

Moreover, with the lord of the east being cadent from its regard,[15] while however the Moon (being placed under the earth) would regard the east, I believe one must pay attention to when the Moon, entering from there into a sign in which she retains some dignity, would support the east with her own aspect: for on that day it introduces liberation. Also, there will not be another judgment with the Moon being cadent,[16] while the lord of the east, being already placed above the earth (or both being above the earth), would regard the east itself. Then, you will note which of them would apply to or regard the other: for it will be allowed to establish that one as the significator.

---

[12] That is, cadent.
[13] But does this mean death if he leaves, or that he will die in the service of his current master (see §6.49 and §6.52 below)?
[14] Probably in §6.32 above (especially if the captive himself is asking), but refer also to §6.33.
[15] That is, being in aversion to the Ascendant.
[16] Probably in aversion to the Ascendant, as the reverse of the previous situation.

Which if they would be deprived of a mutual aspect, while the aspect of each would be directed towards the east, when (I say) they, being above the earth, would arrive into a sign where they take on some power, while (above the earth) they do not deny an aspect to the east, the captive's departure will undoubtedly be revealed on that day and hour.

§6.41: When he would be freed—al-Kindī

§554. Moreover, the degrees of application of that star which recedes from infortunes and applies to the fortunate ones, determine the hour of obtaining freedom—namely, by substituting for hours, days or months, or years for [the degrees] by which it seems to be thus far distant from a fortunate one. For an application in a convertible sign, and its lord in a convertible sign, [and] in the same way the significators (or the majority of them) in convertible signs, suggests hours. Which if the application [would be] in a convertible sign and its lord in a fixed one, it decrees days. In a double-bodied one, months. But in a fixed one, years.

§555. Moreover, the quick course of that withdrawing significator, seems to confirm the same thing. In fact, its quickness sometimes transforms years into months, months into days, days into hours. Likewise, its slowness very often changes hours into days, days into months, months into years.

§556a.[17] Furthermore, the stationing of the significator whose recession and application is chosen, [indicates] what is written above.[18]

§6.42: Whether he is destined to grow infirm in prison—'Umar

The eastern lord and the Moon give counsel as to whether he is destined to grow infirm in prison. For if there is an application of each with the lord of the sixth or the Lot of infirmity[19] (or its lord), from a tetragon or assembly, it portends one who is dead in prison; being remote from an application of this kind, this trouble will be absent. Which if they would apply from a trigon or hexagon, they suggest that he suffers it after his departure. Finally,

---

[17] Hugo mistakenly put this sentence at the beginning of §6.44 below.
[18] I take this to mean it will slow things down, as in §555.
[19] Probably the Lot of chronic illness (*ITA* VI.2.19), taken by day from Saturn to Mars (but by night from Mars to Saturn), and projected from the Ascendant.

once the hour of captivity is known beforehand, it will be permitted to judge fully about everything in this way.

§6.43: Whether he would die in prison—'Umar

The lord of the east and the Moon should be consulted for a question as to whether he would die in prison. For if each would apply to the lord of the house of death from a tetragon or opposition or assembly, they threaten a death in fetters; but without that, not at all. However, with an application from a trigon or hexagon being discovered, it afflicts [him] with the trouble of death shortly after his departure from prison.

§6.44: Whether he would die in prison—al-Kindī

§556b.[20] Likewise, the same [planet][21] being foreign and weak in a sign, testifies to the harshness of prison and the difficulty of faring badly. [But] strong and received, the contrary. Moreover, an application of it with the fortunate ones from retrogradation, means an unexpected departure, particularly [if] received by those fortunate ones.

§557. Which if it would be corrupted by the lord of the eighth while [the lord of the eighth] is Saturn, and if it would apply itself to the aforesaid lord of prison, it promises death in prison. Mars taking up the role of Saturn, destroys him. The lord of the eighth being corrupted by the aforesaid infortune, and [that infortune] in the Midheaven, also the other infortune in the pivot of the earth, threatens hanging. But if it would be corrupted by Mars but not the lord of the eighth, it adds blows and blood. Moreover, corrupted by Saturn, it heaps on the labor of torture.

§6.45: Whether he would be afflicted by blows or torments or tortured in some manner—'Umar

The kind of tortures and an inquiry about them will have to be looked into especially from the lord of the east and the Moon. For the one of them

---

[20] Hugo originally had the first sentence of this paragraph here, but it belongs at the end of §6.41 above, where I have replaced it.
[21] Probably referring to §§6.34-36 above.

which blessed the east with its own aspect, deservedly claims the role of the signification. Which if the one which regards the east would apply to Mars (or with the killing Lot) from a tetragon or opposition or assembly, it demonstrates that he is afflicted by torment or punished by torture in many ways. But the Lot of killing[22] is taken from the point of the Moon to the point of Mars. If therefore you added the degrees of the house of death which have arisen to that, you will have to take away what was collected from that. But where the number left off, the Lot really appears there. Which if an application is absent, all torture will be absent.

§6.46: Whether he would be afflicted by tortures in prison—al-Kindī

§558. If therefore the corruptor and giver of anxiety appeared as the lord of the Ascendant, he earns his affliction in prison [because of] his own crime. Which if [it were] the lord of the second, he incurs this punishment because of money and his clients,[23] [or] even those whose help he hopes for.[24] But if it would be established as the lord of the third, he is punished because of friends and those types, and travel. The lord of the fourth afflicts with blows because of parents and something of antiquity or land. The lord of the fifth, he is punished unjustly because of children.

§559. But if it appeared as the lord of the sixth, it is caused because of a lower order of slaves, and by the impediment of beasts and disease. Which if it would be established as the lord of the seventh, it reprimands him through an attack of adversaries, women, merchants. Placed in the rulership of the eighth, the supporters of the adversaries, women, or business [partners] testify that this wrong is done [to him] because of inheritances or his own captivity or some death.[25]

§560. The lord of the ninth, he is made crooked because of law or travel. In the rulership of the tenth, it brings the king or the duty of his own profession, or his mother, against him. It even being the lord of the eleventh, it

---

[22] I am not sure where 'Umar gets this Lot, but apparently it is taken from the Moon to Mars, and projected from the degree of the eighth. The Lot of the killing planet (*ITA* VI.2.28) is taken by day from the lord of the Ascendant to the Moon (but by night the reverse), and is projected from the Ascendant.

[23] Or, lesser associates and dependents (*clientum*).

[24] Reading with Robert for *quorum spes magni habetur*.

[25] This seems to be a more natural reading of the rulership issue. As written, the text says that the supporters of the adversaries (and so on) testify that *he has committed* his offense because of inheritances (and so on).

afflicts him because of the royal family and money, friends, and hope. Which if it appeared as the lord of the twelfth, he is punished with this suffering because of enemies and prison. And so, in this manner you will remember to indicate it with respect to the fortunate ones and their causes.

§6.47: Whether a tortured man would come to death—'Umar

Moreover, a diligent observation of Mars suggests those who endure the torture of whips, whether they would bring death to a captive. He being placed in Aries or Scorpio, threatens death and the sword; but in Leo or Sagittarius, the blows of whips. Moreover, with Saturn occupying the place of Mars, if he would possess one or the other of the houses, while the lord of the east and the Moon would apply to him or with the Lot of torture[26] and its lord, they afflict with clubs and welts from blows, [and] they designate millstones on the back or neck, or serious burdens of this kind being put upon him. If again they[27] would regard Mars or Saturn (bearing themselves just as we stated), they remove and resolve all things according to their power or weakness. Here, if Mercury regarded them and he was corrupted, it will be said to signify according the manner and nature of the corruption.

However, the Lot of torture must be taken from the degree and point of the Moon to the degree and point of Saturn; also, with the degrees of the sixth being added to it, the whole thing is counted from that same degree of the sixth.[28] Therefore, where the number left off, the Lot itself appears in that same degree and point. If therefore the Moon and the lord of the east would apply to it from the tetragon or opposition, it is dangerous.

§6.48: Whether he would be hung—'Umar

With a question presented about hanging, the eastern lord and the Moon must be consulted, as is usual. For the one which regarded the east will take control of the benefit of the signification. Then, too, it seems that we need

---

[26] See below: from the Moon to Saturn, and projected from the sixth. Like so many of 'Umar's Lots, it does not correspond to other classical Lots. But note below in §6.48, where this Lot is identified with the Lot of death. Perhaps the calculation here should use the eighth and not the sixth.
[27] This probably means the benevolents.
[28] 'Umar's calculation suggests the use of quadrant houses, it being taken from the Moon to Saturn, and projected from the degree of the sixth.

[to see], with no little consideration, whether the significator itself would apply from a tetragon or opposition or assembly to Mars or with the Lot of torture (which is called the Lot of death)[29] or with its lord.

Furthermore, with Mars himself or the Lot of torture or its lord being established in the Midheaven, whenever the significator (being placed in Gemini or its triplicity) applied to them, it really prepares a cross and hanging. Which if they would bear themselves otherwise, it claims nothing is to be feared.

§6.49: Whether a captive or slave would be sold—Sahl[30]

The sale of a captive or slave: once the question is had, it could be investigated thusly: the lord of the east traversing in a pivot, while it applies to no [planet] in aversion to or remote from the pivots, speaks against the sale. Which if there were an application of [the lord of the east] to some [planet] lingering in the ninth or third, it prepares the sale.

Finally, if the lord of the east happened to be found in a pivot and corrupted by the malevolents with a perverse aspect, or entering into scorching, he will let out his [last] breath under the ownership of [his current] possessor.

§6.50: On the number of masters [and his sale price][31]—'Umar

Again,[32] if the master himself asked about the sale of a slave and the number of masters, namely whether he would undergo the slavery of many or few, the east and its lord portends the querent, [but] the sixth and its lord will be in the charge of the captive. Now, we discern the buyer from the second from the east, and its lord. And so, with the Moon and the lord of the sixth being cadent from the east,[33] while however they would apply to the lord of the second, the one who is being held as a captive will depart the slavery of the present master. Also, after the application with the lord of the

---

[29] See above (§6.47), and the traditional Lots of death in §6.12 and §8.3.
[30] Cf. *On Quest.* §6.5 and al-Rijāl II.6 (middle), and read with §§6.52-53 below. Al-Rijāl adds that if the Moon or the lord of the Ascendant commit their disposition to the lord of the eleventh or seventh, it likewise shows that he will go to another master.
[31] See the final paragraph below.
[32] For this paragraph, cf. al-Rijāl II.7. I have added the bracketed material from al-Rijāl.
[33] This must mean something like "flowing away from" (i.e., separating). Al-Rijāl seems to have these planets separating from each other or from the lord of the east.

second, [should each or either one] withdraw from it, and each or either one would then apply to the lord of the third, [the slave] will really cross over from the authority of the second [master] to a third one. And we think that one must judge in this manner with respect to the fourth and fifth, up until the application of each or either one is ended. [Because he will remain in that place where the application is cut off, and he will live with that master with whom the last receiver were found. But if one of these two significators did not have an application with any lord (of the lords of [these] houses), but it had] an application to the eastern lord (from a tetragon or opposition or assembly) were discovered, they wholly deny freedom. But it being had from a trigon or hexagon, [and in one of the angles, and after that application it did not apply to another, it likewise signifies that he will remain in the hand of his master. But if the application from the trigon or hexagon were not in an angle, and afterwards it had another application], freedom is promised.

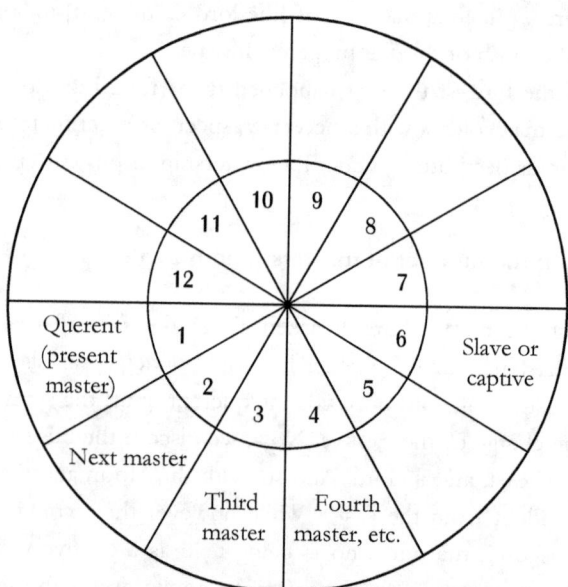

Figure 30: Subsequent masters
(current master as querent): ʿUmar §6.50

If[34] therefore the captive himself asked about his own departure, we give the counsel of the querent to the lord of the east and the Moon, but the in-

---

[34] For this paragraph, cf. al-Rijāl II.6.

formation about the first buyer proceeds from the eleventh, but that of the second (if there were one) from the twelfth. Then, too, this method of judging should be followed just as was stated above about the lord of the east, second, [and] even the third. Nor should one deviate in anywhere from that kind of judging, until the application detains him under the established slavery of some master, or rather it frees him from the yoke of slavery. The sale of a captive was made clear in no other way than above, with respect to the Moon and the lord of the Midheaven.

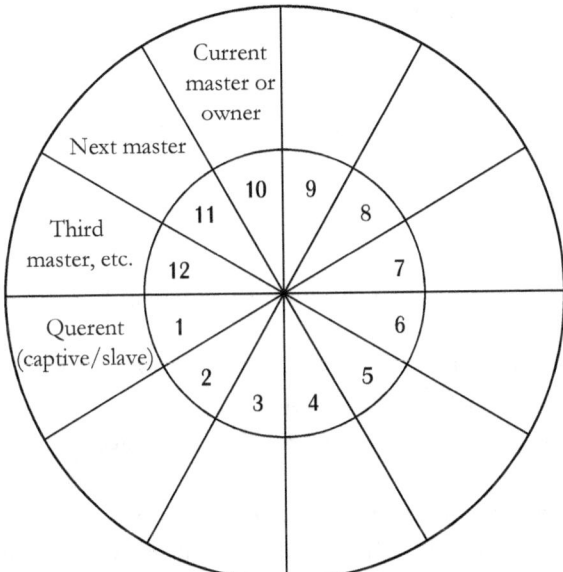

Figure 31: Subsequent masters
(captive or slave as querent): 'Umar §6.50

And finally,[35] [from the lord of the Ascendant, which is the significator of the slave, you will know what the price of the slave is.] [If he is] seeking [to know] for [how much he will be sold],[36] it is necessary that one scrutinize attentively as to what place in the circle [the lord of the Ascendant] claims (namely [its own] house or sovereignty or triplicity), likewise should it be

---

[35] For this paragraph, cf. al-Rijāl II.6. There are just a few sentences there which are relevant, but they do help clear up the issue. That is, this question is really about the sale price of the slave or captive. I have added material in brackets based on al-Rijāl, to emphasize this.
[36] Reading more realistically with al-Rijāl, for Hugo's "for how long or by how many lords he would be held."

eastern or western.³⁷ [And you will give to it according to the number of its lesser years, in terms of single units or multiples of ten, according to the status of that planet, just as we have said in the chapter on assets.]³⁸ Therefore, Saturn always exhibits 30 or some likeness of these units (as is 300). Also, Jupiter [indicates] 120 and [multiples of that], as is 1,200. But Mars has 1,500 or even 15. Venus means 8 and 800. Moreover, Mercury designates 20 and 2,000. Finally, the Moon embraces 25 and 250 and 2,500.

§6.51: On the hour of the sale—'Umar³⁹

However, a tetragonal conjunction of meeting of the significators themselves, or an opposite or from an assembly—a joint reception, I say, of one to the other being discovered, suggests the hour of the sale. Which if reception is absent, it supplies a modicum of delay.⁴⁰

§6.52: Whether he would be sold—al-Khayyāt

Moreover, if perhaps it should come into question whether a slave or captive would pass over to another master (through a sale or in another other way), the lord of the east should especially be consulted. For, it traversing in a pivot, applying to none that is remote from the pivots, [the master] will not sell him nor change him over to another master. But, rendering the counsel of application to a remote star or to the lord of the ninth or third, shows it will happen.

---

³⁷ Reading with al-Rijāl for Hugo's "possess the east or west."
³⁸ Reading with al-Rijāl for Hugo's "For you will give individual units for the quantity of the lesser years, or if it is a greater one of the numbers." For 'Umar's rules on prices like these (with the help of al-Rijāl), see §4.7 above and al-Rijāl I.32-33. Basically, if the key planet is angular and in its domicile or exaltation, it grants the number of its lesser years, multiplied by 100 or 1,000; in its triplicity, only that number or at most multiplied by 10. What follows in the *Judges* manuscripts and edition is a confusing mess of numbers, but this rule is generally followed. I have translated the passage so as to remove the ambiguities, and will not try to explain the manuscript errors and differences. For the table of planetary years, see §1.2.
³⁹ Cf. al-Rijāl II.6 (end).
⁴⁰ Al-Rijāl says it will include labor and be painful.

Moreover, with the eastern lord being corrupted by an assembly or opposition or tetragon, or if Saturn[41] would be scorched, he will die in the rulership of [his current] possessor.

§6.53: Whether a slave would be sold—Dorotheus

Furthermore, with a question given about a slave or captive, if he would be sold, we consult the lord of the east and the Moon. For, they applying to the lord of the ninth or third, or to any [star] placed there, signify being sold. Moreover, their application with infortunes bars it. Which if they would apply to a star drawn back [from a pivot], he will be sold. Being placed in the seventh, they also do not indicate anything else.

Moreover, with the lord of the sixth being corrupted, the slave insists on being sold; but if it were made fortunate, not at all.

Moreover, the eastern lord and the Moon being in a pivot or applying to a star in the pivots, deny the sale. They make the same thing go awry if they were drawn back [from a pivot, but] applying to some [star] in a pivot.

§6.54: If a slave ought to be sold—Dorotheus[42]

Moreover, for considering the sale of any slave, the eastern lord and the Moon are consulted [as to] if he should be sold. For, their application with the lord of the sixth or any [star] placed there, or at least the lord of the sixth applying to [the lord of the east], indicates it will be [so]; without that, not at all.

§6.55: Whether or not it would be better for a female captive to be sold—Dorotheus[43]

Which if there is a question from someone selling a female slave, we put the east in charge of the querent, the seventh over the buyer, the twelfth[44]

---

[41] Sahl and Dorotheus both make this the lord of the east, not Saturn.
[42] I have assigned this section to Dorotheus, as it matches Sahl and al-Khayyāt in §§6.59-60 below.
[43] I have assigned this section to Dorotheus, as it matches Sahl and al-Khayyāt in §§6.59-60 below, and refers to material above.

over the female captive. For all of them, one must pursue their joint status (with that of the first two being as the masters) [and] manner of their bearing, just as was stated in the chapter above.

§6.56: Whether it is better to sell or keep a captive—Sahl[45]

For an inquiry about a captive, whether it is more advantageous for him to be sold or rather retained, we give such counsel: therefore, with the eastern lord being safe and received according to his place, it is more sacred that he remain. But when you should find the lord of the seventh firm and received in his own place, you will judge it more advantageous that he be sold.

But one must even observe the one to which the Moon applies, and from which she is being separated. For with the one from which the separation is, being cleansed [of the infortunes][46] and regarding the Moon, it praises the [current] possessor; but if you learned that she was received in a familiar way by the one to which she applies, the buyer will be preferred.

Of these, if you find neither these significators nor proofs of this kind, one will have to return to the Moon [or the lord of the Ascendant].[47] If therefore she herself were in her own place (either her own house, even sovereignty or triplicity), received, it teaches it is more useful to remain. Which if you learned that she was crossing over into the next sign, [and was] received or enjoying any of the three dignities, this reason encourages him to go over to the other master.

Nor do we give another opinion whenever [someone] brings up a question about changing places.[48]

§6.57: Whether it is better for a captive or slave to be sold—al-Khayyāt

Moreover, with a question presented about a captive or slave, as to whether it is preferable for him to be sold or retained, the lord of the east being received in its own place commends [the captive's] own place and pos-

---

[44] In al-Khayyāt and Sahl below (§§6.61-62), this is the eleventh, suggesting a slave in sexual service (since the eleventh is the fifth from the seventh).
[45] Cf. *On Quest.* §§6.6-6.7, and al-Rijāl II.8. Hugo originally titled this, "On the changing of places," which really refers to the last sentence in the passage.
[46] Or rather, that it is a benefic planet (John).
[47] Adding with John. Hugo reads the rest of this as though we are dealing with the Moon.
[48] See §9.13.

sessor. But the reception of the lord of the seventh in its own place, portends it is better that he be sold.

Then, the star from which the Moon is being separated being a benevolent and lucky, and receiving the Moon, recommends that he stay with his own master. But if she were received by the one to which she applies, it indicates that the one who buys him will be better for the captive.

But if it is evident that these significators are in no way found [to be thus], one will have to consult the stronger between the lord of the east and the Moon. For [the stronger of them] being received in the sign in which it traverses, or if that lodging-place would agree with it (which is that it is in [its own] house or sovereignty, and so on), it commends the grace of the present master, and in addition it settles it that it is preferable for him to remain. But if it is received in the following [sign] to which it will have crossed,[49] or that [sign] is appropriate to it (as was already stated), we will walk no other path with respect to changing places.

§6.58: Whether it would be better for a captive to be sold or kept—Dorotheus

Then, the lord of the east will respond to a question as to what slavery is better for a captive (namely that of the one selling [him] or the buyer). For, being received in its own place, the ownership of the first one, and the place in which he had been, is better. Contrariwise too, the reception of the lord of the seventh praises the ownership of the buyer.

And so, the Lunar withdrawal and application must be noted together: for the star from which the Moon is separating, receiving the Moon herself, commends the prior master; but she being received by the one to whom she applies, prefers the buyer to the seller.

Which if a signification of this kind is not present, the position of the eastern lord and the Moon, and their reception in the signs to which they head,[50] resolve the aforesaid things.

---

[49] That is, see what happens to the lord of the east or the Moon (whichever is stronger) when it transits into the next sign. Its current sign indicates the captive's present situation, while the next sign indicates the possible buyer.

[50] That is, we should compare their situation in their current signs, to that of the signs they are about to enter next.

§6.59: On buying slaves—Sahl[51]

Then, let us approach the path for a question submitted as to whether a slave should not be bought. For, once the application of the eastern lord or the Moon with the lord of the sixth, or [the lord of the sixth] to either of them is discovered, it praises the business of buying. The same thing even happens with the lord of the east or the Moon being placed in the sixth,[52] or even with the lord of the sixth in the east. Moreover, a transfer of light made between the significators conveys no less. But if it were not this, it portends it is not going to be.

§6.60: On buying slaves—al-Khayyāt

The lord of the east and the Moon likewise give counsel for procuring a slave, as to whether it would happen or if it would be useful. For if they would apply to the lord of the sixth or it to them, or rather either of them in the sixth or the lord of the sixth in the east, or if there would be a transfer of light between them, they praise the buyer and testify it will come to be; if not, not.

§6.61: For buying a female captive—Sahl[53]

If some inquirer approached about buying a female captive, we put the east and its lord and the Moon in charge of the querent, and we find the signification of him about whom the inquiry is,[54] from the seventh and its lord; also, the eleventh claims the slave-girl or female captive.

With these things being established thusly, a reciprocal application of the significators or any transfer of light must be noted. But we will even pursue their places according to the above-written method,[55] so that in the end, once

---

[51] Cf. *On Quest.* §6.8 and al-Rijāl II.3 (first part).
[52] I follow Vienna here, but the other sources and John's Sahl read "seventh."
[53] Cf. *On Quest.* §6.9.
[54] That is, the seller of the slave girl. The question is fundamentally about a business deal, and only incidentally about the slave. The assignment of the 11th to the slave suggests that she is being bought for sexual pleasure: the eleventh is the fifth from the seventh (the seller's pleasure), and not labor (which would be the twelfth, namely the sixth from the seventh).
[55] See above, §6.59.

a consideration of all things is had, you would be able to wrench out a definite judgment.

§6.62: For buying a female captive—al-Khayyāt

Now, if someone made a question about buying a female slave, let the east and its lord (or at least the Moon) be put in charge of the querent; we give the seventh and its lord to the [seller] about whom the question arises; the eleventh to the female captive.

For, if you should wish to attend to the mutual applications or transfer of light of the significators (in the way that was stated above),[56] there will be no ambiguity left in this matter.

§6.63: Whether profit would follow from a captive—Sahl[57]

If someone made a question about a captive's profit, we have recourse to the eastern lord and the Moon. For, the application of either one with the lord of the seventh (because it occupies the second place from the sixth),[58] or should it apply with them, is a sign of getting the profit. A transfer of light being discovered, brings forth no other judgment. Should they even occupy each other's place, in the manner described in the method written above,[59] it makes the arrangement clear.

§6.64: Whether he could have the captive whom he hopes for—Sahl[60]

If [someone] asks about having a captive whom he hopes for, [look] in this way: the third and the lord of the third must be consulted, because this

---

[56] See §6.60 above.
[57] Cf. *On Quest.* §6.10 and al-Rijāl II.9. Comparing John's Sahl and al-Rijāl to Hugo makes this question somewhat puzzling. On its face, John and al-Rijāl make it about inheriting from slaves or perhaps even being able to own the descendants of slaves. But then al-Rijāl gives different rules if one is speaking about the assets proper of the slave (see §6.64 below).
[58] Reading with Sahl and al-Rijāl. Hugo has us look at the eighth, which is the second from the seventh.
[59] See above, §6.59.
[60] Cf. *On Quest.* §6.11, and al-Rijāl II.9 (second half). In al-Rijāl, this is specifically about obtaining a slave's assets. But how exactly does this differ from §6.63 above?

place is the tenth of the sixth. In the same way and method,[61] the application of the significators and transfer of light and reciprocal occupation of the houses must be judged. For if the manner and status of the aforestated [planets], and even their order[62] is inquired into with diligent industry, the knot of the whole ambiguity could be dissolved most easily.

§6.65: On a murderer or anyone frightening—'Umar

And so, one suspected of blood or homicide demands a two-fold knowledge. For universally, the king himself or another person instead of[63] the king accuses someone of homicide: whence one must have fear from the king or [from someone else] instead of the king.

If therefore the king himself brought someone up on charges of homicide, we put the east in charge of the querent, the Midheaven the king, and the seventh the one who was killed.[64] And the fourth resolves the end of the whole matter. And so, if the lord of the east and that of the tenth would rejoice in a mutual aspect, or at least should there be some star transferring or collecting the light between them, they expose the one suspected to the hands of the querent.[65]

While someone else instead of the king would accuse [the suspect] of homicide, the east watches over the querent, the seventh the one from whom blood is sought,[66] but the tenth the causes of death, the fourth the end. If therefore the lord of the east and of the seventh regard each other, or there is a transfer or collection of light between them, they bring forth the murderer; but without that, not at all. Here however, if the aspect would proceed from a tetragon or opposition or assembly, while Mars himself regarded the lord of the Midheaven and of the east and of the seventh equally, they condemn to death the murderer who is found. But a regard from a trigon or hexagon,

---

[61] See §6.63 above. For example, the lord of the east or the Moon applying to the lord of the third (or the other way around), or if the lord of the east were in the third (or the other way around), or if there were a planet transferring the light between each.
[62] That is, which planet is applying to or transferring to which.
[63] Reading *ante* for *a*, as in the rest of the sentence.
[64] This does not make sense: it should probably indicate the suspected murderer, as below.
[65] 1509 and Vienna add, "namely, the king." But this does not make sense.
[66] I believe this means "the accused."

while reception or concord is not absent, the conflict[67] is mitigated, because victory is left to the one whom was reckoned as the suspect.

§6.66: On the prison where he is held, whether he could escape—'Umar

Now however, with anyone asking about fear, it is good that the east be put in charge of the querent, the seventh the thing to be feared. Which if the king were the one whom he fears, establish the Midheaven for the king. But if the frightened man were asking about himself,[68] [establish] the east and its lord for him. Now, the signification of the fear or thing which he fears, must be sought from the house of his very lord (namely, the eastern one). If therefore the lord of this lodging-place[69] regarded the lord of death, or would apply to [the lord of death] from a tetragon or the opposition or assembly, while that same lord of the fear[70] would hold onto the second or eighth or sixth or twelfth, it gravely threatens the one who was afraid, being shut up in prison.

Finally, in every affair, the testimonies of the Moon will have to be applied. Which if she would be lingering in the fourth, it threatens an underground and obscured prison.

If however [the lord of the fear][71] is regarded from the trigon or hexagon, while the significator of the thing to be feared possesses none of the five[72] aforesaid places, it prepares escape and promises flight.

§6.67: On someone, whether at some time he ought to be captured—Aristotle

If a question of this kind were presented, we give him such advice. The eastern lord being placed in the twelfth, or the one who is in charge of the

---

[67] *Discessio.*
[68] 'Umar seems to be saying that the east signifies both any querent at all, and the frightened man himself.
[69] Does this mean, "the lord of the east," or the dispositor of the lord of the east?
[70] This must be either the lord of the seventh, or else the dispositor of the eastern lord.
[71] Added by Dykes. The Latin reads *sit respectus*, suggesting either that there simply "is" such an aspect, or a masculine subject that is being aspected. I take this paragraph to be continuing the discussion above, after the brief interruption about the Moon.
[72] Unless this is an error for "four," 'Umar might mean the second, eighth, sixth, twelfth, and the fourth (mentioned in the statement about the Moon).

twelfth being in the east: without a doubt it captures him about whom it is asked. Which if it would bear itself otherwise, not at all.

§6.68: Whether he would be held a long time, or even if the captivity would be hard—Aristotle

The roughness of prison, and the delaying of freedom, can be discovered in such a way. For, Mars in the east or the twelfth, or if he would be staying with the lord of each, makes the captivity worse and warns of death. The Tail of the Dragon has a quite similar judgment. But Saturn being arranged as was stated about Mars, even though the captivity is shown to be difficult and long-lasting, one will in no way have to fear death. But if the Sun[73] in the east or twelfth, or with their lords, it threatens and brings death in that prison.

Moreover, if any lucky one (of which kind is Jupiter, Venus, or the head of the Dragon) would be holding onto the east or twelfth or would be staying with their lords, they both remove the difficulties of prison and accelerate his way out. Nevertheless too, if that same Jupiter or Venus or Head of the Dragon would be traversing in the third or ninth, with the regard of the eastern lord of that of the [lord] of the twelfth, they aid a quick and advantageous way out, because these two places are indicative of motion. Which if these benevolents would hold onto the third or ninth from the lord of the east or of the twelfth, they have a judgment of freedom that is near at hand. But with the malevolents being established there (so namely that they would be lingering in the ninth or third from the lord of the east or of the twelfth), there will be a change from that captivity into another, equally difficult one.

In addition, the regard of the benevolents to the lord of the east or that of the twelfth, from a good figure, makes the captivity easier; the perverse regard of the malevolents makes it worse. The partnership of the lucky ones and the malevolents [together], indicates that the captivity is now hard, [but] more often better.

---

[73] According to Vienna. But perhaps this should be the Tail?

§7: SEVENTH HOUSE

7th House	
Whether a marriage will happen	§§7.1-6
When a marriage will happen	§7.7
Impediments to marriage	§§7.8-10
Marry the desired person?	§§7.11-12
Legal & sexual issues	§§7.13-14, 7.18-20, 7.34-36
Is the spouse beautiful?	§7.15
Background of spouse	§§7.16-17
Adultery	§7.21
Number of spouses	§§7.22-23
Relation between spouses, future	§§7.24-27
Which spouse dies first	§§7.28-29
Missing/runaway wives	§§7.30-33
Controversies: the opponents	§§7.37-41, 7.54
Who will win	§§7.42-47
The judge	§§7.48-51
Will there be peace?	§§7.37-41, 7.52, 7.55
Source of controversy	§7.53
Business deals and trades	§§7.56-59
Commodities & prices	§§7.60-71
Fugitives: be captured or return?	§§7.72-74, 7.77, 7.89, 7.91, 7.94, 7.99-100, 7.117, 7.119-21
Stolen goods: be recovered?	§§7.73, 7.76-78, 7.89-90, 7.92, 7.94-98, 7.101-04, 7.124
When recovered	§7.75
Where the goods are	§§7.79, 7.81-83, 7.87, 7.125-31
Where the fugitive is	§§7.80-82, 7.84-85, 7.122-23
Why it was lost	§7.86
Why/how the fugitive escaped	§7.87
Thief's background/nature/figure	§§7.88, 7.105-16, 7.118, 7.143
What was stolen	§§7.132-38
Name of thief	§§7.139-42, 7.144-45
Name/number of thief/goods	§7.146
Partnerships	§§7.147-51
Outcome of partnership	§§7.152-56
Find a specific person?	§§7.157-59
War: opponents & outcome	§§7.160-66, 7.171-72
Quality of war	§§7.167-69
Rebellions	§§7.170, 7.185-7
Peace and concord	§§7.173-76, 7.191

Origin & justice of war	§§7.177, 7.197
Who will win	§§7.178-80
Injuries of one going to war	§§7.181-82
Those sent to war	§§7.183-84
Besieged cities	§§7.188-90, 7.192-95, 7.198
Allies	§7.196
Hunting & fishing	§§7.199-203

Figure 32: Questions of the seventh house

Marriage & Relationships

§7.1: On those things which pertain to the seventh house—Sahl[1]

Moreover, with an inquiry of the seventh being proposed, of which type is for a betrothal and that kind [of thing], whether it would come to be or not. For this, he even looks to see how it would come to be or about its future status, or if it would be hindered, or what is the occasion for the hindrance— which if perhaps that happened, it would be asked what was going to be with respect to these and the like. The east and its lord and the Moon report the signification of the person of the querent, but we put the seventh and its lord in charge of the spouse.

Therefore, the eastern lord [or the Moon][2] applying to the lord of the seventh. or traversing in the seventh, he attains what he was hoping for through his own effort and labor; but with the order changed around, an application of the lord of the seventh made to the eastern [lord], or its traversal in the east, introduces the desired nuptials through the care of the other party.

With these being denied, a transfer of light [by the Moon][3] being discovered between them makes the above-stated business firm, but through intermediaries.

---

[1] Cf. *On Quest.* §7.1 and al-Rijāl II.14.1 (which is really 'Umar, but is very similar).
[2] Adding with John's Sahl.
[3] Adding with John's Sahl.

§7.2: On a marriage-union—'Umar[4]

Then, with a question made about the business of a marriage-union, the method appended below supplies the counsel. For if the querent would be taking this up with respect to his own person, [look at the Ascendant and its lord, and the Moon, and the planet from which she is being separated, and give those to the querent as significators; and the seventh house and its lord, and the planet to which the Moon applies, as significators of the one about whom it is asked. And if the querent were a male, adjoin the Sun to his significators, and make him a partner in the signification; but if the querent were a woman, adjoin Venus with her significators, and make her a partner in the signification. Moreover, if the querent were a woman, give Venus, with the Moon, and the lord of the Ascendant, and the planet from which the Moon is being separated, to her, and to the man the Sun with the seventh and its lord, and the planet to which the Moon applies.][5]

Then too, one will consequently have to determine how and whence the eastern [lord] would apply with [the lord] of the seventh, but [even] the star from which the Moon separates, and to whom she advances.[6] For while they bore themselves thusly,[7] they consecrate an indissoluble marriage-union. However, from the tetragon or opposition or assembly, they introduce a delay, [and] not without difficulty. And with reception being noted in that place (and if it predicts the marriage-chamber), the path of judgment should be kept just as its power and virtue advices. [Reception] being removed, [and with the applications being from squares], a certain difficulty of labor carries out a delay everywhere. But an application made from the trigon or hexagon, [especially with reception], removes every impediment and blesses with the desired union.

Contrariwise however, with an application being removed,[8] [look at the lord of the Ascendant: which if it were received, judge through it; but if you found no reception in it, look to see if there were a reflection of light, or a

---

[4] Cf. al-Rijāl II.14.1.
[5] Adding with al-Rijāl, instead of Hugo's brisk and incomplete "establish the east and its lord, but even the one to whom the Moon applies, and Venus, for him."
[6] Al-Rijāl adds, "or Venus with the Sun."
[7] See Sahl in §7.1 for a list of the typical configurations that show success here, both when the querent's significators are applying or are in the seventh, and when the significators of the seventh are applying or are in the east. Al-Rijāl's 'Umar lists all of these here, but since Sahl, al-Khayyāt, and Dorotheus do the same thing, I will not repeat them.
[8] What follows in brackets is from al-Rijāl.

transfer or collection, between the significators, and judge what the matter will be through that. But] while a transfer [or] one who collects their light would be absent, it becomes useless.[9]

Also, the testimonies of the Lot written below, and of its lord, resemble what was stated above. For [the Lot] will have to be taken up from the degree of the seventh to the degree of its lord; and with the degrees of the east being added to that, one will take up the beginning of the computation from the east itself.[10] Therefore, with the degree of the Lot, and its lord, being found in the east or the seventh, or at least with the Sun and Venus, or should the lord of the Lot regard the eastern lord and [the lord] of the seventh (or either one) exactly, or should there be a collection or transfer between them, it adorns the marriage-chamber with the dowry of the woman. Which if nothing of the aforesaid would follow, the nuptials are made infirm, or at least it prepares a quick divorce.

§7.3: On establishing a marriage-union—al-Kindī[11]

§519. In establishing a marriage,[12] the lord of the Ascendant and of the seventh should be consulted. For, an application of the lord of the Ascendant with the lord of the seventh, and they being regarded by their own lords, and in the pivots or after the pivots, consecrate the nuptials.[13]

§520.[14] Moreover, a Lunar application with Venus, and she being received by Venus, moreover an application of the Moon with the lord of the seventh, are asked to be noted. For all of these convey that the husband's vow and devotion to marry is present. But if the lord of the seventh or Venus herself would apply with the lord of the Ascendant or with the Moon, or if the lord

---

[9] But instead of saying it is useless, al-Rijāl (like Sahl) bids us to now look at the Moon: "See if the Moon is fortunate or received, and purified of the infortunes: it signifies that there will be a marriage-union, especially if the receiver receiving her were purified of the infortunes." I then omit the following in Hugo: "Which if it is postponed, it is blamed on a result gone awry" (*perverso tamen culpatur effectu*).

[10] That is, measure from the Descendant to the lord of the seventh, and project from the Ascendant. I have not seen this Lot before.

[11] Cf. al-Rijāl II.29.

[12] This has to do with love and relationship questions, not electing a time for the marriage. For the election, see *Forty Chapters* Ch. 20.6. As usual, most of this chapter assumes a male querent, and should be adjusted accordingly. But see also §7.19 and 7.16 below.

[13] Al-Rijāl only has them applying, and omits reception or angularity.

[14] For this section, see also §534 below.

of the seventh [would do so] with the Moon, the nuptial union agrees with the fiancée's wishes.

§521. No less does the application of the Sun with Venus bring about nuptials, particularly while the Sun would obtain some dignity in the Ascendant. Moreover, the Sun being received (namely regarded by his own lord) indicates the same thing. Moreover, the cadency of the one applying and the one to which the application happens, dissolves marriages, especially with the estrangement of their own lords from them, once the hope of nuptials they had is virtually complete.

§522. The Sun and the Moon and Venus, even the lord of the seventh and of the Ascendant, being in the pivots, [even if they do not regard each other but they are][15] regarded by their lords, and strong, [indicate that] the effecting of the marriage will follow a wholly extinguished hope of nuptials—then, I say, [it will be] when the direction[16] of the significator [which shows that the marriage would happen][17] reached a pivot, by appointing days or months or years.[18]

§7.4: On marriage—al-Khayyāt[19]

When inquiries of the seventh occur, such as whether or not he would have the result of a marriage-union or betrothal, we put the east and its lord in charge of the querent. The spouse is handed over to the seventh and its lord.

Therefore, an application of the eastern lord or the Moon with the lord of the seventh being made, it promises that he will get what he was hoping for, through the querent's effort and labor; it is even the same thing should the lord of the east or the Moon be lingering in the seventh. But conversely, the lord of the seventh applying to the eastern [lord] or traversing in the east, denotes that the marriage-union is going to proceed through effort on his part and the consent of the woman, and without much labor.

---

[15] Adding with al-Rijāl.
[16] *Atazir*, omitting Hugo's explanatory *computatio videlicet aut transmutatio*.
[17] Adding with al-Rijāl.
[18] I imagine this procedure could also be followed in nativities.
[19] Cf. al-Rijāl II.14.1.

Which if these things were absent, but while the Moon (or any other [planet]) would transfer light between them, the matter is established through messengers and mediators.

Moreover, the significator[20] managing something in the seventh[21] and rendering counsel to the lord of the east in the tenth, testifies that it happens. Moreover, the Moon in the Midheaven makes his hope arrive according to his pleasure. Now, if she would render counsel to some [star] situated in the tenth ([and] to the Sun is better), he celebrates public nuptials, but through the royal hands.

§7.5: On marriage—Dorotheus[22]

Whenever a question of the seventh would be given (such as is about a marriage-union and what is of this kind), the east and its lord, with the Moon, designates the very person of the querent. But we hand the spouse over to the seventh and its lord, and Venus.

And so, an application of the eastern lord or the Moon with the lord of the seventh (or preferably they being arranged in the seventh), promises he is going to achieve his hope through his own effort. But the lord of the seventh applying to the eastern one, brings about nuptials through the care and pressure and benevolence of the wife. [The lord of the seventh] being in the east, averts difficulty from the wife's side.

Indeed, a transfer of light made from one to the other by means of the Moon or a light star, confirms the matter through intermediaries.

Which if it rendered counsel to the eastern lord, while the significator itself would manage something belonging to the querent,[23] [and] with the eastern lord holding onto the Midheaven, it is a sign of establishing the marriage-union. Moreover, the Moon being received and she being in the tenth, increases in a more lofty way [his] name and reputation. Also, she rendering

---

[20] Undoubtedly the Moon.
[21] Dorotheus has "the querent." But I think al-Khayyāt is probably right. Al-Khayyāt is describing the Moon (either ruling the seventh, or separating from the lord of the seventh, or perhaps from a planet in the seventh), and applying to a lord of the east which is placed in the tenth.
[22] Cf. al-Rijāl II.14.1.
[23] This should probably be "seventh," as with al-Khayyāt. Dorotheus is describing the Moon (either ruling the seventh, or separating from the lord of the seventh, or perhaps from a planet in the seventh), and applying to a lord of the east which is placed in the tenth.

counsel to a star appearing in the Midheaven, likewise lavishes excellence and a name and prosperity. The Sun himself is not otherwise, but that brings it about through the royal hands.

§7.6: Concerning a marriage-union, slaughter, war, controversy, partnership, and a fugitive—Jirjis

Put the east over the querent. The seventh comprehends the aforesaid things, if they should come into question. Therefore, the eastern lord being strong, while the one which is in charge of the seventh would appear weak, promises that the querent is going to get the thing sought.[24] With the eastern lord appearing weak, while the lord of the seventh prevails, it makes the querent subject to the rulership of the thing sought. It will be permitted to judge in this manner about the rest of things.

§7.7: When someone ought to take a wife—Aristotle

With a question being proposed as to whether someone would happen to be blessed with marriage at some time, we give the Lunar counsel. For, her being in the seventh, regarding the Sun or Venus in a good way, or if the eastern lord would be in the seventh or with its lord, or at least if it would support the lord of the seventh with a benign aspect (or the other way around), it consecrates the marriage and the marriage bed. Which if it would bear itself otherwise, affirm that he is going to marry no one in that year (if the question were posed about that year).

But as to when this ought to happen: the application of the degree of the Moon (namely to the Sun or Venus) or of the eastern lord to the lord of the seventh, celebrates the promised nuptials (but if it were from the turning signs, days, if from the common ones,[25] months; if from the firm ones, toward that many years).

But if it was asked about that year (if it is already agreed that he will marry), the lord of the east in the seventh or being with the lord of the seventh, or even the lord of the seventh in the east, accelerates the nuptials. Which if they were not so, but they do regard each other, the one which applies in

---

[24] Obviously this pertains to cases of conflict; one would not want the significator of a potential spouse to be weak.
[25] Reading *communibus* for *mobilibus*, here and in the next paragraph.

firm [signs indicates that] he unites in marriage at the end of the year; in turning [signs], at the beginning of the year; in common ones, there will be a delay of nuptials up to eight months.

In addition, with Venus being found in the ninth or[26] under the Lunar aspect, or if the lord of the seventh would be lingering in the ninth, he will marry a foreigner.

§7.8: What the cause of the impediment is—Sahl[27]

I believe that one must attend to [the one which] gathers the counsel of the other:[28] which if you would find it to be corrupted by a perverse aspect, or cadent or retrograde, it stains and denies the matter, and the impediment of the whole matter proceeds from it. If one is asked about the manner and cause of the impediment, let the status of the corrupting malevolent be sought. For, it having taken up the rulership of the second or eighth, it disturbs the prepared marriage-union on the occasion of the dowry; which if it would rule over the twelfth, the spouse turns him down, and her ignobility will become the occasion of the impediment. Again, with it claiming rulership of the sixth, we note that he is unworthy.[29] But whenever it was the lord of the fourth, it blames the parents, and testifies that the fault lies with them. If the third, the brothers; and through the rest of the houses in this manner.

Finally, if there were some star discovered which cut off the light of the application, we should attend to its domicile with no less effort: for by it we often indicate the occasion of turning the marriage-union awry, according to the status and nature of the things [in that house]. For if it would be have rulership over the fifth, it would lead the offspring of either one into blame;[30] but if over the sixth, a disease or some defect of the body will impede [the marriage-union]. But here, if the star transferring their light would furnish the

---

[26] This should probably be "and."
[27] Cf. *On Quest.* §§7.1-7.2, and al-Rijāl II.14.2.
[28] That is, the one which is receiving the application.
[29] Or, "ignoble, base" (*degenerem*).
[30] John's Sahl suggests that the woman is already married and has children she has not yet disclosed.

cause of the corruption,[31] we believe the impediment will come through intermediaries or bridesmen.

§7.9: Whether an impediment would occur—al-Khayyāt

Next, too, the receiver of counsel and the one which gathers the counsel of the other, must be noted. For, it being corrupted or cadent, or being unlucky from anywhere, corrupts the whole business; and the kind of impediment particularly emanates from it. It being an infortune, if it would rule over the second or eighth, it is necessary that the dowry will be the impediment (from this side or that one). But if it were the lord of the sixth, it disgraces him and he blames the greed of the parents. But if it is in charge over the twelfth, the ignobility of the spouse or the greed of [her] parents does the harm. But if it is the lord of the fourth, the fault of the parents does the harm. But if of the third, it portends the fault of the brothers. But if it would seize the rulership of the fifth, it mixes in the fault and impediment of another's offspring. And one will have to follow through in this way according to the nature of the rest of the houses.

But if a star transferring their light would heap on the corruption, the corruption of matters proceeds from messengers.

But if any lucky one would impede by cutting off the light, while it would agree with [the matter] in nature,[32] the effect will follow after a delay; but the detriment belongs to the one which impedes the light, if it would seize the rulership of the sixth or eighth or twelfth or even the fourth, and if it would be lingering in a firm sign and in a pivot. For in the rest [of the houses] it is believed to be less harmful.

The[33] east being double-bodied, he joins in marriage to another one than the one he was hoping for; but the same statement is given about the wife.

But that one is betrothed first, whose significator walks through a pivot. For the one which is stronger will enter first into the bedchamber of marriage.

---

[31] That is, if it were an infortune and perhaps transferring the light from a difficult aspect. But al-Khayyāt and Dorotheus have this planet as a fortunate one.
[32] That is, if it is a planet that does not hinder marriage.
[33] For this paragraph, cf. also al-Rijāl II.16 (end). But al-Rijāl has both of the significators (while indicating marriage) in common signs.

§7.10: On the cause of the impediment—Dorotheus

Furthermore, the receiver of the counsel being corrupted or cadent, stains a matter which is as though already completed, and it denies and destroys [it]. Which if this [receiver] were the lord of the second or the eighth, it testifies that it will be through the impediment of the dowry.[34] Which if the lord of the twelfth would be the one corrupted, the ignobility of the spouse and the greed of the parents will cause the harm. The corruption of the lord of the sixth disgraces the querent. Moreover, with the lord of the fourth being the one corrupted, the parents. But if it claims the rulership of the third, it portends the fault of the brothers. If this one would seize the rulership of fifth, it portends it is the fault of the offspring of the wife, and likewise the husband.[35] Likewise, with it claiming the rulership of the sixth, a disease or some defect of the body will hinder it. And in this manner through the rest of the signs, according to their signification.

Here, if perhaps some star would cut off the light, in the same way its domicile blocks the results of a marriage-union, just as the nature of the sign demands. For, it being the lord of the eighth or twelfth, brings the dowry into blame; of the third, brothers; and in this manner through the rest of the signs.

If a [star] which transfers light is a fortunate one, and agreeing with the nature of each, after the difficulty and impediment it does not deny the effecting [of the marriage].

I even warn you wholly to beware lest a malevolent cut off the light, nor even that the lord of the eighth or sixth or twelfth or fourth would be found in a firm sign and in a pivot. Which if they would subsist [in a place] lower than that,[36] [their harm] is more slackened.

---

[34] Reading *dotis* for *dotem*.
[35] Dorotheus probably means it is the husband's children, if the wife is the querent.
[36] That is, in a succedent place or preferably a cadent place.

§7.11: Whether he would marry the wife whom he hoped for—Dorotheus

Furthermore,[37] the east being double-bodied blesses the querent with marriage to another person than the one he reckoned on. Likewise, [for a female querent],[38] he couples with another.

On the other hand, the significator of the wife being in a pivot, hastens her nuptials. The eastern lord occupying a pivot puts marriage in front of the man. But with each being established in a pivot, it is necessary for the stronger one, and the one which agrees more familiarly with the pivot, to precede the other [into the bedchamber].[39]

§7.12: Whether someone marries the wife he was hoping for—Jirjis

Therefore, Venus regarding her own proper house and the east at the hour of the question, promises [that woman]. With a regard of this kind being denied, it wholly speaks against it. Now, if she would regard her own house but not the east, he will rather suffer a serious rebuff from the woman asked about.

§7.13: Whether the marriage-union is lawful—'Umar[40]

But whether or not the marriage-union is lawful or unlawful, is resolved by such a method. If therefore the lord of the east or of the seventh, or the one to which the Moon applies (or from whom she withdraws), even Venus and the Sun,[41] would apply to Saturn or Mars [after the application that shows marriage],[42] or there is an application of [Saturn or Mars] with the three significators which belong to the woman, they consecrate unlawful nuptials. Which if, before they apply to the infortunes, there would be an

---

[37] For this paragraph, cf. also al-Rijāl II.16 (end). But al-Rijāl has both of the significators (while indicating marriage) in common signs.
[38] *Sponsam*.
[39] That is, according to Hugo's reading in §7.9.
[40] Cf. al-Rijāl II.17.
[41] Hugo is not being entirely clear: we are supposed to isolate the three significators for each party (the lord of the appropriate house, the planet related to the Moon, and the general significator of the man and woman) so as to see which one is being affected: see §7.2 above for these significators of 'Umar's.
[42] Adding based on al-Rijāl.

application of them with the aforesaid significators of the betrothed (while however they would apply [to the infortunes] afterwards), even though at first it comes to be in a lawful way, in the end they are incompatible with the laws.

§7.14: On the wife's sexual impurity—Sahl[43]

If perhaps a question would be given about her chastity (or rather, sexual impurity), one will have recourse to the lord of the east and the Moon. Either of them traversing in the same degree with Mars, conceals the adultery within her own home. Which if they would hold onto different degrees of the same sign, it hides a neighbor as the seducer. But the separation of either one from Mars calls her back from the adultery. Also, either one applying to a Mars appearing in its[44] own house: she is in love with a lover from outside.[45]

Which if either would apply to Jupiter,[46] she is vexed with the love of a powerful man or prince. [But if the application were to the Sun, say that she loves a man more noble than he is.][47] But if it would apply to Mercury, it marks one instructed in teachings, or some merchant, and a young man. And an application of this kind being made with Venus, she burns for her own sex, against the customary practices of nature. Moreover, with any of them being placed under the regard of Jupiter, she will be corrected of her own accord and not by any counselor.[48]

Which if the Sun regarded either of them, she is called back [from the adultery] out of fear of the prince.[49] Finally, with either of them traversing under the aspect of Venus, it calls her back, being aware of fear lest he hasten to divulge it.

---

[43] Cf. *On Quest.* §7.7 and al-Rijāl II.18.
[44] In al-Rijāl, this clearly means that Mars is in the house of the other planet.
[45] That is, outside of their area; or perhaps, "foreign, from abroad" (*extrinsecus*). But al-Rijāl identifies this as a man who wants to be with her and marry her, but that she has done nothing yet. Perhaps al-Rijāl understands this to be the case if there is no application.
[46] This probably assumes that they are still applying to Mars as well, since he indicates the adultery itself.
[47] Adding with al-Rijāl (John's Sahl also omits this).
[48] John's Sahl credits a religious experience or awakening as the reason for her ending the affair.
[49] Or perhaps, she fears the powerful person she has had the affair with (al-Rijāl).

Moreover, whenever Saturn and Mercury would equally be regarding the lord of the east and the Moon together from the same sign, they reveal sexual impurity with an old man who is putting on the appearance of a young man.[50] Here, if the Moon would apply to a Mercury and Saturn established together, they testify that the boyfriend himself is referred to their manner and nature—and a corresponding judgment will arise about the rest of the stars, according to their own proper status and nature.

§7.15: Whether she is good looking—al-Kindī[51]

§526-27a. Also,[52] [if someone is] worried about [her] form, let a view of the Ascendant be put forth, and the head and face ascribed to it. But to the second the neck, the third the hands and arms; but the chest obtains the fourth; also, the fifth the belly up to the groin; the sixth, the hips and sides; but the seventh, from the lower groin and the kidneys. Also the eighth, the places of longing; the ninth place, the buttocks and upper portion of the legs; but the tenth, the lower [part] and knees; the eleventh, the shins; the twelfth takes the feet. Therefore, it seems that the individual limbs must be noted individually according to the figure of the animal which is designated by them, and the form of its limbs.

§527b. And no little consideration is needed for this: [namely] in what place of the circle the Moon is made fortunate: for that limb ([designated] by that sign which the Moon is holding onto) being lucky, must be noted as being proper, and an appropriate marking is asserted as being there.

§528. But in a sign where a corrupted Moon dwells, it afflicts the limb belonging to its authority with some deformity or ugly sign. Moreover, the augmentation or increase of the Moon[53] designates some augmenting [in that limb] beyond proper measure; decreasing, it suggests something is missing from the body. Moreover, [in] the middle between increase and decrease, it disfigures the skin and surface of the limbs [attributed] to that sign.

§529. But the color of the sign which the Moon is holding onto, and of the star by which the Moon is corrupted, designates of what color the blemish (or rather, mark) consists.

---

[50] Al-Rijāl amusingly says that he wears a hairpiece.
[51] Cf. al-Rijāl II.30.2.
[52] From here through §532, cf. al-Rijāl II.30b.
[53] Al-Rijāl says that this is an increase in her motion, not in her size or phase.

§530. But from what nature this foulness came forth, an earthy sign of the Moon, and her corrupting star being earthy, testify that it is cold and dry. But they being watery, cold and moist. Airy, hot and moist. But fiery, they establish that it is of a hot and dry nature.

§531. Which if the sign which the Moon is holding onto, and that of her corrupting star, consisted of different [natures], it is believed that the nature of each must be united in the discernment of this matter.

§532. However, [if] a fortunate one traverses the sign of any limb, it commends its looks; and an infortune exposes its ugliness. And so, in all things about whose status it is asked, let us remember to respond in a similar way, being instructed in an appraisal of this opinion.

§7.16: Whether she is rich or from a poor home—al-Kindī[54]

§533. Discern[55] thusly whether she is rich or from a poor household. For, if such a question preceded [the engagement] (since the lord of the seventh claims the signification of that),[56] the lord of the eighth applying with the lord of the seventh, and made fortunate, likewise the Moon regarding the eighth and its lord, [but] the infortunes being estranged from the eighth, increase the woman's riches. Which if they bear themselves otherwise, they testify to scarcity. But their middling [quality] brings forth a mediocrity of assets and possessions. If however the significator of the question [were] the Ascendant [because the agreement has already been made],[57] let it be decided

---

[54] Cf. al-Rijāl II.31 (first part).
[55] Cf. al-Rijāl II.31. This question is really directed towards learning the size of the prospective bride's dowry. This is still a very important issue in traditional marriages such as in India.
[56] Namely, of prospective partners *before* the engagement. See §7.19.
[57] Adding based on Robert. But al-Rijāl distinguishes the approaches this way: if a man asks about the woman, look at the seventh and eighth; but if the woman asks about the man, give her the Ascendant and the second. Now, on the one hand, al-Rijāl might simply mean that the querent gets the Ascendant and second in any case, and that the betrothed always gets the seventh and eighth. But on the other hand, if Robert is correct about the text, and the distinction is between agreements that are only potential (seventh and eighth) and those already made (Ascendant and second), the rationale might be this: when asking about a potential dowry, the question is essentially about a business deal: one family is negotiating and contracting with the other. In that case, the seventh and eighth represent the other family as business partners, so as to investigate their wealth. But if the betrothal is already official, then the couple are legally united, and so a question about their enrichment in the marriage is really a question about *their* finances: hence the Ascendant and the second.

from the Ascendant and the second, in just the way that advice is sought from the seventh and eighth for the other [question].

§7.17: Which one is more noble—Aristotle

If you wanted to be certain about this, let there be recourse to the lord of the seventh and the eastern [lord] equally. For, the lord of the seventh walking through the pivots of the seventh, but the eastern [lord] after the pivots of the first, claims she is more noble. Likewise, the lord of the seventh being after its own pivots, but the eastern [lord] in its own remote [places], [means] the same thing. In this way one will have to judge contrariwise through the eastern lord, with respect to a husband. Which if there were an equality of [their] places, neither surpasses the other in [family] background.

§7.18: Whether a suspicion of sexual impurity is true—'Umar[58]

Moreover, for two people, whether they are justly suspected of adultery, grant the east to the querent, and the seventh to the one about whom it is asked; however, the star from which the Moon is withdrawing, designates [the woman] who is being suspected, [and the one to which she applies indicates him who is suspected of having slept with her].[59] And so, here comes something that must be noted: if any peregrine[60] or western[61] stars occupy the seventh, [or] even the one to which the Moon applies, [because they will be significators].

Now, if the eastern lord would approach the lord of the seventh, [or a planet appearing in the seventh house], or the one to whom the Moon applies (by any kind of application), while the infortunes would regard the aforewritten stars from any direction, they really testify that he is justly accused of sexual impurity, and that their bond would come about unlawfully[62]

---

[58] Cf. al-Rijāl II.20 (first half). I have added clarifying material from al-Rijāl in brackets.
[59] The question seems to assume that a suspicious husband is asking about his own wife and another man.
[60] This is like the material on thieves: if there is a peregrine star in the seventh, then it denotes someone who "doesn't belong," namely the paramour.
[61] Reading *occidentalibus* with al-Rijāl for Hugo's "or rather, familiar." But this word can also mean "setting," which suggests planets under, or about to go under, the Sun's rays (which implies concealment).
[62] Omitting *licite* (Hugo) and reading for *legitime* (al-Rijāl).

according to the intention of the querent. Which if the three aforewritten significators would be blessed by any aspect of the fortunate ones, with that of the infortunes being wholly denied, they grant a sound and respectable response, according to the view of the inquiry.[63] But if there is an aspect of each in common, the truth of the judgment will equally deflect to each side.[64]

§7.19: On the chastity or sexual impurity of the wife—al-Kindī[65]

§523a. Furthermore, if someone suggests a question about the purity (or rather, sexual immorality) of the wife, the sign of the Ascendant should be noted—if, I say, it is asked specifically about the self-control of her whom he has arranged [a marriage contract with],[66] [that is, whether she] will be led astray. Which if someone [only] burning with the delight of [possible] conjugal fetters should seek [to know] whether or not he is going to marry a pure woman, let the lord of the seventh be consulted in place [of the lord] of the Ascendant. Venus and the Moon are supportive for both [kinds of questions].[67]

§523b-24a. [The significators] being in firm signs and in the regard of the lucky ones, promise she is pure, with her virginity unimpaired. In fact, the

---

[63] Al-Rijāl says that they will have had sex, but that it was lawful through marriage. Maybe this implies that the querent is some third party, who did not know that the two were properly married.

[64] This does not really make sense either, unless we assume something like the temporary marriages often practiced even today in the Middle East. In many Islamic cultures, sex can be made legitimate through a perfunctory marriage vow that is specified only to last for a certain amount of time (even if for only a few hours), with an immediate divorce afterwards.

[65] Cf. al-Rijāl II.30.1.

[66] Adding based on Robert.

[67] Like Hugo, al-Rijāl simply groups the Moon and Venus along with the other lords; nor does al-Rijāl mention the seventh at all. Robert distinguishes the Moon and Venus, saying: "First one must discern whether the question comes to be after the contract has been made firm, or before. Therefore, after the contract we embrace the lord of the east and the Moon; but before, the lord of the seventh and Venus." (See also al-Kindī's §533 of §7.16 above, and the differences between Robert and al-Rijāl there.) Robert's (or al-Kindī's) rationale seems to be this: the Moon is consulted once the engagement is settled, because she represents a female spouse (or fiancée); but Venus is consulted before it is settled, because she signifies *desire*. But this does not really answer the question as to why the Ascendant is chosen in one case, but the seventh in the other.

infortunes possessing the role of the fortunate ones, do not take away [her] virginity, but they do exhibit sexual immorality.[68]

§524b. But if these significators are holding onto double-bodied signs and are regarded by the fortunate ones, they do convey that she has been violated, but they preserve [her] purity.[69] Moreover, if the infortunes are allotted the role of the fortunate ones, they claim a corrupted and sexually impure woman. (This is affirmed particularly by the regard of Mars.) Moreover, the mutual regard of the Sun and Moon designate public sexual immorality, if they would even be looking at Mars.[70] Which if the Sun and the Moon were deprived of mutual regard, and estranged from Mars, they conceal the crime of longing.

§525. Moreover, should the Ascendant and the pivots be set up in convertible signs, and the infortunes in the same place, they indicate inextinguishable longing. Which if the regard of Mars is present, she will crave the sexual intercourse of each sex against moral [law], to boot. But if the fortunate ones would take over in place of the infortunes, they testify that she is of immoderate [sexual] longing, but [has] a sense of shame[71] and conceals her own crimes, [but] at last everything becomes public.

§7.20: On chastity or sexual impurity —Jirjis

The east being a firm [sign], preaches the man's chastity; a turning [sign] defames him. The firmness of the seventh announces a chaste woman; but a two-parted one speaks against that.

§7.21: On the shape of her with whom someone is having an affair—Aristotle

In order that this may be discovered, the east should be noticed. For, Aries or Scorpio being in the east, or Aquarius or Capricorn, while Venus

---

[68] The benefic or malefic quality of the planets shows conventional moral purity or impurity respectively, while the quadruplicity indicates the extent of actual sexual activity—such that fixed signs show self-control, but the movable signs something more like promiscuity.

[69] In other words, she has some sexual experience but has not lost her virginity.

[70] Mars can mean prostitution (which is what Robert and al-Rijāl identify), but perhaps it simply means there is scandal and gossip involved.

[71] Omitting the puzzling *et ad horam*, which is not reflected in Robert or al-Rijāl.

should happen to be staying in one of these, reveals a young girl.[72] Moreover, with Mercury occupying one of these, while the Moon would go through any of them (it being the east), it testifies that the light of the candle was not absent.[73] This being done at the seventh hour (which belongs to Venus), it is clear that she was chubby and fair and a young girl. But if Venus were together with the Moon, and she is oppressed by [some] power.[74] Moreover, Venus with the Moon in a domicile of Mars: she had really reached menstruation.

Should Taurus or Libra be setting, with Venus lingering there, [it means] he has been acquainted with his wife. With the sign of Gemini arising, he knew her once; with the Moon lingering in her own proper house, she has become pregnant. If Venus would possess the east with the [Head of the] Dragon, it testifies she is noble and of good stock. But if she would be staying with Saturn in the west, it testifies she was someone dependent on him[75] and of a lower rank.

§7.22: Which suspected man a woman has had sex with—'Umar[76]

[If the querent suspects that a women has had sex with some man among many, put these named men in order as the first, second, and third.] With a distinction being made between the lord of the east and the Moon, the one of them which regarded the east deservedly claims the signification for these things.

Therefore, if that significator itself would bless two or three stars with its own aspect, the first [man] is designated by that first star to which it applies. The one to which the second application is, determines the second [man]. Thus then, the third [man] principally responds to the third one which it approaches—namely, according to what we taught above about the regard of the Moon and the eastern lord into the east itself.

---

[72] This seems to mean that Venus in the east suggests someone young, while the signs of the malefics there suggests something sordid (since it is a case of adultery).
[73] *Lumen candelae non abfuisse.* I am not sure what this metaphor means.
[74] *Vi opprimitur.* I am not sure what this means, and it must be some kind of error.
[75] *Clientela.* This would be like a secretary or intern, or someone else whose livelihood or job opportunities depended on him.
[76] Cf. al-Rijāl II.20 (second part). I have rewritten the title to reflect the content of the chapter, and have added material in brackets to clarify the ambiguities in Hugo. Hugo's original title read: "How many men a woman is going to have."

If an application is absent, the first lord of the triplicity[77] suggests the first [man], but the second one the second [man], but the third lord of the triplicity of the east reveals the third [man], and so on after that if there were more.[78]

Afterwards,[79] look at the application which the lord of the Ascendant has towards the significator of any of them, and at the aspects of the fortunes and the infortunes, and just as we stated at the beginning of this chapter.[80]

§7.23: How many men a woman is going to have—Jirjis

How many male signs there were between the seventh up to Jupiter, promise that many men. But if Saturn, Mercury, and Mars regard the seventh and Jupiter (or only one [of them]), they suggest [the men] will be slaves. If not, [they will be] free men.

Conversely, for a man, how many wives he is going to have: how many female signs there were from the seventh to Venus, furnishes the bedchamber with the torch of matrimony that many times.

§7.24: On the future status of the marriage-union—Sahl[81]

With a question proposed about the future status of the marriage, we consult the significators and their applications: [namely, the lord of the east and the lord of the seventh]. For, an application made from the opposition: they sow anger and discord. If from the tetragon, now they disagree, now they are

---

[77] This must mean the triplicity lords of the significator (whether it is the lord of the Ascendant or the Moon, as described above).

[78] I am not sure what this could mean, since there are only three triplicity rulers for each element.

[79] I have omitted a paragraph by Hugo here which must have been intended for another question, such as §7.18 above: "Which if you are aiming to scrutinize their helpers in this matter, the star which possesses the seventh presents the supports for the one about whom it is asked; but the ones which are staying with the Moon (and in her assembly) do so for the other disgraced person."

[80] That is, in §7.18 above. I think 'Umar's method is this: first, identify the possible adulterers from the applications of the Moon or from the triplicity lords of the significator (whether that is the Moon or the lord of the Ascendant). Then, examine each of these planets individually, to see which ones show positive and lawful influences (benevolents) or negative and unlawful influences (malevolents).

[81] Cf. *On Quest.* §7.3, and al-Rijāl II.15 for the end of this section.

called back to peace. From the trigon or hexagon it marks the most firm love.

Moreover, the Lunar reception, or the position of the eastern lord in a pivot (while it takes up the application of the other), shows a firm and constant rulership over the whole marriage, by the husband.

And so, with either of the two significators being retrograde or turned away, or if it is corrupted in any other way, [or if it is the one applying],[82] the one whom it signifies will be subject to the authority of the other one.

But if they hold onto the same sign, they will not share in common, nor do they consecrate the marriage-union in a friendly way.

But this:[83] if the Moon regarded the east and is corrupted, it disturbs the marriage-union itself with blaming and dishonor. If perhaps a corrupting malevolent should occupy the east, it ascribes the dishonor and blame to the husband; one will have to pursue it in this way through the rest of the houses, as they follow one another: for the one in which the malevolent traverses, will illuminate the whole opinion according to the nature and proper quality of it.

But finally,[84] if the Sun happened to be found corrupted, we believe it is harmful and adverse by means of the husband; but a corrupted Venus wholly turns against the wife. The Lunar corruption impairs [both] with mistreatment.

§7.25: Whether they love each other or not—al-Kindī[85]

§534.[86] Once certainty about the marriage has been gotten, let such a consideration be had as to whether one [spouse] would be conquered by the obliged love of the other: for if the lord of the Ascendant and of the seventh would enjoy a common aspect, [and] in the same way should the lord of the Ascendant, and Venus, even the Moon [and] the lord of the seventh be held [together] by a friendly regard, and be received, they signify the common esteem of each. But if the regard of just one of them would be noted, the

---

[82] Adding with John's Sahl and based on al-Khayyāt and Dorotheus below. In a situation like this, the planet which is lighter and applying shows more eagerness and therefore more personal need.
[83] Cf. *Carmen* V.16.37.
[84] Cf. *Carmen* V.16.1-5.
[85] Cf. al-Rijāl II.31 (second part).
[86] Cf. al-Rijāl II.31.

affection is proven to belong only to the one whose receiving comes to be.[87] And so it will be permitted to judge in this way with the rest of [matters] about which a question of this kind proceeded.[88]

§7.26: On the future status of the marriage-union—al-Khayyāt

If therefore the status of the marriage-union came into question, the application of the significators [of the first and seventh houses] must be consulted. Which if [the application] is one of opposition, it disturbs the marriage-union with anger and hatred. But if from the tetragon, it mixes in now peace, now discord, in turn. From the trigon or hexagon, it makes the love firm and introduces concord. Nor does the Moon's reception indicate less.

But the one whose significator was scorched or corrupted or cadent, and[89] if that same one would render counsel, it brings in discord to his companion and threatens quarrels; it even makes the one over whom it is in charge be subject to the other man. But if they would linger in the same sign equally, they do not thus make the concord of marriage firm.

But if the Moon, regarding the east, were corrupted, it threatens disgrace in the marriage-union. An infortune corrupting their places [and] being placed in the east, testifies that the disgrace will be from the husband, and the rest of the domiciles follow each other in this manner too.

Nevertheless, the Sun being corrupted by a malevolent, is thoroughly hostile to the husband, and makes him an enemy.[90] The corruption of Venus is inimical to the wife. A corrupted Moon throws each into confusion.

---

[87] Robert puts this a bit more intriguingly: "if one of the significators conveys, [but] the other refuses." This sounds like a case of "returning" (*ITA* III.19), but also see "not-reception" in my introduction and Sahl §1.1 above, and al-Rijāl I.10. In his own version of this passage, al-Rijāl says, "and if one of their significators received the other, but the other did not receive it, say that the receiving one esteems the other, and that the received does not esteem the receiving one."

[88] Reading *processerit* for *praecesserit*, following the verb in *Judges*.

[89] Reading *et* for *aut* ("or").

[90] *Inimicum ingerit*.

§7.27: On the future status of the marriage-union—Dorotheus

Moreover, the status of the marriage-union is discerned from the application and regard of the significators. Which if it is one of opposition, it sows anger and quarrels in each, and hatred. From the assembly and tetragon, it mixes peace with discord. Moreover, being in the same sign for the most part heaps on quarrels. From the trigon and hexagon, it makes the love firm and they denote mutual benevolence. The Lunar reception also shows nothing else.

On[91] the other hand, that one of the significators which was in a pivot, and if it is the receiver of the counsel, portends that the [person] whom it designates, will be in charge over and dominate the other. But that one of them which is cadent, it subjects that one whom [that planet] watches over, to the command of the other.

Furthermore, if the Moon would regard the east and be corrupted, it signals beforehand the disgrace of the marriage-union. Likewise, a malevolent occupying a pivot imposes crimes upon the husband; and [treat] the rest of the domiciles just as they follow each other, according to their proper quality.

Finally, the Sun being corrupted from somewhere, will harm the husband in the betrothal. Venus being adverse, is inimical to the wife. And the Moon being thus throws each into confusion.

§7.28: Whether the man or wife would die first—Jirjis

For an affair of this kind, it is good to note the lords of the east and of the seventh: namely which one would enter into scorching first. For if the eastern lord would be burned first, it is fatal to the husband. But the prior scorching of the western lord, kills the wife.

§7.29: Which one would die first, the husband or wife—Aristotle

However, so that you might discover which would die first, inspect thusly: for the one which first, heading towards scorching, [actually] enters the solar rays, will be the first to depart the life-giving air. If therefore the one who is

---

[91] Cf. *Carmen* V.16.30-32, where this is presented as a synastry matter. If the Moon of one chart is in the sixth of the other, then the former will subjugate the latter.

being burned up would be lingering in the turning [signs], it accelerates death; in a double-bodied one, not so much; in firm ones, it prolongs it.

§7.30: On a lost wife: whether or not she would return—Sahl[92]

With an inquiry about a lost wife, as to whether or not she would return, we give the counsel of the Sun and Venus.

For,[93] the traversal of Venus in the upper hemisphere (and well placed from the east), while the Sun would be lingering below[94] the earth, brings her back in subjection (however indignant), with the great effort of the man.

But[95] we will even observe the Lunar place at the hour of the flight itself or of a question of this kind. For, the Moon already crossing over the opposition of the Sun, brings the fleeing wife back quickly; she being found on the near side of the opposition,[96] portends a delay.

Moreover,[97] the retrogradation of Venus in either hour, or at least appearing western,[98] calls the penitent [wife] back of her own accord. Being[99] eastern and retrograde, it shows that pain greatly afflicts the man, but she is stubborn in her malice.

§7.31: On a fugitive or dismissed wife—'Umar

Moreover, we hand the signification of the male spouse over to the east, even to the star from which the Moon is separated, and the Sun; but the seventh and its lord, and no less the star to which the Moon applies, and Venus, will be in charge of the wife who was dismissed by the man or who had fled.

Next, if these three significators [of the wife][100] regarded the east from a trigon or hexagon, they lead a cheerful wife back to the husband, in a benign way. But from a tetragon or opposition or assembly, with reception being denied, it seems to be prejudicial against a return. However, if reception is

---

[92] Cf. *On Quest.* §7.4 and al-Rijāl II.22.
[93] Cf. *Carmen* V.17.6.
[94] Reading "under" with John's Sahl, for "above."
[95] Cf. *Carmen* V.17.7-8.
[96] That is, not yet to the opposition.
[97] Cf. *Carmen* V.17.2.
[98] John's Sahl has her both retrograde and western.
[99] Cf. *Carmen* V.17.5.
[100] Added by Dykes, since these are the only ones which make sense.

present,[101] she is brought back both unwilling and coerced. Finally, with the three aforewritten significators being deprived of the aspect already stated, while there is not one who would collect the light or draw it back to the lord of the east,[102] a return is really denied.

§7.32: On a wife who has fled or been sent away—al-Khayyāt

Now, if a question is presented about the return of a lost wife or one fleeing some indignity,[103] the Sun and Venus will have to be consulted.

Venus being above the earth and well placed, but should the Sun and the Full Moon be staying under the earth, she will return unwillingly, [but] not without difficulty and the effort of the man.

In addition, the place of the Moon at the hour of her departure or the question, comes to be noted. If she has already left the opposition behind, it announces she is going to return quickly; before the opposition, it postpones it.

But[104] Venus being retrograde or western at each hour, already leads her back, regretful, of her own will. Being eastern and going out of scorching, it will call her back, moved by regret, to her own household gods.[105]

§7.33: On a missing wife—Dorotheus

On the other hand, if perhaps a question will be given about the return of a missing wife, Venus will have to be consulted, with the Sun.

For, Venus in a pivot, above the earth [and] placed in a domicile of fortunate ones, while the Sun and Full Moon are staying under the earth, they bring back the missing wife with the greatest labor.

Then, the Moon already crossing the opposition of the Sun at the hour of the question or of [the wife's] flight, means a quick return, for the waxing Moon prolongs [it].

---

[101] That is, with the aspect being a tetragon or opposition, or it being an assembly.
[102] Reading *orientis dominum* for *oriens dominum*. That is, a transfer of light.
[103] *Indignatione*. Or, "displeasure, indignation."
[104] Cf. *Carmen* V.17.9-10.
[105] This must be wrong, as the other sources say that an eastern and retrograde Venus brings her back *not regretful*, while *the man* will have pain.

However, the retrogradation or westernness of Venus at each hour, calls her back of her own accord, being led by regret. Being eastern and scorched, it afflicts the man with pain, and means she is protesting, forced, and stubborn.

Furthermore, an infortune[106] being arranged under the earth and in fall, denotes the subjection of the regretful[107] woman to the man. Which if it would happen to the contrary, the judgment will have to be altered.

Moreover, Venus going out from her scorching, and with the Moon being full, slows the return. However, each one having gone out of this scorching, this Full Moon and [Venus being free of] the rays, accelerates it.

Likewise, if Venus is western while going out of scorching, it brings her back more quickly, but moved by regret.

Both[108] the Moon and the eastern lord (or one [of them]) being corrupted at the hour of [their] betrothal, sows constant[109] mutual discords, until either or both of [these planets] are made safe. But a corresponding judgment is given for friends.

But[110] here I warn you to note: the benevolents dissolve the evils of trouble; the infortunes multiply [them].

Comment by Dykes. The views of the Māshā'allāh group on runaway wives are pretty much in agreement, but they do not cover all possible relations of the Sun and Venus. Still, we can make some general statements about what to look for. I note, however, that in no case do the sources imply that the wife gets away (or in al-Rijāl, that the man does). The rules are only concerned with the difficulty of getting her back, how soon, and what mood the husband and wife will be in. In all cases the Sun represents the husband, and the Moon or Venus the wife.

- The phase of the Moon shows the course of her flight and its return: if waxing, she does not return right away; if waning, she returns quickly.

---

[106] This should probably read, "Venus."
[107] Reading *penitentem* for *potentiam*.
[108] Cf. *Carmen* V.17.11-13. *Carmen* has "the two" being corrupted, which Pingree reads as the Moon and her sign, but evidently the other Arabic authors believed it meant the Moon and the lord of the east.
[109] Reading *constantes* for *constant* and *constantur*.
[110] Cf. *Carmen* V.17.14.

- The hemisphere of the Sun shows the condition of the man: if above the earth, he is strong and competent in getting her back; if below, he is weak and has difficulty.
- The hemisphere of Venus shows the wife's strength and pride: if above the earth, she is proud and indignant; if below, she is penitent.[111]
- The cycle of Venus also shows the wife's state of mind, but here the sources differ somewhat. The principle seems to be that the way in which she leaves the Sun's rays indicates her mood and how she will return. If she is leaving the rays while eastern and retrograde, then Venus and the Sun will be mutually separating, and she will have to re-enter them while direct: this suggests a more forceful and indignant departure, and a reluctant return (since moving direct normally indicates someone willful and in control). But if she leaves the rays while western, the Sun will still be moving toward her, and she will have to re-enter them while retrograde: this suggests regret and weakness and penitence.

Al-Rijāl II.22 contains all of the material from Sahl and al-Khayyāt (and most of Dorotheus), but adds much more. Below is his own material, with his extra rules in italics:

"Look at the Sun and Venus. *If you find the Sun in signs above the earth or in a square of the fortunes, and Venus western and retrograde, say that the woman will return to her own house, tamed, poor, and obedient, asking [for forgiveness] and explaining what she did, and [saying] that she will always be obedient to her husband, she will fear him, nor overlook his command, nor after this will she plan anything unless it is good, useful, and respectable.*

"If you found Venus eastern, say that she will return on her own, and that she will not repent having left. And if in addition you found the Sun above the earth, and Venus in the seventh, say that the man will repent it.

"If you even found Venus in the angles above the earth, or in a fortunate sign, and the Sun below the earth or in places cadent from the angles, say the same thing about the man's weakness and the woman's strength, just as you said in the preceding signification for the woman—namely that she is enraged at her husband, and that she will leave, not about to return.

---

[111] I am inferring this based on the material.

"If, in this question about a woman who has left her home, you even found Venus above the earth or in fortunate places, and the Sun under the earth, and the Moon full of light, say that the return will be difficult and slow, or perhaps never.

"And if, at the hour of the question or in which the woman left the home, you found the Moon in a diminution [of light] (after she had crossed the opposition [with the Sun]), say that she will come back quickly and without impediment.

"*And if, at the hour in which she left, you found the Moon cadent from an angle, and* Venus western in that hour, and in her first station or retrograde, say that she will return on her own, and that she will be obedient, being regretful. If even, at the hour of the departure you found Venus to be eastern, and going out from under the rays, and appearing, say that she will return, and that the man will regret throwing her out.

"*But if,*[112] *at the hour of the question, you found the Sun and Venus cadent from the angles, say that she will separate from [the house], and that she will never return to it, because it will be good and useful for her. But if you found the Sun and Venus in good places, say that in leading her back, he will obtain good and advantage.*

"*If you even found Venus direct in her travel, it signifies that the woman will conquer the man, and that he will contradict the injuries [she has done] to him.*

"*But concerning a man leaving a woman behind, you will even judge in this manner.*

"*If, at the hour in which the woman has left her home, you found Venus going out from under the rays of the Sun, and going to the eastern*[113] *region, she will return humble and penitent, and always will bear her departure painfully."*

---

[112] Cf. *Carmen* V.17.3-4. *Carmen* has the Sun above the earth in strong places while Venus is cadent and in a common sign, or else both of them together in a strong place: profit and joy will come to him if he is diligent in finding her.
[113] This should probably be "western."

§7.34: Whether she is a virgin—Sahl[114]

Then, if it is asked whether or not she is a virgin, we will observe the east[115] and its lord and the Moon. For if they would be walking through firm signs (or even the firmness of [the east] itself), they praise her as innocent and carry a judgment of virginity. But if [through] double-bodied or convertible [signs] (or if [the east] is of this type), it is a sign of a corrupted woman or one already betrothed. The same judgment is also given for a female captive.

Again,[116] the Moon walking through a tropical or convertible [sign], while you find the east to be firm and its lord in a firm one, signifies that she was tempted, [but] in vain, and that [someone] ravished her, but with her virginity [remaining] safe. If the Moon would walk with Mars through movable signs, even though [the others] happened to be firm, it judges she is corrupted.

Moreover, with Saturn occupying the east with the Moon, it being double-bodied or even firm, one may judge a use contrary to nature, and that she is spoiled by the shocking practice, but her virginity is not taken. Which if Mars would hold a pivot from the place of Venus, and the Moon being corrupted [by Mars], or both [Venus and the Moon][117] would be in Scorpio or its triplicity, they corrupt the girl. But[118] if Mercury or Jupiter would possess the pivot or trigon of Venus, while however Mars would be in aversion [to her and] linger[119] in a fiery sign, they preach virginity and claim she is untouched.

§7.35: Whether she has already given birth—Sahl[120]

Should it come into question whether perhaps she has already given birth or not, Venus traversing [with Mercury][121] in Aquarius or in Leo speaks against it; walking through Scorpio or Taurus, claims [she does have a child].

---

[114] Cf. *On Quest.* §7.5 and al-Rijāl II.21.
[115] Reading with John's Sahl and al-Rijāl, for Hugo's "seventh."
[116] Cf. *Carmen* V.16.6.
[117] Al-Rijāl has only Venus.
[118] Cf. *Carmen* V.16.22.
[119] Al-Rijāl has Venus in a fiery sign, not Mars.
[120] Cf. *On Quest.* §7.6 and al-Rijāl II.26.
[121] Adding with John's Sahl; later in the sentence Hugo seems to have *de utroque*, which suggests two planets as well.

Which if Mars and Venus and the Moon happened to be staying in two-parted signs (except for Sagittarius), it is a sign she has not[122] already given birth; and[123] if she did give birth, [the baby] will die.

Moreover, the malevolents traveling through the turning signs produce offspring from adultery, [but] the fortunate ones the contrary. For this, even, the benevolents being mixed with the infortunes in signs of the same kind[124] bear a judgment of admirable offspring who even make the parents upset.[125]

§7.36: Whether a pregnant woman conceived lawfully—Sahl[126]

But if there would be a question about a pregnant woman, whether or not [her child] is legitimate and she conceived lawfully, we dissolve the knot of this ambiguity from the fifth and its lord. For if Saturn or Mars or Mercury would be corrupting the fifth itself by their own aspect, they bring forth[127] a signification of a fetus from adultery. But[128] if the fortunate ones would regard it, they bring it forth that [the fetus] is legitimate.

---

[122] Adding with al-Rijāl.
[123] Reading the rest of this sentence with al-Rijāl for Hugo's "in Sagittarius they sometimes deny it, sometimes agree."
[124] Namely, movable ones.
[125] This reading makes more sense than al-Rijāl, who has bad children that bother the parents.
[126] Cf. *On Quest.* §7.6 and al-Rijāl II.28.
[127] Reading *producunt* here and below, for *produnt*.
[128] Cf. *Carmen* V.16.5.

CONTROVERSIES & LAWSUITS

§7.37: On a controversy or legal case—Sahl[1]

An inquiry into controversies (in what result they are ended), is usually observed thusly. For we seek the querent from the east and its lord and the Moon, whereas the whole business of the adversary depends on the seventh and its lord.

And so, an application of these significators being made from a prosperous figure, means future peace; the regard of a perverse figure increases the discord. But if they would be lingering in the same sign, they really want an agreement without a common mediator. But being under the regard of the lord of the tenth—should they apply to it before doing so with [each] other—the business will be brought to an end through the royal hand. Even a transfer of light made between the significators themselves, establishes a pact of peace through intermediaries.

§7.38: On legal cases or controversies—'Umar

Moreover, with a question about controversies being proposed, we put the east and its lord in charge of the originator[2] of the case, but the seventh and its lord watch over the defendant. However, the judgment of the Midheaven and its lord support the kind of case and what division or discord exists between each. But the fourth and its lord resolves the end of the whole controversy. Furthermore, remember to note equally whether there is an application or withdrawal of the Moon. The star from which the Moon separates even belongs to the accuser, [while] the one to which she applies belongs to the defendant. But establish the Moon herself as the significator of the case shared in common between each. But the lord of the Lunar lodging-place claims the signification of the end.

It is even in need of no little consideration, whether the lord of the east and that of the seventh regard each other, or one would apply to the other. For if an aspect or application[3] would proceed from a tetragon or opposition

---

[1] Cf. *On Quest.* §7.8 and al-Rijāl II.35 (first part).
[2] As with so many questions, we assume that the querent is the one originating the action.
[3] 'Umar seems to be distinguishing between a whole-sign regard and an aspect by degrees, but allows both (although certainly an application would be more powerful).

or assembly, but even [should there be] an application of the star from which the Moon is being separated, with the one to which she advances, [and] likewise from a tetragon or opposition or assembly, it indicates squabbles and dissent in the controversy. And the beginning of the cause of the lawsuit is thus generated from the application of either one of them. With [such an aspect] being had as we have said above, I say, it inserts the most serious lawsuits, especially if no reception would be had. Which if [reception] would be present, it will be there in an easier way, and somewhat more relaxed. But an application discovered from a trigon or hexagon portends a humble and unsteady kind of case comes to be between friends.

Furthermore, the second and those peregrine or familiar (or rather, closely related) stars which are staying in it, determine the supports of the accuser (but alien ones,[4] I say, are those which have no dignity, nor sovereignty nor triplicity in it; but closely related ones are those which possess something of the aforesaid).[5] Moreover, the advocates of the defendant are discerned from the eighth and from those stars (alien or familiar) which stay in that same place.

In fact, the Midheaven really introduces the royal assistants and the persons of the judges.

§7.39: On those things which happen between two people—al-Kindī

§150. Those things which are confirmed to happen most frequently between two people, are: controversies, any causes of action,[6] dissensions, wars, friendships, [and] betrothals.[7] Therefore, once a question has arisen concerning these and what is like these, one must note that the Ascendant itself signifies the agent of the whole affair (namely of the cause of action). But the seventh [signifies] him with whom the matter is done.[8]

§151. But the Midheaven suggests the mediator between each. But if a back-and-forth matter of controversy is being undertaken, it claims the judge;

---

[4] That is, peregrine.
[5] That is, one of those dignities.
[6] Especially in the sense of legal causes.
[7] For more on these, see al-Kindī's material on wars, friendships, and marriage here in *Judges*, or *Forty Chapters* Chs. 10-12, 20, and 22.
[8] This description assumes that the querent is the one undertaking the action (or thinking about undertaking it).

if a negotiation, a helper in the matter. If about nuptials, the bridesman;[9] if the action is about war, victory and success; if partnership and friendship, it regulates the cause of their benevolence and esteem. Also, the fourth sign determines the end of the question.[10]

§152. Likewise, the Moon assumes the mediator of the two. But the star from which she recedes, [indicates] the chief of the cause;[11] but the one to which she applies, the adversary. Also, the lord of the Moon decides the end of the matter.

§7.40: On controversies—al-Khayyāt

Moreover, with a question being made about a controversy, as to what end it will come to, we put the east and its lord, and the star from which the Moon is being separated, in charge of the querent. The seventh and its lord, and the star to which the Moon applies, rule generally over the adversary.

If therefore the joint application between the significators is from a trigon or hexagon, it is a sign of entering into peace; but from the tetragon or opposition (which is finally worse), they enter into peace, [but] not unless it is after brawls and quarrels. Now, if they would linger in the same sign, concord will come to be without a mediator.

But if the lord of the Midheaven would regard them or apply to them before they apply to each other, they will debate in the presence of the king and the business will be ended through his hands. A transfer of light [means] they establish peace and concord through messengers.

Finally, one must note among the significators which of them is stronger: for the stronger one commends the men and power of him whose signification it bears. And so, we call that one stronger which holds onto a pivot and is fortified by many testimonies in that place, and who is better received: he rejoices in many allies.

---

[9] Traditionally, this is a man who arranges (and often pays for) the wedding, usually on behalf of the groom; sometimes this is the one who walks the bride down the aisle and presents her.
[10] See §7.175 below.
[11] That is, the querent (assumed to be the one initiating the action).

§7.41: On a trial or controversy—Dorotheus

If a question is given about a controversy between two people, namely to what end it would come down to, we put the east and its lord and the star from which the Moon is being separated, in charge of the querent; but the seventh and its lord and the one to which the Moon applies, in charge of the adversary.

If therefore an application from a trigon or hexagon were discovered, they put peace in between them. From the tetragon or opposition, they sow discord, nor do they want concord unless it is once the arguments of the lawsuit have been brought to a close. (Among all [the aspects] it must be noted that the regard of the opposition is more burdensome.) Also, being arranged in the same sign, with none coming in between, they enter into concord. With them being regarded by the lord of the Midheaven, while they themselves would apply to [that lord] before they do so between themselves, it is discussed or perhaps brawled over under the eyes of the king before peace is concluded.

However, it seems that the place and strength of each significator must be noted. For thusly they designate the stronger one in the trial (the stronger one is he whose significator occupies a pivot). However, the one whom many testimonies favor, and who is received in a more familiar way, will rejoice in [having] many supports.

Furthermore, the origin and commencement of the peace proceeds from the lighter and applying star. Moreover, the one whose significator was in a pivot, is undoubtedly preferred to the other.

On the other hand, the one from which the Moon is being separated, and the one to which she applies, and their places and status, [should be handled] in just the way it was stated above about the lord of the east.

In this place it is necessary to pay attention: for that one of them which happens to be found to be drawn back (or preferably unlucky), brings in detriment to the [man] over which it is in charge. Which if the lord of the seventh were in the east, it will protect the querent's side. Likewise, the lord of the east in the seventh prefers the adversary.

But the retrogradation of either one of the significators, shows the unsoundness and idleness and fear of his side. Moreover, with each one being established in a pivot, that one of them which was received will take control of the victory. The lord of the tenth regarding them, if it is retrograde, prolongs the trial. Also, if either of these would be separated from the other, and it is an opposition or tetragon, this withdrawal (provided that they regard each other) [means] there will be a delay in the lawsuit. That one of these will be called the stronger one, which possesses its own or at least [its] partner's house, or even a pivot.

Either one of the lights applying to one of the significators, or appearing with it, raises up his situation and commends his side—unless it is perhaps scorched.

I think this must be noted: the second sign and the eighth designate advocates or assistants. For the one of them which obtains a pivot, victory is conceded to him.

However, the judge is hostile [to the one] whom the lord of the Midheaven corrupts.

And an application of the eastern [lord] with the lord of the Midheaven stirs up the querent so that he prevails upon the king. Contrariwise, [the lord of the Midheaven] applying to [the lord of the east], administers the king's spontaneous favor [upon him]. And one will have to describe it thusly for the lord of the seventh.

And so, with the power and testimonies of these being looked at in such an order—with the hope of peace, I say, being wholly remote—we will understand the judge from the lord of the Midheaven. This one, therefore, should he regard any of the significators in a familiar way, he will rather favor that one. Which if it would console each with its own aspect, if it would receive either one, he will really adhere to that one. Moreover, with a peregrine star possessing the tenth, while it regards them, [and] with the lord of the tenth being wholly in aversion to their regard, they call in a foreign judge, but a just one.

Then, the eastern lord being scorched, impedes the querent by death or disease—if the burning would be within the east itself. For in the second, he is injured because of money. In the third, brothers; and this method will have to be observed through the rest of the signs.

In addition, the east being double-bodied portends he will grow sick in prison, and it presents an impediment. Likewise, the regard of Mars brings forward blows and fetters. Which if [it were] convertible, there is a disease in the cause. Likewise with it being a firm one, it makes a sign of death, according to its nature and the regard of the infortunes. But if the fortunate ones would regard [it] at the hour of scorching, it is a sign of escaping; nevertheless a perpetual mark from the disease is left.

§7.42: On the same thing, which of them would get the victory—Sahl[12]

In addition, discover which of them would get the victor, or which would have greater power in disputing, thusly. For the one which could be discovered to be stronger, it greatly increases the power (and multiplies the force) of the one over which [that significator] is in charge, and whom it signifies, and it prefers him to the other. We call that one "stronger," therefore, which happens to be found in a pivot and received better (and [a received one] brings more allies).[13] Moreover, the lighter [planet] will generate the source and beginning of the peace.

Likewise, with the lord of the seventh being placed in the east, he who is asking will be preferred to the other. Which if the eastern [lord] would be traversing in the seventh, it extols the adversary.

The retrogradation of each significator afflicts and tramples its side with fear and laziness and ineffectiveness. But if the lord of the tenth would regard these while [the lord of the tenth] is retrograding, it portends the judge is going to be unjust. If either of them would be separating from the other, it prolongs the controversy.

§7.43: Which if them will win—'Umar

In this place it is appropriate to note the lord of the east especially. Which if it were in the seventh, with the lord of the question[14] lingering in that same place, while they are both scorched or retrograde, or corrupted or cadent, it suggests the accusers[15] are overcome by the defendant. Contrariwise, too, the lord of the seventh and of the eighth[16] in the east, while each is scorched or retrograde or cadent or corrupted, prepare victory for the accuser.

---

[12] Cf. *On Quest.* §7.8 and al-Rijāl II.35 (second part).
[13] This means that it has more supporting aspects.
[14] This phrase means "the lord of the matter asked about," in this case the seventh.
[15] In this question, the accuser seems to be the querent and the east, and the defendant the seventh.
[16] *Octavi*. But this should probably be "east," to make the examples parallel.

§7.44: Who would give in, in the situation—al-Kindī

§153. Therefore, the force of the Ascendant and the one from who the Moon recedes (in the way it was described above with respect to strength),[17] provided that the Ascendant obtains some likeness with the nature of the quaesited matter,[18] and if it acquires the comfort of the fortunate ones (namely their presence or regard) or some shared bearing,[19] [and] even [if] the strength and prosperity of the Moon [is present],[20] they convey victory in the cause, and success to its agent—particularly if the weakness and misfortune of the seventh and the one with whom the Moon's application comes to be, is discovered.

§154. Even the lord of the Midheaven and the Midheaven itself seems to confirm this if the prosperity and robustness of each is made clear. And let there be a regard between these and the Ascendant and its lord, or some bearing of this kind. Also, the Moon manages the same thing as the Midheaven does, if sustained by her witnesses.

§7.45: From whom the beginning of peace is taken up—al-Khayyāt[21]

Moreover, the manner and source of peace [proceeds] from the applying one (namely, the lighter one), or from one remote from a pivot; the one which traverses in a pivot [is preferred] to [a cadent] star.

Even the places of that star from which the Moon is being separated, and to whom she applies, must be noted. For the one which was remote from a pivot or corrupted or scorched, portends that the man [that star] is in charge of, succumbs.

The lord of the seventh traversing in the east notes the power of the querent; contrariwise however, the lord of the east being arranged in the seventh, prefers the adversary.

Of the significators, the one which was retrograde shows the weakness and impotence of his side. Which if each would possess a pivot, victory is given to the received one. If however, a retrograde lord of the tenth would

---

[17] See the end of *Forty Chapters* §139, §§63-72, §§77-78, and *ITA* IV.2.
[18] See *Forty Chapters* §142.
[19] See *Forty Chapters* §144.
[20] See esp. *ITA* IV.5.
[21] Mistakenly attributed to Sahl in the manuscripts. Cf. al-Rijāl II.35.

regard them, it portends the injustice of the judge. Which if it would be separating from one, it is a sign of prolonging the controversy.

With one of the lights applying to one of the significators, or if it would be lingering in [a significator's] house, it extols that one and supports it and means he is better.

The supports of each are in the second and the eighth. Therefore, the lord of each being in a pivot, or if a star assuming some dignity in that place were in those places, it blesses his side with the attained victory.

But should the lord of the Midheaven corrupt [a significator], the king or judge treats his side with contempt. Likewise too, if the lord of the eleventh would corrupt them, the friends and supporters of the king are equally hostile to that one. Which if they would bear themselves conversely, it will be permitted to report it otherwise.

Moreover, the lord of the east applying to the lord of the tenth, [means that the querent is] the one who asks compels the king [to get involved]; but if [the lord of the tenth] would apply to [the lord of the east], the king contributes to that side of his own accord. And no other judgment should be given about the lord of the seventh.

§7.46: Who would yield in the trial—Dorotheus

Moreover, with a question given about victory and which of them the judge favors, we put the east in chart of the originator[22] [of the matter], the second in charge of [his] advocates; from the seventh the adversary is designated, from the eighth his supports, and from the Moon the witnesses. Also, the judge claims[23] the Midheaven.

And so, the east being firm confirms the steadiness of the querent, nor does it promise that he will abandon what was proposed. Which if it were double-bodied, he turns between each [extreme]. But it being convertible, changes the controversy over [into something else], nor does it apply steadiness.

Furthermore, Mars in the east (or regarding it) greatly increases the querent's dishonor and disgrace. And Mercury occupying the east (not without the fortunate ones), brings an argument in the trial about books and

---

[22] That is, the querent. Most of these questions imagine that the querent is originating the question.
[23] Reading *vendicat* for *vendicavit*.

money to a conclusion, but afterwards he abandons [the matter]. With Saturn in the east or regarding it, it is the worst.

The infortunes being thus in the tenth, portends that the trial is not discussed before this judge. And since he is disreputable, one will have to make a transfer [to another judge]. Moreover, the infortunes established in the Midheaven prove that the judge and the king are corrupt and liars. Fortunate ones on the contrary praise [their] justice and they profess truth.

Moreover, the malevolents possessing the seventh or at least regarding it, disturb the accused with insoluble anguish.

However, Mercury in the tetragon of the east, being corrupted, will call forth false witnesses of the accuser,[24] saying what they don't know.

And the pivot of the earth resolves the end of the controversy. The lord of the east and equally that of the Midheaven, or the lord of the seventh, being made eastern in the pivot of the earth, establish peace for him whom they designate. Conversely though, with the lords of the fourth and seventh and tenth being corrupted, they make him submit.

The scorching of his star with the lord of the fourth should be noted: [it means that] peace follows with the case being undiscussed.[25] Moreover, the scorching of the eastern lord [and] that of the seventh equally, in a pivot, prolongs the lawsuit. Thus even the regard of the infortunes generates a steadiness of difficulty, and delay.

Moreover, the Moon being in a pivot, so that she is the lord of that lodging-place, conveys advantage, but fraudulently.

Likewise, the supports of the adversary depend on the eighth. If therefore the same star would rule over the tenth and east, or at least should the lord of the Midheaven regard the eastern [lord], it portends that the judge will protect the side of the accuser, and for this reason he will reinforce his advantage. Which if the lord of the eighth would happen to bear itself thusly, this [advantage] will transform to the contrary side.

Among all of these it is necessary to attend diligently to the Moon and her status. For, she applying to infortunes[26] before she undergoes scorching (and should this application be in the east or after the east), grants the trial to the accuser. Which if she would occupy the seventh with an application of this

---

[24] That is, the querent.
[25] Or perhaps rather, "unargued."
[26] I believe this should read, "fortunes."

kind, it shows the same for the adversary; finally it testifies that he[27] will have regret.

If however the action is with respect to the law or those things which pertain to the law,[28] the one whom the waning Moon accompanies, or which she approaches in a familiar way, is really convicted. But the one which is found to be stronger, makes the one whom it designates to be the more powerful one.

In addition, the Lot of Fortune in the east or second prefers the accuser. In the seventh or eighth, it defends the adversary. (The lord of the Lot signifies the same thing that the Lot itself does.) [The Lot] being established in a pivot, with none coming in between,[29] establishes peace. But with it holding onto the Midheaven, the judge calls both back to concord. If however the lord of the east and equally that of the seventh would be in their own proper light,[30] it designates the perpetual hatred of each. In fact, Mercury as the lord of Fortune establishes the lawsuit as being about children or the houses of children. The Lot of Fortune holding onto a house of Venus, brings women or children or brothers into the controversy. It being in the Lunar house, parents and those who are of this kind. But in either house of Jupiter, the law and those who arbitrate the law. Which if it would occupy either house of Saturn, patrimonies and things full of age.[31]

Moreover, the Moon explains the witnesses and their trust. If therefore a fortunate one would possess her place, it designates their eloquence and power and respectable attention. But the infortunes are otherwise.

§7.47: Who will obtain the victory—Aristotle

The method appended below will teach which one ought to be preferred to whom in the matter. If the lord of the east would walk through a pivot of the east, but the lord of the seventh would linger in a pivot of the seventh,

---

[27] That is, whoever has won.
[28] That is, if the controversy is not merely private but involves breaking the law.
[29] I am not sure what this means.
[30] There are two main senses of being in one's "own light": being out of the rays of the Sun and not yet fully connected to another planet, or being a member of the sect of the chart (i.e., a diurnal planet in a diurnal chart, or a nocturnal one in a nocturnal one). Dorotheus might mean something like the former, namely that if the significators are not connecting with each other in any way, the parties will not resolve their problems because they are not relating to each other.
[31] Note that Mars has been omitted here.

since each side is strong, neither will get the victory hoped for. The one which is scorched or cadent or retrograde or conjoined to one of the malevolents, will really succumb in the matter. The infortunes in the east or the seventh, trample the lord of that place.

We give no other counsel if they were after the pivots, but with them being in these places, they dread now conquering, now being conquered, since none would win. Traversing in the remote [places], and both being free and cleansed (so that any wicked one would not be with them nor traverse in their houses, nor any lucky one), it brings about loss on each side (and equally so)[32] in the matter. But one [of the significators] traversing after the pivots, in every way free of the infortunes (both it and its house), [but] the other one after the pivots (estranged from an association of the benevolents), the first one blessed by manifold testimony will rejoice in the victory wished for. But one must note that the pivots surpass the following[33] ones and the remote [places], but the ones which follow the pivots are stronger than the remote [places].

§7.48: On the king or judge: which of them he favors—Sahl[34]

With these [planets] bearing themselves thusly,[35] if you should find the Sun or the Moon applying to either of the significators, or placed in its house, [the judge] will really aid that side with his favor.

But if the lord of the east would apply to the lord of the tenth, the querent will make an appeal to the king on his own. With the order reversed (the lord of the tenth applying to the eastern [lord]), it portends that the king will come to his side on his own. Nor do we give another judgment with respect to the lord of the seventh and of the tenth, and their status of this kind.

But the judge will even be understood from the lord of the tenth: he will defend and apply himself with full intention to the one whose significator he supports by the better aspect. But should a peregrine star traversing in the tenth regard the significators (if, I say the lord of the tenth is in aversion and remote), they will bring their case to a close with an outside judge whom they

---

[32] Reading *partier* for *partes*.
[33] That is, the succeedent ones.
[34] Cf. *On Quest.* §7.8.
[35] Sahl is referring to other rules given §7.42 about the relative strength of the significators in themselves, as well as evidence that a king or other intermediary will get involved.

themselves call. And so, Saturn traversing in the tenth, if he would gain possession of the rulership, portends the injustice and fraud of the judge; he being corrupted by Mars [means that] disgrace and blame will follow from the judgment. But if Mars occupied the tenth, the lightness and sharpness of the judge, and his loftiness, could be discovered. Jupiter brings forth a just and legitimate judgment. From Venus is denoted the man's softness and his benignness. Mercury shows a subtle and sharp-sighted [judge].

But whenever the tenth were of the two-parted signs, in the controversy there will come to be a transfer [of the case from one judge to another].[36]

§7.49: On the king or the judge, which one of them he favors—'Umar

Then, too, I think it can easily be responded thusly to a question as to which of their sides the king would watch over in a more personal way. For, with the lord of the east and of the tenth equally being found in the same [place], or if the lord of the tenth would regard that same lord of the east from a trigon or a hexagon, and be received from its own place, it promises royal favor to the accuser. To the contrary, too, if the lord of the tenth would regard the eastern [lord] from a tetragon or opposition or assembly, while there is no reception present, he is weighed down by reverence for the royal dignity, and fear and even a certain violence. But with reception being had, it is necessary that this be mitigated. It will be good to undergo a special consideration [with] the lords of the seventh and tenth, as we have shown above with respect to those of the east and the tenth.

You will discover the royal supports from that very star which occupies the tenth; but with none being found there, the eleventh itself, as a significator, denotes the royal assistants. Now, with that consideration being had, it will not be difficult to observe whose side the king himself (and his [supporters]) favor.

Therefore[37] it is permitted to observe in a general way that if Mars, being placed firmly, would possess some pivot in the regard of the east, it inserts manifold squabbles in the controversy, especially in any place of his own dignity and in a firm sign: for then he introduces long-lasting and constant dissent. In a double-bodied one, he will be given to discord. But in a convert-

---

[36] Adding with John's Sahl.
[37] In the text, the first part of this sentence (through "general way") seems to be part of the previous one; but to me it makes more sense here, introducing the role of Mars.

ible one, he will renew frequent and already mitigated dissensions. Which if Saturn held onto the place of Mars (in the way that was stated), in a firm sign, it introduces a long-lasting and stable quarrel to the controversy. But in a convertible one, it does it more modestly, and in a double-bodied one it alternates and prolongs the evil. Furthermore, Jupiter in any sign[38] transforms it to the better by mitigating it; Venus in the same way, and likewise the Moon (but [not if][39] placed with Saturn), because they really are fortunate. If Mercury claimed the Lunar place, he being regarded by either of the unfortunate ones, it manages the kind of controversy according to the nature of the infortune by whom he is regarded.

§7.50: On the judge's faithfulness—al-Kindī

§155a.[40] Again, the robustness and luckiness of the lord of the Midheaven [indicates] the kindness of the mediator in those things which pertain to him. But his regard (or some bearing) proves the truth of the judgment.

§155b. Moreover, with the lord of the Midheaven being corrupted, the judge's fraud is diagnosed.

§156. But [if the lord of the Midheaven is] fortunate and weak, it bequeaths trustworthiness to the judge, but removes the effect and power of the judgment. Moreover, it being unlucky and strong testifies to the power of frauds and trickery. The same [lord] being retrograde [indicates] he is uncertain, and wavering [in] what he should do about the judgment, nor does he allow what is suitable to have the power of coming to pass.

§157. Moreover, if Mars is the lord of the Midheaven [and] regarded by Venus, it corrupts the judge with a bribe. Being regarded by Saturn adds that he is underhanded, with one thing in his heart, but another in his mouth. Being in the regard of Jupiter, he wants a just judgment but it shows that he is powerless. In the regard of Mercury,[41] [it signifies] astute orators and those of great counsel, but with no perseverance in it. Regarded by the Sun, it introduces a royal judge.

---

[38] That is, if he were in the same situation that Mars was stated to be above.
[39] Added by Dykes.
[40] This sentence originally appeared at the end of §7.44, but belongs here.
[41] Reading the rest of this sentence with Robert.

§158. Again, with the Moon obtaining the rulership of the Midheaven, [and estranged from the fortunes],[42] although she introduces many changes and wrongfully [introduces] various little annoyances, still she suggests it is brought together [even though] with public bribes—unless the regard of the fortunate ones reinforces [her]. In this way one will even have to judge the mediator according to its counsel.

§159. Also, the lord of the seventh gets a judgment similar to the lord of the Ascendant, in those things which belong to its own signification.

§7.51: Whom the king favors—al-Khayyāt

With these things having been discovered in such an order (namely so that the power of both is understood, and no hesitation is left about entering into peace),[43] we discover the judge or king from the lord of the Midheaven. Therefore, he will really favor that one of the significators whom he regarded; but if he regarded each, he will adhere to the one whom he receives. (And it is in this way for the supporters and friends of kings.) But if a foreign[44] star occupying the tenth would regard them, while the lord of the tenth is diverting its aspect from them, they will apply themselves to a foreign and outside judge.

Moreover, the lord of the east entering into scorching, will inflict an impediment because of death or sickness (if, I say, the scorching were in the east). But if it would be scorched in the second, he undergoes impediment and difficulty because of a wealth or resources. But if in the third, he is impeded because of brothers. One will have to look no otherwise through the rest of the domiciles.

Moreover, scorching being made in the east (and it being double-bodied) conveys the impediment and difficulty of prison. But if the regard of Mars is not absent, it even threatens beatings and blows. But that same [east] being a turning [sign], afflicts with illness. But being a firm one, it afflicts him with death as much as anxiety, the occasion of which undoubtedly proceeds from the nature of the sign. But if the regard of Mars is not absent, it even threatens beatings and blows. It being a turning [sign], afflicts with illness. But a

---

[42] Adding with Robert.
[43] That is, both are strong enough that the case will go before a judge, *without* peace beforehand. See §7.41.
[44] That is, peregrine.

firm one (should it be mitigated in this scorching by an aspect of the benevolents) is a sign of escape, but the vestiges of a disease will be left behind.

§7.52: Whether there will be peace between them—'Umar

However, the lord of the east and that of the seventh equally preserve the manner and end of the concord (or rather, the mutual reconciliation). The regard of either of them from a trigon or hexagon or assembly, and [their] joint reception, establish peace: for reception manages all affairs more quickly and more respectably. Which if they would be deprived of a mutual aspect, while however there is a star collecting or transferring the light of each, it means establishing peace through someone mediating. The proper quality of the collecting (or rather transferring) star demonstrates the nature of the mediator.

If there would be a question about [the mediator's] status, one will have to have recourse to that same star. For, it being eastern [indicates] an adolescent; western, old men. Which if it were neither western nor eastern, it prefigures the middle years [of life]. However, the status of a star of this kind (namely being neither eastern nor western) is discovered whenever it is distant from the Sun by 90° up to 180° (for then it is understood to be in the opposition of the Sun), [up to 90° on the other side of the Sun].[45]

§7.53: Why there is a controversy—'Umar

Therefore, whenever the kind or rather theme of the controversy came into doubt, it is reasonable to turn your attention to the significator of the accuser with more diligent care, [to see] what kind of sign it is holding onto. For in Aries (or at least in its triplicity), while that same triplicity appeared as a partner of the sixth and the twelfth, it calls forth beasts and captives into the trial. In Taurus or its triplicity, it asserts that the trial has to do with lands or agriculture, grain, or livestock. Which if [it is] in Gemini or its triplicity, it introduces living things into the trial: in a human sign, men; in Libra, domestic birds; in Aquarius, flying things of the forest, and one given to a hunt of this kind. Moreover, in the triplicity of Cancer, the controversy is concluded with respect to water or rivers, springs and that kind [of thing], aquatic things

---

[45] Adding based on 'Umar's similar statement in §7.110.

(of which kind are pearls, fish, reeds[46]), and things which derive their life from the water.

§7.54: With whom the lawsuit must be carried out—'Umar

If however you arrive [and] are about to make summary arguments against someone,[47] the lord of the east suggests [with whom it is]. For you will have to observe diligently the one to which it applies by a tetragon or opposition, while there is no reception, namely so that the appropriate truth of the judgment could be discovered, uncovering the cloud of error. For if it[48] would have control of the rulership of the fourth, it testifies that it is the father or grandfather, and that type [of person]. Likewise, if it were the lord of the third, it portends the brother and what is like that. And it will be permitted to judge through the rest of the signs in this manner.

§7.55: On the end of the lawsuit, and the hour—'Umar

The judgment of this matter depends on the lord of the east and of the seventh, and even that of the fourth. For whenever they regarded each other from a tetragon or opposition or assembly, they really impose the end of the controversy.[49] Which if the regard is from the trigon or hexagon, the case and disagreement is broken off in peace.

---

[46] Reading *cannas* for *cannes*.
[47] *Peroraturus advenis*. This sounds like an election, but I believe it is simply a horary question.
[48] This must be the star to which the lord of the east applies.
[49] That is, by transit. I think this means that it will continue to its bitter end, without a chance of stopping before things get too serious.

Trades & Sales

§7.56: On business deals and commerce—Sahl[1]

The application of the eastern [lord] with the lord of the seventh equally resolves inquiries on business deals.[2] A common application being discovered, it accomplishes the business and brings it to the end. The lighter one (that is, the applying star) signifies it will be with [that person's] labor and effort. Moreover, with an application being in no way found, while however there comes to be a transfer of light between the significators, the business will be ended through some middle man.

Likewise, with the eastern lord lingering in the seventh, the one who sells gets the better trade, whereas the lord of the seventh traversing in the east will give the better value to the buyer.

Any lucky [planet] found in the east shows the business will come to be from the seller[3] without fraud and trickery, but a malevolent establishes the reverse. Finally, concerning the seventh, the method demands that one judge [in this way] about the lucky ones and the adverse ones in that same place.

Moreover,[4] the Moon withdrawing from none but applying to another, explains that the thing for sale is bought [but not from that seller];[5] but if she applies to none, while in the meantime she withdraws from some [planet], the thing will be bought under the expected price. Moreover, [if] the star from which the Moon is being separated is traversing [so as to] enter into scorching, it will kill the seller before [he sells at] the acknowledged price.

---

[1] Cf. *On Quest.* §7.9. In this question, the querent is assumed to be the buyer and the lord of the seventh is the seller.

[2] The question assumes that the querent (the Ascendant) is a prospective buyer, while the seventh is the seller.

[3] Al-Khayyāt in §7.58 says "buyer."

[4] This paragraph is hard to understand at first, but John's Sahl allows us to reconstruct it. Since we are talking about goods moving from the seller to the buyer, the planet from which the Moon separates represents the goods leaving the seller, while the planet to which the Moon applies represents them coming to the buyer. So, if she separates from a planet but applies to none, then it shows that while *a* sale may go through, it will not be with the current seller (since his goods are not reaching the querent). Likewise, if the planet separates from none but applies to another, there will be some delay or only an agreement in principle (John's Sahl), or the sale will be made to the advantage of the buyer.

[5] Al-Khayyāt and Dorotheus say this means that it has not been bought before. See below.

§7.57: On business deals and trades—'Umar

A general inquiry into business dealing gives a nod to the Lunar counsel. For if she is waxing in computation and light, ascending toward the north[6] (namely from the east to the tenth, [and] thence to the seventh, and, I say, above the earth), it signifies the easy and advantageous trade of everything sought, and in every category. But waning in both light and computation, if she descends into the south, arranged between the east and the fourth, I say, and thus toward the seventh,[7] it introduces very little or nothing useful, but rather detriment with respect to any kind of thing for sale. Which if these three[8] would mix themselves with the Lunar business, you will note diligently which of them is stronger and more eminent, in order that you may wrench the reason or truth of the judgment from it.

Or otherwise: and so the Mercurial strength and weakness, even being eastern and western, direct and retrograde, a regard or assembly of the fortunate ones or the infortunes, easily reveal the aforesaid.

No less too, will one have to describe it with respect to any kind of thing for sale, according to[9] the application and withdrawal of the Moon, but even according to her prosperous and unlucky status, or power and weakness, wicked and lucky place.

§7.58: On commerce—al-Khayyāt

A question being had about trade and commerce, it is usual to observe the buyer from the east, the seller from the seventh. For if either one would render the counsel of application to the other, it perfects the sale more quickly, with (I say) the effort of the lighter one (namely, the one which is applying). An application being denied, while however there is [a planet] which transfers their light, the sale comes to be through a mediator. Nevertheless, the

---

[6] I believe this actually means that she is ascending in northern *ecliptical latitude* as well as being above the earth.

[7] Again, this probably means being in southern ecliptical latitude, as well as being below the earth.

[8] This probably refers to the chapters which immediately preceded this in the Arabic 'Umar, on selling slaves (in *Judges*, §§6.50-51). If so, then "these three" may mean the lords of the east, the seventh, and the sixth. But the sixth is obviously inappropriate here. Otherwise, I am not sure what exactly 'Umar means by this.

[9] Reading *secundum* for *sed*.

star from which the Moon is separating, and the one to which she applies, must equally be noted.[10]

Moreover, the lord of the east in the seventh shows the buyer to be the one [more] inclined [to make the sale happen]. But if the lord of the seventh would be lingering in the east, it affirms the same about the seller.

A benevolent appearing in the east, points out that the buyer is true and it is without delay; the judgment about the seventh will be no other. For the infortunes heap on delay and harshness.

The greatness of the acquisition and price is usually discovered from the Midheaven.[11]

In addition, one must note that if the Moon, withdrawing from none, would apply to another, it really sells the thing, but one not having been bought before, or [it is] real estate and patrimonies. But she withdrawing [from a planet] but not applying to one, is a sign that the thing is sold under the expected price. But if the star from which the Moon is being separated would traverse in the entrance to 'scorching, it will be wholly fatal to the seller before he accepts the price.

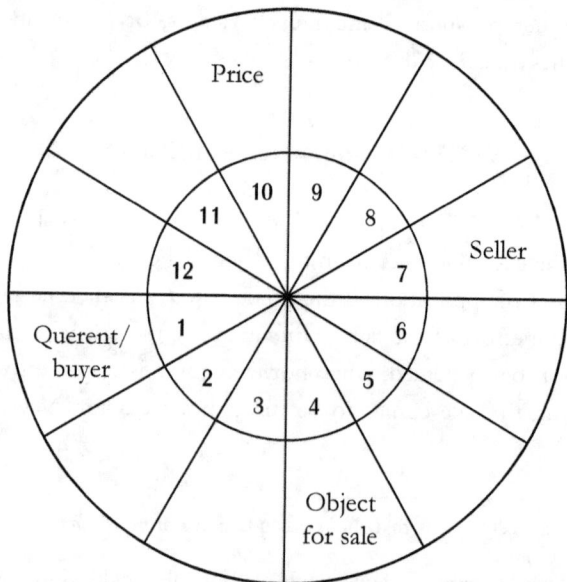

Figure 33: Angular significations for sales (*Carmen* V.9)[12]

---

[10] See my footnote at the end of §7.56.
[11] See for instance §4.6-7 above.

§7.59: On trade—Dorotheus

Moreover, with a question about trade being proposed, let the east be consulted for the seller, the seventh for the buyer.[13] If therefore they should render counsel [to each other] in turn, the sale will be easy for the one whom the light star designates. But with a reciprocal application being denied, while a transfer of light is present, the same thing will be brought about by some mediator. No less must the Lunar withdrawal and application be noted, in the way that was said about the lord of the east and [its] opposite.[14]

Therefore, if the eastern lord would occupy the seventh, the buyer demands [the sale from] the seller. But if would happen contrariwise, it happens to the contrary.

Moreover, a benevolent in the east means an easy and true agreement. On the contrary, infortunes introduce difficulty and lies.

The kind and quality of goods for sale could be discovered from the Midheaven and its lord.[15]

Here, if the Moon, withdrawing from none, would apply to some [star], it reveals a thing not purchased [before] (such as an inheritance and a commercial thing of this kind). Which if she would withdraw [from one] but is applying to none, the buyer purchases it below [his] expectation. Likewise, [if] the star from which the Moon is separating [would be] entering into scorching, it threatens death to the buyer before the price is accepted.

---

[12] The Māshā'allāh group does not address the fourth house, but these attributions are almost identical to those in §4.6-7, on buying land.
[13] The question obviously assumes that the querent wants to sell something, but the Ascendant should be used for the querent in any case.
[14] See my footnote at the end of §7.56.
[15] See for instance §4.6-7 above.

COMMODITIES & PRICES

Comment by Dykes. In the following sections, Hugo describes prices and commodities with two sets of opposing terms that mean expensive (or high-priced) and inexpensive (or low-priced), respectively. Either he calls them "burdensome" (*gravis*) versus "light, easy" (*levis*), or "dear" (*carus*), versus "cheap" (*vilis*).

In what follows through the rest of the commodities/prices material, the methods are rather straightforward. In his general approach (§7.60), 'Umar says we are mainly supposed to observe the lord of the Ascendant at the New Moon, as well as its upcoming exact aspects. ('Umar wants to find a kind of victor, and in his examples he also uses the following: the lord of the Ascendant, its next aspect, and its domicile lord). The following kinds of things show an increase of prices, both in general and specifically for what the planets indicate by nature and sign: planets moving quickly or applying to quick planets, being angular or applying to angular planets, ascending in the apogee, and being received. Conditions which suggest lower prices include: being slow or retrograde or applying to such planets, being cadent or applying to cadent planets, descending in the apogee, and not being received. There are other details here and there, but this captures the core of the method.

But in his discussion of prices throughout he month (§§7.61-63), 'Umar divides the time between three planets, apparently in this order: [1] the lord of the Ascendant, [2] the next aspect of the lord of the Ascendant, and [3] the domicile lord of the lord of the Ascendant. In his examples at least, each of these will govern 1/3 of the month, in order. To these he adds [4] any angular planets, when they are applied to or leave the angles (especially if they are being applied to by the lord of the Ascendant). But there is some ambiguity in the timing. In some of his statements (as presented by Hugo), the increase or decrease in prices takes place *while* planets are angular; but in others, they take place when the aspect becomes exact; then, too, he suggests that they take place after the aspects perfect. My sense is that so long as planets remain in the angles, the changes are steady, while the perfection of an aspect suggests a sudden change in price. I have labeled certain sections and phrases in the text with these numbers, for easier comprehension.

§7.60: On things for sale, and their status—'Umar[1]

Also, a general recognition of all provisions depends on the course of each light. Therefore, for individual months, it is necessary to know the assembly of the Sun and Moon beforehand to the very hour, and that the east be arranged according to the composition of the natural hours,[2] lest the blemish of error should turn up from somewhere in the position of the east and the order of this business.

[Choosing the significators][3]

And so, establish the east and its lord as significators for distinguishing the status of both the common people and the atmosphere,[4] and their supports or rather comforts. The one which is in charge (as lord) of the lodging-place of the eastern lord even resembles these, and a peregrine [star] which occupies the east is in agreement with it by some affinity. Which if [the peregrine star] would wholly differ [from the Ascendant], [and] should it be unlucky or corrupted, it introduces corruption [in that month] according to its nature and testimonies.

On the other hand, if any star should happen to be found [in the angle], [especially] the lord of the eastern sovereignty, we commit its leadership and signification to describing [the status] (namely, if the lord of the east would be drawn back from a pivot).[5] Then, every star in a pivot which assumes some virtue and power there, will likewise show certain things for what was

---

[1] Cf. al-Rijāl VIII.33.2 (first part), which I have used to correct and clarify Hugo's text.
[2] *Iuxta naturalium compositionem horarum.* This does not make sense to me, but does not seem to matter anyway: the point is that we must calculate a chart for the exact time of the New Moon.
[3] The method of this subsection seems to be the following. Calculate the chart for the New Moon, and then compare [1] the lord of the Ascendant, [2] the lord of the lord of the Ascendant, [3] a peregrine planet in the Ascendant, and [4] lastly and only if necessary, other lords of the Ascendant, if they are angular. If the lord of the Ascendant is in a good condition and house, and aspects the Ascendant, then prefer it; if it is not angular, one may also use the peregrine planet in the Ascendant as a substitute so long as it is in it. The other lords of the Ascendant (if they are angular) seem to give additional information but do not override the other significators (such as the exalted lord) is in the Ascendant, one may favor it if the lord of the Ascendant is cadent.
[4] That is, for weather. See the material on weather in §Z.
[5] 'Umar or Hugo seems to mean that we would favor the exalted lord of the east if the domicile lord were cadent.

asked about. With the lord of the east, I say, lingering outside a pivot,[6] the signification of the peregrine star is judged to be appropriate and useful until it has departed from the pivot.

Next too, the eastern lord being arranged in the east itself or the remaining pivots, or in the eleventh, or at least if it would direct an aspect into the east from a lucky place,[7] it will take control of the function of the signification, as being preferable to the rest, especially while the eastern [lord] itself would [be eastern and],[8] having departed scorching, would enter the rays of its own light, walking more quickly (as was already stated).

[Judging prices]

For while [the significator] bore itself thusly,[9] it greatly bestows a price on provisions[10] (nor is an increase of this thing denied in individual faces),[11] namely according to the quantity of the addition which the star has in the quick degrees (be they fewer or many), and the effect and day of this promise is especially designated by the Lunar regard to the east from a tetragon, or with her being placed in [the east], or, at least (with her staying [there])[12] she would bless the lord of the east with her own aspect. But in the opposite (namely the seventh) it is hostile to all of these.

[Moreover],[13] if it were increased in motion, the price of grain and provisions will be increased; and if it were failing and applying to the opposite of

---

[6] That is, cadent (al-Rijāl).
[7] This must be the busy or advantageous places according to either Nechepso *et al.* or Dorotheus *et al.* (*ITA* III.4).
[8] Reading with al-Rijāl for Hugo's confusing and redundant "proceed in a pivot and *azarea* (namely the degrees) or a quick course."
[9] That is, if the lord of the east were the significator and was just as was described in the previous paragraph. From now on, we are dealing with whatever planetary significator was found through the methods above, but 'Umar will speak as though it is the lord of the east.
[10] Al-Rijāl adds that men will make profits from them—so people will buy them at higher prices, enriching the sellers.
[11] This must be a reference to dividing the month into ten-day periods, as in §7.61 below.
[12] Al-Rijāl does not require that she actually be in the east while aspecting the lord of the east.
[13] I am reading this entire paragraph with al-Rijāl, for Hugo's very difficult "If it were adding, or, in the month in which provisions usually grow more burdensome, it regarded its lord, once the opposition of the east has been attained: for thus it signifies diminution; in fact, [when] decreasing it portends an increase. Therefore, this adversity, proceeding from the opposite of the east, [and] moreover, the lord of the east being received, and the one which receives it being an adding [star] and in a pivot, introduces an increase for the

the Ascendant, and it aspected the lord of the Ascendant, it signifies a failure and diminution of the price. Moreover, look and see if you found the lord of the Ascendant received, and the receiver[14] were increased in an angle: it signifies that the price of grain will be increased for that whole month: because the lord of the house of the lord of the Ascendant in the opposite of the luminaries is more firm.[15] Even if you found the lord of the Ascendant to be received, and it and [its domicile lord] were ascending,[16] the dearness [of price] and want [of supplies] will be firmer, and this according to their ascensions.

Furthermore, the lord of the east (or a star in the east) applying to any cadent or subtracting[17] star, brings [the price] down lower. Which if the lord of the east and the one which receives it would both be diminishing [their] course, [the price] will be reduced, namely insofar as the diminishment of each would suggest it becomes, and the more so while both were withdrawing or drawn back [from the angles].[18] If however each one would apply to a withdrawing or subtracting star, it designates [that the price is] much less.

On the other hand, a star [which is] withdrawing or subtracting being arranged in the east, testifies it more expressly.[19] If any star appearing in the east would be blessed in testimonies, it is necessary that it correspond to an increase or diminution according to the quantity or manner of its status, its health or corruption; and it will be enriched by the partnership of the eastern lord. But [if the eastern lord] is not received, [then that planet in the east] takes no partner [and] principally claims the signification and duty.

Also, the lord of the east and the two lights being assembled in the [Ascendant of the chart at the time of their assembly],[20] or if rather they would

---

whole month. However, the one which presides over the lodging-place of the eastern lord after the prevention (that is, the Full Moon), is always found to be stronger. Likewise, with the eastern lord being received, while it and the lord of its domicile are adding, this one will add how much that one added—namely, according to the quantity of the increment of each."

[14] That is, the lord of the domicile in which the lord of the Ascendant is. This was listed as being one of the significators above.
[15] This suggests that we should also calculate a chart for the Full Moon, and look at the lord of the Ascendant in that chart (and its domicile lord). It might also mean, "the lord of the lord of the Ascendant is more firm for the *time period* that follows the Full Moon."
[16] This might be increasing in the circle of their apogee, but perhaps simply adding in motion.
[17] This probably means, "slow."
[18] Hugo adds (but al-Rijāl omits): "for they do not promise it will last much longer."
[19] Al-Rijāl omits this, but it makes sense.
[20] Reading tentatively with al-Rijāl for Hugo's "in the same place from the east."

obtain a pivot from the place of their assembly, they portend the steadiness of the provisions in [their] increase or diminution.[21] But should the lights be received (just as the lord of the east [was]) while they would be adding, [and being placed] in the eleventh or the fifth, they designate the most burdensome increase [in price].

Moreover, if any [planet of the Ascendant][22] would apply to the eastern lord, it introduces the increase of the price on that day. Also, the lights being diminished and the eastern lord [also] decreasing, in the third or in the ninth or twelfth, threaten a not-moderate diminution [of prices]. The pivots prefigure the steadiness of the status.

Furthermore,[23] if a failing planet applied to the lord of the Ascendant, it signifies a similar diminution, and a greater one than if the lord [of the Ascendant] would apply to that planet. Moreover, the eastern lord decreasing in computation, and if the increase of the lord of its house[24] would follow, it could profit nothing: for the root and foundation of the whole business consists in [the lord of the Ascendant], [which is namely] the one which is particularly allotted the signification and power at the same time—unless, I say, it is found to be cadent and another planet were in the angle.[25]

If however, the east would present a house to either of the lights,[26] one will necessarily have to have recourse to [that luminary's] increase in computation or diminution, and place from the east.

---

[21] For al-Rijāl, this seems to mean that the price will remain the same.
[22] Reading with al-Rijāl for Hugo's "star or lord." I believe this means a planet in the Ascendant, applying to the lord of the Ascendant.
[23] This sentence is not in Hugo.
[24] That is, the domicile lord of the place where the lord of the Ascendant is.
[25] Hugo has the lord of the east being in the pivot of another star, which does not make sense.
[26] That is, if it were the domicile of one of the luminaries.

§7.61: When they are going to be more burdensome or easier—'Umar[27]

But whether one would surpass the other (namely increase or diminution), or when it would happen, could be discovered thusly. And so, with it decreasing from the apogee (or rather, orbit),[28] that which is left over from the sixth up to the seventh, is mediocre; but from the seventh to the twelfth, and from one up to the third, the worst.[29] Which if there is a question about addition, it will be good to attend to their computation: for when first added,[30] it is necessary that the provisions be altered. The Lunar application to a quick course especially claims the same thing, and the power of the lord of their domiciles and of their signification.

Therefore, once these things have been diligently observed, one should choose the signification of the present affair from a joint observation of them, with an alert memory. However, in order that a firmer and absolute method be applied to the opinion written above, with a question of this kind being present, I have undertaken to append this example, and to note the ascendant and the places of the stars.[31]

Therefore, Cancer was the east, whose lord, the Moon, was staying outside a pivot. Then, the intention of the mind being drawn back to the east and the rest of the pivots, one finds nothing of the stars there.

[1] Once the eastern lord is taken account of, while I have drawn back its apogee. Furthermore, it is left to 5 signs.[32]

[3] From there, once recourse is had to the lord of her lodging-place,[33] [Venus] is found to be decreasing,[34] and in the entrance to scorching.

---

[27] This section is not in al-Rijāl, so we are more at Hugo's mercy for the next few sections.
[28] *Abside*.
[29] This seems to have to do with the distance from the apogee of the epicycle, but I do not understand it. 'Umar mentions this point again in his example below. Cf. perhaps al-Bīrūnī §§199 and 203.
[30] I believe this means that we must see when the planet actually begins to add in course, for that will indicate the time.
[31] Omitting *consilium*.
[32] Some texts say 6. Again, this seems to refer to the relation of a planet to its apogee, but I do not understand it.
[33] Namely, Venus.
[34] 'Umar must have another, special meaning for increasing and decreasing in this example and the next, because both Venus and Mars (which he claims are decreasing) are actually moving quickly and in direct motion.

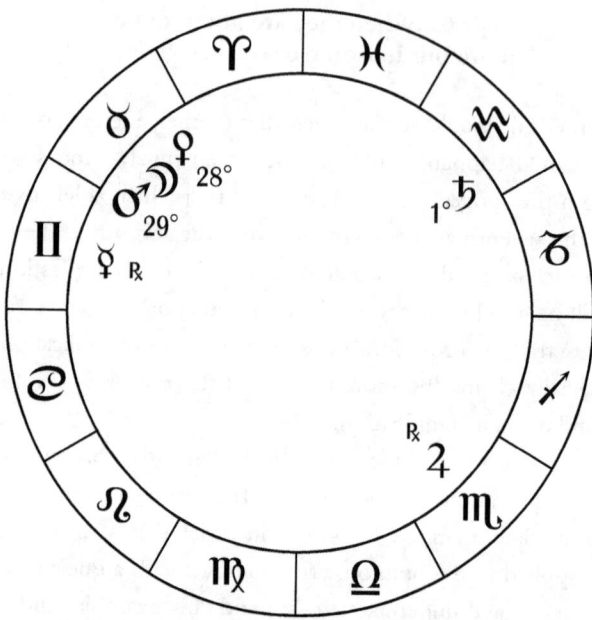

Figure 34: 'Umar's chart for §7.61, based on the 1509 diagram

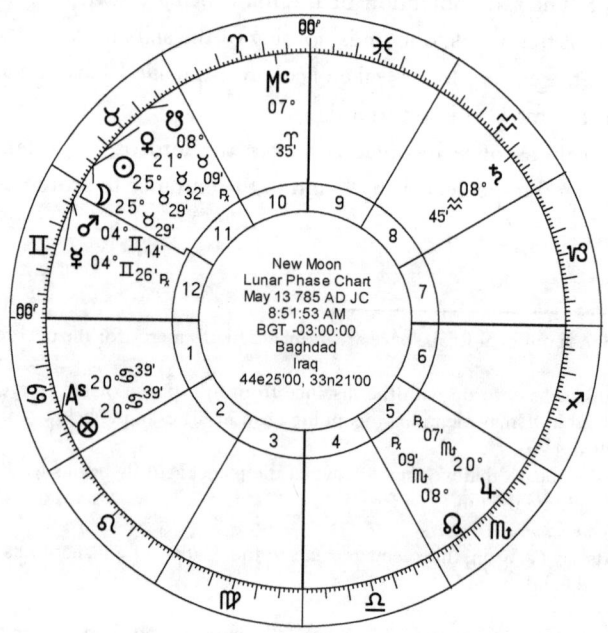

Figure 35: Likely chart for 'Umar's §7.61 (in whole signs)

[2] Considering the status of the Moon, I found her applying to Mars without reception. Therefore, the Moon being in [her] sovereignty or in [her own] house, was portending the steadiness of the burden of things for sale, until she herself crossed the east.[35] Once that has happened, she [will have] conceded the signification to Mars, to which Venus was applying ([Venus] being the lord of [the Moon's] own lodging-place). Thus therefore, both [Venus and Mars are] decreasing, [and] is entering scorching: and so they indicate the greatest increase and diminution,[36] in terms of points in the multitude of each *kardaja*.[37]

And so, their signification in the third part of the month (namely, once ten days have passed by), and in the last of them, testifies that things for sale that are of an easier price will become not-moderately so. It is even agreed that the month is divided into three parts in this way. Because [1] at its beginning, the Moon was enjoying the rulership of the east: whence she, adding in computation, indicates burdensome things for sale. Then [2] Mars, to whom she was applying, takes away from the price, because he is decreasing, and because of [his entrance] into scorching.[38] [3] Venus assumes the signification of the third part, [and is] indicating the same thing Mars does, because she is decreasing and is equally entering into scorching. It will be permitted to observe all of these things through the appended description.

---

[35] I am not sure if this means the degree of the Ascendant, or the entire ascending sign.

[36] This seems to mean that the Moon signifies a good increase, while Venus and Mars signify decrease. See the next paragraph.

[37] A *kardaja* is a unit of measurement, and has two meanings. Originally, it was the sine of 1/96 of a complete circle (3° 45', which is also equivalent to 1/24 of a quarter of the circle), and apparently it was used in measuring planetary motion. But later, it came to be seen as 1/24 of the *whole* circle, and thus equivalent to 15°. Sahl seems to view it as this later value (see *On Quest.*, footnote to §22f), but I do not know what 'Umar thought, nor do I quite understand how it is meant here.

[38] Because the Sun moves faster than Mars, Mars is going under the rays and entering scorching.

§7.62: (More on the same topic)—'Umar[39]

Moreover,[40] just as was interpreted in this figure, it is agreeable to note the east and its lord at the beginning of the month, also to establish the pivots, and to consult the places of the stars, in order.

Therefore, once these have been interpreted in such an order, it seems that an observation of [1] the eastern lord is greatly necessary. No less too, must [2] its application with adding stars (or those which are decreasing in computation) be noted, or their application with it. In addition even, it seems that those stars which are holding onto the pivots must be observed, and their status up until they depart from them, but even the reception[41] of one to another.

[2] Again, in this place it comes to be noted that adding and decreasing stars (namely those which [happen to] apply to the lord of the east, or it to them), if they assume no testimonies with it, they undoubtedly portend an increase or diminution at the time of the application.

[2] Which if a star applying to [the lord of the east] would then possess a pivot (or [it did so in the preceding cycle of the month),[42] [and the lord of the east], I say, being drawn back, and applying to it in a pivot, it does not harm with an increase until it is separated from it. Likewise, with it withdrawing, a diminution follows, namely in accordance with the withdrawal of the applying one which then possesses a pivot.[43] And it signifies the alteration and constancy of the status.

Moreover, the eastern lord and equally [3] that of its lodging-place, if they would apply to a star in the Midheaven, they make things for sale costly, especially while they were adding. For if they would be decreasing, they bring forth a moderate increase, but a steady one.

---

[39] For this section, cf. Dorotheus in §7.67, which has helped untangle some of Hugo's meaning. This material must derive from Māshā'allāh, since Dorotheus credits Māshā'allāh for this whole view, and 'Umar does so in a similar passage in §7.64.
[40] I have brought this sentence up from the bottom of the section, since it connects this section with the previous one, and links with the use of "order" in the next paragraph. I have omitted Hugo's *rationi consentanea omnimodo comprobantur* as not really having a clear role in the passage.
[41] This seems to mean how they apply to one another and receive each other's aspects, not classical reception proper.
[42] Reading for Hugo's "or a cycle of the month preceded."
[43] But according to 'Umar's method, angular planets show increases; so why would it only show an increase *after* it departed the angle?

However, the increase of [the lord of] the east, and the one which is opposed to it,[44] do not convey much addition again, but decreasing they signify harm; still, they are examined and do not lack value. If therefore [the planet to which it applied] would be holding onto the pivot of the earth as was stated, they introduce steadiness (if, I say, they do not recede from [their] average course).

§7.63: [Another example, from the following month]—'Umar[45]

The east was Sagittarius, and its lord [Jupiter] decreasing in computation;[46] the five stars were staying in the opposite [of the Ascendant]. Of them, Mercury was cadent, while [4] the rest occupied a pivot.[47] However, the Sun [is] wholly arranged rightly,[48] the Moon increasing, applying to a decreasing[49] and corrupted Mars. Venus too was likewise adding, with no aspect being conveyed to the lord of the east, until she first gives up the sign which she is holding onto. That portends the same thing which we related above about the eastern lord, the Sun, and the Moon.[50]

The signification of Mars pertains to diminution, until Venus herself gave up that place, once she has applied to the eastern lord (namely after ten days),[51] then finally even the Moon will undergo his assembly.[52] Therefore,

---

[44] This phrase should really read something like: "and of a planet in the house opposed to the east, namely the seventh." In §7.64, 'Umar clarifies that if the lord of the Ascendant or the Moon would apply to planets in the Ascendant or Midheaven, the increases will be more dramatic; but if to planets in the seventh or fourth, it is less dramatic. See the rest of this paragraph.
[45] This example should be easy to follow, with the exception of Mars allegedly decreasing in speed (though perhaps he is decreasing in the circle of his apogee?). 'Umar's point is that, at the beginning of the Lunar month and up to and including the Full Moon, many planets will be angular and moving fast. And, the planets which will perfect aspects to the lord of the Ascendant, will also be moving quickly. So, this suggests a stable increase in prices.
[46] Jupiter is retrograde, so he is moving slowly.
[47] Again, showing that 'Umar uses quadrant divisions to determine angularity.
[48] *Recte*. This word is sometimes used to speak of the angles, and what Hugo means is that the Sun is exactly (or almost exactly) on the degree of the Descendant.
[49] Actually, Mars is increasing in speed.
[50] This might refer to §7.62 above, where it was said that an adding planet will increase prices when it aspects the lord of the Ascendant.
[51] Since 'Umar believes Venus is at 29° Gemini, and Jupiter is retrograde at 12° Scorpio, it should only take her about 10 days to make an exact trine to him.
[52] That is, the Moon will then conjoin with the lord of the Ascendant (Jupiter) while she is still waxing. She will do this a few days after Venus trines Jupiter, and just before the Full

the aforewritten places of the stars, and their positions, designates that things for sale are confined to a suitable status, nor be completely changed in anything, until 13 days of the month are reached. But after that, up until her departure, their adding is noted, but nevertheless it seems an increase of this kind proceeds from the staying of the stars in the pivots.[53]

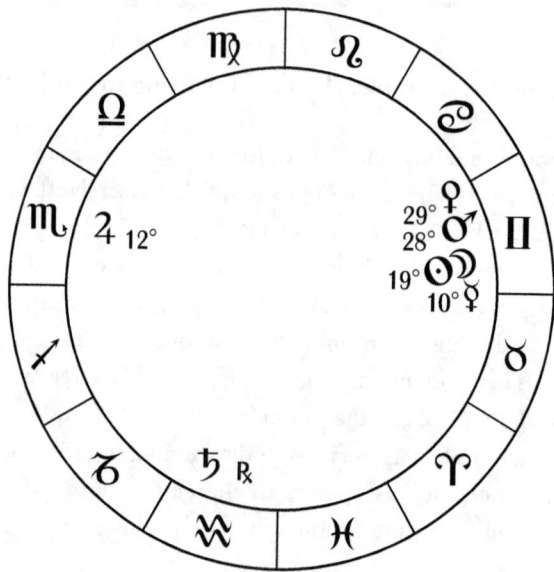

Figure 36: 'Umar's chart for §7.63, based on the Vienna diagram

---

Moon—which is why 'Umar says that this will be the situation for 13 days. On about the fourteenth day, the Moon will be full and will than wane.
[53] 'Umar probably means that just before and during the Full Moon, the Sun and Mercury, and the Moon will all still be in the angles (showing a stable increase).

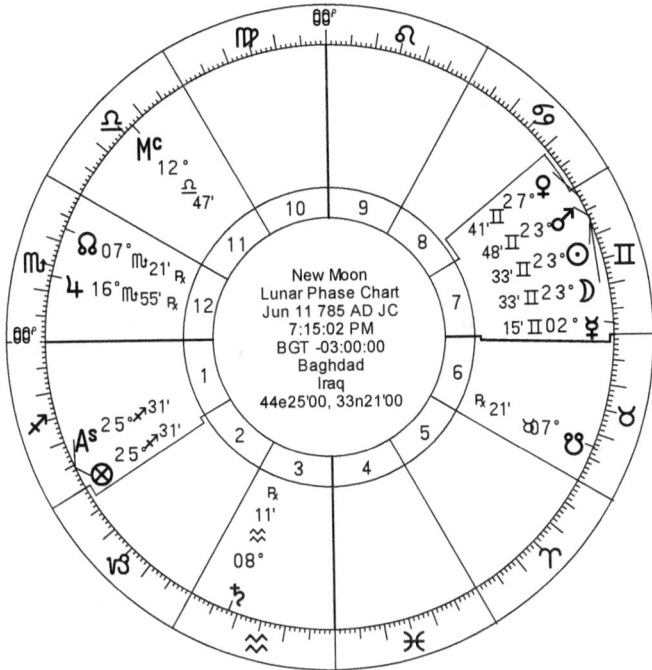

Figure 37: Likely chart for 'Umar's §7.63 (in whole signs)

§7.64: On the price of things for sale—'Umar[54]

Moreover, in this place the opinion of Māshā'allāh (about discerning, I say, the status of things for sale) will have to be written below—namely, whether they would be bought at a burdensome price or the contrary. For he encourages us to attend especially to the lord of the east and the Moon. Which if the stronger of them would apply to some star in the east or the Midheaven, it introduces an increase to the price; but if [to a star] in the opposite[55] or the pivot of the earth, even though it might not go beyond [its] average [price], still it asserts that many will be in need [of it, and things will be sold].[56]

---

[54] Cf. al-Rijāl VIII.33.2 (middle), where this is attributed to Māshā'allāh (as 'Umar states below).
[55] Namely, the Descendant or seventh.
[56] Adding based on al-Rijāl.

Therefore, with these bearing themselves so, it is reasonable to attend to that star which possesses these two places, [to see] if it were received or it would only receive[57] the lord of the east and equally [the lord] of its own house: [because then prices will go up]. If therefore its application would be to a cadent star, nor to one receiving [it], [prices will be cheap and not be sold].[58]

[The worst thing for selling is if the Moon and the lord of the Ascendant applied to a cadent planet not receiving them.] But if they would apply to a cadent[59] star, with the Moon or the lord of the east being received, it multiplies buyers, but these things will not be more burdensome.[60]

§7.65: On the procuring of things for sale—'Umar[61]

Thābit,[62] too, being of no little worthiness among the astrologers of the Egyptians, especially writing a certain book to his student (namely according to the opinion of Ptolemy and of the rest of the sages who were his contemporaries in Egypt, whom he approached in order to counsel them), testifies that he found them to be in agreement (in an affair of this kind) about an observation of each light.[63]

For whenever an inquiry of this kind would come forth into the open, it will have to be resolved from the entrance of the Sun into Aries, [and the conjunction preceding every quarter],[64] but even from the assembly and opposition which happen in individual months. In fact, Ptolemy teaches that

---

[57] Reading with al-Rijāl for Hugo's "regard." *Respicio* ("regard") and *recipio* ("receive") are very close in spelling and easy to mix up.

[58] Adding with al-Rijāl. 1551 says they will not be "sold," while 1485 says they will not be "sought."

[59] Reading with al-Rijāl for Hugo's "received."

[60] This is the opposite of al-Rijāl, who says that goods will not be sought, but the prices will still be high. I think Hugo might be right here: the cadency would show low prices, but the reception shows that sellers will still do all right because there will be buyers.

[61] Cf. al-Rijāl VIII.33.2 (middle), where this seems to be attributed to Māshā'allāh, in a book written for his student; apparently Māshā'allāh credited Ptolemy and other Egyptian sages with this view.

[62] Unless another Thābit is mean, the astronomer and astrologer Thābit bin Qurra (ca. 836 – 901 AD) was born after 'Umar's death, indicating that at least some of this section has been added by another author. But see my footnote above, where al-Rijāl attributes this to Māshā'allāh, who in turn credits Ptolemy and other Egyptian sages.

[63] That is, the two luminaries.

[64] Adding with al-Rijāl.

one must observe it, in the cycle of mundane years,[65] from the assembly or opposition which preceded the Sun's entrance into Aries: because the diversity or alteration of all worldly things seems to proceed from them. For from the assembly comes all generations of things and accidents come to be, but from the opposition their removal:[66] whence, among the philosophers the Moon is said to be the lesser world, because beyond the rest of the seven planets she principally administers those accidents which belong to the lower world, which is said to be the temporal world of generation and corruption. Even the month is said to be found on account of this, because the recognition of increase or diminution depends on that.

Therefore, [so that][67] the temporal world is understood and discovered through a steady method, among the seven the Moon is granted a judgment as being the chief and first one of all the transitory things which she contains under herself (trees, namely, and animals) with respect to increase or diminution. Then, too, it seems one must apply the Sun as a partner, because he furnishes the reason for the Lunar arising[68] or opposition. No less, too, must the Venusian and Mercurial partnership be added (the reason for which matter is the affinity of each of [their] circles with the Solar[69] ones: and they are frequently eastern and western, [and] the motion of their circuit is quick and hastened).[70]

[The value of coinage or money, versus the price of goods]

They[71] even made the Moon and the Ascendant to be contraries, namely one to the other. Likewise too, they made the possession or power of coins and other things which are sold, to be contraries amongst themselves and one to the other: and when one of them is increased, the other is pressed

---

[65] Omitting Hugo's transliteration for the Arabic "revolution of the years of the world."
[66] Reading with al-Rijāl for Hugo's "the renewal of a certain generation, but from the opposition every variety."
[67] Reading for *postquam* ("after, afterwards") to make the meaning clearer. What 'Umar ultimately means is that we will look at the Sun "after" looking at the Moon, because she is the principal planet here.
[68] Hugo must be referring especially to the Moon's arising out of the rays after the assembly. Al-Rijāl says, "because these changes happen through her conjunction and her opposition with him."
[69] Al-Rijāl reads this as the Lunar circle.
[70] See also al-Kindī in §7.66 for Mercury and Venus.
[71] Reading this whole paragraph with al-Rijāl, as Hugo's version is so compressed as to be incomprehensible.

down, such as gold and silver, and grain and clothing. Because for little money they will give much of [one] thing, and for a small amount of a thing they will give much money. The astrologer even said that the more noble places of heaven are the pivots: whenever therefore the fortunate ones occupy the pivots, they make gold costly, and designate that things for sale are neglected. Contrariwise, with infortunes appearing in the same place, gold is cheap, while things for sale are of a greater price. However, if the fortunate ones would be staying in the rest of the domiciles, there is honor in things for sale, while their price grows cheap. But it happens to the contrary if the infortunes would possess the same houses.

And if one of the infortunes were in the angles, and the other in the other houses, judge through the more firm one of them, and pay attention to it, and the cheapness which comes forth through a fortune, could not be great. Likewise, any lucky one being retrograde (or at least in a weak place) exhibits a lesser effect. In this manner too, the infortunes in any of their own dignities are agreed to be stronger.

Furthermore, whenever it would please you to discover the quarter of the year or the middle or the whole year,[72] the Moon should principally be noted, [when she separates from the conjunction or opposition].[73] Which if she would first apply to fortunate ones, they make things for sale more dear. With her encountering the infortunes, they grow cheap. The Moon in a pivot adds to their price.[74] It is not otherwise too, with her being in her own sovereignty, strong and free of the infortunes.

Next, too, the Sun encountering a fortunate one (or it him), such as if Venus would encounter the Sun or the Sun Jupiter, coin will increase and things will be rejected and become cheap,[75] especially while the Sun would be holding onto a pivot or his own sovereignty. Now, he encountering infortunes takes away from the price of gold, especially [with him] possessing a weak place or if he withdrew from a pivot.

However, Mercury principally rules over the aforesaid money (namely gold and silver), and claims a major portion in them, [while] Venus accompanies [him in this].[76] The role of Venus is the respectable look [of the money] and the splendor of [its] color, but to the portion of Mercury one

---

[72] Or probably, the month as well.
[73] Adding with al-Rijāl.
[74] Al-Rijāl reads this as increasing scarcity and want: this would drive up the price.
[75] Reading with al-Rijāl for Hugo's "things for sale will become more burdensome."
[76] I have restructured this sentence a bit in accordance with the meaning and al-Rijāl.

grants any sculpting and the beauty of the painting. However, in gold he claims the greater power, because he is more closely neighboring the Sun.[77] Which[78] if they were eastern (and especially in their own sovereignty), they commend gold; but being western, [coin grows cheap],[79] especially in their depression.

Moreover, Mercury being placed with the Sun strives after gold, and shuts it up in the royal treasure-houses [as being of great value], but it establishes things for sale as being easy [in price]. If however Venus would accompany the Sun, it bestows value on silver, and commends it to the purses of the rich. But, they being far from the company of the Sun, roaming high in the circle of their apogees,[80] they favor the price of gold [but things will be cheap], especially [while] adding or being eastern, or being established in their own domiciles or any dignity of their own. But declining in the circles of their apogees, going towards westernness,[81] being alien or in places wholly devoid of any dignity, they trample gold underfoot, [but] hoard things for sale as being worthy in price.

Moreover, with the east of the year or quarter or month (or rather of the middle [of the year]) being established, and the pivots fixed in place, even with the degree of the house of money being assigned:[82] if the lord of the lodging-place of money would occupy some pivot, especially in a place where it assumes some dignity, while (I say) any fortunate one would be staying in that same place,[83] it renders gold costly. But[84] if it were an infortune in the angle just as we have said before, coin will be esteemed, but will not be respected, because low-class men will handle it.

---

[77] Al-Rijāl reads, "because he is of the distribution [*partitione*] of the Sun." I am not sure what this means.
[78] I have restructured this sentence in accordance with al-Rijāl. Hugo mistook the statement about being eastern as meaning "rising in prominence" (namely, in a good condition) and western as meaning "being humbled" (namely, in a bad condition).
[79] Adding with al-Rijāl.
[80] Reading with al-Rijāl for "roaming alone in their own circles." I have also clarified this using al-Rijāl immediately below.
[81] Reading with al-Rijāl for Hugo's "and not without an increase."
[82] This suggests that 'Umar was using a quadrant-based house system (or perhaps even equal houses, as with his profection method).
[83] Al-Rijāl reads this as though the lord of the second itself is a benefic.
[84] Reading with al-Rijāl for Hugo's "But an infortune occupying a pivot just as we said: of its own corruption, assumes greater testimonies: it does not portend this because of the corruption or defect of gold, but because it is handled by the hands of undistinguished people." I am not sure what this means.

[Prices in particular goods, according to houses and signs]

On the other hand,[85] the worth and lowness of things for sale can be demonstrated (and not idly so) by the infortunes and fortunate ones appearing in the signs.[86] For the fortunate ones being placed thusly, the things for sale which are made subject to the sign which they are holding onto, will not lack in price. Contrariwise however, a sign possessed by the infortunes, whatever they signify, grow cheap, being neglected. Now, a distribution of things for sale through the individual signs, is appropriate: such as sheep and flock-animals for Aries. The rest are conceded by the philosophers to the rest of the signs, by means of an appropriate correspondence.[87]

Moreover, in this place it seems worthy to understand that the east possesses the head of all living things, but the fourth the belly, the seventh the body, tail, and hind parts, and the tenth claims the flanks.[88] If therefore an infortune occupied [one of these], it states that there is a defect in that same place.

But with respect to a man, the head will be ascribed to the east, the neck to the second, the head and shoulders[89] to the third, and no less in such an order through the rest of the twelve domiciles.

But there is a double observation of sprouting things: for it is the first and last appearance.[90] Therefore, the east has what is first and is being released, but the seventh what is last and transmitted. Whenever therefore a question were proposed about sprouting things, establish the east and the Moon and equally the lord of [the east and of the Moon]. All of them being safe and lucky, do not deny increase. But being corrupted, they promise harm. Two of them being free and cleansed, and the perversity of two, introduce a mediocre judgment.

---

[85] Reading *porro* with al-Rijāl for Hugo's "generally, therefore."
[86] Reading with al-Rijāl for Hugo's "in that same place."
[87] Reading less correctly but more clearly than Hugo's *congrua portione*.
[88] Including the upper parts and back of the animal (*costas*). 'Umar is thinking of animals such as cows or pigs here).
[89] Normally this would be the shoulders, arms, and hands.
[90] *Facies*. 'Umar seems to mean that vegetation is observed only in terms of the first planting and sprouting, and the final produce and production of further seed. See the next sentence.

§7.66: On things for sale—al-Kindī

§662. If someone worried would inquire into the price of things for sale, let him note studiously the victor of the degree[91] of the assembly or opposition which preceded the Sun's ingress into the first point of Aries), and let it take possession as the significator. If therefore the significator itself would be adding, or there would come to be an application of it with a star [that is] adding,[92] it seems to signify that the price of things will be more burdensome, and according to the nature of the sign which it is holding onto. No less should the understanding of the lord of the Ascendant of the year and of the Ascendant of the conjunction [or opposition] be judged as necessary.

§663. Moreover, the pivots being blessed with the light of the lucky ones makes the price of things for sale more burdensome; but that of the unlucky ones, the contrary. Moreover, the Sun and the Moon in a pivot declare coin to be costly. And so the Sun designates gold, the Moon silver.

§664. Venus [and] Mercury even testify in this manner: for Venus resembles the Moon in signification, Mercury the Sun. Which if these significators would be cadent from the pivots, they mean the cheapness of gold and silver, but they commend what is bought with these at a greater price.

§665. Therefore, one should note with an ever-watchful mind, what kind of assent the fortunes show.[93] But the fortunes make things more expensive, the infortunes the contrary.

§666. This same thing must be considered in the individual quarters [of the year] for the price of things at that time, and in the individual conjunctions and oppositions (just as done here at the beginning of the year), and a moderating judgment [made] from all of these.[94]

§667.[95] If therefore the significators of things for sale were cadent, they convey low[96] [prices] or a manifold abundance of them. Then the ingress of

---

[91] Reading with Robert. Hugo reads, "the victor, namely the lord of the degree...". But the victor assumes a decision procedure: it is not merely the lord of a place of a degree. Note however that *Forty Chapters* Ch. 3, which lists several victors, does not explain the victor of a particular degree. Perhaps al-Kindī is thinking along the lines of *Forty Chapters* §§699-700, which suggests the most important ruler of the degree which also regards it.
[92] This probably refers to increasing in speed, but I would not rule out increasing in the circle of the apogee (see *ITA* II.0-4).
[93] This probably means that we must keep watching the transits throughout the year, and not only at the ingresses.
[94] Using Robert's more succinct version of this paragraph.
[95] I add Robert's version below, because he gives a slightly different version of the ingresses. Hugo has the lord of the Ascendant or of the assembly/opposition entering the

[the lord] of the Ascendant [of the year]⁹⁷ or of the opposition or the assembly, into the Ascendant itself or into one of the pivots, determines the hour at which these things should happen. The lords of the annual quarters do not even deny what the lords of the Ascendant [of the year] and of the assembly [or opposition] testify to.

[Robert]: The ingress of the aforesaid significators into the places designated above will bring about the time of the foreseen alleviation or burdensomeness [of the cost]: namely, [1] the [ingress of the] victor of the degree of the conjunction or opposition into [that place itself], or [2] the entrance of the ruler of the east of the year, or the lord of the conjunction or opposition, into the east itself.

§668. Moreover, the ascent of the stars into the north,⁹⁸ increases the price of things; but into the south, the contrary.

§7.67: On the signification of the lights with respect to the status of things for sale, through the individual months—Dorotheus⁹⁹

For discerning the quality of the status of things for sale, Māshā'allāh teaches that the east must be noted at the hour of the conjunction of the Sun and Moon.

The east and its lord, and what star possesses it,¹⁰⁰ determine the status of things for sale. Therefore, the eastern lord proceeding quickly in a pivot or in the eleventh, makes things for sale burdensome in that month, namely according to the greatest increase of that star—or [if the contrary], the contrary.

Ascendant of the year or any of the pivots. Robert allows these significators to enter the Ascendant, but also lets the lord of the assembly/opposition enter the place of the assembly/opposition.

⁹⁶ *Graves.* I am a bit unsure about this, because in other places *gravis* and *gravescor* refer to higher and more burdensome prices. But one would expect the price and value of things to go down in the cadent places.

⁹⁷ Adding based on Robert.

⁹⁸ That is, by ecliptical latitude.

⁹⁹ This section should be read with 'Umar's §7.62 above (and secondarily the end of §7.60 and §7.64). The fact that they both credit Māshā'allāh with this view, also suggests their overlap.

¹⁰⁰ This is probably the east (and possibly the Midheaven), by comparison with 'Umar above.

Now when the Moon obtains the Midheaven or the east,[101] things for sale grow burdensome on that very day. But when she attains the seventh, it portends the same thing as it does at the beginning of the month. But it is important [to note] that the beginning of the month pertains to increase, the end looks at detriment.[102] And it is necessary that it happens contrariwise, too.[103]

Moreover, the eastern lord applying to a star in the Midheaven, makes things for sale dearer, especially if each is adding, but [those prices] are lasting. But the diminution of each designates a moderate increase.

If however there is an application [of the eastern lord] with a star in the pivot of the earth, it shows a steadiness in increase.

Especially with both the lord of the east [and the lights] being received,[104] while they [also] possess the eleventh or second or fifth place,[105] and the Moon is applying to a star adding in a pivot, [it indicates an increase in prices]. They especially become cheap, then, when the [lights and the] lord of the east would be lingering in the seventh[106] or twelfth, and is decreasing.[107] Also, the pivots designate steadiness, unless the Moon would apply to a star that is cadent or decreasing in computation: for then things for sale are promoted.[108]

§7.68: On the price of things for sale—Jirjis

For having an understanding of this kind, the lord of the year should be noted. For, this [planet] traversing in a fiery[109] sign, makes gold, silver, and what comes to be through fire, more burdensome. In an earthy one, provi-

---

[101] I believe this is by ongoing transit throughout the Lunar month.
[102] This is probably a reference to the idea that a waxing Moon increases prices, while a waning one decreases them (see *ITA* V.7 and *Forty Chapters* §61, both based on *Carmen* V.43).
[103] I am not sure what this sentence means.
[104] I have read this condition with 'Umar (§7.60) and al-Rijāl, since Hugo has the lord of the east itself being both "cadent" and received, but then in the next clause it is in one of the succedent places.
[105] But by definition the lord of the east was cadent, not in those places. Something seems to have gotten mixed up by Dorotheus or Hugo.
[106] 'Umar (§7.60) reads, "third or ninth."
[107] Reading with al-Rijāl §7.60 and al-Rijāl for "received."
[108] Jirjis (§7.69 below) reads this as meaning that prices will go down: this would lead to more sales.
[109] Reading *igneo* for *aereo*.

sions[110] and germinating things. In a human one, living things and four-footed things. In a watery one, in fish and marine animals.

But[111] so that you may discern the place of this outcome, let the intention of your mind be drawn back to the sign of the Midheaven. Therefore, Aries in the Midheaven [indicates] it is in the middle of the second clime, toward the east. Leo, the last parts of this clime, toward the east. Sagittarius, at the beginning of it, towards the east. Taurus too as the Midheaven, suggests the middle of the second clime, to the south. But Gemini [means] the last parts of the fourth clime, toward the west. But Libra, the beginning of the fourth and toward the west, and likewise Aquarius. But if Cancer, the last parts of the sixth toward the south. But if Pisces, the beginnings of the seventh, to the south.

But these will only endure for a span of three months, up until the Sun undergoes the first degree of Cancer. With the east and the rest of the houses established, just as was done in the first point and degree of Aries, one will have to work thusly whenever he enters the rest of the turning [signs].

§7.69: On the same thing, through individual months—Jirjis[112]

But if you wish to distinguish what would happen through individual months, you will note the assembly of the Sun and Moon at that same point, and you will establish the east at that hour.[113] If therefore the lord of the east were adding in course, the price of provisions increases. But its average progression brings [the price of] provisions down.

Now, if it[114] would be lingering in the Midheaven, it makes the price most burdensome.

It is not otherwise[115] if it[116] would apply to a star appearing in the Midheaven.

---

[110] *Victualia*, here and below.

[111] In this paragraph, Jirjis is associating the signs on the Midheaven with the climes (areas of geographical latitude, from the equator to the north pole). The description here is incomplete and confusing. For different schemes of assigning signs and planets to climes, see Māshā'allāh's *On the Revolution of the Years of the World* (in *WSM*) and Bonatti's *BOA*, Tr. 8.1, Chs. 7-8.

[112] This section is a very abbreviated version of Dorotheus in §7.67 above.

[113] That is, cast a chart for every New Moon throughout the year.

[114] Dorotheus reads this as being the Moon.

[115] That is, prices will go up.

[116] In Dorotheus, this is now the lord of the Ascendant.

[Also, the pivots designate steadiness,[117] unless the Moon would apply to a star that is][118] in its own fall, or in the third or in the ninth: for thus provisions will be easier.

§7.70: On the price of things for sale—Jirjis

Therefore, if the east of the annual cycle[119] were Aries, fish grow cheap but meat grows burdensome. With Taurus as the east, grain is dear, and meat will be cheaper. An east [comprised] of Gemini denotes that all things are burdensome, but wheat is cheap. But Cancer diminishes waters and dews, but multiplies conflagrations. But Leo as the east multiplies revenues and produce, [and] finally all provisions. Virgo makes olive oil very burdensome. Libra has few coins, whence silver is dear but gold grows cheap; finally, all provisions will be dear. Scorpio takes away from heavy rains, and makes moderate rivers, fertilizes trees, greatly increases proceeds,[120] and multiplies the waters of rivers. But Sagittarius stirs up battles, wars, and seditions, but the provisions will be many. Capricorn has the cheapest meats, but fruits or the dates of palm trees are dear; finally, vegetables[121] are cheap. But Aquarius as the east diminishes waters, [and] shows that provisions are more burdensome. An east of Pisces throws in mediocrity everywhere.

§7.71: On the price or status of things for sale—Aristotle

Whenever[122] it is asked about some thing, whether it is going to be dear in that month or year, the whole affair should be sought from the east and the rest of the pivots. For, any star traversing in a pivot will make the things of its own nature and proper quality dearer. But should it be staying after the

---

[117] In Dorotheus, this seems to mean a steadiness of *increase*.
[118] Adding with Dorotheus.
[119] That is, the chart of the annual solar revolution. But I'm sure Jirjis also means this to pertain to the quarterly ingress charts as well (and perhaps the monthly ingresses). The previous section tracked prices based on the lord of the Ascendant, which must be why the sign on the Ascendant is addressed here.
[120] *Fructus*, which can also mean "fruit." I take it to mean "proceeds" here, since Hugo just contrasted it with *frux*, which has the more specific meaning of actual crops, produce, etc.
[121] *Olera*, a variant on *holera*.
[122] In this paragraph I believe Aristotle assumes the querent wants to *sell* something; but in the next paragraph, I believe he means that the querent wants to *buy* something (namely, essentials and provisions for life).

pivots, it calls the things of its nature and proper quality back to a better status. And those in the remote [places] trample their own things with a cheap price.

But if he made the question about provisions, what is of a dearer price should be sought in the east and the tenth. In the second and eleventh the price is not wholly mediocre, because they look more to what is severe.[123] In the third and ninth, the cheapness is greater.

Finally, let us see what things agree with which planets:

Therefore, Saturn has especially claimed lead and worse iron or Indian steel; of colors, the black; of clothing, woolens and what is of monastic (that is, poorly-made) quality,[124] and instruments of agriculture, but even hides.

But Jupiter has olive oil, and silk, raw silver, very white textiles, and white wine.

To Mars belong any arms, red wine and clothing of that color, moreover he has red gold and copper, more expensive or better steel and iron, mustard and pepper, euphorbia,[125] scammony,[126] and horses given to warlike uses.

But to the Solar power responds gold of a citrine color, and wine just like that, and saffron textiles, but even saffron-colored copper, and garnets[127] and *siricae*[128] clothing.

Venus has any fatness (lard, I say, and grease),[129] also sweet-smelling and any odiferous commodities, sweet water, and she has womanly ornaments.

But Mercury possess coins and millet (and middling or small grains), moreover filberts and what is of this kind.

Finally, the Moon has the beasts of common laborers and those that are put out for hire, olibanum, but she even claims milk and cheese.

---

[123] *Gravitatem*. I take this to mean that since they are moving towards the pivots (which indicate higher prices), they are somewhat middling in price, but more towards high or difficult prices.

[124] *Laneas et monachalis, id est, incompositi, ordinis.*

[125] A plant with a hot or stinging sap, used as a laxative.

[126] A plant used as a laxative.

[127] *Carbunculus*, lit. "live coals, embers."

[128] This word has a number of connotations, from red pigments (which might be considered solar) to various kinds of silk and finer textiles like velvet or damask.

[129] *Sepum (sebum)*. This can also include suet and tallow.

Fugitives[1]

§7.72: On a missing captive or any thing gone missing—Sahl[2]

With an inquiry submitted about a missing captive (or if someone would be fleeing), as to whether or not he would be able to be recovered, the [following] observation comes to be [noted]. For the east and its lord, with the Sun,[3] are put over the querent, but the seventh and its lord and the Moon, over the missing thing.

And so, an application of the eastern lord with the lord of the seventh, suggests the one sought[4] is recovered, [but] not without effort and labor. It is even [the same] if that same eastern lord would be lingering in the seventh. But with the order being turned around—the lord of the seventh applying to the eastern [lord] or traversing in the east—it portends he will return on his own.

Then, the Moon being separated from the lord of the east and applying to the significator [of the missing person],[5] announces definite rumors to the querent about the missing captive or fugitive. But if the reverse—should she be withdrawing from the significator [of the fugitive and] be applying to the

---

[1] This topic should be read with the following one (theft), as the entire treatment of fugitives and theft seems to have been divided by Hugo into these two parts (fugitives in §§7.72-88, and theft proper in §§7.89-146). Obviously there is some overlap between these two topics, but we can see from Sahl and 'Umar in particular that different houses and planets were attributed to each topic. For fugitives, Sahl conceives the question as being one of the owner (Ascendant, Sun) initiating a search for the fugitive (seventh, Moon); but 'Umar (following *Carmen* V.36) seems to frame it as an escape initiated by the fugitive (Ascendant, Moon), with the Midheaven and Sun and lord of the Moon signifying the fugitive's master or the goods' owner. In both cases, the Ascendant represents the one initiating the action, the Sun indicates the owner or master, and the Moon the fugitive. Al-Kindī's attributions are from Ch. 7 of his *Forty Chapters*, and seem to be closer to Sahl than to 'Umar or *Carmen*. Some of the ambiguities and differences among these texts could have to do with the fact that a fugitive slave is himself property: so a runaway slave is essentially committing theft by stealing himself, just as much as a robber stealing silverware.

[2] Cf. *On Quest.* §7.10.

[3] John's Sahl does not include the Sun; Hugo may have included it because the Sun indicates recovery, which is what the owner or querent wants. But *Carmen* V.36.1 gives the Ascendant and the Moon to the runaway, and the tenth and the Sun to the master—which is what Sahl might have had in mind as well.

[4] Reading *quaesitum* for *quaerentem*.

[5] That is, the lord of the seventh.

eastern lord—it restores what had fled, into the graces of the owner.[6] Moreover, an application of the significator [of the fugitive][7] being made [later] to the eastern lord, wholly confirms it will return.

But whenever the significator[8] would apply to a malevolent occupying a pivot, it impedes the one fleeing with captivity, and prepares foreign chains. Likewise, nor would the fugitive be able to be concealed with either one of the lights applying to the significator. Moreover, the scorching of the significator suggests that the one fleeing will be apprehended, especially if it regards the lord of the east.

Again, the Moon[9] applying to a malevolent prepares prison for the fugitive. But if she would apply to a fortunate one, it promises freedom and escape, unless perhaps [the fortunate planet] would be entering into scorching itself, or it would come to be retrograde or corrupted: for while it enters scorching it bears a judgment of death, [and] if it happened to be corrupted while entering scorching, [the querent] will find[10] his corpse and remains even after death.

Also, a Lunar application being made to the Sun[11] impedes and denies the escape. But while [she] would apply to some retrograding planet, it leads the one returning back, of his own accord. Applying to a star lingering in a pivot or after a pivot, it impedes the path and journey of the one fleeing, and brings him back, apprehended.[12] But [if that angular or succeedent star is] traversing in [its] first station, made towards retrogradation, it brings the apprehended fugitive severely punished; in its second station, so that it is already moving forward, it apprehends him but he cannot be held long. Moreover, [if] a malevolent[13] is the one to which the application of the Moon is, appearing direct, it brings down the one fleeing, apprehended [but] without severe punishment.

---

[6] John's Sahl is more direct: the fugitive will send someone to the querent in order to arrange a safe return.
[7] The lord of the seventh. But compare with al-Khayyāt and Dorotheus in §§7.77-78 below, where this is the lord of the sixth. I believe Sahl is correct.
[8] Again, the lord of the seventh, throughout this paragraph.
[9] John's Sahl has "the lord of the seventh," but note that Dorotheus and al-Khayyāt below also have the Moon.
[10] Reading with John's Sahl for Hugo's *prosequitur*.
[11] John's Sahl has a malefic planet, not the Sun.
[12] John's Sahl connects this angularity to a planet in its station (as in the next sentence), and not a separate condition.
[13] John's Sahl does not specifically say it must be a malevolent planet, but it does follow the logic of the passage.

Finally, the Moon being scorched [and] applying to Mars, threatens the one who fled with the scorching of fire ([but if] Saturn, with the dangers of waters).[14] [If the Moon aspected the lord of her own domicile, the fugitive's assets will be captured.][15]

The traversal of a malevolent in the ninth[16] captures him for punishment, [while] a benevolent wholly frees him.

With the Moon increasing and adding,[17] whoever fled is especially helped; but decreasing and subtracting will be the contrary for those who flee.[18]

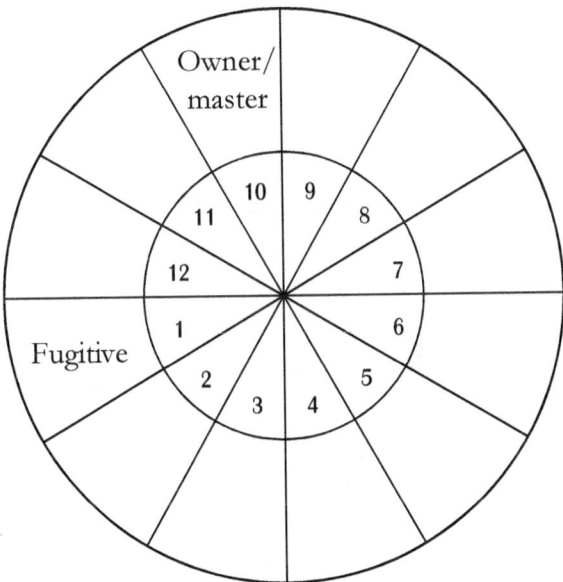

Figure 38: Angular significations for fugitives ('Umar §7.73, *Carmen* V.36)

---

[14] Cf. *Carmen* V.36.29 and 36.35.
[15] Adding with John's Sahl.
[16] Reading with John's Sahl for Hugo's "seventh." To name the seventh again would be redundant, and elsewhere Sahl treats questions about prisoners using the ninth: see *On Quest.* §9.5 and §9.17 below.
[17] According to John's Sahl, this is in light and number.
[18] *Carmen* V.36.23-24.

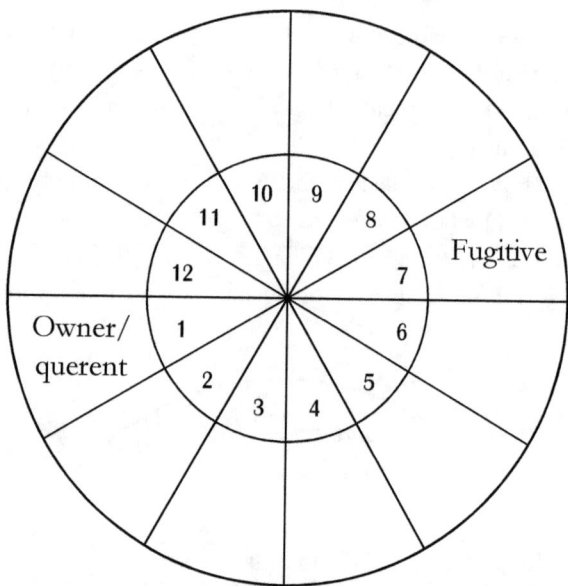

Figure 39: Angular significations for fugitives (Sahl §7.72)

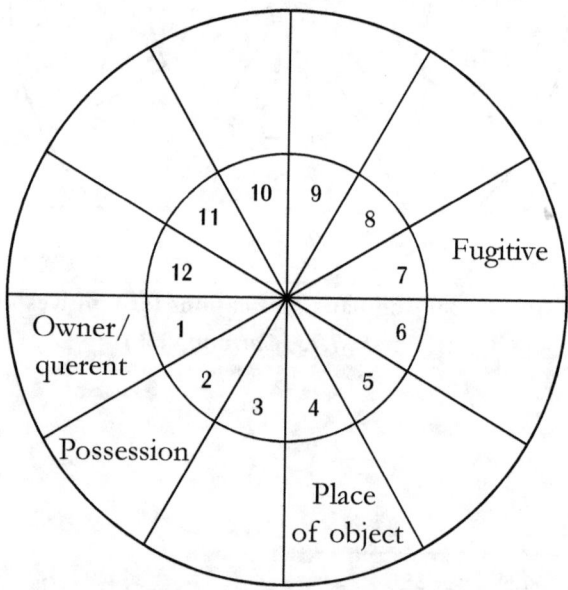

Figure 40: Angular significations for fugitives (al-Kindī §7.76, §7.82)

§7.73: On a fugitive and lost thing—'Umar

If someone would come into doubt about a fugitive or lost things, establish the east and its lord and the Moon as significators of the one fleeing. Then, the Sun himself, but even the lord of the Midheaven and of the Lunar lodging-place, supply the signification for the one who has lost, and those who are seeking, the missing things.

Whenever therefore the eastern lord and the Moon would apply to the lord of the Midheaven or the lord of the Lunar lodging-place, it is a sign of discovery. Which if the application were from the tetragon or opposition or assembly, with the lord of the east and the Moon being established in the east, they bring it forth that the one who had escaped has not yet departed from the region. Now, if the regard of application would come forth from the trigon or hexagon, with the lord of the east and the Moon being cadent or remote (but they are "remote" [when] nearby before the pivot, "cadent" after the pivot),[19] it signifies that the fugitive is found having departed from the region.

However, the Moon waxing in light, while it prohibits him from being caught, it maintains a profitable flight. But she waning, even though it forbids that he be apprehended, it shows an unprofitable flight.[20]

§7.74: On a fugitive, whether he would be found—'Umar

We hand over the counsel for this ambiguity to the Moon. If therefore you would discover her or the lord of the east in the seventh, with an infortune possessing the eighth, before the fugitive is found he undergoes the trouble of death. But contrariwise, the Sun himself or the lord of the Midheaven or at least [the lord] of the Moon being arranged in the seventh (with an infortune, I say, possessing the eighth), they threaten death both for the

---

[19] If this comment is 'Umar's and not Hugo's, it might mean that "remote" means somewhat far away from the axial degree but in a later degree, while "cadent" mean being beyond the axial degree in an earlier degree. That is, if the Midheaven is at 1° Cancer, then maybe being "remote" means being farther away in Cancer (such as 20°), while "cadent" means being beyond it somewhere in Gemini.

[20] This last part must be wrong, since it would mean he is never apprehended no matter what the Lunar phase. See the end of the previous section by Sahl: if the Moon is waxing it should make it easier for him to escape, while waning should make his capture more likely.

one who lost the missing things and the ones seeking them, so that they never find them.

Moreover, with these same [planets] being established in the seventh just as we said before, while Mercury in the eighth would be corrupted by the regard of any infortune, they afflict the one who has lost [the goods], and those who search for them, with death, while they postpone the discovery. In this way too, the Moon and the lord of the east in the seventh, Mercury in the eighth (regarded by an infortune), will really kill the one who had fled before its discovery.

Which if neither the Moon nor the lord of the east would regard the Sun and the lord of the tenth and [the lord] of the Moon, the hope of discovery is wholly removed.

Finally, the Moon applying to a fortunate one, regarding nothing of the infortunes, watches over and saves a certain flight and the security of the flight. But she being unlucky or corrupted, brings back the one who had hidden, as being found. Also, an application with the fortunate ones in the pivot of the Midheaven is not otherwise; or at least, they being blessed with the rulership of the Lunar lodging-place testifies that he can be found.

§7.75: On the hour of discovery—'Umar

Moreover, it will be permitted to observe the most certain hour of discovery, and the exhibited time of the stars (by the fateful day), in this order. For whenever the lord of the east and the Moon, with the Sun, or moreover the lord of the tenth or that of the Lunar lodging-place, or if the one having full control of the seventh with the eastern lord, would either undergo the same assembly, or if the lord of the seventh would be scorched, or should at least the lords of the tenth and of the Lunar house assemble, finally the certain hour of finding him could be discovered.[21]

---

[21] Although Hugo has stated this in a complicated way, note that these are all of the significators of the thief and goods and owner which we have already seen. So, 'Umar is recommending that we watch the transits of the appropriate significators to see when they come together by body. Or perhaps, since assembly technically takes place simply by being together in the same sign, an ingress into the same sign might indicate the time.

§7.76: On missing things and those who slip away due to escaping—al-Kindī[22]

§248. There are two kinds of lost things: for they are either animate or inanimate. An understanding of these seems [both] manifold and necessary. Namely, he broods about: [1] in what place the hidden thing is being held, [2] whether it would be found or not,[23] [3] whether as a whole or in part,[24] [4] in what place it is to be found, [5] what is the reason for finding it and losing it.

[2] Whether it would be found

§249. The Moon, as the significator of the lost thing,[25] restores what was lost if there would be an application of her with the lord of the Ascendant or [with the lord] of the second[26] from the Ascendant, or with the lord of her own house. But if there is no application of her with these, nor is she in the Ascendant or in the second, it wholly denies it. Moreover, the lord of the Lunar house in the trigon or hexagon of the Ascendant[27] makes a sign of finding it, if it applies itself to the degree of the Ascendant [itself].

§250. Again, with her receding from the lord of the twelfth or eighth or sixth, and should there be an application with the degree of the Ascendant or of money (from whatever regard), she brings back the lost things at the hour of the application—if however the lord of the Moon regards her. With her being applied [along with] the regard of [this lord], the judgment is unchangeable.[28]

---

[22] Cf. al-Rijāl II.33 (second part).
[23] See §7.95 below.
[24] See §7.103 below.
[25] This is an important point. One might suppose that the second and its lord signify the missing item. But if we look at al-Kindī's §282 in §7.88 below, I think we can see a rationale for using the Moon. The second and its lord indicate possessions which are actually under one's control—but by definition a missing thing is not directly under one's control. Therefore, the Moon, which indicates changing circumstances, acts as a proxy for the item.
[26] The 1551 al-Rijāl reads "twelfth," which is clearly where Lilly gets his information, and perhaps why he believes this chapter refers to large livestock (*CA* p. 319). But note that the next instructions involve the Moon being in the second, not the twelfth, and the 1485 al-Rijāl correctly reads "second."
[27] Al-Rijāl specifically mentions the third and sixth.
[28] Robert and al-Rijāl put it more directly: "But if you found the contrary of these combinations, judge the contrary" (al-Rijāl).

§251. Moreover, the Moon being corrupted by the lord of the eighth or sixth or twelfth, makes it clear that it can in no way be wrenched from the hands of the [current] possessor.[29] Particularly while the Ascendant is free of the regard of an unfortunate one [and] likewise the Moon being blessed by one of the fortunate ones, it keeps the thing to be returned safe, [and it is] committed to some just and trustworthy man. Moreover, an application or regard of a fortunate one to the Ascendant, [and] in the same way with the Moon applying herself into the Ascendant, they bring the missing things back. Moreover, the Moon in the pivot of the Sun (or better yet, being with him [in the same sign]) will have brought the missing things into royal possession. Likewise, the Sun looking upon the Ascendant by a friendly regard, [and] even an application of the Moon to the degree of the Ascendant, compels the things to be returned.

[3] Whether as a whole or in part[30]

§252. Moreover, an application of the Moon to the Ascendant from a tetragon or the opposition, restores the missing things with difficulty; it being from a trigon or hexagon, peacefully and completely. Again, the Moon in the Ascendant introduces some adversity in finding it.

§7.77: On a fugitive and a lost thing—al-Khayyāt

If someone made a question about a fugitive or any lost thing, whether or not it would be recovered or he would return, we put the east and its lord in charge of the querent, but the lost thing will have to be sought from the seventh and its lord.

And so, if the lord of the east would render counsel to the lord of the seventh, it is a sign of recovering it. But conversely, if the lord of the seventh (especially [if] staying in pivot) would render the counsel of application to the

---

[29] That is, the thief or whoever has it now. I have ended the sentence here, because Robert and Hugo and al-Rijāl all continue with the next clause about the Ascendant. But it does not make sense that the Ascendant being free of the infortunes would *prevent* the object returning, especially given the other conditions in the paragraph. So, I have separated the sentences and connected the clause about the Ascendant to the following sentence.

[30] I believe this is the question as to whether it will be returned in whole or in part: see a similar treatment in §7.103 below.

eastern lord, it brings the fugitive back of his own accord. An application made from the pivots brings him back before he leaves the region.

It is no less if they would apply to each other on the right of the east. In fact, the lord of the seventh applying to the eastern lord from the left of the east, brings him back [after] already having left from the region.

Moreover, if the lord of the seventh would apply to a malevolent occupying a pivot, it apprehends the fugitive. But if that same infortune would regard the lord of the east or the lord of the seventh, it restores him through the owner himself. The lord of the seventh in the east, holds the fugitive before he goes out.

But either of the lights applying to the lord of the seventh, suggests he cannot be hidden.

But if the lord of the seventh happened to rule the sixth or twelfth,[31] it whips the captive and applies chains: for the perversity of each place does harm (but it is more grave with the lord of the twelfth occupying a pivot). Moreover, with the lord of the seventh being scorched, without a doubt the one who had fled will be held (it is better if the lord of the east would regard it).[32]

Likewise, the Moon applying to an infortune detains the fugitive. But if that infortune would be staying in the east, he will be detained before his departure—[but] if it is remote from a pivot, on the journey [itself]. The reception of this malevolent reconciles him to the owner, and he earns leniency. But, she applying to a fortunate one prepares escape, unless perhaps [the fortunate one] would either be undergoing scorching or would be retrograde, or corrupted. In fact, entering into scorching really threatens death. But if instead of the fortunate one, the malevolent would enter scorching, it even reveals his corpse after death.

Likewise, the Moon applying to the lord of her own place, wholly establishes that he will return—if, I say, [that lord] was established in a pivot. For if it is remote from [a pivot], it captures the one fleeing, harshly.[33]

Moreover, the Moon applying to the Sun speaks against those fleeing.

---

[31] In whole-sign houses, this would be the case if the seventh were Aquarius (so that the sixth is Capricorn, both ruled by Saturn) or Scorpio (so that the twelfth is Aries, both ruled by Mars) or Taurus (so that the twelfth is Libra, both ruled by Venus).

[32] This must mean that it is better for *the owner* if the lord of the east also regards the scorched lord of the seventh.

[33] *Graviter*. But Dorotheus in §7.85 below says that he will be traveling alone (implying that he will not be caught).

If the Moon, being separated from the lord of the east, would apply to the lord of the seventh, while however they[34] would apply to each other afterwards, it brings back a definite report[35] about the lost thing to the one who had possessed it. And thusly accepting counsel from the one, and rendering it to the other, [the Moon], (as though a messenger), begs forgiveness from the querent. But the lord of the sixth[36] applying afterwards to the eastern [lord], means he is going to return fully and of his own accord.

But if the Moon, in her own place, would render no counsel of application,[37] she will have to be handed over to the following [sign]. But if then she would apply to some retrograde [star], it leads the fugitive back of his own accord; applying to some slow [star] in a pivot or after a pivot, brings the apprehended one back, slowly; which if it is in its first station, prepared to go retrograde, it afflicts the captured one with severe distress;[38] in its second station, so that it is already moving direct, it captures him but he cannot be held long. Likewise, it being a malevolent [and] appearing direct, he will be led back according to the manner and quantity of its course, but without much distress.[39]

§7.78: On a lost thing or a fugitive—Dorotheus

Then, if it is a question about a lost thing or a fugitive (whether it would be recovered or not), the east and its lord give counsel for the one who has lost it, but the seventh and its lord watch over the lost thing.

If therefore the lord of the east would render counsel to that of the seventh, it brings back the fugitive through [the querent's] own effort. Which if the application were from the pivots, he gets him before he has left the region—especially if it were from the right. Which if the lord of the seventh (imitating [the example of the lord of] the east), would apply to the eastern lord, it promises that the one who has already left will return of his own accord.

Moreover, the lord of the seventh applying to a hostile [star] in a pivot, affirms that he will be gotten before he leaves. That malevolent being drawn

---

[34] That is, the lord of the east and of the seventh.
[35] *Mandatum*.
[36] Sahl in §7.72 has it as the lord of the seventh, which I believe is more correct.
[37] That is, if she is void in course (*ITA* III.9).
[38] Or perhaps, "punishment" (*districtione*).
[39] Or perhaps, "punishment" (*districtione*).

back,[40] brings him back [after] already having left; it is more severe if the eastern lord would regard that infortune or the lord of the seventh.

Either of the lights applying to the lord of the seventh, denies that the fugitive [can be hidden].[41]

Which if the lord of the seventh, and that of the sixth and twelfth, would come together [in one and the same planet],[42] they bring back the one who had run away, and threaten fetters (preferable is a regard of the eastern lord to it.)

Moreover, the Moon rendering counsel to a malevolent brings back the fugitive. But if the infortune would occupy the east, it reports he has not yet left. Which if the malevolent is drawn back, it gets him on his journey. Also, with it being received, it restores the favor and kindness of the owner. Likewise, the Moon rendering counsel to a fortunate one promises escape, unless perhaps that benevolent is undergoing scorching, or is retrograde or corrupted: for thus it wholly captures the one who had run away.

Furthermore, the Moon transferring light from the eastern [lord] to the lord of the seventh, while however they apply afterwards, [means that] the one who had run away is brought back through an intermediary. Now, if the rendering of counsel would happen from the lord of the seventh to the eastern [lord], the return will be spontaneous and without a middle man. Then also, the lord of the sixth[43] applying to the eastern [lord] designates a spontaneous return.

If however the Moon would bar counsel within the sign which she possesses,[44] there will be recourse to the following sign. Furthermore, the one who transfers the light being retrograde,[45] brings back the one who has turned around, of his own accord. Which if it were slow, there will be a delay. Being direct impels it to happen according to the quality of [its] progress [forward].

---

[40] That is, "cadent."
[41] Reading with Sahl and al-Khayyāt for *metuendum*.
[42] Reading with the sense of al-Khayyāt for "with each other." That is, if the lord of the seventh also rules the twelfth or sixth.
[43] Sahl in §7.72 has it as the lord of the seventh, which I believe is more correct.
[44] That is, if she is void in course (*ITA* III.9).
[45] Note the difference with al-Khayyāt: he has the Moon moved into the next sign, and supposes that the Moon is now applying to a retrograde planet. But Dorotheus speaks as if it is any planet that transfers the light. I believe al-Khayyāt is correct here.

§7.79: In what place the fugitive or missing thing is being held—Sahl[46]

Whenever a question is laid down about the place of the fugitive or the lost thing, or a thing taken by theft, it is good to attend to the Lunar place. For if she happens to be found in the east, it suggests the eastern direction. Which if she would be lingering in the tenth, the fugitive tends towards the south. But if in the seventh, he has withdrawn to the west; if she would possess the pivot of the earth, it demonstrates the north. Finally, with her lingering outside of these pivots, the judgment will have to be referred in common to the nature and signification of the places.[47]

Moreover, if [the querent] would make a question as to whether or not the one who has fled would go or rather return: the counsel of the Moon [must be examined] for the return: separated from the infortunes, it bars a return; which if she would be separated from most useful benevolents, it shows a return.

§7.80: To what place he is fleeing—'Umar

The stars to which the Moon and the lord of the east apply, even the place which the lord of the seventh possesses, particularly suggest the place to which he who had fled, has withdrawn. In fact, with the three aforewritten significators (or the lord of the Lunar house)[48] being established equally in the east or in the Midheaven, or rather in a pivot of the Sun, the fugitive has not yet departed from the region.[49] Furthermore, the three aforewritten significators (or the majority of them) holding onto a quarter above the earth (namely between the east and the Midheaven), or the opposite of this under the earth (from the seventh, I say, to the fourth), it testifies that he who had fled has withdrawn to the eastern direction from the city itself. In the remaining quarters (namely the female ones, from the seventh to the Midheaven [and] likewise from the east to the fourth), they invite us to the western[50]

---

[46] Cf. *On Quest.* §§7.11-12.
[47] This simply means that we should take her specific direction into account: for example, if she were between the Ascendant and the Midheaven, then somewhere towards the southeast.
[48] Reading *lunaris domus dominus* for *lunaris domini domus*.
[49] Reading *fugitivus* for *fugitivo*.
[50] Reading *occidentalem* for *orientalem*.

direction from the same place. With them being cadent or drawn back from the pivot of the east, or rather [being cadent from] the three above-named stars (which are the lord of the tenth, and equally the lord of the Lunar lodging-place, and the Sun himself), it portends he has already departed from the city.

Also, the direction which the majority of the significators especially claims (that of the east, I say, and the west, the north and the south), really diverts and turns the look and face and mind of the one fleeing, into that [direction].

§7.81: In what place the lost things would be found—al-Kindī[51]

[Where the missing thing will be found]

§253. Moreover, the place of the Moon identifies[52] where the missing things can be found, according to the nature of the sign in which she appears. For, [the sign] being eastern indicates the eastern direction from the place where the thing had been taken. But in a western sign, it shows the western direction; likewise, a northern sign, the north; a southern sign, look to the southern direction.

§254. Likewise, the Moon's place [in the figure] settles the same thing according to the order of the signs: in this way, the right and left of each pivot are distinguished.[53]

§255. Wherefore, one will have to judge according to the nature of the sign which the Moon is holding onto. The Lunar lord in a human sign indicates the missing things will be in a place frequented by men; in a sign with a sheep-like form (as is Aries and Capricorn), it demonstrates that the place is inhabited by sheep and animals of that kind. In Taurus, it designates a place frequented by cows and heifers and camels. But in a four-footed sign (as Sag-

---

[51] Cf. al-Rijāl II.33 (middle).
[52] Reading *agnotescit* for *ignotescit*.
[53] That is, use the actual cardinal direction in which the Moon is. Al-Rijāl: "If she were in the Ascendant, the lost thing is in the east; if in the angle of the west, it is in the direction of the west; if in the Midheaven, it is in the direction of the south; if in the angle of the earth, it is in the direction of the north, or northern. Likewise even contemplate it from the right and left of any of these angles, and judge by mixing this signification with the signification of the sign in which the Moon is." See the next sentence and Lilly, *CA* pp. 364-65.

ittarius is), it declares a place of four-footed animals.⁵⁴ In Leo, a place of wild animals (namely forests and deserts [and] caverns).⁵⁵

§256. In Scorpio, it shows a place of creeping things (namely locusts, beetles and those which move without wings and are poisonous). In Cancer, it shows ponds⁵⁶ and cisterns, springs and aquatic animals. But in Pisces, it teaches sweet waters and places full of fish. But⁵⁷ in Aquarius, even though it is reputed as being among the human signs,⁵⁸ it indicates mountainous places, rivers and larger streams. At the end of Pisces (namely from the middle onward), it recounts the habitations of birds.

§257. Moreover, it seems best to consider the sign the Moon is holding onto in this way: she being in a fiery sign determines fiery places or those near fire; in a watery sign, it signifies watery places or those near waters and water-based affairs; in an airy sign, it suggests windy places and those [places] whose substance cannot subsist without the benefit of wind; in an earthy one, it is believed to be earthy places and those in which the earth shows an effect and strength.⁵⁹

§258. Likewise, the Moon in a convertible sign or with the lord of a convertible one,⁶⁰ introduces new and recently cultivated earth, neither [wholly] flat nor mountainous. In a firm one, flat and recently inhabited land. But in a double-bodied one, it demonstrates the most ancient earth, already partly desert, here mountainous, there flat, of the nature of one and the other.

---

⁵⁴ Al-Rijāl has this as a sign and place of large animals.
⁵⁵ Reading with Robert for Hugo's "cliffs." Al-Kindī is probably thinking of bear caves or other places near cliffs and mountains.
⁵⁶ Or any hollowed out area such as a ditch or den where animals may hide (Hugo: *lacuna*; Robert: *cavea*).
⁵⁷ All three authors read the rest of this paragraph differently. Robert reads: "But in Aquarius, even though it is enumerated with the human signs, it [indicates] mountainous places, torrents, everlasting rivers; moreover, at the end of *Capricorn*, it must be noted that it imputes the place of the lost thing to be that of predatory birds." Al-Rijāl reads: "If she were in Aquarius, it denotes the same [as Pisces]. Moreover, if she were in human signs, it signifies that the thing is where precipitous places are, high mountains, high rocks, and great rivers. And if it were in the last half of Capricorn, it signifies that it is in the staying-places of ships." I am inclined to think that Robert and Hugo are right about Aquarius indicating high places and rivers, while al-Rijāl is right about the last half of Capricorn and ships.
⁵⁸ Because it is an airy sign.
⁵⁹ Robert: "in an earthy one, earthy [places] and also those producing powers and effects from the earth." Al-Rijāl simply says, "earthy places and where there are houses of earth."
⁶⁰ Al-Rijāl reads, "If the Moon or the lord of her domicile were in movable signs," which makes more sense to me.

[Where it is being held][61]

§259. Moreover, the Moon with the lord of the Ascendant and in the same quarter, if she is distant from him by 30° or less, it permits the missing thing and he who has lost it, to be in the same house. But if the difference were more than 30° and up to 60°, it means it will be in the same city. But if the distance is found to be more than 60° and up to 90°, it portends that so far it is being held in that same region. [But] their being removed from the same quarter, asserts that it is far outside the region.

§7.82: In what place the missing things would be held—al-Kindī

§276. The nature of the fourth, and if a star is contained in it, clearly suggests the place where the thing is contained, namely before it would lead [you] out to the home…[62]

[The home of the thief][63]

§277. Moreover, this same Abū Yūsuf [al-Kindī] designates the home in which the thief is hidden, thusly. Let the place of the Sun be given to the home (just as he instructs), but the Moon claims the door for herself. And so, the Sun in an eastern sign indicates the home is to the east of the home of the one who is missing the thing.

§278. Moreover, he teaches that the place of the thing taken by theft must be investigated in this order: the place of the star[64] established as the significator of the thief should be compared to [that of] the lord of the fourth, and noted whether [its signification] agrees with it. If [the signification] is remote,[65] the place of the thing will be asserted more surely from the place of

---

[61] See also al-Kindī's §206 in §7.121 below, and *Forty Chapters* Chs. 6.5.5 and 6.5.6 generally.
[62] In other words, know what you are looking for before you barge into someone's home, in search of your goods. For this paragraph, cf. *Carmen* V.35.25*ff.* I have omitted the rest of this paragraph because while it mentions the fourth (as the following paragraphs do), the rest of it really constitutes the end of the discussion of an example chart in §7.87 below (where I have put it in full).
[63] Cf. al-Rijāl II.34, and compare with §7.127 below.
[64] Reading with al-Rijāl II.34.
[65] That is, if they do not agree.

the [lord of the]⁶⁶ fourth. For a convertible sign indicates a place that sticks out;⁶⁷ a firm one shows one underground; likewise a doubled-bodied sign calls out to the roof.⁶⁸

§279. Moreover, this same recognition proceeds from the nature of the signs. For in a fiery sign it shows places dedicated to fires; but in a watery one, both watery places and those near watery ones; in an earthy one, places sticking out more from the pavement, near steps and staircases; in an airy one, it portends neither fiery nor airy [places] but mixed of both.

§7.83: On the same thing—al-Kindī⁶⁹

§280. Likewise, when the significator of the thief renders its own power⁷⁰ to another star, it expels the thing from out of his hand and control. But if not, it concedes that he possesses it yet.

§7.84: In what place the fugitive is being held—al-Khayyāt

But, an infortune gathering the counsel of the Moon [while it is] in a pivot, testifies that the fugitive is staying in the same place (namely, not far from the house or family).⁷¹ Now, on the right of the east, it conceals him near the city or a home, and far from the city. But if it would be staying on the left of the east, it suggests he has already departed.

---

⁶⁶ Adding with al-Rijāl. But Robert and Hugo read that the fourth itself should be used, which also sounds plausible: see *Carmen* V.35.27-37.
⁶⁷ Or a "lofty place" (al-Rijāl).
⁶⁸ One would expect the roof to be the movable sign, and the common sign to indicate a place in the middle, between an underground spot (fixed) and the roof (movable).
⁶⁹ Cf. al-Rijāl II.34.
⁷⁰ That is, "pushing power" (see *ITA* III.16). But this could simply mean "pushing management," in which it simply applies to another planet (*ITA* III.18).
⁷¹ Sahl in §7.72 above says he will be caught.

§7.85: In what place the fugitive or lost thing is being held—Dorotheus

A malevolent that transfers[72] the Lunar counsel, being in a pivot, hides the fugitive not far from the house and family. Being in the portion of the east,[73] it teaches he has already set out from the city.

In addition, the Moon rendering counsel to her own lord, he is returning (namely if the lord of the Lunar lodging-place entered into a pivot); [but if the lord of the Moon is] drawn back, he is progressing alone on his journey.

Now, the lord of the fourth being placed in the east, wholly catches him lying hidden up till now.[74]

§7.86: What was the reason for losing it—al-Kindī[75]

§260. But the reason for losing it (which preceded [the question]) is sought thusly. For, the lord of the Ascendant receding from Saturn or dwelling in a house of the same Saturn, testifies that the thing was lost because of forgetfulness or sorrow or a cold infirmity—which [Saturn's] retrogradation especially seems to be a confirmation of. Moreover, if its receding happens from Mars or it dwells in a house of [Mars], it testifies it was because of fear or some sudden impulse[76] or anger, even fire or enemies.

§261. But receding from Jupiter or in [his] house, it confirms that it happened because of prayer or fasting or the observation of some law,[77] even sometimes a child or controversy. Moreover, receding from the Sun or in his house, a king or hunting, or augury, or a friend's sudden and unforeseen arrival, convey the reason for the missing thing. Likewise, that same lord of the Ascendant being in a house of Venus or receding from her, introduces jokes laughed about among the common people, and women delightful to look at, even sexual immorality [or] longing,[78] into the cause.

---

[72] This should probably be "gathers" or "receives," in accordance with Sahl in §7.72 above.
[73] See §7.84 above for al-Khayyāt's version.
[74] *Adhuc latentem omnino comprehendit*. I am not sure if this means he is actually arrested, or whether Hugo is personifying the situation to say that we *mentally grasp* (*comprehendit*) that he is hiding.
[75] Cf. al-Rijāl II.33 (middle).
[76] Reading *impetus* with Robert and al-Rijāl, but Hugo's "journey" (*discursionis*) is also a signification of Mars.
[77] In many medieval astrological texts, "law" can also refer to one's religious code.
[78] The Latin reads literally "the sexual immorality *of longing*," which doesn't really make sense in English; so I have separated them to make clear that both elements are involved.

§262. Moreover, in a house of Mercury or receding from him, it foretells[79] that books, rumors, commerce and the impediment of some affair[80] are in the cause. Likewise, in the house of the Moon or receding from her, it testifies that a messenger or servant was [relevant to] the cause, because the owner wanted to add something to (or subtract from) the thing.[81]

§263. Moreover, if the lord of the Ascendant would be receding from some star, and it would dwell in the house of the other,[82] remember to connect everything, just as their manner of bearing demands.

§264. Likewise, whichever one of the aforesaid significators (namely the one from whom the lord of the ascendant recedes) is direct, makes it clear that the owner—with foresight and free will, namely being deceived by no dream nor drink nor worry nor error, has put the thing in the place where it was left. Retrograde, it confirms that he was deep in a dream or drunk with wine or disturbed by worry or deceived by error, and affected by misfortunes of the soul like these.

§265. Moreover,[83] it seems one must note with the greatest effort when they are situated in the circle of forty-eight figures,[84] [and] with which of them the Moon then finally connects [her] ascent. Which if she appeared closer to the horizon, it will be useful to determine the place where the missing things are contained, according to the nature of that figure which then possesses the Ascendant with her; [but] if the Moon were in the Midheaven or closer to it, from the property of the one which is then approaching the degree of the Midheaven with her. But if two or more would accompany the Moon, the observation must be made from the shared nature of their shapes.

§266. Moreover, with the missing thing being animate but not human, all places and [their] statuses acquire a signification similar to that of inanimate things.

---

[79] Reading the verb *praefor* for *praesum*.
[80] But al-Rijāl reads, "undergoing a legation."
[81] Al-Rijāl: "is missing by reason of an increase of the lost thing, or a decrease of it, or a messenger or slave lost it."
[82] Robert reads: "But with that very star (whence the separation [*discessus*] happens) holding onto the domicile of the other."
[83] This use of the constellations probably comes from a much older source than the rest of this material.
[84] That is, the 48 northern constellations identified by Ptolemy in *Almagest* VII.5-VIII.1.

§7.87: Whether he escaped on his own or through the advice of another—al-Kindī[85]

§267. If it should happen that a question about a human is made, it seems that [the following] come into question: [1] whether he has escaped due to himself or slipped away due to the advice of another; [2] even whether he is living or acquitted the laws of death; [3] even the cause of death.

§268. [1] First of all therefore, the lord of the Moon should be consulted: its withdrawal from some star demonstrates he is free of his own devices. But if another star would be withdrawing from it, it promises he was released by another. With the lord of the Moon being deprived of this evidence, let recourse be had to the lord of the second: it withdrawing from none, nor any from him, so far holds back the one whom we believed had fled, [and] in that same place with which he had been associated.

§269. [2-3] Also, the Moon about to apply with the lord of her eighth,[86] testifies to death. Lacking that, should the Lunar lord apply itself with its own eighth or the Moon's, it claims that he has either already died, or his death must be feared. Likewise, if the lord of the Moon is deprived of this signification, the solution of this fear should be sought from the lord of the second. Which if it [too] discards testimony of this matter, it teaches he is unharmed.

---

[85] For these first paragraphs, cf. al-Rijāl II.33.
[86] That is, the eighth place from her own position.

Example #1:

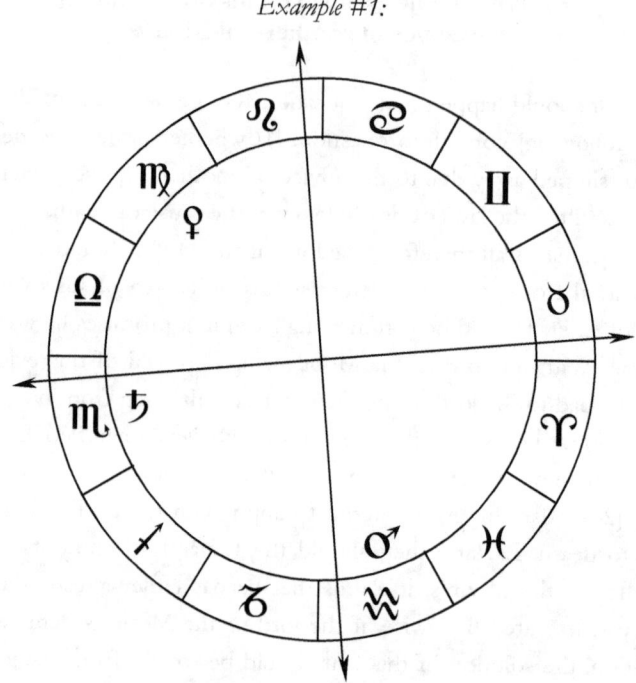

Figure 41: Example of theft #1 (al-Kindī)[87]

§270.[88] An example by Abū Yūsuf [al-Kindī]: a question having been made about a theft, Scorpio was the Ascendant, and Saturn in it, obtaining the signification over the robber. The nature of Saturn and of the sign which he was holding onto, determines the form and status of the robber. Mars in the fourth, and being the lord of the Ascendant, conveys to us a certain knowledge of that matter. Therefore, we say that the signified robber frequents the doorway of the [man] whose role Mars takes, with a certain friendship and familiarity; the unluckiness of each [planet] designates that their friendship was false and fraudulent.

§271. As the lady of the seventh, Venus is consulted: once her status is imparted (along with the nature of Virgo), she is confirmed as [providing]

---

[87] Based on the information for this chart, it would have been around 8:00 AM and after daybreak, from late September to early October, 867 AD. The client must have come to al-Kindī (or whoever the astrologer really was) right after waking up.
[88] This paragraph does not appear in al-Rijāl.

advice for the pilfering of the thing. For she, being the lady of the seventh, always appears adverse to the Ascendant.

Example #2:

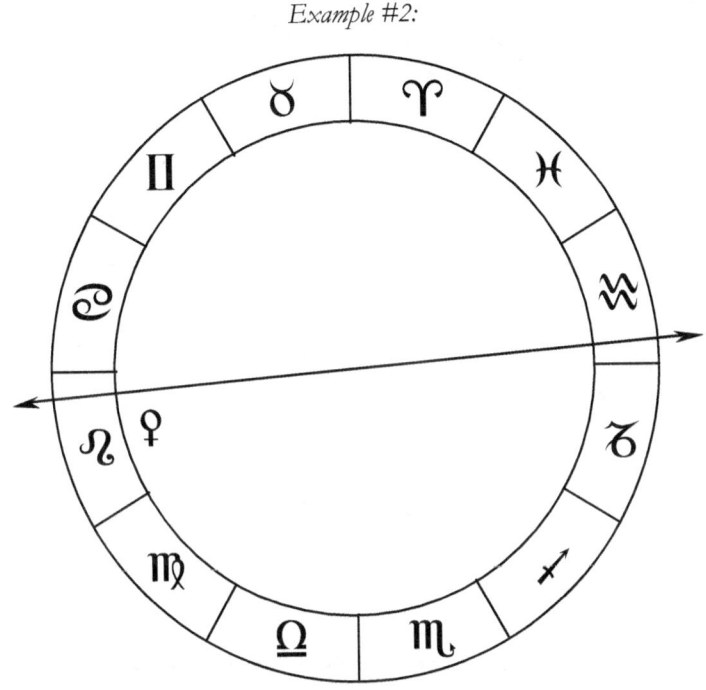

Figure 42: Example of theft #2 (al-Kindī)[89]

§272.[90] Moreover, another example by the same astrologer of a missing thing. The Ascendant was Leo, but Venus in the Ascendant. Therefore, this same judge, Abū Yūsuf [al-Kindī], said the missing money was hidden under the bed and under the covers. In the bed, because Leo is counted among the four-footed [signs];[91] he reckoned it was being kept under the blankets for this reason, that Venus in the Ascendant seemed to confirm that. The appraisal must be balanced in this way in the rest of the matters.

---

[89] I take this chart to be from the same year as the first, which would put it at around 8:00 AM, between late June and early July, 867 AD.
[90] For the following paragraphs, cf. al-Rijāl II.34.
[91] Al-Kindī is really saying that a four-footed sign is like a bed because beds have four feet.

Example #3:

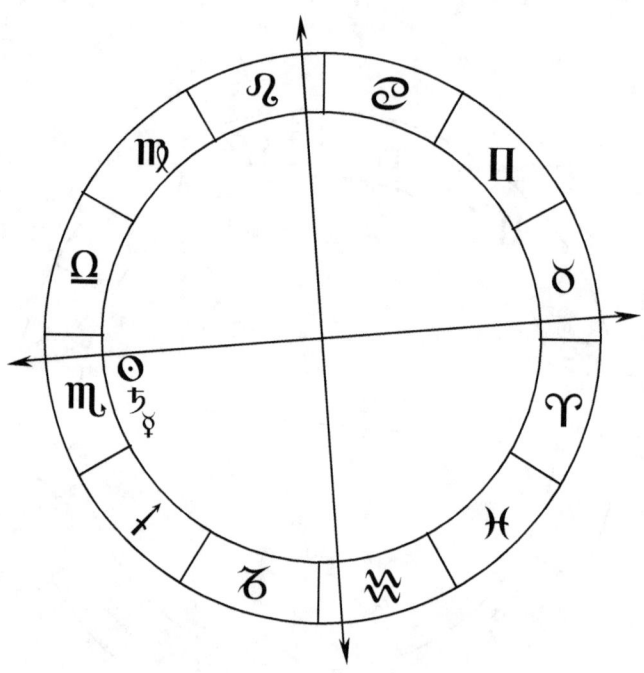

Figure 43: Example of theft #3 (al-Kindī)

§273. Moreover [another] example by the same man, in a question about a theft. The Ascendant was Scorpio, but in the Ascendant the Sun, Saturn and Mercury, all of whose signification tends towards the robber.[92] Therefore Saturn in the Ascendant, and being the lord of the fourth, proves that the robber was a relative of the one who lost [the thing], and Mercury [proves that it was] another friend, because he is the lord of the eleventh.

§274. Moreover, another property of them which comes down from the lords of the bounds: for, Saturn in the bound of Mercury shows that he is a common servant (I say, in Saturnian duties). Mercury in his own bound does likewise.

---

[92] Because al-Kindī takes them to be peregrine planets in an angle. Mercury is technically not peregrine because he is in his own bound (see below), but none of them has domicile, exaltation, or triplicity rulership in Scorpio.

§§7.72-88: FUGITIVES

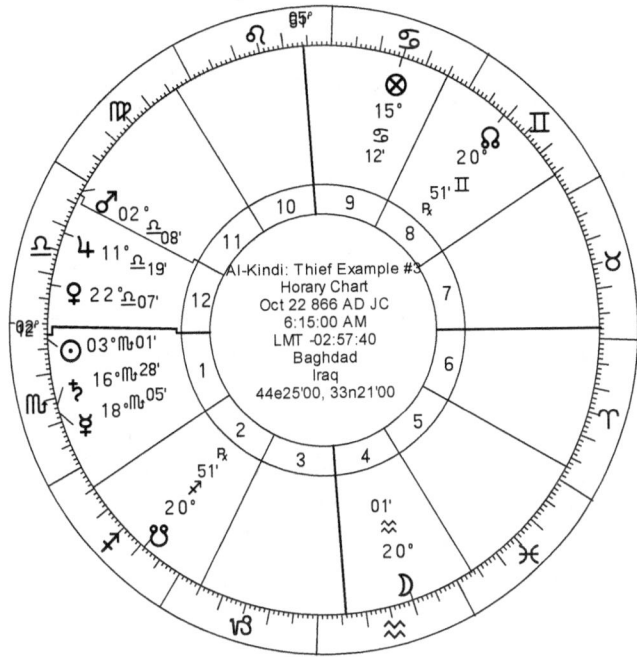

Figure 44: Likely chart for al-Kindī's example #3[93]

§275. For what law he belongs to, take Saturn. The lord of the ninth from his own house (namely Aquarius) lays this out thusly: Libra is in the ninth place [from Aquarius], which is a house of Venus. And so Venus signifies the law of the Christians, [because] their places of prayer are entitled to be decorated with figures and images and even paintings and what is like these.[94]

---

[93] There are a couple of problems in dating this chart. Because of the explicit mention of the planets in the Ascendant and the sign of the Moon, I favor 866 AD. However, al-Kindī then mentions the "nearness of the Martial place to Aquarius": if the chart were from 867 as I assume the others were, then Mars would indeed be in Pisces, neighboring on Aquarius: but then Jupiter would be in Scorpio, and the Moon would not be in Aquarius. Is it possible that al-Kindī is speaking of the nearness of the *trine aspect* of Mars to the degree of the IC in Aquarius itself? Unfortunately, al-Rijāl does not discuss these charts at all in II.33.

[94] Al-Kindī does not explain why we should take the ninth from Aquarius—why not from Capricorn? Perhaps because in this chart it is the angular domicile of Saturn. If we had used Capricorn, the thief's religion would have been Mercurial (Virgo). Also, note that most medieval sources attributed Venus to Islam rather than Christianity, perhaps because Venus traditionally indicated rites of purification, a conspicuous feature of Islamic prac-

§276.[95] The nature of the fourth, and if a star is contained in it, clearly suggests the place where the thing is contained, namely before it would lead [you] out to the home.[96] In the fourth was Aquarius, and it is airy; also the Moon, [who is] moist: it signifies wells and sewers,[97] and that type of thing. But[98] because of the nearness of the Martial place to Aquarius,[99] [it signifies it is] in a related part: the oven or kitchen or a hot bath.

§7.88: Whether he is noble—al-Kindī[100]

§281. Moreover, the significator[101] of the robber being lucky and in the bound of an unfortunate one, describes that he [was of a good family, but][102] has disfigured the nobility of his parents through his own bad reputation. [But if the significator were an infortune and in the bound of a fortune, he is of low stock, but is now in a good condition.][103]

§282. By the authority written above, the lord of the second designates all money, except for that taken by theft, which [the querent] is complaining about: the lord of the Lunar bound principally claims for itself the signification of his missing thing.

---

tice (see *ITA* V.5). But Scorpio (and therefore Mars) was also sometimes taken for Islam, because the Saturn-Jupiter conjunction heralding its establishment took place in Scorpio (see *ITA* VIII.3.2).

[95] Hugo mistakenly put at the beginning of §7.82, when in fact it forms the end of the discussion of the chart above.
[96] In other words, know what you are looking for before you barge into someone's home, in search of your goods. For this paragraph, cf. *Carmen* V.35.25*ff*.
[97] Or, drains (*cloacas*).
[98] Reading this sentence with Robert.
[99] See footnote above on the dating of this chart.
[100] Cf. al-Rijāl II.34.
[101] Reading with Robert for "lord."
[102] Adding with Robert and following al-Rijāl II.34.
[103] Adding with al-Rijāl II.34.

THEFT

§7.89: On something stolen, whether it could be recovered—Sahl[1]

With a question being proposed about something stolen (namely whether it would be recovered or not), the east and its lord and the Moon will answer to the querent; we seek the thief from the seventh and its lord; we put the tenth and its lord over the thing stolen by theft; also, the fourth and its lord will watch over the place of the stolen thing.

And so, the eastern lord applying to the lord of the seventh or existing in the seventh, promises that what had been taken by theft will be recovered, [but] not without his own labor and effort. Contrariwise, if the lord of the seventh would apply to the eastern [lord] or would be traversing in the east, the stolen thing will be returned by the thief on his own and without [the querent's] labor. Once an application of this kind is discovered, if the lord of the second would be traversing in its exit from scorching,[2] it restores a certain portion of what was stolen.

Moreover, an application of the eastern lord to a star lingering in a pivot (and preferably in the tenth), recovers what was stolen.[3] But if it would apply equally to a remote [star] and one in aversion [to the Ascendant],[4] it is unrecoverable; but applying to a remote one that is not however in aversion, it upholds the hope of getting it.

With the lord of the seventh being scorched, the thief cannot escape, especially if it were regarded by the lord of the east, for it brings back the thief by means of the owner of the stolen thing.

Again, should you recognize that the lord of the seventh would be applying equally to the lord of the east and that of the tenth, the thief will restore, of his own accord, whatever he had borne away (out of fear of the king or some prince). But if the lord of the east would apply to each lord (of the seventh, I say, and the tenth), it will be recovered by him, with the king being compelled. Moreover, an application of the eastern lord and the seventh to that of the tenth being discovered, with both of them being in aversion to

---

[1] Cf. *On Quest.* §7.13. At this point we seem to be dealing with the theft of property, and no longer with fugitives.
[2] John's Sahl adds that if he is still fully under the rays, then the goods will not be recovered.
[3] John's Sahl reads this as the thief himself, here and in the next sentence.
[4] Adding based on John's Sahl.

one another, they grant the recovery to a king or prince or someone else, [while] denying it to the one who had lost it.

The lord of the east applying to the lord of the tenth, the king's aid procures it; but with [the lord of the tenth] to the lord of the seventh, the thief himself is defended by the prince's favor and protection.

Moreover, a transfer of light being made by the Moon between the lord of the east and that of the seventh, suggests that the thief can be apprehended. Finally, should the lord of the seventh apply to the lord of the third or ninth, or to a star going through those places, or should it be lingering in them, it portends the thief has already left the whole region. But if it would hold onto a pivot, he has not departed from the place.

Again, the lord of the seventh and its figure of application or regard with the benevolents or adverse [stars], could sufficiently explain the thief's fate.

Moreover, a Lunar application to a malevolent claims that what had been taken by theft is wholly lost. It is even the same if she happened to apply to a scorched or corrupted fortunate one. She applying to some [star] occupying the east or tenth[5] (but a free [star]), judges recovery.

However, the shared regard of each luminary to each other from a prosperous figure, restores what was stolen, and especially while each would hold onto the east or tenth. But if they would be regarding each other from an adverse figure, it brings back what was taken by theft, after already losing hope [but] not unless it is after long spaces of time.

Again, if the luminaries would regard the Lot of Fortune, or either of them would be lingering with it in the same sign, it suggests it can be recovered easily (especially if it were the Sun). Finally, whenever the lights would divert their aspect from each other [and] from the Lot of Fortune and from the east, I reckon it is absolutely unrecoverable.

---

[5] John's Sahl reads, "seventh."

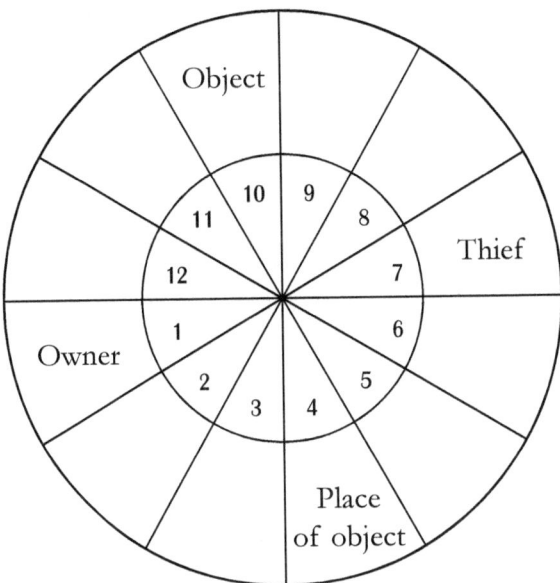

Figure 45: Angular significations for theft (Sahl §7.89, 'Umar §7.91)

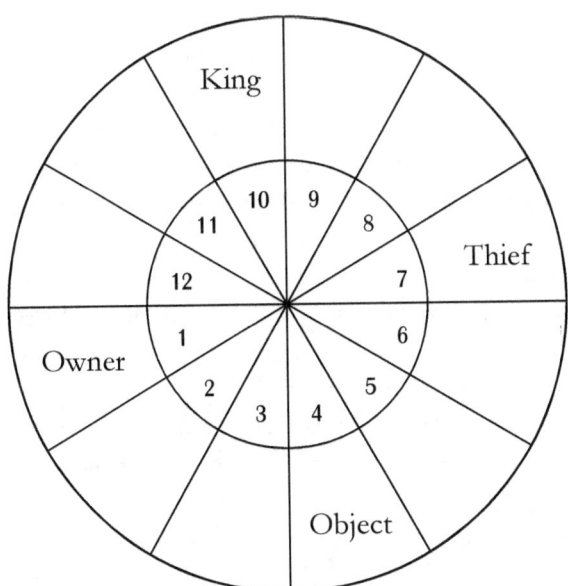

Figure 46: Angular significations for theft (al-Kindī §7.93)

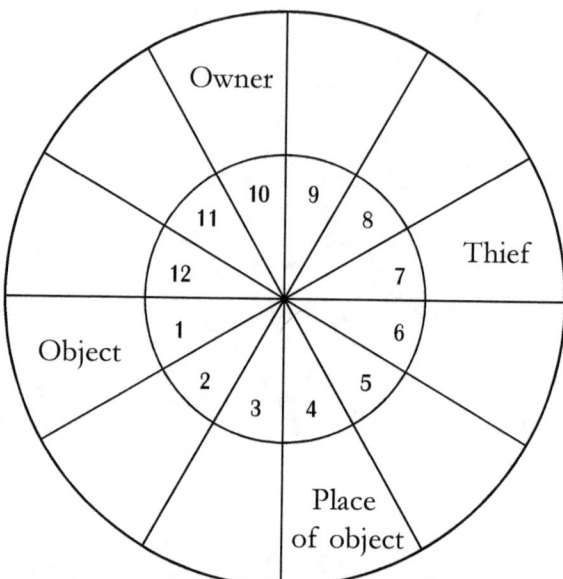

Figure 47: Angular significations for theft:
Carmen V.35 and "Erasistratos"[6]

§7.90: On recovering lost things—Sahl[7]

For recovering lost things (when any inquirer should approach), the lord of the east and the Moon will have to be consulted. And so, with any of these applying to the lord of the second, or if some star would transfer light between them, it is a judgment of recovery. The collection of their light even does the same thing.

The lord of the second traversing in the east portends the same, but with a certain delay being inserted. It is no less if the lord of the second would apply to some [star] placed in the second.

Moreover,[8] the lord of the second being in the eighth, or applying to the lord of the eighth, wholly loses what had been lost. On the other hand, if you

---

[6] For "Erasistratos," see Schmidt 2005, p. 37. Note that in the previous figure, Sahl and 'Umar reverse the attributions of the first and tenth houses—even though the Arabic *Carmen* is 'Umar's own translation.
[7] Cf. *On Quest.* §7.14.
[8] The first sentence of this paragraph reads very differently in John's Sahl: "Likewise if the lord of the eighth from the Ascendant were joined to the lord of the seventh (who is the significator of the robber). And if the lord of the seventh were joined to the lord of the second, it signifies the loss of the assets."

should find the lord of the eighth to be applying to the lord of the second, what had been lost is returned with profit and the harm of the thief, especially if it were regarded by the lord of the east.

But if the lord of the tenth would regard either of them [while] bearing themselves with each other in this way, the whole profit of each is granted to the king. Moreover, an application of the lord of the eighth being made to the lord of the tenth, declares that the thief is fleeing with the stolen goods, under royal protection.

Finally, the lord of the second being cadent from the east and in aversion to the lord [of the east], wholly loses what had been lost. Again, if the lord of the second[9] would apply to the lord of the third or ninth, or to a star occupying either [place], or should it be traversing in either, it shows the stolen goods have been transported from the province.

But whenever both luminaries were under the earth, it cannot be recovered. But whatever goes missing with the Sun and equally the Moon aspecting the east[10] (and more so by a trigon), cannot be lost.

§7.91: On theft—'Umar

With a question about theft being proposed, we put the east in charge of the owner of the lost thing, the seventh over the thief, the Midheaven over the stolen goods, but the fourth over the place of the stolen goods.[11] Moreover, any peregrine star in the east will be principally allotted the signification of the thief. Now, according to the opinion of this chapter, we claim that a peregrine [star] is any one which traverses only outside of its own house: for, it [not] being in [its] sovereignty or trigon or rather any place of its own dignity, it is always judged to be alien.

Furthermore, with the Lunar application or withdrawal being discovered, the star from which the Moon is separated designates the owner of the thing stolen by theft, but the one to which she applies [designates] the thief. But the Moon offers a signification for the stolen goods themselves, and the lord of her lodging-place the place of the stolen goods.

---

[9] Reading with John for Hugo's "eighth."
[10] John's Sahl has the Moon in the Ascendant with its lord, and the Sun aspecting both.
[11] Reading *medium caelum furto, quartum vero loco furti* (following Sahl §7.89 above) for *medio caelo furtum, quartum vero locum.*

Now, this one[12] regarding the lord of the east or applying to it, or rather being placed in the east itself, really brings the thief back to the one whom he had plundered. Contrariwise too, the lord of the east applying to the lord of the seventh, is a sign of the same thing. Therefore, with this application being had from the tetragon or opposition or assembly, reaching him will be difficult and full of labor. But a hexagonal or trigonal application easily brings back the one who has already departed, unless (I say) the lord of the seventh would occupy a pivot: for with it being placed thusly, difficulty and labor is meant. Moreover, with them being deprived of every aspect, it is a sign that it is unrecoverable. And, any star transferring or collecting the light between the lord of the east and of the seventh, does not permit the thief to escape.

§7.92: Whether it could be found—'Umar

For recovering the stolen goods, we especially consult the lords of the second and of the Midheaven. For, each one (or either one) regarding the lord of the east, or rather being placed in the east, promises that it will be found. Contrariwise too, either or both being deprived of the regard of the lord of the east, or of the position and place of the east, or if they would not regard the lord of the seventh, nor would each or either one be staying in the seventh, it wholly removes the hope of recovery.

Moreover, if the one to which the Moon applies would be in the Midheaven, and it would be thought to be worthy of supporting them[13] with its own aspect, they shut the captured thief up in a royal prison. No less, too, the lord of the second, even the star from which the Moon is being separated, and the lord of the Midheaven, being arranged in the Midheaven or regarding it, hand over the thief and the stolen goods to the imperial power.

§7.93: On theft—al-Kindī[14]

§173. Whenever you are eager to investigate something about a theft, you must note that the Ascendant signifies the owner of the thing taken by theft; but the seventh [signifies] the thief, also the tenth the king, but the fourth the

---

[12] The lord of the seventh, based on the opposite situation in the next sentence.
[13] Probably the lords of the second and tenth and first.
[14] Cf. al-Rijāl II.34.

place where the hidden thing is being held. Concerning all of these, we think one must handle it according to the nature [and status][15] of their lords.

§174. But if a peregrine star (namely, one appearing remote from[16] its own house) were found to be in the Ascendant, particularly [if it were] the lord of the seventh, it signifies the robber. If however it were not in the Ascendant but in the tetragon of the Ascendant (namely, it held onto the Midheaven or the fourth, or even the seventh), if, I say, it were in some tetragon of the Ascendant, it will always designate the robber.[17]

§7.94: Whether it could be recovered—al-Kindī[18]

§235-36. Moreover, the lord of the Ascendant with the lord of the Lunar bound, or [with the lord] of the second, or with an application of [either] of them to it, seems to agree [that the object will be found]. For if its application comes to be with either or each of them, or[19] if the Moon would apply with them or with the lord of her own house, or if an application of the Sun would happen with the lord of his own house (while the Moon is being deprived of light)—or, the other way around, [namely] an application of the solar lord or the Lunar bound or even the lord of the house, with the Sun—I say with an observation being had of all of the things above, the recovery of the missing things is confirmed—especially if the stellar significator appears in a pivot or after the pivots.

§237. Moreover, if the lord of the Lunar bound or house, or even the lord of the second, would be applying to the lord of the Ascendant, they restore the lost things to the owner without the expense of labor[ing for it]. Moreover, an application of the Moon and of the lord of the Ascendant (or either of them) with the lord of the second, ([or] even, in imitation of these, the lords of the Lunar bound and house), they grant that he will rejoice in finding the lost things he lamented over, after labor and the difficulties of worrying.[20]

---

[15] Adding with al-Rijāl.
[16] That is, "peregrine."
[17] I.e., a peregrine planet in one of the angles will show the thief more immediately than the lord of the seventh does, even though the latter is still important.
[18] Cf. al-Rijāl II.34.
[19] Al-Rijāl reads, "and."
[20] Al-Rijāl nicely says instead, "the owner of the stolen thing will find the stolen goods through investigating and the quickness of [his] ingenuity."

§7.95: On discovering what was stolen—al-Kindī[21]

§242. Likewise, the mutual regard of the Sun and the Moon from the pivots restores the things taken by theft, but signify that it can be found slowly, after labor and difficulty, [and] it confesses many thieves. But if their regard would happen from a trigon, it restores the lost things very soon.[22] Again, no less does the Moon (being in the Ascendant with either of the fortunate ones) bring back the things which were lost. But she being burned up promises what was stolen is either unrecoverable, or permits it to be restored at some time after difficulties and the harshness of labor.[23]

§243. Moreover, the Sun and the Moon being placed below the earth deny the lost things [to the owner].[24] But they accelerate the return of them [if] in the tenth and in the regard of Jupiter. Likewise, the Moon alone being in the tenth or regarding it, [returns the things] with difficulty but introduces labor and impediment. But with her in the Ascendant it does not postpone the finding of the lost thing or stolen goods. Moreover, the Moon being burned up, nor yet with [her] light being renewed, denies [their recovery]. Likewise, if the Sun and the Moon regard the Ascendant from the pivots,[25] they do not curtail the ability to finding [it, but only] after the work of disagreement, wars, and even at some point duress and clashes.

§244. Dorotheus says:[26] the Sun in the Ascendant restores the stolen goods, except [if the Ascendant is] Aquarius and Libra. Likewise the Moon in the Ascendant, relying on the partnership of Venus and Jupiter,[27] brings back the things that are missing or taken by theft.

---

[21] Cf. al-Rijāl II.34.
[22] See perhaps *Carmen* V.35.42.
[23] *Carmen* V.35.15.
[24] *Carmen* V.35.10.
[25] Al-Rijāl reads: "If both luminaries were nearer to the Ascendant than to another of the other angles….".
[26] Reading with Robert and al-Rijāl for Hugo's *Est etiam haec subscripta super id negotii sententia.* See *Carmen* V.35.17.
[27] Al-Rijāl has only Jupiter. But *Carmen* V.35.19 reads rather differently: if we knew the nativity of the owner of the object, and *at the time of the theft* the Moon was in a sign which had a benefic in it *at the nativity*, then the owner will get it back. Thus *Carmen* has an event chart in mind.

§7.96: Whether the stolen goods could be recovered—al-Khayyāt

For a question about stolen goods, whether they would be recovered or not, we put the east (as is usual) and its lord, and the Moon, in charge of the querent; we hand the thief over to the seventh and its lord. We entrust what had been taken by theft to the Midheaven and its lord, [and] the place of the stolen goods is found in the fourth.

And so, the lord of the east applying to the lord of the seventh (or being in it), [means the querent] will get the stolen goods. But if conversely the lord of the seventh should [be] in the east or apply to the eastern [lord], the thief himself brings back what he had taken, of his own accord. With this application being observed, if the lord of the second is being scorched, it will put fetters on the thief, but it in no way brings the stolen goods back. Here however, the lord of the second having left scorching, restores part.

The lord of the east applying to a star in a pivot (especially one appearing in the tenth), testifies to the obtaining of the stolen goods. But if it would apply to a remote [star], and one in aversion [to the east], so that it does not even regard the east, it portends it is unrecoverable. But [applying to] a remote one that is not in aversion (but rather to one regarding [the east]), it does not wholly take away hope.

Moreover, the scorching of the lord of the seventh[28] apprehends the thief, and better so under the regard of the eastern lord (for thus [the goods] are wholly held).

But if the lord of the seventh would equally apply to the eastern [lord] and the lord of the tenth, it announces he is going to return the stolen goods out of fear of the king.

Now, the lord of the tenth applying to the eastern lord restores the same through the king's own urging.[29]

But with a joint application being denied, while however they would apply to the lord of the Midheaven, they promise the gotten goods to the king or prince or someone else, but they make the one who had lost [them] wholly devoid [of them]—unless, I say, the Sun himself or the lord of the Midheaven or of the seventh, or even the Moon, would render counsel to the eastern lord, or there would be a transfer of their light to it.

---

[28] Reading with Sahl and Dorotheus for "east."
[29] Reading *impellatione* for *appellatione* ("title").

And it affirms [the goods] are recovered according to the nature of the one transferring: for a transfer made from the Sun or the lord of the Midheaven, brings it through the royal hand; from the lord of the seventh, the thief himself restores them.

But whenever the lord of the east would apply to the lord of the tenth, royal aid promises it to the one who lost it. The lord of the seventh applying to it, the thief himself is excused through the royal power.

Now, a transfer made between the significators, apprehends the thief. Moreover, the lord of the seventh applying to the lord of the third or ninth, or to a star positioned in those same places, or [the lord of the seventh] itself appearing there, testifies that the thief has left the entire region. But if it would be lingering in a pivot, it portends he is not far from the place.

Likewise, the Moon applying to an infortune, wholly loses the thing; it is no less if she would apply to a scorched or corrupted fortunate one. For if that unlucky one [which is corrupting the Moon] would be lingering in a pivot, it reveals the thief, but does not return the stolen goods. But an application of her being made with a star in the east or Midheaven, being cleansed of the unfortunate ones, is a sign of recovery.

The Sun in the east restores the stolen goods, unless (I say) Gemini or anything of his triplicity is the east: for then it wholly speaks against [recovery]. But if the lights would regard each other from a trigon or hexagon, they quickly bring back what had been taken by theft, especially while one would be lingering in the east or Midheaven. An application made from the tetragon or opposition, brings it back with difficulty and after he has already lost hope. Moreover, the Moon in the opposition of the Sun, she being corrupted by a strong infortune, [and] with the benevolents being cadent from her, scatters the majority of the stolen goods, and he recovers [only] a moderate amount because of the opposition of the lights.

But if the lights regarded the Lot of Fortune, or either one of them would be in its assembly, he recovers the stolen goods, and preferably if [it is] the Sun; then finally if the Sun himself regarded both the Moon and the Lot of Fortune. But if there is only a regard of the Moon, or she assembles with [the Lot], there will be labor and delay in it. If therefore the lights did not regard each other, nor did they [regard] the Lot of Fortune nor the east, they declare it is absolutely unrecoverable.

§7.97: Whether the stolen goods would be recovered quickly or not—al-Khayyāt

Whenever therefore the [star] from which the Moon is being separated (or, the lord of the seventh) regards the star to which she is applying, he quickly recovers what had been lost.

In addition, the lord of the second in the east, gives a nod to [the same] thing, but more slowly. But if it would apply to a star lingering in the second, the same.

Moreover, the lord of the second or eighth being in the second: he fully loses it. Now, the lord of the eighth applying to the lord of the second, brings back the lost things with profit and the detriment of the thief—preferably if the testimonies of the eastern lord are not absent.

But if the eastern lord or even that of the tenth would gain testimony, it grants the profit over to the royal resources. But if the lord of the eighth applied to the lord of the tenth, it leads the thief (with the stolen goods) into royal custody. The position of each light in a pivot, and [their] mutual application, is a sign of recovery. Which if the application is missing, they lose the thief himself.

Finally, with the lord of the second being cadent from the regard of the eastern lord (and that of the seventh), the stolen goods are absolutely lost. Moreover, the lord of the second applying to the lord of the third or ninth, or to a star positioned in those same places, brings the stolen goods away from the whole region.

§7.98: Whether it could be recovered—Dorotheus

An[30] observation of the Sun and Moon responds to a question about the stolen goods, as to whether or not they are to be recovered. For, one of these (namely the Sun) regarding the Lot of Fortune, finds what was taken by theft more quickly. On the contrary, a Lunar regard or conjunction furnishes difficulty. Moreover, with the regard of the lights being remote from[31] the Lot of Fortune and from the east, and even from each other, wholly speaks against recovery.

---

[30] This paragraph should be read with §7.99, in parallel with the end of al-Khayyāt §7.96.
[31] That is, "in aversion to."

However, [if] the star from which the Moon is being separated, is regarding the one to which she applies (or at least the lord of the seventh), it is a sign of recovering it.

Moreover, the lord of the second traversing in the second or in the east, even if it does not permit it to be found at present, [it does so] at some time [later]. Also, the lord of the second applying to a star appearing in the second [means] nothing else.

Again, the lord of the eighth in the seventh scatters the lost things. And the lord of the eighth applying to the lord of the second restores the lost things, even if a portion has been consumed by the thief; it is better if the testimonies of the eastern lord would be supportive.

The lord of the Midheaven agreeing with them,[32] grants the stolen goods to the royal dignity. Thus even an application of the lord of the eighth[33] with [the lord of] the tenth, portends that the thief himself will fraudulently and with deception take refuge under royal protection.

In addition even, the lord of the second applying to the lord of the third or the ninth, or if preferably it would be established in it, declares that the stolen goods have been exported from the region.

Moreover, the lights being in the pivots do not allow the lost things to be lost [forever], even if they do not bring back the thief.

§7.99: On the same thing, but in another way—Dorotheus

With a question proposed about recovering stolen goods, the east designates the querent, the seventh the thief, the Midheaven the lost things, the pivot of the earth the place of the stolen goods.

And so, the lord of the seventh applying to the eastern [lord], compels the thief himself to bring back the lost things. While these bear themselves thusly, the lord of the second being scorched apprehends the thief but does not save what had been lost; [its] departure from scorching, recovers part [of it]. Likewise, the lord of the seventh occupying the east apprehends the thief.

It is not otherwise, too, with the lord of the east applying to a star in a pivot (especially in the Midheaven). But if it would apply to a star that is drawn back, it portends escape—if, I say, it does not regard the east. For

---

[32] *His accedens.* This means that there is some kind of aspect between the lord of the tenth and perhaps the lords of the second and eighth. Cf. Sahl and al-Khayyāt.
[33] Reading with Sahl and al-Khayyāt for "second."

however it may be drawn back, its application with the eastern lord testifies that he will be apprehended.

Likewise, the scorching of the lord of the seventh does the same, and better if it would regard the eastern lord: for thus it subjects the thief himself to the authority of the one who had lost [the goods].

But in the meantime, with the lord of the seventh applying to the eastern [lord] [and that of the tenth],[34] the thief with the stolen goods is forced to return through fear of the king.

But [the lord of the tenth] applying to [the lord of the east]:[35] he merits recovery for the same reason they were lost.[36]

With such a regard being denied, the king himself or someone else will rejoice in the profit,[37] unless the Sun or the lord of the tenth or seventh or the Moon would perhaps render counsel to the eastern lord, or there would be a transfer present: for thus the thief himself is led back according to the nature of that star transferring the light to the eastern lord.

Which if the light would proceed from the Sun or the lord of the tenth, it is returned with the king doing it; but if from the lord of the seventh, of his own accord.

Thus even an application of the eastern lord with the lord of the tenth, subjects the thief to the command of the owner, with the king supporting [that]. Also, the lord of the seventh applying to it, brings the thief under the royal power. With it even being scorched, the thief himself is being held.

But if a star would transfer the light of the significators, it is likewise. And, the lord of the seventh applying to a star appearing in the third or ninth, or to those lords from those places, carries the thief away outside the region. Its application to a star in a pivot, promises he is detained inside the land.

The Moon applying to the infortunes, scatters the lost things. That malevolent being established in a pivot, gives notice of the thief but does not return the stolen goods. Moreover, a Lunar application with some scorched fortunate [star] (or preferably an unlucky one), wholly condemns the stolen goods.[38] Likewise, the Moon applying to a star possessing the east or tenth (and one cleansed of the infortunes), brings back the lost things.

---

[34] Adding based on Sahl and al-Khayyāt.
[35] Adding based on al-Khayyāt.
[36] I am not sure what Hugo means by this phrase, but it means that the king's own action will help recover the goods.
[37] That is, instead of the owner.
[38] That is, it condemns them to being lost forever.

The Sun in the east restores the same thing, unless (I say) he would be lingering in Gemini or in its triplicity. Moreover, the regard of each[39] of the lights from a trigon,[40] announces that the thief and stolen goods are recovered without difficulty, and better while they possess the east or Midheaven; however, from a tetragon or opposition, it supplies a delay. Moreover, even though the Moon may regard the Sun, while however she is being corrupted by a strong infortune and is cadent from the benevolents, it scatters the majority [of the goods] and restores [only] a modicum.

But a regard or conjunction of the lights to the Lot of Fortune, does not permit the missing things to be lost.

§7.100: On theft—Aristotle

With a question proposed about a theft, one must consult the lord of the seventh. For, it being found in the east or with the lord of [the east], the thief reveals himself of his own accord, not being coerced. But the eastern lord in the seventh shows the thief is sought for a long time. Moreover, the Moon in the east or with the lord of the east, or at least traveling through the fifth or eleventh place from the lord of the east, really reveals the thief. Moreover, with the Sun being arranged in the fifth from the Moon, or the Moon in the fifth from the Sun, the thief is brought back. The Sun even traversing with the Moon within 5°, wholly conceals both the object and the thief.

§7.101: Whether a thing taken by theft could be recovered—Aristotle

If someone would make a question about the discovery of the stolen thing, I follow the path set below. For, the lord of the eighth in the east or with its lord, brings back the stolen thing. The lord of the second in the eighth, denies it. Saturn or Mars or the Tail in the second, scatters part of it and ruins it, nor does it suggest that the whole thing can be recovered. The lord of the second in the east, brings back what had been taken away. The eastern lord in the second, he finds the stolen thing [after] it is sought for a long time.

---

[39] Reading with Sahl and al-Khayyāt for "one." That is, if they regard each other.
[40] That is, a regard *between* the two luminaries.

I advise that you note this with the greatest effort: because if the lord of the second were impeded, or the second itself were impeded, what was stolen can in no way be recovered in full.

§7.102: How much should be recovered, [and how he entered the home]—'Umar[41]

Moreover, the seven movable stars (especially the lord of the second and of the tenth, and the Moon) jointly declare the counsel as to the quantity of the stolen goods: what part should be recovered, and what part would perish.[42]

Now,[43] Saturn regarding both the lord of the second and that of the tenth, and the Moon, indicates that he committed the theft through some trick, like an unlocked gate or an entrance at night, or some hiding place. Likewise, Mars holding onto Saturn's place[44] compels him to steal publicly and violently, such as a broken door or some hole, or the power of his muscles, and with anger. Also, while Jupiter would console the lord of the second and of the tenth, or even the Moon, with its own aspect, [it means] the thief does not come for that reason ([because] neither his nature nor custom is like that), but rather he entered by chance and, fooling [people] with a face of laughter, took it away with him. Moreover, Venus having control of Jupiter's role, reveals a corresponding judgment. Now, the Sun endowed with the place of Jupiter, regarding from a tetragon or opposition or even an assembly, testifies that he had come for that reason, and it claims he is famous, and it commends his bloodline. [Mercury signifies that he entered through trickery and cleverness.][45]

---

[41] I have added the material in brackets, as it more accurately reflects the content of the section.
[42] This does not really tell us how to judge the amount. See §7.96 above and §7.103 below.
[43] For this paragraph, cf. *Carmen* V.35.134-38. *Carmen* has Saturn (and the other planets) aspecting the Moon and the Ascendant.
[44] That is, doing the same thing that Saturn did in the previous sentence.
[45] Adding based on *Carmen* V.35.138.

§7.103: How much should be recovered—al-Kindī[46]

§245. Moreover, the lord of the Lunar house and[47] of the second, and the lord of the bound of the Moon, all of them (I say) decreasing in course or computation (or better yet both), and being regarded by the unfortunate ones, shows that the majority of the lost things will be unrecoverable. Fewer of them being corrupted decrees that less will be missing. Wherefore, we recommend that it be judged—with art and industry being brought to bear—according to the noted consideration of lesser or greater corruption.

§246. Moreover, the amount of the lost thing (which the malignancy of the stars prohibits from returning to the owner's possession) is discovered thusly. Therefore, in the first place, the nature of the star which signifies the loss of the things[48] should be noted, and [the nature] of the sign which it obtains, and place of those in the order of signs with which they bear some correspondence.[49] A consideration of all of them having been discussed, the chosen significator will testify to the nature of the lost thing ([as] laid out above), through the manner of its signification. [And if] the lord of the Lunar bound and the lord of the house of the Moon and of the second,[50] were adding [in motion and number],[51] and safe from the infortunes, they return [the things] intact—if their signification does restore the lost things.

§7.104: When it would be returned—al-Kindī[52]

§238.[53] Moreover, the degrees between the applying one and the one to which it applies itself suggest at what hour it leads back all or part of what they signify to the owner (namely, it brings back the lost things). For the number of their degrees determines hours, days, weeks, [and] months, in turn. But the places of the application lay bare the same thing. For the degrees of the application appearing in convertible signs more frequently

---

[46] Cf. al-Rijāl II.34.
[47] Reading with Robert and the instructions immediately following, for Hugo's "or."
[48] Al-Rijāl (II.35) reads: "look at the planet which signifies that one part will be recovered and the other part lost."
[49] This is probably a fancy way of referring to the domicile of that planet which it aspects most strongly, etc.
[50] Al-Rijāl omits "and of the second."
[51] Adding with al-Rijāl.
[52] Cf. al-Rijāl II.34.
[53] See also §A.133 on timing.

reckon hours [or] days for the delay.[54] In a sign of two bodies, weeks and months. In firm signs, they bring years to bear.

§239. Moreover, the significators for recovering this thing being in a pivot or after the pivots or remote from the pivots, determine the aforesaid. For, being cadent from the pivots, they return the lost things under present circumstances;[55] also, in the pivots they imitate [the cadents];[56] after the pivots they involve the thing in no moderate delay. But the judgment of the planets particularly claims this knowledge about the pivots of this question.

§240. Likewise, whenever the Moon or the lord of the Ascendant would reach the significator for finding the thing with its own body,[57] they give assent to the aforesaid things. For when either one of these would reach the significator (or it would [reach] one of them) they restore the lost things. If however it would reach them while retrograde, the lost things will be restored contrary to hope.[58] Direct, it soothes one's hope for the found things.

§241. Again, whenever the lord of the Lunar bound would reach its own bound, or the lord of the house of the Moon or the lord of the house of money would reach their own houses, or even the ingress of one of them into the Ascendant, it claims the same.

Likewise,[59] look to see if the Lot of Fortune had some testimony with the lord of the Ascendant or with the Moon: because when it applied to[60] any of them, or one of them to it, or the lord of the house of the Moon to the Moon herself, they are times for recovering the hoped-for things.

Even if the lord of the Lot of Fortune would apply to the Ascendant, or to the second house, or to the place in which the Lot itself was, [or] to the Moon, times of recovery are likewise signified.

Likewise, look to see how many degrees are from the planet which signified recovery, up to the angle to which it goes first, and that number of degrees is a time of recovery.

---

[54] That is, the time between the question and the objects' recovery.
[55] That is, quickly.
[56] Al-Rijāl says that the pivots indicate something between quickness (cadents) and delay (succeedents).
[57] That is, by transit.
[58] That is, unexpectedly (al-Rijāl).
[59] For the rest of this section, reading directly from al-Rijāl. Both Robert's and Hugo's versions of these conditions are rather mangled.
[60] This probably means "is directed to."

§7.105: Whether he is an outsider or someone familiar—Sahl[61]

In order that this ambiguity may be erased from the mind (namely whether the thief is an outsider or someone familiar), an observation of the Sun and Moon will have to be made. For if they each would be regarding the Ascendant, they profess that the thief is from the family itself; but with the regard of one being denied, while at least the other regards [the east], it claims a neighbor. Moreover, the traversal of the lord of the seventh in the east judges that he is of the family.[62]

The positions of the Sun and Moon in their own houses, while they touch the east [and its lord][63] with their own aspect, accuse the family, for the lights reveal a relative. Which if each would happen to be staying in its own triplicity, even though it is a blood-relation, still he stays outside of the family.[64] But if they both would hold onto their own faces or bounds,[65] it credits the name of a relation and nearness to the one who had lost [the things]. Moreover, the regard of each to the east but not to its lord, prefigures that the thief had never before entered that house—unless it would be lingering in two-parted signs[66]—but if he had entered, it was in the open and with the family being ignorant. Which if it regarded the lord of the east but not the east itself, [it means] the household was known [to the thief] but in no way had he entered it before.

Moreover, with the lord of the east being in aversion to the degree of the east, while another star was with it but closer to the degree of the east, the thief is being held, hidden, within the home.

The lord of the seventh even traversing in the ninth from its own house, portends an outsider, [and] we usually discover both his condition and profession from this. For, this lord of the seventh going through the sixth or eighth from its own domicile, uncovers a slave. But if this significator would be lingering in its own sovereignty, it accuses a great man. From its own house, [it indicates] one famous and with a great name.[67] Also in this way, its

---

[61] Cf. *On Quest.* §7.15.
[62] John's Sahl has the lord of the east in the east, or the lord of the seventh being with the lord of the east.
[63] Adding with John's Sahl.
[64] That is, he does not live in the house, and probably not nearby.
[65] In most systems, the luminaries do not rule any bounds.
[66] John's Sahl helpfully adds that this is because the common signs show repetition.
[67] John's Sahl simply says he will be of the inhabitants of the house, and known among them.

position in its triplicity, bound, or even face, portends someone of lesser dignity but known in his own neighborhood.

§7.106: Whether he is a stranger or familiar—'Umar

Each[68] of the lights come to be noted in this place. Which if they would regard each other or the east itself, they testify that the thief is close in affinity to the one who has lost the things. The individual aspect of one of them, claims he is known in familiarity, but is not close. Which if [the east] is deprived of the aspect of each, while they fall away from the regard of the east, they bring forth a stranger.

Particularly too, the lord of the seventh [and] a star in the east to which the Moon applies, must be noted: for if they were partners in the house or triplicity or sovereignty in that same place, he is close (as was already stated). But with them being alien to these dignities, they wholly judge a stranger.

§7.107: Whether he is a stranger or familiar—Aristotle

Whenever this were brought into question, the lord of the sixth[69] should be noted. For, it being in the east or the second or with the lord of the second, it claims that the thief was of the family and its dependents; if not, not. If it is asked about associates, the same judgment should be related with respect to the seventh. But otherwise it is said: if it was asked about your [family and intimates], as to whether they committed the theft, consult the east, third, and even the fourth. Therefore, the eastern lord traversing in any of these, leads your people into blame. But if the question comes to be about anyone else (such as about the father, brother, and the rest), let the intention of [your] mind be led back to the domiciles in which they are contained.

---

[68] This paragraph is directly from *Carmen* V.35.75-78.
[69] In this question, Aristotle is imagining that the question is about someone specific: e.g., "did my *servant* (the sixth) take it?"

§7.108: Of what age or sex he is—Sahl[70]

For discovering his age or sex or lineage, we give such advice. This significator being of the benevolents, foretells that the thief is freeborn and of good stock; if of the malevolents, it brings out[71] one serving and discloses an ignoble person. Now, if Mercury or Venus would have a signification of this kind, it designates a woman or boy; but Mars, adolescence; in the same way, Saturn represents the senile years (but if he were eastern, he is not an old man); [Jupiter is older than Mars].[72]

Moreover, with that same signification being taken up by the Moon, at the beginning of the Lunar cycle it accuses a boy, in the middle a youth, at the end it condemns an old man.

Finally, the position of the Sun between the east and the tenth lays the theft on a boy, [but] otherwise there comes to be an addition through the rest of the degrees of age, up until he crosses over the pivot of the earth: for from the tenth up to the seventh, it prefigures an adolescent, moreover from the seventh to the fourth, an adult; from the fourth to the east, it announces the senile age.

§7.109: Whether it is a male or female—'Umar

When however there is ambiguity about the sex, one must consult a peregrine star in the east, [and] even one to which the Moon is applying, and the lord of the seventh. For, these three planets being in masculine and eastern signs, or in a masculine part of the circle, ascribe that sex to him. But in female or western ones, or in a feminine part of the circle, they accuse a woman. We call the virile parts of the circle (I say) from the east to the Midheaven, and from the fourth to the seventh; but the remaining ones are called female.

---

[70] Cf. *On Quest.* §7.16 (second half). This section is a garbled mixture of *Carmen* V.35.108-115, and V.35.123-4. For one thing, in *Carmen* the initial statements about benefics and malefics refers to the planets *aspecting* the significator of the thief. *Carmen*'s basic rules are that eastern planets are younger, western planets older; planets in stations are older, as are planets that are scorched or under the rays.
[71] Reading *depromit* for *deprimit*.
[72] Adding with John's Sahl.

§7.110: Of what age he is—'Umar

It is appropriate to scrutinize the three aforewritten significators above,[73] for the recognition of [the thief's] age: namely, as to whether they are holding onto the earlier degrees of [their] signs, or the middle ones or the latter ones, or if they were eastern or western or neither. For, at the beginning of the signs or being eastern, they indict [a thief with] younger years. But in the latter [parts] or being western, they disgrace an aged person. In the middle of the signs, or being neither eastern nor western (namely so that they are distant from the Sun by [more than] 90° in front or behind, or only 90°), they accuse someone of middle age.

§7.111: Whether it is one or many—al-Kindī[74]

[Whether it will be made public]

§203a.[75] Moreover, the thing will be made public and come out into the open, if the lord of the significator of thief and the luminaries regard each other and the significator, and especially if in addition they regarded each other. But with these aspects being denied, no knowledge of the theft or thief will be given. But if the lord of the significator would regard the lights from any of the pivots, after being hidden and the cloud [of secrecy], it will be uncovered and in the open. And commonly if there were many of these regards from the pivots it will be especially declared [in the open], but from the cadents, not at all.

[The significator of the thief][76]

§203b. And so, the significator of the robber is discerned in this art when an exiled star[77] is situated in the Midheaven; if one were peregrine in the eighth, it should be noted; but if not, a peregrine one which is in the fourth should be appointed. Again, if there were none [there], one which traverses

---

[73] In §7.109.
[74] Cf. al-Rijāl II.34.
[75] This part of the section is only in Robert.
[76] Cf. also al-Kindī's §173 in §7.93 above, whose list of options is somewhat different.
[77] That is, peregrine.

in the second should be taken. With none even appearing in that place, [your] intention should be directed to the lord of the seventh.

[Whether the thieves are one or many]

§204. If therefore it pleased [you] to settle whether it is one [thief] or many, the sign of the above-determined significator should be noted. But [that sign] appearing firm, particularly being straight and of few offspring and a simple form, indicates it was one. Likewise in a double-bodied one or one of much offspring and a manifold form, especially if many peregrine stars would accompany the significator itself, they suggest many thieves.

§7.112: Whether they are one or more—al-Kindī[78]

§247:[79] Again, at the hour of the question, the Moon being in the pivot of the earth and in a double-bodied sign indicates many thieves; the Ascendant in a double-bodied sign[80] builds the same thing onto that.[81] But if the Ascendant were a firm sign, it shows one. However, that same Ascendant and lord of the hour being male, testifies to males; the same being female, to a woman. Moreover, the Ascendant being male and the lord of the hour female, claims that one will be a man, the other a woman.[82]

§7.113: The form of the robber—'Umar[83]

The form and status could be discovered by this method. For, Saturn in possession of the signification of the thief, and being in either of [his own] houses, portends that he is black, with small eyes, lame, bent, with contracted muscles.[84]

---

[78] Cf. al-Rijāl II.34.
[79] When translating *Forty Chapters*, I relied on Robert's version of this paragraph because it was missing in Burnett's critical edition. But here I use Hugo's, which is indeed in *Judges*.
[80] Al-Rijāl omits this point about the Ascendant.
[81] *Astruit*.
[82] That is, there are two thieves, a male and a female.
[83] Cf. *Carmen* V.35.86-90.
[84] *Carmen* V.35.87 says that he is "broken," which might be what Hugo has picked up on here.

The significator being Jupiter and in either of his own houses, commends him as being white, the charm of both his eyes and eyebrows, and stout.

Also, a signification of Mars (and being in either of [his own] houses), indicates a ruddy or red color, gray eyes, and bestows a good look to his body.

Moreover, from the signification of Venus, and being in either of her own houses, a blonde color, a good look to the eyes, and the charm of his eyebrows, largeness of body, large legs, a splendor of the face, [and] beauty of the hair on his head is confirmed.

Finally, Mercury being endowed with the same dignity and function, greatly bestows one thin, pale, sharp eyes, quick motions, a sweetness and eloquence of the tongue, a charm of the hair on his head.

§7.114: The form of the robber—al-Kindī[85]

§175a. The form of the thief is described [according to][86] the figure of stars appearing in these places (namely the pivots), even [the figure] of the sign which holds onto [the pivot].

[Saturn]

§175b-176a. So, Saturn in a masculine sign ([that is], of his own sect),[87] and western, indicates a thief that is an old man, pallid or red or black, whose speech is sparing, a wide forehead, large head, foul face, and cunning. Also, in a female sign and female quarter, it portends a castrated man or poor old woman according to the aforesaid form.

§176b. Being eastern and in the beginning of his easternness conveys an adolescent [in body but] an old man in his mind, and a sweet look. But in the middle of easternness, a young man imitating old people in sense. But at the end [of his easternness], it shows a man of already completed age, and instructed by old men.

§177. Apart from the aforewritten signification, Saturn in Aries bestows a discordant voice, pale and large eyes, eyebrows that stand out, a thick face, a

---

[85] Cf. al-Rijāl II.34.
[86] Reading *describitur* and *secundum* with Robert for *describit*.
[87] Robert: *ḥalb*.

straight nose, sometimes even cheeks bearded in a youthful way, thin hair on the head, large buttocks, slender shins, [and foolish].[88]

§178. In Taurus, apart from his own proper signification, a broad forehead, thick voice and top of the nose, ugly lips, thinness of hair on the head, a curved stature, large eyes, loose skin on the throat, fullness of the hips and sides, and even the feet, an anxious life, making a living with labor—is [all] designated by Saturn, whose unluckiness [in the chart][89] will seem to have added the most extreme misfortunes.

§179. But with Saturn appearing in Gemini: a good mind is designated,[90] [and] a loud voice, respectable counsel, eloquence, broadness of the shoulders, beautiful lips, beautiful hair on the head—unless baldness impedes that (which if this happened, he remains beautiful in the remaining things)—long deliberation, even fraud.

§180. The same Saturn in Cancer connects black pupils to his own proper signification, [as well as] little dark spots on the face,[91] a broad forehead, dry limbs, large and foul feet and hands, unsteadiness of the mind.

§181. Moreover, in Leo an anxious life[92] is designated, [and] sunkenness of the eyes, an even and large nose, broad nostrils, ugliness of the lips, a short and swollen neck, a fat chest and arms, appropriate buttocks, thin ankles, sometimes a swollen belly, hairy shoulders and neck, boldness, authority, steady speech, even gluttony.

§182. Moreover, Saturn in Virgo assigns benevolence, a large head,[93] a hairy body (especially the arms and feet), long deliberation, fawning, evenness of speech.

§183. Also, in Libra it shows a narrow head, length of the nose and neck, black hair on the head, thin shins, narrow sides, high buttocks, long fingers, [long] nails coming from the hands, and nobility on top of that.

§184. Also, in Scorpio Saturn designates straight eyebrows, much thick hair on the head and divided on the forehead, large and foul hands and feet, a saffron color,[94] small eyes, short sides, long feet; besides these, malice.

---

[88] Adding with al-Rijāl.
[89] That is, in a poor condition.
[90] Al-Rijāl: "with morals mixed of crookedness and those who are shifty."
[91] Al-Rijāl: "a small face," assigning marks on the face to Saturn in Leo.
[92] Robert: "a grim face" (*vultu trucem*); al-Rijāl: "marks on the face."
[93] Reading with Robert and al-Rijāl for Hugo's "neck" (possibly a mistaken transposition of *cervix* and *vertex*).
[94] Al-Rijāl: "green-saffronish," possibly a kind of light olive or citrine.

§185. But in Sagittarius, ample eyebrows that stand out are designated, [and] a long face, a broad mouth and nose, fatness of the shins, flowing hair and much of it, a hairy nape of the neck, a somewhat curved neck, large buttocks; and besides this, arrogance [and very lazy].[95]

§186. In Capricorn, a drawn-out face is denoted by Saturn, [and] seriousness of the eyes,[96] a thin voice, narrowness of the eyebrows, foul extremities of the feet and hands, sexual impurity, rare or nonexistent chastity, a black or red color, stiffness of the hair, a hairy body.

§187. However, in Aquarius: a large head, long face [which is] broad above and narrow below. His profession has to do with water and moist things, like sailing and what pertains to ships and the sea (such as being a fisherman or cook or bearer of water, and what is like these).

§188. Also, with the same Saturn occupying Pisces (provided that he is strong and made fortunate by the lucky ones, and received [by them]),[97] it indicates nobleness of the blood, no matter how low and unremarkable [he seems]. [But] being unsound[98] or namely being struck[99] or corrupted somehow by an infortune, it proves his parents have come from nobility,[100] but he is bad; and [it signifies] the beauty of his eyes, a wide mouth, uneven teeth, a rough body,[101] self-control in his speech, but [also] gluttony.

[The Moon showing marks & blemishes]

§189. Also, the Moon in the seventh, while she claims many dignities [over] the place of the peregrine or exiled star which appears in the Ascendant or in one of the pivots, and [provided that] she is lucky, [then], should she be in Aries, it shows a beautiful mark on the head, or the head or face itself is handsome. Also, appearing in Taurus and being as was said above, it bequeaths a mark or ornament to the [neck. In Gemini, the shoulders and arms. In Cancer],[102] the chest and breast. In Leo, it seems to concede one to

---

[95] Adding with al-Rijāl.
[96] Robert reads, "soft eyes" (*mollibus oculis*).
[97] Reading with Robert for Hugo's "namely, ascending or regarded." Al-Rijāl reads, "in the prosperity of good aspects."
[98] Robert reads, "unfavorable" (*aversus*).
[99] Reading *azukt* as a transliteration based on *ßakkata*. Robert reads simply, "harmed."
[100] Al-Rijāl adds that they have lost their noble standing.
[101] Robert says he has an evenly balanced body, al-Rijāl that he has a quick body.
[102] Adding with Robert.

the stomach and the lower belly up to the pubes. But in Virgo it ascribes one to the back and hips.[103]

§190. Also, that same Moon appearing in Libra as we said before, does not remove the mark and ornament from the flanks [and] lower belly up to the male organs. Also in Scorpio, it enriches the male organs and genitalia with this gift. In Sagittarius, the buttocks. In Capricorn, the knees and lower part of the thighs. Also in Aquarius, she is accustomed to bless the shins with a mark or ornament. In Pisces, she does not remove it from the feet.

§191.[104] But on the contrary, the Moon being corrupted or unlucky in the aforesaid places, portends that there is a blemish or deformity in the places enumerated above. Moreover, if the star making this misfortune worse[105] were adding in course, it causes this increase to overflow in that blemish. But if this unluckiness was being broadened by a star which is increasing in computation,[106] the increase descends into the proper limbs.

On the other hand, if a star diminished in course had supplied this misfortune, it does not repel the harm of this ugliness, [or] the diminution of the limbs.[107] [And if it were diminished in number, the foulness will be diminished in the limb.][108]

But if it would be going forward in its average course, it manages the beauty mark or defects, and the limbs, without increase or diminution. [If it were equal in number, the mark will be flat, on the surface of the skin of the member, neither high nor deep.][109]

§192a. This above-written understanding of the form can be observed not only for a thief, but even for other people.

---

[103] Higher up, near the waist (*costis*).
[104] This paragraph is a bit unclear to me, because I am not sure whether al-Kindī's vocabulary matches that of Abū Ma'shar and al-Qabīsī in *ITA* II.0-4. Al-Kindī is opposing variations in *course* versus those in *computation/number*. I suggest that changes in course refer to speed, whereas changes in computation/number refer *either* to a planet is direct or retrograde, *or* to a planet's relation to its apogee (if the latter, then probably being close to its apogee makes the marks raised above the skin, while being close to its perigee makes them sink down).
[105] Reading *demutat* with *Judges* for Burnett's *demittat*.
[106] Al-Rijāl: "number."
[107] *Search* Ch. II.1.8 actually has a clearer reading, based on Robert's version of this section: "But she bears this beauty provided that she is fortunate. For, corrupted, [she signifies] ugliness in those places in terms of the amount and quality of the one corrupting her, [and] in the computation of [her] adding or subtracting [in light]."
[108] Adding with al-Rijāl.
[109] Adding with al-Rijāl.

§192b. In fact, the Moon being found in the Ascendant permits the [same] or something just like what was in Aries; also, if she appears in the second, she reveals the kind of indication such as that in Taurus. And so, one will have to judge for all places, just as in their opposite signs, up until the judgment comes to an end with respect to the feet, just as was done for Pisces.

§193. But that same Moon in a male sign indicates that the mark is on the right side; in a female sign, the left side.

§7.115: On the form of the robber—al-Kindī[110]

[The rest of the planets below Saturn]

§194-196a. Likewise, with some [other] star obtaining the signification of a thief, if Jupiter should have the role of Saturn,[111] it means a white and paleish person. But if it were a man, his beard [is] rounded. But the eyes of each sex [would be] black; [in morals], temperate, peaceful, and noble. However, with Mars taking the place of Jupiter, he is portrayed as red-haired, reddishness in the face (no matter what his color is), a round face, small forehead, a sharp look, eyebrows joined together,[112] thin and shiny hair on his head, a quick tread, and a show-off. Again, the Sun taking on Mars's role teaches he is white, a bright face, ready for hunting or augury, or most famous in the medical art, sometimes even a cook or a water-attendant.[113] But if Venus should perform the Sun's role: a white color, lively, ruddy, beauty of the eyes, large pupils, average stature, benevolent; large buttocks and legs are indicated. But Mercury professes a nimbleness of body, a thin beard, long face, white but reddish, his temples even shorn of hair.[114]

§196b. Also, it is good for the individual things which were said above to be mixed[115] with the signs which [the planets] are holding onto, just as was done above with respect to Saturn.

---

[110] Cf. al-Rijāl II.34.
[111] That is, if he were the significator instead of Saturn (see above).
[112] Al-Rijāl has the eyebrows curving upwards, "like the horns of the Moon."
[113] Al-Rijāl reads, "a singer or diviner, or a physician, or repairer of fabrics."
[114] Robert adds "subtlety" and "honesty." Al-Rijāl says "talkative" and "vehement."
[115] *Obtemperare*, which normally means "submit" or "obey," but the meaning here is mixture.

§7.116: On the robber's form—Jirjis

And so, Venus portends one bright white [colored], adolescent, with a respectable face, straight and smooth hair on his head, black eyes, of middling stature. If therefore she would be lingering between the east and the Midheaven, it suggests the younger years; between the Midheaven and the pivot of the west, the middle ones; from the west to the pivot of the earth, the middle of the whole life; from the pivot of the earth to the east, it makes a judgment of more advanced age. One will also have to judge in this manner with the rest of the stars, whenever they walk through those same places. But whenever Venus, being in the bound or house of Mars, would traverse with that same Mars or under his regard, it foretells a sexually impure woman.

Also, Saturn: a black man with a large body, thick nose, hairy body, slow in his tread and speech.

Moreover Jupiter: a man of middle age, relaxed, peaceful, faithful and trusting, with saffron eyes, thin hair, an unusual tooth,[116] and an average body.

By Mars are described a redness of hair on the head, and whitish eyes. But he will be malicious, a friend of slaughter and quarreling, a hanger-on of the king, a personal attendant, and he loves the partnerships of a robber.

Also Mercury suggests an adolescent and the childhood years, thin, eloquent and reasonable, experienced and of great industry. With Venus, it denotes a proud gait and posture.

Then, the Sun prefigures the middle years, a smooth, level and thick body, bright white and reddish, with saffron eyes and an unusual tooth,[117] his gait always declining to one side.

Finally, the Moon: white, saffron-like [in color], a round face, a thin body, average stature, quick speech, a fast walk. At the increase of the month, a youth; at the end, an old man; from the beginning of the month to its middle, it suggests a bright white body; from thence to the end [of it], a reddish and respectable body.

---

[116] *Dente raro*. But this might really be *dentibus raris*, "widely-spaced" or "few" teeth.
[117] See footnote above.

§7.117: Whether the thief would be found—Jirjis

If therefore you wished to know whether or not the one who committed the theft would be revealed, you will note the eastern lord and that of the seventh, equally. For, the common regard of these [two] makes it public. With a regard being denied, he is hidden.

But the lord of the second lays bare whether the one who lost the thing (which was taken by theft) would be able to recover it. For, it being strong, regarding the lord of the east, brings back what was lost. Being weak and not regarding [the lord of the east], speaks against it.

Even the stars' status and manner of bearing themselves brings some support. Eastern [stars] suggest he is white, strong, and respectable. Western ones [indicate] he is foul, dirty, and black. Thus their easternness and westernness must be blended and mixed together, until you draw out a certain judgment with respect to the form and those things which pertain to the hidden and lost thing.

§7.118: On the form of the robber—Aristotle

In order that you may be able to discover the form of the robber, it seems that such an observation must be made. For, any star traversing in the seventh attributes its own proper form to the robber, and the recognition of the robber's whole figure depends on that. But with none appearing there, if one would be traversing in the east, this describes his figure as a whole. Moreover, with [the east] being forsaken of the course of all stars, it is good to note whichever one would hold the second place from the east, because the figure which we seek could be discovered from that. Which if stars would possess all of the aforesaid places, how many of them would be lingering in the seventh (but even how many would be traversing in the first and second) testify that there are really that many thieves.

And so, because [your] whole intention should be brought back to the figures which the planets signify, Saturn portends one black and marked by some illness; he has a mark or blemish on his temple; an ugly walk and unclean clothes, he bears his anger within, and gets angry with himself.

But Jupiter is beautiful in his look, fat in the face, straight hair, delightful, and walking respectably.

Mars has small eyes and crooked teeth, and a ruddy face often mixed with blackness, but he means mistrusted people, those fond of jokes,[118] and murderers.

The Sun makes sharp eyes, a thick voice, and disorganized and hard speech, and one who is mistrustful. He has a mark in the face, and endures an attack of burning on some part of his body.

Venus designates jesting and affable people, with a curved nose and a mark or blemish on the face, the lower lip thicker than the other one. with straight and light hair on the head, she loves verses and very gladly listens to songs.

But to the Mercurial form belongs young men, skinny, with crooked teeth [and] a [*unclear*][119] eye, he wears away the earth with a quick foot; some attack made by iron or a blow has disfigured his mouth.[120]

Those who are of the Lunar enrichment have half-blind eyes or which are affected by some defect, a flowing beard. The face is often blemished, they are bright white and fat, and this is up to the Full Moon. But from the fifteenth [day] of the Moon up to the thirtieth,[121] she signifies those who are bright white but skinny.

§7.119: Whether the thief could be found—al-Kindī[122]

§197. A star which was found to be in the Ascendant, corrupted by the lord of the Midheaven:[123] if it was Saturn himself who was corrupting [it], it demonstrates the thief is found to be held in prison. But Saturn being slow and in a fixed and straight sign, asserts the long duration of the captivity; regarded by the lord of the house of death, it threatens death in prison.

---

[118] *Iocosos*. This sounds like someone who likes to play practical jokes.
[119] The Latin seems to read *innuit* ("it means, it nods"), but this does not make sense to me. Related texts in other authors do not give consistent information about Mercurial eyes.
[120] Reading *os* with Vienna for *hoc*.
[121] Or rather, from the Full Moon to the New Moon.
[122] Cf. al-Rijāl II.34.
[123] Al-Rijāl reads "if you found the planet which was in the Ascendant, or the lord of the Midheaven, to be made unfortunate..." But the parallel statement in al-Kindī's §200 in §7.120 below does not quite match. Therefore I have retained Robert's and Hugo's formulations.

§198. Likewise, Mars getting the role of Saturn, and either [Mars] being the lord of the house of death (or [its] partner),[124] or (apart from his own misfortune) [Mars] being regarded by the lord of the house of death, and the lord of the house of the star which obtains the signification of the thief being in a sign cut in parts,[125] it adds death.

§199. But that same significator being corrupted by both Saturn and Mars, permits him to be found and tortured until his blood is shed. Likewise if Saturn bore himself in this way [and were slow in motion],[126] he prolongs the captivity. Likewise, the significators of death being observed in this likeness, and moreover retreating or being remote,[127] signifies death in prison after long tortures, or he is going to die through the severity of the torture, under the blows themselves.

§7.120: Whether he would be able to escape—al-Kindī[128]

§200. But the exiled[129] star which obtains the Ascendant being fortunate and lucky, [and] particularly being blessed by the lord of the Midheaven, [signifies] liberation. [If] the luckiness is introduced by the lord of the Sun, it is necessary that he be freed by royal decree.[130] But that same [star] taking this prosperity from the lord of the eleventh, introduces liberation by the friends of the owner of the thing taken by theft, or by royal underofficials. Also, with that luckiness being taken from the lord of the twelfth, he is freed by the enemies[131] of the owner. Moreover, with its welfare being taken from the lord of the Ascendant, he will be released by the personal wish of the owner

---

[124] That is, "having some dignity" there (Robert). Al-Rijāl reads "or a partner of it in the house of death."
[125] Probably the signs sometimes called "defective," such as Aries, Taurus, Scorpio, and Capricorn. Such signs are incomplete, or divided, or show some defect: the neck of Aries is broken, only the first half of Taurus exists, the claws of Scorpio are missing (actually they form the pans of Libra), and Capricorn is composed of two different types of animals.
[126] Adding with al-Rijāl.
[127] Al-Rijāl has them "stable and appearing": I can see stable meaning "in fixed signs," but I am not sure whether "appearing" means "eastern," or what that would even add.
[128] Cf. al-Rijāl II.34.
[129] That is, peregrine (al-Rijāl).
[130] Reading for *inventu*, which means "discovery" or "devising." At any rate, the authorities or the king himself will free the thief.
[131] Reading *inimicis* with Robert for *amicis*.

himself. Also, by the lord of the second, he is freed through the helpers of the owner himself, and his money.

§201. Moreover, should the gift of this prosperity come to be from the lord of the third, the brothers and friends of the owner of the missing thing, or the piety[132] of the owner himself,[133] releases him. By the lord of the fourth, he is made free by the parents or compatriots of the owner, in light of an ancient familial tie. But the prosperity being arranged by the lord of the fifth, the children of the one who has lost [the thing], or things which are bestowed, [and] sometimes even a friendship[134] which has been entered into, introduce the cause of the liberation.

§202. If this same thing happens from the lord of the sixth, he will often escape because of slaves or four-footed animals. Also, from the lord of the seventh, he is freed because of a spouse and commerce or adversaries. By the lord of the eighth, he is made free because of someone's death or inheritance or the assistants of [the owner's] partner[135] or commerce. Likewise, the good fortune being conveyed by the lord of the ninth releases captives by [flight or][136] some foreign journey or judgment of the law.

§7.121: Whether he would have run away—al-Kindī[137]

§205. Again, if a question is had as to whether he is in that same region or has already fled, the significator of the theft itself [or][138] a star in the beginning of some sign (the preceding [sign] already having been left behind), does not deny that his flight has been made very recently. Should the same significator—or any star which enjoys some portion of the signification of the thief—be retreating under the rays, or should any partner of the same duty be separated from the lord of the Ascendant and apply itself to some [star] in the eighth or sixth or twelfth, it suggests the same.

---

[132] Reading with al-Rijāl for Hugo's uninspired "goodness." The third house is a spiritual house in traditional astrology, and so al-Rijāl's term is better.
[133] Reading with Robert and al-Rijāl for Hugo's "thief." If it were the thief's piety it would probably indicate something like an early parole or reduced sentence due to sincere repentance and good behavior.
[134] Al-Rijāl reads "service" or "servitude" (*servitia*), which sounds like working off a debt.
[135] Reading with al-Rijāl. Robert also includes "the allies of enemies," also a proper signification.
[136] Adding with al-Rijāl.
[137] Cf. al-Rijāl II.34.
[138] See the next sentence.

§206. Moreover,[139] with the significator of the thief or its lord being found in [some] quarter of the circle, but not in the [same quarter] in which the significator of the one who lost the thing is, it gives notice that his departure has recently been made (or is currently being made) from the region. Being remote or cadent from a pivot, and being wholly estranged from the significator[140] of the owner of the thing taken in the theft, it asserts the aforesaid flight. Moreover, [if] the companion[141] of the significator of the one who has lost the thing[142] [were] put in that same quarter, it no longer allows him to be absent.

> [Robert]:[143] But, withdrawing from its own sign or from the quarter of the significator of the east, [and] likewise it or the lord of the theft departing or being cadent, also [if] it or any planet which is very powerful in its own place would be going out from under the rays or departing from the east, [and it is] an associate of the lord of the eighth or twelfth or second, it announces the departure of the thief from the region. His distance is perceived by the quantity of the departure and exiting of the aforesaid [planets].

> [al-Rijāl]: If you even found the significator of the robber or its lord in some quarter of the figure, and the significator of the stolen thing in another quarter, say that he has going out from his house; likewise if you found it cadent from an angle and not aspecting the significator of the stolen thing, you will say that he has gone out from his home. But if the significator of the thief were with the significator of the stolen thing in one quarter, say that he is alone in some house.

---

[139] See a similar treatment in al-Kindī's §259, in §7.81 above.
[140] Reading *duce* with *Judges* for Burnett's *vice*. I take this to mean that it is both cadent from the pivots and in aversion from (i.e., not configured by sign with) the lord of the Ascendant. But
[141] This may mean "the domicile lord" of the significator. Compare with al-Rijāl excerpt below.
[142] That is, if some planet which partners with the lord of the Ascendant (probably by an aspect within orbs) were there.
[143] Robert adds much more information, but he departs so much from al-Rijāl I am tempted to think he might have added the extra material himself.

§7.122: In what direction he tends—al-Kindī[144]

§207. Again, the star which shows the signification over his travel (or rather, his flight) manages [the issue of] into what part of the world he is going to take himself, or which has already taken the fleeing man in. Even note the sign in which it traverses, [since] it will not be silent [about this matter]. In a fiery sign, it testifies he is going into parts of the east; in a watery one, the north; in an airy one, the west; in an earthy one too, it suggests the south.

§208. In the same way, discernment of the quarters of the circle is necessary for the same thing. For, if the significator of the fleeing person would appear in the eastern quarter, [it indicates] the east; in the western one, the west; in the northern one, the north; but in the southern one, it decrees the south. Also, the eastern part is bounded by the [space] from the Midheaven to the Ascendant.

§209. The southern one is stretched from the seventh to the Midheaven. Likewise the western one is asserted to be from the pivot of the earth to the seventh. The northern one is left over, [and is] from the Ascendant to the pivot of the earth. And so, with a consideration of the quarter and the nature of the sign being had,[145] we will have to follow through with everything else.

§7.123: In what direction he would head—Aristotle

If therefore a worried inquirer would approach [and ask] in what direction [the thief] would head, the lord of the seventh should be noted, as to which of the twelve signs it holds onto. For, it traversing in the eastern signs, [means] he has withdrawn toward the east, and in this way with the rest.

For example,[146] this [lord] traversing in Aries, invites us to the middle of the east. In Libra, to the west. In Cancer to the north, in Capricorn to the south. If in Taurus, to the part of the south near the east. In Gemini it indicates the part of the west neighboring on the south. In Leo, the part of the east next to the north. In Virgo, it figures the southern [part] toward the

---

[144] Cf. al-Rijāl II.34.
[145] See Lilly's treatment in *CA* pp. 364-65, 391, and 393.
[146] The assignment of signs below is virtually that given by Lilly in *CA* p. 365, although this version is more consistent than his. One may see that the signs of each triplicity occupy the four cardinal directions. However, it seems to me that there is an error in these description: either the fixed signs should all be to the left of the movable signs, with the common ones to the right, or the other way around.

west.¹⁴⁷ In Scorpio, to that which is [toward the north and] near the east. In Sagittarius, to that part of the east that is near the south. But in Aquarius, to the western [part] neighboring on the north. In Pisces, it signifies the part of the north which is joined to the west.

Nor will it be another judgment with respect to the father, brothers, children and slaves and the rest, if one would observe with diligent industry the places which the lords of these would possess.

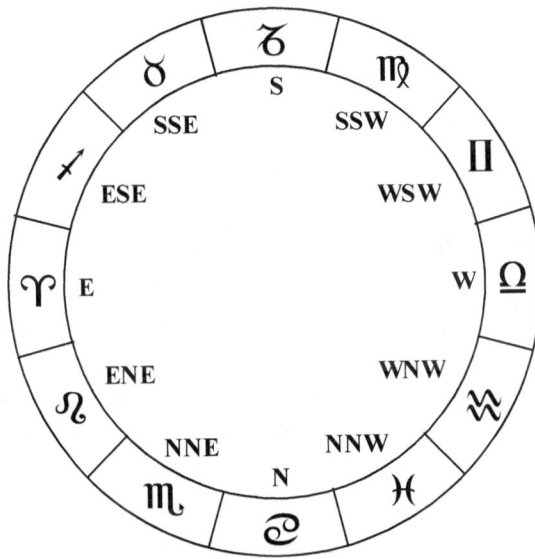

Figure 48: Signs and directions in space, according to "Aristotle"

§7.124: On the thief, if he carried something away with him—Aristotle

Consider¹⁴⁸ whether he carried something with him, in this manner: principally consider the lords of the seventh and the eighth. For if the lord of the eighth would traverse in the pivots which are established from the seventh, so that namely it would be lingering in the seventh itself or the fourth from

---

147 Reading *ad occidentem* for *ab occidente* ("from the west").
148 The logic of this paragraph is as follows. The lord of the seventh indicates the thief's *desire* to take the goods for *himself*, while the lord of the eighth indicates his actual possession of them. These lords' angularity shows the power of the desire or the completeness of the possession. So for instance, if both were angular, he greatly wanted the goods for himself, and took it all for himself. But if the lord of the eighth were angular while the lord of the seventh were cadent, his desire for himself was low, but he took it all anyway.

it, or the tenth, it is clear that he wanted to carry it away.[149] However, with the lord of the seventh[150] lingering in the places already stated, he wanted to and carried it [away]. But if the lord of the eighth would proceed after the already-stated pivots, in the regard of the seventh, with the lord of the seventh (I say) moving through the pivots from the seventh, even though he wanted to, he did not carry [away] the whole thing. But the lord of the eighth in the remote [places] of these, proceeding after the already-stated pivots, while however the lord of the seventh would happen to be moving through the pivots from the seventh, even though he longed for all of it, he took nothing away with him. And in this manner, if the lord of the seventh would be lingering after those pivots, while the lord of the eighth would wander around [in] those pivots, in the regard of the seventh, he snatched it all away, however much he did not have a will to take it all away, so that he [did indeed] take everything. Finally, with the lord of the seventh lingering in the remote [places] from the seventh itself, and also the lord of the eighth would traverse those pivots, he took everything away but arranged to take nothing away [with himself]. If however the lords of the seventh and eighth equally would happen to be staying after the already-stated [pivots], he did not want it all, nor did he take it all. Moreover, with each lingering in the remote [places] of these, he wanted nothing, and snatched nothing. Now if, whenever the lord of the seventh would appear in the remote [places], but the one which is charge of the eighth [would be] after the pivots, even though he wanted nothing, still he placed part of it [at his own disposal].[151]

Nor do we give another judgment about any thing taken by anybody. For a partner, you should consult [the partner's] lord and the lord of his money. For a father, one must consult the lord of the fourth and his money (which is in the fifth), equally. And thus with the rest.

Therefore, Mars being found in that same place[152] has a judgment of a reddish thing or one of those which pertain to fire. Jupiter, too, has precious coins or things varied with a middle color (green, I say, and orange),[153] no less even books and the histories which they read in books, but he even por-

---

[149] This should really read that "he *did* carry it away," with the logic of the rest of the paragraph.
[150] Reading for "second."
[151] *Sustulit*.
[152] Below, Aristotle specifies that he means the east; but one might rather expect this planet to be in the seventh or eighth, since it is supposed to be in the thief's possession.
[153] Hugo or Aristotle means a color derived from the three primary colors (red, yellow, and blue).

tends silver. To Saturn they ascribe black and foul and bad-smelling things, also hides or shoelaces, bones, and heavy and massive things (like lead and what is of this kind). Moreover, womanly ornaments belong to Venus (rings, I say, and earrings, or precious stones, even aromatic things and of a good odor). But round things or coins, and what is carved in a subtle way, and books of teachings, yield to Mercury. Then, the Lunar power claims soft things, and watery ones, even figs and stones. Finally, the Sun has shining pearls and precious stones, also the best gold and things of a citrine color.

Therefore, with none found in the east, the lord of the hour should be consulted. Which if it were Mars, a full and unconditional statement of the judgment will emanate from him. In that manner with the rest, whenever they would happen to have the rulership of the hour.

§7.125: In what place the stolen thing is being held—Sahl[154]

Should an inquiry come to be about the place of the stolen thing, one will have to have recourse to the pivot of the earth, once the east has first been made firm and the rest of the pivots established. For Cancer or any [sign] of its triplicity occupying the pivot of the earth, portends places full of water or those neighboring water, and the stolen thing is kept there. Moreover, Aries or any of its triplicity conceals it in pens or stables or around the hearth[155] and fiery places. Likewise Taurus (because its triplicity is agreed to be threefold) teaches that it is being kept around the stalls of cows, Virgo around places of grain (such as barley), and screened enclosures [for it]; Capricorn gives a token beforehand for sheep pens. Also Gemini and what is of its triplicity, since it is airy, recommends that the stolen thing be sought in entrances[156] or places distant from the ground.

§7.126: On the stolen goods, where they are—'Umar

And so, the lord of the east, but even that of the Lunar house and of the hour, and the one which is in charge over the second, jointly reveal the places of stolen goods. For, the lord of the second being in the east or in a pivot of

---

[154] Cf. *On Quest.* §7.17.
[155] *Lares*, lit. the household gods. The idols of Roman household gods were often displayed near the hearth or on the dining table.
[156] John's Sahl has them in cupboards or other enclosures.

the eastern lord itself, and the lord of the hour claiming any pivot from the east, portend that the stolen goods that were snatched are being held within his[157] own house.

Next, too, let the intention of your judgment be brought back to the fourth sign. Which if it were watery, it designates the stolen goods are stored [in places] such as flowing places or those near waters, such as a brook, and so on. But a fiery one invites us to fiery places, such as are the hearth, oven or kitchen, and that category. Likewise, in an airy one such as Gemini, they are held in a chest or walkway,[158] or in places distant from the ground. In Libra or Aquarius it prefigures higher and highly lit places, such as a throne[159] or bedchamber. Now, Aries [indicates] the places of sheep, but Sagittarius those of arms (such as bows and warlike instruments), and Leo places of hawks, dogs, and deer, and that type. Taurus, the stalls of cows, tilled areas; Virgo suggests the places of grain and barley, as are a threshing floor and a granary; but Capricorn decrees the pens of young goats and larger sheep.

§7.127: In what place it is concealed—al-Kindī[160]

[Where the thief's house is][161]

§210. Moreover, the work of the present observation undoubtedly completes the task of what part of the city the house (which the thief inhabits) would be found in, and the specific location of his habitation. For the sign in which the significator of the thief is staying, in its own part of the circle, promises the house is [there].

§211.[162] Which if perhaps you discovered it in the Ascendant, it confirms that the house is in the middle of the east. In the west, it leads it toward the

---

[157] This probably means the owner.
[158] *Porticum.* That is, a portico or hallway which separates two different parts of a house or other building.
[159] *Solium.*
[160] Cf. al-Rijāl II.34.
[161] See also §7.87 above.
[162] This paragraph offers a rather unusual way of assigning cardinal directions. It seems that the pivots or angles all point to the proper cardinal directions (as they should), while all of the succeedent places indicate the "right" of that, and the cadent places the "left" of that. But this assignment does not make sense to me. One would rather expect, for in-

west. In the Midheaven, in the middle of the southern direction.[163] But in the pivot of the earth, we are attracted to the middle of the north. Again, in the second, on the right of the east. In the twelfth shows the left [of the east]. In the eighth, the right side of the west. In the sixth, its left [side] is noted. But in the eleventh, the right [side] of the southern direction. However, in the ninth the left [side] should be sought. Finally, in the fifth it reveals the right side of the north; but in the third, it uncovers the left [side].

[The entrance to the thief's house]

§212. Also, by this observation, the entrance of the house—[namely] in what part it showed itself to be—will be laid bare. Commend to [your] memory whether the Moon is in a pivot or after a pivot or remote from a pivot, just as we related above with respect to investigating the location of the house. I say that with her being in the sign which designates the theft, it proclaims the entrance to be in that direction which the Moon designates.[164] But if it were a firm [sign], it reveals just one [door]. But with her in a double-bodied sign, it indicates many or at least two [doors]. Again, in a convertible sign, it confirms [that] it is at a height above the earth, and something is missing from it.

§213. Again, Saturn regarding that same sign indicates it is going to be partly broken or locked up, or black. Likewise, a regard of Mars (and not Saturn) portends it is partly burned or has some evidence of fire. But a friendly regard of Mars confirms there is much iron on the entrance. Again, the friendly regard of each (namely of [both] Saturn and Mars]) reveals it is wholly or for the most part iron. The Moon being corrupted or unlucky[165]

---

stance, that the second house would be ENE (east-northeast) and the twelfth to be ESE (east-southeast), as in *CA* pp. 132-33.

[163] Omitting Hugo's "and it is said to be on the right."

[164] But al-Rijāl seems to take this a bit differently: "And judge just as we said before in the judgment about the direction of the door, by taking *eam* from the sign in which the significator of the theft is." *Eam* could mean "her" (the Moon), or the door (*ianuam*). In the latter case, the sign of the significator of the thief/theft shows the direction of the door, but the quadruplicity of the Moon would show where on the house the door is, or what kind of door it is. Lilly (*CA* pp. 347-48) takes al-Rijāl to mean the Moon in both cases.

[165] This probably means an aspect from a square or opposition (or even assembly), but perhaps it includes being in detriment or fall.

means the entrance is worn out with age. But corrupted and defective in light[166] grants that no entrance is prominent.[167]

§7.128: Whether the stolen goods are yet being held in the same place—Aristotle

If therefore you were consulted about this, the seventh and its lord should be consulted. For, the lord of the seventh being in the seventh, or traveling in the fourth or even the tenth or seventh from the seventh place, divulges that it is yet being held in that house or place. Which if it were in the second, fifth, eighth, [or eleventh][168] from the seventh, they signify it is outside it but not transported far. If however in the third, sixth, ninth, and twelfth, in the regard of the seventh,[169] it is plainly far removed already.

§7.129: In what part of a house—Sahl[170]

Finally, once the stolen thing is discovered to be within a house, or should one be able to reach a certain part of a house which has the stolen thing, we will consult the fourth and the lord of the fourth, or a star walking in the fourth. For if this were Saturn, it stores the concealed stolen thing in a stinking and obscure place. Also, Jupiter taking the turn of Saturn, hides it in a church and places of prayer. Mars, around the hearth[171] and the place of foreigners. Moreover, the Sun hides it around the chair of the father of the family, Venus around the beds of women. But Mercury usually invites us to carved or painted places, often even to storerooms of both wine and grain, and cupboards with books, particularly if Virgo is made the pivot of the

---

[166] Robert has the door being inconspicuous only if the Moon is deficient in light, not both deficient and corrupted.

[167] *Imminet.* This must mean that it has no distinguishing features—or perhaps that it is not very visible? Lilly reads this as indicating that the door will be in the back, away from the main road.

[168] Adding based on the logic of the paragraph.

[169] This suggests that Aristotle uses quadrant-based houses, since by definition no planet in the sixth or twelfth can regard the seventh, in whole-signs. On the other hand, this statement is consistent with using whole-sign houses for topics, but the quadrant divisions for stimulation and activity. See my introduction to *ITA*.

[170] Cf. *On Quest.* §7.17.

[171] *Lares.* See footnote to §7.125.

earth. Finally, the Lunar signification holds what had been taken in wells or cisterns, or even washrooms.

And so, whenever benevolents occupy the fourth, it portends the charming quality of the place which contains the stolen thing, or it suggests that it will be held for safekeeping at the house of a noble person. Moreover, the infortunes occupying the fourth designate a horrid place, or they put it down at the house of an ignoble person.

§7.130: To whom he hands it, or with whom he deposits it for safekeeping—'Umar

And so, any star established between the east and the fourth, or rather one being between the significator of the thief and 90°, signifies he has handed it over to someone;[172] which if they would bear themselves otherwise, it portends he has handed it over to no one.

§7.131: What indications would be had in that house—al-Kindī[173]

§214. Again, you will know the indications which are contained within the home, thusly. The place of the Moon designates watery locations in the home (namely a well and where water tends to be kept in reserve). The place of Venus portends the bedroom and places dedicated to pleasures. The place of Mercury guards treasure, chests and where money is hidden away, even cupboards[174] and books. In the same way, the place of Saturn defends hidden places of the home, namely sewers[175] and stinking places. Also, the place of Mars looks after the kitchen and oven and fireplace, and where blood tends to be shed. The place of the Head holds onto ladders, stairs, and instruments for going upwards. Likewise the Tail defends the bases [of things], porches,[176] pillars, and stables.[177]

---

[172] Presumably, the nature and rulerships of such a planet would indicate the type of person.
[173] Cf. al-Rijāl II.34.
[174] Or perhaps, any type of locked cabinet (*armarium*).
[175] Or, "drains" (*cloacas*).
[176] Or perhaps, porticoes (*porticas*), but that word is usually spelled *porticus*.
[177] Or perhaps, any dirty or cheap place on the property, such as a shed (*stabula*).

§215. Again, Mercury in a double-bodied sign [indicates] a storehouse; in a convertible one, its upper room;[178] finally, in a firm one it wholly refuses the house.[179] A corresponding judgment is derived from all the signs [and planets].[180]

[Robert]: The number of these places is perceived from the places of the planets: for example, Mercury in a firm sign says a cupboard [with] one [door]; in a double-bodied one, two connected side-by-side; in a movable one, one above the other. The same goes for the rest of the planets in similar signs.

§216a. Moreover, Jupiter signifies that the house is the palace of the master, and the best [part] of that place.

§216b-217. [On the other hand, in the Midheaven they clarify the interior quality of the place.][181] Again, Jupiter and Venus in the Midheaven show a suitable garden. But Saturn in the Midheaven indicates a well or cistern or some destruction of the flooring in the middle of the home. Also, Mars in that same place testifies that in the middle of the home is a fire vent or where blood tends to be poured out. Likewise Mercury hoards money in the middle of the home, or the beasts of burden belonging to a dependent.[182] But the Sun in the Midheaven means an [elevated][183] well or couch in the middle of the home. Again, the Moon in the Midheaven guards outlets for draining water, even sometimes certain instruments like millstones and that kind of thing, which men tend to have in common use for fulfilling necessary [tasks].[184]

---

[178] *Solium*.
[179] Lilly (*CA* p. 353) reads this as "in a house that has no cellar nor other chamber, as many country houses have not."
[180] Reading more with Robert for Hugo's "derived from all houses of the atrium." My sense is that al-Kindī has added to the confusion, and this paragraph is trying to say two things: (1) that Mercury indicates storehouses; (2) that the quadruplicity of any planet (using Mercury as an example) indicates the kind of hiding-place within that type of room.
[181] Adding with Robert.
[182] *Clientelae iumenta*. But Robert reads: "or the place of one's personal property" (*peculii*, which has particular connotations of someone who is a dependent in the home). Perhaps al-Kindī is thinking of a stable boy or someone like that.
[183] Adding with Robert (*elatum*).
[184] *Quae in usus familiaris rei necessitate supplenda solet homines habere*. Robert adds: "a cellar or crypt of underground passages, and instruments of business."

§7.132: On the quantity and number of what was taken by theft—Sahl[185]

For[186] the quantity and number of things taken by theft, let the signs between the Moon and Mercury be counted: if this number happened to be even, it is clear that they are connected together or are many; but being odd, it claims that it is some one thing.

But if someone came into suspicion (as tends to happen), we will follow the path of responding which we are about to give later (with respect to discovering messengers and instructions),[187] and the testimonies of the Moon must be applied at the same time. So, an application of this[188] with malevolents proves that the one you had held as a suspect is the culprit of the theft and crime; if not, not.

§7.133: On the number of things taken by theft—'Umar

Even the number of the things lost through theft may be easily discovered from the tenth: which if it were a firm sign, it indicates only one; but a convertible one testifies that it was many; a bicorporeal one, two [things].

Then, the lord of the tenth must be consulted. For, it being at the beginning of a sign,[189] portends one or three or rather five, and thus unequal ones below ten.[190] Again, in the second face, 11 or 13 or 15[191] is contained, and from there up to 20, and even up to 100. But in the third decan, it comprehends unequal portions up to 100 [and even] up to 1,000.

---

[185] Cf. *On Quest.* §§7.18-19.
[186] For this paragraph, see *Carmen* V.35.72-74.
[187] Probably referring to §5.68 above, which in *On Quest.* had been in a later section (§13.9). Here, John's Sahl means to look at the lord of the Ascendant.
[188] John's Sahl has the stronger of the two (i.e., between the lord of the east and the Moon) *separating* from a malevolent, which makes more sense.
[189] That is, in its first decan or face (see the rest of the paragraph).
[190] Reading *decem* for *denarium*, which is actually a classical Roman currency. My sense is that we are talking about coins or monetary value here, but as linked to the decans, and Hugo has conflated the size of the decan (which means "ten") and the number ten with the name of the currency.
[191] Madrid reads, "*xii.*"

§7.134: What it is that was taken by theft—Sahl[192]

If what it is which was taken by theft should be sought by someone, the whole affair of this kind depends on the tenth and the bound of the degree of the tenth[193] (the which place signifies the stolen goods).

[The bound of the Moon][194]

Saturn as the lord of [the Moon's] bound, but so that he would occupy the east itself or would be lingering in the tenth or its triplicity,[195] it portends that what was lost, pertains to agriculture and what is necessary for it. If, however, with a rulership of this kind being retained, he would possess the seventh or the pivot of the earth, it brings an indication of an old and long-standing thing. Moreover, he in aversion to the east, while he would be favored by the aspect of neither light, or should he traverse in Aries,[196] means it is something cheap. Now, if he would be staying in Gemini or its triplicity, it prefigures a doubled thing. On the other hand, if Jupiter would regard Saturn from the tenth, it decides that one of these two things which was lost was golden; if from the seventh or the fourth, silver. Jupiter being in aversion and cadent from the east, shows lead and that type.

Furthermore, if Moon would be traversing in Jupiter's bound, we will consider his place, and no less the star which regards him. If therefore that place were Aries or any of its triplicity, it declares gold or silver or something of this kind made through fire. However, Jupiter in the regard of Venus or walking through her bound, has pearls. Moreover, that same Jupiter occupying Taurus or its triplicity, portends kingly clothing. Traversing in Gemini or its triplicity, [something animate or from animals]. In Cancer or its triplicity, a watery kind of gems.[197]

---

[192] Cf. *On Quest.* §7.20 and *Carmen* V.35.44-69.
[193] What follows, however, is a description of the bound of the Moon, in accordance with both John's Sahl and *Carmen*.
[194] For this part, see also al-Kindī's lengthy treatment in §7.136 below.
[195] According to John's Sahl, the Moon is in a bound of Saturn, and Saturn is in the earthy triplicity (just as he goes through the other triplicities below).
[196] Reading *Ariete* with John's Sahl for *oriente*.
[197] See footnote to the next subsection below.

But the Lunar traversal being in a bound belonging to Mars, shows that it is tempered in fire, and wonderful.[198] If however Venus would regard the Moon, it claims that it is stained by dyers.

Moreover, the Moon being in the bound of Venus and going through Aries or its triplicity, signifies gold or silver. In Taurus or Cancer or their triplicities, it portends womanly ornaments and what is of this type. (The price of the thing stolen by theft can be discovered from the rays of the stars which had claimed the signification,[199] namely insofar as there are adding or subtracting in course, or are humiliated[200] or exalted, or are stepping directly in course or retrograde.)

In addition even, if the Moon is placed (as was stated above) in Aries or its triplicity, [and] would run in the bound of Mercury, it describes coins. But from Gemini or its triplicity, designates things stolen from a chest or a letter box, and that type (that is, red purses).

[The sign of the Moon]

Then, it is proper to observe the Lunar place. She traversing in Aries, portends something suitable for and fitted for an ornament of the head or face. In Taurus, ornaments of the neck (ladies' necklaces, I say, or [other] necklaces). Traversing in Gemini in the regard of Mercury, it means coins. She being in no way regarded by him, something leather or red.[201] In Cancer, something that can be handled in waters. In Leo, regarded by the Sun, it is a sign of gold or silver. Not regarded, it suggests something bright.[202] In Virgo, regarded by Mercury, a kind of coin (as was stated above). Not regarded, fabrics. Moreover, in Libra, under the regard of Venus, something odiferous and manufactured and fit for womanly luxuries but sold by the pound. Not regarded, something of animals. In Scorpio, regarded by Mars, gold or silver. Not regarded, something bright [and] from any other metal. In Sagittarius and regarded by Jupiter, something manifold, or dyed. Not regarded, something of that kind but of a lesser price. In Capricorn and in the regard of Saturn, something cheap or something earthen, or of things sprouting from

---

[198] *Mirificatum*.
[199] This is probably true, but John's Sahl specifically mentions Venus—probably because we are speaking of Venus at the moment.
[200] That is, in their own fall.
[201] Or more likely, something bound in red leather.
[202] John's Sahl suggests other bright metals.

the earth. But in Aquarius, regarded by Saturn, something of animals. But in the regard of Jupiter in that same place, gold or silver. Regarded by the Sun and Mercury there, coins in red purses. Traversing in Pisces, in the regard of Jupiter, a watery kind of gem.[203] With the regard denied, something separated by manifold colors.[204] In this manner too, she must be observed with all the rest, by means of [their] natural property.

§7.135: Concerning the thing taken by theft: of what kind [it is]—'Umar

The second domicile from the east (which is the house of money), the tenth and its lord, likewise the Lot of Fortune, and the lord of the Lunar bound, watch over an indication of this kind. For, it is necessary that that one of the signs which many testimonies support, obtain the signification over the nature of the stolen goods. Then, the natural property of that sign which the significator holds onto (namely whether it is watery or rather airy)[205] must be observed. For an observation of this kind determines the kind of thing taken by theft.

§7.136: On the kind of stolen thing—al-Kindī[206]

§218. Further, from what is written below let a judgment be made about the kind of lost thing which is sought. [But the quality of what is stolen is indicated by the lord of the Lunar bound, and the one looking at her.][207]

And so, if Venus would rule the Lunar bound and is regarded by the Sun, it signifies coins or gold carved in some way, even fine fabrics and costly clothing of the best color, and that type of thing.

Moreover, Venus regarded by the Moon means a silver and sculpted object, or something of the best color, moreover linen or hemp fabrics, and what is of this kind.

---

[203] John's Sahl has: "pearls or amber, or something brought forth from out of the water."
[204] John's Sahl has silk that is in manifold colors. Perhaps a scribe mistook *sericum* for *separatum*.
[205] *Potius aereum*. 'Umar is not limiting the kinds of triplicity here, but is simply giving two examples.
[206] Cf. al-Rijāl II.34.
[207] Adding from Robert.

§219. But she being regarded by Mercury indicates things of the best craftsmanship, namely clothing for which the wool of animate beings presents the material, such as purple fabric,[208] silk, and what is put together among the Arabs from the wool of sheep or goats with fine skill and calculation.[209]

In the regard of Mars, it declares the works of a goldsmith and that which is formed with the benefit of fire and iron.

She being regarded by Saturn indicates ancient things and those of an old form, and blotted[210] and a pale color—namely earthenware and what is sculpted in stone.

In the regard of Jupiter, it shows what is composed of the pelts[211] of animals, and what is like this.

[Mercury as the bound lord]

§220. Moreover, Mercury as the lord of the Lunar bound takes on the signification of books. Regarded by the Sun, it introduces legal books with precepts written in them, or the manners and customs of kings, moreover golden things or books enclosed in gold.

But in the regard of the Moon, it means written papers of commerce, profit and those things which proceed from just profits in agriculture, recollections, sometimes even silver things.

Likewise, regarded by Venus he guards over books, painted or sculpted things and those of respectable form, often even golden or silver ones, and books enclosed in silver or gold.

§221. Moreover, to the above-stated things the regard of the Sun and Jupiter [together] add costly pearls in the treasures of kings, and things dedicated to the superstitious[212] ornaments of women, moreover good-smelling things (namely musk) and lapis lazuli, lignum aloes and what is just like those.

---

[208] Tentatively reading *tyrium* for *tiriacium*. Hugo's *tiriacium* resembles *tiriaca* (from the Latin *Gr. Intr.* VII.4), which means "antidote," but does not make sense in this context.
[209] My gloss for *rata cautele...industria*. Al-Rijāl reads, "through geometry." Some exact method of piecing is meant here.
[210] Reading for *pene deletae*.
[211] Probably leaning more towards the use of fur, since Saturn usually indicates leather itself.
[212] This is probably refers to pendants or charms with saints' images and that sort of thing.

Likewise, the regard of Mars possesses the silver containers for books, and those same things inscribed with red-colored figures, and that kind of thing.

The regard of Jupiter indicates healing images[213] and books having the praises of the laws and the memorials of ancient forefathers.

Also, a regard from Saturn commends books of black magic inscribed with incantations, talismanic [images], augury, prophecies and what is like these, and those things with no truth;[214] moreover it shows that their container is iron or stone.

§222. Likewise, the regard of Venus and Mars [together] presents musical instruments (namely a lyre, psaltery, drum, symphonia and chorum, even the melodies of the tibia;[215] likewise vessels fit for drinking (namely chalices), and so on; and sometimes even wine itself.

Moreover, the regard of Venus and Jupiter [together] asserts the ornaments of women, namely clothing and things whose odor and color is the best, even healing images, necklaces, ladies' necklaces, earrings, collar-necklaces and ornaments which belong to them, namely clothing and what smells good.

§223. The regard of Mars with the rest divulges bronze vessels which are sculpted very well, which kings and other powerful people tend to import for their own use.

Likewise, a regard from Mars and the Sun [together] indicates royal arms and those which nobles tend to use.

§224. But a regard coming forth from the Moon and Mars introduces instruments of agriculture, namely a plowshare, hoes, and that type of thing.[216]

In the same way, if a regard should proceed from Jupiter and Mars, it produces those things which royal dependents[217] tend to use: iron or jagged arms, and whatever borrows its form from the benefit of fire, and what sailors and soldiers take up in their own defense.

And so, in this way it seems the virtue of the regarding [planets] must be imparted according to their nature, whether it is one or more.

---

[213] *Species medicas*. Robert and al-Rijāl have theological books.
[214] Reading *nulla veritate*.
[215] A kind of reed flute.
[216] Al-Rijāl has simply, "an instrument adapted for war."
[217] This could mean something like the royal guard or personal retinue.

[Saturn as the bound lord]

§225. Saturn retaining the rulership of the Lunar bound [indicates] something earthen or akin to the nature of earth, or sculpted in stone, even put together with lead or iron.

Again, with him in the regard of the Moon, part of the things (taken by theft) which are sought supply maintenance for an attendant of water or a job in agriculture.

With him being regarded by the Sun, a certain part aids kings.

§226. A regard of Jupiter even concedes a certain part to the rest of the nobles.

Moreover, a regard of Mars leaves part for use in the kitchen, baths, furnaces, ovens, even often something necessary for use on a journey.

Likewise, the regard of Venus takes something left for the use of women, like seamstresses and so on.

If Mercury would make a regard with him, it brings about arrows, hunting spears, and the rest suchlike.

[Jupiter as the bound lord]

§227. Again, Jupiter in possession of the rulership over the Lunar bound, names unsculpted money and beautiful things made of the pelts of animals, [and] what tends to serve the uses of sages or judges.

Also, in the regard of the Sun it particularly demonstrates precious money which customarily enriches the treasures of kings and decorates their ornaments; sometimes even animals of that kind.[218]

§228. Likewise, the regard of the Moon shows money of lesser value which commonly provides for the needs of the common people, even certain instruments made by men for the practice of justice,[219] often even animals (namely sheep and cows and that kind).

Also, the regard of Saturn denotes ancient money and that of no value, even instruments of agriculture, even cheap animals and their pelts, and the limbs of animals (like elephant teeth and everything of the class of ivory, not to mention even rope made of hair).

---

[218] That is, animals that kings tend to have. Perhaps something like peacocks or elephants or stags? Al-Rijāl reads, "noble animals."
[219] Probably instruments of punishment and torture.

§229. In the regard of Mars, [it indicates] the defenses particularly of those who, with all hope of returning having been lost, enter into wars, and what is like these. Even those kinds of [instruments] of punishment which avenge certain people's wicked deeds and transgressions of the law or justice.

Also, the regard of Venus introduces the ornaments[220] of women by which they are adorned when entering temples because of lawful observances or prayer.

Likewise, the regard of Mercury does not leave behind divine books [and] instruments of books.

[Mars as the bound lord]

§230. In the same way, Mars having full power over the Lunar bound assigns iron, arms and what is put together with the help of fire.

Regarded by the Sun, he takes care of the military instruments of kings or the equipment of the royal kitchen.

Also, the regard of the Moon identifies everyday arms and those which pertain to messengers and traveling merchants.[221]

In the regard of Venus, it commends things painted and [what is] beautiful in decor.

§231. [Mars] even in the regard of Mercury confesses instruments for singing, catapults for walls and fortresses, and what is like these.

Likewise the regard of Saturn claims bows and clubs with which wicked deeds are punished, and what is like these.

The regard of Jupiter brings forth everyday arms, hard and harsh—namely breastplates and shields, and suchlike.

[The quality of the object, from the bound lord of the Moon & the lord of the hour]

§232. Finally, every star obtaining rulership over the Lunar bound, if the bound is being regarded by that lord,[222] it is believed to confirm the best nature of that same thing. Being eastern, a new thing; but western claims an old one. Near retrogradation or in its second station,[223] affirms [it is] in the middle, neither new nor old. Also, being direct conveys evenness of form and a

---

[220] Reading for *ditamenta*.
[221] Or itinerant officials (*discursores*).
[222] Reading with Robert, and also Hugo's reiteration below.
[223] Reading with al-Rijāl for Hugo's *longe post a retrogradatione remota*.

good condition; retrograde, it will confess an uneven and distorted shape, and its breaking or corruption and blemish, and already being in conflict with its proper condition.

§233. Again, in a pivot [it indicates] the strength of its nature and good craftsmanship; [if] remote from a pivot, the unsoundness and ugliness of [its] nature is designated. But after a pivot settles it as being in the middle of strength and unsoundness, good composition and being ugly.

But being lucky, good, useful, proper; unlucky, the contrary.

Moreover, dwelling in a place proportionate to itself,[224] it renders a thing appropriate and agreeable in its category; but being foreign [to such a place], the contrary—or it renders it harmed[225] because of some accident.

§234. If therefore the aforesaid bound seems to be situated otherwise than with a regard from its own lord, the judgment must be changed according to the variation of the regard.

The lord of the hour seems to confirm this same thing as well, from its own direct motion or retrogradation, [just as] the lord of the Lunar bound does. For everything which it introduces into this judgment, imitates the manner of the lord of the bound of the Moon.[226]

§7.137: What it is that was stolen by theft—Jirjis[227]

But if someone made a question about a thing taken by theft, you will discover the thief himself from the lord of the seventh and its status; it will be permitted to recognize the stolen goods from the bound where the Moon is staying.

And so, the Moon traversing in a bound of Jupiter suggests gold or silver. If however Venus regarded her, it means gold or pearls. Even the Mercurial regard testifies to an inscribed or sculpted thing. But if she would be linger-

---

[224] Robert says "*alb*," which is undoubtedly correct, but we should also consider its dignities.
[225] Reading with al-Rijāl for Hugo's *praeditam*.
[226] Rewriting Hugo's awkward *Omnia quoque quae in aliquid huic iudicio probationis inducunt, praedictam ipsius Lunae terminalis domini modum immitantur.*
[227] This section should be compared with Sahl (§7.134) and al-Kindī (§7.136). Although the structure of the section looks more like Sahl, there seems to be constant confusion about which planet is in which bound. I have indicated some changes I think are required to make the passage more plausible.

ing in a bound of Jupiter[228] in the same way, it means admirable things or costly clothes, and those things which perhaps are agreed to be found only in the houses of kings.

Moreover, she lingering in a bound of Venus [means] it is of womanly things (of which kind are gold, silver, the most costly pearls, or embroidered clothing, or any odiferous things, and the ornaments of women, perhaps anointed with some scent; and it will be gold or silver if, I say, Venus would be lingering in Aries or its triplicity. For, she traversing in Gemini or its triplicity, it denotes clothing made of the hides of animals. From Cancer and its triplicity, it suggests decorated and dyed clothes, or those embroidered with a needle.

The place of Venus wholly portends their price or form, according to the nature of the signs. For, Venus in the first departure from scorching, [means] something new. But retrograde and proceeding most quickly, or decreasing in computation, it suggests something ancient and old.

Mars regarding the Moon[229] in Aries and its triplicity, portends gold or something bright. But in the regard of Saturn, a broken or jumbled[230] thing is meant. In the bound of Mars, it foretells iron or arms. Venus regarding her, portends there is silver in it. From a regard of Saturn, a disorderly and dark thing is meant. Now, Mercury regarding the Moon in a bound of Mars, states that it will be something of those which come to be through fire, namely sculpted or put together through some art. But if Venus and Mercury equally would regard [her], with the aspect of Mars, I say, being denied them, it claims something of stones and pearls and compacted of stone (of which kind are glass vessels).[231] The Moon traversing in a bound of Saturn, hides or animals. In the aspect of Jupiter, pearls. In the aspect of Venus, silver. The Mercurial regard suggests what is sculpted or painted forms. But if she would traverse in an airy sign, it testifies there are animals in it. Moreover, with the Moon lingering in a bound of Mercury, it suggests the books of sages and philosophers. In Gemini[232] and its triplicity, coins and money.

---

[228] Instead of "bound of Jupiter," this should probably read "aspect of the Sun," as with Sahl.
[229] Reading for "Venus," since Jirjis later has Venus doing the aspecting and it is clear that he is concerned with the Moon's position.
[230] *Quassata.*
[231] Jirjis must mean that glass is formed by melting down silica and other minerals and crystals.
[232] Reading more with Sahl for Hugo's "an airy [sign]."

But in a sign of germinating things, it introduces something of things germinating in the earth, according to the nature of that star. For in an airy one, it indicates something of the substance of animals, of which kind is a feather or something light, or a costly thing. But from a watery one, it portends watery things. Moreover, in a bound of Saturn, camels or birds or even fish. Then, in a bound of Mercury, a donkey or a cat or even a fox is designated. Moreover, in a Martial bound, it indicates a pig or lion or from some kind of wild beast.

Finally, I estimate it is appropriate in the stated place lest, being led by the trouble of forgetfulness, you neglect the mutual aspects of the stars. For if you would link them together, it will be permitted to judge about the thing which was taken by theft, in terms of their nature and manner.

§7.138: Of what type the stolen thing is—Aristotle

You will have thusly what kind of thing it is that was taken by theft. Any star traversing in the second principally lays out the nature and proper quality of the thing taken by theft. The method appended below describes what things agree with what planets.

And so, Saturn claims iron and lead and black things. But Jupiter [signifies] bright white things and raw silver and white things mixed with green and saffron. Mars even possesses reddish things (such as copper or gold) or things polished smooth (like a sword), finally all burning things. The Sun has gold and things worked with gold, or copper ore of a golden color. Belonging to Venus are womanly ornaments and what pertains to women (of which kind are rings and vestments). But Mercury [signifies] things engraved or painted in a subtle way (namely books and coins and what is of this type). But to the Moon we will ascribe horses and other beasts, and also glass and vessels of this kind, moreover olive oil, wax, and such wares.

§7.139: On recognizing the name of the robber—'Umar

Comment by Dykes. The following few sections by 'Umar (and §7.146 by Jirjis) outline some methods for identifying the name (or type of name) of a thief, as well as what his nationality or religion is. (Jirjis also seems to include methods for identifying the names of objects.) Some of these methods bear a resemblance to the *Yavanajataka* Chs. 71-72, and there may be a common inspiration for the general approach. The fact that 'Umar's method attributes letters to the Nodes also suggests an Indian origin.

The core of the method is the identification of a significator, and from its location and aspects a series of letters is derived. Other methods suggest how many letters there are likely to be and in what order they will appear, while cultural knowledge and planetary conditions may also guide us to identifying specific names. I must admit that I do not understand all of the methods, and probably only a translation of 'Umar's Arabic will reveal how they were meant to be used. Of course, 'Umar may also be reporting a hodge-podge of methods from his own time, without really committing to one or another. I find some of these approaches intriguing and astrologically more likely than others, and it would be worthwhile for contemporary astrologers to experiment with them.

Identifying the significator. In William Lilly's presentation of these methods (*CA* pp. 340-42), the significator for the name is the significator of the thief itself, ideally a peregrine planet in the seventh. Because the seventh normally indicates a thief, this makes more sense to me than 'Umar's approach, which is to find a victor over the Ascendant, or else use the sect light or the degree of the Ascendant itself (§7.139).

Identifying the range of letters. After identifying the significator, 'Umar finds the Arabic names of the significating planet, its Lunar mansion, its sign, and even the signs of the entire triplicity (§7.141). The letters which are most represented in this group, are more likely to be letters of the name. He also seems to suggest that the last letter in the Arabic name of the planet (perhaps including an aspecting planet) can be added. On the other hand, he also suggests a puzzling Lot-like method which manipulates the longitude of the significating planet (§7.145). To my own mind, this use of the Arabic is questionable because 'Umar does not appear to have any systematic or symbolic way to associate the Arabic letters with the signs and planets. In the *Yavanajataka*, certain classes of letters (sibilants, etc.) are attributed to various planets, and in Qabalism the Hebrew letters are likewise individually assigned to elements, planets, and signs, according to certain rules.[233] But 'Umar's reliance on the accidental spellings of Arabic seems flimsy, and his attribution of individual letters to the planets (§7.141) lacks both completeness and obvious organization.

---

[233] See for example Appendix G below.

Number of letters and structure of name. 'Umar presents a number of methods dealing with the number of letters and the structure of the name. For the number of letters, he considers the following:

- The whole-sign aspect between the significator and another planet (§7.139).
- The number of signs (or perhaps the number of crooked signs) between the Lot of Fortune and the Ascendant (§§7.140, 7.145).
- The number of the letters most represented in the grouping of Arabic letters (§7.141).
- The number of letters in the name of the significating planet, and perhaps also the aspecting planet (§7.141).
- The number of letters in the name of the significating planet's sign (§7.141).
- If the Ascendant is the significator, one might use a planet in its angles (§7.141).
- The number of (any of?) the above, but adding the last letter in the name of the planet (§7.141).

On the other hand, the significator's quadruplicity indicates the general structure of the name, such as being a compound name or more likely a single syllable or something simple (§§7.139, 7.141).

Order of letters. This is the most difficult part to understand. Of the methods, 'Umar suggests one based on decans (§7.142), the Lot-like method mentioned above (§7.145), and a way of attributing letters to the houses which is probably mistranslated by Hugo (§7.145). To this, Jirjis adds a different way of assigning letters to the triplicities and houses (§7.146), as well as determining amounts of things and perhaps the names of objects (§7.146).

The name by planetary condition and cultural knowledge. Finally, the significator may indicate, through its nature and place and condition (taking the cultural context into account), the kind of name and its social prestige (§7.141-44). For example, Saturn might indicate a slave; but for Jewish names,[234] if he is in a good condition it might be Moses; or if he is in the second house, some name whose fundamental meaning has to do with wealth or livelihood; or if he were close to a royal fixed star, that star's nature might be related to the meaning of the name.

---

[234] Saturn traditionally signifies Judaism.

For having the discernment of this business, an observation of the east seems to be highly necessary—namely whether it is ascribed to the slanting or straight signs. Those arising in a straight manner are from the beginning of Cancer to the beginning of Capricorn; but those arising in a slanting manner or rather indirection, are from the beginning of Capricorn to the end of Gemini.[235]

Then, one must convey, among the lords of the east and that of its bound and sovereignty, triplicity, and even that of the hour, which of these five significators is principally assumed into the worthiness of the signification. Which if the east does not exhibit the rulership to any, let the intention of the mind be brought back to the diurnal (the Sun) and nocturnal (the Moon) lords—namely, that one of them which possesses its own house or sovereignty or triplicity or bound. (Here however, should either of them possess a masculine sign, or if it regarded the east from a masculine one—[but] since a regard of this kind would seem to be not very or not at all useful, I believe it should be overlooked.)[236] Now, while any of these[237] would regard the east in the way we have said before, that one deservedly claims the signification. Therefore, once it is discovered, the truth of the judgment should be sought according to its proper quality. Which if a complete understanding is not yet free of the ambiguity of error, one will have to ascribe the dignity of the leadership and signification to the lord of the east itself, (provided it is free from fall), once all the rest have been given priority. Moreover, with it being cadent from the regard of the east, remember to establish the east itself as the significator, so that the number of letters which come together in the name may be discovered in full.

Then too, it portends that we must note whether it regards any of the stars, or how many of them it is [which it regards]. It seems that even its withdrawal and application must equally be noted. Namely, with those having

---

[235] 'Umar returns to the straight and crooked signs in §7.140 below, but I do not really understand what it means. It may be a separate method.

[236] In this awkward sentence, 'Umar is apparently reporting the view of others about whether the luminaries (or perhaps any of the candidate significators?) is in a masculine sign. But he seems to stop short of completing his thought, because he immediately states that such a rule is not important.

[237] As I pointed out just above, I don't believe that 'Umar is actually rejecting the role of the sect light altogether, just the rule about the gender of its sign. So, I think he is including any of the lords of the Ascendant here, or, if none of them aspects the east, the sect light (if it is in one of its own dignities).

been discovered, if you recognized that the degrees of separation were fewer, the beginning will be from them; which if you would discover [that the degrees of separation] were more [than those of the application], you would take the degrees of the application: for one must always start from the fewer ones.

Therefore, once their number has been diligently observed, one is in need of no little consideration as to whether the application or withdrawal which you had observed, would regard [them] from a trigon or hexagon, tetragon or opposition.[238] Now, if the significator itself would assemble with a star by any admixture of affinity,[239] or rather would it apply to it from a tetragon, four letters will have to be taken; which if from the opposition, seven or four;[240] but from the trigon, five; if from the hexagon, three.

Moreover, the significator being placed in a firm sign designates that the name is simple, whole, and one. In a double-bodied one, it is composed of two letters. In every convertible one, it means it is shortened in both voice and writing.

§7.140: On the number of letters—'Umar

Therefore, once the descent from a fortunate sign[241] to the east itself has been had, how many slanting signs lie between them undoubtedly affirms that that many letters come together for the formation of the name. But the slanting ones are as was already stated: from the beginning of Capricorn to the end of Gemini.

On the other hand, these testimonies, and those of this kind, are applied according to the greater effectiveness and strength of the aforesaid.

---

[238] The idea in what follows is that each whole sign stands for a letter. For example, if the significator is in Gemini and its closest aspect is to a planet in Leo, there are three signs involved (Gemini, Cancer, Leo), and so three letters.

[239] This simply seems to mean by any assembly (i.e., bodily conjunction in the same sign) whatsoever.

[240] An assembly, square, and opposition may each get four letters because they form the whole-sign angles from the significator, and there are four signs forming these angles.

[241] *A fortunato signo.* That is, from the sign of the Lot of Fortune (see §7.145 below). In the last sentence of this section, 'Umar probably means that this method is less effective than that in §7.139, but that it might give extra details.

§7.141: On the letters of the planets—'Umar

These things having been interpreted in such an order, with respect to the number of letters:[242]

Mars assumes ي [*i*], و [*u*].
But Venus [has] ب [*b*], ذ [*dh*], ر [*r*],
Likewise Mercury: ج [*j*],[243] ل [*l*], ش [*sh*].
But the Head, د [*d*], م [*m*], ت [*t*].
Moreover the Tail, ه [*h*], ن [*n*], ث [*th*].
And Saturn, و [*u*], س [*s*], ح [*h*].
Jupiter, ز [*z*], ع [*ʿ*], د [*d*].
In the same way, the Sun [has] ح [*h*], ف [*f*], and ض [*d*].[244]
Finally the Moon: ط [*t*],[245] ض [*d*], ط [*t*], ع [*ʿ*].

If therefore the lord of the east would have control over the role of the signification, adjoin the collected letters of that Lunar mansion which that same star would then be holding onto, to the letters of the sign in which Mars traverses, so that, therefore, if Capricorn were in the Midheaven, and [it][246] regarded the east, one will have to have recourse to the mansion which is meanwhile possessed by Mars.[247]

For example with the lords of the Ostrich [*al-nʿāim*],[248] the letters of this are taken as being such: ن [*n*], ع [*ʿ*], ا [*ā*], م [*m*].

No less too, do we note the letters of the stellar significator itself (namely, Mars), which are: م [*m*], ر [*r*], ي [*i*], خ [*kh*].[249]

---

[242] Vienna clearly assigns 24 letters to the planets and the Nodes, but there are some repeats (which may be errors), and some letters left out. At present I do not know the rationale for these letters. But when assigning letters to the signs and planets below, 'Umar draws on the letters of their Arabic names themselves. See Jirjis's alternative approach in §7.146 below, and alternative assignments of letters (in Hebrew) to the planets, signs, and elements, in Appendix G.

[243] Although the Vienna manuscript gives this letter (*jim*), the scribe adds *h* above it. So 'Umar might have meant خ [*kh*].

[244] In Persian, this last letter has a *z* sound, and the Vienna scribe adds *z* above it.

[245] Note that this letter appears twice for the Moon.

[246] I take this to be Mars.

[247] I believe 'Umar is describing a hypothetical example, which I reproduce below.

[248] Reading for Vienna's *aninaaim*. This is the 19th or 20th Lunar mansion (depending on how one counts).

[249] I have added the م [*m*] from below, where it was mistakenly added to the spelling of Taurus. I have also read خ [*kh*] as the correct spelling for the Latin scribe's ع [*ʿ*].

Returning to the signs of that triplicity, we commend the letters of the first one (namely Virgo) to memory. But these are: س [s], ن [n], ب [b], ل [l], ه [h].²⁵⁰

Thus even [those] of the second one, which is Taurus: ث [th], و [w], ر [r].
And likewise those of Capricorn: ج [j], د [d], ي [i].²⁵¹
It is appropriate to observe all of those placed separately.

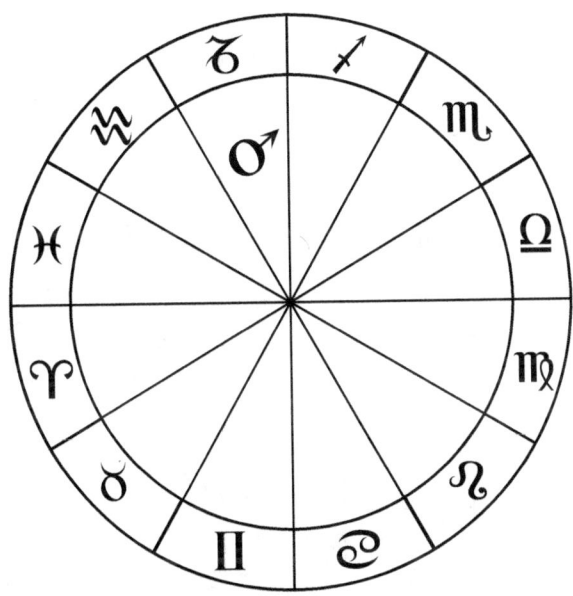

Figure 49: Chart suggested by 'Umar for determining names (§7.141)

Then, you will scrutinize diligently what place in the circle that star is holding onto, especially in what mansion it is then dwelling in, but even [the place] of its triplicity: we likewise lump the noted letters together with the lord of the east.

Therefore, with the Moon holding onto Virgo (the first one; the other sign is Taurus, the third one Capricorn),²⁵² once they have been established in this order, the testimonies should be deduced from the majority of the

---

²⁵⁰ Reading more accurately with the Arabic spelling for the Latin scribe's م [m], ن [n], ر [r], ب [b], ل [l], ه [h].
²⁵¹ I have correctly substituted ج [j] for the Latin scribe's ح [h].
²⁵² Reading *priore* for *priori* and in the order of signs stated above, for the following awkward remark: *alterum priori ternarii signum, Capricornus tertium quidem erit Taurus*.

letters of this kind. Therefore, attending to the form of the name from what was written above, we claim it is established from four letters, [namely: ن {n}, م {m}, ر {r}, ي {ī}].[253]

Likewise, Mars holding onto the signification, designates four letters.[254]

Here, if the Moon would be staying in Virgo (in the triplicity, I say, of Mars), her letters will be described. Which if Jupiter would be in that same place, we also arrange the letter ي [ī] in the name.[255]

Planet	Arabic Name	Letters	Last letter
♄	زحل Zuḥal	3	ل [l]
♃	مشتري Mushtrī	5	ي [ī]
♂	مرّيخ Mirraykh	4	خ [kh]
☉	شمس Shemesh	3	ش [sh]
♀	زهرة Zuhrah	4	ه [h]
☿	عطارد ʿUṭārid	5	د [d]
☽	قمر Qamar	3	ر [r]

Figure 50: Letters of the Arabic planetary names

Sign	Arabic Name
♈	حمل, Ḥamal
♉	ثور, Thawr
♊	جوزاء, Jawzāʾ
♋	سرطان, Saraṭān
♌	أسد, ʾAsad
♍	سنبلة, Sunbulah
♎	ميزان, Mīzān
♏	عقرب, ʿAqrab
♐	قوس, Qūs
♑	جدي, Jadī
♒	دَلو, Dalū
♓	حوت, Ḥūt

Figure 51: Arabic names of the signs

---

[253] If we put all of the letters of the above names together, these four letters are each represented twice, and so will be the basis of the name.
[254] See below.
[255] This is because the last letter of the Arabic name for Jupiter is ي [ī]. See the table immediately below.

(But any star holding onto the triplicity of the significator, is a significator of five letters.²⁵⁶ It is appropriate for it to be put as the last of them in the formation of the name, whether it has another witness in the name, or not.)

Moreover, with Mercury staying in that same place, we suggest that د [*d*] should be applied.²⁵⁷ With him observing no testimony (just as it did not with Jupiter), but if the east itself would assume the role of the signification, one will have to operate in just the way as we said above about the lord of the east, but with [Mercury] being wholly neglected.

Furthermore,²⁵⁸ with Saturn claiming the rulership of the east, it will be a name of three letters, frequently mixing ر [*r*] or ز [*z*].²⁵⁹ But Jupiter being endowed with the gift of that dignity, establishes a name of five letters. Mars as the lord of the east, indicates it is formed with four letters, most often granting ح [*ḥ*] or خ [*kh*]. In fact, Mercury being endowed with that same rulership, teaches that it is composed of five letters, without a doubt setting ع [*ʿ*] next to the name.

Once more, I believe one must pay attention to this: because a certain portion of the above-named stars holding onto a double-bodied sign, or applying to any [star] in a double-bodied one (especially in a pivot),²⁶⁰ suggests a double name or one constructed of paired names: like Abdullah²⁶¹ and Abd al-Rahman.²⁶² Which if it were of the Latin names, it is good to render it either as a family name known more by its own proper term, or perhaps the fathers' name with its own familiar term,²⁶³ based on what is supported by the greater authority of testimonies. Moreover, the significator being in a convertible sign attributes one and a simple name, for the most part diminutive or shortened.

On the other hand, in this place it seems not inappropriate to suggest the signification of the signs for discerning the letters of names. And so, [for]

---

256 I think what ʿUmar (or Hugo) really means is that since Mars signifies four letters, any star in that triplicity would add its letter onto the end as the *fifth* letter.
257 This is because the last letter of the Arabic name for Mercury is د [*d*].
258 See the table above, where I have listed the number of letters in each Arabic name.
259 ʿUmar (or Hugo) might be saying this because the difference between the letters is only a dot indicating a different pronunciation.
260 Based on the statements below, I believe this means that the significator is in the double-bodied sign, not the planet to which it applies.
261 *Abdalla*. The name عبدالله means "slave/servant" (ʿ*abd*) "of God" (*Allah*).
262 Lat. *Abdarahmen*, sometimes in English spelled Abdulrahman. The name عبد الرّحمن means "slave" (ʿ*abd*) "of the Merciful One" (*al-Rahman*).
263 *Propria familiarius appellatione*. I am not sure what this means. This is probably a comment by Hugo, as I doubt ʿUmar concerned himself with Latinate names.

Aries, Taurus, Leo, Sagittarius, Capricorn, Aquarius, [and] Pisces, the name is established from three letters.[264] But Gemini and Scorpio teach that it is constructed from four. Moreover, Cancer, Virgo, [and] Libra assert that its structure is of five letters.

Therefore, Mercury[265] holding onto the signification, not in a double-bodied sign but rather in a firm or convertible sign, invites us especially to a simple and single name, such as ʿAli or ʿUmar.

In addition though, turn the eyes of your mind to the inhabitants of that region which you then inhabit—namely whether [a name] worthy of greater veneration by them is had. And so, Mercury traversing a prosperous place of the circle, while the name was of three letters, highly esteems ʿUmar as being more worthy among the people of *al-Baẓara*.[266] But in Kufa, it judges that ʿAli is to be preferred, as being more excellent.

Then, too, it seems that the star to which [the significator] applies should be brought to bear as a partner, especially if it would designate five letters.[267]

Now, without a doubt the name itself requires the last letter of the star, such as ى [*ī*] for Jupiter or د [*d*] for Mercury.[268] If therefore Mercury would possess his own proper sovereignty with Jupiter, it attests that the name is Ishmael or *Aliusmaiel*.[269] Moreover, Jupiter being the significator in the east and in a fortuitous place, frequently claims it is Abū Muhammad or Muhammad, or ibn Muhammad.[270]

Which if Venus, being endowed with the signification, would be in that same place, it suggests a Latin name. Which if she would hold onto her own sovereignty or would regard Jupiter or apply to him, or at least she would be lingering in an optimal place of the circle (of which kind is the tenth or ninth), being lofty[271] and made fortunate, it claims it is of the family and lineage of prophets, like Ahmed or Muhammad. Which if the majority of the

---

[264] In Arabic, all of these names have three letters. Likewise, Gemini and Scorpio (below) each have four letters, and Cancer, Virgo, and Libra have five letters. See the table above.
[265] I am not sure why ʿUmar has switched to considering Mercury, which he began to do a few paragraphs above.
[266] Place unknown at this time. Evidently, ʿUmar represented a distinguished name in that area.
[267] Because Mercury was said to indicate a five-letter name.
[268] See the table above.
[269] Perhaps ʿAli Ishmael?
[270] Hugo might have gotten these names reversed: the latter names attributed to Jupiter all have a *d* (the Mercurial letter), while the names attributed to Mercury have an *ī* (the Jupiterian letter).
[271] This probably means being high in the circle of her apogee (*ITA* II.1).

§§7.89-146: Theft

stars, or at least half,[272] would be in agreement with one appearing in a double-bodied [sign], it portends a double name or one constructed from two names, such as is Abū Muhammad or ibn Muhammad.

But if Saturn (having assumed the signification) would be in the east, it grants a servile name, or Scythian[273] or belonging to Ethiopia.[274] Which if he would be staying in his own sovereignty, it prefigures the name of Moses; less than that, Aaron; but the lowest is David or Ishmael.

Generally therefore, both here and with the rest, one must have a power of discernment as to the common parlance of the customs of different peoples,[275] just as is made clear in the names of the signs. The *Arachitae*[276] and the eastern people call the sign of Pisces *al-Samakah*;[277] but Egypt and Africa, even *Samir*[278] and the westerners, [call] it *al-Ḥūt*.[279] Among the Babylonians, for Virgo it is called *al-Sunbulah*;[280] in *Samir* and the west, *al-'Adhrā'*. But the Persians [use] *Bahram* for Mars, but further people [say] *al-Mirraykh*.[281]

Likewise, the signification of Mars conveys a name from Persia or a pagan.[282] However, when the Sun is in control of the signification, should [the Sun] settle down on the east, it grants a designation of kings. The Moon even taking the role of the Sun, introduces one like the names of kings or prophets, [and] often messengers. Which if Mercury would fill the place of the Moon, it professes a name of a little girl,[283] or an Egyptian one. Moreover, the signification of Saturn indicates a name of three letters, such as Sayyid [سيّد] or[284] Mazen.[285]

---

[272] Reading tentatively for *multitudo medietas aut saltem medietas*.
[273] *Sciticum*. Scythia was anciently a country north of the Black Sea. In the medieval period the Slavic regions were raided for the slave trade, which could be the connection with servile names.
[274] Probably due to Ethiopians being black.
[275] *Iuxta alios et alios usitatio (res inquam diversarum gentium ritus) habenda erit discretio*.
[276] Unknown at this time.
[277] *Azamacha*.
[278] Probably Sumer. In his section on Virgo, Allen attributes the *Samir* name to "early Arabs."
[279] This is the standard Arabic name.
[280] This is the standard Arabic name.
[281] This is the standard Arabic name.
[282] The Persians, probably due to the fire-worshipping of the Zoroastrians. I am not sure about pagans, unless it suggests a hatred of or dissent from (Mars) the monotheistic religions.
[283] Reading as *puellulae parvulae*.
[284] Omitting *zied* as an alternative transliteration of Sayyid.

In this manner too, Venus being found outside her own proper and more worthy place, [and] no less each light, indicates a name put together from three letters, and it receives no increase in pronunciation, even though it might happen to be written [that way].

Finally, if the east itself would be enriched by the gift of the signification, it seems that [the letters] both of it and its own mansion, even that of a star placed there or in the fourth sign, [and] of the two signs tetragonal from that (if a star would traverse in them), should be collected into one. One will have to do it not otherwise with the lord of [the east],[286] if it would obtain the signification.

In addition to all of this, if the Lot of Fortune regarded the east, a letter is superfluous in the name and [should] be taken away, such as is [the name] Suleiman and what is of this kind: for the letter ا [ā] can be taken away, or its addition can happen.[287] Some letters of this kind are had among the Arabs, namely which they use as necessary in pronunciation, but they in no way represent in writing,[288] as is made clear in these names: 'Umar, I say, and *Sumair*.[289]

And the lord of its triplicity being in a double-bodied sign, conjoins the name from two parts or names.

Thus it will be good to take the letters of the lord of the eastern bound or of the east itself (of that one, I say, which earned the signification), moreover [the letter] of the sign where it is staying. For some portion of the signification and indication is contained in these.

§7.142: On the order of letters in names—'Umar

On the other hand, the place and position [of the significator] demonstrates the order of the letters (namely which is put first, [and] which ones should be adjoined next). For, it being in the first decan of the sign places the

---

[285] Reading for *mazid*, taking the *d* as a misread for the Arabic *n*. This name is apparently derived from the Arabic for "storm clouds," which are an attribution of Saturn in weather prediction.
[286] Added by Dykes, as this seems to be what 'Umar means.
[287] 'Umar must be thinking of the name Suleiman (سليمان, 6 letters) being spelled as Suliman (سلمين, 5 letters). In fact, he might specifically have the long vowels in mind, as it is harder to have virtually identical names with consonants missing.
[288] This may be a comment by Hugo, referring to the short vowel markings which are frequently omitted by fluent speakers in Arabic script.
[289] 'Umar may be referring to alternate spellings of Samir.

first letter of the mansion first in the name. But it lingering in the second [decan], the middle [letter] of the mansion [is put down] as the first one of the name. But in the third face, the one which comes first in the name is like that of the last [letter] of the mansion.

Which if perhaps the significator itself would be staying in the assembly of one of the fixed [stars],[290] such as are *al-Qalb al-'Asad*[291] and *al-Qalb al-'Aqrab*[292] (namely, the Heart of the Lion and of Scorpio), or Aldebaran and the Lucky One,[293] and what are of this kind, it seems that the name itself imitates the structure[294] of the star; and its proper quality depends principally on the composition and signification of both it and the mansion.

§7.143: Of what law or nation he is—'Umar

Then, with a question presented about his law and nation, one must enter into the counsel of the lord of the hour. Therefore, the Sun being in control of the gift of this dignity, testifies that he has converted, namely from law to law. Which if Venus would obtain the rulership of this, it signals the Arabian law. But Mercury denotes a Hindu and the legal institutes of the Indians. The Moon even being put in charge of the rulership of the hour, portends a Persian or, if more important, a Tyrian.[295] Which if [the hour] were Saturnine, it ascribes him to the Jewish confession. Moreover, Mars being in full control over the hour, indicates a Roman and puts him under Roman laws. But if the rulership of the hour is ascribed to Jupiter, it introduces a pagan—unless, I say, he would claim the east or his own sovereignty: for thus it commends his lineage and nobility.

§7.144: On the etymology of the name—'Umar

Looking to the etymology or rather signification of the name, you will principally note the significator and its place in the circle. For, it being placed

---

[290] The following major fixed and "royal" stars are in the constellations corresponding to the fixed signs.
[291] *Kalbalaced*. That is, the royal fixed star Regulus or *Cor Leonis*.
[292] *Kab alacrab*. That is, the fixed star Acrab. But the royal star *Cor Scorpionis*, is Antares.
[293] *Assaare*, probably Sadalmelik (*sa'ad al-malik*), the alpha star in Aquarius.
[294] *Compaginem*. That is, its associations and nature.
[295] *Vel si maius Tyrium/Tirium*. I take this to be one from the region of Tyre, Lebanon, and not the river region in Greece.

in the east, signifies a name of general and complete signification, such as what is taken from life, [such as] *Seviahie*,[296] that is, "live-giving."

But in the second house, it portends a name of money and with the signification of support, such as Wealth, Increase, Indigenous Ally.

But in the third even, one like a blood-brother, such as Beloved and Famous Little Brother.

But with the significator being placed in the fourth, a name of antiquity is derived, such as [First?] Born or David, even sometimes descending from fathers or old men, often from a term belonging to lands, such as Hyspanus, Briton, Frank, Andigovia, and so on.

Moreover, the significator in the fifth claims a diminutive or delicate [name], such as is Little Son, and so on, or rather a poor one like Strange Portent.[297]

No less indeed in the sixth or eleventh,[298] [it is] a diminutive one, such as is Slave and the rest of the rank of an inferior and undistinguished person, like Client, Slave-girl, and what has to do with this category.

But concerning the seventh, it puts terms [indicating] manly things for women, [and] womanly things for men, contrary to custom, [and names] such as Adversary, Exile, and Perverse.

In the eighth, one like Unfaithful, Unjust, Hoarder,[299] Greedy.

Likewise in the ninth, it grants names of the law and obedience, such as those of just prophets (both for men and women), such as Male Pilgrim or Female Pilgrim, Religious Man or Religious Woman, Abbot, Abbess, and what is of this kind.

Now, in the tenth it decrees a name of advancement and excellence, such as seems to pertain to rulership and dignities.

---

[296] The last part of this name is probably Hayah, which corresponds to the name "Eve." Like many older Greek and Latin (and even indigenous medieval) names, Arabic names have literal meanings that are still clearly understood as such. In the modern West, we generally only recognize these in last names (such Shoemaker or Goldsmith), and have to look up the meanings of first names in baby name books. In what follows, Hugo seems to be translating Arabic first names directly into Latin rather than finding their indigenous equivalents. For example, the name Palmer means "pilgrim" in modern English, but Hugo uses the Latin *peregrinus*, even though no one in Latin would actually be named Peregrinus. Baby name websites are available which allow searches by meaning, such as babynamesworld.parentsconnect.com.

[297] *Alieni portenti gracile simile.*

[298] The eleventh does not make sense to me.

[299] Or, "concealer."

It being in the eleventh grants a term with a certain relationship of esteem, such as Friends, Beautiful, Faithful; often, it retains a signification [for] a vow [or] desire.[300]

Finally, the significator being placed in the twelfth generates a name of enmity, namely one which looks to harm and negligence, even whatever can be thought of as being hateful and detestable.

§7.145: On the composition of the name and the joining of the letters—'Umar[301]

In this place, the composition of the name and how the letters should be conjoined in it, remains to be observed. Wherefore, with respect to the order of the stars, the significator and its strength comes to be elicited, namely as to whether it [would have] any dignity in the east, then whether it would be holding onto its own house or sovereignty. If therefore Saturn were in his own domicile or sovereignty, he administers the whole affair. Which if he were wholly estranged from the house or sovereignty, Jupiter (being endowed with that same dignity) would be [his] successor. But if not, seek the signification of Mars. But with him appearing unworthily, the Sun will have to be brought to bear. Which if he would bear himself otherwise, Venus should be consulted. Afterwards, one will have to enter into the counsel of Mercury, [then] finally the Moon.

After you have carried out all of this, the degrees of the significator-star that have been run through in the sign where it is staying, being multiplied by the degrees of the east, should be subtracted from the rest of the degrees of the star which it has not yet crossed. The number of degrees which is left, makes a sign of the first letter. Moreover, multiply those parts which the star is going around, by the degrees of the second house (which belongs to money). The collection of those must be subtracted from the remaining ones which it has not yet gone through, in just the way as was done first. For the remainder designates the second letter. Again, with the degrees of the star being multiplied by the parts of the third house, what is collected from thence must be subtracted from the remainder of the significator. But what is

---

[300] *Voto desiderio significationem retinet.*
[301] This section introduces several methods for determining the order of the letters (and includes a reference to the Lot of Fortune method for the number of letters), but I confess I do not understand how these methods work. Perhaps with a translation of the Arabic original they will begin to make more sense.

left over portends the third letter. And so, the sequence of this progression will have to be pursued through the twelve houses, until one reaches the east, [and] moreover from the east itself [according to] the order of the disposition set out before, until you recognize the heap of letters (however many was would be agreeable). Remember to extend those in the wrong order, in the contrary way.[302]

Which[303] if some worried inquirer would approach in order to discern the name of a man or woman, with respect to the number of their letters, it is good to consider how many signs lie between the east and the Lot of Fortune: for the number of them introduces a precise calculation of the letters.

Furthermore,[304] once all ambiguity about the number of letters is removed, in order that you may decide in what place they should be taken up, do not let the number of degrees of the east slip from memory, For it being one or eleven,[305] portends that the letter is *a*. Which if it were found otherwise with respect to the degrees, let the intention [of your mind] be drawn back diligently to the seventh: for if you would discover [the degree to be] two or twelve, it represents the second letter (namely, *b*). Moreover, with these bearing themselves, otherwise, you will note the sign of the Midheaven (namely, the tenth): the third or thirteenth degree of which indicate the third letter. Which if again they would be different, it will be good to attend to the lower sign (the fourth, I say): for [the degree being] four or fifteen, they denote the fourth letter.[306] Furthermore, seek the fifth letter from [the one following] the east, the sixth from the one following [the seventh], the seventh from the one following the Midheaven, the eighth from the one following the fourth; but the ninth from the third from the Midheaven, the tenth too from the third from the pivot of the earth, but the fourth from the

---

[302] Reading tentatively for *econtrario et ratione praepostera/praepostere continuare memento*. It might mean simply that we must subtract the lesser from the greater, so that the order of subtraction might have to be reversed.

[303] Cf. §7.140 above, which had us count only the crooked signs, not all of them.

[304] This method is odd and seems inconsistent. At first, 'Umar seems to want the cusps to fall on certain degrees, but later this does not seem important. The ordering of letters and houses does not seem to follow a clear pattern, either. At any rate, it does seem as though perhaps the letters here are those of the alphabet, not the letters of the name. My conjecture is that if a given house contains (say) the first and fifteenth letters of the Arabic alphabet, then if a key planet is in that house, then the name should somehow contain those letters. See the similar method of Jirjis in §7.146 below.

[305] Reading with Vienna for *duo* ("two"). Medieval texts often confuse ordinal and cardinal numbers, so I am not sure if this means the "first or eleventh" degree, or "1° or 11°." Likewise for the rest below.

[306] Reading *quartam litteram* for *quartum elementum*.

east signifies the thirteenth, but the seventh will indicate the fourteenth. Likewise, the fourth from the Midheaven decrees the fifteenth. But the fourth from the pivot of the earth reveals the sixteenth. No less, too, the fifth from the east supplies the seventeenth. Likewise, the fifth from the Midheaven means the eighteenth.[307] But the fifth from the pivot of the earth opens up the twentieth. Then, the sixth from the east indicates the twenty-first. After this, the seventh designates the twenty-seventh. After that, the Midheaven itself exhibits the twenty-third. Finally, the sixth from the pivot of the earth teaches the twenty-fourth.[308]

§7.146: On finding the number and name of a concealed thing—Jirjis

But in order that a first and principal understanding of this matter may be had, it will be good to distribute the letters [of the alphabet][309] by 12, according to the natures of the signs. Therefore, Aries, Leo, and Sagittarius, which are in the first triplicity, are allotted the first letter. Taurus, Virgo, and Capricorn (which are of the second triplicity) assume the second [letter]. But we give the third [letter] to Gemini, Libra, and Aquarius (which bring forth the third triplicity). To Cancer, Scorpio, and Pisces (namely the fourth triplicity) is left the fourth [letter]. Moreover, the first triplicity takes up the fifth [letter] in order, the second [triplicity] the sixth[310] [letter], the third [triplicity] the seventh [letter], the fourth [triplicity] the eighth [letter].

Not otherwise will it be good to distribute these 22[311] letters through twelve triplicities,[312] so that the first two triplicities take groups of six, the others only groups of five,[313] as is written below:[314]

---

[307] The nineteenth letter is missing in the text.
[308] This is an indication that 'Umar's method derives from an alphabet of 24 letters (probably Greek). Below, Jirjis relies on 22 letters (probably Hebrew).
[309] Reading for the unknown *abiiciet* or perhaps *abivet*.
[310] Reading *sextam* for *secundam*.
[311] This is an indication that Jirjis is using the Hebrew alphabet, which has 22 letters.
[312] Reading *ternarios* for *terminos*.
[313] See the table below. If we distribute 22 letters through the triplicities as he has described, the first two triplicities will indeed have 6 letters apiece, with the other two having only 5.
[314] I note that some of the Arabic letters are missing, while others are repeated. A couple are uncertain: for example, the second instance (from the right) of ف has the dot below the letter, and in 'Umar's section this letter was said to be a *p*. Also, the ى in the manuscript has the top curve facing the other way. So I am not at all confident either that Jirjis

ا ب و س ج ح ف ه ص و ف ر ع ح ص ط ز ي م ت ل ك

Figure 52: Apparent order of 24 Arabic letters in Vienna manuscript

Fire	Earth	Air	Water
1	2	3	4
5	6	7	8
9	10	11	12
13	14	15	16
17	18	19	20
21	22		

Figure 53: Distribution of 22 letters through the triplicities

Fire	Earth	Air	Water
א [a]	ב [b, v]	ג [g, j]	ד [d]
ה [h]	ו [v, w, ŭ]	ז [z]	ח [h, kh]
ט [t]	י [y, ī]	כ [k]	ל [l]
מ [m]	נ [n]	ס [s]	ע [ʿ, gh]
פ [f, p]	צ [tz, x]	ק [q]	ר [r]
ש [s, sh]	ת [t]		

Figure 54: Example distribution of Hebrew letters

Therefore,[315] for extracting the name, once the degree and minute of the east is established, let the rising sign be apportioned by means of the afore-

---

was using a 24-letter alphabet (see the 22-letter version below), nor that it was really Persian or Arabic.

[315] In what follows, the method seems to be this. Find the rising sign, and see what triplicity it is: the first letter will be among those letters attributed to that triplicity. Then, look at the sign on the Midheaven (which is probably assumed to be in the tenth sign), and the second letter will be among those attributed to that triplicity. Do the same for the signs on the Descendant and the IC. Then, if you need more letters, continue with the succeedent places (probably in this order: 2nd, 11th, 8th, 5th). These placements will give you the range of possible letters for the spelling of the name. So for example, suppose Jirjis really is using Hebrew (see table). If the Ascendant were a fiery sign, the first letter or sound in the name would be one of the fiery ones: a, h, t, m, f/p, s/sh. If then the degree of the Midheaven were on an earthy sign, the next letter or sound would be one of the earthy ones, and so on.

said letters. Next too, once it is discovered what letter the eastern degree is, let the number be distributed by means of the heap of the name. In this manner too, the letter of the Midheaven and [of the west and][316] the one which belongs to the pivot of the earth.

But afterwards, taking the letters of the east and the Midheaven, likewise the west and the pivot of the earth, once you have added those which appear after the pivots,[317] you should try with the greatest effort to avoid error in this place, so that finally you may elicit the complete name from their appropriate orderly arrangement. (However, if letters still existed, such as what belongs to the family name, they should be left behind as though superfluous.)

You will have to do this in no other way if it is asked about the name of the mother or father, so that namely you take the letters of the Midheaven and the east, even the pivot of the earth and the west, [and] strive to arrange them by the method stated above, and by extracting every name in this manner from the four pivots and the four triplicities.

[A question about amounts?][318]

Now, whenever someone gave a question about drawing out the number, one must note diligently how much (by number) the east has. And as it is a method of the Indians, put 1 for 10, and establish 10 for 100, and 100 for 1000. Therefore, with the east being a turning [sign], put 1 [for] 1. But if it were double-bodied, put 1 for 10. Also, a firm one demands 100 for 10.

---

[316] Adding based on the repetition of the list immediately below.
[317] Reading *existentes adiectis* for *existentium abiectis*. It makes sense that one would add the letters of the succedent places, not ignore them.
[318] I am rather uncertain about the following method and its purpose. It seems to refer to questions about the amounts of something, but I do not understand how it relates to the letters, and something about the numbers seems mixed up. The part about different quadruplicities indicating different amounts might relate to how many zeroes we are adding in Indian numerals. This little section reads (in Vienna): *Nam quotiens de numero eliciendo quis dederit quaestionem, quantum de numero habeat oriens diligentius notandum. Et ut est indorum ratio, unum pone × et × constitue c atque c pro mille ponito [posito?]. Oriente igitur tropico existente, unum pone unum. Si vero bicorpor fuerit, unum pone ×. Firmum quoque pro × expostulat c.*

[A question about multiple people/objects?][319]

Moreover, for another question being presented, you will take the letter of the Midheaven, so that you would establish [that letter] as the number of the second, in the way that was stated above. But if it is asked about a third one, you will give the letter of the west to it. If [about] a fourth one, it will have to be ascribed to the fourth (which belongs to the pivot of the earth) as the number.

The order of the circuit of the signs must be followed in this manner, namely whenever an interrogation is given about a concealed thing:[320] after [a letter][321] with respect to the number, after the number with respect to the thought, after the thought with respect to the name, even after the name, up to a thousand times.

---

[319] Again, this method does not quite make sense to me, because I am not sure what the question is. My sense is that this refers to questions about finding the names of multiple people or multiple objects: thus the letter of the Ascendant would identify an important letter for the first person/thing, that of the Midheaven an important one for the second person/thing, and so on.

[320] I am not sure what Jirjis means by putting letters, numbers, thoughts, and names in this order.

[321] *Aliam*.

Partnerships

§7.147: On the status of a partnership—Sahl[1]

With a question proposed about a partnership and partaking together [in something], we observe the affair of the querent from the east and its lord, but the seventh and its lord comprehend the partner. We seek the partnership of each of them itself in the tenth, but both the fourth and the lord of the fourth resolves the end of the whole affair.

And so, if the lord of the east and the Moon would be stepping through movable or turning signs, they dissolve the partnership more quickly, and it is unstable. Their traversal in firm ones conveys steadiness and portends that it will last. But going through a two-parted [sign] brings acquisition and success with trust and esteem.

The traversal of malevolents in the east corrupts their association from the side of the querent, while should they possess the seventh, the occasion for the corruption will proceed from the other side.

The Lunar application to her own lord will report a profitable and peaceful end, with the greatest diligence. But with the regard of each being denied, there will be suspicion in it.

But if the infortunes would be staying under the earth, the same thing is given to be understood. On the other hand, with the benevolents established in the tenth, a judgment of great profit arises; the infortunes in that same place promise the converse.

This also: if the Moon, being conjoined to her own lord, would apply to benevolents, the shared partnership (as was already stated) continues up to death.

---

[1] Cf. *On Quest.* §7.23 and al-Rijāl II.37.

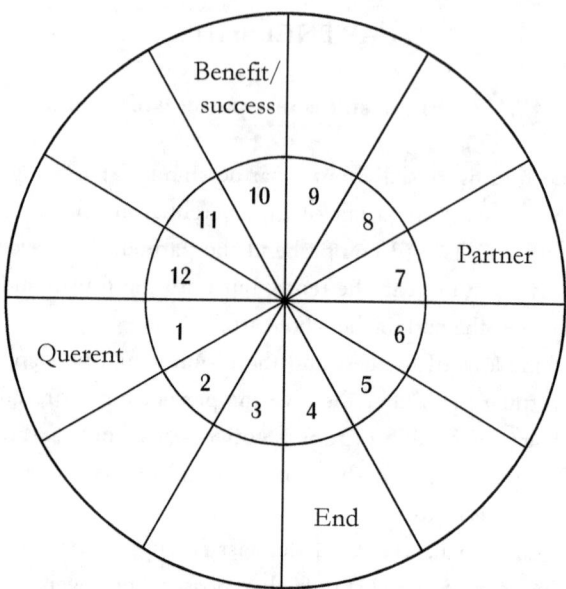

Figure 55: Angular significations for partnerships

§7.148: On the association or hatred or love of two people—'Umar[2]

And so, an observation of this kind proceeds from the east and the seventh and their lords, even from the stars which appear in them, and their application and withdrawal. However, the Moon must be applied as a partner, if she had an application or withdrawal.

Which if they bear themselves thusly, you will apply the star from which the Moon is being separated as a partner of the lord of the east, but the one to which she applies, [as a partner of the lord] of the seventh. Then, too, it seems one must note of what kind the application is (namely from a trigon or hexagon or assembly), and whence the regard proceeded; no less, whether there is some reception. Which if they would bear themselves thusly, it signifies the joint, respectable, and firm concord of each. But a regard from a tetragon or the opposition (with reception, I say, being denied), they testify

---

[2] Cf. al-Rijāl III.30. This section is identical to §11.7, drawing on the same chapter in 'Umar.

to mutual hatred and dissent. Which if reception would be present, it makes them scornful towards one another.[3]

But once it is discovered to what the Moon applies (and how), or from what she is withdrawing (just as was said above), one will have to judge in the way one did with the lord of the east and of the seventh. It is not otherwise with those stars which you will find in the east and the seventh.

Moreover, if the Moon would apply to none, nor would she be withdrawing from any, you will bring into view the lord of the east and of the seventh equally, as you do with the rest. If therefore they would be deprived of a mutual aspect, nor would they apply nor withdraw, nor would there be a transfer or collection between each by some star, it wholly denies peace and concord.

§7.149: On the status of the association—al-Khayyāt

But if a question would be proposed about an association or partnership, whether it would come to be or what success would result, the east and its lord will be in charge of the querent, but the seventh and its lord over the partner. Moreover, the joint business will be placed in the Midheaven, [and] finally the end in the pivot of the earth.

And so, the lord of the east and the Moon traversing in turning [signs], denies steadiness and they quickly dissolve what partnership had been there. But if in firm ones, they portend it will last longer. But in a double-bodied one, even though they may convey profit and success, it is unstable.

The infortunes in the east testify that disagreement and fraud and lies are there on the part of the querent. They being places in the same way in the seventh, the corruption comes to be from the other side of the association.

The Moon applying to her own lord, finds the end to be with esteem and profit. But if a regard of this kind will not be present, it will be with mistrust and disagreement.

With the malevolents being placed under the earth, it is the same. Which if fortunate ones would be lingering in the Midheaven, it is a sign of manifold success. But if malevolents, it happens contrariwise.

This must even be noted: if the Moon would be staying in the assembly of her own lord, while she does not apply to the infortunes, there will be no

---

[3] I take this to mean they will *only* be scornful, and not hateful (as in the case of a square or opposition without reception).

separation up until death; but applying to fortunate ones, it pronounces the status of the partner to be proper.

§7.150: On a partnership or association—Dorotheus

However, if a question is presented about the status of an association, the east and its lord respond to the querent. But from the seventh and its lord, the associate is determined. The Midheaven lays bare the joint association, the pivot of earth its end.

Which if the lord of the east and the Moon would be holding onto convertible signs, they are hostile to an association, and they dissolve it quickly. In a firm one, they establish a steady partnership, and make it long-lasting. Being thus in a double-bodied one, in introduces concord and trust and profit to each [partner].

But either of the significators being a benevolent and lucky, urges him[4] to trust and truth; but the other one being corrupted invites him to fraud and illicit things.

The infortunes which occupy the east, warn that one must beware of theft and fraud on the part of the querent; being placed in the seventh, they threaten it from the other party.

But the Moon applying to her own lord, determine the association to be with love and profit; she diverting her aspect from him, stains the end with mistrust.

Infortunes placed under the earth, hurl in the same thing. Fortunate ones in the tenth signify profit, the infortunes the contrary.

Likewise, the Moon being adjoined to her lord, denies a parting; applying to fortunate ones, makes a respectable and steady association.

§7.151: On any association—Aristotle

If perhaps a question about entering into a friendship or some association, or even establishing a marriage-union, would be brought into the open, we should consult the east and the seventh. For, the traversal of Jupiter or Venus or [the Head of the] Dragon in the seventh, either consecrates nuptials or establishes an association or prepares friendship, in that year—namely,

---

[4] Reading *illum…impellit* for *reliquum…depellit*.

whichever one [of these associations] the question put forth. But with none lingering [there], when however any of them would happen to be entering into the seventh,[5] finally then will the effect of the thing asked about be given.

§7.152: On the stability of the association—Aristotle

You will learn the status and faithfulness of the association through this method. For if the eastern lord and equally that of the seventh would support each other by a benign aspect, the association will be firm and friendly. But the sign of the querent being indirect,[6] will make him subject to the other; conversely, with [the querent's sign] being direct[7] and the other appearing indirect, he about whom it was asked will be made subject to the querent.

§7.153: On the success or harm of an association—'Umar

The benefits of the association, or rather the trouble of loss, remains to be disclosed in this place. And so, diligently pay attention to the lord of the tenth: to which it applies or which one to it, even which peregrine or familiar stars traverse in it, [and] no less to which one they (namely the lord of the east or of the tenth) apply, or which one to them: for they[8] signify the success and promise profits. And so, the lord of the east applying to any of those appearing in the tenth (or they to it or with the lord of the tenth), or if [the lord of the tenth] would apply to stars placed in the east (or they to it), while the application would be from the trigon or hexagon or assembly, it watches over profits and benefits, and brings them back to them. (The lord of the seventh, too, brings forth no other judgment when they bear themselves thusly.) An application from the tetragon or the opposition prepares discord, introduces loss, [and] presents moderate or no success.

---

[5] That is, by a later transit.
[6] Normally called "crooked." See *ITA* I.9.1 or *Forty Chapters* Ch. I.1.11.
[7] Normally called "straight." See the previous footnote.
[8] Reading *ipsi* for *ipsis*.

§7.154: On the usefulness of the association—Jirjis

With a question of this kind being had, if the Moon would traverse with a Saturn or Mars that is lingering in the Midheaven, or should [the malevolent star] even occupy the seventh, it reveals a deceiver, and he will defraud [the querent] of the money that was handed over for [the purposes] of trade.

§7.155: On the result and reward of the association—Aristotle

In addition, consider the result of the friendship, and the acquisitions of the association, in this manner. For if the lord of the second from the east (which pertains to you), but even the lord of the eighth (which comprehends [the friend's] profits) appearing free, should bear themselves well, each one will be enriched with the greatest profit. In the same way, with both bearing themselves badly and placed perversely, each one will mourn the troubles of the association. However, so that I might comprehend all things more briefly, the lord of whichever one's second [being placed] in the second [house] of the other, or even were it placed well anywhere at all, that one will rejoice in manifold reward. Also, I praise no other opinion if you would attend to the eleventh with respect to a friendship that was under question.

§7.156: On the hour of attaining the advantage or disadvantage (or rather, the harm)—'Umar

Moreover, the hour of the future advantage or rather disadvantage, can easily be discovered from the adjoining, in the same sign and degree, of the significator of each ([that is], of the querent and the one about whom it is asked): for, such a conjunction of them which is had, introduces the aforesaid things. Which if an open (not a hidden) question were set out before—so that it is asked specifically about a blood-brother or father or child, or a slave or his own wife—I think one should pay attention with diligent observation and care to the house which retains the signification of the quaesited thing, and its lord, [and] even if a star is found in that same place.[9] After that

---

[9] That is, if the partnership is about a specific person whose relationship is better described by another house (the father, brother, and so on), then use that house instead of the seventh.

too, he[10] warns that in this place one will have to judge just like the statement given above[11] with respect to the seventh and its lord.

---

[10] That is, ʿUmar.
[11] Probably in §7.148 above, but perhaps also §7.153.

Journeys to Find Someone

§7.157: On a journey established by someone—Sahl[1]

With a journey to some man being established, if it were sought by someone as to whether or not he would be able to be found in that place, the lord of the seventh will have to be consulted. For, this [planet] occupying a pivot portends he is in that place; traversing after the pivots decides that he is nearby; traveling through the remote [places] claims he is far removed.

§7.158: On a journey established [to meet] someone—al-Khayyāt

But once someone has established travel to someone, if someone would ask whether he would be found in that place, the lord of the seventh should be consulted. For if it would traverse in a pivot, it suggests he could be found in that place. But if he would be lingering after the pivots, it means he is not far from [there]. Traversing in the remote [places], it detains him in faraway parts.

§7.159: On a journey established [to meet] someone—Dorotheus

Moreover, with a journey to someone being proposed, as to whether or not he would happen to be found in that place, we should consult the lord of the seventh. For, it traversing in a pivot declares that he is staying there. After a pivot, nearby. But in the remote [places], it removes him far away and testifies that he is absent.

---

[1] Cf. *On Quest.* §7.24, and al-Rijāl I.15 and II.38. Al-Rijāl reminds us that a connection of some sort is needed between the lords of the first and seventh, to ensure the querent will actually find the man.

WAR

§7.160: On war—Sahl[1]

It is allowed to observe the production of wars and the successes of those fighting, in this order. For if the king himself, or at least some leader (namely of an army) or prince—having no lesser concern about this kind of affair—came as a worried inquirer, the east and its lord, [and] even the star from which the Moon is being separated, assume the signification of the querent. But we hand over the enemy to the seventh and its lord, even to the star to which the Moon is applying. Which if there were no application or withdrawal of the Moon, an expert in this business will leave [her] alone. But generally in all affairs of wars, the power of the superior stars is discovered to be greater than that of the inferiors.

Therefore both significators, [that is], of each side, must be consulted: their joint aspect and reception, and from a prosperous figure, is a sign of securing peace (but the lighter star brings forth the movement and origin of the peace), while if the application should come to be from an adverse figure with reception, the peace is finally made firm after long gestures of discord. On the other hand, the retrogradation of either significator, or [its] position in a perverse place, or if it is in no way received, threatens betrayal for that side. And it portends that the trouble of his betrayal is going to come in terms of the nature and signification of its place: for if it would be traversing in the second, he will guard what belongs to him, but the enemy will scatter his wealth and resources.[2] But if it were in the sixth or twelfth, he will afflict [him], being detained and tortured, with the most severe imprisonment. Traversing in the eighth, it is wholly fatal. Moreover, the mutual separation of each significator [indicates] conflict and discord.

Moreover, should a significator happen to be one of the superior stars, in a pivot and received, it would attain victory unless it is in the entrance to scorching.

Also, the lord of the east being of the superior ones, even though it may be in aversion [to the Ascendant] and if you should find the significator of the other side (namely the seventh) in a pivot [and it also being an inferior planet],[3] you must not immediately lack confidence in the querent's side be-

---

[1] Cf. *On Quest.* §7.25. For this section and also §7.167 below, cf. al-Rijāl II.42.2.
[2] Reading as *ipsum custodit ille suum, eius tamen opes atque facultates dissipabit hostis.*
[3] Adding with John's Sahl.

fore you discover, with a more subtle examination, to whom the lord of the seventh is applying: for, they being positioned in this way, [should there be] an application made to a star lingering in a pivot, [with reception],[4] then it blesses [the enemy's] side with the desired victory. And the manner of winning will be referred to the power and nature of the star to which it applies. For, the lord of the seventh being strong, even though its application to a cadent[5] star may be discovered, still he will overcome [the querent] so long as it[6] is established as being well-placed. But as soon as he would be first removed from that place, he will become weaker until namely he finally succumbs to the trouble of corruption or scorching. But, existing in that place, if it should apply to none, its ingress into the following sign should be noted, as well as to whom it ought to apply in that place, or in what way it happens to bear itself.

To the extent that it pertains to this business, with no regard [existing] among the inferiors, let confidence in the superiors be had—unless perhaps [the inferior planet] would hold onto a place familiar to the east, and be free, and be supported by the aid of the superiors.

On the other hand, the eastern lord traversing in the seventh (and more powerfully if regarded by the lord of the seventh), it seems that [the querent] is already as though a captive, undergoing and suffering the forces and power of the enemies. Which if it happened the other way around (namely the lord of the seventh in the east, especially placed under the regard of the eastern lord), let the same judgment be given about him.

Moreover, the position of the eastern lord in the eighth, or its application with the lord of the eighth, announces death; nor is it allowed to affirm something else about the significators of the enemies, whenever the lord of the seventh would hold onto the second or at least apply to its lord. It is worse while it would be without reception.

Moreover, the lord of the east in the tenth or applying to its lord, or the other way around (so namely that the lord of the tenth would hold the east or apply to its lord), prefers and extols those who belong to that side, and more powerfully if the receiver[7] would be lingering in a pivot: for thus it indicates in advance that the general of that side will be unconquered. Likewise

---

[4] Adding with John's Sahl.
[5] Hugo says "averse/in aversion," but John says "cadent." I follow John because he is less committed to a specific kind of cadency.
[6] John's Sahl understands this to be the angular lord of the seventh.
[7] Reading *receptor* with John for *receptorum*.

with the order reversed, if you should find the significator of the other side (namely the lord of the seventh) being placed thus in the fourth, or applying to its lord, and more powerfully so with the receiver moving through a pivot, the same judgment should be given about him.

But whenever any of the significators is applying to a star possessing a pivot or to the lord of a pivot (and better yet, with it appearing in a pivot), it extols the powers of its side and prefers it to the rest. Moreover, should either of the significators, although it appears in a pivot [and] free, if [the sign] were a turning one, [then] after the victory given by it, it hastens him into ruin and loss.[8]

Should either of the significators happen to be found in its own twelfth,[9] it is a sign of fleeing.

Moreover, if any of these would appear retrograde, it shows the impotence and weakness of his side.

Likewise, were the lord of the tenth in the domicile of one [of the parties],[10] it will convey royal aid to that side. Nor is another judgment given with respect to the lights (namely, the Sun and Moon), to whichever significator they render the counsel of application.

The Moon even conveying light between the significators (so that, I say, she withdraws from one and applies to the other), promises victory to the one to whom she applies.

However, in every question of wars, whenever Saturn would be lingering in a pivot without the testimony of benevolents, it prolongs the quarrels and discord, and more so if he appeared retrograde: for thus he greatly increases it and frequently it is repeated. The Moon traversing with Mars, being in aversion to the fortunate ones, threatens death or captivity to the querent. The Sun with the Head or Tail at the imminent hour of war, will mix the greatest devastation without future peace. Moreover, both significators being with the Head or Tail at that same hour of war, allow few or none on each [side] to escape.

---

[8] But a fixed sign would make a lasting and secure victory, according to John's Sahl.
[9] Hugo says "in the sixth or the twelfth," but John's Sahl reminds us that the sixth is the twelfth of the seventh. I have opted for this short phrase which encapsulates the meaning of both texts.
[10] That is, in either the Ascendant or the seventh.

§7.161: On war—'Umar[11]

Whenever (as Valens claims) a question will be given about the affairs of kings, he produces counsel for kings from the Sun and the Midheaven and their significators equally (namely from the greater assent[12] of either one): and so it is necessary to establish that. Also, one will have to perform its releasing in the same way as with the [longevity] releaser, with the degrees of ascensions.[13] But one must take up the releasing for the peoples and common subjects from the lord of the year[14] and the place of the Moon, and the degrees of the east. Moreover, the Mercurial releasing (or rather, "leading forth") in the cycle of the year, or at the hour of the question, watches over the scribes of the king and prince, and his counselors. Also, [the releasing] of Mars is in charge of the army and the generals of the military, and aristocrats.[15] However, Saturn and his releasing merits the care of the sentries of the common people, [and] the citizens and soldiers of the masses. To Venus we commit the king himself[16] and the wives of kings.

§7.162: On war—al-Kindī

§383. Also, concerning the combatants [one may] imitate the above-written judgment. For the Ascendant signifies him who is provoking [a fight], and the seventh his adversary.

[Robert]: And so, since the lord of the east signifies him whence it is asked, and the lord of the seventh the one who is resisting, a conjunction of these (and its manner) should be noted with the utmost effort. For, these regarding each other in a hostile way, or joined in any way through an unlucky [planet] in a pivot, with all conditions of favor being removed, war will undoubtedly take place. But with them being

---

[11] This chapter really pertains to mundane charts, just as in §10 'Umar examines the lives of kings through mundane charts.
[12] *Assensu.* This might be a misprint for *ascensu,* but in any case it sounds somewhat like the "greater condition" of a native (i.e., by profections) in 'Umar's *TBN* II (in *PN* 2).
[13] That is, directing these places around the chart and through the bounds. 'Umar seems to prefer the rougher (but more easily calculated) ascensional directions instead of Ptolemy's more complicated proportional semi-arc directions. See *ITA* Appendix E.
[14] This is obviously a reference to a mundane chart.
[15] In earlier periods, nobility and military service were closely linked.
[16] This seems odd.

joined in a friendly way, and particularly when received, and likewise with them being united together, peace will intervene. And if the Moon, leaving one of these behind, joined herself to the other, here it wholly portends the same thing about a legation that it did in the preceding chapter.[17] The signs, and the places of the circle, and the natures of the significators, clarify both the size of the war's circumstances and its difficulty.

§384. Therefore, the lord of the seventh being mixed together with the lord of the Ascendant by a perverse aspect, but with each being in a double-bodied sign, it increases his army by the number of each.[18] The lord of the second and of the eighth in a similar bearing suggests the same. But the corruption of one being made toward the other, confounds him whom the corrupted one seems to watch over or signify.

§385. Moreover, the one of them which holds onto the pivots, indicates that his army is stronger than the other. But with each one in pivots, the virtue of both is confirmed, and their endurance for wars.

§386. Likewise, the one whose easternness is discovered to be stronger: his vigor, steadiness, [and] eagerness for war is highly praised. But a stronger westernness of either makes him known as being unsound, timid, not wanting to fight. Moreover, the one of them which obtains a peregrine place: it takes away his diligence and counsel for wars.

[*Allies & support*]

§387. In addition, he in whose second [place] Jupiter appeared, shows his money to be much; it multiplies the faith of those assisting, first by love of money [but] then by reason of the law. Moreover, he in whose second place Saturn dwells (or should he become the lord of the second, and regarding it), it indicates less money, mistrusted allies; even the distorted will of its master and his mistrusted mind provokes [the allies] to fraud. Moreover, should the lord of the second corrupt one of them, it warns that his allies might abandon him.

---

[17] See §7.191 below.
[18] Hugo is probably trying to say that his army will be twice as big. At any rate, it seems a double-bodied sign will increase the army's size.

§388. But if the corruption comes to be from Mars and from a perverse aspect, particularly from a pivot of the Ascendant, it threatens destruction from an attack by his own soldiers. But if a regard of some fortunate one would reinforce [it], after the wounds it promises hopes of living: the strength or weakness of the regard of the one making it fortunate will teach a definite experience of that judgment.

[Capture & death for the querent's side]

§389-390a. Furthermore, the lord of the Ascendant in the seventh and corrupted by the infortunes, or scorched or retrograde, pursues the chief [person] of the city.[19] Corrupted by Mars, it hands him over to the enemy in captivity, or afflicts him with death. But this corruption proceeding from Saturn, frightens him with long-lasting captivity [among] the enemies.

§390b. Moreover, the lord of the second being with the lord of the Ascendant in the seventh, and corrupted by Mars, taints the chiefs of those who convey aid to the citizens with captivity or death through the hands of the enemies. Mars in particular, as the lord of the eighth and [placed] in the second, multiplies the massacres of the citizens and allies, no less even than with him in the eighth. Moreover, Saturn corrupting the lord of the second [while] he is in the seventh, ushers the city combatants and allies into captivity. The same [planet] as lord of the eighth, or at least being in the eighth or second, explains the killing of citizens.

§391. Moreover, if the lord of the second is being corrupted by Mercury, [and] he is the [lord of] the house of death, and in the bearing of Mars, it contaminates the supporters of the citizens with sudden mortality and plague.[20] In the regard and aid of Saturn, that same Mercury disseminates blisters which we say are a type of smallpox, [and] compels many to die because of that disease.

§392a. Moreover, it seems one must conclude that, should the lord of the Ascendant in the seventh be tainted by Mercury, and he is in the eighth or [is] the lord of the eighth, it afflicts the captured citizens with the aforesaid evils. Which if the lord of the Ascendant [were] in the Ascendant, tainted by Mercury—provided that he does not lose the [aforesaid conditions]—it cor-

---

[19] In other words, the person on the querent's side will be chased and in trouble. (It is not important here that he runs a city.)
[20] Or perhaps simply, "death" or "destruction" (*peste*).

rupts those presiding over the city and the citizens with the aforesaid infortunes and similar evils within his own city and tents.

[Capture & death for the enemy's side]

§392b. Contrariwise, the lord of the seventh in the seventh, abused by Mercury (and [Mercury being] mixed with Mars and Saturn), weighs down the princes of the enemies and their battle line, with the above-written adversities—provided that Mercury would have possession of the rulership[21] of the second.[22]

§393. Moreover, the lord of the eighth being mournful (by means of the aforesaid improsperity), and it being in the eighth or seventh, destroys the enemy hand and his allies by means of the aforesaid plague—with Mercury, I say, claiming the rulership of the second.

[Victory]

§394. Moreover, Mars himself staining the seventh, but being estranged from the lord of the seventh [and] likewise from the Ascendant and the lord of the Ascendant, and he [also] being in a fiery sign, introduces fire into the tents of the enemies. Conversely too, Mars corrupting the Ascendant itself, [and] also estranged from its lord and the seventh and the lord of the seventh, proclaims the burning of the [querent's] city. Which if he would be regarding the lord of the seventh, and from a fiery sign, it threatens that the burning of the city will come to be by the enemies.

§395. Moreover, the lord of the Ascendant being in the seventh, strong, eastern, direct, aided by fortunate [planets], [but] with the seventh and its lord being corrupted by infortunes (particularly with the lord of the seventh being cadent), likewise with the lord of the Ascendant in its own *ḥalb* (that is, its fortification) or triplicity or bound or face, and that same [planet] regarding the Sun or Mars in a friendly way, [indicates] an attack or assault by the princes of the city upon the enemy army; it afflicts some with death, [and] leads others away as captives.

---

[21] Reading *dominio* for *domino*.
[22] Or that he would be in it, in order to parallel the opposite conditions above for the lord of the Ascendant.

§396. Moreover, if the lord of the seventh is cadent (that is, remote), even scorched or in the pivot of Mars or with his body (namely in [his] assembly), it kills the enemy prince.

§397. And so, in this way, the lord of the seventh being strong, while the lord of the Ascendant is turned away from it and from the fortunes,[23] [and], I say, the lord of the seventh being in the Ascendant, aided by the fortunate ones, eastern, free from the infortunes, with the lord of the Ascendant cadent (particularly in its own depression),[24] it opens the city to the enemies, [and] encloses some by death, others by prison. Which if Mars would be situated with the lord of the Ascendant or in its pivot, it kills the prince of the city.

§398. If however the lord of the seventh and of the Ascendant appear to be equal in virtue and power, the one of them which was in possession of the assent[25] of Mars and Mercury is enriched with the triumph. Moreover, he whose partner appeared to be Venus [likewise] has possession of joy and victory: for she signifies joy and exultation, also joy and glory in wars, victory, and exultation.

§399. But he who claimed the testimony of Mercury for himself, will shine with the prudent management of the fighting, and in counsel. For, Mercury being fortunate, strong, cleansed of the infortunes, increases the success of victory, pillaging, spoils and arms, by his own acquired care and counsel—by all of which, the harming and trampling of the enemy is brought about.

§7.163: On war and its outcome—al-Khayyāt

Whenever therefore the leader of an army (or at least someone equally worried about an affair of this kind, and who is very pertinent to it) gave a question, we entrust the querent to the east and its lord, and the adversary and enemy to the seventh and its lord. But if there were an application and withdrawal of the Moon, the star from which the Moon is being separated bears the supports of the east, but the one to which she applies, [bears] the

---

[23] Reading *fortuniis* for *infortuniis*: it would be a good thing for the lord of the Ascendant to be in aversion to the infortunes.
[24] That is, "fall" (and omitting "or death").
[25] That is, "is in the best relationship with" them. For example, regarding them from a trine with reception would be more favorable or show more assent than being in a square without reception.

auxiliaries of the seventh. And in all of these things (namely the business of controversies and wars), the superior stars assume greater efficacy.

Therefore, we command that the two significators of each side be pursued more eagerly. The stronger of them, and the one placed in a more familiar way, will rejoice in the victory attained.

But that one of these significators which was in a pivot and received, really overcomes, unless perhaps it is in the entrance of scorching, or the lord of the eighth would apply to it.

But if the lord of the east happened to be of the superiors, however much it may be adverse and cadent,[26] even though the lord of the seventh may be lingering in a pivot, you must not judge about the querent's side as though without confidence, namely before you have discovered attentively to whom the lord of the seventh applies. For, it applying to a star lingering in a pivot, and [the lord of the seventh] being received, grants victory to his side, in accordance with the manner and strength of the one to which it applies. That same lord of the seventh even being strong, [but] applying to a cadent star and one corrupting it, he overcomes just so long as it was well placed. And so, as soon as it first withdraws from there, it will really be weaker, namely until the time that it becomes corrupted or scorched: for then he will really succumb. But if [the lord of the seventh] would apply to none in the sign in which it is, let it be transferred over to the next sign: once an ingress of this kind is discovered, one must note to what it applies in that place.

[Mars][27] appearing in a double-bodied sign, more often repeats the war; but from a turning [sign], it declares the fervor of wars. Which if he were in his fall, he will wage war in a more slack way, and one will have to judge about a short time in this manner. But even the power or weakness of Mars will give birth to a certain method of judgment.

Moreover, it will be permitted to attend to the army and support of each side, from the aspect of the stars to the significators, in terms of their position in their own proper houses. In fact, the lord of the second has the querent's army and allies, while the lord of the eighth grasps the supports of the contrary side. Therefore, a lucky one being found in the second, or regarding it or its lord, or if the lord of the second were placed in an optimal way, it denotes the trust and power of the querent's men and allies. And in this way for the lord of the eighth.

---

[26] According to Sahl in §7.160, this means being in aversion to the Ascendant.
[27] The rest of this section corresponds with Sahl in §7.167 below.

Whenever therefore the significators would regard each other from an opposition or tetragon, they portend the harshest war.

Moreover, the eleventh and its lord embraces the personal attendants and supports of the king. And so, a malevolent traversing in the eleventh, brings out the laziness of the royal army, nor does it portend that faithful people will be there, especially if [a malevolent][28] would traverse in the second from the Sun, or at least should [Mercury and] the Tail be staying with the Sun. For thus it indicates the greatest ruin for his side, from fraud.

§7.164: On entering into war—Dorotheus

Now, if anyone gave a question about advancing to war or entering into a dispute, [asking] how it would go for him, we put the east in charge of the querent or the one invading, [and] the seventh over the enemy. Which if there would be an application or withdrawal of the Moon, the star from which the Moon is being separated suggests the assistants of the east; but the one to which she applies, portends the supporters of the seventh. Moreover, the superior stars give greater effectiveness to this business than the inferior ones do.

But of the two significators, the one which appeared stronger will seize the victory.

Likewise, if either of the significators were of the superiors, holding onto a pivot and being received, it will overcome (unless perhaps it would be in the entrance to scorching, or apply to the lord of the eighth).

§7.165: On war and a marriage-union, and the rest of what is like that—Jirjis

Whenever it was asked about war or slaughter, let the intention of your mind be led back to Mars and his status, just as was stated above about Mercury with respect to papers.[29] But if a question is posed about a marriage-union and the rest of those things which pertain to women ([such as] pleasures and love), in the manner that Mercury does so for papers and legations,

---

[28] Adding this and "Mercury and" below, with Sahl. Hugo also adds "and with that same infortune," but that seems to be a mistake.
[29] Cf. §5.46 and 5.70 above. Jirjis simply means that Mars is a natural significator of war, as Mercury is for papers.

so Venus assumes a corresponding signification in an affair of this kind. Then, for peace and honesty, law, and humbleness, and dignities and religion, Jupiter should be consulted. But for fields, waters, and harvests, Saturn responds. Moreover for messengers and rumors, the duties of matrons and aristocratic ladies, one will have to have recourse to the Moon.

Also, for money the lord of the second assumes the whole affair. If someone made a question about brothers ([or] parents and children, sickness and marriage, and the rest of the things which are arranged throughout the twelve domiciles of the heavenly circle), one will have to make a partnership with the lord of that house and the rest of the stars which follow the nature of the interrogation.

Even for the hour [of the outcome] in all matters of this kind, one will have to do no otherwise than with papers: namely, a well-founded method demands now hours, now days, here months, there years, according to the nature of the signs.

§7.166: On a future war between two cities or peoples—Aristotle

With an inquiry of this kind being proposed, we give the east to the querent and what belongs to his side, but the seventh is ascribed to the adversaries and enemies. Therefore, benevolents traversing in the east, with the wicked ones established in the seventh, [and] the lord of the seventh being arranged badly while the lord of the east bears itself well—the victory is given to the querent's side. If this whole situation bore itself in the converse way, the enemies really triumph over the querent's side.

Now, if the eastern lord and equally that of the seventh would be staying in their own sovereignties, while however the lucky ones would be traversing in the east or tenth or from the tenth itself to the east, [and], I say, with the malevolents in the seventh or from the seventh toward the ninth or in the ninth itself, or under the earth, the querent's side will rejoice in the victory [that is] sought. With these bearing themselves to the contrary, namely so that instead the lucky ones would hold onto the places of the malevolents, but the wicked ones would do so to those of the lucky ones, so that they would even reign above, with the good ones being discovered under the earth (and badly so), the triumph will be given to the side of the adversaries.

Which if both (namely the lords of the east and of the seventh equally) would be burned up, or in their own fall, or they would become retrograde, if the benevolents would support the eastern side but the wicked ones would follow the side of the adversaries, each side will be afflicted with the greatest trouble, but the querent in a more mild way.

However, so that I might speak openly, it is good to make note of all helps or detriment belonging to each side, and whom they seem to turn against, so that you could undoubtedly draw out to which side it happens, and to whom it does so better. Moreover, with the benevolents and unlucky ones being equal to each [side] in power, the triumph will be given to neither side.

How long it should last, you will have thusly: the east being a firm [sign] portends it will last a long time; if a turning [sign], not very much; if double-bodied, it is between both.

In addition, if the eastern lord regarded the lord of the seventh by a prosperous figure, they will be called back to concord after the war. A perverse regard involves all things in disagreement and discord. With every regard being denied, it is neither the one nor the other.

§7.167: On the quality and manner of the war—Sahl[30]

But so that you would be able to discover the manner and quality of the war, you will have it thusly. Mars himself and his place from the east, and the star regarding [it],[31] settle the whole thing. Also, the quantity of the slaughter could be discovered from the Moon and her place. Now, each army follows the proper quality of its significator. Therefore, the star from which Mars is being separated, takes the role of the querent or the one attacking; likewise the one to which the application of Mars happens, manages the signification of the other side, both of the army and the combat.

And so, that significator which happened to be found in a turning [sign], portends that its side is weaker and is going to submit; in a double-bodied one, it is stronger; in a firm one, it is wholly going to stand firm.

But you will judge the significator which lingers in its own sovereignty as being stronger than one in [its own] domicile. The domicile is stronger than the triplicity, while the triplicity comes before the bound. Moreover the bound is preferred to the face of decan. That one should be judged stronger whose lord will support it by its own aspect, because it especially gathers to-

---

[30] Cf. *On Quest.* §7.25.
[31] Neither John nor Hugo explicitly say whether this star is regarding the east or Mars.

gether the forces and power of its side. It will be weakness and the most extreme detriment while it would linger in its fall or in an inimical place,[32] traversing outside of the regard of its own lord. However, that one of the significators which possesses its own sovereignty, portends that the one whom it signifies is a king; traversing in its own house, one born of royal stock; in the triplicity, it prefigures one of the lineage of magnates and princes; and it will be appropriate to go down [in rank] in what follows, in this way. Nevertheless the face is a lower dignity than the bound.

On the other hand, [for] either of the significators, whenever its own lord would regard it, it designates he is bold and courageous, and is a sign of the greatest vigor.[33] With the regard being denied, it portends contrariwise. But should either of the significators come to be retrograde or adverse[34] or corrupted, he is asserted as being unjust, [and] to depend on lies. Moreover, being direct and lucky on the other hand, he struggles in a just and appropriate cause.

Finally, it is good to investigate the status of Mars with the greatest effort. For, traversing in his own sovereignty (or at least that of the Sun), he will rejoice in the greatest and renowned devastation of those fighting. But if he would thus hold onto the tenth, it will spread his reputation about the slaughter we stated, to the outer parts and up to the ends of the earth. Being placed thusly in the east, he will not prevail to that extent. But in the west, it prolongs the military situation and events. Outside the pivots but while he walks through firm signs, it will be less harsh; in a double-bodied one on the other hand, he will jump eagerly at the chance for war; in a convertible one, it stirs the combatants up with warlike fervor, and incites them to struggle. But if he would be lingering in his own fall, [the sides] struggle more lightly. And beyond that, the greatness and timing of the war could be discovered from the position and status of Mars, in this manner.

And so, whenever Mars regarded the Moon from the seventh (she being found in the east), or contrariwise should Mars do so to her from the east (she being placed in the seventh), it contrives the destruction of the one attacking.

Moreover, the regard and reception of the significators more fully resolves the [question of] resources and the assistants and supplies. For, the querent's

---

[32] I take this to mean the sign of its detriment, but it might be something else, such as being peregrine in a sign belonging to a planet of the opposite sect.
[33] John's Sahl adds that an aspect to its lord implies loyalty to the king.
[34] But this might also be *aversus*, "in aversion" to the Ascendant.

army will be sought from the second and its lord, the eighth and its lord have the hands and battle of the enemy side. In the eleventh you will see the allies of the king,[35] but in the fifth you will seek the city or province. Therefore, with benevolents being found in the second, or regarding it, or at least with the lord of the second being well established, it is a sign that the hand of the one engaging is robust and steady; no other judgment emanates from the eighth and its lord for the contrary side. And so, if benevolents would hold onto the second (as was stated above), and it was a two-parted [sign], or at least a fertile[36] one, [or convertible],[37] it declares the multiple resources of that side. For this, even, should that lucky [planet] which happened to be found in the second, [be eastern],[38] or the lord of the second would appear eastern and direct, it indicates the faithfulness and steadiness of his side; its retrogradation suggests flight. Which if malevolents would possess the eleventh, or its lord retrograde, it indicates one should trust in the king's[39] resources less, and especially if an unlucky one would possess the second from the place of the Sun, or if Mercury and the Tail would equally be conjoined to the Sun.[40]

§7.168: On the misfortune and success of wars—'Umar

If this came into question, the lord of the second, but even those lords who are in charge of its triplicity, watch over the side of the combatant;[41] moreover we entrust the enemy power to the eighth and the lords of its triplicity. And so, the lord of the second being fortunate or lucky, or any fortunate one traversing in the second, or at least they[42] being found strong, prefers the side of the one attacking.[43] The eighth and the ones who are in charge of its triplicity demand no other judgment with respect to the enemy hand.

---

[35] Following John's Sahl, as Hugo has the redundant "In the eighth you will see foreign resources."
[36] Reading with John's Sahl for Hugo's "eloquent."
[37] Adding from John's Sahl.
[38] Adding from John's Sahl.
[39] Reading with John's Sahl for Hugo's "foreign."
[40] John's Sahl has a malevolent planet *or Mercury* in the *eighth* from the Sun, and the Tail alone with the Sun.
[41] *Congressoris.* That is, the querent.
[42] This must refer to the triplicity lords of the second.
[43] The querent.

§7.169: On the vigor or laziness of those fighting—'Umar

Now, the significators of those fighting must especially be noted, or if [there is][44] one which bears supports from any direction. They being eastern and in some one of their own dignities, strong, favor with boldness and commend [their] strength.[45] But they bearing themselves otherwise, neither the eagerness for fighting nor faith is designated, but rather fraud and surrender.

But[46] the testimonies of the Lot of Fortune and of the warlike Lot should come into view. And so, the Lot of war,[47] being invested by Mars, means the heat of the fight. Its lord being eastern and strong, greatly increases the warlike uproar. Moreover, the Lot of Fortune falling on the east, intends to prefer the sharpness of the initiator of the conflict.[48] But in the seventh, it strengthens the enemy hand. It professes no other opinion with respect to the lord of each.

This even comes to be noted: whether it[49] would possess the quarter between the east and the Midheaven, or the opposite one (namely, between the fourth and the seventh), [or] rather it would be staying from the Midheaven to the seventh or in the opposite (namely between the east and the fourth): for these two,[50] I say, fall to the enemy portion. No less, too, [if] the supports of each of these would appear to hold onto each quarter.

Likewise,[51] the Lot of war is even taken by night and day from the degree of Mars to the Lunar degree. Then, with the degrees of the east being added, and the beginning having been led down from the east, where the number will be ended, this Lot could be discovered in that same place. Then, however, one will have to diligently observe in what place it and its lord would be. For if it would hold onto an optimal place of the initiator of the conflict, it promises the victory to him. It being established in a safe place of the de-

---

[44] Omitting *maius*, which is probably a misprint but does not (I think) change the meaning.
[45] Or, "men" (*vires*).
[46] This paragraph is similar to one in al-Rijāl I.42.2.
[47] See below.
[48] *Congressoris*. Or rather, the querent: 'Umar assumes that the querent is initiating the hostilities.
[49] This might still refer to the Lot of Fortune in the previous paragraph.
[50] That is, the so-called western quarters just mentioned. The other two, so-called eastern quarters, are favorable to the querent.
[51] For this paragraph, cf. al-Rijāl II.42.1. This Lot is probably the Lot of kingdom and authority (*ITA* VI.2.38), which is however reversed by night.

fender, it blesses that one with the desired victory. After that, it falling between each, it unites each battle line with the peace that is established.

Moreover,[52] a certain Lot whose name is "concord," must be consulted in this place. And so, we prescribe that you take it up from the Lunar degree to the Mercurial one. Then, an addition of the degrees of the east being made, and beginning from the east, it suggests that at its ending, is the place of the Lot written above.

§7.170: On those who have left the king and become rebels against him—'Umar

However, once anyone who has left [the king], and their rebellion, has been discovered, if someone gave a question about their status, we put the east in charge of those who have left, but [also] the star from which the Moon is separated; and [we put] the Midheaven, [and] no less too the Sun and the one to which the Moon applies, [in charge of] the king.

And so, with these being established, one will have to judge in the same way as above, with respect to the east and the seventh.[53]

But the Midheaven manifestly reveals what would happen to the royal side, and the fourth [what would happen] to [the king's] adversary. The eleventh comprehends the royal supporters, but the second from the east the assistants of the enemies.

§7.171: Again on war—al-Kindī

§160. Again, with a question being made about war, should the lord of the Midheaven or the Moon be seen to rejoice in (or rather support) the lord of the Ascendant or of the west, or the star from which the Moon recedes, or the one with whom her application comes to be (I say, whichever one of these two [it was])—without a doubt it enriches [that side] with the triumph of victory. Even the friendly support of Mars means the same thing. But the equality of each [significator] introduces the hope of peace, if their lords en-

---

[52] For this paragraph, cf. al-Rijāl II.43. This is the same as the Lot of friends according to al-Andarzaghar (*ITA* VI.2.45), and the Lot of peace between among soldiers (*ITA* VI.3.3). This should probably be reversed by night, as al-Qabīsī says that al-Andarzaghar reversed his Lot of friends.

[53] I am not sure exactly what passage in 'Umar this refers to.

joy the regard (and a friendly one) of the other.⁵⁴ But the degree of the mutual application makes manifest the time of making the peace firm (likewise the Moon assumes [the role of] the mediator between the two).

§161. Moreover, if Mars could corrupt either of [these places] or their lord, particularly from an adverse aspect, it threatens death in the present war, but [the degrees of] their mutual application asserts the terminal point of death. Again, Mars in a pivot indicates a public death in the war. Again, Mars corrupting either one from the eighth, frequently teaches he is going to die while sleeping at night.⁵⁵ But if the corruption by Mars were made from the second, it introduces the death of the masters [of the war] and their co-helpers, with fraudulence—especially with Mars [not]⁵⁶ holding onto a share or possession⁵⁷ in the second.

§162. Also, the figure of the sign which Mars possesses, describes the murderer. But with Mars corrupting [a significator] from the sixth, provided that the sign represents a wild animal, he incurs death from a beast of that kind. But corruption made from the twelfth threatens destruction after difficulties from enemies. Again, [corruption] from [the four] signs which naturally make a regard to others ([that is], from the pivots), [he will in no way escape the danger of destruction].⁵⁸ Should the corruption by Mars proceed from the ninth, it testifies he achieves death by a public judgment of the law, or some journey or foreign travel, sometimes a hunt or some plundering⁵⁹ or what is like these.

§163. But if [Mars were] in the ninth [and] the house of the Moon would be exhibited [there], law and social custom give a capital sentence. And so, the same house being that of Venus, the law indicates death because of [his] libido or joking, and sexual immorality carried out with women. If the same [place] would be found to be a house of Mars, it confers destruction on some journey. If however [it is] a house of Saturn, he incurs death by fraud and flattery. Again, if the house of Mercury comes to be in the same [place], he will lay down [and die] because of words and books.

---

⁵⁴ For more on peacemaking, see §7.191 below.
⁵⁵ Robert adds: "and the time of it will be perceived from the quantity of the degrees of their conjunction."
⁵⁶ Adding with Robert.
⁵⁷ *Faciem* (drawing on Niermeyer's medieval usage). That is, if Mars is peregrine in the second.
⁵⁸ Adding missing parts from Robert.
⁵⁹ *Depraedatione*. Or, "devastation." The sense is of marauding soldiers traveling from place to place.

§164a. Mars corrupting [a significator] from the fifth: he meets death because of children [or a change of affection].[60] Also, from the eleventh[61] it signifies that he dies from the king's underofficials or his own friends, [and this apart from what was hoped for].[62] Again, the misfortune of Mars being recognized from the third, brothers or some journey or a common judgment of the law introduces the cause of death.

§164b.[63] Even the lord of the seventh (with the attacking stated above), being unlucky in all things which belong to its signification, gets a similar judgment.

§164c. The retrogradation of either one of them teaches that the man whom that significator indicates, is going to be conquered.

§7.172: Whether the combatant would meet death—al-Kindī

§403. Likewise, the Moon comes to be noted to the greatest extent. For, she being made fortunate, is very advantageous to the one who commences the beginnings of the war. But made unfortunate, she presents trouble to him and the harm of the whole affair. In fact, corrupted by Mars and from a pivot, she threatens death and blood, especially if Mars were harmful to the Moon and the Ascendant [at the same time], or he himself were the lord of the eighth or of the eighth[64] from the Moon.

§404. With these bearing themselves thusly, and the lord of the Ascendant being direct, it prepares a death to be feared when hostilities are initiated. Also, being retrograde kills [him while] fleeing. But it warns that he must beware of death in his own bed and tent, [if] the same [planet is] in one of the wells[65] or in an obscure place or in a nocturnal sign. But in a diurnal sign and in a shining degree,[66] it threatens death in the day and among his own battle lines (or not far from them). But if some unfortunate and pivotal

---

[60] Reading with Robert for Hugo's "or his own will." Hugo repeats *propriae voluntatis* in the eleventh house as well, which leads me to believe there has been a manuscript error.
[61] Reading with Robert for *decimo*.
[62] Again, reading with Robert for Hugo's "an attack of his own will, [or] because of some expected thing."
[63] So far, al-Kindī has described Mars's effect on the lord of the Ascendant (namely, the querent); here he simply means that the same rules apply to harming the lord of the seventh (the opponent).
[64] Reading *octavi* for *octavus*.
[65] That is, one of the welled degrees (see the next sentence). See *ITA* VII.9.1.
[66] See *ITA* VII.7.

[planet] would corrupt it, and it was Saturn, and he in a moist sign, it tramples him with the feet of horses, and humbles him, often in a river or the mud of a river, or it kills him at the seashore and what is like these in terms of causes.

§405. Moreover, an eclipsed Moon introduces an opening in the earth, or the collapse of a bridge, or the falling of some ruin, into the cause of death.[67]

§406a. Likewise, the lord of the fourth or of the Moon being corrupted by Mars and from a pivot, pollutes the end of the affair with death, once victory is had. Moreover, the lord of the end[68] being made fortunate by another, conveys health and prosperity after the business of war is accomplished.

§7.173: On peace and concord—Sahl[69]

If a question would arise with these [planets] bearing themselves thusly, one must observe this order: for the significator of peace or concord[70] holding onto its own house, shows someone among them who is concerned to convey peace. Which if it were foreign,[71] a foreign person is brought in to establish peace. And so, Saturn prefigures an old man, but Jupiter shows a magnate, but Mars has the judgment of some powerful man, fraudulent and a liar, the Sun brings in a prince, Venus a prince and gentle person, Mercury

---

[67] I omit here a garbled sentence which only appears in Hugo's version of *Forty Chapters*, and which appears differently here in *Judges*. It refers to the Moon being free of the infortunes and lucky, and being either of the sect of the significator of the one who is attacked, or perhaps if it is simply at night. I cannot easily determine what Hugo means. In *Forty Chapters* it reads: *Luna quoque ab infortuniis libera et felix, in adaulahu ipsius quem agressus iste est videlicet in fine regiae prosperitatis, illud autem audaulahu solatio forte iuxta terram victoria privat.* But *Judges* reads (underlining indicates differences): *Luna quoque ab infortuniis libera et felix, in admunitione ipsius quam iste aggressus scilicet in fine regiae prosperitatis. Illud autem adaulahu solatio et adminiculo forte iusta terram victoriam privat.* The word *adaulahu* is probably the Ar. *al-dawlahu*, "its shift" (i.e., "sect"), but *Judges* reads the first instance of this as *admunitione* (prob. *munitione*) or "fortification," which is Hugo's normal synonym for the condition of ₁*alb* or "sect." The passage seems to be saying that if the Moon is unharmed and is somehow more favorable to the one attacked, then it deprives the attacker of victory.

[68] That is, the lord of the fourth.

[69] Cf. *On Quest.* §7.25. John's Sahl is more complete on this topic, adding several sentences at the end to explain more about Mercury: "And look, for betrayal and cunning, to Mercury. If he were impeded under the rays from both planets [which signify the combatants], there will be betrayal and cunning toward them (namely, from each one of them toward his associate). And if Mars were with Mercury, the cunning and betrayal will appear, for it will be publicized and will not be able to be concealed."

[70] This would be a planet transferring or collecting the light of the two main significators.

[71] That is, peregrine.

some learned person and one given to commerce, the Moon brings together true messengers between them.

Moreover, with fear or suspicion about the peace being had, Mercury will have to be consulted. For if he happened to be equally corrupted and scorched, each one will be judged suspect by the other. His being adjoined with Mars has the judgment of firm and manifest fraud, and future betrayal.

But meanwhile, if the Moon would bear testimony to Saturn and the east,[72] it hastens the betrayal. If that testimony of the Moon would be with [Jupiter or][73] Venus, it will wholly remove the fraud. But if Mercury would be regarding the east and the Moon, he mixes fraud in and supplies trickery.

§7.174: On the end of the war—'Umar

And so, the lord of the east and equally that of the seventh, even Mars himself, moreover the star from which the Moon is being separated, and the one to which she applies, or the one to which Mars's application is, or from which he is being separated, wholly resolve the end of the war. For, the weakness of these three significators[74] (or at least the majority of them), impose an end to the war. However, they possessing a place of their own strength, contrives the steadiness of the fight, namely up until the harm of corruption stains them jointly.[75] Therefore, the last hour and end of the war is determined thusly.

§7.175: On the end of the war—al-Kindī

§165. Also, the status of the fourth and its lord, even the lord of the Moon, will not be silent about the end of the affair. For, they being made fortunate, and forceful, grant a glorious end for the victor. Moreover, their unluckiness and lack of forcefulness [signifies] the contrary. Also, the corruption of the fourth, even a corrupted lord of the Moon (namely so that they would be cadent), signify he is deposed from [his] honor. Moreover, being

---

[72] Reading *orienti* for Hugo's *orientali*, following John.
[73] Adding with John's Sahl.
[74] These must refer to the situations of (1) the lords of the first and seventh, (2) the Moon and her separations and applications, and (3) Mars and his separations and applications.
[75] Probably, when they reach their own falls or detriments by transit.

corrupted by an assembly,[76] they promise death or deposing, [or] poverty, and because of this he will flee from his fatherland.

§166. But corruption made from another place leads harm into the body according to the nature and place and [bodily] part belonging to the one making it unfortunate. Also, the lord of the fourth and of the Moon being affected by these evils, leads these evils into the soul, while they present the fear and anxiety of these things. Likewise, the forcefulness[77] of the lord[78] of the fourth [and] even [the lord] of the Moon being strong (namely that they would be eastern), declares his promotion and long deliberation.

§167. Likewise, Saturn as the lord of the fourth, being eastern, robust and strong, even the lord of the sign which the Moon is holding onto being likewise eastern and strong, promises to render long premeditation, slaves, steadiness, tolerance, the building of cities, the inhabitants of wilderness.[79] Also, Jupiter signifies his justice, piety, firm counsel, introducing respectable ceremonies, [and] enriching the people when he survives. Likewise, Mars retaining the power of the fourth and the rulership of the Moon,[80] [indicates] he is bold, a leading person in society, an effecter of affairs. Also, the strength of Mars conveys fear [of him] to his enemies, and their flight.

§168. Again, the Sun being in full control (and not Mars), establishes many people subject to him, glory, power, being feared, a prominent position, and steadiness of [his] command. However, Venus obtaining this place instead of the Sun ([and] being strengthened by the aforesaid supports) shows that he reigns over the benevolence of strong people,[81] dramatic roles,[82] gifts, drinking parties. Moreover, should Mercury be considered strong (instead of Venus) as was stated before, it makes him excel over [legal] cases, studies, ingenuity, handling tools,[83] writings, and better yet incentives for learning.

---

[76] Probably with a malefic planet (especially Mars), but possibly with the Sun, too.
[77] *Valetudo*, which has connotations of being robust and healthy.
[78] Reading *domini* with Robert's meaning, for *dominus*.
[79] Or, "deserts."
[80] This probably should not read that he rules both, but that he rules the fourth and *in addition* that the lord of the Moon is strong.
[81] *Fortium benevolentiam*.
[82] Reading *operibus ludicris* with Robert for Hugo's *officia* ("jobs, duties").
[83] *Exercitium* (following a medieval meaning). But this could also refer to various spiritual or intellectual exercises and disciplines. Both tools and these other things are equally Mercurial.

§169. Also, the [if] the Moon assumes this [role] instead of Mercury, she manages power, legations, the discourse[84] of messengers, the transmitting of services,[85] even the gratitude of the whole people.

§170. Also, the weakness of one [or another] of these lessens the causes of the aforesaid as well as the quantity of the matter.

§171. Again, the quickness of the one who corrupts the fourth and the lord of the Moon, asserts that [the end] is near, but [its] slowness that it will happen late. But if it is direct, it means [the directness] of it or of the matter; but retrograde, it signifies disagreement in matters and that one of them is in conflict.[86] Also, if fortunate ones would perform in the role of the unfortunate ones, you will judge the promised things in terms of luckiness just as was stated above about the unfortunate ones.

§172. If however it happens otherwise than as was said above with respect to what the fortunate or unfortunate ones carry out, and the strength [of the significators] is diminished—namely so that it would sometimes happen to be more, sometimes less—in whatever way these [planets'] difference bore itself, remember to judge it in the way their admixture (shown above) has taught.

§7.176: Who, and of what type, is the mediator—al-Kindī

§414. Moreover let the lord of the Ascendant and of the seventh be noted, as to whether they are holding onto the same sign, and if any star would be situated between each. For, that middle one being lucky describes a man who labors to bring about peace on both sides. It being situated in a place of its own authority, indicates a native and noted man.[87]

---

[84] Or perhaps, "traversals."
[85] Or perhaps, "gifts, duties, benefits" (*munerum*). Robert reads, "generosity."
[86] This might also mean "diversity in the things, and that one of them is conflicted" (*rerum diversitatem et alternum earum conflictum*).
[87] Robert specifies: in its own exaltation or domicile or triplicity, a man native to the area; but in its bound or face, a well-known one.

[The nature and status of the mediator]

§415a. Also, the nature of the star by which [this mediator] is signified (namely, its advancement or retreat,[88] moreover whether [it is] eastern or the contrary, [direct or retrograde, well-protected[89] or the contrary]) will declare his nature and status, lineage and fortune. For, it being in a peregrine and an exile place, indicates he is foreign-born. The same [star] being an exile and foreign [only] from its own house and sovereignty, but [still being] in its own triplicity, bound or face,[90] he is known by all even though he is foreign.

[Whom the mediator favors more]

§415b-16. Moreover, you will note what side he seems more likely to favor. Therefore, what sign [the star] resembles with a greater commonality of property (namely, the Ascendant or the seventh), he commends that one's side in a more familiar way, [and] strives to pursue those affairs with greater feeling.

[The mediator's style and position]

§417a. Moreover, a fortunate star as the mediator [between] the aforesaid [two stars] lays bare his status, nature, and moral qualities. Which if it were Jupiter, it signifies a minister of the law, honest, respectable, [and] venerable. Venus brings forth one liberal, proper, polite,[91] elegant in [his] bearing.

§417b-418. Moreover, it seems the nature of the fortune and its lord[92] must be combined, just as we have already taught above. For, Saturn as the lord of that fortunate one, indicates an old man, and that type. Jupiter: one experienced in law, or a minister, [or] generous judge. Mars: a bold man, a prince of wars. However, the Sun shows he is from a royal house and family,

---

[88] That is, whether it is in a pivot or succeedent (advancement) or a cadent (retreat): see *ITA* III.4.
[89] That is, in its own *ḥalb*.
[90] Reading with al-Rijāl. Hugo has the star being peregrine from domicile, exaltation and triplicity, but in either its own bound or face. Robert omits this part.
[91] Or, "clean" (*mundum*).
[92] In this paragraph, Hugo mixes in the mediating planet's domicile lord; but al-Rijāl mixes in any planet *aspecting* the mediator. I tend to think al-Rijāl is right, but since astrologers do also mix the qualities of planets with those of their domicile lords, I cannot be sure which represents the true al-Kindī.

or of royal blood. Venus: pleasant and delightful. Likewise Mercury introduces [someone] skilled, a master of succinctness, modest, a writer or most wealthy businessman. Also, the Moon involves a messenger and underofficial of some legation, and what is like these.

§419. Moreover,[93] you note which one of its houses (which it obtains in the circle) it would be looking at with a familiar aspect. For, combining the nature of that house[94] with the proper quality of that star will be useful.

§420. [Now] it remains to relate such a judgment of this matter. Which if the mediator happened to be the lord of the Ascendant,[95] it denotes a relative or greatest and bosom friend of the one who has claimed the beginnings of the war. Which if the mediator of the aforesaid appeared as the lord of the second, [it indicates] an assistant. The lord of the third, a brother and this type. But the lord of the fourth, from the paternal stock or that of forefathers.

§421. It being even the lord of the fifth, [indicates] a child or one whom he has adopted in place of a child. But the lord of the sixth portends followers of lower rank. Moreover, the lord of the seventh claims he is of the stock of the adversaries. The lord of the eighth, a supporter of the side turned against him. Also, [the lord] of the ninth brings forth a minister of the law or a partner in his own travel and the roads,[96] into view. But the lord of the tenth establishes a friend of the kingdom and of his own profession. Finally, the twelfth testifies to an enemy.

§422. Conversely, with the mediating star being corrupted, it indicates a bad man who personally taints and corrupts each side with the poison of unfaithfulness and poison of fraud, and leads [them] into dissension. Which if this were Saturn, it claims he will be an old man of long-lasting deliberation, a cautious man, fraudulent. Mars, a plunderer, eager for blood just as the nature of Mars and his lord seems to demand. It even seems that [the nature of the planet which the mediator][97] consoled by a friendly aspect

---

[93] In this paragraph I follow al-Rijāl's reading. Hugo seems to be confused as to which planet should be aspecting whose domiciles. We should be identifying that domicile of the *mediating* planet, which it aspects best and most strongly.
[94] Reading with al-Rijāl for Hugo's "its lord."
[95] And if it aspected the Ascendant better and more strongly, etc., than its other domicile.
[96] This seems only to pertain to travel, but it is intriguing to think that "path" could be meant in terms of a spiritual paths, such as belonging to the same religion or sect.
[97] Reading with al-Rijāl. Hugo has us mix it with the nature of the lord of the domicile which it had aspected; but by definition, this would be the same planet.

(namely in the square arrangement of the signs) should be considered in the same way.

§7.177: On the origin of the war and which side is more just—Sahl[98]

Moreover, the cause and origin of the war is sought from the Moon and Mars together. Their separation from benevolents suggests the side of the querent is just, but if they would be separating from malevolents they prove it is unjust. But a corresponding judgment should be given about the contrary side, just as it bears an application with the fortunate ones or the infortunes.

Moreover, the traversal of Mars in the east testifies that the war is happening because of the means of subsistence.[99] If he would traverse in the second, wealth and resources are allotted the origin of the war. In the third, some sect of laws will be the occasion of the fight. In the fourth, an estate or inheritance. Likewise resources in the fifth, but so that he joins with enemies who are his kin, and it signifies the hope of concord; it even proposes cities or the class of women as the cause of the war. In the sixth, [because of a weak thing, and there will be much killing or wounding.][100] In the seventh, ancient enmities and without the hope of gain. In the eighth, an old memory of blood. Here however, if the Moon would regard the lord of the tenth, a cause pertaining to a kingdom, and the powerful increase of litigation, and of slaughter on each side. Mars in the ninth, a diversity of laws. Moreover, the Moon applying in the tenth to Mars (from a tetragon or the opposition or by assembly), testifies that some kingdom comes to be the cause of the war. Mars in the eleventh, the riling up of friends and royal patronage. In the twelfth, old enmities.[101]

---

[98] Cf. *On Quest.* §7.25-26. Much of this material is distributed throughout al-Rijāl II.42.2-43.
[99] Or perhaps, "because of their ways of life" (*victualium*).
[100] I have rewritten the houses between the sixth and eighth in accordance with John's Sahl, since Hugo omits the eighth and it seems reasonable that there was merely a scribal error. Hugo himself reads: "In the sixth, ancient enmities and without the hope of gain. In the seventh, an old memory of blood. *[Eighth missing.]* Here however, if the Moon would regard the lord of the tenth, a cause pertaining to a kingdom, and the powerful increase of litigation, and of slaughter on each side."
[101] John's Sahl now inserts a comment that Hugo may have omitted because it is somewhat contradictory: "But there will not be a war, because Mars in the twelfth does not signify war, since he is cadent from the angle." But the point of the paragraph is to show

The greatness or multitude of the army could be discovered thusly: namely so that the number of signs from the place of the Moon to the place of Mercury would be collected. Which if it were equal, it multiplies the army; but being odd, it diminishes it and is a sign of scarcity.[102]

Finally, in all the events or wars, I instruct that these things be observed universally and with an alert mind, all of which are comprised briefly [here] in a certain summary [form]. Therefore, the east is put in chart of the one engaging, from which the cause of his side is easily understood. Likewise from the second is usually discovered what manner there is between what is advantageous and disadvantageous.[103] From the third we gather the kind of arms and what they need so that victory can be gotten. From the fourth we discern the place of the war, whether or not it is desert or cultivated, isolated or populous, mountainous or flat, wooded, near water or the sea. But the fifth lays bare the spirit of the fighter's army—its vigor, I say, or laziness. The sixth declares what will be ridden (namely, beasts of burden and the kind of beasts). The seventh brings in the enemies and adversaries, but it even engineers the instruments of war and cleverness and the kinds of tortures. The eighth signifies the slaughter of the conquered side, and its manner. But the ninth has the [work of scouts and the knowledge of the enemy's affairs],[104] and the cunning of the fighters. The tenth comprehends the tenor and advice of any prince. The eleventh comprehends the power and minds of the allies [of the king or the chief commander], and the industry of going to war. The twelfth designates the outcomes of those who are maintaining and guarding the camps, whether they would be besieged or would flee.

Therefore, in all of these it will be wholly good to consult these twelve places in order, and the position of their lords, and the figure of the aspect, and the occupations of the places (both of the benevolents and the malevolents), and one will have to respond through every individual one, according to the manner and quality of the heavenly state. For should benevolents possess or regard any place, or should they bless its lord in any way, they are believed to support that place and its lord according to [their] strengths and

---

why there *is* war. Perhaps Sahl means that the war will not be very strong or will end quickly.

[102] This was probably a Pythagorean notion: even numbers are related to the principle of the Indefinite and the Limitless, whereas odd numbers are related to the principle of Limit.

[103] Hugo means this in a financial sense (*utile vel inutile*), as does John's Sahl.

[104] Reading with John's Sahl for Hugo's odd "beginnings" (*initia*).

power, but even [their] position and state. The infortunes, however, respond in a contrary way. For the one they either occupy or regard by an adverse figure (or should they corrupt its lord), they are inimical and speak against it according to [their] state and position.

§7.178: To whom victory would be given—al-Kindī

§400.[105] That one of the warriors who commences the beginnings of the war by night, being stronger than the one who went out by day, is crowned with the victory. And we call the "beginnings of the war" the hour at which he heads to the path against the enemy (once all things are arranged, [there is] a call with the clamor of trumpet and clarion, [and] the battle lines are arranged). For even though the lord of the seventh and the Ascendant may appear to be equal in virtue, the one who goes out by day is conquered and confused; but he who [does so] by night is confirmed as the victor.

§401. Moreover, the overall equality of the lord of the seventh and of the seventh [itself], generates peace. Likewise, whenever the lord of the seventh would be deprived of the regard of the Ascendant and its lord at the beginning of a war, and Mars in a cadent [place] and being estranged from them, it means the delay of the war, scatters the battle lines, sometimes produces peace, [and] reduces all things to quiet. But if they did regard each other, especially from the pivots, [and] likewise Mars in a pivot, and the signs are convertible, it portends a public and immoderate war, [and] declares that aristocrats and the most famous people, and those of a widely-known name, and those eager for a reputation, will get involved.

§7.179: Whom would the people of note would favor—al-Kindī

§402. Again, the lord of the second and of the eighth will declare what side [such people] will follow. For the one of them which was in a pivot or its own house or sovereignty, or being eastern from the Sun, or in a convertible and pivotal sign (or at least its lord), likewise the one of them whom the

---

[105] This paragraph does not seem right to me, and I think it is better read as with Sahl's *On Elect.* §90a and Bonatti's Tr. 7, 7th House Ch. 3 (p. 762): the general who was *born* at night, and in whose nativity Mars played an [important] role, will win—otherwise, every attack at night would be favorable, all other things being equal.

Sun and Moon support by an appropriate aspect, that one will keep for himself the company of the aforesaid powerful people, the final triumph and glory of the war, [and] the parade and advantage.

§7.180: At what hour the combatant or adversary would begin to fight, or when they ought to flee—al-Kindī

§406b-407a.[106] Furthermore, I warn the king (namely him against whom the other has raised up) to the utmost degree, lest he should ever go into war with the Moon made fortunate. But one must observe that with her being corrupted, he should not flee. But he who begins the encounters of war with the Moon being corrupted, should refuse the war. But he should advance and be about to fight with the Moon being safe, especially with the lord of the Ascendant [also being made fortunate and in the Ascendant].[107] Moreover, with the Ascendant and its lord being corrupted with the Moon, he should never presume to attack.

§407b. Moreover, [if] the first of the aggressors is about to attack in the parts of the east, he should establish the Moon in the west; but going towards the west, he should establish the Moon in the east; but if in the south, in the north; which if [he advances toward] the north, let him consider her in the south.[108]

§408. Likewise, Mars in the eastern part of the circle (namely from the tenth degree of Taurus to the tenth degree of Leo, and from the tenth of Scorpio to the tenth of Aquarius) warns him that it should be fought[109] in the direction of the east. In the western part (namely from the tenth of Leo to the tenth of Scorpio, likewise from the tenth of Aquarius to the tenth degree of Taurus), it encourages him to fight in the parts of the west.

---

[106] Remember that the Moon's condition belongs to the initiator of the conflict. So, if the rebel has initiated hostilities under a good Moon, it is unwise for the king to respond; but if under a bad Moon, it is right for the king to respond, since the Moon indicates a less effective attack by the rebel. On the other hand, if the king were initiating hostilities, he should do so under a good Moon, but it would be unwise for the rebel to respond, etc.
[107] Adding with al-Rijāl; omitted by Robert.
[108] In other words, the Moon should be at his back.
[109] According to al-Rijāl, the "rebel begins the battle" in that direction (Burnett 1993, p. 91).

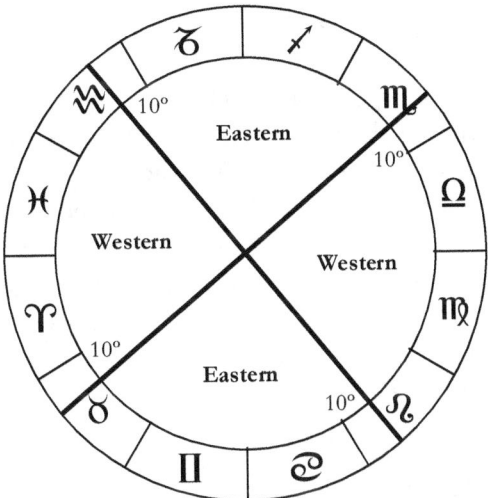

Figure 56: Al-Kindī's directions for fighting

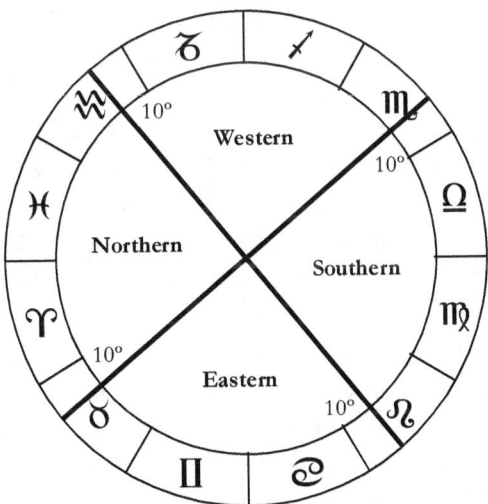

Figure 57: Al-Rijāl's proposed correction to al-Kindī[110]

---

[110] Al-Rijāl (II.2) points out that al-Kindī's division of the zodiac would only allow the armies to advance from the east or west, rather than from all directions. So, he proposes a different division, apparently also based on the four royal stars and the seasons: the Sun is in Taurus at the middle of spring, which is associated with the east, etc., and the constellation Taurus (with which the tropical sign Taurus used to correspond) contains the royal star Aldebaran; likewise for the other seasons and royal stars: summer and Regulus (Leo), autumn and Antares (Scorpio), and winter and Fomalhaut (really in Piscis Australis, but close to Aquarius). In II.43, al-Rijāl attributes this view to Hermes.

[*Election: The* bust][111]

§409. Moreover, let the general or prince of each cohort take care to observe with the greatest diligence not to enter into his own affairs in the wicked and bad hours which they call "scorched": namely, from that [hour] in which the Moon enters the assembly of the Sun on the same spot, until the completion of twelve hours. The principal affairs of the significators and princes of kings wholly abhor the malice and perversity of these hours.

§410. But the subsequent twelve [scorched] hours should also not be put out of one's memory: the beginning of which is drawn out once eighty-four have been crossed after the assembly of the Sun and Moon on the same spot. But the end [of this second group of hours] accompanies ninety-six hours after the assembly: once the eighty-four have been drawn out in sequence, the following twelve hours from the beginning of those whose name is "scorched" begin at[112] ninety-six. Therefore, a discernment of the hours should be observed in this sequence up to the end of the month.

§411. For example, let an assembly of the Sun and Moon, being discovered on Sunday at its first hour, be noted—namely when the Sun arises by half of his body. I say that from the beginning of that hour up to the subsequent setting of half the solar body, the hours which we call "scorched" should be noted. But next, we set apart the subsequent twelve hours of that day (namely, the first day), its nocturnal ones, [and] even the diurnal and nocturnal ones of the second day, [and] in the same way both the diurnal and nocturnal [hours] of the third day, [and] the diurnal [hours] of the fourth day.

§412. Moreover, the beginning of the scorched [hours] is stretched out from the outset of the nocturnal hour of the fourth day, up to the morning (namely the beginning) of Thursday. The rest of the [hours] of Thursday, both diurnal and nocturnal, lead to those of Friday, even to Sunday, in order. Whence likewise the beginning of the scorched [hours] are bounded from the beginning of Sunday to its end. And so it will have to be done in this way until all the hours of the [Lunar] month reach the end of the counting.

§413. Once again, let the assembly following the beginning of the subsequent [Lunar] month be described: so, the scorched ones take their beginning from the first hour of the assembly (namely at which the Sun and

---

[111] For this section, cf. al-Rijāl VII.57a. See also *ITA* VIII.4. *Bust* is an Arabic rendering of the Sanskrit *bhukti*, an ecliptical distance covered by the Moon in a certain time.
[112] Omitting "the end of," in order to make the sequence work.

the Moon embrace on the same spot), until twelve [hours] are completed. Therefore, whatever prince undertook the beginnings of a fight in these scorched hours, chooses the greatest loss: the death or severe harm of his own body or of those whom he has [in his power]. But the first four[113] prepare death while the beginnings of the war are advanced in that space [of time]. The following four infest the body, the last four [his] money, and they condemn his subordinates when they hold onto the same sign.[114]

Day	Hours	Scorched/Burnt
1 – Sunday	Diurnal 0-12	**Scorched**
	Nocturnal 12-24	Unscorched
2 – Monday	Diurnal 24-36	Unscorched
	Nocturnal 36-48	Unscorched
3 – Tuesday	Diurnal 48-60	Unscorched
	Nocturnal 60-72	Unscorched
4 – Wednesday	Diurnal 72-84	Unscorched
	Nocturnal 84-96	**Scorched**
5 – Thursday	Diurnal 96-108	Unscorched
	Nocturnal 108-120	Unscorched
6 – Friday	Diurnal 120-132	Unscorched
	Nocturnal 132-144	Unscorched
7 – Saturday	Diurnal 144-156	Unscorched
	Nocturnal 156-168	Unscorched
8 – Sunday	Diurnal 168-180	**Scorched**
	Nocturnal 180-192	Unscorched

Figure 58: Time-based scorched period, from New Moon on Sunday morning

Comment by Dykes. This time-based approach to the scorched (or "combust") period is very close to the method of determining the crisis hours in decumbiture charts, and may in fact be related to them. Since the hours are calculated according to uneven seasonal hours (that is, dividing the period of daylight or nighttime by 12, instead of using a regular 60-minute hour), the

---
113 That is, the first four of the scorched hours.
114 This probably means, "if the Sun and the Moon are in the same sign during the last twelve hours."

actual distance of the Moon from her original position will change according to the season and latitude. So, in al-Kindī's example, if the days were very short and the nights long, then the scorched hours would last for less than 12 of our standardized hours, and the distance traveled by the Moon in that time would be less than at other times of the year.

But if we used an idealized 60-minute hour and her average daily speed (13° 10' 36"), the Moon will be in her idealized Quarters and Semi-Quarters, because she will have traveled approximately 45° between the beginning of each period of scorched hours. For example, if the scorched hours began on Sunday at dawn, they would end at sunset after the Moon had traveled 6° 35' 18". The next period would begin on Thursday at dawn, when the Moon had traveled about 45° from her original position; the next period of scorched hours would take place at about 90° from her original position (i.e., an idealized First Quarter Moon); and so on. *However*, since seasonal hours are uneven, and because the Sun also moves, these scorched hours will not always coincide strictly with the true Quarters and Semi-Quarters: for by the time the Moon reaches, say, 270° from her original position (an idealized Third Quarter), the Sun will already have moved about 21°, and so the Moon's position will fall short of the true Third Quarter. This means that calculating the actual time of the scorched hours a bit complicated, since one cannot simply look at the Moon to tell just when they begin and end: one really needs tables of sunrises and sunsets, or an astrology program which lists the times of the planetary hours.

A distance-based version of the scorched hours is given in Māshā'allāh's *Book of Aristotle* II.4. There, the scorched period is defined as 12° of *distance* traveled by the Moon (close to her average every day), instead of 12 seasonal *hours*. This version makes a bit more sense, if we remember that the Moon is often taken to come out of the Sun's rays at a distance of 12°. If we use a non-scorched distance of 84° instead of 84 hours, then the Moon's position at the beginning of the scorched hours will coincide almost exactly with her Quarters: the next scorched period will happen at about 96° from her original position—but since the Sun will have moved about 7° in the meantime, they will be almost exactly 90° apart, i.e., the true First Quarter. The next period will put her at 192° from her original position, but since the Sun will have moved about 14° in the meantime, this also puts her at almost exactly 180° from him: the Full Moon. And so on with the rest.

And so, the time-based scorched period is an idealized division of the zodiac into 8, using the Quarters and Semi-Quarters, and is more complicated to reckon. The distance-based scorched period uses only the actual Quarters, and is relatively easy to reckon (in many cases one may do this from sight alone).

§7.181: About someone going to war—Aristotle

If it is asked whether he should return [safe and] sound, the lord of the east should be consulted. Therefore, with it bearing itself well, while the Sun or Jupiter or Venus or [the Head of the] Dragon would be traversing in the east, they declare a sound and unharmed return. However, the Sun being placed with the lord of the east does not presume he heads out eagerly (because [the Sun] scorches it thusly). Moreover, the lord of the east with the fortunate ones, while however it bears itself badly, even though it is not fatal it does not take away an impediment. The same [lord of the east] bearing itself badly, but with the lucky ones placed in the east, afflicts him with impediment but not to death.

Saturn being in the east or with a lord of the east that is bearing itself well, prohibits him from going, because he will tumble down from a horse or another place, not without a serious impediment. Which if [the lord of the east] would bear itself badly, and Saturn [were] with it or at least occupied the east, he should fear a serious fall, or he is struck with a stone or wood. Moreover, Mars or the Tail in the east or with its lord (it bearing itself badly), a fatal blow will not be absent; [but] with it bearing itself well, it will not be to death.

It seems this must be noted with the greatest effort: because when the lord of the east is bearing itself badly, whether the malevolents are in the east or even with it or without it (but outside the east), he could in no way avoid an impediment. In addition to all of this one must look: because if the wicked ones traverse in the eighth, one must fear death; no less, if the Sun should traverse in the eighth or with the lord of the eighth, do we prohibit the journey. Moreover, with the malevolents being established in the tenth, we prohibit him from going. Mars and Saturn in the east afflict equally with ruin.

§7.182: In what limb he is struck—Aristotle

But so that you are able to discover in what part someone is struck, consult the eastern lord, and understand him to be wounded through that, and the extent to which one is distant from the other.[115] Therefore, that same [planet] being placed with the lord of the east, shows the head as wounded. Traversing in the second from it, the neck and throat. In the third, the shoulder-blades up to the hands. In the fourth, the chest. In the fifth, around the stomach. In the sixth, the intestines and belly. In the seventh, the buttocks. In the eighth, the haunches. In the ninth, the legs. In the tenth, the knees. In the eleventh, the shins. In the twelfth, the feet. You will note the blow thusly.

Whichever one of the number of the malevolents were in the east or the eighth or with their lords, they signify those striking blows. Saturn does not strike but breaks; Mars and the Tail strike. Malevolents in the pivots denote strikers. Therefore, whichever it was, you will note which place they hold onto from the eastern lord: so that namely you will discover, by how many places [they are from the eastern lord], in what places he is attacked.

But the Moon traversing with Mars in the east or fourth, or even the tenth, while the lord of her place runs through the fourth or seventh or tenth, has a judgment of a wound or some attack. But without this, not at all.

§7.183: On partners and those whom they prevail upon, and on sending generals to war—'Umar

On[116] partners and those whom they prevail upon, and on sending generals to war, choosing those who are going to be more useful, also beasts of burden or two things which come to be compared, whether they are two or three, which one is stronger or the strongest, and on the racing of horses.

[1] The prudence of the astrologers untie the knot of this question, with the benefit of the east. They propose the first sign for the first one, the second for the second, the third to the third. And so, once the power and strength of their lords is discovered, a consideration of these proceeds according to the position of the places (namely a perverse or lucky one).

---

[115] Aristotle means the location of a malefic that threatens harm, from the place of the lord of the east. See what follows.
[116] For this paragraph, see Sahl's *On Quest.* §13.13.

[2] Moreover, there are some who want to ascribe them to the lords of the eastern triplicity (to the first, I say, the second, and the third), and thus in order until the method of the judgment makes it clear.

[3] But others[117] choose it from the Lunar application, so that the first star [to which she applies] watches over the first one, the next one the next one, the third the third one.

But I judge that you should conduct[118] this with an appraisal among the rest, and especially through a more related[119] method.

Moreover, no one thriving in discretion would fear to ascribe a position of first place in philosophy to Ptolemy, since he comprehends the teaching of all science with the lockbox of his heart, and especially and principally (beyond the rest) has revealed the secrets of the whole teaching and the mysteries of truth.[120] [And] he gave a definite judgment about an inquiry of this kind, whose opinion I imitate as being preferable.[121]

This[122] chapter is very necessary and useful with all men, and especially besides that for kings observing and examining the faithfulness of their own men who are put in charge and appointed, and when they desire to know which of their seneschals is more faithful and complete in the discharging of the function he has taken up. Of course they must do this with much skill and diligence when they make someone the general over an army or over some multitude, for knowing which one among many is going to manage what was given and accepted more skillfully and prudently and completely.

[2] Moreover, with a question about kings being presented (namely about sending princes to war), as to which of them one should believe is preferable in mind and faith, we consult the lords of the eastern triplicity. For, the first of them claims the signification of the first [man who is named, the second one the second man, the third one the third man].[123] Sometimes it even happens [that] one is fortunate, the other unlucky, with the proper quality of the triplicities examining [their relative condition]. Because either of these being

---

[117] Sahl, *On Quest.* §13.14. See below.
[118] Reading *magistrandum* for *magistra*.
[119] *Affinius*. I am not exactly sure what this means.
[120] This long statement of praise for Ptolemy is phrased parenthetically after Ptolemy's name in Hugo, so I am not sure if this reflects a belief of 'Umar's or Hugo himself.
[121] Evidently a pseudo-Ptolemy, source unknown at this time.
[122] I have substituted al-Rijāl's paragraph from his VII.85 for Hugo's, which contains some uncertain words and convoluted sentences. For the next few paragraphs, see al-Rijāl VII.85.
[123] Adding and reading with al-Rijāl for Hugo's *tertium quidem non minus beare convenit*.

stronger in its own place (be it fortunate or unlucky), [means that it is] necessary to scrutinize [that one]. Then, once its misfortune is discovered, it will be right to attend to the power of a fortunate one regarding it. For the truth of the judgment is elicited according to its strength in the possessed place, and according to the moderation of the fortunate one: namely because [the truth] is generated[124] from its power. Therefore, [if the triplicity lord is][125] Mars, and the Moon [is also made unfortunate], and they[126] being [deprived] of the fortunate ones, also the remaining lords of the triplicities being weak, they strengthen the virtue [of the one signified by Mars]; moreover, [although he is] stronger than the rest, even though they save that one who would be sent, still they deny the whole effect to the affair asked about.[127] But Saturn being in the same place, heaps on delay. [Afterwards, consider if the fortunes aspect that infortune which was ruling over one part of that triplicity, and what kind of power that infortune has in its own place, and in the bound of what fortune or infortune, and consider the fortune aspecting it, what kind of power or dignity it has in its own bound, and judge in this path according to what you find.][128]

Moreover,[129] with the lords of the triplicities being equal in power and luckiness, judge the first one to be stronger. Especially, any fortunate one appearing in that same place (nor corrupted) promises victory, prepares the faith of the allies, and allegiance and benevolence. But if infortunes would convey the victory, they indicate in advance their enmities and frauds, and that they are unjust men obeying a royal command. Moreover, infortunes being placed there, if they would be blessed by the aspect of the fortunate ones, in closely related[130] places and those agreeing with the infortunes, it is a sign of victory after labor and the malevolence of their military supports. A fortunate one being found in that same place, with the infortunes being ca-

---

[124] Reading *generatur* for *generat*.
[125] Adding and reading with al-Rijāl, else the passage would not make sense.
[126] Al-Rijāl has only the Moon being in aversion to the benefics, which might be important because a further sentence by al-Rijāl below refers to benefics aspecting the malefic triplicity lord.
[127] The idea seems to be (following al-Rijāl) that because the man is represented by a malefic and the Moon is corrupted, he may be the best one to send but he will not finish the job.
[128] Adding with al-Rijāl.
[129] For this paragraph, al-Rijāl differently enough to warrant putting his text below.
[130] *Propinquis*.

dent from it, signals a not-moderate victory, with the humiliation and surrender of the enemies.

[al-Rijāl VII.85] If even the three lords of the triplicity were equal in power and the goodness of their own places, and in the fortunes which they have, and none of them were of a better status than another, judge that the first one [is better than] the second, and the second one [better than] the third. And if the planet which was more powerful than [the other] two lords of the triplicity were a fortune, and it were not made unfortunate, it signifies they he will easily complete the dispute for which he goes, or that thing on account of which he was sent, and that he will be lawful and of good obedience, and pure will towards the one who has sent him. But if it were an infortune, and it had a better status than its associates, it signifies that the man will go beyond the command of his master, and that he will do things which will not be to the pleasure of his master. If even fortunes aspected it from strong and good and appropriate places, it signifies that he will conquer and complete it, but through violence and bad deeds. If even the planet were made fortunate and the infortunes [were] cadent from it, and it were in a good and strong place, it signifies that he will conquer and easily fulfill [his duty] in a good manner, and that he will be obedient to his master, and will complete his will.

Furthermore, the regard of Mars [to the triplicity lord] from a trigon or hexagon in a question of this kind (but even that of the Moon), will not be unuseful. Which if the first lord of the triplicity, and equally the second one, would happen to be found corrupted (but the third one lucky), while [the fortunes] bestow the power of their regard to [the two malefic triplicity lords from an angle],[131] and especially [if] Mars [is involved], it commends the warlike boldness of the partners.

[4] If[132] therefore a question is given about sending or handing over money for any kind of purchase, the fortunate ones are stronger in this affair, even a star regarding the Lot of Fortune, and the Moon: she being fortunate in any [affair] of this kind, is understood to be stronger.

---

[131] Reading with al-Rijāl for Hugo, whose account does not really make sense in context.
[132] I do not find this in al-Rijāl.

[5] However,[133] the establishment of the east responds to an inquiry about the number and multitude of these. Therefore, the beginning of this observation is conducted from any star favored by having many testimonies in the east.[134] Thence, one will have to pursue it from the second-[best] one in the way which was stated above, after that from the third one, [and] finally from that one which possesses something of dignity in that place.

[6] Māshā'allāh[135] too (being of no lesser dignity among astrologers), promises that he can open up a question of this kind and its knots, so that he seems to report that a complete consideration of this kind depends from the east. For, the eastern lord being in a pivot, free of the infortunes and received, bestows the highest favor on the one about whom it is asked first, before the rest. Being unfortunate[136] [while] positioned in a pivot, afflicts that same affair of his with harm. Also, [the lord of the east] being alien from the pivots [but in the succeedents],[137] while however it is free of the infortunes, should it regard the east and be received, extols the reputation and name of the second one. Which if it is asked about any affair, the second [option] is conveyed as being preferable and more excellent, [but again] if they would bear themselves just as we have said, and they [were] unlucky, they announce a good beginning but a bad conclusion. Moreover, with its regard into the east being denied, and it being cadent, while however it is free of the infortunes and received, it shows victory for the third one. With that place bearing itself as was stated before, and they are infortunes,[138] they corrupt the question, with every pleasantness being removed.

[3] Also,[139] the Lunar application suggests otherwise. For, she applying to any fortunate one (and [she being] in a pivot) at the beginning of the matter, or at least [if she would apply] to a star receiving her, it advances the first one about whom we have spoken, by making him better, or it conveys victory to the first affair. Which if the beginning of her application would not bear itself thusly, let the intention of your mind be led from star to star according to the manner of her application, and according to the number and multitude of the things inquired about. Moreover, if the application is not yet ended in the

---

[133] Al-Rijāl VII.85 says that this is for cases when the choices are more than three.
[134] Reading more with al-Rijāl for "a star in the east, whom more testimonies favor."
[135] See Sahl's *On Quest.* §13.13.
[136] Reading with Sahl for "An infortune being positioned...".
[137] Clarifying with Sahl.
[138] Or perhaps, "impeded" or unfortunate (Sahl).
[139] Cf. al-Rijāl VII.85 and *On Quest.* §13.14. But in Sahl, this has to do with answering multiple questions, not deciding between candidates subject to the same question.

sign in which they are,[140] let recourse from star to star be had to the second [sign] from that one in the same way, until she regards it or would encounter any star in a pivot [by assembly].

Likewise,[141] here we enjoin you to watch over her more diligently: for, she being cleansed of the infortunes, lavishes a victory (God willing), or blesses the affair with truth. However, she being unlucky, wholly abolishes [the matter], or at least it corrupts it after hope and the best condition of having [it].

Moreover, the Moon being established in an optimal place from the east, applying to a star possessing an unlucky place and receiving her, is profitable, nor could the perversity of the place be harmful, while reception is present. Conversely, the Moon possessing an unlucky place, and being received, wants her to be blessed in those things which we said by the testimony of the eastern lord. But if her place is unlucky, while she would apply to a star established in an optimal place, it is useful. Which if reception is absent, the pivots will be stronger than the rest [of the places], and[142] they bestow the effect upon the affair, unless, I say, another would corrupt the aforesaid star, however the other one [would be aspected][143] equally by the eastern lord and that of the question, and by that one which receives the star.

Also, the worst is an infortune applying to it, and the Moon [applying to it]. If therefore, the Moon would apply to the lord of the twelfth or sixth or eighth, or even the second, is wholly [bad],[144] namely while the inquiry is about money or about death.

§7.184: On riders sent to plunder—al-Khayyāt

Finally, if someone gave a question about riders sent to plunder, as to whether or not they would meet hostile [forces], we put the east in charge of the querent, the seventh that of the contrary side. For, the application (or transfer of light) of one [to the other] being found, establishes it. But if Mars would neither be lingering in the pivots, nor would he hold onto the fourth of the pivotal lords,[145] it portends that they have met them, but not gone to

---

[140] That is, if she is void in course and cannot complete the application while they are both in their present signs. This relates to the notion of "escape" (*ITA* III.22).
[141] I do not know the source of the rest of this section, although it may simply be ʿUmar.
[142] Reading *atque* for *ut qui*.
[143] Tentatively supplying the verb for this clause.
[144] I cannot quite read this smudged word in Vienna.
[145] That is, the fourth house from any of the lords of the pivots.

war. Moreover, with an application or transfer being denied, the one did not encounter the other.

§7.185: On those whom we reckon to be rebels, wanting to turn against their masters—al-Kindī

§423.[146] Being consulted about someone as to whether he would rise up against his own king: if you found the Moon remote from the east,[147] or the lord of the east retrograde, or a retrograde star in [the east], you should confirm that he is resisting his own king and is rising up against him. But the east and its lord obtain the signification of him whence the question comes. The south and its lord belong to the king, the seventh and its lord to the man sent by the king to fight him.

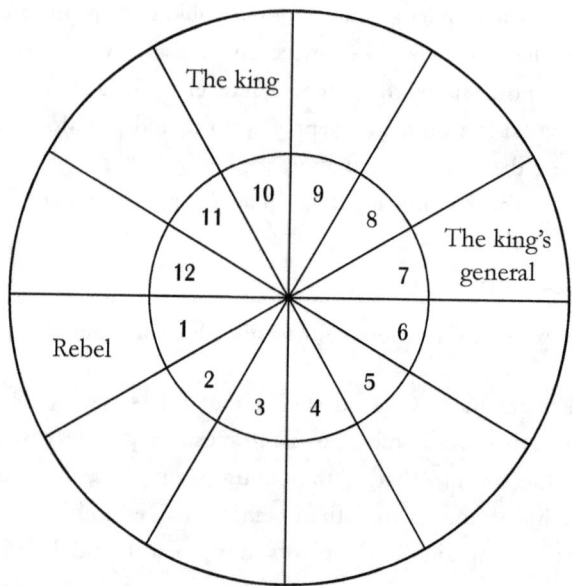

Figure 59: Al-Kindī's scheme of angles for rebellion

---

[146] Reading this paragraph with Robert, as his version is more complete.
[147] This is probably more accurate than Hugo, who has the Moon cadent from an angle. If the Moon is cadent from the Ascendant, then she is in aversion to it: such places are traditional spots of secrecy.

§424. Therefore, with a question as to what end the matter of each is going to have, the lord of the Midheaven [and] even the Sun himself being lucky and fortunate—but the lord of the Ascendant unlucky—convey victory to the king. Moreover, the eclipsing of the Sun or Moon in the Ascendant, or [should this eclipsing happen][148] with the lord of the Ascendant, it ruins the hostile cohort [and] afflicts the [rebel] soldiers with death. The Tail of the Dragon in the Ascendant, [and] likewise Mars as the lord of the second corrupting the lord of the Ascendant from a pivot, promise that the enemy who has risen up will die by iron at the hands of his own family, soldiers and supporters, and even the common people.

§425. Moreover, the Tail in the same place [but] Saturn occupying the role of Mars: he will be overwhelmed by his own soldiers and beset by stones at the hands of the common people, or led as a captive to the king. Moreover, the retrogradation of the lord of the second (and he being in a perverse place, namely lacking the regard of the Ascendant), provided that there is no star in the second, banishes[149] his family, brings his cohort down, and leaves him as though alone.

§426. While they bear themselves in this way, and Mars as the lord of the seventh is corrupting the Ascendant and its lord, the general sent out by the king to fight this kind of enemy rebellion, kills him. Also, With Saturn holding onto [this] role of Mars, and being in the rulership of the seventh, he incurs death (but without iron) from that same general or powerful man.

§427. Furthermore, the lord of the eighth corrupting the Ascendant and its lord explains that the enemy, being deceived by some art, will be killed by the family of the general himself or friends or scouts or the wife of the general. Furthermore, if the Moon and [her] lord would assume the roles of the Ascendant and its lord, namely so that [they] would be corrupted by Mars as the lord of the seventh or eighth (or by Saturn in possession of the same rulership), they will bestow the same misfortunes which the enemy got from the Ascendant and the lord of the Ascendant being corrupted.

§428. Also, if the above-written arrangement of stars taints the enemy side and denies victory to him, the scorching of the lord of the Ascendant kills him by royal decree, as a captive. Likewise the Moon or the Lunar lord being peregrine and exiled in the seventh hands the enemy (being captured by the above-stated general) over to the royal authority as someone about to die.

---

[148] Reading the meaning with Robert, for Hugo's puzzling *annuit*.
[149] Reading *amovet* for *amovit*.

§429a. Moreover, the lord of the Midheaven strong, even the strength of the Sun, [and] with the Ascendant and its lord being corrupted from the eleventh, affirms the enemy's death.

§429b. Which if the lord of the seventh were situated as an exile in the Ascendant, or Mars himself would corrupt that same lord of the seventh—or the seventh itself—it leads the general (whom we said had gone out to resist [them]) as a captive to be killed at enemy hands.

§430. Moreover, the lord of the seventh peregrine in the Ascendant, with no corruption of it or of the seventh by Mars having been incurred, if an application of it to the lord of the eleventh or tenth would come to be, [and] meanwhile the lord of the Ascendant is unlucky, it shows the escape of the general (who was already losing hope for his life) and the king's consequent victory. Likewise, the lord of the Ascendant being corrupted by the Sun or by the lord of the Midheaven or the eleventh, after the achieved victory the enemy will meet death.

§431. But next, the lord of the Ascendant being direct, pivotal and eastern, [but] with the Sun and lord of the Midheaven being cadent, particularly Mars tainting the Sun from a square or opposition, makes a confused king submit to an enemy gloating over victory. Moreover,[150] with the lord of the Ascendant not suffering this misfortune of the Sun, but [Mars] attacking the Midheaven and its lord [while the lord is] cadent, it indicates the king is subdued and killed by the enemy.

§432. But the lord of the Ascendant in a pivot, eastern, direct, in the place of its own *ḥalb*[151] or authority, blessed by the fortunate ones with a friendly regard, or in their assembly, moreover with the Sun or the lord of the Midheaven or of the eleventh being corrupted by Mars, it kills the king by an assault of the hostile cohort, [and] leaves victory to the enemy. But Saturn entering the role of Mars captures him or confines him, besieged.[152] But [if] he [is] the lord of the eighth, it kills him [while] besieged.

§433. Moreover, with the lord of the Ascendant being defended by the aforesaid strength, likewise the lord of the eighth being strong, also the lord of the Midheaven being somehow weak (namely retrograde and that kind [of

---

[150] Reading this sentence more with Robert, and emphasizing Mars as the corrupter instead of the Sun. Hugo reads: "Moreover, with the misfortune of the Sun being remote from the lord of the Ascendant, while the Sun himself attacks the lord of the Midheaven and the Ascendant itself…".

[151] Reading with Robert for Hugo's synonym *munitione*.

[152] Omitting *cuilibet*.

thing]), and likewise the lord of the eleventh, while the lord of the Ascendant or of the second would corrupt the lord of the eleventh (they regarding it from a square), they conquer[153] the king in a fight, [and] attack his [people] with much slaughter.

§434. Also, the lord of the second or of the Ascendant corrupting neither the lord of the eleventh nor that of the Midheaven, but with each one retrograde and cadent, they disturb the cohort, stimulate the flight of the king, [and] free the fleeing one from death. Likewise [if] the lord of the Midheaven [is] cadent, retrograde, scorched.

§435. Also, an Aries or Leo Ascendant, likewise the lord of the eleventh being unlucky and cadent, but the Sun being regarded by the lucky ones, and [also] the lord of the second in their regard, [and] the lord of the Midheaven, I say, corrupted from a square after its initial emergence from scorching, it threatens death to the king ([who is] deprived of victory), [and] confounds his [people] with much slaughter.

§436. But besides this, the Midheaven itself being corrupted from a tetragon devastates the kingdom, it is deserted by the inhabitants, the citizens are left abject and despised. Again, the lord of the Midheaven being corrupted in the Midheaven itself,[154] means a most famous and public death, such as cutting off the head, and [the rebel] sets [the king's] head up in public view of the people for them to understand.

§437. Moreover, the lord of the Midheaven corrupted by [the lord of][155] the eleventh, and the lord of the eleventh regarding the lord of the Ascendant in a friendly way, [and] with the lord of the Midheaven, I say, cadent and retrograde and scorched as was said, the princes and powerful men of his own cohort will slaughter the king and offer his head to the enemy as a gift. Again, the lord of the fifth place from the Ascendant being scorched and corrupted from a square, exposes the king's son to be killed.

§438. But if the lord of the Midheaven (being cadent, particularly in the twelfth) would be enclosed[156] between the two infortunes (with one preceding it, the other following behind), [and] should it traverse by sign [with][157] or in the same way apply to the lord of the twelfth, it shuts the king up in prison

---

[153] *Convincunt.*
[154] But Robert reads: "if one found the one making the [Midheaven] unfortunate to be in the south," which makes somewhat more sense.
[155] Adding from Robert.
[156] That is, "besieged" by degree (*ITA* IV.4.2).
[157] That is, "be in the same sign as," i.e., be in an assembly with.

as a captive. If it would reach an infortune (Mars, I say), it warns that death in prison is to be feared. But if it reached Saturn, it especially reveals the same thing if that infortune to which it is said to come, has possession of the rulership of the eighth.

§439. Moreover, the lord of the Midheaven being cadent and remote (or rather, retreating), [and] the lord of the Ascendant being strong, but there being an application of it made with some fortunate one in the Midheaven, and the same [planet] being free of the pivots of the unfortunate ones,[158] after flight and disturbance and conquering, it restores the kingdom to the king, but the enemy perseveres for a long time in the malice of his rebellion. If these are bearing themselves in this way, [and] the lord of the Ascendant is applying to a cadent and corrupted star, it confounds the enemy rebel, and after getting the kingdom from the king and reinforcing [it], it takes away his hope of fighting [more].[159]

§440. Moreover, the lord of the Midheaven in the seventh, or the lord of the seventh itself, or likewise the Sun, and they being strong, pivotal, it signifies the king will enter into a duel [in order to] fight it out with the enemy through his own hand. Wherefore, the lord of the Ascendant being cadent and weak grants victory to the king. Moreover, the lord of the Ascendant being strong produces dissension, and strengthens the enemy's rebellion. Likewise, an application of the lord of the Ascendant with the lord of the eighth harms the enemy [while] persisting in his malice.

§441. Which if Mars appeared as the lord of the eighth, and in a pivot of the lord of the Ascendant,[160] it beheads the one who is thus far rebelling, and pours out his blood. Moreover, Saturn in possession of the rulership of the eighth and in a pivot of the lord of the Ascendant, destroys the enemy with trickery or drowns him in water, or tramples him under horses' hooves, and—so that I might speak more truthfully—he loses his life without iron.

§442. Moreover, while the lord of the Ascendant bears itself thusly, its application with a cadent star means the enemy's flight. Again, if the star to which the application of the lord of the Ascendant comes to be, is applying with the lord of the seventh or the Sun, the enemy demands a truce after fleeing, [and] he greatly desires discussions with the king. Which if the lord of the seventh or the Sun would receive that star to which the application of the

---

[158] That is, not being in their whole-sign angles.
[159] That is, his victory is only temporary.
[160] That is, in his whole-sign angle.

lord of the Ascendant is made, after the truce and with many gifts being accepted by the king, he is made into a friend.

§443. But an unfriendly or perverse application, [and] the Sun not received, even the lord of the Ascendant in possession of a pivot of the infortunes, he is killed after [his] pledge is received by the king.

§444. Moreover, an application of the lord of the Ascendant with the lord of the seventh or with the Sun, or with the Sun in the seventh, or if the lord of the Midheaven or the lord of the seventh [is] in the seventh (this application, I say, being friendly and received), it denies the enemy's flight but he demands a truce and observes things given [to the king]. [But if],[161] in the midst of all of this, the lord of the Ascendant would be retrograding and estranged and absent from[162] the Sun or the lord of the Midheaven,[163] likewise the Moon or the lord of the Ascendant being in a double-bodied sign, he violates the accepted truce, throws peace into confusion, and once again hastens to rebellion.

§445. Moreover, the lord of the Ascendant in possession of a tetragon of the infortunes[164] (particularly of Mars), the end of the enemy's whole affair is ended in death.

[The relation of the rebel to the king]

§446. While these bear themselves thusly, the lord of the Ascendant or the Moon in the second from the Sun, or in the second from the Midheaven, or if either of them would rule over those same places, it suggests the enemy is going to be a near to the family of the king. On the other hand, either of them as the lord of the third from the Sun or from the Midheaven, shows he was a brother of the king or one having the role of a brother, and that type [of person]. Moreover, either of them as the lord of the fourth from the Sun or from the Midheaven, or at least dwelling in the fourth from the Sun or from the Midheaven, it adduces that the enemy is a parent of the king or of the parents' stock.

---

[161] What follows is a case of revoking (*ITA* III.20), in which a planet preparing to complete a connection goes retrograde. It is stated a bit more clearly by Robert.
[162] That is, "in aversion to," i.e., not regarding it by sign.
[163] Robert omits this part about being in aversion to the Sun and the lord of the Midheaven, which makes sense because the lord of the Ascendant would have to regard them by sign in order to be in an application with them.
[164] Again, being in their whole-sign angles; but probably more intensely if close by degree.

§447. Either one as the ruler in the fifth from the Sun or from the Midheaven, or established in those same places,[165] it admits that the royal children or those accepted in place of the children are in dissension with the king. Moreover, while either one would rule over the sixth from the Sun or the Midheaven, or should it appear in that same place, it brings in royal slaves and that type. Which if either would rule over the seventh from the Sun or from the Midheaven, or be found in that same place, it adduces that the enemy is numbered among the king's adversaries, very often even his sisters.

§448. Likewise, should either of them be the ruler in the eighth from the Sun or Midheaven, or with it holding onto that same place, the servants and followers of the adversaries or sisters come forth, or those who previously were held in the king's prison. Either of them as lord of the ninth from the Sun or from the Midheaven, or if it were in that same place, it compels a doctor or underofficial of the law, or a partner in travel, to dissent with the king.

§449. Also, either one in the tenth from the Sun or from the Midheaven, or as the lord of that same place, it picks out the rebel as being a king or someone of royal stock, or an advisor or counselor of the king, or in the administration of [royal] affairs, engaged with the royal authority. Also, in the eleventh from the Sun or from the Midheaven, or either of them being the lord of that same place, [it indicates] an intimate of the king, and a secretary, and it especially reserves a friend in the greatest distress of necessity.[166]

§450. But either of them as the lord of the twelfth from the Sun or from the Midheaven, or dwelling in the twelfth from the Sun or from the Midheaven, it testifies the rebel will be an ancient enemy of the king, of a great name.

§451.[167] If however the lord of the east and the Moon held a different place and [were in] a different[168] regard of the Sun and the lord of the south, the judgment must be moderated from the nature of each place.

§452. For example, the lord of the Ascendant being in the eleventh from the Sun (and in the second of the Midheaven),[169] portends the enemy will be from the rank of the king's friends and his underofficials. For the second

---

[165] Robert simply has them in these places, not ruling them.
[166] That is, the friend feels that (for some reason) he must rebel, but feels anguish about it.
[167] Reading this paragraph with Robert, as it is clearer and more succinct.
[168] Reading *alio* for *alium*.
[169] This would put the Sun in the Ascendant.

place from the Midheaven denotes the royal family, but the eleventh from the Sun decrees the royal friends. And so, if the lord of the Ascendant would bear himself thusly, but the Moon would occupy the sixth place from the Sun, once the nature of the above-written place has been observed, the Lunar place and status and what she signifies in that place, comes to be combined: whence the enemies would be said to have revolted against[170] the king from among [his] friends and the rank of underofficials and the company of slaves.

§7.186: On someone, whether he would strike against[171] the king—Dorotheus[172]

And so, the east is in charge of him about whom it is asked.[173] Therefore, the significator being retrograde wholly strikes against the king. It does the same [if] placed in the twelfth. Moreover, in the pivots and traversing with Mars, it generates offense and war. But if otherwise, not at all.

§7.187: On those having left the king—Dorotheus

But with the king asking about someone who has left him, the east presides over the querent, the seventh over him about whom it is asked, the Midheaven over the king, but the eleventh over [the king's] supporters. And so, Mars withdrawing from one and applying to the other, indicates open war. Which if [Mars] would possess their pivots or those of their lords, it portends the same thing. The assembly of each[174] designates victory, but the one which will be more lofty and powerful will seize the victory. It is necessary for it to happen likewise in the opposition.

---

[170] Reading *decidisse* for *decivisse*.
[171] *Offendat*. This can range from merely giving offense, to actually striking or injuring.
[172] Cf. the end of §7.160 above (Sahl).
[173] Like Sahl, Dorotheus assumes that the querent is the king or someone working on his behalf.
[174] I believe this refers to the two significators, not Mars.

§7.188: On the status of a besieged city—'Umar

It[175] is especially good to note the significator of the besieged city (namely, the lord of the Midheaven), and its sign. For, Mars occupying it, being strong, eastern [and] in a dignity of his own, [means the besieger] enters the city with the sword, but with the assent of the citizens. If however he were devoid of all dignity in that same place, the city itself will succumb violently and with no fraud. Likewise, Mars occupying its tetragon or opposition, does not depart from the prior judgment. Moreover, he being invested with the fortunate ones,[176] compels the citizens to surrender after the warlike motions, with peace already being established.

The fourth and its lord demand the same judgment about the besieged city of the combatant, as we stated above about Mars.

§7.189: Whether he would be overcome by surrender or war—'Umar

Furthermore, if there would be an indeterminate question about storming some city, with war threatening, the east and the Moon and its[177] lord watch over the city. Then, too, it will be good to attend to whether Mars himself would invest the east or the eastern [lord] or the Moon or the Lunar lord, with a tetragon or opposition or assembly. Which if [it would be so] invested, nor [would there be] reception, nor would it rejoice in the aspect of the fortunate ones, the city is forced to come to a surrender, being conquered violently and by the sword. But reception, or a regard of the fortunate ones coming after, [means that] after the devastation of wars, once peace is already established, the beaten city is unbarred. However, with a regard from a trigon or hexagon being had, or rather should Mars be invested by the fortunate ones, a surrender will happen with peace. With [an aspect] that is to be invested by the fortunate ones being denied, even though it is overcome, with peace being made, it signifies a short and not effective rulership.

---

[175] In this question, 'Umar seems to assume that the querent wants to besiege someone else's city. Thus, the tenth is the fourth from the seventh.
[176] That is, "being assembled with or in aspect to."
[177] This probably means the lords of both the east and of the Moon, since each is mentioned later.

§7.190: On the besieging of cities—al-Kindī

§348. For a question as to whether enemies are going to besiege a city, he[178] consults the Ascendant. For, infortunes or adverse stars in the twelfth and second,[179] claim the besieging is [already] in the present circumstances, but being remote from those places they do not permit it to happen yet. Moreover, the infortunes in the eleventh and[180] third denote that the enemies are nearby, however they do not liberate the city from besieging. The same [planets] in the fourth and tenth they mean it [will be] besieged, but they do not release it from the enemies' entrance.

§349. Moreover, with a question being made as to whether or not it would be occupied, infortunes in the Ascendant testify to it. Being removed from the Ascendant but still in the pivots, the same. If therefore Saturn, [being the lord of the twelfth or sixth],[181] would enter the Ascendant or the pivots, it impairs very many in prison, [but] few by death. Mars in possession of this role of Saturn's, and being the lord of the eighth, the other way around.[182] Moreover, Saturn and Mars doing this in common, bind very many with each misery. Also, the Sun as the ruler of the Midheaven, being a partner of the Ascendant by no bearing, but nevertheless holding onto the Ascendant itself or the pivots with the unfortunate ones, reveals the entrance into the city [by the enemy] to the king or authority.

§350-51. In addition, with all doubt about the besieging being removed, if the truth is sought about the city's assault and the status of the citizens, it will have to be noted that the greater infortune being in [the Ascendant's] first trigon (namely in the fifth) or even in the eleventh or in the Midheaven, [and] moreover Mars being associated with the Ascendant by some proper quality,[183] promise the comfort of friends [and] the expulsion of the enemies by the citizens. The [greater] fortune, namely Jupiter, in the Ascendant, removes enemy harm to the citizens, and announces their well-being, especially with the lord of the Ascendant being cleansed of the infortunes and regarding the Ascendant itself. Moreover, the Sun and Moon in the trigon or hexagon of the Ascendant confirm the same. Venus taking the role of Jupiter brings in

---

178 This must be Hugo referring to al-Kindī.
179 Reading "and" for Hugo's "or": namely, a case of besieging by sign (see *ITA* IV.2).
180 Again, reading for "or."
181 Adding with Robert.
182 That is: many dead, a few injured.
183 This probably includes rulership.

the same joy to the citizens from the enemies in that campaign, that Jupiter does. Moreover, one of the fortunate ones being under the rays and in the beginning of its exit [from out of them], should it even consider the Ascendant by a friendly aspect, it brings forth the friends of the citizens and the allies from out of traps, pursues the enemies, throws the army into confusion, disperses the assembly [of soldiers], restrains their powers, [and] tramples the arrogance of the proud.

§7.191: What is the condition of peace—al-Kindī

§360a. In addition, the Moon receding from the lord of the seventh, and an application of her[184] with the lord of the Ascendant, [and] the receding and application being friendly, brings about peace with the consent of the citizens, once messengers have been sent over from the enemies.

Moreover, the Moon's friendly recession [but] perverse application, portends the enemies will demand peace in vain from the reluctant citizens, and especially with the lord of the Ascendant being retrograde.

§360b-361. On the other hand, the Moon's recession from the lord of the Ascendant and application with the lord of the seventh, signifies that the citizens on both sides rejoice in a friendly way, peace having been obtained with the assent of the enemies.

A friendly receding but adverse application, the citizens are disappointed in the peace that is desired through messengers, but particularly with the retrogradation of the one with whom the application is happening.[185]

Again, the [recession] unfriendly and the application safe, [indicates] the citizens fraudulently demand peace from the enemies.

Moreover, perversity in both the application and recession, indicates the trickery of the messengers (on both sides) sent to obtain peace.

§362. Likewise, if the lords of the application and recession were considered,[186] [and] even the Moon (but likewise the infortunes)—if they would be regarding those places into which the application comes to be, and from

---

[184] Omitting Hugo's incorrect parenthetical explanation: "([namely], the star from which the Moon is receding, [that is,] the one assuming the rulership of the seventh)." The Moon is doing the separating and applying in this subchapter, not the lord of the seventh.
[185] Namely, the lord of the seventh.
[186] I take this to mean the domicile lords of the planet from which she recedes, and of the one to which she applies.

which the receding comes to be—they testify that a virtually forced peace is made, with those on each side being invited. But the regard of the infortunes into the same [places], breaks off the peace. For the receding and application of [the Moon] bears the signification of legates.

§363. Which if this unfortunate one were Saturn or a Saturnian [fixed] star,[187] it captures the messengers. But Mars or a [fixed] star similar to Mars threatens death.

§364. Furthermore, the nature or moral qualities, and even the form, of the messenger could be discovered by this method. For the Lunar lord and its nature demonstrates the moral qualities. Moreover, the sign which the Moon is holding onto describes the form. Also, the Lunar lord's place or house in the square arrangement of signs (namely the one which is in its stronger regard), reveals [the messenger's] kind.[188] About all of these, one will have to relate it just as was stated above with respect to corresponding [types of people].

§365. In addition, the Moon settles the faithfulness of the messengers, namely [in terms of] whether they show a stronger assent towards those from which she [recedes], or those to which she goes. For whether the familiar bearing is found to be with the one whom she leaves behind or the one to which she applied herself, the messenger seems to look after the side of the one whose signification that star claimed.

§7.192: When [the city] would be stormed—al-Kindī

§366. Moreover, if an infortune would hold onto the pivots, it will declare when the city does not deny entrance to the enemies. If the application reached the degree of the Ascendant itself, the city will be unlocked for the enemies on that day.

§367. Likewise, by how many degrees the degree of the Ascendant is distant from the rays of an unlucky star, [then] if the significators promise delay, the assault on the city will be set aside for that many days or months or years. Moreover, by how many degrees the Ascendant was distant from an infortune,[189] you will note that many [increments] of 12 1/6 days.[190]

---

[187] Robert reads this as though the Moon is on one of these planets or fixed stars.
[188] *Genus*. That is, the type of social role (slave, sibling, *etc.*).
[189] Or more likely, including its rays as well.

§368. Moreover, the Moon receding from an infortune or from the lord of the seventh, and applying with the degrees of the Ascendant, threatens the most severe attack by the enemies on the citizens. Moreover, the Moon receding from Saturn and applying herself with the degree of the Ascendant, threatens the undermining of the walls, and hurling mechanisms,[191] and tortures, and even frauds and things of this kind. Also, Mars taking over for Saturn produces fire and arrows and flying missiles. [Mercury being dressed in the nature of Saturn, tricks and frauds.][192]

§369. [Mercury] sharing in the nature of Mars, prepares the fraud of tricks and more prominent tortures for the citizens, the drawing of arrows, and walls being undermined from below.

In addition, the Tail of the Dragon applying itself to the Ascendant, [indicates] a common[193] cohort of foot soldiers and vassals, [and] compels the projecting of scorpions, lizards, poisonous things of this kind or stinking corpses, and that kind within the walls.

§7.193: From where one should have fear—al-Kindī

§370. Moreover, the sign in which the star (which besieges and attacks the city) was, will denote from what direction the citizens would incur harm. In an eastern [sign], it warns that one must beware of it from the east; in a western one, from the west; but in a southern one, from the south; also, in a northern one, from the north.[194]

§7.194: On the citizens' courage—al-Kindī

§371. Moreover, the lord of the Ascendant will indicate the courage and status of the citizens, and in what frame of mind they are protecting the places devoted to their defense. For, it being direct increases their courage in

---

[190] This is a profection. Here, each degree of the zodiac is equated with 12 1/6 days, which makes each sign (or increment of 30°) almost exactly equivalent to one year.
[191] *Fundibula*: that is, catapults. The difference between Saturn and Mars here must be that the catapult works by brute force to smash things (Saturn), while Mars's missiles are designed to burn and kill.
[192] Adding with Robert.
[193] That is, of unprofessional soldiers, the general public.
[194] See the diagram and discussion in §7.122 above.

defending [them], [their] steadiness, even [their] faith and vigor. But retrograde, the contrary. Eastern, it tends to their cunning and powers, and claims they will be young men, for the most part. Western, the contrary.

§372. But in a pivot, it shows steadiness in assaulting the rebellious, and that they are courageous against the assaults. After the pivots, they are for the most part supported. But remote from a pivot, it deprives them of everything which pertains to the defense. In its *ḥalb*[195] and in some place of its own proper quality, it brings the strength of forts, and defenses, and ramparts to bear. But remote from these places, it renders them impotent and inexperienced in protection.

§373. Moreover, the fourth place and its lord should be noted. For if the lord of the fourth would make the Ascendant or its lord fortunate in a friendly way, and the lord of his Ascendant would enjoy a manifold analogy[196] with the fourth, it presents an end to the whole war, and the victory of the citizens over the besieging. Contrarily, with the bearing of the lord of the Ascendant being remote from the fourth, and with the companionship of the lord of the seventh being taken up with the [lord of the][197] fourth, victory is granted to the enemies.

§7.195: What was the reason for surrender—al-Kindī

§374. In addition, Saturn in an earthy sign (if he would be corrupting the Ascendant) and his lord in an earthy sign, also the Ascendant being earthy and its lord in an earthy sign, provided that the significators promise [the enemies'] entrance into the city, it defeats the city decisively through thirst and a lack of water. But apart from this, the lord of the second being western,[198] and there being no application of him with the Ascendant and its lord, and being in a fiery or earthy sign and in the regard of Mars, makes the citizens surrender to thirst and starvation.[199]

§375. Also, the ascending sign being watery and its lord in a watery sign, and likewise those who participate with his Ascendant, moreover should Sat-

---

[195] Following Robert for Hugo's synonym, "shelter."
[196] Robert reads, "it had manifold power in the fourth."
[197] Adding with Robert.
[198] Omitted by Robert.
[199] The second normally signifies wealth, but in particular it indicated the provisions and sustenance of one's livelihood, one's immediate means of support: *victus, quaestus* (which is

urn corrupt the Ascendant from a watery sign (especially Cancer and Scorpio), they bring about an assault on the city through an onrush of waters and [their] immoderate impact.

§376a. In addition, the slow course or even stationing of the infortunes which attack and are besieging, generate a pause in the besieging and the anxiety of the citizens.

§7.196: For whom are there more allies—al-Kindī

§376b. But, [many] stars in the second give over very many allies to the citizens. With the lord of the Ascendant [joined] in a friendly way to these, or [if they had some power in the Ascendant],[200] they testify to their faith and steadiness in attacking the enemies.

§377. [But] just one [star] in the second, and it being a partner of the Ascendant or regarding its lord in a friendly way, promises the help of few [allies] for the citizens, but [it also promises] their faithfulness and steadiness. Finally, with no [star] appearing in the second, if the Ascendant itself and even its lord would be lacking the friendly regard of all, they affirm that the citizens will be altogether destitute of aid.

§378. Conversely, the lord of the eighth being blessed by the friendly regard of many, [and] also the lord of the seventh and the eighth [sign] itself, or if [many planets] would be holding onto the eighth, they console the enemies with the aid of many. But if they bore themselves otherwise, the judgment will have to be changed. Again, those stars being friendly to the seventh or the lord of the seventh, no less too to the eighth or its lord, indicate [the enemy's allies] are strong in war, prudent, even faithful. Also, an alteration of how they bear themselves makes the other judgment.

§7.197: Whose cause is more just—al-Kindī

§379. Moreover, the lord of the seventh being lucky, in some place of his own analogy,[201] in a firm sign, indicates the cause of the enemies is just; but

---

[200] Reading with Robert for Hugo's line, which seems to refer to the lord of the Ascendant instead.
[201] *Proportione.* Again, Robert reads "powers."

being unlucky and in a convertible sign, they are worthless and unjust and moreover foreign to what is true.

§380. Moreover, if in a double-bodied and fiery sign,[202] and it being lucky, it denotes that the part of the cause which he gives as a pretext, and by which he frees himself from blame, is just; but [his own real motive] is unjust, and that he is hiding that [fact], and that he is a show-off. In a watery [and double-bodied] sign,[203] [it means] the enemy cause is just, but [he has one motive inside, and another in his speech];[204] he even defends the humble and the religious, it means deep counsel, but covers up minor secrets, [and] he takes no partner or confidant.

§381. Moreover, the lord of the seventh in a double-bodied sign and an airy one,[205] indicates twin enemies, and reveals two men or brothers unanimous in counsel, that they exhibit much foresight in matters, and less popularity or sympathy in [their] subjects, but public ambition for victory. The same [lord] in a double-bodied and earthy sign[206] portends their evenness, justice, piety, advantageous power of discernment, care in administering things, benevolence toward men.

§7.198: On storming fortresses—Dorotheus

If there were an inquiry about storming some fortress, the pivots that are established will be in charge of the besieged town. Which if malevolents would enter [them] or be in them, an entry [into the city] through war is being prepared; fortunate ones in the same place bring about peace. Moreover, if the infortunes possess them,[207] there will be a giving over [of the town to the enemy], with the assent of the citizens.

---

[202] Namely, Sagittarius.
[203] Adding with Robert. By definition this would be Pisces.
[204] Reading with Robert.
[205] That is, Gemini: note the reference to twin enemies.
[206] That is, Virgo.
[207] In this case, I believe Hugo means "if the infortunes *rule* the pivots" in addition to being in them.

HUNTING & FISHING

§7.199: On the hunt—Sahl[1]

With an inquiry about a hunt being proposed, consult the east itself and the lord of the hour (since it is principal and strong in this matter). For in every election (or rather, question) of this kind, one will have to inquire into the east and the seventh with the greatest diligence (as to whether they are of the four-footed [signs] or of this type), and their lords (what places they are holding onto). For, an application of each lord being made from a friendly aspect, brings in the catch that is sought without any difficulty. But it being had from the tetragon or opposition, throws in labor and exhaustion. With an application being removed, the thing wished for will be completely frustrated.

But if the seventh were four-footed, with the hour of Jupiter being near, or at least with any of the pivots being goat-like, he should hunt.

Moreover, the lord of the seventh being of the malevolents, cadent from the fortunate ones, tortures him while hunting, and he acquires little, but it even threatens loss or impediment to his own body (if, I say, this were Saturn). Mars having taken the rulership of this kind, and he being strong in that place, brings the catch[2] but introduces harm from a certain one of his associates, and finally frees him[3] (because the hunt itself belongs to Mars). Moreover, Jupiter regarding Mars (and being the lord of the hour or of the east), saves him from fear and removes all labor and exhaustion in hunting, for the good.

Which if it happened that the seventh is going to be airy or earthy,[4] with a benevolent occupying it, while its lord or that of the hour was of the unfortunate ones, it watches over him and protects him, but after many difficulties and troubles, it speaks against what he wished for, and frightens away the prey—unless, I say, Jupiter or Mercury would be traversing with that malevolent which we put as the lord of the hour: for thus it breaks its malice and

---

[1] Cf. *On Quest.* §13.15.
[2] Reading *venationem* for *venatorem*.
[3] Neither John nor Hugo is clear as to whether this is the hunter being freed from difficulties, or the prey being freed from his trap.
[4] Suggesting birds (airy signs) or land animals (earthy signs).

blocks the flight of the prey. In fact, Mercury has a powerful partnership with Mars on a hunt.[5]

§7.200: On the multitude or scarcity of the catch—Sahl[6]

For inquiring into the discernment of many or scarce prey, we should consult the Midheaven at his departure.[7] For, Mars being the lord of the Midheaven, or being there and under the aspect of Jupiter and Mercury, or [if he is] lingering [under the aspect] of either, while one of them would rule over the hour or the east, the catch will be much, and so much that it will come into the hands of the one capturing it, without the labor of all. But if, I say, Saturn would regard Mars from a pivot, or would be lingering in the tenth or would assume its rulership, it afflicts the one hunting in hope and wishing, with much sorrow. However, with Jupiter being cadent from and in aversion to Saturn (while Saturn bears himself as was said above), and Mars would occupy a pivot, it threatens impediment and loss to the body, and likewise slows down the affair, and finally all hunting is denied: for delay and harm proceeds from Saturn if the hunt is by land.

§7.201: On hunts—'Umar[8]

Now, the east and the Moon, moreover the lord of the eastern bound (namely where the degree of it is) but even [the lord] of the hour equally (which assumes no moderate power in this judgment, with the east[9]), generally reveal the status of the one hunting. But we commit the hunt to the seventh and its lord.

Then, too, one must inquire as to whether the east is of the four-footed signs, or it is airy or earthy: for these are in charge of hunting. No less do the lord of [the east] and that of the hour equally need no little consideration, as to what place they are in, whether they are fortunate or the contrary, even

---

[5] Reading *Martis namque potentem Mercurius* for *Martis namque potentiam Mercurium*.
[6] Cf. *On Quest.* §13.16 and cf. al-Rijāl II.47, which is also very close to the last part of 'Umar in §7.201 below.
[7] Al-Rijāl adds that we should see what relationship the lord of the tenth has with the lords of the Ascendant and of the hour.
[8] Cf. al-Rijāl II.46.
[9] Al-Rijāl says, "when it is *staying in* the Ascendant, and the ascending sign is of the four-footed ones."

whether they regard each other or rather are placed next to each other [in the same sign], or one would be cadent from the other. But even the seventh, whether or not it is four-footed, possessed (I say) by its own lord or at least that of the hour, or if at last they, being fortunate, would hold onto the pivots: for placed in such a way, they denote the certain obtaining [of the prey].

In fact, the lord of the seventh being corrupted or unlucky, or the Moon being corrupted in the same way, with the fortunate ones being cadent from her, profits [only] a moderate amount, nor does that supply [the prey] without labor: for they threaten an attack upon the body of the one hunting, especially with Saturn occupying the east,[10] [and the situation was] in the same way as was shown above with respect to the seventh.[11]

Moreover, the Moon occupying the seventh or the pivot of the lord of the seventh, and she being lucky, promises the catch.[12] Likewise, Mars being the lord of the seventh and traversing in [the eighth, or in any place in which he claims something of power],[13] even though it presents the thing hunted, it wounds some one of his partners, but it is not dangerous. Mars even claims greater power for hunting in the wilderness than the rest do. The regard of Jupiter and of the lord of the hour and equally of the eastern [lord],[14] save from fear and made an easy catch.

Which if the seventh is airy or earthy, and the fortunate ones possess it, and with its lord and equally that of the hour being corrupted, even though they instill nothing of fear, they disturb and scatter what is hunted, tire out the hunter, [and] finally make the work disappointing—unless, I say, Jupiter or Mercury would accompany that infortune or the one which claims the rulership of the [seventh or the][15] hour: for thus it breaks the malice of the one making [the situation] unfortunate, nor does it take away or deny the thing hunted, [on account of] Mercury or Jupiter.[16] In fact, Mercury is a partner of Mars in this affair, nor does he exhibit a moderate signification in it.

Moreover,[17] the lord of the Midheaven at the hour of the departure, [and] even the regard of a star which is in the tenth, decide the quantity of the

---

[10] Al-Rijāl has him ruling the east, but this makes more sense.
[11] Namely, that a four-footed sign was on the seventh (al-Rijāl).
[12] *Venationem.* That is, the prey.
[13] Reading with al-Rijāl for Hugo's "traversing in it, claiming something of power in that same place."
[14] That is, to that same Mars (according to al-Rijāl).
[15] Adding with al-Rijāl.
[16] Reading with al-Rijāl for Hugo's odd *Mercurii quidem aut Iovis loco faciente.*
[17] For this paragraph, cf. al-Rijāl II.47.

catch. One must even watch over what place [the lord of the tenth] holds onto, from the lord of the east and of the hour: therefore, Mars as the lord of the Midheaven, and appearing there, regarding Mercury or Jupiter while each or either of them would possess something of dignity in the hour or in the east), with Saturn, I say, being cadent, first saves [and] he will even rejoice in much game without difficulty, unless Saturn would regard Mars from a pivot or he would appear strong in his own place, or he would possess something in the tenth, corrupting Mars himself: for thus anxiety and not-moderate labor oppresses the one hunting. But if Jupiter would be falling down, with Saturn being established as we have said, with Mars occupying a pivot, it introduces fear and conveys an attack on the body of the one hunting, and difficulty on the journey, and the labor of hunting will wholly bring about a fall. For Saturn corrupts his effort and slows the one hunting; in fact, it especially seems to harm those hunting in the desert.[18]

Finally, it is necessary for the prosperity or corruption of Mars to be everywhere known, as the one which merits the signification of the hunt.

§7.202: On fishing—Sahl[19]

For if someone would question you about fishing, the lord of the east and the Moon (not without the lord of the seventh) will have to be consulted. Therefore, with the east being watery, the Moon or the lord of the hour applying to Mars, while Venus is in aversion to and cadent from the regard of the Moon, it wholly warns that you should desist [from fishing], since nothing could be gotten without the greatest labor. But if the Moon would be applying to Saturn, and should Venus be aspecting her, the haul will be great, because in this kind [of hunting] Saturn does not impede the Moon, unless Mars aspects her. Venus is even weakened for this [purpose], since Mars is adverse to Venus while she walks under his aspect: for it threatens shipwreck, and the qualities that are of this kind are heavy rains and flooding, and so on.[20]

---

[18] Or rather, on land (al-Rijāl, Sahl).
[19] Cf. *On Quest.* §13.16.
[20] John's Sahl reads this last sentence differently: "...because Mars is the enemy of Venus. If Saturn aspected her, then shipwreck will be feared...".

§7.203: On fishing—ʿUmar

First of all, once the east is established, its lord and equally that of the hour, even Venus and the Moon, should be consulted. And so, the east being watery, while Mars would corrupt the Moon and the lord of the hour, with the regard of Venus being wholly denied, it stands in the way of the catch, instills fear, [and] brings in nothing useful (or very little). The[21] evil will be greater and worse if the sign were not watery, because then Mars is worse and introduces greater loss or is more harmful, unless you found Venus to be strong in its[22] place, or having some rulership in the Ascendant or in the hour, and she were in some angle of the Ascendant, and the Moon would be aspecting Venus or would be joined with her: because Venus is powerful in a hunt on the sea.[23]

Also, Saturn being in the regard of the Moon, but Venus being strong, possessing something of the dignity of the hour, and with the Lunar strength being discovered in her own places, weighs down the nets with many fish, in accordance with Saturn's not-difficult adversity. Even Venus and especially the Moon (as was already stated) claim a not-moderate signification over the fishing, unless, I say, Mars would regard the Moon from a pivot or an assembly, and Venus is weak:[24] for it threatens the fishermen, and perhaps not without the danger of death. [But if Saturn aspected her, it signifies an impediment for the master of the hunt.][25]

Likewise, for watery fishing, among the rest it is healthful that Venus, the Moon, Mercury [and] Jupiter would have control over the rulership of the east and the hour [and] the Midheaven, while the Moon would apply to Venus and each would be in the aspect of Mercury, with Jupiter occupying a watery sign: for thus they save from every danger, and make a copious haul without difficulty.

---

[21] Reading the rest of this paragraph with al-Rijāl, because Hugo's choppy sentences do not always make it clear who is doing what.
[22] This probably means that she is strong in the place where she is.
[23] Medieval texts consider fishing to be a hunt on the water.
[24] Al-Rijāl reads more plausibly and simply: "Because Saturn's harm towards Venus and the Moon in hunting by sea is small, unless Mars would aspect the Moon from an angle, or he were joined with her, and Venus [were weak]: for this signifies loss in hunting, and evil, on account of Mars (who is the enemy of Venus)."
[25] Adding with al-Rijāl.

The[26] preferable signs, I say, are the watery ones, and they being remote from the aspect of Mars, because he harms this affair in a difficult way, unless (I say) Jupiter is regarding or rather would have the rulership, being not retrograde nor scorched or descending:[27] for thus the perversity and malice of Mars is broken.

Likewise, Mercury being regarded by Saturn, while [Saturn] would govern something of the matter,[28] is by no means attacked by the partnership [of Saturn]: for Saturn is hostile to this affair [in only] a small way.

---

[26] In this paragraph, al-Rijāl has the Ascendant in watery signs, and Jupiter saving the matter if he aspects the Ascendant, and if the *victor* of the Ascendant is direct (and so on).
[27] That is, in its fall.
[28] Al-Rijāl has Saturn "having some rulership there," which suggests that he is receiving Mercury.

§8: EIGHTH HOUSE

8th House	
Death	§§8.1-5
Fear	§§8.6-7

Figure 60: Questions of the eighth house

DEATH

§8.1: On those things which pertain to the eighth house—Sahl[1]

If perhaps an inquiry about the eighth would occur (as there often is about some exiled person), as to whether he is living or dead, it is rightly solved [in this manner]:[2] we give the counsel to the eastern lord and the Moon. For if they would possess the fourth or eighth, or if they would be scorched or are falling,[3] or rather should they be conjoined to the lord of the eighth, they convey a certain decree [of death]. Which if either one alone would bear itself in this way, one will have to observe with respect to the status and position of each significator, even how they are in the aspect of the benevolents and the infortunes. And so, the just testimonies of good or evil are maintained in the method[4] of judging.

In fact, with the eastern lord being retrograde or falling,[5] or at least moving through the eighth, or withdrawing from a retrograde lord of the eighth,[6] it claims nothing of death is to be feared—unless perhaps in retrograding it would be scorched: for thus it declares death is going to come soon.[7] The Lunar application to some [star] staying under the earth, is fatal; above the earth, the contrary. Moreover, the eastern lord being in the twelfth[8] and con-

---

[1] Cf. *On Quest.* §8.1.
[2] Reading *iure exsolvitur* for *iura exsoluverit*.
[3] That is, in their own fall.
[4] Reading *ratione* for *ratio*.
[5] Again, being in its own descension.
[6] Or perhaps this should be read as "withdrawing from the lord of the eighth *while* retrograding," as with al-Khayyāt below.
[7] Hugo seems to be stating this a bit too forcefully. John's Sahl has: "If the lord of the Ascendant were in the fourth, retrograde, or retrograde in its own descension, or retrograde in the domicile of death, or separated through retrogradation from the lord of the house of death, look to see if it turns back to the degree of being burned up: he will be dead."
[8] Reading with John's Sahl and al-Khayyāt for "[being with] the lord of the twelfth."

joined to malevolents, or being regarded by them, where at the same time one of the lights is being corrupted [without an aspect of the benevolents],[9] it is mortal. The Moon traversing with Mars in the fourth, the benevolents being wholly in aversion, threatens and conveys the same thing.

Nevertheless, the Lot of Fortune being with the wicked ones, should it possess the fourth and sixth or twelfth, without any aid and testimony of the fortunate ones, [signifies death].

But generally, an inquiry of this kind is resolved by the hemisphere. For stars stepping through the upper hemisphere have a judgment of vital breath, and those which traverse in the lower one are allotted judgments of death. And so, with the eastern lord being scorched, and the benevolents in aversion [to him], so that equally the Moon (she appearing under the earth) would be walking through a remote[10] sign, has a judgment of death. And this is more powerfully so, and with all ambiguity being removed, if the Moon, being placed thus, [and] within the third degree of Scorpio,[11] would be corrupted by Saturn (whose nature is to bring death).

§8.2: On the life or death of an absent person—al-Khayyāt

When inquiries of the eighth happen, such as for the life or death of an absent person, it is good to note the lord of the east and the Moon. If they happened to be found in the fourth or the house of death, or in their own fall, or with the lord of the eighth, it will be an indication of death. Which if either one alone would bear itself in this way, one must consult the testimonies of the fortunate and unfortunate ones. For, the lord of the east being in its own fall, or being retrograde in the eighth or fourth, or withdrawing from the lord of the house of death by retrograding, speaks against death, unless perhaps it would undergo scorching from that retrogradation: for thus it will then be wholly fatal. Even the Moon applying to some [star] under the earth is equally fatal. Moreover, the lord of the east being in the twelfth with the infortunes, or they regarding it,[12] and with either of the lights being corrupt-

---

[9] Adding based on John's Sahl.
[10] A cadent sign, which would include the third and sixth (which John's Sahl specifically mentions).
[11] This is the actual degree of her fall.
[12] Reading *respicientes* for *respiciens*.

ed, it is mortal. If a malevolent would corrupt one of the lights without the testimony of the fortunate ones, it is the same.

Never should there come to be a judgment about death, unless either one of the significators is first being corrupted, or one would weaken the other, with even the fortunate ones first being cadent from an angle.

§8.3: On someone, whether he is living or dead—Dorotheus

If perhaps an inquiry of the eighth would happen, such as about some man as to whether or not he is living or dead, we consult the lord of the east and the Moon. For, being in the fourth or in the house of death or in [their] own fall, or being conjoined to the lord of the house of death, they really declare death. For if either one is placed so, the testimonies of the fortunate ones and the infortunes (namely of those in the regard of the lord of the east),[13] are taken. Also, the lord of the east being retrograde in the fourth or in its own fall, or entering into scorching, is mortal. It is not otherwise [if he is] under the earth, applying to some retrograde [star] in that same place. But the Moon being placed thusly, and the lord of the east being corrupted, signifies the same thing: namely while that same lord of the east, on account of its own corruption, would hold onto her tetragon or opposition. Which if it happened otherwise (namely that the lord of the east would be lucky or would withdraw from the degree of the house of death), it speaks against death.

Moreover, one will have to take up [the distance] from the Moon to the degree of the house of death, and once that number is drawn back from Saturn,[14] one must note where it ends. And the bound of its place, if it should fall to a malevolent, or the receiver is unlucky, it is fatal to the one about whom it is asked. But if the significator[15] is Mercury, and he is far removed from the Sun, and in the regard of the malevolents, it really threatens death. Venus and the rest of the stars signify in this way, too.

---

[13] Reading *domini* for *dominium*.
[14] Reading *Saturno* for *oriente*. This is one version of the Lot of death (*ITA* VI.2.27), actually found in *Carmen* IV.1.158. Al-Rijāl (V.7) gives two others. According to Zaradusht, it is by day and night from Saturn to the Descendant, and projected from the Ascendant; according to Hermes, from Saturn to the degree of the eighth (but not indicating from what point it is projected).
[15] This may mean the lord of the bound of the Lot, because Mercury is not normally one of the infortunes. Nevertheless, I do not understand how Mercury and Venus could indicate by being *far* from the Sun's rays.

Moreover, the Moon possessing the pivot of the earth with Mars, they being cadent from the eastern lord and the benevolents, denotes an indication of death.

§8.4: What is the cause of death—Dorotheus

If the cause which will have preceded his death is sought, we advise you to consult the eastern lord or the Moon (namely, the one which bears the signification of death).[16] And so, it being scorched generates death from heat, and prefigures a hidden disease. But at the extreme point of a pivot,[17] it suggests the worst kind of death, for then it will possess a hot place; and in the same way if the significator were one of the wandering stars.[18]

And so, the significator being corrupted by Saturn, with Saturn (I say) appearing in the east or its triplicity, really threatens death from slipping (namely from a prominent place), or from a beast. Which if that same Saturn would possess Taurus or its triplicity, he will perish from melancholy or a condition of the head,[19] [since] cold and dryness would furnish the cause. Also, in Gemini or its triplicity, if he does not leave the tenth [place] behind, it declares a fall from a high place. But in the pivot of the earth, he dies either by slipping, or something tumbles down upon him. In the same way, in Cancer or its triplicity, he will die through drowning or dysentery, unless perhaps Saturn would be ascending:[20] for thus it means a death because of apoplexy and that kind of thing.

Which if Mars would corrupt [the significator], with [Mars] being in the east or its triplicity, it threatens a fall or impels a heavy thing upon him. After that, it is necessary that he die through the sword or iron. [Mars] being established in the tenth, prepares a cross and hanging. In Cancer or its triplicity, he incurs death through water.

---

[16] That is, once you have used them to determine death in the previous section.
[17] *Extremo.* I believe this means exactly on (or at least virtually on) the axial degree.
[18] *Erraticis.* I am not sure what distinction Dorotheus is trying to make here.
[19] *Cephalia.*
[20] This must mean either in zodiacal longitude or in the circle of his apogee (*ITA* II.0-1).

§8.5: What kind of death ought to end his life—Aristotle

But whenever it was asked by what kind of death he would end his life, the knot of the question will be dissolved by the eighth and its lord. For, Leo being in the eighth, he really incurs death by some beast. Scorpio in that same place, he dies by means of poisoning.[21]

Moreover, Saturn traversing in Scorpio, Pisces or Cancer, and with the lord of the eighth, threatens death by waters.[22] But Mars being in the eighth or with its lord: he breathes out his spirit by means of some feverish heat and often even iron. Moreover, the Tail being equally arranged there (in the eighth, I say, or with its lord) prepares iron.

Finally, wherever the lord of the eighth would traverse alone, it warns not of another kind of death, but its own.[23]

---

[21] *Veneficiis*. This also includes evil magical practices.
[22] For this sentence and the next, cf. *Carmen* IV.1.147 and IV.1.150. In both cases, *Carmen* has Saturn or Mars *being* the lord of the eighth (which makes more sense); nor do they have to be in the eighth.
[23] That is, according to its own planetary nature.

FEAR

§8.6: On fear—'Umar[1]

However, with a question about fear being proposed, the eastern lord regarding the east, being free of the infortunes, claims an empty command of fear, for it frees the querent from every trouble. Moreover, it traversing in the perverse places (which are the second, sixth,[2] but even the eighth and the twelfth), testifies that he has incurred fear according to that place which the lord of the east claims. Which if the testimonies of infortunes from the pivots are present, the whole affair and the fear declines to what is worse, while he will really lie under [a cloud of] terror.[3] With the favor[4] of these [infortunes] being discarded, he will undergo no trouble apart from fear. But, [the lord of the east] being established in a pivot, [and] likewise under the aspect of the infortunes from the pivots, it is serious; it is most serious if that [corrupting] star would have control of the rulership of the eighth from the east: for thus it introduces ruin and death. But if it rules over another rather than the eighth, [it indicates] death, but after the worst he escapes the danger.

Furthermore, the proper quality of the convertible signs come especially to be noted here: for they signify that the harm will be changed quickly.[5] Likewise the double-bodied and firm ones signal constant and anxious danger, under the favor of the aforesaid.[6] Then, too, an infortune placed in the twelfth saves from every trouble.[7] But in the second, it leads him as a captive, not without money.[8]

Moreover, the lord of the east occupying the twelfth, while it regards neither the lord of the seventh nor that of the twelfth, prepares flight and means an escape. If however it would apply to an infortune, he incurs loss from the

---

[1] Cf. al-Rijāl I.22 (second half).
[2] Reading with al-Rijāl for "seventh."
[3] *Dum is profecto formidini subiacebit.*
[4] Hugo is being ironic here: obviously the infortunes are not providing anything favorable.
[5] Reading with al-Rijāl for *adiuta testimonio graviter minatur.*
[6] That is, if the malefics indicating the fear are in them.
[7] This runs somewhat contrary to the general trend in traditional astrology, which says that infortunes in the twelfth are generally bad for the native. 'Umar says that an infortune there will be bad *for the enemies*; Abū Bakr II.14.2 (in *PN2*) says that infortunes there indicate harm for the enemies, provided that the lord of the twelfth is also harmed—but that a dignified infortune there signify the enemies are evil. Abū Bakr is based on al-Khayyāt's *JN* Ch. 36 (in *PN2*).
[8] Perhaps 'Umar means he will be held for ransom.

flight; but[9] if the infortunes had the rulerships over the house of the lord of the east, or they ruled the east itself, he will suffer no evil besides flight, and the turmoils which were threatening will happen on the flight.

§8.7: On security or worry—Dorotheus

But here, if it is asked about someone's security or anguish, or whether the worry would be long-lasting, one must note the status and power of the malevolent corrupting the Moon, [and] even what virtue it is allotted in that house.[10] If therefore it were Mars, it denies what is feared[11] but he will die through fire or blows. But Saturn prolongs prison to the utmost moment of life, namely according to the nature of the dignity assumed in that same place. But if any lucky one would stain[12] the Moon, the one who was afraid is being held, but afterwards he will escape.[13]

Moreover, [the Moon] being cleansed of the infortunes and being in a pivot, nor applying to a cadent [planet], declares it is true. Being in a pivot and applying to a cadent infortune (nor one receiving [her]), even though there is truth to what was said above, he incurs nothing besides fear. She being placed outside a pivot, applying to a fortunate one in a pivot, and received, it manifests and claims that it is true. Which if [she were] unlucky or corrupted by anyone, [and] would apply to it, it promises detriment.

---

[9] Reading the rest of this sentence with al-Rijāl.
[10] This must mean the sign in which he is; but it could mean the sign in which the Moon is.
[11] *Metuendum negat.* This does not make sense, unless Dorotheus is only saying that the fear will not be long-lasting.
[12] *Inficiat.* Normally Hugo only uses this for aspects that have a negative role.
[13] Remember that we are assuming that the Moon is being corrupted and that there is a real threat, so Dorotheus is really describing a situation where both a malevolent and a benevolent are aspecting the Moon.

§9: NINTH HOUSE

9th House	
Travel: will it happen	§§9.1-8
Length of travel	§9.9
What will happen on the journey	§§9.10-12, 9.15-16
Should one travel	§§9.13-14
Ships: their cargo & condition	§§9.41-43
Absent persons: their status and return	§§5.49, 8.2, 9.20-35
Leaving one's current condition	§§10.25-26
Dream interpretation	§§9.36-37
Alchemy & other knowledge	§§9.38-40

Figure 61: Questions of the ninth house

TRAVEL

§9.1: On those things which pertain to the ninth house—Sahl[1]

When inquiries of the ninth happen, of which kind is [a question] about travel, whether or not it would happen or if it would be denied, [and] what is the occasion for hindering it, let these paths to judgment be held. And so, the lord of the east and the Moon determine the querent; but the ninth and its lord assume the signification of travel. If therefore the lord of the east or the Moon should happen to be found in the ninth or applying to the lord of the ninth, he about whom it had been asked will undertake the journey according to his own will. But contrariwise, whenever the lord of the ninth would be in the east or would apply to the lord of the east, it portends he is going to undertake the journey with a reason forcing [him to do it]. With an application being denied, while however there is a transfer of light, it definitely establishes travel. And so, if you understood this to be absent, while a collection of their light was not absent, but so that the one which collected [the light] would be regarding the ninth,[2] it is a sign of establishing travel. But with a regard being denied, the travel is denied.

---

[1] Cf. *On Quest.* §9.1.
[2] See reflecting light #2, in *ITA* III.13.1. But it is not clear to me whether Sahl requires the two significators to be actually in aversion before this kind of collecting/reflecting can take place, or simply that they are not applying to each other by degree.

On the other hand, the lord of the east being in a pivot and cleansed of the unfortunate stars, and free, applying to [a star] placed on the left of the east, consoles with respect to travel, and makes it be present. (But the left of the east is from the Ascendant[3] up to the third).

Moreover, once an application of the eastern lord or the Moon to some [star] positioned in a pivot is discovered, it speaks against travel.

Also, [if] infortune possessed the east, [then] however much the significators may apply to each other, while however you find each being corrupted by that infortune, it wholly resists travel. Even the traversal of any malevolent in the seventh blocks travel from happening, because it brings an impediment from the region toward which he heads. If however an infortune would be lingering in the tenth, it declares that the reason for the impediment is going to come from a lord or prince.

In addition to all of this, if the lord of the east would apply to the lord of the ninth, but so that it would be[4] corrupted afterwards by the assembly or perverse aspect of a malevolent, then once the travel is accomplished he cannot avoid the harm of adversity (in terms of the status and nature of the corrupting [planet]). With it having the rulership of the sixth, it afflicts him with disease; but if it would rule the fourth, it prepares tight spots and captivities; but if the eighth, it claims that death must be feared; which if [it rules over] the seventh or twelfth, it threatens robbers or the attack of enemies. Moreover, for this infortune: it regarding[5] the east from the figure of a tetragon, threatens iron. But whenever it would regard the second, it assails his wealth and resources.

Which if you would find the lord of the east in the seventh or eighth, it has the judgment of a laborious journey, and more powerfully so with it being unlucky; but contrariwise, if the lord of the east is already beginning to be eastern or if it would be withdrawing from an infortune, it makes it easy and unhampered.

The reception of the Moon makes the travel easier; but not being received renders it complicated [and] unprofitable.[6]

---

[3] Reading with John for Hugo's "eleventh." Sahl must mean from the degree of the Ascendant to the degree of the IC.
[4] Omitting *nec* ("not"). The connection between the significators shows travel, but the subsequent connection to malefics shows trouble after the journey.
[5] Omitting *iterum* ("again").
[6] John's Sahl adds: "the lord of the Ascendant signifies likewise if it aspected her from the opposition."

Again, if the lord of the east would be lingering in the east or in its other house, it rejects travel, particularly if what it was holding onto was a firm [sign].

Therefore, concerning the four pivots, the east is put in charge of the querent, but the tenth comprehends the manner of the business, the seventh not undeservedly possesses the region to which he heads, the fourth resolves the end of the whole thing. Therefore, the traversal of fortunate ones in the east preserves him himself; going through the tenth, they consummate the business; in the seventh, they prepare profit in that region; in the fourth, they bring forth the desired end. The infortunes operate contrariwise.

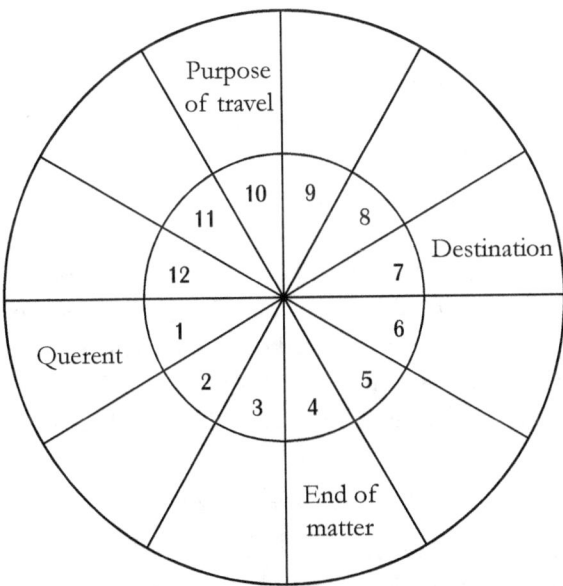

Figure 62: Angular significators for travel (Sahl §9.1, al-Kindī §9.15)

§9.2: On travel, whether it would happen or not—'Umar

On the other hand, the lords of the Lunar lodging-place and of the domicile which is in charge of travel appearing in the pivots, hastens travel. No less too do they establish travel if they support the lord of the east with their own aspect. Now, if an aspect of this kind is absent, while there is a star between each collecting their light, or should there be a transfer of their light to the eastern lord, it is a sign of setting out [on the journey]. Contrariwise, too, if neither collection nor transfer is present, nor do they regard the lord of the east, it speaks against travel. Likewise, with reception being denied while however there is a regard and application from a tetragon or assembly or opposition, they indicate travel after a difficulty; but a regard from a trigon or hexagon, even though reception would be absent, threatens travel but does not prevent it.[7] Finally, reception with an application removes the difficulty and blesses with joy.

§9.3: On travel—al-Kindī

§283. For a question on travel, as to whether or not counsel of a stellar nature would permit it to happen, the Sun and Moon and lord of the Ascendant and the [lord] of the Lot of Fortune, even the lord of the assembly or opposition [of the lights], come especially to be considered.[8] All of them being remote from the pivots confers the effecting of travel, particularly if there would be an application of the lord of the Ascendant with the lord of the ninth or third, or even [with] Mars, and Mars is remote from a pivot.[9]

§284.[10] Moreover, if the lord of the third or ninth, or Mars, would apply themselves with the lord of the Ascendant, [and] moreover should an application of the Moon with her own lord or that of the ninth or third or even with Mars be noted, [and] moreover [if] the lord of the house of travel [would be] in the Ascendant (I say, a little bit drawn back or nearly remote from the Ascendant),[11] or the lord of the Ascendant itself [would be] in the ninth or third—all of these, I say (and an observation of them being thus

---

[7] I take this to mean that there will be travel, but with some trouble.
[8] Note that these are all derived from the list of releasing places for the weighted victor over the querent in Ch. 3.2 of *Forty Chapters*.
[9] In which case, Mars would be in the angles of the ninth.
[10] For this section, al-Rijāl first seems to say that the lords of the third and ninth should be cadent, too (if the lord of the Ascendant should apply to them, as at the end of §283). Then he continues: "And should Mars be cadent from the angle of the Ascendant, or as though he is falling from the Ascendant by entering into the twelfth, and the lord of the Ascendant would be in the ninth or third, all of these signify that the travel is completed and happens; but if you found the contrary of this, judge the contrary." By Mars being cadent, he could mean being cadent from *the* angle of the Ascendant (i.e., in aversion to the Ascendant), or cadent from *an* angle of the Ascendant (namely, simply cadent, in the third, sixth, ninth, and twelfth).
[11] I believe this means he is dynamically cadent: in the rising sign, but more than about 5° earlier than the rising degree itself.

noted), confirm that the travel will undoubtedly come to be. But [if they were] foreign to this arrangement,[12] they wholly deny travel.

§285. Moreover, [if] the five releasers[13] [are] in the pivots or after the pivots, [then] even though the lord of the Ascendant or the Moon may apply with certain ones of the afore-stated (namely those which obtain the signification of travel), he will never acquire the effect, even though he seems to be able to complete the travel without any hindrance.[14]

[Timing of travel]

§286. Moreover, if the generosity of the celestial circle already confirms the effecting of the travel, the number of the degrees of application determines how long the delay[15] is: namely, the space of their hours or days or months. An application of [1] the Moon in her own course with the lord of travel;[16] or [2] of the star whose signification we follow in travel with the degree of the Ascendant or of the Moon or of the Lot of Fortune; even sometimes [3] the exit of some star[17] from under the rays, or [4] the transit of the lord of the Ascendant from its own sign into another, or [5] the advancement of either of these to the Lot of travel[18]—I say all of these determine the time when the hope of carrying out the travel is had.[19]

§9.4: On travel—al-Khayyāt

With a question presented about those things which pertain to the ninth house, such as for travel, whether it would happen or not. We put the lord of the east and the Moon in charge of the querent, the ninth and its lord over

---

[12] This must mean that *none* of the above conditions are met.
[13] See Chs 3.2-3 of *Forty Chapters*, but note also the modified list above in §283. Al-Rijāl seems to indicate that only the primary releaser. See also al-Kindī's §311 in §9.15 below.
[14] That is, if all of the releasers are angular or succeedent, they will override the usual indications of travel.
[15] *Dilatio.* I read this as the time between the question and the actual date of travel. But Burnett (1993, p. 81) believes it means the length of the whole trip.
[16] Al-Rijāl: "the planet which signified travel: that is, the planet which demonstrated that the journey is completed."
[17] Robert: "one of the aforesaid stars."
[18] The Lot of travel is taken by day and night from the lord of the ninth to the ninth, and is projected from the Ascendant.
[19] It seems to me that we should probably consider the real-time transits of these planets as well, and not just convert their degrees into units of time.

the journey. A joint, mutual application of all of these equally, establishes travel. In addition even, the lord of the ninth placed in the east accelerates the same; no less too with the lord of the east and the Moon being placed in the ninth. Moreover, the lord of the ninth being in the east or rendering counsel to the lord of the east: he undertakes the travel on some occasion befalling [him]. But if to the contrary, should the lord of the east be in the ninth or render counsel to its lord, he jumps at the chance to travel of his own accord. Moreover, a transfer of light made from the eastern [lord] to the lord of the ninth shows the certainty of travel. Likewise, the lord of the east being received, brings about a profitable journey. Which if it would bear itself towards the inimical and adverse lord of its own place, it impedes travel and mixes in something other than his hope. Therefore, with these things which we said before not being found, while the eastern [lord] and the lord of the ninth would equally apply to some heavier [planet] which however regards the place of the affair, travel is certain. But if it does not regard it, nor would it be lingering in the ninth, it wholly speaks against [travel].

Moreover, the eastern lord rendering counsel to some [star] placed on the left of the east, [the lord of the east] being free of the infortunes, favors travel. In fact the lord of the east, not without the significator, rendering powers[20] and counsel to a star lingering in a pivot, bars travel from happening. But if it applied to a malevolent on the right of the east, it complicates travel, and threatens labor and difficulty. Likewise, the lord of the east being in the ninth or on the left of the east, receiving the powers and counsel of both significators, portends that the travel will happen. It is even the same if it, from the right of the east, it would receive the counsel of the significator staying on the left—however, there will be labor and difficulty in it. Likewise, the lord of the east rendering counsel to a star on the right[21] of the east (nor one having testimonies), shows easy and unhampered travel. An infortune in the east, even though a mutual application of the significators may be discovered, while however it would be hostile to each [of the significators], he will get nothing of what was proposed. For if the lord of the east would be corrupted, he himself will inflict the impediment upon himself.

A malevolent in the east generates some impediment apart from his hope. Which if it would be lingering in the seventh, the occasion of the hindrance comes from the region to which he heads. Moreover, the lord of the east

---

[20] That is, "pushing power."
[21] This should probably read "left," with the logic of the paragraph.

rendering counsel to the lord of the ninth, but afterwards it would apply to a hostile one by assembly or a tetragon or opposition, once the travel is completed he will incur the trouble of adversity according to the nature and powers of the corrupting [infortune], through the twelve houses.[22] If that malevolent would rule over the sixth, it prepares an infirmity. But if the twelfth, it threatens prison and afflicts with anguish. If the eighth, death. (It is more severe if the star to which it is being joined, were an infortune: for then it heaps evil onto evil, and is finally fatal. But it being a fortunate one, promises escape.) The lord of the seventh or twelfth being the infortune [that is] receiving the counsel of the eastern lord after the lord of the ninth, warns that one should beware of robbers, and the attacks of enemies are to be feared. Should that same infortune regard the east from a tetragon, it threatens a sword and slaughter for the querent, if however [that sign] would have the signification of a person.[23] But if the second, it seizes wealth and scatters resources; regarding the third from a tetragon, it supplies anguish and fear. The reception of the significator[24] alleviates the travel, [but] not received it complicates and aggravates and removes success.

But it is appropriate to note the significator, as we taught about the lord of the east. For, it being peregrine [in] its place, rendering counsel to a star placed in the ninth or twelfth, makes the travel spontaneous and hastens it—if, I say, the Moon would be lingering in a pivot. But if it would apply [to infortunes?] in those same places, while however it renders counsel to the lords of those places (they being peregrine where they themselves are traversing), it is opposed to travel and supplies something apart from his hope. Moreover, the Moon rendering powers and counsel to the lord of the third and ninth equally, with they being peregrine, or at least [if she does so] to a peregrine star in those places, it bestows the outcome upon the travel. It is no less too, with the Moon transferring light from a star positioned in a pivot, to another one [that is] remote.

§9.5: On travel, whether it would happen or not—Dorotheus

Whenever questions of the ninth are brought out into the open, such as for travel (whether or not it would have an effect), we consult the lords of

---

[22] Reading with Sahl §9.1 above for Hugo's confusing wording.
[23] That is, if the image of the sign has a human form, or perhaps if it is a humane sign.
[24] According to Sahl in §9.1, this would be the Moon.

the east and of the house of travel equally, and the Moon. For if they bear themselves just as was said,[25] and the lord of the ninth is placed in the east, it quickly establishes the travel hoped for. But the lord of the east and the Moon possessing the ninth, [means] the same. The lord of the ninth in the east: he undertakes travel with his own urgency (but not a harmful one) compelling him. Which if there is a transfer of light from the eastern [lord] to the lord of the ninth, it persuades [him to undertake] the journey. Moreover, the lord of the east being received, declares the travel is useful; but outside its own house, it complicates it with labor and difficulty. But with these things which have been said before being denied, while however the eastern lord and that of the ninth would apply to a star regarding the place of the affair,[26] it is a sign of establishing travel. Which if no star would possess the house of travel,[27] it speaks against travel.

If however the lord of the east, with the other significator, would render counsel to a star situated in a pivot, it is believed to obstruct travel. But[28] if this rendering [would be to an infortune on the right of the east], it mixes in impediment and difficulty. While the lord of the east would be taking up [a position in the ninth or on the left of the east], it declares travel. No less too, the lord of the east rendering counsel to the right side where it rejoices in no witnesses, he carries on with the travel [but] not without the trouble of adversity; and the Moon in the same way.

Which if a malevolent would transfer [light] between the significators, it spoils travel or involves labor, and leads the owner of the question into [a bad] situation. This malevolent being in the pivot [of the east],[29] necessarily spoils the travel. But it being in the seventh, brings in impediment from the region to which he advances, and stains the affair. But if in the tenth, the king or a prince is going to be the impediment.

But this must be noted: the lords of the twelfth and of the seventh being the corrupting [malevolents],[30] if they gather the counsel of the eastern lord, it warns that one must beware of robbers and ambushes. Now, if they regard [the eastern lord] from the east, they threaten death. But if in the second,

---

[25] This must mean, "if they are all applying to each other," as with al-Khayyāt in §9.4 above.
[26] That is, to a collecting planet which itself aspects the ninth.
[27] Adding based on al-Khayyāt in §9.4.
[28] For this sentence and the next, reading with al-Khayyāt in §9.4 for Hugo's confused wording.
[29] Adding based on al-Khayyāt in §9.4.
[30] Reading with al-Khayyāt for "being corrupted."

they snatch away resources. Finally there will be a progression through the rest of the signs with such a reckoning.

Nor do I believe one should overlook that the Moon in a pivot accelerates the affairs of the querent. Likewise, with her blocking counsel from those places,[31] while however she would render counsel to the lord of the ninth or the third (they being established in that same place), it will really support travel.

§9.6: On travel and any change [of place]—Jirjis

With a question of this kind being proposed, the east that is established embraces the querent and his first steps. Also, the Midheaven is in charge over the travel, the land to which he heads is distinguished in the seventh, but the pivot of the earth resolves the end of the whole affair and even [his] return.

And so, the eastern lord being strong, strengthens the querent in the journey, and protects him. Being weak judges to the contrary. But the one which is in charge over the Midheaven, [if] a lucky one and free, adorns the journey with every prosperity. A malevolent appearing in that same place introduces trouble and loss. Which if Saturn appeared as that malevolent, it threatens death on the journey; but Mars prepares slaughter and scatters wealth.

Nevertheless, with recourse having been had [to the east and the Midheaven], it will be permitted to attend to the seventh and the fourth: for where a lucky and benevolent [planet] happened to be found, remember to describe good and joys; but where [you find a malevolent, report] trouble and loss on the journey.

But if someone made a question about travel (whether it would happen or not), the equal and joint aspect of the eastern lord and the one which is in charge of travel,[32] establishes the journey; with an aspect being denied, this speaks against travel. Once the certainty of travel has been discovered, if the day when it would happen is sought, [see] on what day the eastern lord would reach (by regarding it)[33] the degree where the lord of travel is staying, and it testifies that the travel will happen on that very day.

---

[31] See my tentative reading of al-Khayyāt in §9.4, which has her applying to infortunes.
[32] Namely, the lord of the ninth (or perhaps third, for shorter journeys).
[33] But surely this also includes an assembly by body.

§9.7: On travel, a marriage-union, or kingdom—Jirjis

With a question being presented about travel or a marriage-union or even a kingdom, one must note equally the lord of the seventh, ninth, and tenth. If therefore they would apply to the lord of the east, they will attain [the matter]. But do as we said above at the beginning of the chapter on this category,[34] even though the shortest method resolves the greatest bit of the science.

But for travel, the lord of the east being in the east (and it being a firm sign) in no way establishes travel. But if it would be holding onto a turning [sign], he does it. But in the east, he advances toward the east; in the second, after the east;[35] in the third, toward the middle of the earth; in the Midheaven, it calls him to the south and to foreign nations; in the seventh or eighth, it threatens death or prison; in the pivot of the earth, toward the north.

§9.8: On travel—Aristotle

With a question being proposed about travel, let the intention of your mind be led back to the east and the ninth (which announces a long journey). If therefore Saturn would traverse in the ninth (he having a house or sovereignty in that place), there occurs no doubt about the prosperity of the journey; moreover, he being deprived of each dignity and traversing in that same place, speaks against travel, for it disturbs all things with a squabble and quarrel and supplies impediment, while it even threatens [a strong] wind]. The contrary [situation] often even happens so that the journey is successful, but someone detaining him[36] there slows his return and inflicts a delay.

With the lord of the ninth bearing itself badly, namely so that it would be cadent or retrograde or scorched or even burned up, or at least with the bad ones and in a foreign house, it conveys the most burdensome impediment, because in such a way it confines the ship or him himself, so that it instills the fear of death.

Moreover, with Saturn lingering in the ninth, with the lord of the ninth (since the lord of that place has greater power in the ninth than Saturn does), it will be permitted to recommend travel.

---

[34] I am not sure what Jirjis is referring to.
[35] That is, in the direction of the second house: east-northeast.
[36] Reading *eum* for *eos* ("them").

Jupiter traversing in the ninth, with the lord of the ninth bearing itself well, favors travel; but while it bears itself badly, it signifies impediment: in order to avoid that, the journey should be deferred.

The presence of Mars in the ninth announces that enemies are to be feared on the journey. In addition however, with the lord of the ninth bearing itself badly, he is captured; if not, not. If it were a journey by boat, the boat will be stormed [and] captured; if not, not. But if the lord of the ninth would linger in its own proper house, where Mars brings robbers, it will hit him with no loss at all.

The traversal of the Sun in the ninth introduces nothing beyond fear. But if it is common and in the middle,[37] it is more praiseworthy and propitious, and for that reason it makes the journey profitable—with the lord of the ninth, I say, bearing itself well: if otherwise, otherwise.

The steadiness of Venus in the ninth, while the lord of the ninth would be lingering in an optimal way, [puts him] in the good grace and favor of women (because Venus is feminine), and makes the journey profitable.

Now, if Mercury were in the ninth, and with the good ones, so that however the lord of the ninth would be arranged in an optimal way, the journey will be praiseworthy but not profitable enough.

Moreover, the Lunar progression in the ninth, and if the lord of the ninth would be bearing itself well, recommends a prosperous journey; nevertheless, they do not progress in a straight path, just as the Moon does not.

The Tail in that same place makes it wholly bad, for it prepares ambushes or wrecks the ship. The [Head of the] Dragon in the ninth, so that the lord of the ninth would traverse prosperously, it is certain that aristocrats will be found whom he will please (for the Head of the Dragon bears the signification of powerful people and magnates).

But we give no other judgment about a short journey, than we do about with the ninth.[38]

---

[37] *Mediocris.* This probably means only that it is in a common sign.
[38] This could either mean that both short and long journeys are decided through the ninth, or else that short journeys are handled through the third house but using a similar method.

§9.9: What the journey is, in days—Aristotle

Finally, the present method will teach about the span (or rather, the time) of the journey. For if you wish to attend more diligently to the years of the planets,[39] you will assign that many days to their number. Namely as an example of the teaching: whenever therefore Saturn will have claimed the rulership of the ninth, you will establish the journey as being for 30 days, and thus with the rest. Also in this manner, how long he ought to stay.[40]

In addition even, one must note: should the lord of the ninth possess a strong place from the ninth (namely, a pivot),[41] you will judge the journey to be for the lesser days of that planet. If it would linger after the pivots, you will assign the middle days.[42] With it traversing in the remote ones (namely, the weak ones), remember to attribute the greater ones.[43] But in order that we may speak in an ordinary way: appearing in the strong [places] indicates he is going to go immediately; in middling ones, not so much; in the weak ones, more slowly.

No matter if none would be traversing in the ninth, should however the lord of the ninth be bearing itself well, let there be no ambiguity for you about the prosperity of the journey.

Finally, in all things I warn that you should beware with the greatest effort, lest while impediment be promised from anywhere, you recommend to anyone that he jump at the chance for a journey, unless it will be deferred until the travel could be freely accomplished. And then the question be answered thusly.

---

[39] See the table in §1.2.
[40] Omitting *vel qualiter* ("or how").
[41] I take this to mean the whole-sign angles from the ninth. So for instance, the ninth itself, the third, the sixth and the twelfth would indicate the pivots of the ninth. But there might be an error here, and Aristotle might simply mean the normal pivots (the first, tenth, seventh, fourth).
[42] That is, days corresponding to the middle years.
[43] The reason for this is that the cadent places generally indicate travel and something far away, while the pivots indicate something present: so, being in the pivots indicates a shorter trip, and therefore fewer days.

§9.10: Whether a premeditated journey would be brought to its end—Aristotle

Before all else, it will be good to attend to the east, but even the third and the ninth, and their lords. For, with any of them appearing retrograde, while the Moon would traverse with that same one, it speaks against a successful journey. Moreover, she traversing with any one of them (which however is proceeding directly), even though the retrogradation of the others would render the intention of the one going as being ambiguous, it grants the travel with the [desired] effect. Moreover, the Moon being estranged from every association of theirs while two are retrograde, they wholly prevent the goal of the journey, and they take away the effects that ought to be. But the two of them being direct, present a certain judgment about effecting it.

§9.11: To what men he heads, and what would happen to him on the journey—Sahl[44]

If therefore certainty about travel is had, if one seeks [to know] to whom he is going to go, it is good to investigate the Moon. For, she applying to the Sun guides him to kings or princes; but if to Saturn, the journey is directed to some of the common people; if to Jupiter, to magnates; if to Mars, he proceeds to someone of the rank of knights; which if she would apply to Venus, he is arranging travel to some kind of woman; but if to Mercury, to sages or those given to commerce. Moreover, with her proceeding in a solitary way, he enters into travel because of conducting trade. Now, withdrawing from Saturn, it frees him from a debt; if she is being separated from Mars, it protects him from a tight spot and captivity.[45]

Nor is it good to make note in any other way of the stars to which she applies, and their position: which if they would hold onto their own houses, they call him to someone native [to the area]; appearing in their triplicities, to strangers but inhabitants of his land. Now, if the lord of the star to which the Moon is applying, regarded that house, he heads to a man notable in that land; [but if it did not, he is not known in that land].[46] If the aspect were

---

[44] Cf. *On Quest.* §9.1.
[45] John's Sahl makes it seem like he is fleeing these things, not that he has really been freed from them.
[46] Adding with John's Sahl.

from the tetragon, it occupies him[47] in that place to a moderate extent; from a trigon or hexagon, it suggests he will be loved in that place; from the opposition, it makes him hated; from an assembly, it suggests he is a moneylender and squanderer.[48]

Moreover, the lord of the east or the Moon applying to a malevolent in a human sign, cautions him to beware of robbers. If in a watery sign, it encourages him to flee ships. If in a sign of trees, you will flee high places and *aconita*.[49] In a four-footed sign, it counsels that the attacks of wild beasts must be avoided. Moreover, an infortune occupying Leo [threatens] cruel wild animals; and [in Scorpio],[50] poisonous reptiles; in Pisces, it threatens sea beasts and the dangers of waters. In addition, I believe one should note: Saturn is more serious in waters than on land, but contrariwise the wickedness of Mars is more pernicious on land than in waters.[51]

§9.12: On the return of the one traveling, even what would happen to him (and how) while he goes—Sahl[52]

Again, I think one should note by an equal method what [sign] is arising [when] he entered that region. If at that time the lord of the second[53] would proceed by retrograding, it portends he is going to turn back quickly and without profit. Which if it would be lingering in its first station, it brings him back with no further delay, but still it profits nothing. In its second station, it draws him back with profit that had not been hoped for.

Moreover, the lord of the second walking through the east or tenth or even the eleventh, suggests the journey is useful and unhampered. It being in the seventh, brings it about to the contrary. Which if it would be lingering in the ninth or third, it portends it is unstable in that region, [and] the journey is

---

[47] We still seem to be discussing the person to whom the traveler is going, based on the type of aspect the domicile lord of the planet is making to the sign.

[48] John's Sahl: "he will be of those who take away the assets of men by force."

[49] Unknown word. John's Sahl (§9.1) has "Indeed if it were in the signs of seeds, he should beware of trees and thorns, and a higher place, or from food in which there is poison."

[50] Adding with John's Sahl.

[51] This sentence is from *Carmen* V.35.42. That is, Mars is harmful to prey on land (and so is good for hunters), and likewise for Saturn while fishing. See §7.199-203.

[52] Cf. *On Quest.* §§9.2-3, and al-Rijāl III.7-8. Al-Khayyāt's version is in §9.16 below.

[53] As the first sign signifies the entrance into the city, the second signifies "what happens next."

changed [to another one]. But if it would traverse in the fourth, conjoined to a malevolent or at least regarded [by one], but so that Mars himself would be regarding the ones conjoined thusly, he will acquire drudgery, and it will afflict him with an inborn abscess of the brain.[54]

[The Moon being assembled with or aspecting the second, or being with Mercury, or if Mars aspected her, he will have illnesses and troubles.][55] The Moon at the same time occupying the fourth, [indicates it is] fatal; which if she would occupy another pivot, it prepares escape [from the illness], but it designates that the abscess will be with him perpetually. In addition, if the Moon even regarded Mars, it afflicts the body itself with a trouble of that kind. But she being placed meanwhile under the regard of benevolents, brings forth medicines; but if she were [only under the regard of] a perverse one, it is mortal.

[To examine] travel for a king or any prince or magnate setting out, and their authority[56] or family [whom they left behind], we look at the second. For if any malevolent would possess this [sign] without testimony, it threatens a difficult status for those who are left behind. And if it is Mars, it will mix in disputes or cause fires to rise. But if Saturn, it contrives thefts and designs piracy. The reception of this malevolent [means it is] not so serious. But the most serious is if it would traverse in its own fall (the greatest pinnacle of evils is if in that same place it would also be retrograde). But on the contrary, fortunate ones walking in the second please and reinforce.

Generally therefore, the lord of the east and the Moon being corrupted, is inimical to travel. The malevolent corrupting each, being established between the east and the tenth, will harm one who is returning; between the tenth and seventh, it threatens one who is going out; with it going from the east to the fourth, it is inimical to those whom he had left behind him;[57] between the fourth and seventh, it disturbs one who is returning.

---

[54] But this might be better read as "numerous abscesses in him." Al-Rijāl says (more plausibly) "blows and wounds and fractures."
[55] I have separated this from the previous sentence along with John, as Hugo's Sahl runs them together.
[56] *Potentatu.* Sahl is referring to the various ministers and substitutes and supporters who are trying to manage things while the powerful querent is gone.
[57] John's Sahl says it will affect things he has acquired in his departure; likewise in the next clause, things he has acquired while returning.

§9.13: On changing [one's] place—Sahl[58]

If someone would pose a question about a change of place, namely whether or not he should rather stay or go over to what he proposed, the Moon's counsel should be chosen. For if she would be separated from infortunes, it praises the change and testifies it is better to go. But on the other hand, withdrawing from benevolents chooses that he should rather remain. Moreover, this ambiguity is resolved by the lord of the east and of the seventh. For a stronger eastern [lord] commends staying; but if the one which is in charge over the seventh is greater, it gives assent to leaving.

§9.14: On something proposed—Sahl[59]

Also, if it was sought about someone's proposal as to whether it is useful to undertake [something else], the lord of the east and the Moon equally respond. Withdrawing from infortunes, if they apply to benevolents, it reinforces undertaking it. Which if it happened the other way around, the method of judgment is turned to the opposite way.

§9.15: What would happen to him on a journey, and how—al-Kindī[60]

[Planets in the Ascendant (beginning of travel)]

§287. If therefore there is no hesitation about travel left, the stars which hold onto the pivots reveal how it will go, and what will happen to him on the road. Finally, if a lucky star is situated in the Ascendant, it anticipates a journey with much prosperity before he exceeds the border of his home.[61] In the Midheaven, it no less happily hastens the travel. But if in the seventh, the land entered by him furnishes him with many riches. But in the fourth, he is entitled to pray for a return with much glory of resources.[62]

---

[58] Cf. *On Quest.* §9.4, and al-Rijāl III.9.
[59] Cf. *On Quest.* §9.4.
[60] Cf. al-Rijāl III.5.
[61] That is, before he leaves, or perhaps near the beginning of travel.
[62] That is, the benefits will come more while on his way back.

[Planets in the Midheaven (prosperity during travel)]

§288-89. But if a fortunate Jupiter is established here [in the Midheaven],[63] it will bring the generosity of money to bear according to the dignity which its lord obtains in the circle. For, [if Jupiter is] in the house of the Sun, it is promised that he will be ennobled by kings and magnates and those of this kind, or by hunting or augury. In the house of Saturn, it does not deny that he will be enriched by old men or because of some ancient thing, or some land. In the house of Jupiter, the law or a magistrate of the law, [and] sometimes even children or just men increase riches for him. Moreover, in the house of Venus illicit sex, games, exulting, [and] love do not take it away [but rather give it]. In the house of Mercury even, the aforesaid cause attributes [wealth] because of writing or business or eloquence or books. In the same way, in the house of the Moon, it forces clients and servants, sometimes even messengers, to be conveyed to him.[64]

§290. Moreover, if a lucky Venus has control over the tenth, it really brings in joy and exultation and Venusian things and things delightful to practice. Moreover, the Sun as the prince of the Venusian house designates it is from kings and the rest, just as was stated above about the Sun in the judgment of Jupiter. Moreover, [Saturn as] the lord of the Venusian[65] house consents to those things which were stated about Saturn in that same judgment of Jupiter. Therefore, with respect to the [rest of] the individual stars, you should follow the judgment about them written above in the heading [pertaining to] Jupiter.

[Planets in the seventh and fourth (prosperity at the destination and while returning)]

§291. Moreover, a lucky star in the seventh enacts, what was said before about the causes, and prepares for him [something] of that kind in the region [to which he goes]. In this way, even, if some lucky one would be inhabiting the fourth, one will have to affirm about it what was laid out for the tenth and seventh. If it should hold onto the Ascendant, a good of the same kind (and by similar things of those causes), is promised to take place, just as was stated in the rest of the pivots.

---

[63] Adding with Robert.
[64] Al-Rijāl adds gambling as a source of income, which one would normally expect to come from Venus.
[65] Reading *veneriae* for *saturnalis*, with Robert and the logic of the paragraph.

[Planets in the quarters]

§292. But with no fortunate [star] appearing in the fourth or tenth, while one does traverse between the tenth and the seventh,[66] in the middle of his departure while on the journey, he should be secure in expecting good according to the distance of that star from the seventh—in proportion to the corresponding distance from the region that is sought. And so in this way, [if there is a fortunate one] between the fourth[67] and the Ascendant, it undoubtedly rewards him with the promised goods in the middle of his return, according to the distance of the Ascendant from the fortunate one, and of his home from the region he has left. Likewise, it appearing between the Ascendant and the fourth, you will note[68] the distance of the Ascendant and fourth, according to the nature of the stars and the signs of their places which are allotted in the circle.

[Events according to planetary signification and rulership]

§293. Every place of the circle is entitled to claim a signification for itself according to the place of the sign in the quadrangular[69] disposition of the signs, and [according to] the nature of its place.

§294. For example, let one of the unfortunate ones be the lord of the twelfth, and let it be Saturn; also, let the sign have no likeness to an animal: it signifies a cold and dry illness, according to the claim of the astrologers. But in an animal sign, it testifies that that same cold and dry danger will come upon[70] him because of some animal. In a human sign, it encourages him to beware of murderers and that type of thing.

§295. Moreover, Mars having acquired this role of Saturn (if he took on the rulership of the twelfth), warns him that acute diseases, robbers, fear of his own body, often four-footed animals, and poisonous reptiles are to be avoided. Also, Mercury taking over for Mars, and Saturn being in his regard

---

[66] Reading "seventh" with al-Rijāl for "fourth." But generally in this paragraph, the logic has to do with the distance from the Ascendant and the Descendant, not so much with the particular quarter.
[67] Reading "fourth" for "tenth."
[68] Reading *notato* for *notata*.
[69] This reference to square charts seems to be Hugo's own, as Robert and al-Rijāl omit it.
[70] Reading instead of *discedere*.

or being a partner to him in some bearing,[71] teaches worthless men and violent lawsuits and reproaches are to be avoided.

§296. Moreover, Mars being related to [Mercury] by some companionship, claims there are going to be plunderers and those who set traps around roads, [and] the tricks of certain fraudulent men should be feared. In the same way, if a link is had [between] Mercury and some fortunate one, it seems the signification of each must be mixed in their natures.

Moreover, if Venus takes over for Mercury, it makes prosperous things available from women, jokes, drinking, but [also] by those who are enemies to him, or who play the role of enemies.[72]

§297. Jupiter summons profit, money, dignity, from[73] men who present the likeness of enemies, or they are enemies of his sect and his lineage.

Also, the Moon brings profit from the public treasury and one's livelihood, [and] from heralds and couriers."[74]

Finally, the Sun joyfully extols a lofty magnate, also the hunt; or it demonstrates that he acquires many things from those whom we said before, through the gift of prediction.

§298. Finally,[75] should any star corrupt or save the lord of the Ascendant, if this [star] would be situated in the eleventh, it wholly supports the judgment stated before, except that (with an assessment being made [of this]), it confirms this will emanate from friends or the king's servants, or from his own profession[76] or the teachings of his job.

§299. But if it would rule the Midheaven, it everywhere resembles the aforesaid, but he would be entitled to get it because of his profession, even his mother or from the king.

---

[71] One of the standard types of planetary configurations or connections, such as an assembly by body, or a close connection by aspect.
[72] This still assumes that the planet indicating success and wealth is the lord of the twelfth: al-Rijāl appends this statement about enemies to the rest of the planets below, to emphasize the point.
[73] Reading the rest of this sentence with al-Rijāl for Hugo's *a vulgo si inimico vel inimici vice potito.*
[74] Reading with Robert for Hugo's *censum et totius adquisitionis profectum ab eisdem.*
[75] From here through §302, our sources are somewhat vague as to whether we are dealing with the rulerships or locations of the planets. I'm sure both should be considered, but most of the delineations have the planet ruling these houses.
[76] The eleventh is the second (wealth) from the tenth (profession).

In the rulership of the ninth it does not withdraw from the aforesaid, but he is entitled to be enriched by the pretense of law or honor or travel or some change.[77]

But if it enjoys the rulership of the eighth, it does not differ from the prior [statements], but concedes riches because of inheritances, prison or some death, or because of the money of adversaries or the spouse, or some hidden affair.

§300. Moreover, if the aforesaid judgment changes to the rulership of the seventh, it enriches him by adversaries or commerce or that business because of which he applied himself to that region, or by grandfathers or the money of slaves.

Also, the lord of the sixth makes the above statement firm, but slaves or another's anxiety tend to honor him, or a disease or weakness or prison or some hidden affair, and sometimes the paternal money or that of children.

§301. But the lord of the fifth does not flee the aforesaid reasoning, but he will possess the riches of children or gifts or paternal money, or of those who turn against their friends.[78]

Moreover, the lord of the fourth praises the aforesaid highly, but does not neglect to make him be revered by fathers and the money of brothers or sisters, [or] a revived memory of an estate or fief or some ancient thing.

§302. But the lord of the third responds to the same things, nevertheless it adds a benefit belonging to the brothers or travel or some change [of place] or the enemies of the father.

Also, in the second it agrees in every way with what was said above, but greatly bestows money or the benefits of the father's friends.

[Other considerations]

§303. Moreover, the degree of the seventh being in the face of Jupiter[79] shows that he is to be feared[80] by the inhabitants of that region, [but] praised in the attentiveness of his speech. Moreover, if Venus would rule the face of

---

[77] Or "shift" (*transmutationis*), but probably a change in place is meant.
[78] The fifth is the seventh from the eleventh.
[79] Al-Rijāl only has the Descendant being on *a* or *the* dignity of Jupiter (or Venus, see below); the fact that both Robert and Hugo mention the face leads me to think that they are right. The use of faces for travel is old and may go back to the original Egyptian uses for decans. See *Carmen* V.25 for the use of the Moon in the faces for electing travel by water.
[80] Probably in the sense of awe and respect.

the seventh, it portends that he is loved by the same [people], listened to thankfully, [and] what is sought is procured, particularly while Venus is situated in the aspect of the lord of the Ascendant by a trigon.[81]

§304. But Jupiter regarding the lord of the Ascendant from a pivot of the lord itself,[82] strengthens his own signification. Moreover, [if in addition] Jupiter [is] in a pivot, it professes he will obtain it from those who are powerful among the common people or who are brought forth as being advanced; but after the pivots, from the rank of someone lower; remote from a pivot, from the lowest people. One will have to make a judgment just like it with respect to Venus.

§305. Moreover, the lord of the fourth and even [the lord of] the Moon[83] should be consulted, [and] likewise the star with which the Moon's application comes to be: namely as to whether they are lucky [by nature], made fortunate, whether strong, whether in pivots or after the pivots, whether retrograde or direct, whether eastern or western, whether burned, whether in their *ḥalb*[84] (namely, enhanced)[85] or outside it, whether in their own power or place of proper quality, or peregrine and exiles.

§306. A consideration [which is] had of all of these determines the extent to which [what they signify] is in the end of the journey. Therefore, [1] a fortunate partner in the fourth or with the lord of the fourth in some bearing, or [2] [with the lord of the Moon's house],[86] or [3] should the star to which the Moon's application is coming to be, bear itself in some way with a fortunate one, it claims that good will ensue at the end of the whole affair, in accordance with the nature of that fortunate one, or of the house in the circle which it possesses,[87] just as was said about those things which seem to happen on a journey or [in] a region.

§307. Likewise, an unfortunate one declares evil conclusions to the journey, according to the nature of that infortune and of its house in the circle which it claims, namely in what house of that unlucky one its regard would appear to be more robust.

---

[81] Reading with Robert and al-Rijāl for Hugo's "tetragon."
[82] That is, being in a whole-sign angle of it.
[83] Reading *Lunae* with Robert and al-Rijāl for Hugo's *Luna*.
[84] Al-Rijāl uses "domain" (*ḥayyiz*). See *ITA* III.2.
[85] *Ornatae*.
[86] Adding with Robert and al-Rijāl.
[87] Certainly by its location, but also whichever of its own domiciles it happens to be regarding more strongly (see the next paragraph for this explicit statement).

§308. Moreover, a judgment of those things which resolve the last parts of the travel: a retrograde [significator of the end of travel][88] heaps error and disturbance into the whole matter, wherefore it permits something to be exacted from him at the end of the journey. Direct, it preserves all things to the contrary. All [of them] being direct, they accomplish[89] everything justly, gladly and evenly.

§309. Moreover, the majority being direct [means] you will judge the majority of the whole matter to likewise [move forward], especially that [part] which seems to pertain to the nature of the direct significators;[90] moreover, [judge] more or less with respect to error or disturbance and hindrance, according to the [nature] of the retrograding ones, just as we told [you] about the direct ones.

§310. Likewise, all [of them] being eastern, they accelerate the effecting of the matter without hindrance, according to the signification of that easternness, and according to the nature and kind of the matter itself. Western, the contrary. Moreover, they (or part of them) being in the pivots or after the pivots, they show the advantageous end of the matter without divergence[91] or hindrance. But cadent or remote, they throw into confusion and pervert and block. And so, in this way those which are in their own *ḥalb*[92] (namely, in their own fortifications) [show] evenness and aid in the matter; remote from that fortification, they rob it of the same.

[*On returning from travel*]

§311.[93] But concerning [his] stay or quick return, the significator of travel (namely, the minister of those things which happen on a journey)[94] should be consulted. For, this one being quick of course and western, indicates a quick but hidden and laborious return. Being quick and eastern, it means a fast but

---

[88] Adding with Robert and al-Rijāl. That is, either the lord of the fourth, or of the Moon's domicile, or of the planet to which the Moon is applying.
[89] Reading *consummant* for *consumant*.
[90] Again, of the three listed above.
[91] Reading for *divorcio*.
[92] Again, al-Rijāl reads "domain."
[93] For this paragraph, see al-Rijāl III.6 (first part).
[94] Al-Rijāl reminds us: "the one which has the rulership in the causes of it, and makes the matter, and the victor among the five releasers." See the footnote to al-Kindī's §285, in §9.3 above.

public return, and one impeded with minimal labor. But being slow, it throws a delay into the stay.

§312.[95] Moreover, the star which shares some bearing of partnership[96] with the significator of travel should be noted, for no less does it manage the manner of the return. But that star from whose bearing the significator recedes, ascribes corresponding things and significations of this kind to the beginning of the journey.

§313. Likewise, the firmness[97] of the sign[98] of the seventh, and having many ascensions, testify that the stay in the [foreign] region is not middling [but rather long]; but in a double-bodied one, it shows a changed journey; also, a convertible sign signifies a moderate stay on the journey.

§314. Moreover, [1] the retrogradation of the lord of travel,[99] or [2] its application with lord of the seventh (and with [the lord of the seventh][100] being retrograde), even [3] the Moon applying with some retrograding [planet], portend that he returns from the journey before he arrives in the desired place. Moreover, the significator of the return (and the one which snatches away [his] pursuit of travel)[101] being fortunate, shows the return to be useful and healthful. Also, an unlucky one [shows] loss according to the nature of the star which impedes the journey and of the sign which it is holding onto, and according to place of it and its sign in the circle.

§315. Likewise, the lord of the seventh being lucky, and taking in[102] the lord of the Ascendant with a friendly regard, prepares good in the region which was visited, with exultation and friendliness. Moreover, a bearing being shared between the lord of the seventh and of the Ascendant, [but] with [the lord of the Ascendant] not being received, [but nevertheless] being fortunate and strong, wrenches good from the inhabitants of the region, although they are unwilling.[103] The lord of the seventh being received by the

---

[95] For the rest of this whole section, cf. al-Rijāl III.6 (last part).
[96] That is, if the significator is applying to it.
[97] That is, being in a firm or fixed sign.
[98] Reading with Robert and al-Rijāl for Hugo's "lord."
[99] Probably the victor from among the five releasers as described in al-Kindī's §283, in §9.3 above.
[100] Following Robert and al-Rijāl for Hugo's "it."
[101] That is, one of the retrograde planets just mentioned. Al-Rijāl: "the planet which signified impediment and the destruction of the travel."
[102] That is, "receiving" (al-Rijāl).
[103] The lack of reception seems to indicate their unwillingness.

lord of the Ascendant conveys his success with the cities and inhabitants, with generosity and benevolence.

§316. Moreover, the lord of the seventh being unlucky, but associated with the lord of the Ascendant from a friendly regard, greatly bestows good from the inhabitants, but acquired dishonorably. But being unlucky[104] and conjoined to the lord of the Ascendant from a perverse aspect (or in its assembly), conveys harm according to the place and strength and manner of its bearing. Moreover, the lord of the Ascendant corrupting the lord of the seventh, corrupts the inhabitants of the region with its own evil according to its own place and virtue.

§317. Moreover, the lord of the bound[105] of the Ascendant being lucky, makes him be rewarded by powerful and famous men—whose status is determined by the lord of its bound. Also, the lord of the degree of the Ascendant being lucky, promises things will be obtained according to [its] nature, status—and the strength or unsoundness of that status.

§318. Furthermore, the reception[106] of the lords of the triplicity of the seventh denotes steady, faithful friends in the region that is sought,[107] and those blocking many adverse things, particularly [if] the lord of the Ascendant and of the seventh are safe from the infortunes. Also, the lords of the triplicity being cadent and remote show them to be unfaithful and weak, and they deny the hope of all help. The lord of the Ascendant being cadent seems to assent [to this] just like these [triplicity] lords do.

§319. Then, it seems the ninth[108] place should be noted. For if it were in a double-bodied sign, and its lord with some star in a double-bodied sign, or associated in some bearing with the lord of a double-bodied sign,[109] or [the ninth sign is] regarded by its own lord, the journey will be doubled, or he will have to go on a very similar one next (that is, consequently), especially while the lord of the ninth [is] after the pivots. [But] being in a sign remote from a

---

[104] Reading with Robert for Hugo's "lucky."
[105] Reading with Robert and al-Rijāl for Hugo's "degree," here and throughout this paragraph.
[106] Al-Rijāl speaks of their being in pivots or succeedents, not reception.
[107] Reading the verb *peto* with Robert for Hugo's *repeto*.
[108] Al-Rijāl reads "eleventh" throughout this paragraph, instead of the ninth; it is probably a mistake.
[109] Al-Rijāl has the lord of the ninth applying to a planet *in* a double-bodied sign, which makes more sense than it being the *lord of* a double-bodied sign (which would by definition only include Mercury and Jupiter).

pivot demonstrates that he has already gone out previously on a journey just like this one.

§9.16: What would happen to him, and how, while he was there—al-Khayyāt

Therefore, in order that no ambiguity be left concerning his return, [namely] one must note with the greatest diligence at what hour and with what Ascendant he will have entered the region. If therefore the lord of the second happened to be retrograde, the return will be quickly present, without gain and success. It traversing in its first station, even though he might linger longer, still it profits him nothing. In the second stay, he stays for a moderate amount, but it will grant an advantage not hoped for; it is also no less if it were direct. In the meantime, the aspects of both the fortunate ones and the malevolents should be noted.

Whenever therefore the lord of the second would happen to be found in the east or tenth or even the eleventh, it is a sign of an unhampered journey and success. But it traversing in the seventh, supplies impediment and difficulty. In the ninth [or] third, he is not going to stay fast in the region for long, but [will travel] to another. Likewise, it being under the regard or assembly of malevolents, afflicts the last parts of the journey with death, or he will never rejoice in the safety had before.

Likewise, the Moon in the assembly or aspect of [the lord of][110] the second or perhaps Mercury, while however the regard of Mars is not absent, afflicts him with the wounding of sores[111] and the loss of wounds or the troubles of fractures. Meanwhile, if the Moon would possess the fourth, it makes an indication of death or a wound for him. Which if she would linger in another pivot, it prepares escape, but it leaves the scars and marks and vestiges of wounding. Even this must be noted: which benevolents or infortunes regard the Moon, as was first stated above. Moreover, the Moon being regarded by Mars, with the benevolents in aversion, wounds his body with the already-stated problems, namely according to the nature of the place in which it is staying. Worse is if she were in the assembly of Mars. If the fortunate ones did regard her, [then] even though he escapes, they are not useful, [and] he will lose value. We give no other opinion about a sick and wounded

---

[110] Adding with Sahl.
[111] Or, "ulcers" (*ulcerum*).

person. Now, with [the fortunate ones] being in aversion, this trouble will not recede until the last moment of life.

IMPRISONMENT

§9.17: On imprisoned people and their liberation—Sahl[1]

But if it were asked by someone about imprisoned people and their liberation (or rather, [their] departure), [this] observation responds most certainly. Above, we taught about travel (whether or not it would happen), but we believe that this alone is important: because if any lords of a pivot (even if not all) would be lingering in the pivots,[2] they in no way release the one held fast and imprisoned in that year.

Among all of them, it is especially good to note the lord of the east: which if it would possess a pivot, it prolongs prison and defers [his] departure, more so in the pivot of the earth. If meanwhile the lord of the twelfth[3] or any of the malevolents would regard [the lord of the east], it introduces other punishments in prison. Moreover, an application of the lord of the east (he being in aversion [to the Ascendant]) to a star occupying a pivot (and if hope of freedom was had), retains him still longer in captivity. Conversely, if [the lord of the east], being in a pivot, applied to a remote [star], it opens up an unexpected departure. Finally, that same lord of the east applying to some [malevolent star] appearing in the fourth, or to the lord of the eighth,[4] really brings death in prison.[5]

An application of the eastern lord and of the Moon to some [star] placed in the third[6] or ninth is a sign of escaping, especially if that star has no rulership in a pivot. Moreover, either of them applying to the lord of the third or ninth, but not receiving it (should it be sitting on the left of the east),[7] prepares escape through the effort of the one being detained. Contrariwise, while the lord of the third or ninth would apply to the eastern lord, it frees the captive unexpectedly.

The lord of the east applying to the lord of the twelfth, but so that meanwhile it[8] would run through the left of the east, is a promise of escaping. Nor

---

[1] Cf. *On Quest.* §9.5.
[2] John's Sahl prefers that they also be in their own domiciles.
[3] Al-Khayyāt has the second, Dorotheus the eighth.
[4] Here and below, reading with John's Sahl for Hugo's "fifth."
[5] John's Sahl has the application to a malefic planet in the fourth, *or* that the lord of the eighth is in the Ascendant.
[6] Reading with John for Hugo's "twelfth."
[7] John reads this as though they may apply either to the lord of the third or ninth, *or* to a planet placed on the left of the east.
[8] This is probably the lord of the twelfth.

is another judgment given if the lord of the third or ninth would be conjoined to the lord of the twelfth.

Moreover, if you should find the lord of the east applying thusly to the lord of the third or ninth, so that the one who is receiving [the aspect] would hold onto a pivot, it promises escape, but not before leaving that sign and it [then] happens to be remote from the pivots.

But this: the [lord of the][9] Moon applying to the lord of the east, declares difficult exits.

In fact, the Moon will have to be pursued for greater evidence. For she, walking through a turning sign, accelerates the flight unless she is in Cancer;[10] still, however, it is quicker in Aries and Libra than in Capricorn. For if she would be in these two, he cannot remain; but in Capricorn he will labor for a while longer, [and] finally he is going to escape. Moreover, she being in firm signs signifies being held for a long time, and more so in Aquarius. The Moon being found in a double-bodied [sign], provided that he has not [already] left while she is staying there, he will be held for a long time, and more so in the Jupiterian lodging-places (if that same Jupiter is in aversion); but in Mercurial ones, it conveys joys within the prison.

Then it seems one should note the star to which the application of the Moon is happening. For if, [while she is] occupying a pivot, she should apply to a star placed on the left of the east, so that even the lord of the east would bear testimony of this kind, it has a judgment of escaping. Moreover with the Moon being remote, applying to a star holding onto a pivot, it is a sign of prolonging the captivity, unless (I say) [that star] would rule the third or ninth lodging-place: for thusly, before it[11] exits that sign, he will escape. In addition, with the Moon being remote from a pivot, applying to a remote star, but so that it would rule a pivot, there will be hope[12] of escaping until that star returns to a pivot and enters into it. Then, it will snatch away all hope (unless, I say, that star is in the ninth or third). And should she apply to the lord of any pivot, it really impedes flight.

Finally, the lord of the east entering into scorching, with an infortune meanwhile occupying the fourth, prepares death inside the prison. But if that malevolent were Mars, he is led out for beheading. Moreover, if the eastern lord has already left scorching behind, even though up until now it was lin-

---

[9] Adding with John's Sahl.
[10] Since Cancer is her own domicile, it suggests staying where one is.
[11] This probably refers to the lord of the third or ninth.
[12] Reading *spes* with John for *ipse*.

gering under the rays, he is afflicted with disease, but finally he will get better. But an application of the eastern lord being made to the lord of the eighth or to a malevolent placed in the fourth,[13] is declarative of death. That same [lord of the east] being either conjoined to Saturn or regarded [by him] in an unfriendly way, portends he will be held for a long time. But if the lord of the east[14] would bear itself in the same way with Mars, it seriously impedes[15] him who is being held. [And if the Moon were then impeded, distress will find him and he will not be whipped. And if the Moon aspects the lord of her own house, it will be easier; but if she did not aspect, it will be harder.][16]

Which if they would bear themselves so, the lord of the seventh exposes the one who led him in as a captive. But if it would support the lord of the east with a benign aspect, it suggests he is going to demand what was owed with a sweet and peaceful attitude; but from a wicked figure it portends he is going to demand it sharply and strictly.

§9.18: On incarcerated people, whether they are about to escape—al-Khayyāt

With a question being presented about incarcerated people (whether they are about to escape), Māshā'allāh bids us especially to observe what we taught above about travel (whether or not it would happen).[17] In fact, the occasion for the departure of [each kind of person] follows the same path. But in an inquiry about a captive, it seems only this is different: that if the lords of the pivots would be lingering in the pivots and their own proper places (even if it is not all of them), or if a certain portion of them would hold onto the houses of the others, they portend that the incarcerated person will be held for the whole year—unless, I say, another star, traversing quickly, possessed the pivots, [and] it would apply to a remote star on the left of the east, or even to the lord of the third or ninth: for thusly there is a certain promise of escape (but preferable to all is an application with the lord of the

---

[13] Reading with John for Hugo's "fifth."
[14] Reading with John for Hugo's "seventh."
[15] Reading with John's Sahl for *affugit*.
[16] Adding from John's Sahl.
[17] See §9.4 above.

third or ninth). After the departure of the second or eighth, they threaten labor and difficulty.[18]

In addition, even the east and the place of the significator[19] (and more so the [place of] the lord of the east) must be noted. Which if it would be lingering in a pivot, it prolongs the captivity, especially in the pivot of the earth. But if the lord of the second[20] or any of the infortunes would regard it, it introduces manifold punishments in the prison according to the figure of the regard. Moreover, that same lord of the east being remote from a pivot, applying to a star occupying a pivot, makes an indication of prolonging the captivity after hope of escape is had. But [the lord of the east] traversing in a pivot, if it would apply to a remote star, promises escape. Moreover, it applying to the lord of the eighth or any malevolent staying in the fourth, threatens death in that prison.

Which if the lord of the east or the Moon should apply to a star placed in the third or ninth, it brings comfort to the one escaping. But if that same star would rule over one of the pivots, nor did it regard it, escape will be certain; [but if it did regard it, it indicates a burdensome departure.][21] Then, that star especially means a promise of escape, which brings back counsel to the lord of the third or ninth by applying [to one of them], namely so that the significator[22] which receives from the left of the east would traverse remotely.

Moreover, an application of the eastern lord with the lord of the twelfth, or being in its assembly, afflicts[23] the captive with labor and difficulty. [The lord of the east] applying to the lord of the sixth or holding onto its assembly, while it is being regarded by hostile stars, is a sign of infirmity; no less indeed the lord of the eighth, whose place signifies death. The same lord of the east applying to the lord of the twelfth (while it[24] is holding onto the left of the east) is a sign of escaping. The same thing is asserted if the lords of the third or ninth would be making a stay[25] in the twelfth, or they would be joined with its lord.

---

[18] Based on Dorotheus in §9.19 below, al-Khayyāt must mean that the application is to planets *in* the second or eighth, but perhaps to their lords as well.
[19] This must be the Moon.
[20] Sahl reads this as the lord of the twelfth, and Dorotheus as that of the eighth.
[21] Adding based on Dorotheus in §9.19 below.
[22] The lord of the third or ninth, based on Sahl's clearer explanation in §9.17.
[23] Reading *afficit* for *efficit*.
[24] Probably the lord of the twelfth.
[25] Hugo normally uses this word (*mora*) to mean a planet making a "station." But here he must mean "being in."

Also, an application of the eastern lord made with the lord of the third or ninth,[26] while the one which receives [the counsel] would possess a pivot, promises escape after it goes out of [its] sign, with the pivot being left behind.

But[27] if the one which receives the [counsel of the] Moon or the eastern lord were Saturn, and he [were] in a pivot, it declares a hard exit because of his severity. A Lunar application with the lord of the east [means] nothing else. Which if the lord of the east were in the rendering of counsel,[28] it prepares freedom. With no supporting [aspect], he will look out for himself. But if it would linger in the reception of the second, another [person] is proven to have concern for him, with him not being consulted [about it beforehand].

§9.19: On imprisoned people and their liberation—Dorotheus

For imprisoned people, whether or not at some time they would be liberated, the opinion which was given above about effecting travel[29] resolves the question. For a departure is noted in each case, but I believe this alone is important: if the lords of the pivots do not give up their own places, or should one possess the place of the other, they portend that the imprisoned man will be held for the whole year. Moreover, the lord of the east regarding the lords of the ninth or third, is a sign of escape—better indeed while there is an application to them or at least to a star placed in those same places.[30] But in the second and the eighth, they prolong imprisonment but do not take away the liberty that will follow.

Moreover, among all things the place of the eastern lord and even of the significator[31] especially comes to be noted. For in a pivot they make a long-lasting captivity, especially in the pivot of the earth. Which if [either] would be under the aspect of the lord of the eighth[32] or either malevolent, over and above the trouble of prison, it heaps on the harshness of [his] difficulty, according to the proper quality of the infortune. Being cadent from a pivot and

---

[26] Reading with Sahl and Dorotheus, for "fifth."
[27] This final paragraph has no clear parallel in Sahl or Dorotheus.
[28] I am not quite sure what al-Khayyāt means here.
[29] See §9.5.
[30] That is, planets in the third or ninth.
[31] Probably the Moon.
[32] Sahl reads this as the lord of the twelfth, al-Khayyāt as that of the second (which seems unlikely).

applying to a cadent star, it promises escape. But rendering counsel in that same place to a [malevolent] star appearing in a pivot[33] or to the lord of the eighth, it denies his departure and afflicts with death.

Moreover, the eastern lord and the Moon rendering counsel to the lord of the third[34] or ninth, do not deny escape. Which if that star would rule a pivot, and diverts [its own] aspect from it, it prepares flight and escape; but regarding [the pivot it rules], it designates a burdensome departure. Among all of this, as was already said, it is preferable if counsel is rendered to the lord of the third or ninth, and let the receiver [of it] be on the left of the east.

Moreover, a conjunction of the eastern [lord] with the lord of the twelfth,[35] threatens punishments and torments within prison. [The eastern lord] being regarded by the lord of the sixth or any pivot [of that planet], afflicts him with a disease in his fetters.

Finally, an application of the eastern [lord] with the lord of the third or ninth—if the receiver [of the counsel] would hold onto a pivot]—impedes his departure.[36]

---

[33] According to Sahl and al-Khayyāt, this should be the fourth.
[34] Reading *tertii* for *octavi*.
[35] Reading with Sahl and al-Khayyāt, for "second."
[36] But according to Sahl and al-Khayyāt, it does not ultimately prevent it.

ABSENT PEOPLE

§9.20: On the return of an absent person—Sahl[1]

With a question being proposed about the return of an absent person, and when he is going to come, an exposition of this kind depends on the eastern lord, according to its place and position. For if it would be walking through the east or the Midheaven, or at least should it apply to some star appearing in them, it declares the quick return of the absent person.[2] But being placed in the seventh[3] or fourth, it throws in a signal of slowness, nor has he left the land in which he is, but it signifies he is so far staying in that same place. Which if it would be traversing in the ninth or third, applying to some [star] in the east, it portends he has undertaken the journey of the present return, and he is already on the way. It even indicates the same thing if it would apply, from the eighth or second, to a star placed in the tenth.

[If however the lord of the Ascendant were cadent and was not joined to some planet in an angle, nor did it aspect the Ascendant, it will be bad because it signifies slowness.][4]

Moreover,[5] an application of the eastern lord or of the Moon being made to some retrograde [star], so that the east would be deprived of every aspect, signifies the impediment of the journey and path. Furthermore, that same lord of the east or the Moon applying to a retrograde [star], so that the retrograde one would regard the east,[6] promises a hastened arrival, unless, while it bears itself thusly, it is corrupted: for then it delays and shows it is difficult.

Once these things have been [looked at], if these things did not happen to the eastern lord, one will have to have recourse principally to the Moon. For while she renders the counsel to the lord of the east, [the lord] being [also]

---

[1] Cf. *On Quest.* §9.6.
[2] Omitting a sentence from John's Sahl that seems redundant, especially since it does not match al-Khayyāt and Dorotheus.
[3] Reading "seventh" with John's Sahl, al-Khayyāt, and Dorotheus.
[4] Adding from John's Sahl.
[5] This paragraph is significantly different in John's Sahl: "And if the lord of the Ascendant or the Moon were joined to a retrograde planet, or were the lord of the Ascendant retrograde and it aspected the Ascendant, it signifies his arrival. And if the lord of the Ascendant were impeded, it signifies duress and the prolonging of the arrival." See John's Sahl for my suggested alternate readings of these statements.
[6] Vienna reads, "or if that retrograde one would regard the east…".

placed in the east or near the east,[7] it accelerates the return. [The lord of the east being] in the seventh or even after the seventh, will slow the return.

Moreover, with the Moon withdrawing from the lord of the fourth or seventh or ninth or third, while however she applies to the eastern lord, makes a judgment of a most speedy return.

But she withdrawing from a star on the left of the east (that is, from the lower hemisphere), [and] applying to a star placed on the right of the east, portends a hastened return. With her being in aversion,[8] and applying in the Midheaven to a star on the right of the east,[9] it prepares a return but more slowly, because it was possessing the right of the east.

But this: should the lord of the east happen to be corrupted or unlucky, it is a sign of a slower return, because the man himself is overwhelmed and the journey is impeded.

§9.21: On the return of an absent person—'Umar

With someone calling the return of an absent person into question, we put the east in charge over the querent, and its lord over the quaesited matter—unless it is specifically asked about the father, for then the east and its lord present the signification for the querent, while the fourth and its lord will watch over the father; but if the inquiry proceeded with respect to the brother, we commit the third and its lord to him; also, the fifth and its lord should be deservedly preferred for the child, if about a woman, the seventh and its lord; for a slave or captive, the sixth and its lord.

Generally therefore,[10] the east will watch over the querent, and its lord over that domicile about whom the question comes to be. However, establish the Moon, with the lord of the east as a partner, for every inquiry. However, one must note in what way it[11] applies: for if its application and

---

[7] Reading with John's Sahl, as Hugo has her rendering the counsel *of* the lord of the east, with *her* being in the Ascendant.

[8] John's Sahl says "cadent."

[9] John's Sahl reads this as though she is joined on the right of the Ascendant to a planet in the tenth.

[10] This seems to be 'Umar's version of the claim in §§9.20, 9.24, and 9.25 that most questions are resolved in the same way. To me, the fact that 'Umar echoes the other three (which he rarely does) strongly suggests that the core of this material on absent people comes from a single source.

[11] This seems to be the lord of the east, since the Moon is referred to with the feminine later in the sentence.

regard comes to be from the pivots, with the lord of the question occupying a pivot with [the Moon], he returns; but they being cadent and drawn back from the pivots, they hinder travel and divert [him] from what was proposed.

§9.22: On the status of an absent person—al-Kindī

§567. If someone would propose a question about the status of an absent person, namely as to what would happen to him on his journey, and whether he would be able to complete what he proposed: the lord of the Ascendant, and the Moon, likewise the Sun and the Lot of Fortune, even the degree of the assembly or opposition, necessarily seem to reinforce [the matter].[12] Therefore, you will note the victor (namely the stronger star) in all of these: which if it would be situated [and be] fortunate between the Ascendant and the Midheaven, it testifies he is staying in the first half of his journey.

§568. But if it would be receding from the fortunate ones, between the Midheaven and the west, or at least should [its] receding come to be from none of the infortunes, you will report that he is unharmed [and] in the second half of the proposed journey, but not yet in the region [he has] considered [as his destination].

§569. But receding from the infortunes in the aforesaid places, but applying to fortunate ones, it declares he is unharmed [and] in the corresponding places of the journey, but he has had fear or grown ill according to the nature of that unfortunate one from which it recedes, and of the sign [the infortune] is holding onto, and of that house in the circle in which it is situated. Which if it would be receding from one of the fortunate ones, you should not doubt that he has achieved good according to its nature and its house and place in the circle, just as was said above about an infortune.

§570. But if you would discover that it was applying with the lord of the seventh, between the seventh and the Ascendant itself, and was received by it, in any event he has completed what was proposed in the journey. Finally, dwelling in the seventh, he is in possession of the proposed thing he wished, in the land to which he was going.

---

[12] These are virtually the five releasing places described in *Forty Chapters* Chs. 3.2-3 for finding a weighted victor for the querent, and the releaser for the whole chart. But since al-Kindī (or his sources) wants to analyze this victor as a planet, he uses the *lord of* the Ascendant and of the degree of the assembly/opposition, instead of simply those degrees themselves.

§571. Moreover, it seems that the proper quality of the star to which it applies must be combined, just as its nature and its dignity in the circle seems to demand.

§9.23: On the return of an absent person—al-Kindī

§572. Also, with a question made about [his] return (once you were certain about his life),[13] if [the victor or significator] would be established in the seventh, it detains him thus far in the region [whence he had gone]. Also, being drawn back from the seventh, it does not permit him to have departed for very long.[14] Retrograde, it leads him back without question. Drawn back from the four pivots, likewise. Which if it would appear fortunate (or [else] unlucky), you will remember to affirm it in the same way, and in the corresponding places of the path,[15] just as was said about his departure.

§573.[16] In discerning the hour of [his] arrival, you will note how many degrees [it is] from where it began to go retrograde, up to the one in which its step will go forward. For, the individual degrees insert hours or days or months or years, just as was said in a heading above.[17] Or, more strongly, [giving] days for individual degrees from the degree of the significator up to the Ascendant. Sometimes the degrees of its application with the Ascendant suggest the same. In all of these, the Moon and the lord of the Ascendant present no little evidence.

§9.24: On the return of an absent person—al-Khayyāt

With a question about an absent person, as to when he is going to come, the lord of the east will give counsel according to its place. For, it traversing in the east or the Midheaven, or applying to a star appearing in that same place, indicates a return. With [the lord of the east] appearing in the fourth or seventh, the slowness of difficulty will be present, [and] it even declares he has not yet left the land in which he is. Which if it were in the seventh, it

---

[13] That is, if you knew he was still alive. See below.
[14] *Nondum longius abscessisse permittit.*
[15] That is, in the diurnal path down from the seventh, through the fourth and back up to the Ascendant.
[16] For this section, see also al-Kindī in §5.52 above.
[17] See §A.133.

shows he will stay for a long time (according to the heaviness [of the lord of the east]). But it appearing in these two places,[18] should it apply to a star positioned in the east or tenth, they portend that he is already coming back.

Moreover, the lord of the east being remote or cadent, nor would it render counsel to a star in a pivot, is the worst: for it shows slowness and impedes the way.

Moreover, the significator rendering counsel to the eastern lord, it[19] being in the east or at least not far, absolutely hastens the return. But [if it renders to the eastern lord] in the seventh or after the seventh, it makes it worse and slows it down.

Again, the Moon withdrawing from a star from the left of the east,[20] applying to a star on the right of the east, means a quick return. She withdrawing from the eastern lord, while however she applies to the lord of the seventh, makes an indication of one returning, Which if there would be an application in the east or on the right of the east, to a star positioned in the ninth, it prepares a return, but more slowly.

§9.25: On the return of an absent person—Dorotheus

In addition, a question proposed about the return of an absent person demands a judgment of the eastern lord and its place. For, it being placed in the east or Midheaven, or at least should it render counsel to a star placed there, means a quick return. However, the lord of the [east] holding onto these places (the seventh or the fourth),[21] slows down and does not yet assert that he has left. The [lord of the east] in those [two] places,[22] applying to a star in the east, means a return. But an application of it to a star appearing in the tenth, [means] likewise.

Moreover, the eastern lord being cadent, rendering counsel to no [planet that is] in a pivot, slows down.

---

[18] Cf. Sahl, for whom these two places are the third and the ninth (applying to a planet in the east), or the second and eighth (applying to a planet in the tenth).
[19] I am not sure if this is the lord of the east or the significator.
[20] Sahl seems to understand this as though the first star (not the Moon) is on the left, and she is applying to one on the right. But Dorotheus makes it seem as though the Moon is on the left.
[21] Reading with Sahl and al-Khayyāt for "the lord of the seventh or the fourth holding onto these places."
[22] Cf. Sahl, for whom these two places are the third and the ninth (applying to a planet in the east), or the second and eighth (applying to a planet in the tenth).

Likewise, with the significator rendering counsel to the eastern lord, [and] it being placed in the east, is a sign of a hastened return. In the opposite [of the east] or after it,[23] it heaps on a delay.

But the Moon on the left of the Ascendant, receding from a star,[24] [and] applying to another on the right of the east, supports a return. Moreover, her withdrawal from the eastern [lord], and application with the lord of the ninth, wholly prepares a return. An application made in the east with benevolents, announces the healthy state of the absent person.

§9.26: On anyone's status—Jirjis

A malevolent in the east warns of a most grave condition; a lucky one in the same place, the contrary. Moreover, a malevolent occupying any pivot is unfavorable; a lucky one in the same place is successful. The benevolents neighboring on the east, the same; malevolents being near [it], the contrary.[25]

§9.27: When an absent person would return—Jirjis

The lord of the east in the east, signifies one who is coming; traversing in the twelfth, it reveals one already having left, and who is coming; in the eleventh, it means he is already approaching; in the tenth, he has already left the region to which he headed; traversing in the seventh, it yet detains him there; in the eighth and ninth, the same; in the sixth or fourth, it is a sign of a dead person or one incarcerated, or rather of one growing infirm; but for the fifth, it signifies one returning.

§9.28: When someone would return to his own nation—Aristotle

A question of this kind being brought into the open demands the counsel of the east and fourth, but even the seventh. For, the lord of the east in the east, or the fourth or seventh, testifies he is going to turn back this year; it being estranged from these places, defers the return by how many signs [the

---

[23] That is, the seventh or the eighth, based on al-Khayyāt in §9.24.
[24] Al-Khayyāt and Sahl seem to read this as though the Moon is separating from a star on the left, but Hugo's Dorotheus makes it seem as though the Moon herself is on the left.
[25] I believe Jirjis is referring to how closely the planets aspect, or are bodily near, the degree of the Ascendant itself.

lord] is distant from any of them, until that many years. Moreover, that same eastern lord traversing with the lord of the seventh or fourth, brings him back within a year. But if the lord of the east would be walking through the fifth or eighth, he will turn back in the following year.

§9.29: On the return of an absent person—Aristotle

With anyone asking about the return of an absent person, the lord of the east responds. For, it traversing in the east announces a speedy return. Moreover, with it traversing in the second: by how many degrees distant it is from the east (but one must even note it from the fourth, fifth, and sixth),[26] it prefigures that many days if it is lingering in turning [signs]; if in a double-bodied ones, that many months; if in firm ones, it signifies that same number of years.

That same [lord of the east] being in the seventh, has a judgment of one year or month or day according to the aforesaid method. With it lingering in the eighth, and the benevolents turned away, he will die there. It being in the ninth, while any of the benevolents would possess the east, it announces a present and quick return. In the tenth and eleventh, more quickly so.[27]

§9.30: On the hour of turning back—'Umar

On the other hand, the hour of turning back could be discovered by this method: namely, whenever the lord of the domicile of the quaesited manner, or of the Lunar lodging-place, would apply to the pivot of the east, or at least to that of the eastern lord. And so, one must note that the types[28] of pivots are two: for some pivots are of the signs, others are [pivots] of the stars. Whenever therefore any star would occupy the pivot of another star, it urges the effecting of the affair.[29]

---

[26] I believe this means that if it is in the fourth or fifth or sixth, we reckon the degrees from the IC.

[27] Notice that the cadent places (which often show travel) are omitted in this method, with the possible exception of the sixth. I have a feeling that the sixth should not have been included.

[28] Reading as *species*.

[29] This kind of approach is also used in transits and profections.

§9.31: Whether he is healthy or infirm—'Umar

However, it is good to scrutinize the sign of the matter about which it is asked, and its lord, but even the Moon, [to see] how it bears itself. Being cadent or corrupted, but the Moon decreasing in light [and] even with the significator of the question being retrograde [and] descending,[30] threatens a difficult [situation] for the absent person. Contrariwise too, being direct or eastern, or in its sovereignty or rather possessing any place of its own dignity, or being lucky, or with the Moon increasing in light, she being placed in anything of her own rule and outside her own fall, cleansed of infortunes, it portends the absent person's health in all respects.

§9.32: Whether he is living or dead—'Umar

Moreover, with a question being made about life, it is especially appropriate to consult the significator of the absent person. For, the lord of the question and the Moon being placed under the earth, while the lord of the eighth regards them—or if [the lord of the eighth] would acquire the signification of the question, it really threatens death. Which if the lord of the eighth would not regard them, it is not yet fatal. Also, with them being arranged above the earth, the lord of the eighth being cadent from them, it gives a life-bearing sign. Likewise, being in [the lord of the eighth's] regard, with the fortunate ones being cadent from them, it is mortal. But if the fortunate ones would not fall away from them, it introduces good health after the difficult troubles of death and losing hope of life.

§9.33: Whether he is living or dead—al-Kindī

§574. Furthermore, [if] being asked about [his] death or life, a strong and fortunate significator, and strengthened by the seventh,[31] and free of the troubles produced by the lord of the eighth, preserves him as living. If it is corrupted by the lord of the eighth, it designates he is dead. Receding from [the lord of the eighth], he is dead, [and] it will be permitted to describe the

---

[30] Probably being in its own fall.
[31] Robert reads, "and should it give aid to the seventh." This probably means being in a favorable aspect to the seventh sign and particularly the Descendant.

death according to the nature of each (namely the corrupter and the significator) and [its] place in the circle.

§575. Moreover, the significator itself being placed between the two infortunes,[32] and in a fixed sign (particularly being arranged in the eighth or twelfth),[33] claims he is a captive. [Besieged] by the lord of the eighth, but corrupted in its own place, threatens the death of prison.[34] But being scorched in that same place, it claims he has met death at the very hand of the king. Which if the lord of the Midheaven would be corrupting it, he is killed [when] found by the king.

§576. Moreover, being corrupted by the lord of the house of death, or scorched, and in the seventh, it confirms he has undergone death in the region to which he has gone. Also, being free of these infortunes and what is like them, brings him back to his own family.

§577. Moreover, being tainted by the lord of the house of death, namely [while the significator is] between the Ascendant and the fourth (particularly being scorched with another infortune), prepares death during [his] return, unless [the significator] would be freed, sustained by no [merely] moderate prosperity of some one of the fortunate ones[35]—provided (I say) that the lord of the Ascendant appeared stronger than the corrupter, and the decreasing light of that infortune would be reduced.[36] For in such a way, he would be able to avoid death, [but only] after bringing no [merely] moderate care and intention to bear.

§9.34: Whether he would head eagerly for diverse journeys—'Umar

When these bear themselves thusly, once the significator of the absent person has been known diligently beforehand, you should attend with one mind [to see] whether they would hold onto peregrine places (namely, signs in which they are deprived of a house or sovereignty and triplicity). No less do I think one should pay attention to whether they would merit being en-

---

[32] That is, besieged. See *ITA* IV.4.2.
[33] Robert adds, "or the sixth."
[34] This sentence could also be read as, "Being corrupted by the lord of the eighth, but in its own place…". But if it were in a sign which it ruled, it would not be in so difficult a position.
[35] That is, having the siege broken. See *ITA* IV.4.2 and my comment to that section.
[36] That is, that it would be decreasing in light. Perhaps this means that the infortune is about to go under the rays of the Sun?

riched by any of the three dignities (which we said before) in the house which they possess. If therefore they transfer themselves to houses wholly devoid of what was said before, they teach that the one about whom it is asked, is being changed from place to place.

§9.35: Whether he would undertake to turn back by day or night—'Umar

Moreover, the significator of the absent person and the star which the Moon is leaving behind, or at least either one, serve a question given about an unknown hour of return. For if [the significator][37] has withdrawn from a nocturnal and feminine [star], and thus it[38] would [also] possess a nocturnal and female sign, the departure will be nocturnal. Which if a diurnal star would be staying in a diurnal sign, it means a diurnal departure.

Furthermore, whether it would be at the beginning of night or day, or in the middle or at the end. Being placed[39] in the first [decan], at the beginning of both the day or night. In the second face, the middle. In the third decan, it decrees the last space [of time].

---

[37] *Recessus*, but surely the same goes for the Moon as well.
[38] This seems to mean the star from which the lord of the east has withdrawn, as implied by the next sentence.
[39] *Locatus*, the masculine ending again suggesting the significator of the absent person.

Dreams

§9.36: On dreams—'Umar

Also, the truth of dreams emanates especially from an observation of the east. And so, with the twelve domiciles being established just as their order demands, one will have to make the beginning of this observation from the ninth house.

Saturn, however, being placed with the Tail in the ninth, shows what must be feared (like serpents), [and] finally whatever generates terror, and it suggests that what has a Saturnian signification and nature is dreamt about. Also, one must note the lord of its lodging-place: what it is holding onto. For it introduces certain horrendous things and what has a perverse signification. It does not happen otherwise in the other houses.

Jupiter even being in that same place, [pertains] to kings and aristocrats or princes, and what pertains to kings (as are magistrates and judges and people of advanced rank), and signifies whatever pertains to the Jupiterian nature.

Mars placed in the same place, [pertains] to hunting, killings, wounds, quarrels, wars, even meats, or iron, blood, and the sword, and what are of Martial signification.

However, Venus shows odiferous things and what are of a respectable form (like pearls), even nuptials, and what the nature of Venus demands (such as are singing and dances).

But by Mercury are designated books, temples, a people given to prayer, and the offices of painting pictures, the common people running about and laboring, and a seditious person, and what pertains to Mercury.

The Sun, even, traversing in the same place, portends whatever is flying between heaven and earth, or a distinguished king, or some light, and what goes forth from the Solar nature (like gold, *et cetera*).

Also, the Moon designates an old man or a woman with a round face, or the water of rivers or a well.

However, with none appearing in the ninth, it is necessary to observe the pivot of the earth and [see] if any stars appear there, so that one may obtain the same judgment as that about the ninth. Which if nothing were found there, one's intention being drawn back to the east and the seventh and the Midheaven, even the third, wants to imitate no other order of judging than with the rest. If therefore you would take the beginning of this observation from the east and the seventh and the Midheaven, I advise you to note, with the greatest effort, the lord of them and equally that of the ninth, [and] even the one to which it[1] applies, or which one to it.

No less too, should the Moon and her application and withdrawal [be examined], even the nature of the sign which she is holding onto, so that from all of these (once the significator is known beforehand), the method of judgment that is relied on would [follow] according to both its status and place.

Finally, if nothing would happen to be found in the pivots or the ninth or third, it will be good to attend to the lords of the aforesaid lodging-places, namely which place in the circle they would be holding onto. For, they being in the pivots agrees with the aforesaid method; cadent ones, somewhat more loosely so (whether it is good or bad).

§9.37: On the nature of dreams—Dorotheus

The eastern lord and the domicile of law, moreover the status of the fortunate ones and the infortunes, lay bare the nature and signification of dreams. Therefore, infortunes in the east or the domicile of law, portend evil and anguish. But the fortunate ones possessing those same places of vision, testify that the signification is going to be favorable, and they conclude the end [of the matter] with joy.

---

[1] That is, the lord of the ninth and the lord of whatever other house you are examining.

ALCHEMY & OTHER KNOWLEDGE

§9.38: On alchemy—Sahl[1]

If someone would presume to confess the knowledge of alchemy, [and you are] wanting to discover whether a true teaching would be had with him, you have a certain judgment of such a great matter from the lord of the east and the Moon. For if each one appeared cleansed of the infortunes and free, it testifies it is true, and not without reward. The corruption of these suggest it is false and he is a liar. Which if it were about gold, the testimonies of the Sun must be looked for; for silver, we consult the Moon.

§9.39: On alchemy—'Umar[2]

But with a question being had [about] the discipline of alchemy, whether it would be established as certain or firm for someone, establish [the east and its lord for the querent],[3] the seventh with its lord for the one about whom one has doubt;[4] but the ninth sign from the seventh demonstrates his knowledge.[5] [See if the lord of the ninth][6] would be lucky or rather corrupted, eastern or western, in a pivot or drawn back from a pivot, even whether it would regard the lord of the seventh.[7] If therefore it would regard the lord of the seventh, and it is fortunate, it indicates one who is experienced—especially from a trigon or hexagon, while their application would not be without reception. But from a tetragon or opposition, it testifies he has attained this with difficulty and after the troubles of much labor—if, I say, the regard of the fortunate ones is not absent. For if [only] the infortunes would regard [it], even though he will have studied with difficulty, the labor has ceased, ineffective.

---

[1] I do not find this in *On Quest.*, but something similar appears in *On Elect.* §41.
[2] Cf. al-Rijāl III.16.
[3] Adding with al-Rijāl.
[4] Namely, the would-be alchemist.
[5] Al-Rijāl has the ninth itself. I can see the rationale for each.
[6] Adding with al-Rijāl, and reading singular throughout.
[7] These instructions seem odd, because grammatically they indicate the sign itself, but the reference to being eastern, western, pivotal and so on, really pertain to planets.

§9.40: On the knowledge of something—'Umar[8]

Moreover, if a question of this kind about someone's knowledge came forth, the east denotes him, but the ninth sign his knowledge. And so, any fortunate one in the ninth, or if the lord of the ninth[9] (being lucky) regarded the lord of the east, it presents a firm knowledge. Contrariwise however, with an infortune occupying the ninth, or the lord of that ninth being unlucky, while the lord of the east would be in the aspect of each, they speak against knowledge.

Here, even the testimonies of the Moon resemble the lord of the ninth. Their[10] application with the fortunate ones confirms the truth of the knowledge. Which if each would apply to infortunes, it testifies it is nothing. Likewise, one of these applying to fortunate ones, the other to unfortunate ones, [means you should] pay attention as to which one would possess a stronger place, so that the truth of the judgment would come down from that one (as being the stronger one). Furthermore, with either one applying to the infortunes, while the other would be deprived of an application, it wholly removes his knowledge. [If one would apply to a fortune and the other to none, there is truth in it.][11]

If therefore the ninth and its lord would offer testimonies, [but] if the lord of the east would not regard [them], it commends the knowledge, but portends that he is ignorant. Again, with the ninth and its lord being corrupted, while [they][12] would be deprived of the aspect of the eastern lord, [it means] it is not knowledge, nor that he has knowledge, nor has he attained anything: and thus they wholly deny both the effecting of it and its fruit.

---

[8] Cf. al-Rijāl III.15.
[9] Reading with al-Rijāl for "seventh."
[10] That is, the Moon and the lord of the ninth.
[11] Adding with al-Rijāl.
[12] *Hic*, implying the lord of the ninth in particular.

SHIPS

§9.41: On a ship or the status of those sailing—'Umar[1]

And so, [if] you will want to discover the status of a ship or of those sailing, and their certain departure, [then] once the east has first been placed, and the rest of the pivots established, [and] no less with the arrangement of the stars being added, it is reasonable to observe (with the greatest industry and an alert mind) the established portions of the ship, and which one the earlier philosophers ascribed to each sign.

In fact, Ptolemy took care to distribute the individual parts of the whole ship among the signs, through this method, so that one might expect trouble or soundness in those places, [and so that] anyone might discover it more easily. Therefore, Aries claims the prow, Taurus too the lower parts (namely, it occupies from [the prow] to the waters); [Gemini has the rudder or helm, Cancer the bottom];[2] to Leo is ascribed the highest part that sticks out over the waters,[3] and thus to Virgo is ascribed the belly; the forward part of Libra responds especially to what is now lifted up, now pressed down;[4] Scorpio the place of the tree or mast, Sagittarius the mast itself,[5] Capricorn the ropes, sail, and yard-arm; Aquarius the sailors;[6] also the sign of Pisces comprehends the rowers and places of refuge.[7]

Therefore, once this kind of distribution of the parts [of the ship] has been carried out, what advantage or trouble, or what kind it is, could be discovered without difficulty, and whence and where it warns that you should have fear, both for the ship and the cargo. For, a fortunate one being discovered in any of the aforesaid places, or should the Moon and the Lunar lord be blessed in [any place], it introduces soundness. Moreover, with any infortune occupying those places, or if the Moon would happen to be found

---

[1] Cf. al-Rijāl III.14 (first part). See also Jiménez 2007 for more on the history of attributing parts of a ship to the houses or signs.
[2] Adding with al-Rijāl.
[3] This seems to be the upper sides of the ship.
[4] I am not sure what this means.
[5] But al-Rijāl's version suggests the place of the chief sailors (Scorpio) and the chief sailors themselves (Sagittarius).
[6] Al-Rijāl: "the master of the ship."
[7] *Subsidia.* That is, the safe places inside.

corrupted with her own lord, while the sign[8] is unlucky or corrupted, it is the worst.

Furthermore, the Moon and the east have control over the signification of the whole cargo, but the eastern lord is in charge of all the men. The perversity of all of these shakes the boat and sinks the cargo, unless perhaps [one of them][9] is received by the infortunes [which are corrupting them]: for thus, with the craft [itself] being unharmed, they threaten prosperity for the one, detriment and danger for the other. Contrariwise, the luckiness of all, especially with reception, promises soundness for all in common (namely for the ship and the cargo). Moreover, with the east safe and the Moon cleansed, while the eastern lord is corrupted, it saves the ship but sinks the men.[10]

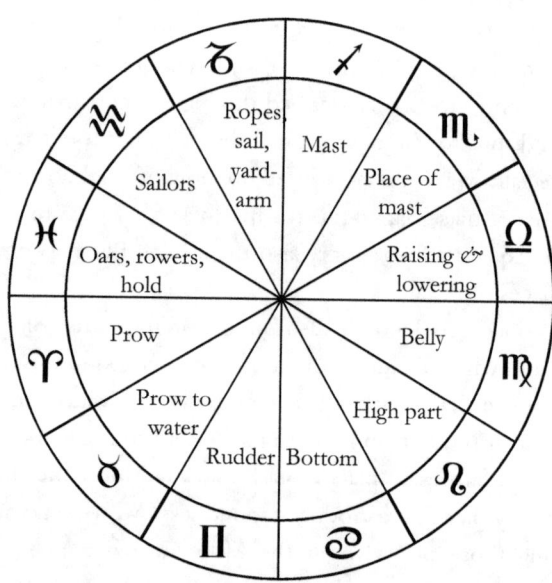

Figure 63: Parts of ship attributed to signs ('Umar §9.41)[11]

---

[8] That is, the sign of the Moon or her lord or both. Al-Rijāl has "the lord of that sign," but that would already seem to include the lord of the Moon.
[9] Reading with al-Rijāl for "they are."
[10] Reading with al-Rijāl and the logic of the passage for "sinks the ship but saves the men."
[11] The version by Demetrius (Schmidt 2005, p. 64) has these roughly reversed, so that Aries is the stern and Libra the prow. Lilly (CA p. 158) follows 'Umar.

§9.42: On constructing ships—al-Kindī[12]

§490. For organizing the construction of ships, let comfort of this kind be conveyed. Therefore, in the first place the Ascendant should be made firm, and the rest of the pivots established as immovable, nor drawn back[13]—but we should ascribe these to the fixed and straight signs. Also, let the Moon and the lord of the Ascendant be set up in a pivot and received by the lucky ones. Moreover, let a strong fortunate one,[14] in [its] easternness and in a place of its own authority and in quick step, strengthen and defend the Midheaven. Also, let the Moon be borne by her greater and faster course, and raised up in the ether.[15] Also, let her and the lord of the Ascendant be cleansed of the infortunes.

§491-492a. And so, Mars in a pivot, corrupting the Moon and lord of the Ascendant (or at least one [of them]), burns the ship up—especially from a fiery sign. In an earthy sign, it shakes and breaks the ship by a small bump or collision with a mountain or rocks.[16] In an airy sign, it sinks it through the loss of the oars and the blowing of winds. Moreover, with him appearing in a watery sign, it is sunk through the carelessness of those navigating, or the amount of the cargo. Which if Saturn would perform the role of Mars, it is believed to be harmful through a corresponding misfortune. However, he being in a fiery sign brings the wrecked ship down to the depths, but on account of those things which we established above with respect to the signs. Mars being in a human sign [means] the calamity of sinking, an assault of robbers, and an assault by enemies seem to follow.

§492b-493. In addition, the prosperity of the ship comes to be discerned in this ranking. For, Jupiter in the Midheaven preserves the full and general health of the cargo and of those sailing, and multiplies the profit and reward. If however Venus would favor and comfort the ship from the Midheaven, it greatly increases the common safety of the ship and cargo (though it happens more powerfully from Jupiter), [and] multiplies the joys of the captain or [the one who acts] on behalf of [its] owner.

---

[12] Cf. al-Rijāl III.14 (middle).
[13] I believe this means that the degree of the Midheaven should not fall on the ninth sign.
[14] Reading the singular with Robert; Hugo begins with the singular but uses verbs in the plural.
[15] Ascending in the circle of her apogee.
[16] *Montis et saxorum.* Or perhaps this should simply be read as "a mass of rocks."

§494-95a. Further, the lord of the assembly or opposition should be noted [and] established in the way it was stated before in the above chapter.[17] Moreover, let the application of the Moon (after she leaves the assembly or opposition of the Sun), come to be or happen with a fortunate one.

§495b. Likewise, let the lord of the second make the lord of the Ascendant fortunate, and also establish the lord of the Midheaven in its own sovereignty, if it is permissible, and [make it] everywhere strong; also let the infortunes fall down from[18] the Sun and Moon, but let the Lot of Fortune be situated in a more powerful[19] aspect of the Moon.[20]

§9.43: On ships, what good or bad should happen to them—al-Kindī

§497. With the Ascendant being noted first, let the rest of the pivots be established with a precise method of computation. For the Ascendant designates the front part of the ship (namely the prow), but the seventh the stern, also the Midheaven the mast;[21] the underside is left to the pivot of the earth. In addition, four parts are reckoned as being on the right side, and that many on the left.

§498.[22] For example, with two parts on the right bordering on the water, [we give] the second to the forward one, the fifth to the rear one. To the two upper ones near the mast [we give] the third to the forward one, the sixth to the rear one. Of the two next to the water on the left side, [we give] the eleventh to the forward one, the eighth to the following one. Of the two lofty [parts], [we give] the twelfth to the leading one, the ninth to the rear one.

---

[17] Perhaps referring to al-Kindī's §483 in §4.14 above.
[18] That is, be "in aversion to."
[19] Robert: "friendly."
[20] Robert: "And let the Lot of Fortune and the lights regard the east at the same time, in a friendly way; and let the infortunes be cadent from the pivots."
[21] Reading with Robert for Hugo's "each edge."
[22] Using Robert's more succinct paragraph for Hugo's.

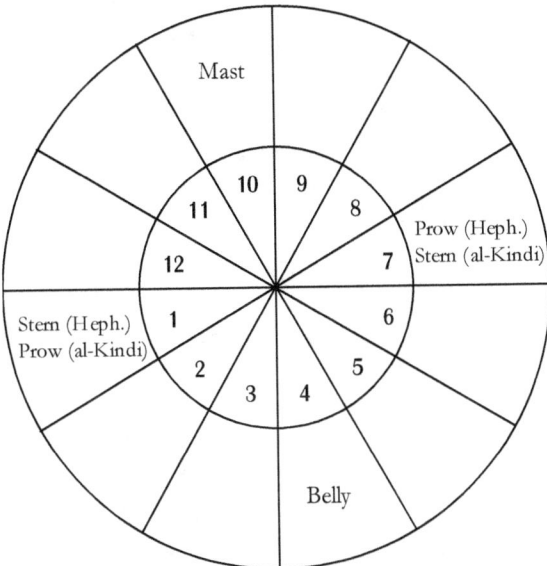

Figure 64: Angles of the chart & ship:
Dorotheus-Hephaistio *vs.* al-Kindī

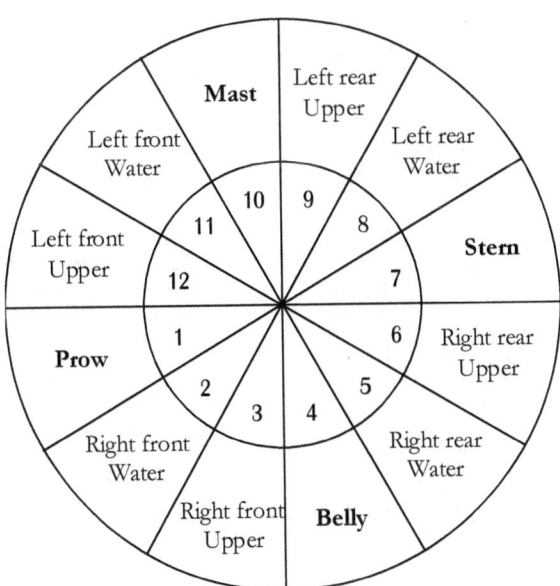

Figure 65: Al-Kindī's ship-house associations (Robert & Hugo)

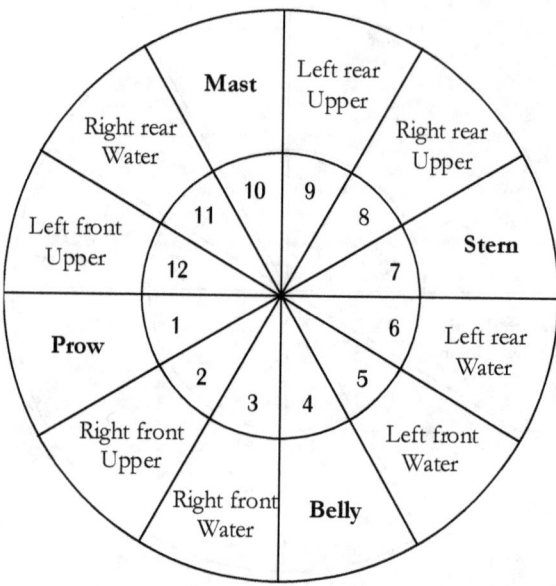

Figure 66: Al-Kindī's ship-house associations (Latin al-Rijāl III.14)

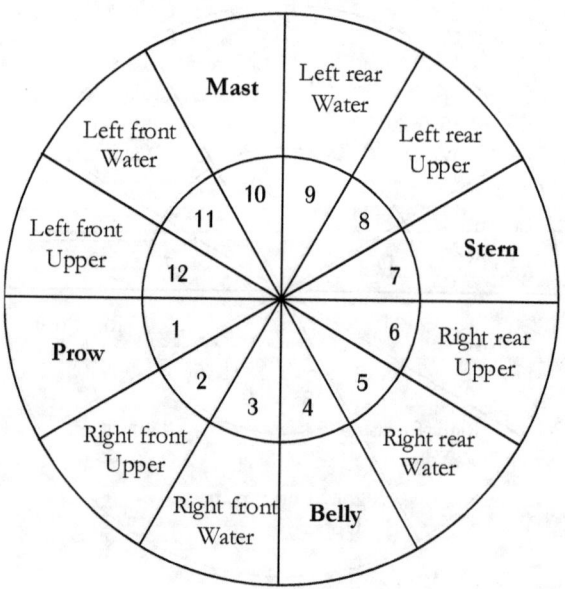

Figure 67: Proposed correction to al-Rijāl (Dykes)

Comment by Dykes. The attributions of houses to the parts of a ship are somewhat troubled in the literature.[23] In this comment I will only address the house-based attributions, derived from al-Kindī and Dorotheus-Hephaistio. Two types of differences are shown here: [1] in the assignment of the angles, and [2] the assignment of the rest of the houses.[24]

[1] The version according to Dorotheus (in Hephaistio III.14) gives the prow to the seventh and the stern to the Ascendant, as though the ship is sailing toward the 7th and the west. But the version according to al-Kindī reverses these, as though the ship is pointed towards the Ascendant and the east. What accounts for this difference? On the one hand, the seventh is usually envisioned as the destination of a journey:[25] in that case, Dorotheus imagines the ship *sailing away* from home (the Ascendant) *into* other waters (seventh), while al-Kindī imagines the ship *returning to* home (the Ascendant) *from* other waters (seventh). In that case, the attributions would really depend on the kind of question: "Will the ship reach its destination" (Dorotheus), and "Will the ship return home" (al-Kindī)—and indeed, al-Kindī's §§499 and 506 below suggest just this. But it seems to me that the disagreement is probably not intentional, and that the extent of the differences in the various versions are due to an error by al-Kindī or his sources—which brings us to the second difference:

[2] Robert and Hugo give a different attribution to the other parts of the ship than even al-Rijāl does, though both Robert-Hugo and al-Rijāl have their own kind of logic (and provided that one accepts my proposed correction to al-Rijāl above).

[2a] For Robert and Hugo, everything above the horizon is the left side, and everything below it is the right side (which does *not* make sense if the ship is pointed eastwards, as they claim); likewise, everything in the eastern hemisphere is the front half of the ship, and everything in the western hemisphere is the rear part (which *does* make sense if the ship is indeed pointed eastwards). From there, the succeedent places all pertain to the lower sides of the ship touching the water, and the cadent places to the upper sides of the ship. I do not see why succeedent and cadent places should be divided in this way.

---

[23] The zodiacal signs are also attributed to parts of a ship, as we see in §9.41 above, where 'Umar credits Ptolemy. Lilly also uses this zodiacal scheme (*CA* pp. 157-58).
[24] As Jiménez (2007, p. 29) points out, another and apparently jumbled and unclear version is attributed to Rhetorius in *CCAG* VIII.1, p. 265).
[25] See for example *Forty Chapters* Ch. 29, and al-Kindī's §§604*ff* in §5.48 below.

[2b] Al-Rijāl (III.14) has a much more logical scheme for the non-angular parts of the chart. One may refer above to the scheme as actually written in the Latin version), which seems to mix up several of the attributions in ways that do not make sense. But I believe my own correction is probably what al-Rijāl intended: like Robert and Hugo, my corrected al-Rijāl gives the upper and lower, eastern and western parts of the chart to the left, right, front and rear parts of the ship, respectively. However, from there, the attributions of the parts near the water or upper sides follow more logically: the places on each side of the Ascendant-seventh axis are higher up, near the upper points of the prow (Ascendant, second, twelfth) or the stern (seventh, sixth, eighth). The places flanking the Midheaven-IC axis are closer to the water. In this way we can follow a semicircular path around the ship on each side: from the point of the prow (Ascendant) we can trace from the upper part (second) to the lower part near the water (third) to the belly below (fourth), then up again to the water's surface again (fifth) and then to the upper side (sixth) toward the top of the stern (seventh)—and likewise down and around on the other side (provided that the fourth indicates the belly itself, no matter what side we are on).

[2c] However, my correction to al-Rijāl not answer the puzzling problem of the sides and direction of the ship itself. For in my corrected version, if one stands and faces the prow, toward the east, then the southern side of the chart (to one's right) indicates the left side of the ship, and vice versa—which does not make sense. But, the sides of the chart and ship *would* be consistent and logical if we adopted the Dorothean attribution of the angles and switched the stern and prow around. And so, I propose the following attributions, using the following: Dorothean angles, corrected al-Rijāl sides and upper/water distinctions, and switching the front/rear attributions to match Dorotheus:

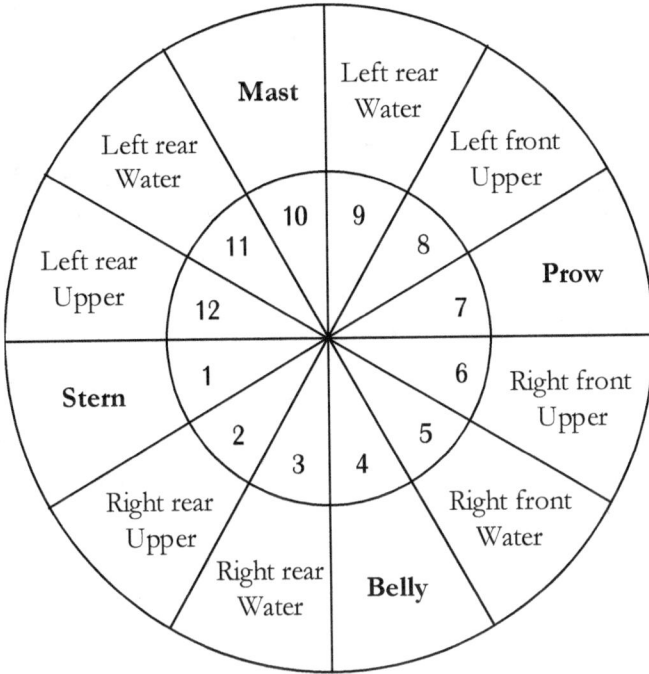

Figure 68: Proposed correct attributions (Dykes)

[The safety & harm of the ship]

§499. Therefore, with a question proposed about the course of a ship, if the pivots would gleam with the fortunate ones' own proper light,[26] but with the infortunes being estranged and cadent and scorched, they promise a safe and longed-for [return to] port without impediment, for both the ship and the cargo. But the infortunes in a pivot or after the pivots introduce danger into that part of the ship designated by the sign which the infortune is holding onto.

§500. Saturn [as that infortune] sinks it, wrecked. Moreover, Mars being in some place of his own dignity or in its regard,[27] and in an earthy sign, indi-

---

[26] That is, if the fortunes were bodily in the pivots (al-Rijāl).
[27] Reading with al-Rijāl and Robert: that is, if Mars is in one of his own dignities or aspects a place of his own dignity (presumably this would only include his domiciles). A problem with this interpretation is that there is no sign in the zodiac in which Mars will not aspect at least one of his domiciles.

cates the same as Saturn, but warns that one should fear an excessive collision of waves and overturning by rough seas.

§501. Also, with the infortunes bearing themselves thusly, if the regard of fortunes would be brought to bear, even the pivotal lords being safe and clean [of the infortunes], [and] particularly the Ascendant [and] the Lunar lord, [then] after the aforesaid threats of rough seas and seething waves, they look after the integrity of the ship, and for the most part the cargo. But if Mars himself would corrupt the lords of the pivots and the lord of the Moon, it brings in the trouble of excessive storms and various attacks of enemies.

§502. If however unluckiness would accompany this corruption of the signs, it generates war, afflicts with wounds, pilfers goods through theft, particularly while the infortunes appear in signs defending the upper parts of ships (namely those adjacent to the edges [of the ship]). Also, the perversity of Saturn and Mars [together] inserts death and captivity. However, Saturn as the sole author of this corruption expels death [itself], but binds captives together and squanders the money.

§503. Which if Mars would hold onto the Midheaven, it being corrupted ([for the Midheaven] takes the signification over the upper parts of the ship, with the rest), it brings flashing [and] lightning down from above, and[28] what the fiery adversity of clouds tends to bring. He being in the pivot of the earth scorches the lower parts of the ship. Moreover, in a human sign it burns the ship by an enemy hand, and it attacks[29] the part possessed by that corrupted sign, with iron. But if Saturn would enjoy the role of Mars in the Midheaven, it tears down the mast (namely the "tree" of the ship), shaken by the force of the winds, it shatters the sail, and induces danger according to the nature of the infortune and the estrangement of the fortunate ones, or even [according to] their testimony.

§504-05a. Also, an infortune (namely Saturn) being in the seventh, shocks the rear of the ship [and] breaks the ornamental stern. Which if Mars would be taking up that position, it incites enemies and renews the fires and lightning strikes just as was said before. Moreover, an infortune in the Ascendant contaminates the forward part of the ship with loss, just as I think has al-

---

[28] Omitting *si*, which may have been *etsi* but still does not help.
[29] Reading *afficit* for *appetit*.

ready been said enough with respect to the nature of the danger with the effectiveness of the infortune [in the seventh].[30]

§505b-506. But the retrogradation of the lord of the Ascendant impedes the journey and leads the ship back with it being incomplete. Likewise, with the lord of the Ascendant in a convertible sign, and it[31] retrograding, it brings it back to the place whence the ship had set out, with the journey being cut short. Which if retrogradation of [the lord of the Ascendant] would happen, and it is fortunate, it promises a useful return; being unlucky, it makes a return with loss.

§507. Then, the lord of the eighth (particularly with it being in the seventh) corrupting the lord of the Ascendant, threatens harm to the ship according to the manner and nature of the one harassing [it]. Moreover, the lord of the eighth (it being in the eighth) corrupting the Moon and the Lunar lord and [the lord] of the Ascendant, exposes the master of the ship (and very often all of those whom he takes [on board]) to harm. The Lot of Fortune corrupted, and the Lot of money (and their lords)[32] corrupted, testify to the loss of the cargo according to the nature of the one making it unfortunate. If however fortunate ones would take up this role of the infortunes, they convey profit.

[Speed]

§508. Also, the slowness of the lord of the Ascendant and of the Lunar [lord], particularly with their lords bearing themselves that way, suggests a delay in completing the journey. The quickness of their course leads it more quickly to the destined place.

[Death]

§509. Which if the unfriendliness of contrariety would be found between the lord of the Ascendant and the Lunar [lord], namely so that one would be situated in the seventh of the other without mutual reception (but rather if one would taint the other), it inserts mutual dissension [between] those sail-

---

[30] Again, all of this assumes that the Ascendant really does signify the prow and the seventh the stern (unlike with Dorotheus-Hephaistio).
[31] Reading with Robert for *eiusdem signi domino*. But al-Rijāl reads, "the lord of the fourth sign."
[32] Reading with al-Rijāl; Robert and Hugo include only the lord of the Lot of money.

ing and the one whom the infortune afflicts with its own nuisance of adversity, will meet death, conquered.

[Supplies & food]

§510. Moreover: [1] the lord of the second being estranged from the second, likewise [2] the lord of the second from the Moon standing back from[33] the Lunar second, moreover [3] the lord of the Lot of Fortune being estranged and absent from the Lot of Fortune, afflicts the cohort of those sailing, with a lack of food and supplies and those things which pertain to the sustaining of life.

§511. But if this should happen in watery signs, they are restricted by a lack of water. In airy or fiery ones, they are vexed with anxiety over starvation. Also, in fiery signs they are pressured by starving for those things which generally have the essence of sustaining [people] through the benefit of fire.[34] And so, remember to consider it for the rest in this manner.

---

[33] Again, "in aversion to."
[34] In other words, cooked foods.

§10: TENTH HOUSE

10th House	
Attaining honors	§§10.1-10, 10.33, 10.36
Rulership & its course	§§10.11-16, 10.20-22, 10.34-35
Underofficials	§10.17
Predecessors & successors	§§10.18-19
The return of absent rulers	§§10.23-24
The life & death of kings	§§10.27-33
Others' relationship to the king	§§10.37-38
Trades	§10.39

Figure 69: Questions of the tenth house

HONORS

§10.1: On those things which pertain to the tenth house—Sahl[1]

If perhaps an inquiry about the tenth were presented by someone (for more often it is asked about the obtaining of dignities and the rulership of kingdoms), as to whether someone would be able to attain it, one must first engage the counsel of the lord of the east and the Moon. For, the application of each with the lord of the tenth (but so that [the lord of the tenth] would regard the Midheaven) bestows what was asked about, through his own effort and labor. The position of both together in the tenth will even confer the same, provided however that they happened to be free and cleansed. With the order changed around, the lord of the Midheaven traversing in the east or applying to the lord of the east, will confer the dignity which he had hoped for, without the expense of his own labor. Nor does the application of the lord of the tenth to a fortunate one holding onto the east, mean something else.

With these things not being found to be so, so long as there occurs a transfer of light between each significator, he will obtain the gift of the dignity that is asked about, by means of someone mediating. But if the one who receives [the management][2] happens to be cleansed and free, and should it regard the tenth, it promises that he is going to get what he was hoping for.

---

[1] Cf. *On Quest.* §10.1.
[2] That is, the disposition or application.

Moreover, its corruption carries off the things which were sought after hope [had been] certain. Here I think one must even note: should the malevolents corrupt from a tetragon or opposition, he who was asking will give up because of a severe and indignant rebuff; but their corruption proceeding from a trigon or hexagon [means that] the sought gift of honor is denied with patience.

In addition, with these things being denied, should there be a collection of light between the significators, and the one who collects traverses in the east or tenth, [then] it is good to take note of the Moon. Because she, applying to either of the significators, [means] he will rejoice in the honor that is sought; but with an application not being found, if at least she happened to be cleansed and received, he will get what he had sought, by means of many helping. But if the Moon happened to bear herself otherwise than what we said, we will follow up with the star that collects the light. For, it[3] being arranged in the tenth, or regarding it, even so that it is not remote from the east,[4] and is cleansed of the infortunes, so that before it hastens to leave the sign, both significators (or either one) would apply to it or they would assemble with it, it in no way stands in the way of having the dignity.

§10.2: When he would attain the honor—Sahl[5]

In addition, whenever it was asked about the term of the promised honor, it seems the application of each significator must be noted. For if you find both applying to each other, and the Moon conveying [her management] to one, [while she is both received and cleansed of the infortunes],[6] it accelerates achieving it. Which if she conveyed it to neither of them, while however in her own right she is received from elsewhere, it is a sign of delay. Which if she happened not to be received, but she were however cleansed, we will follow up with each significator (namely the eastern lord and that of the tenth). For that one of the two which gathers the counsel of the other, being free, if it would support its own house with an aspect, he achieves less than

---

[3] In the rest of the paragraph, the Latin does not clearly distinguish between the collecting star and the Moon. John's Sahl seems to read as though we are talking about the Moon here, while Hugo clearly means the collecting star. I think Hugo is probably right.
[4] That is, in aversion to the Ascendant.
[5] *On Quest.* §10.2.
[6] Adding with John's Sahl, since it seems to be required by the logic of the passage.

what he aspired to. If you learned that this one [is impeded in the way]⁷ the Moon is impeded, it wholly speaks against his wish.

On the other hand, provided that the lord of the tenth would apply to the lord of the fourth, but so that the one who receives [the management]⁸ would convey it to the eastern lord, it promises he is going to get it [even though] he is already losing hope.⁹ Moreover, the lord of the east gathering the counsel of the Moon, with every difficulty being removed, means [getting] the dignity that is sought.

§10.3: Over which region he would be in charge—Sahl¹⁰

In addition, if nothing ambiguous would be left over about attaining an honor, this other observation comes to be. If the lord of the east would be holding onto its own house, he is put in charge over his native region. Traversing in its sovereignty, it sets him up [over] many lands, magistrates, and great dignities. If however it would be lingering in its triplicity, he ought to be lifted up to the greatest office of command, but outside his born fatherland. Meanwhile however, if the lord of the east were devoid of all dignity in the sign where it is staying, he earns a position of dignity over a region unknown [to him].¹¹

Moreover, it often happens that the same star claims rulership over the tenth and the east. And so, it being cleansed and well-placed (not, however, without reception), will bestow a certain portion of the dignity that is sought. But with reception being not at all found, and the Moon appearing impeded, it is a sign that [the dignity] is contradicted.

And it can even happen thus, that the lord of the eastern lord cannot¹² apply to the lord of the tenth. For example, with Leo rising, [and] so that the pivots are upright, we should consult the Sun and Venus [separately]. For, each one being received and regarding the tenth, confirms the matter. But if

---

⁷ Adding with John's Sahl.

⁸ Namely, the lord of the fourth.

⁹ John's Sahl adds that this transfer can also work in the other direction: from the lord of the east, to that of the fourth, to that of the tenth.

¹⁰ *On Quest.* §10.2.

¹¹ John's Sahl puts it that he will be unknown in the region, but I suppose that would amount to the same thing.

¹² Adding *non* with John's Sahl. The idea seems to be that the Sun has fewer opportunities to aspect Mercury and Venus, because they are rarely able (and in the case of Mercury, never able) to aspect from the sextile.

one of them happens to be received, but the other is in no way received, one will have to have recourse to the Moon. Which if she conveys [her management] to the one which is not received, [and] with there being hope, it does not fail. Moreover, with both being in no way received, and the Moon is [not][13] conveying it to either one, while the one who receives [the management] is free [and] regards the Midheaven,[14] it bestows part of the thing sought.

But if a star traversing in a pivot would collect the light of each, nor is it going to leave behind the sign it is staying in until both are joined with it, [it indicates] the establishment of the matter.

Finally, the Moon being received and regarding the Midheaven, is a complete sign of prosperity in that matter. Moreover, with her being conjoined with the lord of the tenth by the light of her own body, regarding the tenth, it brings forth the hope to an effect; nor is it otherwise with her being received by her own lord, equally regarding the tenth with [her lord]. In addition, the Moon applying to none in the sign where she is staying,[15] stands in the way of what is sought, unless you should find both the lords of the east and of the question strong, nor foreign[16]—provided, however, that they regarded the place of the question in a friendly way.

Moreover, one must note that the Moon's hindrance, and the lord of the question being not very firm, take away from the matter sought. But if the receiver of the Moon's [management] would be corrupted, they wholly turn [the matter] aside and contradict it. However, the Lunar application with either of the significators helps very much.

Whenever the star which receives the [management of the] Moon is also the one who is in charge of the tenth, should both (I say), be rendering counsel to one and the same [star], but so that the receiving one would bear testimony to the Midheaven without a regard,[17] they lead the matter to effect [but] without all counsel and opinion of the querent.

---

[13] Adding with John's Sahl.
[14] Omitting *dominum* ("lord") with John's Sahl, because by definition the lord of the tenth is already involved in this situation.
[15] That is, being void in course (*ITA* III.9). John's Sahl specifically notes that she will not complete a connection while in her current sign.
[16] That is, peregrine.
[17] According to John's Sahl, this means that it has some strength in its own place and in the tenth.

But[18] if the significator and its lord should happen to disagree and be inimical, it disturbs the matter and contrives the heaviest labors. But this disagreement is that one would be remote from or in aversion to, the other. Moreover, the regard of each from the opposition brings about nothing different.

Moreover, note that you should attend with the greatest effort [to this]: because the lord of the east principally lays out and embraces whatever future good, evil, or any difficulty (or contrariwise, good opinion) looms over the good person of the querent. The lord of the seventh is put over subordinates in the magistracy or dignity. Seek future events after the dignity is acquired, from the Midheaven and its lord. In the eleventh it establishes his successors, wherefore the ninth and its lord prefigure those who came before him, and their status. From the fourth and its lord, the end of the whole matter is resolved. The second and its lord, but even the Lot of Fortune (not without its lord) determines his livelihood and resources, but we even observe [his] secretaries and chancery-clerks from that. The eleventh, with its lord, comprises the revenues of the acquired dignity. From the third depends the knowledge of friends.[19] We judge slaves and beasts of burdens from the sixth and its lord. Finally, from the twelfth we bid you to attend to enemies.

Since[20] these bear themselves so as to [indicate] complete knowledge of what was written before, one ought to scrutinize the places we described above with diligent observation, so that finally the regard and position of their lords, [and] the benevolents or their opposites behave, manage a certain judgment: if good, good; if otherwise, [bad].

---

[18] In this paragraph, John's Sahl reads it as a difference between the significator and its own *house* (*domus*), not its own *lord* (*dominus*). Clearly one of the manuscript traditions is wrong. I can see reasons for both being appropriate.
[19] John's Sahl has friends in the eleventh, and brothers in the third; on the other hand, friends are also an attribution of the third (i.e., friends who are so close so as to be kin), and I do not necessarily see the relevance of brothers in this question.
[20] Reading rather freely from Hugo's rather tortured sentence, and in comparison with John's Sahl.

§10.4: On anyone, whether he would be able to get a kingdom or dignity—'Umar[21]

At the hour of an inquiry or nativity, the Sun holding onto the tenth or his own house, or being arranged in the degree of his own sovereignty, while Jupiter (being cleansed of scorching) appeared as his partner, or Venus would possess a pivot, with the regard (I say) of the infortunes from a tetragon or opposition or assembly being denied, it is necessary that the querent himself (or one who is then born) will rule the whole world. Now, the Sun being deprived of both [his] house and sovereignty, takes away from the aforesaid, unless (I say) he would originate from a royal family or one of magnates. For, being placed thusly, he subjects the ends of the kingdom and his clime to his rule.

Moreover, with Mercury being found in the east, while it is his sovereignty, but should the Sun be holding onto his own house, yet Jupiter the tenth, [and] Venus in his assembly, with the aspect of the infortunes (I say) from a tetragon, assembly, or opposition being frustrated, it generates a secretary or scribe of the king.

But if Libra is rising, should Saturn possess it, and Venus in the ninth, [and] should even Jupiter and the Sun be lingering in the tenth, it establishes a tributary of money and of the royal resources, a distinguished guardian, or dignitary.

Which if the east would present a sovereignty to Jupiter,[22] with Jupiter being placed there, however the Sun and Venus being in the tenth, he is made a general of the military and having power over blood, especially with the Moon occupying the pivot of the earth.

Furthermore, the Sun being placed in the east, in his own sovereignty, should Jupiter occupy the tenth, Venus the east, [and] the Moon the pivot of the earth,[23] while they are deprived of both the tetragonal aspect and opposite of the infortunes, they present an unharmed kingdom.

---

[21] I have not been able to identify this passage in al-Rijāl, but it presents no translation problems. Some of these configurations also satisfy conditions for bodyguarding (and therefore eminence), as described in *ITA* III.28.

[22] That is, if it is Cancer (Jupiter's exaltation).

[23] In this case, the Sun would be exalted and the Moon in her own house, but Jupiter in his fall in Capricorn and Venus in detriment in Aries. It seems that the planets' presence in the angles is more important than their dignity. But 'Umar might also be considering that each of these signs (Aries, Capricorn, Cancer) is the exaltation of a superior planet.

Figure 70: A few eminence configurations ('Umar §10.4)

Now, every star being found in its own house or sovereignty, signals a royal dignity, if, I say, the fortunate ones do not leave the pivots behind. Moreover, any star means what is of its own nature and proper quality.

Likewise, if Leo is arising, but the Sun in his own sovereignty, Venus and Jupiter in the tenth, they being free (I say) of the tetragonal aspect or opposite and assembly of the infortunes, they bless with royal power.

Moreover, if each light would apply to the eastern lord (appearing in a pivot) from a pivot, especially in the tenth, it claims he is going to obtain whatever is demanded from the king. But if either of the lights would have control over the rulership of the Midheaven, applying (I say) to the eastern lord, it grants the greatest increase.

§10.5: Whether he would obtain an honor sought from the king—'Umar[24]

And so, the east and the lord of the east, but even the Midheaven and the Moon and their lords, should be consulted if (I say) someone, coming to the king or any aristocrat, would be eager to obtain some gift of dignity.

Therefore,[25] the lord of the east being established in the east or any pivot, in some place of its own power, applying to the lord of the Midheaven, it promises the honor sought. Also, it happens not otherwise whenever a star would transfer or collect each light—with the significator,[26] I say, being arranged in the degrees of the Midheaven; it traversing in the degrees of the east, too, claims nothing else. Which if they would be deprived of a mutual aspect, and the significator itself tumbling down,[27] they wholly deny the same. No less, too, whenever the infortunes would hinder each.

Moreover,[28] if the lord of the Ascendant were an infortune, and the lord of the Midheaven a fortune, and both aspected each other in places in which

---

[24] For parts of this section, cf. al-Rijāl III.20 and III.25, as well as 'Umar's §10.36 below. These sections (§10.5 and §10.36) were paired together in 'Umar's own text.
[25] Compare this paragraph with the Hugo/al-Rijāl version in §10.36.
[26] This may be the Moon.
[27] *Corruens*. Based on §10.36, this means "in aversion to," namely that the lord of the Ascendant is in aversion to the lord of the tenth, and that the lord of the tenth is in aversion to the tenth.
[28] Reading this paragraph with al-Rijāl. Hugo's more abridged and confused paragraph reads: "Moreover, with the eastern lord being unlucky, while the lord of the Midheaven is fortunate, and between them—as we have said, with respect to the strength of the place, with them being in places of dignity or power—one is stronger, one must attend even to that one of them which possesses the pivot of the east. A fortunate one claiming the

they have dignity and power, and each was in its own place, look to see which of them is more powerful, and which one [has more power] in the angle of the Midheaven. And if perhaps the one of them having greater power in the Midheaven were a fortune, and more powerful in its own place, and it was applying to an infortune, judge that he will quickly have the office and will be sent to it; [but] afterwards he will engage with one who will resist him, and trouble will happen to him in this, and he will be expelled from it in a bad and shameful way, especially when that rulership and power would decline to an infortune after a fortune. But if the infortune had greater rulership in the Midheaven, and were more powerful in its own place, it signifies that he will speak about the matter, and it will be thought to happen, but it will not happen.

The[29] Lunar aid must be scrutinized in this kind of question, and in what place she is staying. For, she being arranged in the house of hope, and applying [to her own lord],[30] he is consoled by the expected honor. Which if the significator itself, the lord of the east, claimed a strong place in the circle, and the Moon [would be] applying to it from these places, it does not deny the effect. But she being corrupted by the lord of the house of hope, wholly abolishes the hope. Moreover, the lord of the house of hope being a fortune,[31] possessing a strong place from that house, with the Moon being cadent from it and from the fortunes,[32] it conveys some portion of the request; but then it declares that [the matter] is corrupted and thrown into confusion by his subjects. Finally,[33] every question of this kind (namely, about obtaining some dignity, and about the succession of someone of power in it, or whether someone is going to obtain what he demands), is resolved by such a method. For, she being corrupted by Mars in this question, and

---

Midheaven, is indicated as being stronger in its own place. Therefore, it applying to the infortunes, even though it advances him quickly to an honor, still it does not drive away trouble: it strips away the dignity that was given, namely when the two lights first apply to an infortune after any fortunate ones. Which if it would have control over the rulership of the Midheaven, holding onto its own strong place, even though it bestows a gift of dignity (so that there already seems to be no ambiguity present), still the matter itself will lack an effect, but rather will introduce rather loss and persecution."

[29] For this paragraph, see the more complete version in §10.36.
[30] Reading with al-Rijāl, based on the more complete version of this paragraph in §10.36.
[31] Reading with al-Rijāl for Hugo's "placed."
[32] Reading with al-Rijāl for Hugo's "it is fortunate."
[33] The rest of this paragraph had originally been put after the next paragraph by Hugo, but it belongs here. Still, it is incomplete and should be compared with the fuller version in §10.36.

Mars (being in a strong place) would corrupt the east, and equally its lord and [the lord of the eleventh or the lord of] of the Midheaven, it wholly denies the desired dignity. Furthermore, the domicile of hope being corrupted in an inquiry of this kind, with the Moon and the eastern lord, and [the lord of the eleventh or the Midheaven] being corrupted, it stirs up adversaries and finally afflicts with death.

Furthermore,[34] the greatest recognition of this question depends on the bound of the tenth. For if a fortunate one would be staying in it, or would be regarding it from bound to bound, or the lord of the house of the star would collect [the light of it] and of the bound of the royal lord,[35] it blesses with the desired gifts. Which if this fortunate one were unlucky, and arranged in [its own] sovereignty, it bestows the same thing to him.

If however a question would happen about a king—namely whether, while he is still living, [someone else] would have control of the royal scepter, the royal Lot[36] will have to be consulted. For if the lord of [the Lot's] own lodging place, or of the bound or face (or rather both) would regard it, they advancing in direct course, it is a sign of attaining the kingdom. Then, the hour of the matter could be discovered thus:[37] for one must attend to the Sun and Jupiter, [and see] which one is stronger; how many degrees are between it, makes the distance of the Lot of the king; once they have been drawn down from Mars, where the number is ended [indicates] the place [of the Lot]. The Sun himself or Jupiter being cleansed, [and] entering [into that place], leads the dignity to its worthy end.[38]

§10.6: On the attainment of an honor—al-Kindī

§320. With a question made about the obtaining of some dignity, the star which was the victor (namely, the more powerful) for the Ascendant, and the [victor for] the Midheaven, should be consulted. For, their mutual applica-

---

[34] I have been unable to locate the rest of this section in al-Rijāl.
[35] Tentatively adding the material in brackets, and reading *termini* for *terminus*, otherwise the sentence would make less sense. As it stands, I am not sure of the meaning: perhaps ʿUmar is really looking for a planet (perhaps even the fortunate one in the tenth) which collects the light of the domicile lord and bound lord of the Midheaven?
[36] See for instance *ITA* VI.2.37-40.
[37] This Lot seems to be calculated from the stronger (of the Sun and Jupiter) to the weaker, and projected by Mars. Since strength and not sect is the deciding factor, it would not be reversed by night.
[38] Reading for the awkward *dignitatem ipsam ad finem et dignum perducit effectum*.

tion, or with them being regarded by their own lords—[and] moreover the Sun and the Moon (or at least that one which obtains the shift) being in the regard of their own lords, grant the benefit of the honor. Moreover, with the common regard of the Sun and Moon being taken away, nor [would they be] regarded by their own lords, they deny the hope of honor.[39]

§321. Moreover, with all doubt about obtaining the honor being taken away, the strength and weakness of the lord of the Midheaven should be noted: namely, whether it is direct or retrograde, whether appearing or being hidden, whether eastern or the contrary, whether fortunate or unlucky, even the luckiness or misfortune of the Midheaven itself, would settle the judgment. For, all things which are considered to befall the Midheaven itself or its victor-lord (namely the stronger one), these same things do not abandon the master of that honor.[40]

§322. And so, the Sun being the one to save and bless the Midheaven or its lord more strongly, and being its very powerful supporter, introduces honor from a superior king. But the Moon taking this role of the Sun, [it will be] from the common people. However, Saturn introduces aristocrats and old men, the cultivation of deserts, the spring waters of lands, streams and rivers, and he brings back that kind [of thing which is] in the common use of citizens, into the reason for conferring honor.

§323. Also, Jupiter greatly bestows it from the aristocrats of the people, and those of a more prominent name, and the just. Moreover, Mars brings in the leaders of the army, people powerful in war, [and] masters of booty and plunder into the benefit of the bestowing of this honor. Venus obtains the dignity by means of women and the benefits of women, [and] dug-up materials of gold and silver. Also, Mercury gets the honor in turn through writing, advice, commerce, administrating the royal provisions,[41] reason, [and] eloquence.

§324. Moreover, with the Sun being the very lord of the Ascendant,[42] he acquires a kingdom with labor. He being the lord of the house of money,

---

[39] In this paragraph, the domicile lords of these planets seem to stand for the authority who is granting the dignity or position.

[40] In other words, those qualities will also attach to the quality of the honor itself, or the experience of the person possessing it. It is possible that they also pertain to the authority figure who is granting the honor.

[41] *Census.*

[42] That is, while he is also the best and most powerful planet making the Midheaven fortunate, etc., as above. Al-Kindī is using the Sun here as an example of what to do with all planets.

brings it through underofficials and through his own money. But as the lord of the third, he testifies that [the querent] gets it from brothers and much traversing. With him appearing as the lord of the fourth, he climbs up to the honor because of some land or estate, or a city or some hidden and ancient affair. But as the lord of the fifth, children or the friends of brothers or the paternal money revere him with this gift.

§325. Moreover with him as the lord of the sixth, slaves or animals or someone's disease conveys it to him. Likewise, in the rulership of the seventh, he is promoted by the inhabitants of the land, [and] sometimes even because of adversaries or women or commerce. But as the lord of the eighth, it establishes the cause of the honor as being the money of adversaries and women or merchants, sometimes even inheritances or provisions acquired through someone's death, or the besieging of cities or someone's long captivity, or treasure. In the same way, with him as the lord of the ninth he is entitled to obtain it by law, travel, or some change.[43]

§326. Also, as the lord of the tenth advances him to an honor because of the king and the benefit of royal counsel, or his own profession or the mother or a woman who performs the role of a mother. In the rulership of the eleventh, friends or the hope of some matter, and [his] reputation and the prosperity of fortune, even the royal family and its money, are believed to greatly bestow it. Also, as the lord of the twelfth, he is entitled to attain this from enemies and because of someone's departure and remoteness, sometimes even with anxiety.

§327. And so in this way, one will have to consider it by the individual signs, if the fortunate ones[44] would hold onto them or [the signs] would be made prosperous by them.

§328. The eleventh sign denotes the royal money:[45] which if it would be blessed by some fortune, it indicates it will be much and very advantageous, according to the nature of that fortune. Likewise, it signifies the royal underofficials and it releases the accepted luckiness into them according to the proper quality of the one making [it] fortunate. Also, the twelfth sign being lucky, since it means the brothers and friends of kings, shows its luckiness to

---

[43] *Transmutatione* (Robert: "movement," *motione*). This most likely refers to moving from one place to another.
[44] Reading *fortunatae* for *fortunata*.
[45] From here through §332, al-Kindī considers the houses as derived from the tenth, so topics relating to the king. If the Sun were the lord of the eleventh it could certainly also denote the friends of the querent.

them. Again, the Ascendant denotes royal parents and their estates, mansions, and treasures. But the second [denotes] children by [the king], whose prosperity brings forth many benefits of the kingdom to him.

§329. The third contains the king's captives and beasts and disease. Therefore, they take on whatever [kinds] of prosperity are in them, according to the nature of the one blessing [it]. Also, the fourth designates the royal wife, but one which he takes [as a wife] *after* accepting rule; it even indicates the king's adversaries and business partners.[46] Likewise, they incur whatever [types] of prosperity or loss [there is], according to its signification. Once more, the fifth claims the king's adversities and loss, disturbance [and] corruption. Which if some luckiness would attain it,[47] it applies what is signified by it, to those [things].

§330. But the luckiness of the sixth[48] watches over royal travel and [the king's] treaties, testimonies, faith, and these [things]. Also, the seventh (namely the tenth from the kingdom or the house of the king) suggests (and defends with its luckiness) the affairs of the king and his counsels, by means of which the stability of the kingdom endures. But the eighth [indicates] the heads of the military and underofficials of the kingdom, and those great men among the leading people of society or lords, who make him [king], commending his acts, [and who] try hard to obtain what is useful for him. And its benignness looks after those things which belong to its signification.

§331. Finally, the ninth place takes the enemies of the kingdom, and the envious, and those who gloat over its confusion; and it mitigates these same things with its good fortune.

§332. If therefore they bear a signification of improsperity, remember to judge in the same way concerning unfortunate [stars] as was stated above with respect to the fortunate ones.

§10.7: On acquiring kingdoms and dignities—al-Khayyāt

With a question of the tenth being proposed (of which kind is one about a kingdom or some kind of inheritable tenancy,[49] [namely] whether someone would merit getting it), the east and its lord, with the Moon, [and] no less too

---

[46] *Negotiatores*.
[47] That is, if a benefic planet is in it.
[48] Reading *sexti* for *sextum*.
[49] *Haereditatum*.

the tenth and its lord, will have to be consulted. And so, an application of the eastern lord with the lord of the tenth, so that the receiver of counsel[50] from both [of them] would regard its own house, conveys the acquired dignity through his own labor. This is so even [with] the Moon applying to it (especially with the lord of the east lingering in the tenth, cleansed of the infortunes), even should it not be received by its own lord, or if the significator, applying to it, rendered powers and counsel to it: and in this way the gift of the dignity will be greatly bestowed. It is even the same if it[51] would apply to fortunate ones in the tenth or at least in the eleventh, but even the east and the rest of the pivots [should be treated] in this manner. Likewise, with the converse order—the lord of the tenth placed in the east and the Moon applying to it, or if that same eastern lord or [the lord of the tenth] would apply to a benevolent occupying the east—it conveys the dignity sought, on its own.[52]

But with these things being denied, while however there is a transfer of light, it introduces what had been asked about, [but] not from him, unless it is by other middle men. But if the receiver, being cleansed and free, would console the lord of the tenth with its aspect, it indicates he is going to get it. But corrupted nor regarding, it stains and denies, or destroys, the hope that had been had for a long time.

But this must be noted with the greatest effort: what is the distance in degrees between the receiver and the corrupting infortune, but even between it and the one giving [the counsel]. For if that same receiver were in front of the infortune, it speaks against the dignities. Also that same [receiver] being a lucky one, applying from an infortune, shows no other [result].

But if a star collecting the light of each significator would traverse in the east or Midheaven, it is appropriate to note the Moon. For she, applying to the lord of the east or of the tenth, perfects the things sought. But applying to none, while however she is cleansed and received, he finally gets it with the resources of many people. Likewise, the Moon bearing herself otherwise than what we said before, while the collecting star would be lingering in the tenth or would regard it, being free nor cadent, it conveys the dignity sought—unless it would leave that sign before it receives the application of each.

---

[50] Namely, the lord of the tenth.
[51] Probably the lord of the east.
[52] *Sponte*. That is, without having to do anything special to get it.

Nor should the judgment about attaining [the dignity] be made firm unless you inspect the Moon first, even though the application of the eastern [lord] and that of the tenth has equally been discovered. For she (as was already stated) rendering counsel to either one, in no way resists the things sought. Which if she does not render, but she is received, [then it means] the same thing, even if it is after a delay. She not being received, while however she is cleansed, an observation of each significator must be consulted. For the one which was the receiver of the other's counsel, being cleansed, if it would regard its own house, will confer less than what was hoped for. But it being corrupted (as was said about the Moon): he is wholly deceived in his wish. Which if it applied at the end of a sign, while the Moon would then be lacking in all testimonies, nothing is conceded [to him], especially, if the corruption of the Moon is present.

Also, the lord of the tenth applying to the lord of the fourth, so that the lord of the end would convey it to the eastern lord, is a sign of getting it; it is better if the testimonies of the significator would help out. But if the lord of the end does not regard the eastern lord, it denies it; it is worse if it happened[53] to be corrupted. But if, on the contrary, the lord of the east, applying to the lord of the end, would donate counsel, so that [the lord of the end], receiving it,[54] would convey it to the lord of the tenth, it blesses one who has already lost hope with the attained dignity. Moreover, the lord of the fourth being received, while it would possess the east or the Midheaven, nor being remote, but even should a star regard the significator from a pivot (especially from the east or the Midheaven), it promises he is going to get it. Now, the receiver of counsel being corrupted, corrupts the whole business. But if a malevolent would regard it from a trigon or hexagon, he will get it quickly; but from a tetragon or opposition, not unless it is with difficulty and impediment; [then] even with hope already being destroyed, he will get what he was striving at. Moreover, once that regard is discovered, if it would regard the lord of the east from the opposition, he will not get it, unless [the lord of the east] would be helped by the lord of the Midheaven. With these bearing themselves thusly, if the infortune regarding the significator would be lingering in the pivot of the earth, he would not be able to get it except after some interval of time.

---

[53] Reading *contigerit* for *consiterit*.
[54] Reading *recipiens* for *respiciens*.

Moreover, the star receiving the lord of the east and the significator, if then it would regard the Midheaven, being aided by testimonies, [and] if the pivot were a firm sign, it will agree with the things sought. But a turning [sign] administers difficulty.

But this comes to be noted: the lord of the east traversing in its own lodging-place, puts him in charge over the land in which he is. But if it would hold onto its own sovereignty, he will obtain magistracies and honors and many provinces. But if it would linger in [its own] triplicity, he merits being raised to the not-moderate dignity of a prefect, but outside his native place. But if it would happen to be found devoid of all testimony[55] in the sign in which it is lingering, he is put in charge of an unknown region.[56]

§10.8: On kingdoms and dignities, whether they could be obtained—Dorotheus

With a question of the tenth being proposed (of which kind is one for a kingdom or some dignity), as to whether someone would be able to obtain it, let the eastern lord and that of the tenth, and even the Moon, be consulted. For, the eastern lord being in the tenth or applying to its lord, lavishes the things sought, [but] through his own effort. The Lunar application [means] no other thing. Moreover, the lord of the east being in the house of kings, free of the infortunes and their regard, but the lord of the Midheaven and even the significator itself applying to [the lord of the east], rendering [their] power and counsel,[57] confers the dignity sought, but preferably with fortunate ones in the house of kings or an application in the eleventh. And the effect in the remaining pivots [should be] noted thusly.

In addition, [the lord of the east] applying to the lord of the tenth in the east, and the Moon [doing the same] to it, while there is a transfer of light between each: he gets control over the gift, not through himself but some intermediary.

Moreover, one must note by how many degrees the receiver [of the application] is distant from an infortune and from the one rendering.

The receiver being corrupted at the hour of the question, removes the things sought and deprives him of the effect.

---

[55] That is, "dignity."
[56] Or perhaps, in a land in which he has no connections and is not known.
[57] That is, "pushing power" and "pushing management." See *ITA* III.16 and III.18.

§10.9: On attaining an honor—Jirjis

If someone would ask about the obtaining of a dignity or kingdom, attend equally to the eastern lord and that of the Midheaven. With a joint aspect of each being discovered, there is no ambiguity about attaining the honor; but if not, not at all.

But with a question had about when this would happen, it is necessary [to see] how many degrees of application are between the lord of the east and of the Midheaven: they put down the distance as being so many days or months or years, according to the turning or double-bodied or fixed signs.

§10.10: On the acquisition of an honor—Aristotle

The method written below will declare with respect to the attaining of an honor. With the east being made firm and the pivots established, if the eastern lord would traverse in the ninth with Jupiter or Venus or the Head (or at least should the lord of the ninth [be] with one of these in the east), or whenever Jupiter or the [Head of the] Dragon (Venus being left out) would regard the lord of the east or of the ninth, they advance him to an ecclesiastical dignity. Moreover, the lord of the ninth being found in the pivots from the first, it will enrich him with a gift of honor within his native region. Appearing after the pivots, next to his own land. But in the remote [places], it sends him to a remote region.

Kingdoms & Rulerships

§10.11: How it will go with him, or if he would be deposed—Sahl[1]

Also, I think one must note with the greatest effort, at what hour the new prince enters his rule, or, sitting down in the imperial seat, he first manages the royal affairs.

[Diurnal charts]

For if the entrance were diurnal, and the Sun would be lingering with Saturn, it portends that he steps down sooner. Moreover, the Sun being regarded by benevolents, while he and the lord of the east are established in an appropriate place from the east and in a firm sign, they indicate a long-lasting rulership, and according to his wishes. Moreover, the Sun traversing in the east and in a turning sign, if the other of the malevolents (namely Mars), occupying the tenth, regarded him, sometimes it suggests that he will be turned against and plotted against by his citizen subjects, or it threatens death at the end. With even Jupiter appearing fortunate in the Midheaven, while the Sun himself would possess an optimal and strong place, it greatly increases the kingdom, multiplies his name and reputation, and collects wealth and resources. But while you find the Sun in the eighth or sixth, if the lord of the east (it being of the benevolents) should walk through the east itself or the Midheaven, [then] even though it supports the prince in all things, still it portends the death of him from whom he had accepted the rulership.

[Nocturnal charts]

On the other hand, if he took up the already-stated dignity by night, we give the Lunar counsel in this place, just as was stated about the Sun above. For, she being cleansed of the infortunes and in a safe place preserves his body unharmed. Which if she would traverse with the wicked ones, or she would apply to them, he will be deposed sooner, confined by the severest difficulty. Moreover, the Moon traversing by 4° or less distant from the Head or Tail, shows a useless rulership. But a distance of more than 4° is less harmful. But having passed 12°, he will escape the already-stated evils, free.

---

[1] Cf. *On Quest.* §10.6.

[Primary significators]

In all of these things, it is appropriate to note the Moon and the east and their lords, even the regards of the benevolents and wicked ones to them. For if the fortunate ones would regard them and their lords (they being established in optimal places), with the malevolents being cadent [but] the fortunate ones placed in the tenth, all pleasing things will happen to the new prince. Finally, if the Moon and her lord would hold onto the perverse places, they prepare evil and anguish in the subject region.

Moreover, at the hour in which this [man] is advanced [to active rule], if the degree of the east were in a bound of the malevolents, and it was regarded by the infortunes, it designates the prince's impotence and laziness, and that he is blamed in a serious way. But if the degree of the east happened to be of the bounds of the benevolents, so that however the fortunate ones would regard it, the rule and office will be praiseworthy: for once the dignity is left in an honorable way, not only will he merit a good name but he will even be thanked by manifold profit.

[The Ascendant]

A wicked one traversing in the east, turns everything around with distress and detriment, since it perhaps threatens death in that dignity. A benevolent in the same place, with an infortune going through the fourth, praises the beginning but threatens perverse departures. [But a malevolent in the east and a benevolent in the fourth suggests the beginning will be bad and the end good.][2] In addition, the Tail being placed in the east, if you should find the lord of the east in a bad place and a malevolent in a pivot, and even with the Moon being corrupted by the infortunes, it testifies to ignoble and the lowest-class underofficials, and those ruinous to the kingdom. It even suggests he is worried and sad until [the end].

In the same way, at the hour of the accepted dignity, a benevolent in the east or the lord of the east in the tenth, and also the lord of the tenth being established in a strong place and free of the infortunes, makes not only the prince but even the kingdom long-lasting. Contrariwise too, with a malevolent occupying the east, while you find the lords of the east and the

---

[2] Adding with John's Sahl.

Midheaven equally placed perversely,³ it is a sign of quick stepping-down. Now, if the eastern lord and even that of the Midheaven would be lingering in the twelfth or sixth, he will tumble down sooner, unless (I say) Jupiter, being eastern, holds onto the east or the Midheaven: for thus it blocks and defers a little bit of his future deposing.

[The Midheaven]

Then, in all of this, you will note the tenth and where its lord is, and even under whose aspect. For, it being in a pivot and regarded by the fortunate ones, commends the prince. Moreover, a lucky one in the tenth advances him beyond what he was hoping for, to better and more worthy things. For it makes him worthy and respectable, strengthens the kingdom, [and] greatly increases resources and profits. Infortunes placed in that same place give rise to difficulty, it even torments what had been acquired, and he is borne off in fetters; he will be deposed with the anger of the king who had promoted him. The unfortunate ones being remote from the Midheaven, while the benevolents regard it, suggest a restful and peaceful reign. But the regard of the malevolents into it disturbs and destroys the rule. With the regard of the fortunate ones and the infortunes being equally discovered, the one which advances in more degrees will trounce the other, but it will not otherwise wholly take up [every]⁴ portion [of the meaning].

Moreover, Mercury walking through the Midheaven with Jupiter, preserves, increases and amplifies the attained dignity in wisdom and counsel, cleverness, and even reason, it will spread his name and reputation wide, particularly if they would support the Moon with a corresponding aspect. Likewise with the Sun holding onto the tenth (in addition to what was said before), without any aspect of the malevolents, the reputation of his name is amplified (as was stated), all things will flow together with his desire, his life in the rulership will be long-lasting. Nor is another judgment given when Jupiter and the Moon are established in the tenth, and Venus is found to be in a safe place. Also, whenever any of the benevolents was in the Midheaven, it diminishes anguish and sees things through to something better. Moreover, with malevolents in that same place, [and] the lord of the Midheaven and of the east being cadent,⁵ it is a sign of an unstable and very short dignity.

---

³ For John's Sahl, this also includes the lord of the Ascendant being a malevolent.
⁴ Reading *omnem* (following John) for Hugo's *qualemcumque*.
⁵ This probably means that they are in aversion to the Midheaven.

[The seventh]

But generally, the traversal of Mars in the seventh (while no lucky one would walk through the east) threatens death in that reign. With Saturn in that same place, while Jupiter has the east or the seventh, it wholly removes slaughter and death. For, that same Jupiter in the seventh deposes him respectably enough, to his own honor.

[The fourth]

[A benevolent] traversing in the fourth preserves the body unharmed, and he will arrive to his desired end. A malevolent being placed in that same place, after stepping down he undergoes the trouble of torture and long-lasting incarceration. But while a benevolent is regarding the fourth, it promises escape after the long difficulties of prison. If a fortunate one would [not][6] regard the malevolent in the fourth, it claps fetters on him, and after the difficulties in the prison, he will die. But if the lord of the fourth would occupy the east or the tenth, or the rest of the places which are appropriate, being free of the infortunes, and likewise the lord of the house of the Moon, all things are called back to a prosperous end.

§10.12: On the steadiness of the reign, or if he would be deposed—Sahl[7]

With someone asking about the steadiness of the reign, or if perhaps the prince would be deposed, the matter advises us to consult the lords of the east and of the tenth equally. For, a joint application of them being discovered, while the one receiving [the management] would be lingering in a pivot, firms up the accepted dignity. Which if the one who receives it would be traversing under the earth on the left of the east, even though he would be deposed, it leads him back. Its reception accelerates his return, not without honor.

But if the lords of the east and of the Midheaven would happen to be separated from each other, he is deprived of the royal dignity. If the Moon would render counsel to a slow star (and one proceeding in a pivot), it pre-

---

[6] Adding based on John's Sahl.
[7] Cf. *On Quest.* §10.7.

serves the steadiness of the reign until the one to which the application happens undergoes scorching or is impeded in its own place or withdraws—and then it casts aside the dignity that was had.

Moreover, the eastern lord applying to the lord of its own fall, argues that he will perish by means of his own undertaking. But if the lord of its fall would happen to be applying to the eastern lord, he is accused falsely. Which if the same thing would happen to the lord of the tenth, namely so that it would apply to the lord of its own fall, it is necessary that he be ruinous to the kingdom over which he is put in charge; their contrary application portends that the contrary[8] will come to be.

Moreover, the eastern lord rendering counsel to a star appearing in a pivot, preserves the steadiness of the reign, and more powerfully so while the one who receives [the management] possesses a pivot (except for the fourth, I say, because it is opposed to the Midheaven).

Likewise, an application of the eastern lord being made to some star in the ninth or third, or at least with their lords, really deposes him. Now, if it would apply then to some [star] appearing in a pivot, it will restore the lost dignity. However, with the lord of the Midheaven lingering in the tenth, [and] the Moon applying to it, it makes the reign stable, nor does it promise that he will leave.

But Jupiter being in a pivot where he has some dignity, or at least should he be receiving the Moon or the lord of the east, it keeps him in his reign until [Jupiter] is either corrupted by the common-company[9] of the infortunes, or more strongly so if he would be scorched, or withdrew from his own place.

Besides that, one must note that if the eastern lord and that of the Midheaven would equally apply to each other, while the one who receives [the management] would walk through an optimal place, but while it would not regard the Midheaven, it sets up the one about whom we are speaking, as a prince over a foreign kingdom. But if it would support the Midheaven with its own aspect, it makes the reign stable.

Also, with the eastern lord and the Moon being found in a turning sign and in a pivot, while however a Lunar reception would [not][10] take place, it portends the departure of the king.

---

[8] That is, instead of destroying the kingdom himself, someone else will ruin it.
[9] *Consortio*, which implies an assembly (i.e., a conjunction in the same sign). John's Sahl says it is until he "encounters" a malefic.
[10] Adding with John's Sahl.

Moreover, the Moon rendering counsel to some [star] in a pivot, [and] with the lord of the Midheaven gazing upon [the tenth], it preserves a stable reign and keeps the king.

Likewise, an application of the Moon being made with the lord of the east (but [the lord being] remote from a pivot), [then] before the Moon would be separated from it, should it be hampered by infortunes, it makes him who had been put in charge step down. But the Moon applying to some peregrine [star] from[11] the ninth or third, or if their lords are agreed to be peregrine, it drives him out of his reign. But if it[12] would hold onto the fourth (it being a turning sign), he will be deposed; [and] more firmly so with the Moon applying to the lord of the end (namely, the fourth), unless perhaps [that lord] happened to possess its own house (the pivot of the earth, I say), because this promises something better.

The Moon will be stronger for this [bad effect] if she would apply to a star moving through her fall (the Moon's, I say), or at least should it be lingering in the opposite of her house. Finally, here, if the Moon would be wandering, strong, in her own place (but void in course), it deprives him of the royal dignity.

§10.13: For how long he is going to reign—'Umar[13]

Moreover, Valens expresses such an opinion about an affair of this kind. For if, according to his claim, it should be ambiguous as to how many years some king or all-powerful man would be strengthened in a rulership or dignity, one must observe diligently by how many degrees the Sun himself is distant from the eastern degree: the steadiness of the reign demands years or months or days in accordance with the number and manner of these.

The Lot of the office and king reveals the same thing. For, being taken up from the Jupiter to the degree of the Midheaven, one will have to draw down what is collected from the degree of the Ascendant.[14] Where therefore the

---

[11] This should probably be "in."
[12] I am unsure whether this is the Moon or the other planet.
[13] Cf. al-Rijāl VIII.22 (middle part).
[14] Reading with al-Rijāl for "Jupiter." This Lot is probably the Lot of a job and authority according to Valens (*ITA* VI.2.42), which according to al-Qabīsī is taken from the Sun to the Midheaven. On the other hand, the Lot of the cause of a kingdom (*ITA* VI.2.43) is taken from the Sun to the Midheaven and projected from Jupiter, just as 'Umar projects from Jupiter.

number will be ended, the Lot really appears. If therefore the lord of the bound where the Lot is staying, would be holding onto its own proper house or sovereignty, it really bestows [its own] lesser years. Which if [the lord of] the bound would be under the rays or rather unlucky, or be in the sign or bound of infortunes, or even be scorched,[15] [according to] how many its lesser years are, it lavishes that many months or days. Moreover, the lord of the house and of the face equally advancing in a direct course, if they would both regard the house and bound where the royal Lot is, they will watch over the life of the king just as was stated above.

Furthermore, if someone would work to know when the one about to reign would arrive, and for how long, how many degrees are from the lord of the Midheaven[16] to the lord of the pivot of the earth should be taken up: for according to their number, they preserve the status of the reign [for that many] years or months (and so on).

Now, if it is asked when he will take control of the dignity of rule, let your response proceed in this way.

§10.14: For how long he would possess the honor attained, or when he would be driven out—'Umar

Once the sign of the Midheaven and its lord have been diligently observed, if the infortunes would be made firm in that same place, once the degree of the Midheaven is reached by them, and they would possess a peregrine place in that same sign, but even with the lord of the Midheaven being cadent from it, while no star would bring[17] its light to the Midheaven nor collect it, and it[18] would apply equally to the lord of the seventh and [to the lord] of the third from the east, or at least to one appearing in the ninth or third, in that same hour, I say, they depose him (about whom this is done) from the honor.

In this place, the testimonies of the Lot which is said to be of an office or carrying out orders,[19] and those of its lord, come next. For, it is taken up from the degree of the Sun to the degree of Saturn, and thus one must draw that down from the degrees of the Midheaven: and where the number will be

---

[15] Al-Rijāl adds, "or retrograde."
[16] Al-Rijāl has it from the Midheaven itself.
[17] That is, "transfer."
[18] Probably the lord of the Midheaven.
[19] *Ministrandi*.

ended, it really establishes the Lot in that place.[20] Concerning the degree of the Lot, it conveys no other judgment than the degree of the Midheaven does. Moreover, a different statement does not emanate with respect to the lord of that same Lot, and likewise that of its own Midheaven.[21]

Even this Lot—that of the resources of a man of power or rather of a minister (namely, those which he has acquired)—is taken into testimony. But this one, being drawn down from the degree of the lord of the house of money of the man in power, to the degree of his lord (the one which is in charge of the man in power), one takes the added degrees of the east, [and] therefore what was collected is thrown down from the east: where the number left off, the Lot is found in that same place.[22] Therefore, [the Lot] being lucky, and its lord being blessed in the same way, if they would regard the Midheaven and its lord, they portend the good condition of the business that is taken up. Not otherwise do they introduce harm, [if] the Lot and its lord are corrupted by the infortunes, [and] are cadent from the aspect of the house of money of the man in power. But with them remaining safe, it establishes these things as safe.

Again, the statements of Valens[23] come to be examined in this place. For whenever (he says) someone wished to be assured about the expulsion of a man in power, we suggest that one attend diligently to the degree of the Midheaven and what corruption of its own lord there is. Now, when the Moon will reach the degree of the infortune which is corrupting the Midheaven or the lord of its lodging-place, or she will assemble [with it] in the same degree, it finally deprives [him] of the dignity that was collected, unless (I say) that same infortune will have crossed through to another [bound], once [it has] left that bound[24] behind. But if Jupiter or Venus would reach that same degree, with them bearing themselves thusly, they preserve him in his prior status, but it could not avert the harm of groaning or stinging cares.

---

[20] This seems to be another version of the natal Lot of power or kingdom or sovereignty (*ITA* VI.2.39), which is taken from the Sun to Saturn by day (but the reverse by night), and projected from the Ascendant (not the Midheaven).

[21] *Sui medii caeli.* I am not sure if 'Umar means the lord of the Midheaven of the chart, or the lord of the tenth place from the Lot, or the lord of the tenth place from the lord of the Lot. Remember: 'Umar regularly includes whole-sign angles of planets in his rules.

[22] In other words, we measure from the lord of the eleventh to the lord of the tenth, and project from the Ascendant. But as with so many of 'Umar's Lots, this is strange and not reported (so far as I know) in other sources.

[23] *Welitis.*

[24] Perhaps 'Umar really means "sign" here and a few words earlier.

It even claims the same thing with an infortune holding onto the Midheaven, or if it would regard it: it declares the king's trouble in that hour.

Moreover, in this place another interval[25] comes to be noted, namely so that (once the four pivots have been placed) the intention of the mind should be directed to the degree of the Midheaven. Once the degrees from it to the infortune have been calculated, the individual degrees change [into] years, months, or days—and this must be done with the degrees of ascensions.[26] No less will it be allowed (once the individual degrees[27] have been made right)[28] to multiples of two: two days or years [for every degree],[29] so that the quality of the judgment proceeds from this indication.

There is even another Lot, which you will take from the lord of the twelfth place to the degree of the twelfth. Therefore, however much the number of degrees is found to be, it preserves the status of the dignity as being unharmed, through that many years.[30]

§10.15: For how long he is going to reign, or if perhaps he would be deposed—al-Khayyāt

It seems that a question of this kind must be treated with the greatest intention. Wherefore, whether he is going to reign for a long time or if perhaps he would be deposed, the testimony of the star[31] or significator must be consulted in no other order than as was stated in the previous chapter.[32] And so, with the application of the eastern lord and that of the Midheaven equally being discovered, while the one which receives the counsel would be lingering in a pivot, it portends the tireless steadiness of the kingdom. But if that same receiver would be traversing on the left of the east, the man, being expelled or deposed, will return to his own proper honor. It even being received, declares a quick and prosperous enough return.

---

[25] Reading for "Lot," since this is not really a Lot.
[26] Reading for "east." In several places, Hugo has mistaken ascensions for the Ascendant.
[27] Vienna reads, "hours."
[28] *Rectis*. Hugo's 'Umar seems to be referring to degrees of right ascension—again, this is a kind of direction.
[29] Reading somewhat loosely for *dies aut annos, duabus semper, duos dies aut annos*.
[30] Again, this is not really a Lot, but is the interval that starts the calculation of the Lot of enemies according to Hermes (*ITA* VI.2.48). 'Umar must mean that this interval represents the time *until* enemies or some other disaster brings his rule to an end.
[31] Reading *stellae* for *stella*.
[32] See §10.7 above.

But if a mutual separation of the significators would be noted, it strips him of the previously-had dignity. (Here however, the testimonies of the Moon must be consulted: for, she traversing in a convertible [sign], being in no way blessed with light or received, or at least being corrupted, deposes him.) Moreover, with the eastern lord and [the lord] of the Midheaven equally bearing themselves as was stated, if the Moon would apply to a star advancing slowly, it has an indication of letting go of the kingdom. In addition even, she rendering the counsel of application to some remote [star], she being received, will even bless the one who has left with much advantage in dignity. But not being received, even though he may be good, he is wholly disgraced.

But if the lord of the east would apply to the lord of its own fall, it will devastate the whole region over which he presides. Which if that lord[33] of its fall would be lingering in a pivot, it pursues him and attacks him up to death. However, the method of this chapter [does not][34] make a judgment of deposing if, I say, the lord of the east (not being received, in a pivot), would render counsel to a star already receiving [it].

The lord of the fourth applying to the lord of the tenth, devastates the kingdom which he possesses. Conversely, the lord of the tenth applying to the lord of the fourth, with the eastern lord and the significator being corrupted, strips him of the dignity that is given. Moreover, the lord of the east applying to a star positioned in a pivot apart from the fourth (rather, in the east or tenth) makes the kingdom firm.

Moreover, with an application of the eastern lord and that of the Midheaven being discovered, while the one which receives [the application] is placed in the best way, even if it does not regard the tenth, it shows the kingdom to be long-lasting. Often it even promises something other than what he was aspiring to, [even] if it does regard it. Likewise, the lord of the Midheaven regarding the tenth [makes the reign stable].[35]

While the one which receives the Moon[36] (it being unlucky) would linger in a pivot, it establishes that the honor is unuseful and with harm. But if the

---

[33] Reading *dominus* for *domina*.
[34] Adding *non*, or else the sentence would not make sense. This sentence does not have a parallel in Sahl or Dorotheus.
[35] Adding based on Sahl. Hugo ran this sentence together with the next one (which does not appear in Sahl), so that it did not make astrological sense. There may be more missing from al-Khayyāt here.
[36] I take this to mean the planet to which the Moon is applying.

unlucky one would in no way receive the Moon, it denotes his impotence, whence it even encourages him to beware of death (if, I say, the malevolent would occupy the pivot of the earth). The malevolent being in the seventh [means] he speaks against his citizens and subjects, but he succumbs in the conflict,[37] whence he will be afflicted by much trouble. Which if they would bear themselves thusly, and the lord of the east [would be] in a pivot, victory is given to him over his subjects. But if it were cadent, he will be overcome.

The Moon applying to the eastern lord [when it is] remote from the pivots, so that namely before the Moon would be joined to it, any malevolent would catch it (even after the question), it really deposes him from the honor. Moreover, a Lunar application being made with a peregrine star in the ninth or third, or at least with their lords, shows an unstable dignity. It being in the fourth, while it is a turning [sign], and what is more applying to its lord, it denotes an unstable kingdom. It is the worst whenever the Moon would apply to a star that is cadent from the pivots (even if to the lord of the tenth), unless, I say, [that planet] would have control over the rulership of that same place: for thus it conveys some support.

The Moon is worst [if] applying to Mars from her own proper house; or, traversing in a house of Saturn, she would apply to the Sun; or if she would linger in a house of Jupiter, applying to Mercury or Mars;[38] [or] rather, however, application with Mercury from a house of Jupiter, as well as if it would come from the sovereignty of Jupiter to Mars.

§10.16: On the kingdom's prosperity or troubles—al-Kindī

§333-34. It is well known that whatever good or prosperity, fortune or misfortune he would incur, is plainly understood thusly. And so, one will have to make a direction[39] of the Ascendant and the Moon: and should it arrive at some fortunate degree, without a doubt he will rejoice there (being put in possession of prosperity), according to the degrees of the direction—by taking hours, days, months, [and] years in turn, according to the manner

---

[37] *Causa*.

[38] I do not think Mars should be included here, because all of the other applications are implied to be from the fall or detriment of the planet receiving the application (or from a planet whose signs are opposite it): an application to Mars from Cancer, to the Sun from Aquarius or Capricorn, from Gemini or Virgo to Jupiter, from Pisces or Sagittarius to Mercury, and from Cancer (the exaltation of Jupiter) to Mars.

[39] Reading for the transliteration *atazir*, here and throughout.

of the signs which are in the direction (namely if they are double-bodied or convertible or fixed), in the way it was stated above with respect to the instruction on times.[40] And so, the type of the prosperity in all modes will be changed according to the very blessedness of the lucky one itself, or [the blessedness] which is taken up from another. In this way, even if the order of the direction reached an improsperous degree, harm will be reported (with, I say, the forcefulness, places, portion, [and] causes of the unlucky one being noted, just as was said before).

[The affairs of kings][41]

§335. Moreover, for royal affairs the degree of the Midheaven should be distributed by direction. Which if it reached a fortunate degree, declaim goods; if an improsperous one, the contrary. Likewise, its application to a fortune [which] blesses, and it is receiving it, portends the increase of the kingdom, the strength of the king, victory. But to an infortune and what is dissimilar [with what we said before], the contrary.

§336. If therefore that infortune would enjoy the rulership of the fourth, or some bearing of it, it threatens the king from adversaries. Also, [if it is] the lord of the eleventh, it brings in a sudden attack or assault by his underofficials and their partners. Moreover, as the lord of the twelfth it compels the enemies of those executing [his orders] into the harm of the kingdom.

§337. But the same [infortune being] the lord of the Ascendant, the king or prince himself releases the causes of corruption and the losses into his own kingdom. Performing the rulership of the second, it corrupts the kingdom because of money. With it appearing in the rulership of the third, brothers and those whom he embraces in the role of brothers attack the kingdom, or [it is] because of some law or journey. Again, while it would manage the rulership of the fifth, the kingdom is pressed down by [his] children.

§338. With the rulership of the sixth being occupied, slaves, disease and animals introduce the cause of the corruption. Moreover, while it enjoys the rulership of the seventh, it warns he should beware of adversaries and those whom he incites through the injury of [his] underofficials, and his own business [partners], and women. Moreover, in the rulership of the eighth, because

---

[40] See §A.133.
[41] This section assumes that the king or an authority is the querent.

of some death or inheritances; sometimes even the spouses of underofficials and adversaries taint the kingdom. With the rulership of the ninth being attained, it perverts the kingdom because of law or some road or journey.

§339. No less does it seem that the rest of the pivots should be noted, and the leadership or signification of every matter should be chosen by means of their decree.

§10.17: On underofficials—al-Kindī

§340. The[42] direction of the degree of the seventh clarifies what happens to the underofficials of the king or those who are in charge of lands. The direction of the degree of the fourth, what [happens to] the ends [of things]. Wherefore, with it reaching a prosperous [planet], good will be judged; but an unlucky one,[43] the contrary, according to the nature and strength of that fortunate or unlucky one which it claims in the circle (or in the square arrangement of the signs),[44] just as has already been said enough before.

§10.18: On his predecessor—al-Kindī

§341. Moreover, if a star were found in the ninth, it sufficiently declares him who preceded the minister, powerful man, or king, and his nature and status and manner; but if [there were none in it], the lord of the ninth does so. Again, if there were a star in the eleventh, it accurately suggests what kind of successor he should expect; but if [one were] not [in it], the lord of the eleventh itself does so. Therefore, whatever strength or weakness, fortune or misfortune (and so on) the lord of the eleventh would convey, do not fear: it indicates the same about his successor. Also, with respect to [his] predecessor, remember to affirm [it] according to the nature of the star which holds onto the ninth place, or according to the lord of the ninth itself.

---

[42] Reading the first two sentences with Robert.
[43] Reading *infelicem* for *infelix*.
[44] This must also include the domicile of its own which it aspects most powerfully and favorably, as has been said before.

§10.19: On his successor—al-Kindī

§342. Moreover, you will note the kind and fatherland of the predecessor or even the successor, thusly. For Saturn shows he is going to be an Indian or Arab (or of their lineage) if [Saturn] enjoys some bearing of Venus. Also, Jupiter suggests a Babylonian or Persian or one of their tribes. But Mars grants a Roman or the progeny of Rome. But Venus introduces an Arab, Mercury someone from the western parts or what neighbors these. The Moon, from Thrace.[45] The Sun confirms he is going to be from the east or from a royal family and house.

§343. Therefore, whichever one of these significators appeared in a house of Saturn, advances an ignoble or old man. Moreover, in a house or bound of Jupiter, it claims he is of the sages, or numbered among merchants, or the rank of the law. In a house or bound of Mars, it advances a leader of armies or chief of wars or a victor, even one by whose hand blood is somehow in the habit of being shed, even one whose works frequently demand fire.

§344. In the house of the Sun, it conveys he is an underofficial of the family of the royal house, even an augur or astrologer, or a hunter, or of some excellent profession. Even in a house or bound of Venus, it introduces a singer, a lover of women, or one who, being of this type, greatly delights in jokes. In a house or bound of Mercury, a writer,[46] courier or teacher of children or a man of respectable counsel and appropriate succinctness is introduced. In the house of the Moon, it commends some courier or one given to messengers and legations and that class of the common people.

§345. If however it were in a house of some star and the bound of another, it seems the virtue and signification of each must be united in the inquiry of a matter of this kind.[47]

§346. Moreover, at the limit of easternness (or even in its beginning), it testifies he is an adolescent; western, one already of advanced age.

§347a. Moreover, it seems that the manner and nature of all of the stars generally which represent the signification of the past or future leader, must be considered.

---

[45] Robert: "a Parthian."
[46] Following Robert and omitting *aut alidbe aliquis videlicet*. *Alidbe* is probably a transliteration of Arabic.
[47] Perhaps the domicile indicates things such as origin and personality, while the bound indicates physical appearance.

[His rule, from event charts or elections]

§347b. The hour at which the honor and power of ruling is ascribed to him, describes his strength or weakness in [his] rule. Also, the hour at which he enters the honor, elicits the discretion of ruling, and [his] counsel, and the care of the kingdom. But the hour at which he arranges his official duties, supplies his precepts, [and] begins to rule, undoubtedly lays bare his vigor or how long he is going to rule.[48]

§10.20: On kingdoms and dignities—Jirjis

For the day on which the underofficial or prince enters the region subject [to him], let the degree of the Midheaven be drawn forth to the fortunate ones and the malevolents, and let its progression to them happen,[49] and with your whole intention consider how many degrees are between it and them, by any application.[50] The degrees of application to the fortunate ones or infortunes undoubtedly lay out the hour of [his] promotion or when he would cast off the dignity. In a turning sign, it suggests days; in a double-bodied one, months; in a firm one, years.

An application made with the benevolents portends good, good health, and an increase of honor in that hour. But if it would happen with the malevolents, while that malevolent would rule over the eighth (which is the lodging-place of death), it means death must be feared in that hour. An application being discovered with a benevolent, while that lucky one would rule over the seventh, he will be blessed with a worthy marriage-union in that dignity. But, it assuming the rulership of the house of money [means] he will have influence over great means[51] in that affair and in that same hour. Which if it would gain control over the lodging-place of brothers, it claims brothers and friends. It appearing as the lord of the house of children, in that same hour he will rejoice in the production of children. If therefore you follow an

---

[48] In the United States, these three moments probably correspond to the moments of: (1) the election results; (2) swearing the oath of office; (3) making the first decisions after the celebrations of Inaugural Day are over.
[49] This is probably just the distance by zodiacal degrees, but Jirjis might be referring to primary directions or ascensional directions.
[50] Reading *application* for *applicationis*.
[51] *Copiis*, a very generic word referring to influence, supplies, opportunities, wealth, and so on.

order if this kind through the rest of the domiciles, you will stumble into no scandal of error.

§10.21: If he would shed the dignity given, and if perhaps he would happen to come back—Dorotheus

The method of the previous chapter[52] responds to this question (namely that there is an equal and joint application of the eastern lord and that of the Midheaven). Once the application is discovered, while the one of them which is the receiver of counsel would regard the tenth, [but] with the eastern lord being corrupted, he will return to his own proper honor, having been expelled. With these bearing themselves in this way, and the Moon in turning [signs], it prepares a return. If however the eastern lord is not retrograde, while however it would be lingering in the tenth, it resembles the things said above. Also, the Moon means nothing else [if she is] rendering counsel to the lord of the east.

Moreover, the lord of the tenth applying to the lord of its own fall, strips off the given dignity. Likewise, with the lord of the tenth in a turning [sign], while it applies to a star in the house of kings, it preserves the honor that was taken up. Which if there is mutual reception, he is brought back, having been expelled. Which if the significator of the kingdom[53] and the lord of the end happened to apply [to each other], it is a sign of his being deposed.

§10.22: How long he is going to reign—Dorotheus[54]

It seems that a question of this kind must be treated with the greatest attention. For when someone is promoted to some honor, or sits down on the tribunal chair for the first time, at the hour of the question one must note what star claims the sovereignty of the sign where the Moon is staying.[55] For, [that star] being cleansed of the infortunes preserves his reign for a whole year and beyond. Which if none[56] would take hold of the rulership of [her]

---

[52] This probably refers to §10.8 above.
[53] That is, the lord of the tenth.
[54] Cf. *On Times* §12, which is attributed to Māshā'allāh.
[55] That is, look at the exalted lord of the Moon's position.
[56] Reading *nulla* for *Luna*, and omitting *non*. Otherwise the sentence would read, "if the Moon would not take hold of the rulership of her sovereignty...".

sovereignty, one must enter into the counsel of the star to which the Lunar application is. For, it being an unlucky one or being near scorching, how many degrees distant it is from scorching should be sought: for the individual degrees suggest that many months. Moreover, the Moon being well arranged, whenever a malevolent would reach the degree of the star receiving the [application of] the Moon—with that star remaining scorched, I say—it is a sign of being deposed.

Furthermore, while someone who was promoted enters into the principal seat, at the hour of either the election or entering into counsel,[57] or even that of the question, if the lights would hold onto the east or the Midheaven, while either of the unfortunate ones also meets with their places, they deprive him of the dignity that was conferred.

But Saturn being placed in the east or the Midheaven, under the aspect of the fortunate ones,[58] will protect the gift [of honor] that was accepted for as long as his lesser years are (namely 30); on the contrary, being established in a wicked place or in his own fall, he preserves it for 30 months. Which if Jupiter would thus occupy the east or the tenth, he would know to distribute 12 years; but corrupted, he lavishes that many months. Moreover, Mars in that same place, he gives 15 years; corrupted, it transforms into months. On the other hand, while the Sun[59] would hold onto the aforesaid places, it will last for 8 years; but badly placed, he commands for 8 months. Likewise, Venus traversing in either of these places, and she being eastern, in her own sovereignty or house, he will hold onto the scepter for 10 years; also, being cadent or applying to infortunes, he will reign for that many months. However, Mercury in that place, while he would possess [his own] sovereignty or house, protects a safe reign for 10 years; likewise, being cadent or applying to the infortunes, it will be a rulership of 10 months. Finally, the Moon being thusly placed, manages 25 years; contrariwise, that many months.

Generally therefore, any star in the east or the tenth, while it would possess the sovereignty (or a dignity of this kind) in that place, being cadent from[60] the infortunes, and in the aspect of the benevolents (or should there

---

[57] *Consilii.* I am not sure what this means, unless it refers to taking part in a council or body of advisors for someone important.
[58] See the final paragraph for a fuller list of the best conditions.
[59] The years for the Sun, Venus, and Mercury below are not their lesser years. The lesser years of the Sun are 19, Venus 8, Mercury 20. I do not know the source of these alternate numbers.
[60] That is, "in aversion to."

be any kind of application between them), it really lavishes the lesser years. But appearing in its own fall in that place, and should there be some application [to the infortunes], with the regard of the fortunate ones being denied, it transforms the above-written number into months.

§10.23: About a king who has left his place or reign, or an absent king: whether he would return—Sahl[61]

On the other hand, if someone made a question about someone who has left his reign, or about an absent king, [namely] whether he would return or not, one must pursue this not otherwise than how it was stated in the chapter set out above.[62] For if the eastern lord would apply to the lord of the Midheaven (or contrariwise, [the lord of the Midheaven] to it), while the one who receives [the management] regards the tenth, it promises his return. With the regard being denied, and the Moon applying to a star in the tenth, [it means] the same. In addition, the retrogradation of the eastern lord does not suggest anything else. With these bearing themselves thusly, if the Moon would walk through a turning sign, it hastens the return.

Moreover, if [the lord of the east] were not retrograde, but the Moon would be applying to some [star] in the east or the tenth, it makes a certain judgment of turning back. Nor is it otherwise with the Moon applying to the lord of the east.

But if the lord of the ninth would apply to the eastern [lord], he withdraws of his own inspiration and with no one persuading him.

Likewise, the lord of the Midheaven applying to the lord of its own fall (even if it is in a pivot) means the withdrawal of the prince. The application of the eastern lord to the lord of its own fall testifies to the same.

Now, the lord of the Midheaven being in the tenth, leads back one who had already been removed.

Likewise, the lord of the tenth withdrawing from the lord of the fourth or its rays, indicates a return; but if he would apply to it, he will be deposed. On the other hand, the lord of the fourth applying to the lord of the tenth, prepares an entrance to his kingdom through his own labor, and he deserves to be enriched with another kingdom. But if the lord of the fourth would apply to the eastern [lord], it does not signify he is removed, but he will even be

---

[61] Cf. *On Quest.* §§10.8-9.
[62] Probably referring to *On Quest.* §10.7, in §10.12 above.

given a dignity not asked for. And the withdrawal of the eastern lord from the lord of the fourth brings about a stable reign. Nor is another judgment given for one who had been deposed, if the lord of the fourth would apply to it. Which if there were an application made of the eastern lord and [the lord] of the tenth equally, so that the lord of the tenth did not regard the tenth, he is put in charge of another kingdom than the one he is in charge of [now].

But if the significator (that is, the Moon) would apply to the lord of the tenth [while] it is regarding the tenth, there is no ambiguity about returning; it is more firm with the Moon going through a turning sign. Which if she would render counsel to a peregrine star on the left of the east, the king will be deprived of the dignity. The reception of the significator[63] promises a return, but not received, it deposes him.

Moreover,[64] the Moon applying to a star in the ninth, portends he will [not][65] return. Which if the one to which the application happens is of the benevolents, [then] should it walk through a [common sign, but not a][66] turning or even a firm sign, it leads him back. For with it appearing in a common[67] [sign], he will take a kingdom different from the first one, over which he will be in charge for three years—unless, I say, the receiver of the counsel would fall before it reaches the twelfth.[68] For in the second year he will be advanced to something better and will handle all things according to his wish, unless some one of the malevolents, reaching the Midheaven, would go retrograde in that same place before the aforestated hour. For a wicked one occupying that place is ruinous to the reign and destroys it.

The Moon applying to benevolents or being received, makes him praiseworthy in his reign. Her application to malevolents predicts he is disgraced.

[And if the Moon would apply to a star in the tenth, he will not withdraw, and he will reign for two years.][69]

---

[63] According to al-Khayyāt (§10.24), this is the Moon.
[64] This paragraph and those following describe a kind of profection defined by transits. If the key planet is in the ninth (and in the appropriate conditions), then the ninth, tenth, and eleventh signs describe the next three years in order. Thus Sahl describes the transit of a malevolent through the tenth as indicating the second year.
[65] Adding with John's Sahl.
[66] Adding based on John's Sahl.
[67] Reading with John's Sahl for Hugo's "turning."
[68] I believe this means, "unless it would transit the sign of its own fall, before it reaches the twelfth."
[69] Adding with John's Sahl.

Which if she would apply to a star in the eleventh, he will reign through a year, unless (I say) a malevolent, reaching the eleventh,[70] would become retrograde in that same place.

That[71] same Moon applying to a star in the fifth, he commands for two years and withdraws in the third. But while she applied to a star in the fourth, the reign is for a year and he is deposed in the second [year].

Which if the Moon and the lord of the tenth would equally be found to be corrupted and applying to each other,[72] he is deposed. For both made fortunate and lucky and in common signs, they heap kingdom on kingdom, and make him strong and powerful, so that if perhaps he happened to be deposed, he would return.

In addition, with someone asking whether he would reach the dignity of a kingdom, the eastern lord and the Moon must be consulted. For, their application to the lord of the tenth [or the Sun],[73] or at least should they be lingering in the Midheaven, [means] he is crowned with the royal diadem. But if otherwise, not at all.

§10.24: On an absent king, or anyone in exile, whether he would return to his original dignity—al-Khayyāt

With a question of this kind being proposed, the judgment of the chapter above[74] will have to be pursued, namely so that the application of the lord of the east and of the tenth equally should be noted. If therefore one would receive the other, while the one receiving regarded the tenth, without a doubt it indicates a return. With a regard of this kind being denied, while the Moon would transfer light to the lord of the Midheaven, or to a star positioned in [the Midheaven], it is the same. But with this being denied, it must be known that the lord of the east being retrograde signifies his turning back, and better and more quickly if the Moon would be walking through a turning [sign].

---

[70] John's Sahl says "the Midheaven," but I believe Hugo is probably right, since the malevolent planet would be transiting the sign corresponding to that year.
[71] I do not quite understand how the profection symbolism works in these cases. Perhaps these places mean fewer years because they are below the earth.
[72] John's Sahl adds, "in a pivot."
[73] Adding with John's Sahl. I think the use of *saltem* derives from a misread for *Solem*.
[74] Probably §10.15 above.

But if the lord of the east is in no way retrograde, while the Moon would be applying to a star in the east or the Midheaven, it confirms a return; even rendering counsel to the lord of the east is the same.

Moreover, the lord of the tenth applying to the lord of its own fall,[75] even though both may traverse in pivots, threatens deposing. Nor is an application of the eastern lord with the lord of its own fall, otherwise.

Likewise, with the lord of the tenth staying in a convertible [sign], while however it would apply to a star in the Midheaven, he will not be deposed. But if one would receive the other, the one which was retrograde will return.

Moreover, the significator of kingdoms[76] withdrawing from the light of the lord of the fourth, wholly brings back the exile or expelled person. But if it would approach [the lord of the fourth], it drives him out. (It is no less with that same lord of the tenth applying to the lord of the ninth.) But contrariwise, the lord of the fourth applying to the lord of the tenth, conveys a dignity without labor, and makes it entirely stable. It is no different with [the lord of the fourth] applying to the lord of the east.

Moreover, the lord of the tenth applying to the one which rules over the fall of the eastern lord, proposes another prince as a substitute. But if the lord of the east and that of the tenth would apply one to the other, it promises he is going to return. But if the lord of the tenth does not regard the tenth, it renders an honor, but another one.

Moreover, the Moon (the significator), applying to the lord of the tenth (so that it regards the tenth), returns him to honor, especially if the Moon would be lingering in a turning [sign]. Likewise, the Moon rendering counsel to a star placed on the left of the east (it having nothing [of dignity] in that place), if the Moon is received, portends an increase in honor; not being received, it deposes him. The Moon traversing in a turning [sign], regarding the lord of the tenth or a star placed [in the tenth], and being received, calls him back to his own proper dignity.

Indeed, with respect to the significator, one should imitate no other opinion than the one about the eastern lord.

---

[75] That is, to the ruler of the lord of the tenth's fall, such as Mercury (whose fall is in Pisces) applying to Jupiter (who rules Pisces).
[76] That is, the lord of the tenth.

§10.25: On those who are parting from the king or their family, slaves, friends, partners, or the region, or a wife from her man—'Umar[77]

With an affair of this kind being brought into question, the eastern lord gives counsel. Being received, it prohibits a parting, namely while the star will possess a pivot.

Then, too, one must observe to whom it applies while it occupies that sign. Moreover, it departing from thence, applying to any [star] appearing in a pivot, wholly denies a parting for as long as it is in that same place.

Furthermore, an application of any star with the eastern lord, if [that star] would hold onto its own house, or at least should it rule over [some] pivot of the east, it does not praise leaving in that year. Therefore, with the cycle of another year being noted, you will give no other judgment.[78]

Moreover, with the eastern lord being drawn back, but applying to any [star] appearing in a pivot, even though the owner of the question would be staying unwillingly, still he will not withdraw while that star will possess a pivot from the east.[79]

Which if [the lord of the Ascendant][80] rendered its own counsel to another star ruling any pivot,[81] he can nowhere depart, unless [it was the lord of] the pivot of the earth. Therefore, it being corrupted, stains the end [of the matter]; it is worse too, [if the lord of the fourth] is bad and unlucky.[82] And so, an application of the eastern lord with the lord of the fourth, if it is corrupted, is judged to be the worst; but more serious, with it appearing remote.

Moreover, the lord of the east being in a pivot, should it apply to a star that is drawn back [but] not receiving [the lord of the east], [or][83] one must note whether [that star] would rule any pivot from the east ([and it is] appear-

---

[77] Cf. al-Rijāl III.22. I have organized the paragraphs here and in al-Khayyāt (§10.26 below) in accordance with al-Rijāl's ordering. I have also added clarifying material in brackets from al-Rijāl. These two sections (§§10.25-26) should be read along with the material on travel and imprisonment in §9 above).

[78] That is, look at upcoming solar revolutions to see if things change. See below.

[79] Hugo's 'Umar adds another, almost identical paragraph: "Likewise, the eastern lord being remote from a pivot, applying to a star appearing in a pivot, nowhere permits one who is prevailed upon [to leave], to depart from friends and friends and comrades."

[80] Reading with al-Khayyāt and al-Rijāl for Hugo's "it would direct its own aspects to the lord of the east."

[81] Deleting Hugo's "but one drawn back, while the eastern lord would occupy the pivot of the star."

[82] Al-Rijāl simply says that the lord of the fourth will show removal, especially if it is an infortune.

[83] Adding based on al-Khayyāt.

ing in a remote sign): for it portends that the one about whom the question is, wants to depart [but] not without worry and fear; nevertheless one is not allowed to do it until that planet[84] would arrive at a pivot: once it is arranged in a pivot, he takes no action, and the care and fear about departing will be absent.

Wherefore, a revolution of years will always have to be done first, for greater knowledge of these things. Now, if [in the revolution] the lord of the east would be occupying a pivot, applying to the lord of the ninth or of the third, the originator of this question—being about to leave behind that part of his authority which was given to him—will go away. Which if perhaps the lord of the east is received, it leads him back (with God's favor). With reception being denied, no return is made clear for this [matter]. But with the one to which [the lord of the east] applies being unlucky or corrupted, trouble or adversity will not be absent after the departure.

And a quick and speedy exit [should not be][85] judged if the lord of the east is one of the superior [planets], but applying to none. Therefore, the standing or stay of [such] planets in the pivots, and their application with [another planet] from the pivots or outside [them], must be noted with the greatest effort, as was stated above.

Likewise, in this place the eastern lord is taken into testimony. Now, if the two infortunes do not leave the pivots behind, being less remote (I say) than [the lord of the east], they impel the matter under consideration in the same way—if namely they would be peregrine in that same place. The Moon advances into the testimony in the same way. For if she would willingly bestow favor, it saves the whole affair. And so, should the Lunar assent be given to the eastern lord,[86] and with her being received, it grants steadiness.[87] Which if reception is absent, but she would apply to a star appearing in a pivot (and it being received), or one in its own house, or to a fortunate one lacking rulership over a pivot, it really heaps on a delay[88] while this star would be staying in that same sign. Which if it were unlucky, it prepares a parting and after the good condition which is had, it introduces detriment.

---

[84] Reading with al-Rijāl. Al-Khayyāt seems to read this as the lord of the east, which also makes sense.
[85] Adding based on al-Rijāl, who says that an angular superior planet will indicate he is content and not want to leave.
[86] Al-Rijāl reads this as her applying to any received planet.
[87] That is, he will not move around, but stay in one place.
[88] That is, the person will stay in one place for the time being.

If however the one to which the Moon applies would rule over the ninth or third, anxiety and labor and the heat of adversity do not abandon the affair under consideration.[89] But the Moon being received by it, brings him back without fail, and blesses with a preferable dignity. But she being deprived of reception, and she being unlucky, brings him into difficulty after [his] departure.

Moreover, with the Moon applying to any star from the left of the east, while it does not regard it,[90] nor would it have control of a pivot, [it prepares][91] a hastened departure for the querent.

But otherwise too, the lord of the east and the Moon applying to a star occupying a pivot (or to one in control over its rulership), [but] to an unlucky and corrupted one, they provoke him to a bad status and desolation after a respectable one, and after a worthy expectation they wholly deny it—unless, I say, that infortune would receive the applying star.

§10.26: On recovering lost patrimony, or if it is good to withdraw from friends or the fatherland—al-Khayyāt[92]

In addition, if someone were seeking with respect to the command of resources or a lost patrimony, or rather if someone would be forced to withdraw for some reason from family or friends, even from his fatherland or associates, the eastern lord should principally be consulted. For, being received, it bars and denies his departure. In a pivot [but] not received, the same—namely, while it possessed the pivot.

Then, [look at] the one to which it applies in the meantime (namely, while it will be staying in that same sign, and before it leaves it behind). If it would apply to a star positioned in a pivot, the departure is denied while [that star] would be in that place.

Likewise, that star (namely the one to which the lord of the east applies) traversing in its own house, or if it would rule some pivot, it makes the steadiness of the command or dignity. Wherefore, the cycle of the year comes to be noted.[93]

---

[89] *Subditum*.
[90] I am not sure what planets or places are meant by this phrase.
[91] Reading with al-Khayyāt for what seems to be *solatur*.
[92] This should be read with ʿUmar in §10.25 above, and al-Rijāl III.22.
[93] That is, one must look at further solar revolutions to see how matters unfold.

The lord of the [eastern] sign being remote, while it would apply to a star positioned in a pivot, the owner of the question would stay [in his current place], even though unwilling and negligent: while [that star] held onto the pivot, it completely denies his parting.

[If the lord of the Ascendant were the lord of an angle, he will not be removed unless it is the lord of the fourth.][94] And so, the application of the eastern lord with the lord of the fourth, if [the lord of the fourth] were corrupted, is judged to be the worst, because it warns of a bad end (it is even worse with it being remote).

Moreover, attend diligently to whenever there was an application of the eastern lord [while it is in a pivot], with a cadent planet (nor one receiving it), or [that planet] would rule over some pivot and would walk through a remote sign: for it portends that the one about whom it is asked, wants to withdraw, [but] not without fear, care, and worry. Nor however do you do this until it[95] reaches a pivot: and then the dread will quiet down, and the care, departure, and anxiety will be gone.

Therefore, for greater knowledge, the cycle of years will have to be made. But when [in the revolution] the lord of the east occupies a pivot, applying to the lord of the ninth or third, it prepares for the owner of the question a departure from the honor or business that was asked about. But the one to which it applies being an unlucky one, afflicts him after the departure with much inconvenience.[96]

Still, the eastern lord should be taken into testimony of this kind. [If you found an infortune in an angle],[97] then one must apply the testimonies of the Moon. Which if [she would apply to the lord of the east and][98] she were received, it makes an indication of steadiness and firmness. With reception being denied, while she applies to a star in a pivot (and one received), or to one appearing in its own house, or at least to a fortunate one lacking rulership over a pivot, it denies his departure while this star lingers in that same sign. Which if it would rule over a pivot, it [make him stay] firm, unless (I

---

[94] Adding with 'Umar and al-Rijāl.
[95] 'Umar reads this as an infortune, but that does not really make sense.
[96] Now al-Khayyāt omits a paragraph about the lord of the Ascendant being one of the angular planets. See 'Umar above.
[97] Adding based on al-Rijāl. Hugo's 'Umar reads this as though the malefics are more angular than the lord of the Ascendant.
[98] Adding based on 'Umar. Al-Rijāl reads this as her applying to any received planet.

say) it is being corrupted. For a corrupted [star] prepares his parting and introduces detriment after the recovery is undertaken.

Moreover, the Moon applying to a star occupying the east or the Midheaven, or to one receiving [her], but which obtains no rulership over a pivot, prepares a quick departure for the querent.

But even an application of the eastern lord and the Moon to a star occupying a pivot, or to one having seized its rulership, indeed to an unlucky and corrupted one, provokes him to evil and parting after [having] a respectable status and appropriate hope—unless, I say, the infortune would receive the applying star.

§10.27: On inquiring into the life of kings through interrogations—'Umar[99]

With a question being proposed about the life of kings, the east and the victor of the east should principally be consulted.

The victor resembles a dignity, so that the lord of the east should be preeminent over[100] the rulership of the east, the Solar lodging-place, but [even] of the Moon and the Lot of Fortune; no less too should it have control of the supervision of the eastern sovereignty, triplicity, bound, [and] face. Which if all of the testimonies do not favor the lord of the east, then recourse should be had to the ruler of its sovereignty; likewise, with it lacking these gifts, the lord of its triplicity would come into the open [for consideration]; moreover, with it being deprived of the gifts, I think one must pay attention to whether the lord of the eastern bound or face would merit being enriched with them. If therefore [more than one][101] equally happened to enjoy the dignities of the aforesaid mansions, should either one claim more power in the aforesaid places, that one will be enriched with the gift of [being] the victor (namely the excellent[102] significator), beyond the rest.

---

[99] I have not been able to locate this passage in al-Rijāl. But see also §10.32 below.
[100] Hugo's wording suggests that we should initially see if the lord of the Ascendant has many or the most number of rulerships in these other places as well as in the Ascendant itself; if not, see if the exalted lord of the Ascendant does, and so on. But this method should be compared with the similar one in §A.129. The approach here is similar to finding the longevity releaser.
[101] Reading for *eosdem* ("they"). 'Umar is describing what to do if two or more candidate victors seem to be equally viable.
[102] *Excellentis*, namely the preeminent one.

But after that we believe that one must note to whom it applies, or which one to it.[103] The Moon even, being made its partner, bears no other signification than the victor does.

Which[104] if the victor (or rather the significator) for watching over the king's life happened to be found lucky, cleansed of the infortunes, it is good to look at what place in the circle it is holding onto. For, it being arranged in a pivot, lavishes the greater years;[105] but after the pivots, the middle ones; being cadent, too, it concedes the lesser ones. Moreover, it being retrograde or scorched or depressed,[106] or enclosed between the two infortunes,[107] months will have to be granted according to the greater quantity of years. But if it were after the pivots and in the way we have said, [it grants months] according to the number of middle ones. But it being cadent [and in the way we have said], it changes the lesser years into months, sometimes months into days, [and] frequently days for hours.

Moreover, with the Moon being found lucky, it is reasonable that they be attributed according to the quantity of the lesser years: namely, if they were years, years; if months, the same; if days, days. And what was collected, really terminates the king's life.

Furthermore, I believe it should be noted whether the victor is in the aspect of fortunate ones or infortunes. For the victor-significator conveys an increase according to the lesser years of the fortunate one [which is] regarding it, while being regarded by an infortune takes away from that, just as its lesser years encourage it to do.[108]

---

[103] Omitting the puzzling *vel quae*.
[104] This paragraph is very similar to 'Umar's version of attributing years in his *TBN* I.4.3 (in my *PN2*) and al-Khayyāt's in his *JN* Ch. 3 (in my *PN1*).
[105] That is, the planetary years. See the table above in §1.2.
[106] This certainly means being in its fall, but may include the sign of detriment as well.
[107] That is, besieged: see (*ITA* IV.4.2).
[108] That is, aspecting benefics will add time-units according to the number of their lesser years, while aspecting malefics will decrease time-units based on the number of their lesser years.

§10.28: On discerning the life of kings from the cycle of mundane years[109]—'Umar[110]

And so, whenever it would be agreeable to investigate the royal years from a cycle of the mundane years, establish the east of the cycle[111] for the common people, but the Sun for the king; but the seventh portends the adversaries of the common people, the fourth its end and outcome; the ninth from the east of the cycle [indicates] the royal enemies;[112] the second from the east shows the house of the money of the whole people; the eleventh from the east (namely the second from the Midheaven) watches over the royal money; and the lord of [the Midheaven, and] equally the Sun with its lord, [are significators of the king].[113]

With these being divided up so, the lord of the eighth from the east of the king (which is the Midheaven)[114] should not slip from memory, as to how it regards the lord of the Midheaven or the Sun, or applies to them. Which if would lack both a regard and an application, it is equally appropriate to observe whether there is a collection or a transfer of [their] light. For[115] if you found a transfer of light or collection between them, and you found the planet which is making the transfer to be aspecting the sign of the Midheaven, it signifies death in that year. But if it did not aspect there, it signifies no death.

However, a Lunar application with the fortunate ones and the infortunes, resembles the aforesaid. But she applying to fortunate ones, [indicates] good health; to the infortunes, death, [unless other significations would liberate him—in which liberation, hindrance and labor will happen to him, but he will escape. On the other hand, the signification belongs to the Moon][116] if, I

---

[109] That is, from mundane solar ingresses.
[110] Cf. al-Rijāl VIII.18.
[111] That is, the Ascendant of the solar revolution.
[112] The ninth is the twelfth (enemies) from the tenth (the king).
[113] Reading and adding with al-Rijāl, for Hugo's "and its lord, [and] equally the Sun with its lord, watch over the royal money."
[114] That is, the Ascendant of the king is the Midheaven; thus the eighth from his Ascendant would be the fifth house of the chart.
[115] Reading with al-Rijāl for Hugo's more confused "[or] even one which would transfer or collect that [of the lord of] the Midheaven and of the house of death equally, from the sign of the Midheaven. In fact, their joint regard threatens death in that year. But lacking that, not at all."
[116] Reading the material in brackets with al-Rijāl for Hugo's "however, she being received by them introduces good health after the most serious disease."

say, the Moon would possess something of dignity in the sign of the Midheaven (namely, the house or sovereignty or triplicity or face).

§10.29: Likewise on obtaining the life and dignity of the king—'Umar[117]

And so, once the Sun's entrance into Aries is noted (if someone would be advanced to any dignity in that same year), Saturn especially comes to be noted in the hour of that entrance [into Aries]. For, he being in his own house or in the lodging-place of any of the superior stars, suggests [the king] is going to reign for a long time, namely to a completed assembly,[118] especially [with Saturn] being arranged in the tenth or in the eleventh from the Sun: nor [in that case] would there be any ambiguity up to the completed conjunction.[119] Which if he would bear himself otherwise, [something] of this dignity will be missing, being taken away [according to] the amount of [Saturn's] power which is taken away.

Next, in this place one must note that the first portion[120] is said to be Saturn. If therefore the second portion (namely Jupiter) [aspected the first portion], the matter suggests an increase of life: which if [Jupiter] would be in a strong place,[121] it lavishes months in increase according to [his] lesser years and their number, if, I say, he obtains something of his own dignity [where he is]. After the pivots, he attributes the same thing according to one-half of the lesser years.

Furthermore, the first portion possessing the house of any inferior star (in the year of the dignity that was conferred), while he does not regard the Sun (especially in Virgo),[122] one must note how many degrees of the sign [Saturn] has transited. And with them being discarded, you will grant years according

---

[117] Cf. al-Rijāl VIII.20.
[118] That is, to a completed planetary "conjunction" (*conventum*). This probably means the lesser years of Saturn (30).
[119] *Alkiren*, a transliteration of Ar. *al-qirān*. That is, he will reign until then, *provided that* there are no other mitigating circumstances.
[120] *Pars*. I am not sure what Arabic word this translates, but here and in §10.33 below it seems simply to designate the fact that Saturn and Jupiter each grant something to the length of the king's rule.
[121] Namely, in an angle.
[122] The Sun is in Aries during the ingress, so by definition any planet (here, Saturn) in Virgo cannot regard him by sign.

to the degrees which are left, and you will judge that the one who is advanced will live that many years.

On[123] the other hand, if that boundary has been crossed,[124] direct by releasing from the place of the first portion to the place of the first infortune which you find: and if, when the revolution applied to that sign in which he had been crowned, he will die then; and in this case, you will give one year to each sign. You will even do it in this way: take from the lord of the house of the portion up to the portion itself, and see how many signs there are in between. By giving one year to each sign, judge that the crowned man will last that long.

§10.30: Likewise on obtaining the life and dignity of the king—'Umar[125]

Moreover, the opinion of Valens presents a model in this place: so that, as he claims, with a question posed about the affairs of kings, one must enter into the counsel of the Sun and the Midheaven and their lords. For, that one whom the most testimonies favor, or especially the one which was arranged [better], deservedly claims the signification beyond the rest. And one will have to perform its direction[126] in the way that the conducting[127] of the releaser is, with the degrees of ascensions.[128]

What belongs to the commoners and the people, should be sought [by directions] from the lord of the year, and the place of the east, and the degree of the Moon.

---

[123] Reading this paragraph with al-Rijāl, for Hugo's "Moreover, let recourse be had to those which have been crossed, from that place to the first one which an infortune blocks; and once the circle is completed, and recourse is had to that sign where it had been advanced, it is a sign of his ruin, so that you should take years for individual months. And it could be discovered to that extent in a different way, namely from the lord of the house of the portion to the portion itself: having taken the degrees which are in between, while the individual degrees lavish individual years; and this number really determines the time of reigning."
[124] Namely, if he lasts longer than the years just described.
[125] Cf. al-Rijāl VIII.21.
[126] *Atazir* (Ar. *al-tasyīr*). Literally, "dispatching, setting out"). That is, primary directions.
[127] *Ductus*. That is, primary directions.
[128] Reading with al-Rijāl for Hugo's "the Ascendant."

Likewise, the Mercurial conducting at the cycle of years (or rather at the hour of the question), denotes the letters of kings or powerful people and those of secretaries.

Now, the conducting of Mars watches over magistrates and the leaders of a militia or army.

Belonging to the Saturnian advancement are[129] treasurers and those who govern estates and villas, plains, and they are the guardians of the greater royal houses in any city.

The direction of Venus comprehends the wives of kings [and the vices of kings].[130]

And so, the status of the individual [planets], and how they bear themselves, and their application with the fortunate ones and the infortunes from a trigon or hexagon, likewise from the tetragon and opposition or assembly, come to be noted. For, good and bad are announced in that signification according to the manner of the nature [of the house and sign in which it is].[131] Moreover, it seems we must note how the fortunate ones and the infortunes mix with each other in those same places. Therefore, if the fortunate ones possess these signs, they bring good, joys, and profit (namely according to the nature of the sign itself), without labor and fear. Likewise, the signs being possessed by the infortunes, introduce on the contrary losses and fear, and finally he is stripped of the dignities. However, with a question proposed about those things which are confined to a king,[132] if the harm were in the Ascendant or concerned its lord and they were unfortunate, it signifies that the harm will be in the life of the king and in his body, because he will have infirmities and pains and killings, and perhaps he will be killed at the end of his rule. If even the harm and infortune were in the angle of the earth, it signifies that he will have a bad end and loss at the end of his affairs and business matters, and perhaps he will die on the occasion of that.

---

[129] For the rest of this sentence, reading with al-Rijāl for Hugo's "sentries, the inhabitants of country villas, the peoples of camps, and the citizens of cities."
[130] Adding with al-Rijāl.
[131] Reading with al-Rijāl. Hugo seems to have thought one should consider the culture and location of the people involved.
[132] Hugo is pointing out that 'Umar has recommended directions for all sorts of planets and people; but at this point 'Umar only wants to talk about what harms will come to the king. From here to the end of the paragraph, I am reading with al-Rijāl, because Hugo has mixed up a couple of the sentences and I cannot understand part of what he is trying to say.

(Moreover, if a prelate or underofficial were accused, it is necessary that he will be deposed from that honor, and perhaps he will undergo the danger of death in that business.)[133]

Which if the bound of the east[134] would be corrupted, he will expect that misfortune from his own family.

With the degree of the Sun being corrupted, the one who is going to accept [the honor] will rejoice to modest extent.[135] Now, the lord of the day[136] being corrupted, lavishes no more than the eastern lord does. Likewise, the face[137] being corrupted, he will accept harm from the dependents[138] of his own house, because[139] he will not be feared, but they will despise him in his deeds and commands, and he will be weak, nor would he be able to demand payments and his rights.

The Lot of Fortune applying [by direction] to fortunate ones, returns the dignity that was taken up, and [brings] all things back to what is better and to his pleasure, and it will be subject to his own will. An application with the infortunes, calls the aforesaid back to harm and to violence.

§10.31: On inquiring into the hour of the king's death—'Umar[140]

And so, the regard of the royal significator with the lord of the eighth [from] the Midheaven, or rather with the Sun,[141] or their tetragonal [regard] or from the opposite, really indicates the hour of the royal death as understood beforehand, from the cycle of mundane years. No less too, the lord of the eighth[142] in the sign of the conjunction[143] or of [its] tetragon or the oppo-

---

133 This sentence is not in al-Rijāl.
134 Al-Rijāl has the lord of the bound of the east.
135 Al-Rijāl says he will not be feared.
136 Al-Rijāl has the lord of the sign of the Sun, which might mean, "the lord of the *significator* of the day," namely the Sun.
137 Al-Rijāl has the lord of the face of the Sun.
138 *Clientela*. This includes anyone who counts on him as a patron.
139 Reading with al-Rijāl as being more direct and simple.
140 Cf. al-Rijāl VIII.19. It should be read with §10.32 below, as these follow each other in 'Umar's own text.
141 Probably because the significator of the king would be burnt by the Sun in that situation (as al-Rijāl says in his VIII.16). This part is a little ambiguous because the Sun himself is supposed to indicate the king. So 'Umar might also be referring to the following: the conjunction of the royal significator [the lord of the Midheaven] *or* the Sun, with the lord of the eighth from the Midheaven.
142 That is, the eighth from the Ascendant.

sition, being in any dignity of its own and in power, namely so that it is not scorched nor retrograde, nor western nor cadent. For if they bore themselves thusly, they undoubtedly threaten death.

§10.32: On the death of the king, through interrogations—'Umar[144]

For discovering the hour of his death through a question, it is plainly adequate that it be discovered from the victor[145] of the aforesaid conjunction or opposition or tetragon, with the regard of the lord of the eighth. For if the lord of the eighth would possess the sign in which it is conjoined, or their tetragon or opposition, it grants assent to those things which we said before.

The Lot of death presents its own discrete favor from a question or from the cycling of mundane years. For this, being taken up from the degree of the house of death to the degree of its lord, once the degrees of the east are added, will have to be drawn from the degree of the east itself.[146] But where the number will be ended, is the Lot that is sought. If the significator itself[147] would regard this [Lot], either [by being] joined to it or being opposite or tetragonal, while there is no reception between each,[148] even though it indicates the most serious trouble of disease, it declares that good health will follow.[149] Also, a regard from the trigon or hexagon drives away a not-difficult disease through health, especially when you are ignorant of his nativity. For with [his nativity] being known beforehand, it is necessary that the

---

[143] This must refer to the sign of the New or Full Moon which most recently preceded the revolution. But al-Rijāl reads this as though the lord of the eighth is in a dignity of its own and is also in one of the conjunctions, squares, or opposition just described—unrelated to the New or Full Moon. I can see reasons for both interpretations.

[144] I have not located this passage in al-Rijāl. It should be read with §10.31 above, as these follow each other in 'Umar's own text.

[145] *Mubtazz*. If al-Rijāl is right in his interpretation (see footnote to §10.31 above), this is the victor over the place in which the lord of the eighth is, when it assembles with or makes a hard aspect to the lord of the Midheaven (or perhaps even to the Sun). In most cases, such a victor would be that same lord of the eighth itself.

[146] In other words, from the eighth to the lord of the eighth, and projected from the degree of the Ascendant. I have not heard of this formulation before. A common version (attributed to Hermes in *ITA* VI.2.27) is from the Moon to the eighth, and projected from Saturn.

[147] This must be the victor mentioned above.

[148] This does not quite seem right, as Lots are not received.

[149] This does not quite make sense. Perhaps 'Umar means that a hard aspect will indicate death, but if there *is* reception, he will recover.

degree of the releaser be dispatched (namely, led out) from its place to the terminal place, so that your work would be more exact.[150]

§10.33: On anyone advanced to an honor, from the cycle of mundane years—'Umar[151]

Whenever notice is required about advancing anyone to a kingdom, it will be good to consult first Saturn (who is the first portion),[152] but even Jupiter (which is said to be the second portion). One will even have to observe diligently by how many degrees and minutes they are distant from one another (wholly disregarding whether they regard each other mutually or not). Then too, the lord of the Midheaven: once it is known beforehand, what sign it would be holding onto, and with the ascensional degrees of that sign being added to the aforesaid, the number which is gathered from that suggests it is that many years or months or days. Now, if they[153] would possess their own houses or supremacies, they bring forth years; but after the pivots and peregrine, months; [otherwise], days.

If, I say, an application [of the Sun] with a Mars that is roaming alone (not even with Saturn) is noted, then it portends that[154] soldiers will be moved against the crowned man, [and] even those who were driven out will come upon him, and perhaps they will catch him. Moreover, the application of Mars with Saturn bestows the nature of each [planet], and he will suffer no rebel.[155]

However, with the Sun applying to a Jupiter that is roaming alone, while [Jupiter] does not apply to Saturn, it is a sign that the common people and certain people from [his] family become rebels against the prince: whence, because they have broken allegiance with him, he is shaken by the stimulation of [his] cares. However, Jupiter applying to Saturn will really bless with [their] double nature, here vanquishing the wicked, there pressing down his subjects; blessed, I say with a double category, so that namely neither his

---

[150] In other words, if you know the person's nativity, perform primary directions of his or her natal longevity releaser as described in 'Umar's *TBN* I and elsewhere.
[151] Cf. al-Rijāl VIII.22 (first part).
[152] *Pars.* I am not sure what Arabic word this translates, but here and in §10.29 above it seems simply to designate the fact that Saturn and Jupiter each grant something to the length of the king's rule.
[153] Probably referring to Saturn, Jupiter and maybe even the lord of the Midheaven.
[154] Reading the rest of this sentence with al-Rijāl, as Hugo has gotten some of it mixed up.
[155] The idea seems to be that Saturn squashes any rebellion.

household intimates nor strangers will be hostile. Which if perhaps that did happen, they are shaken.

Furthermore, with the Sun applying to neither Mars nor Jupiter, while however his application with Saturn is seen, he subjects the rebels to his own rule, especially if Saturn would possess his own house, and he appearing free of misfortunes.

If however the Sun would be separated from Jupiter, [applying] first to Mars [and] then to Saturn before [the Sun] leaves behind the house where he is staying, [then], stirring up certain people from the royal household or those neighboring on him (as though they are familiar) against him, it renders him anxious and worried, but he will wholly shake them, especially with Saturn lingering in his own house, while he appeared cleansed of misfortunes. Which if the Sun did not apply to Saturn before he has gone out from the house he is holding onto, it leads the king into the most severe danger, so that he even fears for his own reign.

Moreover, Mars withdrawing from Jupiter, applying to Saturn, prepares accusers from his own family.[156] [But if in addition Jupiter applied to Saturn, those who were cast out will obey the king, and he will avenge himself with them.][157] Likewise, Mars withdrawing from Saturn and an application of [Mars] with Jupiter, provokes household intimates against him, with him making it his own fault. But, Jupiter applying to Saturn makes them totally humble and surrendering to him, especially if Saturn (being cleansed) would possess his own house. Indeed, Jupiter proceeding in a solitary way, and being safe, placed in his own light and nature, multiplies[158] adversaries and accusers [and] heavily weighs down his authority, so that with human counsel wholly withdrawing, the whole thing must be handed over to divine power.

Therefore, with a question being presented principally about an affair of this kind, one must enter into the counsel of Saturn and Jupiter, namely as to whether the first one would possess anything [of dignity, and also be][159] in the Midheaven or the eleventh or the east (but preferably in a pivot). Then, one will have to expressly attend to how many degrees are between [Saturn and Jupiter]: for by how much they are distant (in terms of the number of degrees), they administer that many years or months. (One must even ignore

---

[156] Al-Rijāl says, "a man of great justice."
[157] Adding with al-Rijāl.
[158] Al-Rijāl reads totally differently, saying that he will be avenged, strengthen his own cause, and will do what he wants.
[159] Adding with al-Rijāl.

how much of the sign it is transiting, or how much is left.) Now, if you should find Saturn at the end of a sign and in its last degree, wanting to go out [into the following sign], that degree really establishes one year in that place. Then, Saturn wholly lavishes [the time] according to the greatness of each of the places in the circle,[160] and according to his distance from Jupiter.

§10.34: On estate managers and supervisors, and their authority, acts, and life—'Umar[161]

And so, establish the east and its lord for the querent (namely the prominent person), in terms of his power [and] acts. But the dignity that is accepted is judged from the Midheaven and the Moon. Also, the fourth [indicates] the land in which he is staying, and resolves the end of the whole affair. But from the seventh depends knowledge of the remaining underofficials who are obedient, and of the common people who are subjects.

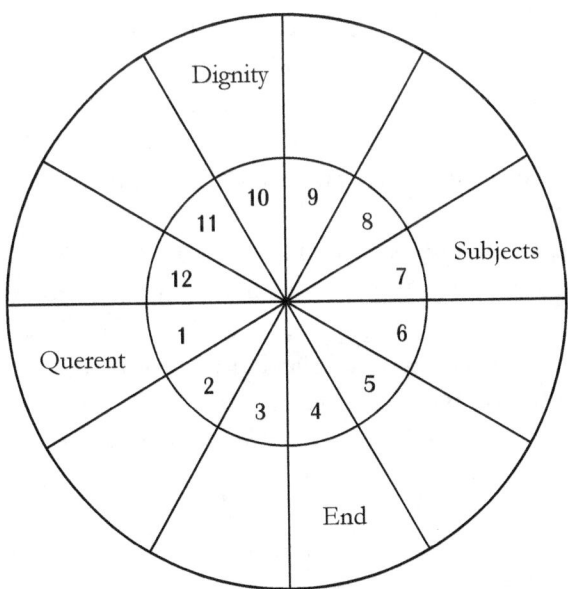

Figure 71: Angular significations for attaining a dignity ('Umar §10.34)

---

[160] That is, whether they are in pivots or succeedents or cadents, or perhaps even dignities, as has already been suggested (see also §10.29 above).

[161] I have been unable to find this passage in al-Rijāl. But it should be read with §10.35 below, as they follow each other in 'Umar's own text.

Once these have been divided up, with recourse being had to the sign of the Midheaven, one must foresee what fortunate ones or infortunes are holding onto it, and even where its lord is: namely whether they would be holding onto a pivot from [the Midheaven] or from the lord of the Midheaven, or they would be falling away[162] from each. And so, infortunes being established in the Midheaven, while they are estranged from[163] their own places, and they would touch both the lord of the Midheaven and the eastern [lord] with their own rays, being corrupted in dignity, afflict his very body with some trouble. If, however, being placed there, they would support the lord of the Midheaven with their own aspect, while however they would fall down from[164] the lord of the east, they introduce soundness, both for his office and his body. Contrariwise, too, with the infortunes placed in the east, if they would regard the eastern lord, they being cadent from[165] the lord of the tenth, they afflict the body with a disease, but save the attached office. Which if they did not regard the eastern lord, and the Moon is corrupted, it is mortal. Moreover, the eastern lord being received by the infortunes, and the Moon being safe, promises good health after the trouble he gets from the disease.

Moreover, with the sign of the Midheaven and its lord (but even the east and its lord) being fortunate and lucky, while they would enjoy a mutual aspect in common, and there is a collection or transfer of light between them, it presents a good condition for each: namely for the body and the affair that is accepted.

Moreover, the lord of the second from the Midheaven[166] applying to the eastern lord, and being received by it, and free of the infortunes, conveys money from the king, namely according to the nature of the star holding onto its own sovereignty. For, it being in its fall, or retrograde or scorched, or in some place of its own corruption, his resources and the affluence of riches will prosper just as the nature of that star promises: if it is unfortunate, unjustly, but if it were fortunate, justly.

---

[162] Reading *decidant* for *decidat*. This seems to mean being in any sign that is succeedent to, cadent from, or in aversion to, those signs.
[163] *Alienentur*. I am not sure if this simply means they are peregrine, or that they are in aversion to the domiciles they rule. I think Hugo and 'Umar mean "peregrine."
[164] This probably means "be in aversion to."
[165] That is, in aversion to.
[166] That is, the eleventh (the king's money).

§10.35: If someone in power would please the people—'Umar[167]

With anyone seeking into the affairs of people in power and the status of the subject common people, the seventh and its lord agree with [the Midheaven and its lord].[168] If therefore the infortunes occupied the seventh, with its lord being cadent from it, and in the sign of its own depression or fall, while they do not regard the east, nor is there an application or transfer between them, nor one who collects their lights, or if it would be retrograde or scorched or at least unlucky, it suggests a bad status for the common people; and it testifies that this comes forth from the prince, while it wholly postpones their care and benevolence. Also, with a regard from the opposition or assembly or tetragon, while there is no reception present, it declares the severe detriment of the masses, reporting the anger and injustice of the prince. But with reception being had, what was stated above is a bit more relaxed. A regard from a trigon or hexagon with reception, professes the faith and piety of the prince: nor, if there were adverse things, do they come down from him, but from elsewhere. Which if the fortunate ones would support the places of the infortunes, they suggest steady and certain, even manifold, profit from the dignity he took up.

§10.36: On the household intimates[169] of kings, whether they would obtain something good from them—'Umar[170]

And so, with the east being established, it is necessary to attend to its lord and the Lunar status, [and] no less too to what place from the east the fortunate ones and infortunes are holding onto.

Therefore, the lord of the east being established in a strong place in the circle, and applying to the lord of the Midheaven [by] either a trigon or hexagon, while each would be made fortunate from a place of reception, they

---

[167] I have been unable to find this passage in al-Rijāl. But it should be read with §10.34 above, as they follow each other in 'Umar's own text.
[168] Reading a complete phrase for Vienna's *medium*. I believe I am justified in this, because this section follows on the previous one, which dealt with the Midheaven and now treats the seventh in a similar way.
[169] *Familiaribus.* This would probably include close staff in addition to family members and friends. But there is no indication in the text (here or in al-Rijāl) to indicate that the querent is such a person.
[170] Cf. al-Rijāl III.20 and III.25. I have rearranged some of the paragraphs to fit al-Rijāl's account, as Hugo's distribution of paragraphs makes certain points unclear and does not follow a clear order.

present the benevolence and respectable partnership of the king, and they lavish what is useful. Which if they would rejoice in a joint application or regard [while] being arranged in the pivots, they will bless with not-trivial success, especially holding onto some place of their own dignity: namely, according to the quantity of power taken in those same places. [But if the lord of the Ascendant were cadent from the lord of the tenth, nor did it aspect it, and likewise the lord of the tenth were cadent from the tenth (nor did it aspect it), nor was there a powerful fortune which would convey the light to the lord of the Ascendant and aspect it, judge that he will not obtain the matter or office.][171]

If[172] the Moon were made fortunate in the eleventh, and were free of the infortunes, and the lord of her house aspected her, it signifies that the matter will be brought about well and powerfully. But if the lord of the eleventh were an infortune, and the Moon were made unfortunate by it, it signifies that the matter that is thought about will not be perfected, but will disappear into nothing. If the lord of the eleventh were a fortune, and an unfortunate Moon were cadent from the eleventh and from the fortunes, it signifies that a certain portion of the matter sought will come to be, [but] which will later be denied. But if the diminishment of the Moon were from Mars, and Mars were powerful in his own place, harming the Moon, even harming the lord of the Ascendant and the lord of the house of trust[173] or the lord of the Midheaven, it signifies that he will be killed in that office; but if some fortune improving him aspected him, he will not be killed, but he will be removed from thence, and expelled from the region or city. If the lord of the tenth and eleventh were both fortunes, and in places in which they have dignity, and the Moon were harmed by Saturn, it signifies that he will get the dignity,

---

[171] Adding from al-Rijāl. After this paragraph, al-Rijāl adds another which is found above in §10.5.

[172] I am using al-Rijāl for this paragraph, as Hugo's version is hopelessly abridged. He reads: "Again, the usefulness and success is distinguished from the lord of the eleventh (which is the house of royal money). For, [the Moon] being regarded and received by the lord of the eleventh (namely, her own), so that the regard is from a trigon or hexagon, he will obtain it diligently and without difficulty. But from the tetragon or opposition or assembly, he acquires it [but] not without anxiety. With reception being denied, likewise. Moreover, they being deprived of a mutual regard, while there is no transfer nor one which would collect their light, they lavish absolutely nothing. Stars appearing and established in the eleventh do not show another judgment, if, I say, they would support the east with their own aspect. But everywhere, the testimonies of the Lot of Fortune should show assent."

[173] That is, the eleventh.

and that he will be powerful in it, of bad morals, and fraudulent, and that those whom he has to give orders to will be weakened by him and his deeds, and that they will complain bitterly about him and will hate him.

The[174] Moon applying to an eastern lord that is fortunate and lucky, while there is no intervention by either[175] of the infortunes, it portends a cheerful partnership (as was already stated), even profits and joys (namely just as it is allowed to be derived from the place of the Lot of Fortune and the regard of its lord to the lord of the east).[176] [But if one of them did not apply to the other, or some planet intervened between them],[177] but her lord was placed with the lord of the east itself (and it was lucky), it wrenches out something of honor from the king, after a modicum of labor and difficulty. However, he is made sad at one time when stripped of [that honor], and will rejoice at another with it being returned.

Likewise, with the eastern lord and the [Moon and the lord] of the Moon being equally corrupted, it is not a sign of attaining it. But Mars himself corrupting the east and the Moon, means a liar and fraudulent man.[178] The corruption proceeding from Saturn, introduces delay from the king: [the king] promising something by his word but not in his heart, he deters [the client] from the desired partnership. If however Venus and Jupiter would bless each, supporting the eastern lord (I say) and the Moon with their own aspect, [or Venus and Jupiter were] both the lord of the east and of the Moon, they equally commend a part of the expected success, namely according to the moderation of each and the strength of the authority of the office.[179]

§10.37: Whether they would be his household intimates for a long time—'Umar[180]

Moreover, [for knowing the time of his stay in the dignity],[181] you will note the degrees possessed by the fortunate ones, and one will have to make

---

[174] Omitting Hugo's opening "with these bearing themselves thusly...", as it was based on a bad understanding of the order of topics.
[175] Reading with al-Rijāl for Hugo's "governance among each."
[176] This part is not in al-Rijāl.
[177] Reading with al-Rijāl. Hugo begins, "Moreover, the Moon being corrupted...".
[178] That is, the king.
[179] Hugo is being unnecessarily fussy: what 'Umar means is that if both of the benefics are doing this, then there will be success and increase.
[180] Cf. al-Rijāl III.20 and III.25.

a direction of their degree to that of the lord of the east, [and between] the infortune which corrupts the east and the Moon. For the number of these really establishes months.

Also, the Lot of Fortune decides the manner of success and obtaining its advantage. Therefore, if it would regard the Moon, or she would apply to it, and each would be lucky, it means many successes, according to the power of each which they have in the circle. Which if it would happen otherwise, another judgment should be given. Moreover, each one being corrupted by Mars, snatches away the money of the powerful person, and designates flight.[182] But Saturn corrupting each, introduces frauds in buying and concealing [things]: whence he is made sometimes anxious, sometimes free (but hardly so).[183]

§10.38: Whether it is useful to keep close to the king—Dorotheus

Here, if any of the magnates posed a question about some connection to the king (such as about a partnership with him or mutually receiving money, and that kind of thing), or about attending his son, we hand the querent over to the eastern lord and the Moon, [but] the king to the Midheaven. Then, one must note to whom (among the lords of the domiciles) the eastern lord applies. For, the star that does not deny a reception, claims that [that person's] partnership is useful.

---

[181] Reading with al-Rijāl, as being more simple and direct. I have also restructured this sentence following al-Rijāl, as Hugo's is garbled.
[182] Al-Rijāl makes it clear that this means the *querent* will steal once he is in office.
[183] Again, al-Rijāl explains that while his secret thefts will cause labor, he will ultimately escape.

TRADES & PROFESSIONS

§10.39: On trades—'Umar

And so, the staying[1] of Mercury in the domiciles of the stars, and their regards to him, particularly reveal the kinds of offices. He being in his own proper house or sovereignty, free of the aspect of the infortunes, and arranged in a pivot or after a pivot, generates a scribe or astrologer. In [a house] of Mars and in his regard, it produces a shoemaker[2] of some kind. He appearing in a lodging-place of Venus, [means] no other [judgment], if however Mars would regard him. And so, Mercury generally distributes the kinds of all the trades.

If (I say) Jupiter would possess the Midheaven, traversing in the aspect of Mars or Venus, regarding the lord of the tenth, he will thence be mixed with Mercury: for, stars being in the Midheaven agree with a certain mixing of works or affairs, and participate in them.

Moreover, with Mercury and the one who rules over the Midheaven being placed under a mutual aspect, it is finally necessary then to observe the nature of the trade.

---

[1] Hugo often uses this word to speak of planetary stations, but here he undoubtedly means that Mercury "is in" various domiciles.

[2] *Sutor*. Or rather, any profession involving weaving and sewing (*suere*).

§11: ELEVENTH HOUSE

11th House	
Attaining something hoped for	§§11.1-5
Friendships, loves & hates	§§11.6-12

Figure 72: Questions of the eleventh house

THINGS HOPED FOR

§11.1: On those things which pertain to the eleventh house—Sahl[1]

Whenever an ambiguity of the eleventh occurs, [namely] what kind of thing it is that he hopes for and believes he will get, let the affair be sought from the lord of the eleventh. For, this [planet] applying to the eastern lord (or [the lord of the east] to it), leaves no hesitation about attaining the thing which he hopes for. An application made from the [assembly or][2] trigon or hexagon, promises he will get it easily; but from the opposition or tetragon, he will acquire it [but] not without difficulty. Moreover, the lord of the eleventh being in a pivot and received,[3] affirms the hope.

But [the planet] receiving the [application of the] Moon traversing in a double-bodied sign, will bestow a moderate portion of the thing which he was hoping for; with it walking in a turning sign, difficulty even occurs in this; but if it would walk through a firm sign, it fully completes whatever he was hoping for. Which if that same receiver of the Moon happened to be impeded, it will forsake whatever was attained, after [getting it]. The one who gathers the Lunar counsel being received, will convey everything according to his wish.[4]

---

[1] Cf. *On Quest.* §11.1 al-Rijāl III.28.
[2] Adding with John's Sahl.
[3] John's Sahl (like §§11.4-5 below) has it in a pivot, with the *Moon* being received. But the reading above matches al-Rijāl.
[4] John's Sahl adds that if the lord of the Ascendant were received, he will have everything wished for.

§11.2: On those things which someone holds back in his mind, nor does he want to name it—Sahl[5]

If however it is sought with respect to what someone holds back in his mind (namely whether he would be able to attain it), nor however [does he want it] to be named, an observation of this kind must be had, so that you imitate the counsel of the eastern lord and the Moon. For if they would apply to benevolents from the pivots (or at least after the pivots), it will be a judgment of getting it; but if not, not at all.

But [if] he was worried about the attainment of something, [and] if he would lay it out with an explicit designation, you will seek it diligently according to the signification of the twelve houses described above—[namely, according to] what place in the circle [that topic] possesses, as its solution.

§11.3: On hope—'Umar[6]

Moreover, we give the counsel of the significator proper (namely the Moon) for an inquiry about hope. For, she rendering her counsel to a star occupying a pivot, really makes the hope true. Also, with the star possessing the tenth, [it makes it] truer, for it wholly reveals it more manifestly. And it will be permitted to claim it in this way with respect to the east. However, if this [star] would happen to be found in the opposite,[7] it means it is first public, but finally concealed. Being found in the fourth, it similarly hides it.

The lord of the hour being arranged in the way which was said, reveals the truth of the hope.

§11.4: On the hope of a promised honor—al-Khayyāt

When inquiries of the eleventh happen, such as is about hope or a promised honor, the lord of the east and the eleventh equally, and the Moon, are consulted. And so, the lord of the eleventh applying to the eastern lord, or these [doing so] conversely with the Moon, or at least should either one apply to [the other], while none hinders the light between them, it is a sign of achieving the hope. That same lord of the eleventh in a pivot, and the Moon

---

[5] Cf. *On Quest.* §11.3; it is also in al-Rijāl III.28 (last part).
[6] Cf. al-Rijāl I.22.
[7] That is, in the seventh.

being received, convey all things according to his wish. But the one receiving [the application of] the Moon being in a two-parted [sign], promises part. It being in a turning [sign means] the same thing, [but] with difficulty and anguish. With respect to a firm one, it introduces the things hoped for, intact. But that same receiver of the Moon being corrupted, after achieving it, it corrupts and bears away all things. Which if [the receiver of her application] is received, it brings them in beyond what he was hoping for. The reception of the eastern lord, too, brings no other [result].

§11.5: On the hope of a promised gift—Dorotheus

With a question of the eleventh happening, such as about a hope or some gift promised by a king, the eastern lord and that of the eleventh should be consulted (with the Moon as a partner). [The lord of the eleventh] applying to the eastern [lord], or the eastern lord and the Moon to it, while there is not a star present[8] who is cutting with [its] light [between them], it declares he is going to get his hope. The lord of the eleventh in a pivot, and the Moon being received, confers it according to his desire. Which if the receiver of the Lunar counsel would be holding onto a two-parted sign, it is the same, but [only] in part. But in a convertible [sign], it portends he is fooled by flattering words. In a firm [sign], it undoubtedly consoles him with the expected gift. Its reception conveys the gift, and lavishes it, beyond what was promised.

---

[8] Reading *adsit* for *absit*.

FRIENDSHIPS

§11.6: If a friendship is true, or even should someone come together with a friend—Sahl[1]

In addition, with a question proposed as to whether someone should come together with a friend, it will be good to consult the eastern lord and the Moon. For, an application of these with the lord of the eleventh promises what had been sought. Which if they would apply from a trigon or hexagon, they receive each other well and with joy. But from the opposition or tetragon, it means contrariety or there will be discord (though it is worse from the opposition).

§11.7: On love and hate—'Umar[2]

And so, an observation of this kind proceeds from the east and the seventh and their lords, even from the stars which are in them, and their application and withdrawal. However, the Moon must be applied as a partner, if she had an application or withdrawal. Which if she bore herself thusly, you will apply the star from which the Moon is being separated, as a partner of the east; but the one to which she applies, to the lord of the seventh.

Then, too, it seems one must note what kind of application this is[3] (namely from a trigon or hexagon or assembly), and whence the regard proceeded; no less [too] whether there is some reception present. Which if they did bear themselves thusly, they signify the joint and respectable and firm concord of each. But a regard from a tetragon or opposition, likewise with reception being denied, testifies to mutual hatred and dissent. Which if reception is present, it makes them [less] contemptible to each other.

But with the one to which the Moon applies (and how), or from which she withdraws, having been discovered just as was said before, one will have to judge just as with the lord of the east and of the seventh; not otherwise, too, with those stars which you will find in the east and the seventh.

---

[1] Cf. *On Quest.* §11.2, and al-Rijāl III.28 (middle).
[2] Cf. al-Rijāl III.30. This is identical to §7.148 and derives from the same Arabic chapter of 'Umar's.
[3] In this paragraph, 'Umar is only addressing the relationship between the lords of the east and of the seventh. The Moon's application and separation is described in the next paragraph.

Moreover, if the Moon applies to none, nor withdraws from any [star], you will bring the lord of the east and of the seventh equally into view, so that you can do this with them. If therefore they are deprived of a mutual aspect, so that they neither apply nor withdraw [from one another], nor is there a transfer or collection between each by some star, they wholly deny peace and concord.

§11.8: Concerning anyone, whether he would come together with a friend—al-Khayyāt

If someone made a question about someone, whether he would come together with [his] friend, one will have to follow up with the eastern lord and the Moon. For, an application of them with the lord of the eleventh, portends that they would come together. From a trigon or hexagon, it announces joy and love. But [the application] of an opposition and tetragon conveys fights and discord. And in this way, too,[4] for children one will observe the fifth; for patrimony, the seventh; for brothers, the third; the fourth answers for parents (for the most part even for them we follow the Sun and Moon).

§11.9: On friends, brothers, and relatives: whether they would come together—Dorotheus

Now, with anyone being uncertain as to whether someone is going to come together with a friend, it demands the evidence of the eastern lord and the Moon. Wherefore, their application with the lord of the eleventh testifies that he does come together [with the friend]. One of them even being received by the other, promises that the one whom [the received planet] designates will be received, not without success and happiness. With reception being denied, they do not come together.[5]

---

[4] Al-Khayyāt means, "If you asked this question about coming together with someone else, like children, *etc.*"

[5] But Dorotheus had just said that simply by the planets connecting, they would come together. Maybe he means that it will not be very firm or long-lasting without reception.

§11.10: On the concord or love of two people—al-Khayyāt[6]

For a question about the concord or love of two people, the lord of the eleventh, but even that of the seventh and the third, and the lord of the east, respond. If therefore the lords of these places would apply to the eastern lord from a trigon or hexagon, they denote the firmest love. [But if from the square or opposition, they do not esteem each other, especially if one of them were the lord of the twelfth.][7] But if one (but especially the lord of the eleventh) regarded in the same way, it means the same; but the regard of two is judged to be more effective. But if all would come together, it will be an indication of the firmest esteem, and more so if they regarded each other from a firm [sign].

§11.11: On the concord of two people—Dorotheus

The lord of the seventh and eleventh, but even that of the third, resolves the knot of this question. Which if they would regard the eastern lord from a trigon or hexagon (especially the lord of the eleventh), they signal joint benevolence. [But if from the square or opposition, they do not esteem each other, especially if one of them were the lord of the twelfth.][8] The regard of two [of them] is more effective [than just one]. But if a regard would proceed from all of the signs, it denotes greater esteem.

§11.12: Concerning someone, whether it is a friend or flatterer—Jirjis

A benevolent traversing in the east or Midheaven, affirms he is a friend, [and] it introduces benefit from him. But if each or at least one unlucky one would walk through it, it brings forth a liar and [someone] unuseful.

---

[6] Cf. al-Rijāl III.29.
[7] Adding with al-Rijāl.
[8] Adding with al-Rijāl.

§12: TWELFTH HOUSE

12th House	
Horse racing	§§12.1-3
Revenge	§12.4b
Enemies	§§12.4a, 12.5-6
Corruption of matters	§Z.1

Figure 73: Questions of the twelfth house

HORSE RACING

§12.1: On those things which pertain to the twelfth house—Sahl[1]

When inquiries of the twelfth happen, if someone asking about his own horse or even about some other specific one,[2] would ask how it is with a horse race (namely of two [horses] or many), it will be good to attend to the lord of the hour of that question. If you should find it in the east, [the horse] about whom it is asked will rejoice in the victory that is attained. Traversing in the Midheaven, it will occupy the designated goal of being second from first [place]. [And likewise in the eleventh.][3] But while it would be lingering in the seventh, [it will be the middle one. And if it were in the fourth],[4] it will be the last one.

Moreover, the lord of the hour traversing in its own fall, frightens the one sitting on it, and threatens a fall. In addition to all of this, if the malevolents would regard it, it smashes the part of the body ascribed to [the sign]. Which if this aspect proceeded from an assembly or opposition, and this lord of the hour would be walking through the eighth from its own house, it suggests death is going to come from the fall; it is more certain if the lord of that same place or the Moon happened to be impeded.

On the other hand, if he who had no horse running among them would make the aforestated question concerning the color of the winning horse or [its] kind (or rather, breeding), if we should have recourse to the lord of the hour, such information could be had. For, it being placed in the east, or if

---

[1] Cf. *On Quest.* §§12.1-3 and al-Rijāl III.33.
[2] See below for general questions about which horse will win.
[3] Adding with John's Sahl. Al-Rijāl adds, "or in the third," but this is probably a misread for "in the third place," as al-Khayyāt says in §12.3 below.
[4] Adding with John's Sahl.

you find any other star in that same place (or at least in the tenth or in the eleventh), the color of the winner is discerned according to the nature of it, and what colors pertain to it.[5]

If the [significator of] the victor[6] would be lingering in its own [house or][7] sovereignty or triplicity, bound, or even face, it prefigures a noted horse of good stock; better and more worthy is the house or sovereignty. But [if it is not] in the rest of the dignities, it portends it is bad and lower than these places which we stated: a stranger [and] unknown. While these bear themselves thusly, should it even be lingering in its own fall, it suggests a rebellious and unruly [horse]. Concerning the house or sovereignty (as was stated above), it will be of good stock. Concerning the triplicity, it will not be born in that land nor be of good stock. Concerning the bound or face, it is noted in its own land, but in no way of good stock.

Moreover, for knowing its proper quality, the method submitted [here] will give the advice: for if the aforewritten significator were eastern, it has shed its first teeth. Appearing western, it suggests it will be of a completed age, and an adult. Placed between each, it is already middle-aged.

Finally, if you happen to find nothing of what was stated above, let the full attention of your mind be drawn back to the east. For if this were the house of the Sun, it assumes the victor to be of the royal horses. But if it were the lodging-place [of Saturn], it testifies it is of an advanced age, but not of good stock, unless (I say) Saturn is placed very well in a pivot. Moreover, Jupiter having assumed the rulership of the east, blesses a man of great and royal dignity (who is assisting [the king]) with the victory.[8] But if Mars would have the house there, it bestows the same on some general and a bellicose man. If however Venus or Mercury, it will be ascribed to a king or noble, and often even a woman. But if it were the house of the Moon, some businessman has brought [a horse] to run it, in order to sell it.

---

[5] See al-Kindī's description in §12.2, or better yet his full version in *Forty Chapters* Ch. 36.2.
[6] Reading this phrase with John's Sahl.
[7] Adding with John's Sahl.
[8] Reading more with John's Sahl for Hugo's *virum magnae dignitatis et regio semper assistentem aspectui currentis equi habeat victoriam*.

§12.2: On the racing of horses, and their victory—al-Kindī

§649. The arrangement of the Ascendant and the pivots manages the racing of horses and the status of those running [in it]; whence, the Ascendant and its lord designates the master of the whole cohort.[9] Moreover, seek vigilantly for any star which claimed the rulership of the hour for itself: for it signifies the horse [who wins], but the lord of the second [hour] the following one, that of the third [hour] will indicate the third, and the lords of the rest of the hours take the rest, in whatever order they were.

[Identifying the winner by color & markings]

§650.[10] Therefore, if the nature and manner of whatever ruler of the hour [it was] would be diligently looked for, they indicate his horse as a whole. For example, [if the color is that] of Saturn as the significator, a dark horse is expected. Jupiter, blonde or whitish; Mars, red; the Sun, white, more consistent with bright white; Venus, intensely black and glittering;[11] Mercury, less black; the Moon, white verging more into blackness.

§651. But once the significators distinguish these colors, if there were a commixture of the stars with them, the commixture of their colors with those of the applying ones, will follow—but the color of the significator will always prevail in it. For example, if Jupiter applied to the significator Saturn, the majority of the hair will appear dark, [but] a lesser blonde [amount] will be mixed in with it. With Mars being mixed with [Saturn], it exhibits a color of dark and red, verging more to blackness. With the Sun joined to [Saturn], middling white; Venus, middling black; and likewise Mercury, but going more towards the dark. Finally, the Moon joined to [Saturn] will be dark, [but] consistent with brightness.

§12.3: On the racing of horses—al-Khayyāt

If someone would ask about those things which pertain to the twelfth house (of which kind is one for the racing of horses, would one come in first

---

[9] *Cohortis.* This seems to mean the person who is hosting the race: see §661 in *Forty Chapters.*
[10] From here through the rest of the chapter (in *Forty Chapters*), the paragraphs are all from Robert, as Hugo is missing most paragraphs.
[11] Reading *renidens* for *renitens.*

and who is going to have the reward in victory), while the one who asks has a horse in the race (whom he fears will be overcome), one must note the lord of the hour. For, it being placed in the east, [the horse] which he feared would be beaten, and which was sent by him into the race, will overcome the rest of them in the victory that is achieved. But if that same [lord of the hour] would walk through the Midheaven, if there is nothing in the east, it either overcomes or runs second after the first [horse]. Being placed in the eleventh, it arranges it in third place. In the seventh, he runs in the middle among the rest. But concerning the fourth, it shows he is the last.

Moreover, the lord of the hour traversing in its own fall, threatens a fall and slipping to him who will run[12] the given horse, for he[13] will crash, forced by fear. But if the malevolents would regard it, they break some limb (over which that sign presides) of the one crashing. But a regard of the infortunes of this kind (from the opposition or assembly), namely so that the lord of the hour would walk through the eighth sign from its own house, means a deadly fall (it is even worse if the lord of that sign or the Moon would be corrupted).

But if someone who is going to send no horse in the race made the question (I say, having no part in it), the lord of the hour is consulted in the same way. For it or any other [star] traversing in the east, or if it would possess the tenth or eleventh, portends that the horse of that same color which the star represents, will win.[14] Moreover, the significator of the victor traversing in [its own] house or sovereignty, triplicity or bound or face, shows the horse has a great name[15] (and preferably the house or sovereignty; the rest, not so much). But if it would be lingering outside places of this kind, devoid of a dignity of this kind, it brings forth one ignoble and unknown. In addition even, if it would traverse in its own fall, it manifests one not only ignoble, but even deformed and unmanageable. From the house and sovereignty it will be of middling fatness;[16] from the triplicity, it will be famous among the [local] natives, but is ignoble and unknown.

It will be permitted to observe the knowledge of its age, from that same significator. For, the significator being eastern portends it has shed two

---

[12] That is, "ride."
[13] Or perhaps "it," referring to the horse.
[14] See for example al-Kindī's description in §12.2, or better yet his full version in *Forty Chapters* Ch. 36.2.
[15] That is, a great reputation.
[16] This may be an error. For Sahl in §12.1, it means being of good stock.

teeth;[17] western, showing that it has shed all of them, it demonstrates a mature age. But if it were between both [easternness and westernness], there will be a shedding of four teeth.

Which if [these things] did not happen thusly, counsel should be sought from the east. Which if it is the house of the Sun, it signifies the horse will be of the royal horses. But if it shows the house of Saturn, it settles it as belonging to some old man, but ignoble—unless, I say, Saturn would be lingering in a pivot or were well placed. But if it were a Jupiterian domicile, [it belongs to] some prince or magnate. Being the house of Mars, it portends it belongs to some leader of an army, or one fighting, or who is usually dressed in arms. But it being a house of Venus or Mercury, ascribes it to some prelate or one given to letters, or some woman. But with it claiming the Moon for the house, some businessman has introduced him [for the purposes of] sale.

---

[17] That is, as horses' and other animals' ages are sometimes measured by how many milk teeth they have lost.

REVENGE & ENEMIES

§12.4A: On enemies—Sahl[1]

Generally, whenever there were an inquiry put forth about any enemies, counsel should be sought from the twelfth and its lord. But you would be able to elicit a certain response according to its applications and figures of application with the rest (or of theirs with it), and the ways in which they bear themselves, in the way that has often been laid out [before].

Therefore, having enumerated these things which pertain to the twelve houses (in as full a method as I was able), [since] the ancient astrologers want to ascribe the kinds of general questions to the twelve signs and their proper qualities, below I will append, in its own separate treatise,[2] those things which are taken up outside of the twelve houses, lest an error be able to disturb you who are already sailing into port.[3]

For[4] their nature in no way proceeds in a certain order of progression from the natures of the planets and their signification, nor will they be taken up undeservedly. Some want to ascribe [questions about] letters and legates to the fifth, [but] others [to the ninth] on account of the reason for travel and roads which it describes; on revenge, to the twelfth, on hunting to the seventh.

§12.4B: On revenge—Sahl[5]

Concerning revenge for someone dead or an inflicted injury (namely in any way it may be satisfied),[6] we should consult the east and the fourth (because it indicates the end). For if the east and the fourth were turning [signs], and the Moon is walking [in] a turning [sign], there will be no satisfaction. But if the lord of the east regarded the east itself, [and the lord of the Moon

---

[1] Cf. *On Quest.* §12.4, and al-Rijāl III.36. This had originally been found incorrectly at the end of Sahl's horse-racing material in §12.1.
[2] Sahl is referring to *On Quest.* §13 (which immediately followed), which does contain a variety of questions. Some of these questions have already been used by Hugo in other parts of *Judges*.
[3] This is a lovely image for the student—it has been quite a journey so far.
[4] This paragraph may be a note by Hugo, as it is not in John's Sahl.
[5] Cf. *On Quest.* §13.11.
[6] This includes financial compensation.

the Moon],[7] everything is restored quickly. But in addition to what we have said, if the lord of the fourth regards the seventh, [he accomplishes] the thing itself and even pours out the blood of the killer, unless (I say) the Moon would apply to benevolents. Nor should that benevolent apply afterwards to an unfortunate one, for that threatens death after the concord that is made. Which if the application of that benevolent to the malevolent would come to be from a trigon or hexagon, it removes death but still it introduces punishments and fetters. With that malevolent traveling through a fixed sign,[8] he will die in prison. Traversing in a turning [sign], while its lord (being quicker) aspected its own house in a friendly way, it frees him who was being held, for nothing. The regard being had from a perverse figure, he escapes by means of a battle or what is like that. But from an assembly, he will either be sent away or will even disappear in flight.

And if a benevolent is found in the east, all things will be called back to peace and concord through his friends. In addition to all of this, the Moon applying to a strong malevolent in its own place, it promises that the revenge is not [through] friends, but the king. Moreover, if a malevolent would occupy the east, with the Moon being fortunate, [then although] the friends of him who died are straining to surround the killer, the king supports him and strives to snatch him away. Whence, if the lord of the east would regard the east, it submits him to the hands of the avengers, while the king is indignant. Moreover, with the aforesaid aspect being denied, while the lord of the house of the Moon aspects the Moon, the king will take him while [the friends] are unwilling.

Finally, whatever punishment and anxiety the madness of Mars signifies will be through iron and whips; but Saturn has the blows of sticks, anguish, and long-lasting imprisonment.

§12.5: On enemies—al-Khayyāt[9]

With a question presented in the open about enemies, let the intention of [your] mind be drawn back to the twelfth and its lord. But the extent to which the difference between the twelfth and the seventh pertains to this

---

[7] Adding with John's Sahl.
[8] Reading with John for Hugo's "pivot."
[9] Cf. al-Rijāl III.35. This question seems to be about whether the querent has enemies, and the level of their hostility and power over the querent.

affair, [is this]: if a general question comes to be about enemies indifferently, one looks to the twelfth; but if it is asked determinately about someone [in particular], the seventh and its lord must be noted.

Therefore, this general observation will be for both cases: namely, that one must note what application there is between the lords of the twelfth or seventh and the east (namely, a prosperous one or the contrary), and what manner of bearing there is (in terms of the greatness of the places),[10] with diligent observation being had as was stated about the rest, [and] even vigilant care, so that thusly the reason of the one judging would come to a corresponding conclusion.

§12.6: On enemies—Dorotheus

With a question proposed about a magnate, or two or three, or among peoples or enemies, which of them is stronger, one must consult the application of the Moon with the stars. For, that one to which the Moon applies, portends the first one about whom it was asked. Which if it were cadent, it wholly shows his cowardice and leads him to desperation, and denies [his] supports. Which if she would apply to a star after the pivots, or after an application of the first one, one observes the dignity of the next [person mentioned], but not his powers. Which if, after the first application, there is an application of her with a star in a pivot, it commends the power of the third one among all of these.

---

[10] This probably refers to whether the planets are in pivots or remote places, or else the meanings of the houses they are in.

§Z: WEATHER & DISASTERS

Z: Weather and disasters	
Predicting rains	§§Z.2-14
Disasters	§§Z.7, Z.9

Figure 74: Mundane questions on weather and disasters

§Z.1: On the corruption and detriment of things—'Umar[1]

The detriment and corruption of all matters is brought about in eight[2] ways. [1] Therefore, whenever the significator itself (of money, I say, or of any other affair) would apply to a star said to be mistrusted or ambiguous—or rather, should the Moon [apply] to it, whether the significator itself is of their number or not.[3] [2] A star is [also] said to be mistrusted [if] its application is of no account,[4] [or] it is either [3] retrograde, or [4] cadent, or [5] peregrine (namely, possessing no house or sovereignty or triplicity in that same place), or [6] it would be wholly hostile to the affair and its nature,[5] or [7] established outside a place[6] of dignity (but this is that it would have control over neither a bound or face),[7] or [8] it is unlucky, without a benevolent, [such as when] it is held, pressured between the two infortunes,[8] or [9] at least appears scorched, or [10] in a sign outside the ascensions of its own proper house (of which kind are [Jupiter in] Aries, and Pisces, whose arising is the same; likewise the ascension for [Venus in] Aquarius is the same as for Taurus): thus it seems that there is a common partnership of all [such signs].[9]

---

[1] Cf. al-Rijāl I.23, which I have used to clarify parts of the list below. It seems to me that this chapter properly belongs in the twelfth house, but I have put it here in accordance with Burnett's accounting of the chapters. For alternative lists, see *ITA* IV.3 and IV.4.1.
[2] According to my count, there are ten ways, which I have labeled below.
[3] I am not sure what this means. Al-Rijāl reads, "if the significator itself were in a place contrary to the matter itself, and applies itself to some planet, or that the Moon would be in such a status, or that the significator would not apply itself to some planet."
[4] According to al-Rijāl, this means it applies to no planet.
[5] This probably means something like an application to Saturn in matters of romance. But al-Rijāl has it in its own Node, or perhaps in the South Node of the Moon.
[6] Reading with al-Rijāl for "pivot."
[7] It seems strange to me that this would be listed apart from peregrination above.
[8] Also known as "besieged." See *ITA* IV.4.2.
[9] So, we prefer that a planet be in a sign with the same ascensions as one of its domiciles. See *ITA* I.9.5.

Comment by Dykes. The following passages present a variety of weather prediction methods, from understanding the general character of the year (also broken down into semesters and quarters and months), to the prediction of daily rains and winds (usually from specific applications and separations). The methods fall roughly into two groups: the 'Umar-al-Kindī group, and the Māshā'allāh group (since Dorotheus is actually drawn from Māshā'allāh's *Chap. Rains*).[10] Following are the chief features of the groups.

'Umar-al-Kindī group.

(1) For a general appraisal of the year as well as shorter periods, 'Umar and al-Kindī look at the assembly (or assembly and opposition) and individual ingresses. 'Umar looks at the angular planets in them and their natures and aspects, especially with the malefics (and what signs the malefics are in). Al-Kindī provides a variant, in which Saturn has indications for the whole year, but Jupiter for individual quarters at the relevant ingresses. Neither 'Umar nor al-Kindī explains the real distinction between the chart of the assembly and that of the ingress.

(2) 'Umar adds a Lot of rain, and another commentator has added a Lot of daily rains or winds.

(3) The "opening of the doors" and the "foundations/posts" of the Moon. The opening of the doors is a metaphor for opening up the heavens to let down rain. Astrologically, it refers to a relationship between an inferior planet and the superior planet which rules the signs opposite it (such as Mercury and Jupiter). 'Umar and al-Kindī speak both of the Moon separating from one and applying to the other, and the two planets themselves aspecting each other. The "foundations" or "posts" of the Moon are specific degrees relative to the New Moon (see diagram below), in much the same way that critical days in illness are measured from the place of the Moon at the time of someone taking to bed or asking a question (see §§6.19-23). Now, there seem to be two variations on this method, but the basic idea is this. At the New and Full Moons, cast the chart and identify the degrees of the foundations or posts. Then, look to see on what day the Moon is in each of them: if she is transferring between a pair of planets as described above, or if the lord of the Ascendant at the time of the New or Full Moon is joining with

---

[10] The sole section attributed to Jirjis (§Z.14) is a mixture of Māshā'allāh and generic considerations from many sources.

the lord of the seventh of that chart, then that period should have rain. So for instance, suppose that at the New Moon, Mercury was the lord of the Ascendant. If at one of the foundations, either the Moon transfers between Mercury and Jupiter (or a similar pair of planets), or Mercury himself is connecting with Jupiter, there should be rain.

Now, although the diagram of the foundations depicts the whole circle of a Lunar month, 'Umar instructs us to recalculate at every Full Moon as well. Why is that? It could be for the following reason. In critical days, the phase of the Moon is not important, because we only want to measure her position from the time of the decumbiture or the question. But this weather prediction method *is* sensitive to the Lunar phase, since it is calculated from the New and Full Moon. If you look at the diagram below, you will see that the foundations are distributed symmetrically around the circle, relative to the Moon's position at the New Moon and her idealized relations to the Sun. For example, there are foundations at 12° on either side of the Sun (where she goes under and leaves his rays), and at corresponding places on either side of the idealized opposition (at 168° and 192°). But these positions are not really accurate, because the Sun moves as well. So for example, when the Moon is at 180° on the diagram, she will not really be at the Full Moon yet, because the Sun himself will already have moved about 15°. Actually, because of the Sun's motion the Full Moon will occur almost on the next foundation, at 192°. Likewise, the Lunar month will not end when the Moon returns at 360°, but when she has gone about 28°-30° more and caught up with the Sun in the following sign. My sense is that the people who developed this method really wanted us to pay attention to the *actual* quarters and semi-quarters, and the *actual* positions at 12° on either side of the assembly and opposition, and that the list of degrees was only meant to illustrate that. 'Umar might have had this in mind when he instructs us to look at both the New and Full Moons, for if we recalculate the foundations every two weeks, the degree positions will not be as far off the actual Lunar phases, than if we used one set of foundations for the entire month.

Māshā'allāh group. In this group, the general appraisal of the year is similar to 'Umar and al-Kindī, but focuses on the lord of the Ascendant of the ingress, along with specific observations of individual planets. For the quarters and months and days, Māshā'allāh-Dorotheus emphasizes the inferior planets and the Moon, both by application and the signs they occupy.

All agree generally on: the chart of the Sun's ingress into 20° Scorpio, which must have been the location of a special Lunar mansion or fixed star in ancient times. All of the planets should be noted, but especially the inferior planets and the Moon, the lord of the Ascendant, the malefics in the angles, and the triplicity of the signs the malefics occupy.

Category	ʿUmar	Al-Kindī
Character of year, from ingresses	§Z.2	§Z.8
Lots of Rain/winds	§Z.2	
Weather from 20° ♏ ingress	§Z.3, §Z.6	
Opening doors & foundations of ☽	§§Z.4-5	§Z.8
Timing by lord of Ascendant of year	§Z.6	
Disasters by ingress and assembly	§Z.7	§Z.9
Timing by other means		§Z.8
General indications: signs & planets		§Z.8

Figure 75: Weather prediction in ʿUmar and al-Kindī

Category	Māshāʾallāh *Chap. Rains*	Dorotheus
Character of year, from ingress	§1	§Z.10
Weather from 20° ♏ ingress	§1	§Z.10
Individual planets	§1	§Z.10
Quarters of the year	§2	§Z.11
Months of the year	§3	§Z.12
Days of the year	§§4-5	§Z.13

Figure 76: Weather prediction in Māshāʾallāh and Dorotheus

§Z.2: On the quality of the air and the seasons—ʿUmar[11]

[General appraisal of extremes or balance]

And so, the judgment of this depends on the assembly or opposition,[12] even from the [Ascendant at the] Sun's entry into the first degree of Aries, and from the places of the lights (which ones they claim in the circle).

---

[11] For ʿUmar's material on weather in §§Z.2-6, I have relied on Burnett's critical edition of the Latin in Burnett 2000 (Appendix IVB), comparing it with his translation of the Arabic in the same place. For this section in particular, cf. al-Rijāl VIII.26.

Therefore, Saturn in any pivot of the east or rather in that of the eastern lord, holding onto some one of his dignities (particularly in the Midheaven), transforms and corrupts the atmosphere, stains with a harmful obscurity, and wholly converts it into the nature of another season; now, from the hot he generates [what is hot, and in a time of cold he generates][13] the coldest. Being drawn back from a pivot, all things are moderated through an evenness of status.[14] But with him being arranged in any of the pivots of the eastern lord[15] (as we have stated), it teaches that what was said is [made] a little bit more relaxed.

If however Mars himself would occupy the place of Saturn in the way which we have said, especially in the Midheaven, if the season is hot, it shows an increase of heat. But if [the season] were cold, it is necessary that it undergo cold. But with an evenness of the weather being discovered, it everywhere supplies a proper measure but goes rather to the side of heat.

Furthermore, while Jupiter or Venus or the Moon would undergo the places of the aforesaid (not otherwise than what had been said), they commend the evenness of the air and its proper mixture, [and] an increase is really lavished upon planting and sowing.

Moreover, Mercury being assembled in the Midheaven from the east [of the conjunction],[16] and in an airy sign, while he would possess a pivot which either of the infortunes [is also in], it disturbs the air, generates corruption, [and] multiplies the adversity of the winds. In this manner too, with any of the infortunes possessing a pivot of Mercury, while Mercury himself would occupy a fortunate pivot,[17] he works nothing else than what each infortune does in the sign of the assembly.

[General indications for weather]

Whenever, therefore, [a planet] would happen to be found in any of the pivots of the east of the assembly, or after [such a] pivot, it will deservedly

---

[12] The Arabic has only the assembly.
[13] Adding with the Ar.
[14] That is, he will have little or no effect.
[15] The Arabic has him in a pivot of the east, not its lord. Yet it seems to me that Hugo is probably right: a pivot of the eastern lord is not going to be as significant as a pivot of the east.
[16] That is, in the Midheaven. 'Umar might feel compelled to specify this because he also allows planets to be the pivots of the lord of the Ascendant.
[17] That is, the pivot of a fortunate planet.

take control of the role of the signification. One must even note whether it had any affinity of mixture with Saturn or Mars. Whenever therefore it would be reported as being in any bearing from a tetragon or opposition or assembly with Mars ([Mars] appearing in a fiery sign—but the fiery signs are Aries, Leo, [and] Sagittarius), with the season being hot, they confer an increase of heat. But if it were cold, it suggests the harm of coldness. But it being regarded from a trigon or hexagon, [and] in the same way Mars holding onto a fiery sign, it stirs up the aforesaid in a more modest way.

On the other hand, Saturn regarding the significator-star, being admixed [with it] in any way from the tetragon or opposition or assembly, while Saturn himself would hold onto a cold and dry or cold and moist sign, the coldness is augmented in a cold season; but it takes away from a hot one if the heat of the season prevailed. Now, if the significator itself would comply [with Saturn] from a trigon or hexagon in the aforesaid signs (in the way in which it was said), these things will be less. Then too, with Saturn appearing in a hot and moist sign, should the significator itself be admixed, from the opposition, I say, or the tetragon or assembly (as was already stated about a dry one), it shows the worthy and balanced blending of the air: and thus it manages the moderation [and] solace of the air, together with things sprouting [from the earth]. Also, an admixture made from a trigon or hexagon and in the same signs, is pretty much the same,[18] but it brings everything back to something better.

Furthermore, Mars himself being a partner with the significator (or it to him) in any bearing, within the cold and dry or cold and moist signs, while this admixture would be from a tetragon or opposition or assembly, it wholly calls back the airy nature (as we was already said) to evenness, lavishing a required increase upon planting and sowing.

[Lot of Rain]

And so, the testimonies of this Lot (which is said to belong to rain and the winds) resemble the significators written above. However, if either Saturn or Mars appeared as a partner to this or to its lord, no other judgment is given than if they were arranged in the pivots, even though they may be remote from their own proper houses. Therefore, this Lot, being taken up from Mercury (if he would be staying outside his own proper lodging-place) to the

---

[18] Lit., "not otherwise" (*non aliter*).

degree of the lord of his house, takes up the degrees of the east which are added. Therefore, the whole being drawn down from the east, where the number is ended, it testifies that his Lot really falls there.[19] Moreover, with Mercury being established in his own house, [take his degree and minute, and][20] the degrees of the east will have to be applied. Therefore, if the number of the whole collection is taken down from the east, by its termination it suggests the place of the Lot already stated.[21] Even the entrance of the Sun through the quarters of the circle demands that it come to be in no other way; even just as with him entering the individual signs, a not-dissimilar observation will be present.[22]

[A Lot of daily rains or winds]

Moreover, the matter warns that we should insert another Lot handed down from the Babylonian Abū Ma'shar (overlooked by 'Umar).[23] And so, they say this Lot is one of days, being taken up from the degree of the Sun to the degree of Saturn, we throw it down from the Lunar degree around the rising of the Sun on individual days.[24] If therefore Mercury regarded it, or rather should he be in there with it, it is necessary that winds be prepared on that day, and stronger ones with the Moon accompanying [the Lot], especially if Venus appeared as a partner to them. In this way too, [see if at this time] the Moon is arranged at first point of any sign:[25] for that one which will support her with its own aspect, deservedly claims the office of signification for the investigation of matters of this kind.

---

[19] In other words, if Mercury is not in his own domicile, measure from Mercury to his domicile lord, and project from the Ascendant.
[20] Reading with the Ar. for Hugo's *ab eiusdem puncto et gradu parti assumptae*.
[21] This seems to mean that if Mercury is in his own domicile, then take the number of degrees which he has traveled in that same sign, and add it to the east.
[22] In other words, calculate this Lot for all of the Sun's ingresses.
[23] This last paragraph was evidently added to the Arabic by someone else, since Abū Ma'shar was still a young man when 'Umar died.
[24] That is, from the Sun to Saturn, and projected from the Moon—but calculated on a daily basis at sunrise.
[25] Slightly altering the sentence according to the Arabic, and omitting Hugo's "follows by night." Hugo evidently thought one should calculate the Lot at sunset and examine the Moon.

§Z.3: On rain and lightning and thunder and wind—'Umar[26]

Therefore, the Sun entering the twentieth[27] degree of Scorpio (and even [to the] minute), presents the greatest notification of heavy rains, thunder, lightning, and winds. Therefore, with the east being established at that hour, the pivots must be established in order and the arrangement of the stars must be applied. Finally too, it is reasonable to attend to Venus, Jupiter, [and] Mercury. Whenever therefore these three were western or slow or retrograde, they bring in dews and multiply heavy rains in that year. But being eastern or direct or adding in course,[28] they portend the contrary.

However, Mars being in any pivot (especially in the Midheaven), in airy signs, invested by Mercury, designates many thunderings, flashings of light, and harmful [but] inconstant heavy rains, even multiplying locusts [and] the corruption of the air. Moreover, with him being in the pivot of the earth and in an earthy sign, with the fortunate ones being cadent from him, while Mercury would invest him, it declares an earthquake, produces fires from the earth, greatly increases terrors and disturbances, [and] corrupts minerals and sulphurs of the earth. But he being in a fiery sign and in the pivot of the earth (in the way it was said) generates conflagrations, [and] burns up whatever is earthy (minerals, I say, and crops).[29] Furthermore, Mars being arranged in watery signs and in the pivot of the earth (as has already been said), portends the defects of waters and their diminution, and threatens detriment to all watery things (both the animate and everything else). He being invested with the fortunate ones, or if they should apply to him, indicates that the adversity of both thunder and lightning in that year will be [only] moderately harmful. Which if he would be bereft of each, so that he would neither be invested by the fortunate ones, nor would they apply to him, it makes all of these harmful and multiplies the lightning.

Therefore, with Saturn occupying the place of Mars (especially in the Midheaven) and in airy signs, while Mercury would invest him, with the fortunate ones being cadent from [Saturn], it is a sign of obscurity and corruption [in the air], for it signifies continuous and harmful rains. Likewise, Saturn being in earthy signs and in the pivot of the earth, moreover being invested by Mercury, in aversion to the fortunate ones, renews earthquakes

---

[26] Cf. al-Rijāl VIII.27.
[27] Reading with the Arabic and other texts for Hugo's "tenth."
[28] That is, moving faster than average.
[29] The Arabic adds that crops will be harmed because of mildew.

and from the earth it brings forth the blackest waters and what is of this type. On the other hand, being in watery [signs] and in the pivot of the earth, with the fortunate ones being in aversion, while Mercury would invest him, it dries out the waters of wells, [and] bears harm to all watery things (of whatever kind they may be). Occupying fiery signs and the pivot of the earth, under the investiture of Mercury, with the fortunate ones being cadent from him, it corrupts the sulphurs of the earth and what is of this kind, [and precious stones].[30] Which if the Mercurial benignness is absent, it is necessary that all of these things be a little bit more relaxed. Furthermore, if neither the cadence nor perversity of the fortunate ones is there,[31] it completely calls back whatever has been said to an evenness of moderation in that year.

Finally,[32] here one must generally note that the superior stars, jointly with the inferior ones, are described in terms of the general renewal of things, with the Sun appearing as a judge and teacher in the middle, as though with a chain of some bearing. For the superior ones fulfill the role of souls, but the inferior ones that of bodies, while for every generation which happens in the world, the moderation of their application is necessary, as though through a certain maternal rearing.[33]

§Z.4: On the hour of rain and winds, heat and cold—'Umar[34]

A timely observation of heavy rains, winds, even heat and cold, could be discovered by this method. For, the Lunar withdrawal from Venus and application with Mars (or if she would be separated from Mars and apply to Venus), unlocks the cataracts [of heaven]. Which if she would withdraw from Jupiter, applying to Mercury, or rather being separated from Mercury should she proceed to Jupiter, this likewise opens the portal. Furthermore, applying only to Saturn while she withdraws from none, or if [her] withdrawal from that greater one would be granted, the cataract is loosened. I even believe this should be paid attention to: to the extent that the aforewritten are bear-

---

[30] Reading with the Arabic for what seems to be "what is less than a proper mineral" (*infra propriam mineriam*). Could this relate to the prices of precious metals?
[31] That is, if the benevolent planets *do* regard him and they are *not* in a poor condition.
[32] This seems to be a reference to the opening of the doors in §Z.4 and §Z.8.
[33] Hugo's paragraph is more elaborate and evocative than the Arabic. The Arabic says that each superior planet is bonded to an inferior planet in the position of soul to body, and that things on earth only exist according to their mixtures.
[34] Cf. al-Rijāl VIII.28.

ing themselves thusly, and the Moon is arranged in the places of foundation[35] (namely, those secured in a uniform way), it bears a certain[36] signification of heavy rains or winds, likewise of heat or cold. Which if she possessed a moist place, applying to a moist star, even though there is no opening of the portal in that place, still [you should] undoubtedly expect rains.

§Z.5: On the places of the foundations[37]—'Umar[38]

And so, whenever the Moon occupies the same point with the Sun, she is said to possess a certain one of the places which they call a "foundation" in the Persian language. Moreover, whenever the distance between each were one of 12°, this is called a foundation. Now if they were distant by 45°, this again is allotted the word "foundation." But if she preceded the Sun by 90° or 135° or 168°,[39] or even 180°, it is really necessary that she be undergoing places of foundations. And this last place is one which unties the knot. Moreover, she going before the Sun by [192° or][40] 225° or 270° ([which] indicates the second half-phase).[41] Now, if she would precede by 315° [or 348°][42] this [last] place of a foundation ties the knot.

If therefore any of the portals had to be opened, first of all one must arrange the east of the assembly or the opposition.[43] [Then look at the lord of the seventh sign from the assembly or opposition.][44] Then too, [see] whether there is an [application between the lord of the east and the lord of the opposite sign], or there is a returning[45] there, or there is a reception or one who would collect the lights, or the Moon [is in the places of the openings]: in its

---

[35] *Atteciz.* See §Z.5 below.
[36] Reading *certam* for *certa.*
[37] Lat. *atteciz,* a transliteration for the Arabic *ta'sis,* itself originally a Persian transliteration of the Gr. *phasis* or "phase." These are the twelve phases of the Moon described as "posts" by al-Kindī in §Z.8 below.
[38] Cf. al-Rijāl VIII.29.
[39] Reading with the Arabic for Hugo's "100° or 170°."
[40] Adding with the Arabic.
[41] That is, when she is half-full during the third quarter. Hugo's Latin uses *atteciz* but the Arabic indicates the half-phase, so I have used that here.
[42] Adding with the Arabic.
[43] That is, the Ascendant at the time of the Full or New Moon.
[44] Adding based on the Arabic, here and in the other brackets of this paragraph.
[45] I am following the Arabic, but "returning" is a specific condition which indicates a failed application (*ITA* III.19). Actually I have a feeling that this should really be understood simply as a transfer of light between these lords.

own time it denotes useful and fruitful rain. With Venus, I say, and Mercury being western or retrograde or slow, or rather should one or two of the superiors be retrograde or slow, they undoubtedly promise rain.

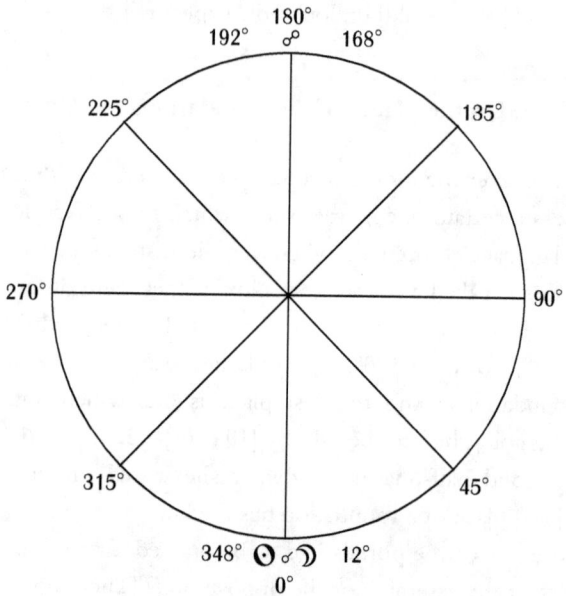

Figure 77: The twelve "posts" (al-Kindī §Z.8) or "foundations" ('Umar §Z.5) of the Moon

§Z.6: On the hour of rain—'Umar[46]

And so, the significator and minister of rains[47] is in need of the greatest consideration, as to whether it would possess a pivot [of the Ascendant in the chart], whenever the opinion stated above shows that future heavy rains are foreknown—namely, when the Sun enters the twentieth degree and minute of Scorpio. No less indeed [if at the same time it would aspect] the stars which designate many rains in that same year, whether they are received [by it] or not. For while they bear themselves thusly, [and the Moon forms an

---

[46] Cf. al-Rijāl VIII.30.
[47] According to the Arabic, this is the lord of the Ascendant of the year.

assembly or tetragon or receives it],[48] they introduce heavy rains; but [if not received, there will still be rains but] not harsh ones. Even in the aforesaid hour—namely in which they demand that it be in a pivot—if an assembly of the Moon with it is not absent, [that time] will abound in earthquakes and thunder and flashings of lightning.

§Z.7: On pestilence, war, submersions, conflagration, and earthquake—'Umar[49]

However, in the resolution [of a question] of this kind, it must be noted that the Moon (namely, the victor) being blotted out,[50] and with [the luminaries] being established in the twelfth but a watery [sign],[51] while however they would apply to infortunes appearing under the earth, they portend that plague or earthquake will descend in that same region on that same day; no less, too [if they are] cadent and after the meridian, if there is an application to a cadent infortune under the earth:[52] it signifies the drowning of two men[53] on that same day. Moreover, the Moon being blotted out, applying to an unfortunate one under the earth, and in a fiery sign, threatens a conflagration in two places in that same hour and that same region, namely if the two lights would possess the twelfth or the ninth. If however [it were] in the twelfth, they afflict the beginning of the day with the aforesaid troubles; but occupying the ninth, the end of the day. Moreover, if she would be blotted out in the evening [and doing the same thing], it warns us to beware of these in that hour.

Likewise, the Moon being blotted out and descending in the south and in the circle (traversing in Libra, I say, or Scorpio),[54] decreasing in both light and computation (she is decreased in number [or computation] whenever she would proceed less than her average course by day and night), should she

---

[48] Based on al-Rijāl, this is the significator of rains above. But I think that by "receives," 'Umar might mean "by opposition" (which is one meaning of the Arabic), as with Māshā'allāh in his *Chap. Rains* §3 (attributed to Dorotheus in §Z.12 below).
[49] Cf. al-Rijāl VIII.32.
[50] *Deleta*. That is, being at the New Moon, as al-Rijāl makes clear.
[51] Al-Rijāl omits this, but it makes sense for the prediction below. Probably the infortune is supposed to be in a watery sign, not the luminaries.
[52] Or perhaps, "to infortunes falling under the earth."
[53] I am not sure where Hugo is getting his statements about two men here, or two places below.
[54] In these signs, the Moon is entering southern declination.

even be deprived of the aspect of the fortunate ones [while undergoing these misfortunes], it testifies that it threatens a conflagration or any kind of plague or earthquake to that same city: therefore one should not stay in that place, because the corruption will slip over to many regions.

Moreover, I believe this must be paid attention to: because the assembly of each infortune with the Tail in Aries, corrupts flock-animals and is hostile to princes and aristocrats,[55] and in this manner according to the order and position of the signs. And so, the proper quality of the signs by position is wholly necessary. For the first [sign], Aries, [is] eastern; Leo is the middle one, Sagittarius the last[56] of each.[57] Moreover, Gemini is the first western one, and [thus] its triplicity. Likewise, Cancer [and its triplicity are northern. Capricorn] is the first southern one, from which its triplicity differs in nothing [from what we said].

Therefore, once the Sun's entrance into Aries is discovered, the star which is found to be eastern [or is going to be eastern more quickly],[58] deservedly claims the signification of the year. Therefore, Jupiter being eastern will recall all things to a healthful, and the best, status. But a signification of Venus multiplies produce, fertilizes all things, [and] makes an abundance of provisions. Also, Mercury brings back all things to a [proper] measure.[59] Saturn indicates[60] evil and the raging of all trouble, a scarcity of provisions, and excessive cold. But Mars embraces the sword and wars, disgrace and fear, and what is of this type.

Nor should one desist from this kind of observation whenever the Sun hastens to enter the four individual quarters[61] of the year. But that star which was eastern is principally allotted the signification of the quarter itself; and first, one must always note the status or application of the Sun and Moon [to each other, and which of them is the lord of the time],[62] and everywhere one must judge according to the condition of the stars.

---

[55] The fiery signs are also called the "royal" signs.
[56] Reading *posterior* for *potior* ("preferable, stronger").
[57] Al-Rijāl makes these pertain to eastern regions: the beginning, middle, and last part of the east (and likewise with the other triplicities).
[58] Adding the phrase in brackets based on al-Rijāl. ʿUmar must mean the planet which will rise out of the Sun's rays first, while in direct motion.
[59] Reading *ad modum* for *admodum*. Al-Rijāl reads, "the year will be in the middle."
[60] Reading *indicat* for *respondet*.
[61] That is, the quarters of the zodiac (Aries, Cancer, Libra, Capricorn).
[62] Adding with al-Rijāl. I am not sure if this refers to the sect of the chart, or if ʿUmar is assigning the Sun to one part of the month, and the Moon to another.

§Z.8: On the quality of the air through individual years—al-Kindī

§669. For a complete recognition of those things in the atmosphere which are renewed[63] through individual years, it is good that the Ascendant of the assembly or opposition[64] which came before the Sun's ingress into the beginning of Aries, be established. Therefore, whatever sign Saturn claimed in that hour, the year seems to imitate its nature: for a hot one means heat; cold, cold; dry, aridness; moist, moistening.

§670. Moreover, when the Sun enters the individual quarters or seasons of the year,[65] Jupiter comes to be noted: one will have to judge about him in that same quarter of the year, in the way it was stated above [about Saturn]. But the consideration that is made of the signification of a quarter, and the signification of the year, will exhibit the truth in revealing the judgment.[66]

§671. Moreover you will note [1] with whom the application of the lord of the assembly or opposition[67] (preceding the beginning of the year or quarter) comes to be. For the sharing [of indications] that is made of that star (just as was stated above) lays bare what will be.

§672. Moreover, with no less attention should you care [2] with whom the application of the lord of the Ascendant of[68] the assembly, or [3] of the lord of the Ascendant of the year, comes to be. For once a discernment of all of them is had, they suggest what must be said. Moreover, [4] the lords of the assembly and opposition in every month should be noted. In this way, let there be a report about those future things which are imminent.

§673. In addition, if the significator and giver of hail (or heavy rains or dryness) is regarding the [Sun or Moon at the][69] assembly or opposition of the month or year—the Sun for planets of the year, but the Moon for the planets of the year and the months[70]—it signifies that those things which

---

[63] Hugo means the revolution or cycle of years: the Sun's return to Aries every spring.
[64] The Ar. has only the assembly/conjunction.
[65] That is, his ingresses into the other movable signs: Cancer, Libra, Capricorn.
[66] That is, by combining the indications. Burnett's translation of the Ar. makes it seem that we should also look at Saturn at every quarterly ingress, but to me the sense is that Saturn is for the year as a whole, and Jupiter for the quarters. Certainly Robert and Hugo read it that way.
[67] Again, the Ar. has only the assembly/conjunction.
[68] Adding with Robert and the Ar.
[69] Adding with Robert and the Ar.
[70] Adding with Robert and the Ar. The sense seems to be that planets examined at the beginning of the year (Saturn, planets at the annual assembly just before the ingress) should aspect the Sun, but any of them may aspect the Moon when looking especially at

follow its nature are imminent—especially [if] placed in a bound or house of its complexion.[71]

[Individual planets' indications]

§674. And so it seems one must note that Venus principally signifies wetness, Mercury stirs up winds, Saturn multiplies clouds and the darkness of the air, and hail, Mars incites the southern winds [and heat] (but especially in Capricorn [or its pivots]);[72] moreover Jupiter in a house of some authority of his own (but especially in Cancer) sends in the northern winds. The Sun introduces heat and dryness.

[The posts[73] of the Moon, the opening of the doors]

§675. Moreover, let the [Ascendant of every assembly of the Sun and Moon][74] be principally established. But no less will you note, with the equal attention of your mind, [the following] twelve points, for they are these: the assembly, opposition, the two squares (namely the tetragons), and the cross-quarters of the tetragons, the 12° before the completion of the assembly and opposition, [and] the same amount after their completion.

§676. Therefore, when the Moon is found in any of these, if any of the inferiors would apply to a superior by an opposition,[75] it testifies that what is in agreement with its nature will happen, if a common regard of the Sun and

---

monthly times. But this does not really make sense, since by definition any planet aspecting one luminary at the New or Full Moon will also be aspecting the other.

[71] Reading with Robert (Ar.: "according to its nature"). Hugo reads, "in agreement with the nature of the one to which it applies," but in this paragraph we are not considering applications.

[72] Adding bracketed material with the Ar.

[73] Ar. *marākiz*, which comes from a verb (*rakaza*) very similar to the Arabic (*watada*) and Greek (*kenteô*) verbs used to derive the words for the pivots or angles: "to ram into the ground, set up a pole, position or fix firmly." Burnett plausibly translates it as "centers," but I do not believe this really captures the sense of a firm position, or point of concentration, so I have used the English "posts," in the sense both of a pole and an organizational position or rank (these are also acceptable readings in the Arabic dictionary).

[74] Adding based on the Arabic.

[75] The Ar. reads as though any inferior can apply to any superior, but al-Kindī is describing the "opening of the doors/portals," in which an inferior must apply to the superior planet which rules the domicile opposite its domicile: Mercury to Jupiter, Venus to Mars, and the luminaries to Saturn. Here, al-Kindī says the *aspect* must be an opposition. Cf. 'Umar in §Z.4-5.

Moon would be present, and if the Ascendant of the region or city does not lack their regard,[76] [and] even should they be supported by a regard of their own lords.

§677. In addition, if the Moon would advance and apply from some inferior to the superior opposite it,[77] both as mediator and key-bearer, it indubitably forces the natural [qualities] of its superior to come about. Which if this administration is ascribed to Mercury, in addition to heavy rains he begets winds; and if to Venus, it multiplies rain clouds; and if to Saturn, it sends down hail, covers the atmosphere, and prolongs [destruction],[78] putting clouds over clouds. Moreover, the Moon brings about a multitude of rain clouds. Finally, in the same way the Sun taints the atmosphere alternately: now with fire, now with clouds.[79]

§678. The significators (or [especially][80] the Moon) being individually in the regard of Mars, stir up thunder and send down lightning strikes. Moreover, Saturn as the author of this administration, even [indicates cold and][81] overturns buildings. [The judgment must be made analogously for all qualities.][82]

[Other indicators]

§679. Furthermore, the moistening places of the circle seem to be worthy of consideration, because they multiply waters.[83] Moreover, the retrogradation of significators furnishes an overflowing of waters.

§680. And[84] this happens at the hour of the Moon's separation from an indicator of [rain], and likewise at the hour of the inferiors' departure from

---

[76] This may mean the Ascendant of the founding of a city or country. In modern times we have assumed Ascendants for the formal establishments of nations, but how could medievals have known this for virtually any city or nation besides Baghdad (whose founding was determined by an electional chart)? Perhaps it could include the annual Ascendant of the year at the Aries ingress, or some other epochal Ascendant.
[77] The Ar. only says that the Moon is applying to an inferior planet. But this is identical to 'Umar's intention in §Z.4.
[78] Adding with the Ar.
[79] Ar.: "air, and darkness."
[80] Adding with the Ar.
[81] Adding based on Robert and the Ar.
[82] Adding with Robert, mirroring the Ar.
[83] Apparently, if significators are in them. There are several versions of these places (see Burnett and Bos 2000, Table III). Al-Kindī's two *Letters* on this topic mainly agree on Cancer, Scorpio, Pisces, and add Leo, Aquarius, and Capricorn (or the end of Capricorn). See also Jirjis §Z.14 below.

the superior significators. [By separating from an indicator, it means] the Lunar departure from the four principal [posts],[85] which tends to alternate and vary any quality of the air [from one] to another. The Sun's [standing] there [does] likewise, but more powerfully so the Moon.

§681.[86] Furthermore, the rest of the stars imitate the Sun in this, but not so manifestly nor with such effectiveness. For example, they operate their own effects in their own orbits [of the apogee and perigee] and the rest of their own places, just as the Sun does in corresponding places, even though they do it more secretly and known to fewer.

§682. Finally, a studious reader should not neglect to scrutinize this attentively: any [star] traversing in north [latitude] seems to enlarge the effects of its own peculiar signification and indication; also, in the south [it is] weaker. Moreover, ascending into the north is more powerful than if it is descending in the [north]. But declining in the south [is] more slack than if its ascent in [the south] would be happening.

§Z.9: On years of pestilence and good health—al-Kindī[87]

§683. First of all, with the Ascendant of the year being placed, then too will follow an awareness of the Ascendant of the assembly or opposition which precedes the Sun's ingress into Aries. And so, let those Ascendants and the Moon be made clean of the infortunes, and no less should the lord of the assembly or opposition appear free [of them]. An application of [that lord] having been made with fortunate ones, or that same [lord] being in the regard of the Sun and Moon (or at least the one which obtains the shift), introduces a healthful year and one without disease.

§684. Moreover, the lords of the [two] Ascendants, and the Moon, and also the lord of the assembly or opposition (or the majority of them), being unfortunate and unlucky, convey the pestilence of disease, and this is agreed[88] to happen according to the manner and harshness of the corrupting

---

[84] This paragraph is a *pastiche* of Robert, Hugo, and the Arabic. The Arabic, however, does not speak of the inferior planets separating, but only that the Moon's departure from the four principal quarters indicates changes in weather.
[85] That is, at the Lunar quarters.
[86] Reading this paragraph with Robert.
[87] Cf. al-Rijāl VIII.31.1.
[88] Reading *constat* for *constans*.

[planet], and the nature of the infortune, and the place in which the corruption comes to be.

§685. Which if there would be an application of those which rule the Ascendants, and of the Moon (the aforesaid infortune having been observed), with the lord of their eighth,[89] a plague is designated which will kill many. But if it happened otherwise, [it will kill] very few. Which if a manifold disease[90] is present, still it will oppress few.

§686.[91] Furthermore, these significators (or one of them), retreating from scorching, and applying with the lord of its own eighth, introduces a sudden kind of ruin but without disease. But if any lord of them would apply with it, once a signification of disease would already be had, the slowness of its natural course multiplies the disease and renders it long-lasting; but the quickness[92] of [its] course removes the steadiness of its long-lastingness.

[al-Rijāl VIII.31.1]: On the other hand, if the planet which was more strengthened among all of these significators, applied to the lord of its own eighth house, many sudden deaths will happen, without any long sickness. If even the lord of the sixth house of any of these significators would apply to that significator, there will be diseases among the people, with long infirmities. But if the significators applied to the lords of their own sixth [houses], the infirmities will not be long.

§687. Which if this corruption would proceed from Mars, it generates acute diseases, particularly [assuming] the quickness of his course, [and] he even being strong and dwelling in a hot and dry sign. But Saturn arriving as the corruptor, indicates the steadiness of the disease, particularly [with him being] slow, strong, and arranged in a cold and dry sign.

---

[89] That is, of the lords with the eighth from that Ascendant, or of the Moon with the eighth from her own position. See a similar treatment in §692 below, and §403.
[90] Robert: "much and difficult." Al-Kindī could mean a serious illness that kills few, or perhaps many diseases that kill few.
[91] I have added the version from al-Rijāl below, because it departs so radically from Hugo's version.
[92] Reading *celeritas* for *caelestis*.

§Z.10: On heavy rains—Dorotheus[93]

Moreover, of the Arabs, a certain most experienced astrologer, Abū ʿAli [al-Khayyāt], claims thusly with respect to the inundation (or rather lack) of rains through the whole year. Whenever (he says) you were eager to know whether at the beginning of the year there would be many rains, [and] at the end fewer, or the other way around, it is necessary to attend to what place Venus is holding onto once the Sun's ingress into Scorpio is discovered. For, she being eastern declares many heavy rains in the beginning of the year, [but] at the end, few; being western, the contrary. She even being conjoined to the Sun in the same sign, [means that] the beginnings of the year and month in which they assemble, pour down with heavy rains.

[To know more, see when the Sun][94] enters the beginning of Aries: once the east is established, and the rest of the pivots are made firm, [see] what star claimed the rulership of the bound of the eastern [lord], and this one manages the benefits of rains through the whole year.[95]

And so, an application by assembly of Venus and Mercury and the Moon (or a portion of [them]) with that same [lord of the bound of the eastern lord], while these three stars would be staying in watery signs,[96] [and] the Moon applying to one of them while she applies to none of the two [infortunes], it multiplies heavy rains. Mercury even, being corrupted by Mars or being under scorching, and the Moon applying to [Mercury], introduces few rains in the first [part of the year], many in the middle—not however, without lightning and thunder and the corruption of the air. Moreover, rains become rare in that year whenever the Moon were with Mars, or Venus would apply to [him], or perhaps she is scorched.

---

[93] From §§Z.10-13, the sections attributed to Dorotheus are essentially identical to all of Māshāʾallāh's *Chap. Rains*, which is translated in *WSM*. Note that these sections are formally attributed to Dorotheus, but mirror Māshāʾallāh, and are attributed in the first paragraph to al-Khayyāt, once again emphasizing the close relationship between these texts. For §Z.10 in particular, cf. *Chap. Rains* §1.

[94] Reading with Māshāʾallāh for Hugo's misleading "Which if it happened otherwise with respect to Venus…".

[95] There is ambiguity among the texts as to which lord is meant here. Hugo speaks of the bound lord here, but later uses the domicile lord; likewise, Māshāʾallāh begins with the domicile lord (or perhaps the best relevant lord), and then switches to the bound lord.

[96] Māshāʾallāh has the lord of the Ascendant connecting in any way with Venus or Mercury, and the Ascendant in a watery sign.

Likewise, once the Moon is with the Sun or Mars,[97] and if Mercury would apply to Saturn, and the Moon would apply to either [Mercury or Saturn], rains will abound at the beginning of the year; but without that, they are diminished, with a density of clouds being made and the air being corrupted.

Now, with Jupiter in a watery sign, while Venus and the Moon would apply to him, one expects many but healthful rains in that year. Likewise, with him occupying a fiery sign, and should there be an application of Mars with him, the heavy rains will be few.

In addition, the eastern lord (who rejoices in the rulership of rains that whole year), in a pivot, applying to fortunate ones,[98] renders the whole year rainy. Now, it being corrupted by Mars, holding onto the same sign with him, while however the Moon would apply to Mars, it will pour with many clouds and few heavy rains. Likewise, the sign in which they are assembling being an airy one, and the Moon applying to him thus, multiplies dew and clouds.

Which if Mercury would enjoy the rulership of heavy rains, and he is corrupted, it declares severe and many rains in that same year, and the corruption is generated from winds and clouds.[99]

If however this [ruler] were Jupiter, however much he may be corrupted, even though [rains] are few, there will be no corruption of the air.

However, Venus claiming this dignity[100] and with Mars, [she] being unlucky or scorched, [this] star greatly increases clouds and dew, [but] without heavy rains.[101]

Likewise, Mars being in possession of that dignity, brings in few rains, fewer dews.

In the same way Saturn, although he moistens with few heavy rains, he frequently will mingle in clouds. Traversing in a watery sign, he will apply some rains. In addition, the benevolence of the aforewritten lord approves of rains.

Also, it is necessary to attend with some industry to Venus, Mercury, and the Moon, and their aforewritten effects. Moreover, their mutual application multiplies or takes away from dew, with the Lunar application with the for-

---

[97] Māshā'allāh omits Mars.
[98] This phrase could also be read as, "applying to fortunate ones in a pivot." This seems to be more in line with Māshā'allāh, but *Chap. Rains* has a lacuna precisely in the middle of this phrase.
[99] For Māshā'allāh, the corruption comes from winds and clouds, and from moisture *other than* rain.
[100] That is, if she were the special weather significator (and so on with the rest below).
[101] Reading *imbribus* for *imbrium*.

tunate ones and the infortunes being discovered.[102] The blocking of heavy rains proceeds from Mars and the Sun and Saturn. But Saturn introduces rains in watery [signs].

§Z.11: On rains throughout the quarters of the year—Dorotheus[103]

And so, once the Sun has entered the first point of [Cancer and][104] Libra and Capricorn, let the east be established. It is no less necessary too, that the places of the stars be examined thoroughly. They having been examined carefully with diligent observation, and it must be noted with an ever-watchful mind if there is an application of Venus and Mercury and the Moon, (but even the place of Mars and the one to which he applies). For the veiling of clouds, and the benefit of dew, and the manner of rains, could be discovered according to the joint application of the stars, just as was said about the beginning of the year.

§Z.12: On the knowledge of heavy rains through individual months—Dorotheus[105]

If however an inquirer worried about the knowledge of heavy rains through individual months would approach [you], it is necessary that the east be established at the hour of the assembly and opposition of the Sun and Moon, and that the places of the stars, and also the Lunar application with the rest, be scrutinized attentively.

For, with [the Moon] applying to Venus or Mercury, this will be rainy. Then, for greater evidence of this matter, one must note: the Moon entering a pivot, applying to Venus and Mercury, introduces rains on that day, unless perhaps at its beginning an application were made with Mars. Which if you judge that it has happened differently, it greatly increases lightning and thunder, but declares few heavy rains, unless perhaps the Moon would be in [his] opposition.

---

[102] This means that the application (or not) with fortunes and infortunes is a key indicator of having rains or not.
[103] Cf. *Chap. Rains* §2.
[104] Added by Dykes.
[105] Cf. *Chap. Rains* §3.

Which if the Moon, withdrawing from the Sun in the first part of the month, would apply to fortunate ones, it pours out not-moderate heavy rains. It is not otherwise around the opposition, with [its] east being established: the Moon applying to fortunate ones while she withdraws from the opposition [with the Sun], will fill up the other part of the month with copious heavy rains. Moreover, she being with Venus at the assembly or opposition, applying to a Saturn that is holding onto a watery sign, these two places will abound in many heavy rains, unless perhaps he would be lingering in a fiery sign.

Likewise, the application of Mars with Saturn [in the above situation][106] multiplies clouds and winds, takes away from heavy rains and corrupts the atmospheres.

Moreover, Mercury applying to Venus at the hour of the assembly or opposition, will rejoice in an inundation of rains.

§Z.13: On daily heavy rains—Dorotheus[107]

Moreover, the Lunar progress through the individual signs could reveal daily heavy rains. Therefore, her entrance into the pivots, [while she has] her application with Venus and Mercury, or [with] that of the rest of the stars [which she had connected to] when she crossed the assembly[108] or its opposite, should not flee recognition. In fact, she entering the watery signs and applying to the stars stated above, generates rain on that day. For greater evidence of this matter, it is necessary to know the watery signs. [Know that the rainy signs are Scorpio, Cancer, Aquarius, and Pisces.][109] Of a moist nature, even, are Venus, Mercury, and the Moon, but Venus and the Moon are more expressly friendly to heavy rains than Mercury is. And so, Venus holding onto any of these signs, and the Moon applying [to her] in that same place, signifies heavy rains. Likewise, Venus with Mercury in the watery signs and moreover the Moon, but [the Moon] applying to either of them at the end of a sign, although it professes many heavy rains, still they will be fewer than at the beginning [of the sign]. Moreover, the Moon with Venus in wa-

---

[106] Adding based on Māshā'allāh.
[107] Cf. *Chap. Rains* §§4-5.
[108] *Alestima*, a transliteration of the Ar. *al-ijtimāʿ*, "assembly." That is, the New Moon.
[109] Adding from *Chap. Rains* §5.

tery signs ([but] not Mercury), the same. The Moon with Mercury in the same place, with Venus being removed [from the rainy signs], it is not otherwise.

Furthermore, the Moon in any of these signs, applying to Venus and Mercury, while they hold onto signs of rain, they denote a steadiness of rains, up until the Moon would withdraw from them. Likewise, Venus, Mercury, and the Moon not applying to malevolents nor being conjoined to them, introduce rains on that day. For, applying or conjoined [to malevolents], they deny [rains].

Venus being placed with the Sun,[110] while each is being joined to Mercury and the Moon, they abound in heavy rains on that day. Mercury or Venus occupying Capricorn, and the Moon in Taurus or Scorpio[111] or Pisces, [indicate] the same.

Likewise,[112] the Moon in Taurus or Virgo,[113] applying to Venus and Mercury from the opposition,[114] it is the same, especially while the Moon would be staying with the Tail in Taurus, and would be withdrawing from Saturn, or Venus with her, [and] with Mars in Aquarius and Mercury in Pisces or Capricorn, the atmosphere is honored with heavy rains on that day.

Nor[115] even do I think it must be overlooked that while stars cross over from sign to sign, threatening rain, one must determine the east of that hour most exactly. For if it were a watery sign, it designates rains, and it is better with the Moon possessing a sign of that kind. Whichever star the Moon will apply to, even manages a signification of rains. Whence it seems one must note the Moon and the applying star,[116] and the one to which she applies, in order that someone would be able to discover the days and even the hours of imminent rain, without the blemish of complete error. For whenever the Moon would reach the star to which she applies, it means an inundation of rains. Moreover, Venus and Mercury, whenever each or either one would possess a watery sign, and the Moon would be adjoined to them, it greatly

---

[110] This makes more sense than Māshā'allāh, who repeats the relation to Mercury and the Moon.
[111] Māshā'allāh reads, "Cancer."
[112] Omitting Hugo's restatement of Mercury and Venus being in Capricorn, as Māshā'allāh omits it for this sentence.
[113] Māshā'allāh adds, "or Capricorn."
[114] Māshā'allāh seems to say, "reception," but Arabic is ambiguous as to oppositions and receptions. Hugo is probably right here.
[115] The rest of this section is not in *Chap. Rains*, and may reflect extra comments by al-Khayyāt or "Dorotheus."
[116] This might be added mistakenly by Hugo.

increases rains, unless perhaps they would linger in the regard or conjunction of a malevolent.

Furthermore,[117] the Moon entering Cancer[118] at the hour of the Sun, Virgo at the hour of Venus, Sagittarius at the hour of Mercury, Taurus at the hour of Mars, but entering Libra and Leo at the hour of Jupiter,[119] is believed to signify heavy rains everywhere, but even winds and lightning. But her entrance into Aquarius and Pisces at any hour throws the air into confusion and wholly perverts that.

§Z.14: On rains—Jirjis[120]

Therefore, whenever the Sun enters a turning sign,[121] Venus being in a watery sign, regarded by a Moon that is traversing outside a watery one, it suggests moderate rainstorms at that time. But [the Moon] regarding from a watery sign portends their excess.

Or otherwise: with the Sun wandering through the eighteenth[122] degree of Scorpio, Venus in watery [signs], generates rains to the level of flooding.[123] She appearing in a moist sign, middling [rains]; in a dry one, moderate ones. Moreover, the Moon dropping off from Mars means rains on that day, especially in a watery sign. But through individual days, the determination will be through the signs which are devoted to rainstorms (but they are Cancer, Scorpio, Aquarius and Leo, especially Aquarius and Leo).

Moreover, the stars significative of rains are Venus, Mercury, and the Moon (especially Venus and Mercury. Venus occupying any of the aforesaid [signs],[124] while she lingers at the end or middle of the sign, moreover should the Moon apply to Venus while [the Moon is] crossing through watery signs, it means an excess of rains on that day. Moreover, Venus and Mercury, while

---

[117] This paragraph seems to describe a planetary hour-based version of the opening of the doors.
[118] This should probably be "Aquarius."
[119] This should probably be "Saturn."
[120] This section is a mixture of *Chap. Rains* with other material not clearly identical with what we have already seen.
[121] That is, his quarterly ingresses into the movable signs.
[122] This should probably be 20° Scorpio, as with the earlier accounts. But medieval texts are often unclear as to cardinal and ordinal numbers, so this might refer to the Sun's ingress into 19° Scorpio.
[123] *Submersionem*. Technically this should be "drowning," but that does not seem quite right here.
[124] The signs just mentioned.

they walk through signs of that kind, and likewise the Moon applying to either one, and it[125] holding onto the end of a sign, conveys rains, but less than the prior ones [just described]. Moreover, the Moon and Venus in watery signs, with Mercury being removed from [the watery signs], has a judgment of rains. Nor is it otherwise while Mercury and the Moon would reach signs of this kind, even though Venus is not walking through a rainy sign.

Moreover, the Moon being in those same signs, applying to Venus and Mercury (while they step in similar [signs] or traverse with her), renew rains until the Moon is separated from them.

---

[125] As in §Z.13, I am not sure whether this is the Moon or one of the others, but they would all have to be there for the application to perfect.

GLOSSARY

This glossary is an expanded version of the one in my *Introductions to Traditional Astrology* (*ITA*), with the addition of other terms found in *Judges*. After most definitions is a reference to sections and Appendices of *ITA* (including my introduction to it) for further reading.

- **Adding in course.** See **Course**.
- **Advancing.** When a planet is in an **angle** or succeedent. See III.3 and the Introduction §6.
- **Advantageous places.** One of two schemes of **houses** which indicate affairs/planets which are more busy or good in the context of the chart (III.4). The seven-place scheme according to Timaeus and reported in *Carmen* includes only certain signs which **aspect** the **Ascendant** by **whole-sign**, and suggests that these places are advantageous for the *native* because they aspect the Ascendant. The eight-place scheme according to Nechepso (III.4) lists all of the **angular** and **succeedent** places, suggesting places which are stimulating and advantageous for a planet *in itself*.
- **Ages of man.** Ptolemy's division of a typical human life span into periods ruled by planets as **time lords**. See VII.3.
- **Agreeing signs.** Groups of signs which share some kind of harmonious quality. See I.9.5-6.
- *Alcochoden.* Latin transliteration for **Kadukhudhāh**.
- **Alien** (Lat. *alienus*). See **Peregrine**.
- *Almuten.* A Latin transliteration for *mubtazz*: see **Victor**.
- **Angles, succeedents, cadents.** A division of houses into three groups which show how powerfully and directly a planet acts. The angles are the 1st, 10th, 7th and 4th houses; the succeedents are the 2nd, 11th, 8th and 5th; the cadents are the 12th, 9th, 6th and 3rd (but see **cadent** below). But the exact regions in question will depend upon whether and how one uses **whole-sign** and **quadrant houses**, especially since traditional texts refer to an angle or pivot (Gr. *kentron*, Ar. *watad*) as either (1) equivalent to the **whole-sign** angles from the **Ascendant**, or (2) the degrees of the **Ascendant-Midheaven** axes themselves, or (3) **quadrant houses** (and their associated strengths) as measured from the degrees of the axes. See I.12-13 and III.3-4, and the Introduction §6.

- **Antiscia** (sing. *antiscion*), "throwing shadows." Refers to a degree mirrored across an axis drawn from 0° Capricorn to 0° Cancer. For example, 10° Cancer has 20° Gemini as its antiscion. See I.9.2.
- **Apogee.** Typically, the furthest point a planet can be from the earth on the circle of the **deferent**. See II.0-1.
- **Applying, application.** When a planet is in a state of **connection**, moving so as to make the connection exact. Planets **assembled** together or in **aspect** by sign and not yet connected by the relevant degrees, are only "wanting" to be connected.
- **Arisings.** See **Ascensions**.
- **Ascendant.** Usually the entire rising sign, but often specified as the exact rising degree. In **quadrant houses**, a space following the exact rising degree up to the cusp of the 2nd house.
- **Ascensions.** Degrees on the celestial equator, measured in terms of how many degrees pass the meridian as an entire sign or **bound** (or other spans of zodiacal degrees) passes across the horizon. They are often used in the predictive technique of ascensional times, as an approximation for **directions**. See Appendix E.
- **Aspect/regard.** One planet aspects or regards another if they are in signs which are configured to each other by a **sextile**, **square**, **trine**, or **opposition**. See III.6 and **Whole signs**. A connection by degrees or orbs is a much more intense of an aspect.
- **Assembly.** When two or more planets are in the same sign, and more intensely if within 15°. See III.5.
- **Aversion.** Being in the second, sixth, eighth, or twelfth sign from a place. For instance, a planet in Gemini is in the twelfth from, and therefore in aversion to, Cancer. Such places are in aversion because they cannot **aspect** it by the classical scheme of aspects. See III.6.1.
- *Azamene*. Equivalent to **Chronic illness.**
- **Bad ones.** See **Benefic/malefic.**
- **Barring.** See **Blocking.**
- **Bearing** (Lat. *habitude*). Hugo's term for any of the many possible planetary conditions and relationships. These may be found in III and IV.
- **Benefic/malefic.** A division of the planets into groups that cause or signify typically "good" things (Jupiter, Venus, usually the Sun and Moon) or "bad" things (Mars, Saturn). Mercury is considered variable. See V.9.
- **Benevolents.** See **Benefic/malefic.**

- **Besieging**. Equivalent to **Enclosure**.
- **Bicorporeal signs**. Equivalent to "common" signs. See **Quadruplicity**.
- **Blocking** (sometimes called "prohibition"). When a planet bars another planet from completing a **connection**, either through its own body or ray. See III.14.
- **Bodyguarding**. Planetary relationships in which some planet protects another, used in determining social eminence and prosperity. See III.28.
- **Bounds**. Unequal divisions of the zodiac in each sign, each bound being ruled by one of the five non-**luminaries**. Sometimes called "terms," they are one of the five classical **dignities**. See VII.4.
- **Bright, smoky, empty, dark degrees**. Certain degrees of the zodiac said to affect how conspicuous or obscure the significations of planets or the Ascendant are. See VII.7.
- **Burned up** (or "combust," Lat. *combustus*). Normally, when a planet is between about 1° and 7.5° away from the Sun. See II.9-10, and **In the heart**.
- **Burnt path** (Lat. *via combusta*). A span of degrees in Libra and Scorpio in which a planet (especially the Moon) is considered to be harmed or less able to effect its significations. Some astrologers identify it as between 15° Libra and 15° Scorpio; others between the exact degree of the **fall** of the Sun in 19° Libra and the exact degree of the fall of the Moon in 3° Scorpio. See IV.3.
- *Bust*. Certain hours measured from the New Moon, in which it is considered favorable or unfavorable to undertake an action or perform an **election**. See VIII.4.
- **Busy places**. Equivalent to the **Advantageous places**.
- **Cadent** (Lat. *cadens*, "falling"). This is used in two ways: a planet or place may be cadent from the **angles** (being in the 3rd, 6th, 9th, or 12th), or else cadent from the **Ascendant** (namely, in **aversion** to it, being in the 12th, 8th, 6th, or 2nd). See I.12, III.4, and III.6.1.
- **Cardinal**. Equivalent to "movable" signs. See **Quadruplicity**.
- **Cazimi**: see **In the heart**.
- **Celestial equator**. The projection of earth's equator out into the universe, forming one of the three principal celestial coordinate systems.
- **Choleric**. See **Humor**.
- **Chronic illness (degrees of)**. Degrees which are especially said to indicate chronic illness, due to their association with certain fixed stars. See VII.10.

- **Cleansed**. Normally, when a planet is not in an **assembly** or **square** or **opposition** with a **malefic** planet, but possibly indicating being free of *any* **aspect** with a malefic.
- **Clothed**. Equivalent to one planet being in an **assembly** or **aspect/regard** with another, and therefore partaking in (being "clothed in") the other planet's characteristics.
- **Collection**. When two planets **aspecting** each other but not in an applying **connection**, each apply to a third planet. See III.12.
- **Combust**. See **Burned up**.
- **Commanding/obeying**. A division of the signs into those which command or obey each other (used sometimes in **synastry**). See I.9.
- **Common signs**. See **Quadruplicity**.
- **Confer**. See **Pushing**.
- **Configured**. To be in a whole-sign **aspect**, though not necessarily by degree.
- **Conjunction (of planets)**. See **Assembly** and **Connection**.
- **Conjunction/prevention**. The position of the New (conjunction) or Full (prevention) Moon most immediately prior to a **nativity** or other chart. For the prevention, some astrologers use the degree of the Moon, others the degree of the luminary which was above the earth at the time of the prevention. See VIII.1.2.
- **Connection**. When a planet applies to another planet (by body in the same sign, or by ray in **aspecting** signs), within a particular number of degrees up to exactness. See III.7.
- **Convertible**. Equivalent to the movable signs. See **Quadruplicity**. But sometimes planets (especially Mercury) are called convertible because their **gender** is affected by their placement in the chart.
- **Convey**. See **Pushing**.
- **Corruption**. Normally, the harming of a planet (see IV.3-4), such as being in a **square** with a **malefic** planet. But sometimes, equivalent to **Detriment**.
- **Counsel** (Lat. *consilium*). A term used by Hugo and other Latin translators of Arabic, for "management" (III.18). An **applying** planet **pushes** or gifts or grants its counsel or management to another planet, and that other planet **receives** or gathers it.
- **Course, increasing/decreasing in**. For practical purposes, this means a planet is quicker than average in motion. But in geometric astronomy, it re-

fers to what **sector** (or *nitaq*) of the **deferent** the center of a planet's **epicycle** is. (The planet's position within the four sectors of the epicycle itself will also affect its apparent speed.) In the two sectors that are closest to the planet's **perigee**, the planet will apparently be moving faster; in the two sectors closest to the **apogee**, it will apparently be moving slower. See II.0-1.

- **Crooked/straight.** A division of the signs into those which rise quickly and are more parallel to the horizon (crooked), and those which arise more slowly and closer to a right angle from the horizon (straight or direct). The signs from Capricorn to Gemini are crooked; those from Cancer to Sagittarius are straight.
- **Crossing over.** When a planet begins to **separate** from an exact **connection**. See III.7-8.
- **Cutting of light.** Three ways in which a **connection** is prevented: either by **obstruction** from the following sign, **escape** within the same sign, or by **barring**. See III.23.
- *Darījān*. An alternative **face** system attributed to the Indians. See VII.6.
- **Decan.** Equivalent to **face**.
- **Declination.** The equivalent on the celestial **equator**, of geographical latitude. The signs of northern declination (Aries through Virgo) stretch northward of the **ecliptic**, while those of southern declination (Libra through Pisces) stretch southward.
- **Deferent.** The circle on which a planet's **epicycle** travels. See II.0-1.
- **Descension.** Equivalent to **fall**.
- **Detriment** (or Ar. "corruption," "unhealthiness," "harm."). More broadly (as "corruption"), it refers to any way in which a planet is harmed or its operation thwarted (such as by being **burned up**). But it also (as "harm") refers specifically to the sign opposite a planet's **domicile**. Libra is the detriment of Mars. See I.6 and I.8.
- **Dexter.** "Right": see **Right/left**.
- **Diameter.** Equivalent to **Opposition**.
- **Dignity** (Lat. "worthiness"; Ar. *ḥazz*, "good fortune, allotment"). Any of five ways of assigning rulership or responsibility to a planet (or sometimes, to a **Node**) over some portion of the zodiac. They are often listed in the following order: **domicile, exaltation, triplicity, bound, face/decan**. Each dignity has its own meaning and effect and use, and two of them have opposites: the opposite of domicile is **detriment**, the opposite of ex-

altation is **fall**. See I.3, I.4, I.6-7, VII.4 for the assignments; I.8 for some descriptive analogies; VIII.2.1 and VIII.2.2f for some predictive uses of domiciles and bounds.

- **Directions**. A predictive technique which is more precise than using **ascensions**, and defined by Ptolemy in terms of proportional semi-arcs. There is some confusion in how directing works, because of the difference between the astronomical method of directions and how astrologers look at charts. Astronomically, a point in the chart (the significator) is considered as stationary, and other planets and their **aspects** by degree (or even the **bounds**) are sent forth (promittors) as though the heavens keep turning by **primary motion**, until they come to the significator. The degrees between the significator and promittor are converted into years of life. But when looking at the chart, it seems as though the significator is being **released** counterclockwise in the order of signs, so that it **distributes** through the bounds or comes to the bodies or aspects of promittors. Direction by **ascensions** takes the latter perspective, though the result is the same. Some later astrologers allow the distance between a significator/releaser and the promittor to be measured in either direction, yielding "converse" directions in addition to the classical "direct" directions. See VIII.2.2, Appendix E, and Gansten.
- **Disregard**. Equivalent to **Separation**.
- **Distribution**. The **direction** of a **releaser** (often the degree of the **Ascendant**) through the **bounds**. The bound **lord** of the distribution is the "distributor," and any body or ray which the **releaser** encounters is the "partner." See VIII.2.2f, and *PN3*.
- **Distributor**. The **bound lord** of a directed releaser. See **Distribution**.
- **Diurnal**. See **Sect**.
- **Domain**. A **sect** and **gender**-based planetary condition. See III.2.
- **Domicile**. One of the five **dignities**. A sign of the zodiac, insofar as it is owned or managed by one of the planets. For example, Aries is the domicile of Mars, and so Mars is its domicile **lord**. See I.6.
- **Doryphory** (Gr. *doruphoria*). Equivalent to **Bodyguarding**.
- **Double-bodied**. Equivalent to the common signs. See **Quadruplicity**.
- **Dragon**: see **Node**.
- **Drawn back** (Lat. *reductus*). Equivalent to being **cadent** from an **angle**.
- **Dodecametorion**. Equivalent to **Twelfth-part**.
- *Duodecima*. Equivalent to **Twelfth-part**.

- ***Dustūriyyah***. Equivalent to **Bodyguarding**.
- **East** (Lat. *oriens*). The Ascendant: normally the rising sign, but sometimes the degree of the Ascendant itself.
- **Eastern/western**. A position relative to the Sun, often called "oriental" or "occidental," respectively. These terms are used in two major ways: (1) when a planet is in a position to rise before the Sun by being in an early degree (eastern) or is in a position to set after the Sun by being in a later degree (western). But in ancient languages, these words also refer mean "arising" or "setting/sinking," on an analogy with the Sun rising and setting: so sometimes they refer to (2) a planet arising out of, or sinking under, the **Sun's rays**, no matter what side of the Sun it is on (in some of my translations I call this "pertaining to arising" and "pertaining to sinking"). Astrological authors do not always clarify what sense is meant, and different astronomers and astrologers have different definitions for exactly what positions count as being eastern or western. See II.10.
- **Ecliptic**. The path defined by the Sun's motion through the zodiac, defined as having 0° ecliptical latitude. In tropical astrology, the ecliptic (and therefore the zodiacal signs) begins at the intersection of the ecliptic and the celestial equator.
- **Election** (lit. "choice"). The deliberate choosing of an appropriate time to undertake an action, or determining when to avoid an action; but astrologers normally refer to the chart of the time itself as an election.
- **Element**. One of the four basic qualities. fire, air, water, earth) describing how matter and energy operate, and used to describe the significations and operations of planets and signs. They are usually described by pairs of four other basic qualities (hot, cold, wet, dry). For example, Aries is a fiery sign, and hot and dry; Mercury is typically treated as cold and dry (earthy). See I.3, I.7, and Book V.
- **Emptiness of the course**. Medievally, when a planet does not complete a **connection** for as long as it is in its current sign. In Hellenistic astrology, when a planet does not complete a connection within the next 30°. See III.9.
- **Enclosure**. When a planet has the rays or bodies of the **malefics** (or alternatively, the **benefics**) on either side of it, by degree or sign. See IV.4.2.
- **Epicycle**. A circle on the **deferent**, on which a planet turns. See II.0-1.
- **Equant**. A circle used to measure the average position of a planet. See II.0-1.

- **Equator (celestial)**. The projection of the earth's equator into space, forming a great circle. Its equivalent of latitude is called **declination**, while its equivalent of longitude is called **right ascension** (and is measured from the beginning of Aries, from the intersection of it and the **ecliptic**).
- **Escape**. When a planet wants to **connect** with a second one, but the second one moves into the next sign before it is completed, and the first planet makes a **connection** with a different, unrelated one instead. See III.22.
- **Essential/accidental**. A common way of distinguishing a planet's conditions, usually according to **dignity** (essential, I.2) and some other condition such as its **aspects** (accidental). See IV.1-5 for many accidental conditions.
- **Exaltation**. One of the five **dignities**. A sign in which a planet (or sometimes, a **Node**) signifies its matter in a particularly authoritative and refined way. The exaltation is sometimes identified with a particular degree in that sign. See I.6.
- **Face**. One of the five **dignities**. The zodiac is divided into 36 faces of 10° each, starting with the beginning of Aries. See I.5.
- **Facing**. A relationship between a planet and a **luminary**, if their respective signs are configured at the same distance as their **domiciles** are. For example, Leo (ruled by the Sun) is two signs to the **right** of Libra (ruled by Venus). When Venus is **western** and two signs away from wherever the Sun is, she will be in the facing of the Sun. See II.11.
- **Fall**. The sign opposite a planet's **exaltation**. See I.6.
- **Familiar** (Lat. *familiaris*). A hard-to-define term which suggests a sense of belonging and close relationship. (1) Sometimes it is contrasted with being **peregrine**, suggesting that a familiar planet is one which is a **lord** over a degree or **place** (that is, it has a **dignity** in it): for a dignity suggests belonging. (2) At other times, it refers to a familiar **aspect** (and probably the **sextile** or **trine** in particular): all of the family houses in a chart have a **whole-sign** aspect to the **Ascendant**.
- **Feminine**. See **Gender**.
- **Feral**. Equivalent to **Wildness**.
- **Figure**. One of several polygons implied by an **aspect**. For example, a planet in Aries and one in Capricorn do not actually form a **square**, but they imply one because Aries and Capricorn, together with Libra and Cancer, form a square amongst themselves. See III.8.

- *Firdārīyyah* (pl. *firdārīyyāt*). A **time lord** method in which planets rule different periods of life, with each period broken down into sub-periods. See VII.1.
- **Firm.** In terms of signs, the **fixed** signs: see **Quadruplicity**. For houses, equivalent to the **Angles**.
- **Fixed.** See **Quadruplicity**.
- **Foreign** (Lat. *extraneus*). Usually equivalent to **peregrine**.
- **Fortunate.** Normally, a planet whose condition is made better by one of the **bearings** described in IV.
- **Fortunes.** See **Benefic/malefic**.
- **Free.** Sometimes, being **cleansed** of the **malefics**; at other times, being out of the **Sun's rays**.
- **Gender.** The division of signs, degrees, planets and hours into masculine and feminine groups. See I.3, V.10, V.14, VII.8.
- **Generosity and benefits.** Favorable relationships between signs and planets, as defined in III.26.
- **Good ones.** See **Benefic/malefic**.
- **Good places.** Equivalent to **Advantageous places**.
- **Greater, middle, lesser years.** See **Planetary years**.
- *Ḥalb*. Probably Pahlavi for "sect," but normally describes a rejoicing condition: see III.2.
- *Ḥayyiz*. Arabic for "domain," normally a gender-intensified condition of *ḥalb*. See III.2.
- **Hexagon.** Equivalent to **Sextile**.
- *Hīlāj* (From the Pahlavi for "releaser"). Equivalent to **Releaser**.
- **Hold onto.** Hugo's synonym for a planet being in or **transiting** a **sign**.
- **Horary astrology.** A late historical designation for **Questions**.
- **Hours (planetary).** The assigning of rulership over hours of the day and night to planets. The hours of daylight (and night, respectively) are divided by 12, and each period is ruled first by the planet ruling that day, then the rest in descending planetary order. For example, on Sunday the Sun rules the first planetary "hour" from daybreak, then Venus, then Mercury, the Moon, Saturn, and so on. See V.13.
- **House.** A twelve-fold spatial division of a chart, in which each house signifies one or more areas of life. Two basic schemes are (1) **whole-sign** houses, in which the **signs** are equivalent to the houses, and (2) **quadrant houses**.

- **Humor.** Any one of four fluids in the body (according to traditional medicine), the balance between which determines one's health and **temperament** (outlook and energy level). Choler or yellow bile is associated with fire and the choleric temperament; blood is associated with air and the sanguine temperament; phlegm is associated with water and the phlegmatic temperament; black bile is associated with earth and the melancholic temperament. See I.3.
- **In the heart.** Often called *cazimi* in English texts, from the Ar. *kaṣmīmī*. A planet is in the heart of the Sun when it is either in the same degree as the Sun (according to Sahl bin Bishr and Rhetorius), or within 16' of longitude from him. See II.9.
- **Indicator.** A degree which is supposed to indicate the approximate position of the degree of the natal **Ascendant**, in cases where the time of birth is uncertain. See VIII.1.2.
- **Inferior.** The planets lower than the Sun: Venus, Mercury, Moon.
- **Infortunes.** See **Benefic/malefic.**
- *ʾIttiṣāl.* Equivalent to **Connection**.
- **Joys.** Places in which the planets are said to "rejoice" in acting or signifying their natures. Joys by house are found in I.16; by sign in I.10.7.
- *Jārbakhtār* (From the Pahlavi for "distributor of time"). Equivalent to **Distributor**; see **Distribution.**
- *Kadukhudhāh* (From the Pahlavi for "domicile master"). One of the lords of the longevity **releaser**, preferably the **bound lord**. It is also equivalent to the **distributor** when directing any releaser through the bounds. See VIII.1.3.
- *Kaṣmīmī*: see **In the heart.**
- **Kingdom.** Equivalent to **exaltation**.
- **Largesse and recompense.** A reciprocal relation in which one planet is rescued from being in its own **fall** or a **well**, and then returns the favor when the other planet is in its fall or well. See III.24.
- **Leader** (Lat. *dux*). Equivalent to a **significator** for some topic. The Arabic word for "significator" means to indicate something by pointing the way toward something: thus the significator for a topic or matter "leads" the astrologer to some answer. Used by some less popular Latin translators (such as Hugo of Santalla and Hermann of Carinthia).
- **Linger in** (Lat. *commoror*). Hugo's synonym for a planet being in or **transiting** through a **sign**.

- **Lodging-place** (Lat. *hospitium*). Hugo's synonym for a **house**, particularly the **sign** which occupies a house.
- **Lord of the Year.** The **domicile lord** of a **profection**. The Sun and Moon are not allowed to be primary lords of the Year, according to Persian doctrine. See VIII.2.1 and VIII.3.2, and Appendix F.
- **Lord.** A designation for the planet which has a particular **dignity**, but when used alone it usually means the **domicile** lord. For example, Mars is the lord of Aries.
- **Lord of the question.** In questions, the lord of the **house** of the **quaesited** matter. But sometimes, it refers to the client or **querent** whose question it is.
- **Lot.** Sometimes called "Parts." A place (often treated as equivalent to an entire sign) expressing a ratio derived from the position of three other parts of a chart. Normally, the distance between two places is measured in zodiacal order from one to the other, and this distance is projected forward from some other place (usually the Ascendant): where the counting stops, is the Lot. Lots are used both interpretively and predictively. See Book VI.
- **Lucky/unlucky.** See **Benefic/malefic**.
- **Luminary.** The Sun or Moon.
- **Malefic.** See **Benefic/malefic**.
- **Malevolents.** See **Benefic/malefic**.
- **Masculine.** See **Gender**.
- **Melancholic.** See **Humor**.
- **Midheaven.** Either the tenth sign from the **Ascendant**, or the zodiacal degree on which the celestial meridian falls.
- **Movable signs.** See **Quadruplicity**.
- *Mubtazz*. See **Victor**.
- **Mutable signs.** Equivalent to "common" signs. See **Quadruplicity**.
- *Namūdār*. Equivalent to **Indicator**.
- **Native.** The person whose birth chart it is.
- **Nativity.** Technically, a birth itself, but used by astrologers to describe the chart cast for the moment of a birth.
- **Ninth-parts.** Divisions of each sign into 9 equal parts of 3° 20' apiece, each ruled by a planet. Used predictively by some astrologers as part of the suite of **revolution** techniques. See VII.5.
- *Nitaq*. See **Sector**.

- **Nobility.** Equivalent to **exaltation**.
- **Nocturnal.** See **Sect**.
- **Node.** The point on the ecliptic where a planet passes into northward latitude (its North Node or Head of the Dragon) or into southern latitude (its South Node or Tail of the Dragon). Normally only the Moon's Nodes are considered. See II.5 and V.8.
- **Northern/southern.** Either planets in northern or southern latitude in the zodiac (relative to the ecliptic), or in northern or southern declination relative to the celestial equator. See I.10.1.
- **Not-reception.** When an **applying** planet is in the **fall** of the planet being applied to.
- **Oblique ascensions.** The **ascensions** used in making predictions by ascensional times or primary **directions**.
- **Obstruction.** When one planet is moving towards a second (wanting to be **connected** to it), but a third one in a later degrees goes **retrograde**, connects with the second one, and then with the first one. See III.21.
- **Occidental.** See **Eastern/western**.
- **Opening of the portals/doors.** Times of likely weather changes and rain, determined by certain **transits**. See VIII.3.4.
- **Opposition.** An **aspect** either by **whole sign** or degree, in which the signs have a 180° relation to each other: for example, a planet in Aries is opposed to one in Libra.
- **Optimal place.** Also called "good" and "the best" places. These are probably a subset of the **advantageous places**, and probably only those houses which **aspect** the **Ascendant**. They definitely include the Ascendant, tenth, and eleventh houses, but may also include the ninth. They are probably also restricted only to houses above the horizon.
- **Orbs/bodies.** Called "orb" by the Latins, and "body" (*jirm*) by Arabic astrologers. A space of power or influence on each side of a planet's body or position, used to determine the intensity of interaction between different planets. See II.6.
- **Oriental.** See **Eastern/western**.
- **Overcoming.** When a planet is in the eleventh, tenth, or ninth sign from another planet (i.e., in a superior **sextile**, **square**, or **trine aspect**), though being in the tenth sign is considered a more dominant or even domineering position. See IV.4.1 and *PN3*'s Introduction, §15.

- **Own light.** This refers either to (1) a planet being a member of the **sect** of the chart (see V.9), or (2) a planet being out of the **Sun's rays** and not yet **connected** to another planet, so that it shines on its own without being **clothed** in another's influence (see II.9).
- **Part.** See **Lot**.
- **Partner.** The body or ray of any planet which a **directed releaser** encounters while being **distributed** through the **bounds**. But in some translations from Arabic, any of the **lords** of a place.
- **Peregrine.** When a planet is not in one of its five **dignities**. See I.9.
- **Perigee.** The position on a planet's **deferent** circle which is closest to the earth; it is opposite the **apogee**. See II.0-1.
- **Perverse** (Lat. *perversus*). Hugo's occasional term for (1) **malefic** planets, and (2) **places** in **aversion** to the **Ascendant** by **whole-sign**: definitely the twelfth and sixth, probably the eighth, and possibly the second.
- **Phlegmatic.** See **Humor**.
- **Pitted degrees.** Equivalent to **Welled degrees**.
- **Pivot.** Equivalent to **Angle**.
- **Place.** Equivalent to a **house**, and more often (and more anciently) a **whole-sign** house, namely a **sign**.
- **Planetary years.** Periods of years which the planets signify according to various conditions. See VII.2.
- **Possess.** Hugo's synonym for a planet being in or **transiting** a **sign**.
- **Prevention.** See **Conjunction/prevention**.
- **Primary directions.** See **Directions**.
- **Primary motion.** The clockwise or east-to-west motion of the heavens.
- **Profection** (Lat. *profectio*, "advancement, setting out"). A predictive technique in which some part of a chart (usually the **Ascendant**) is advanced either by an entire sign or in 30° increments for each year of life. See VIII.2.1 and VIII.3.2, and the sources in Appendix F.
- **Prohibition.** Equivalent to **Blocking**.
- **Promittor** (lit., something "sent forward"). A point which is **directed** to a **significator**, or to which a significator is **released** or directed (depending on how one views the mechanics of directions).
- **Pushing.** What a planet making an **applying connection** does to the one receiving it. See III.15-18.
- *Qasim/qismah*: Arabic terms for **distributor** and **distribution**.

- **Quadrant houses.** A division of the heavens into twelve spaces which overlap the **whole signs**, and are assigned to topics of life and ways of measuring strength (such as Porphyry, Alchabitius Semi-Arc, or Regiomontanus houses). For example, if the Midheaven fell into the eleventh sign, the space between the Midheaven and the Ascendant would be divided into sections that overlap and are not coincident with the signs. See I.12 and the Introduction §6.
- **Quadruplicity.** A "fourfold" group of signs indicating certain shared patterns of behavior. The movable (or cardinal or convertible) signs are those through which new states of being are quickly formed (including the seasons): Aries, Cancer, Libra, Capricorn. The fixed (sometimes "firm") signs are those through which matters are fixed and lasting in their character: Taurus, Leo, Scorpio, Aquarius. The common (or mutable or bicorporeal) signs are those which make a transition and partake both of quick change and fixed qualities: Gemini, Virgo, Sagittarius, Pisces. See I.10.5.
- **Quaesited/quesited.** In **horary** astrology, the matter asked about.
- **Querent.** In **horary** astrology, the person asking the question (or the person on behalf of whom one asks).
- **Questions.** The branch of astrology dealing with inquiries about individual matters, for which a chart is cast.
- **Reception.** What one planet does when another planet **pushes** or **applies** to it, and especially when they are related by **dignity** or by a **trine** or **sextile** from an **agreeing** sign of various types. For example, if the Moon applies to Mars, Mars will get or receive her application. See III.15-18 and III.25.
- **Reflection.** When two planets are in **aversion** to each other, but a third planet either **collects** or **transfers** their light. If it collects, it reflects the light elsewhere. See III.13.
- **Refrenation.** See **Revoking**.
- **Regard.** Equivalent to **Aspect**.
- **Releaser.** The point which is the focus of a **direction**. In determining longevity, it is the one among a standard set of possible points which has certain qualifications (see VIII.1.3). In annual predictions one either directs or **distributes** the longevity releaser, or any one of a number of points for particular topics, or else the degree of the **Ascendant** as a default releaser. Many astrologers direct the degree of the Ascendant of the **revolution** chart itself as a releaser.

- **Remote** (Lat. *remotus*). Equivalent to **cadent**: see **Angle**. But see also *Judges* §7.73, where 'Umar (or Hugo) distinguishes being **cadent** from being **remote**.
- **Render**. When a planet **pushes** to another planet or place.
- **Retreating**. When a planet is in a cadent place. See III.4 and the Introduction §6, and **Angle**.
- **Retrograde**. When a planet seems to move backwards or clockwise relative to the signs and fixed stars. See II.8 and II.10.
- **Return, Solar/Lunar**. Equivalent to **Revolution**.
- **Returning**. What a **burned up** or **retrograde** planet does when another planet **pushes** to it. See III.19.
- **Revoking**. When a planet making an applying **connection** stations and turns **retrograde**, not completing the connection. See III.20.
- **Revolution**. Sometimes called the "cycle" or "transfer" or "change-over" of a year. Technically, the **transiting** position of planets and the **Ascendant** at the moment the Sun returns to a particular place in the zodiac: in the case of nativities, when he returns to his exact natal position; in mundane astrology, usually when he makes his ingress into 0° Aries. But the revolution is also understood to involve an entire suite of predictive techniques, including **distribution, profections**, and *firdārīyyāt*. See *PN3*.
- **Right ascensions**. Degrees on the celestial **equator** (its equivalent of geographical longitude), particularly those which move across the meridian when calculating arcs for **ascensions** and **directions**.
- **Right/left**. Right (or "dexter") degrees and **aspects** are those earlier in the zodiac relative to a planet or sign, up to the **opposition**; left (or "sinister") degrees and aspects are those later in the zodiac. For example, if a planet is in Capricorn, its right aspects will be towards Scorpio, Libra, and Virgo; its left aspects will be towards Pisces, Aries, and Taurus. See III.6.
- **Root**. A chart used as a basis for another chart; a root particularly describes something considered to have concrete being of its own. For example, a **nativity** acts as a root for an **election**, so that when planning an election one must make it harmonize with the nativity.
- **Safe**. When a planet is not being harmed, particularly by an **assembly** or **square** or **opposition** with the **malefics**. See **Cleansed**.
- **Sālkhudhāy** (from Pahlavi, "lord of the year"). Equivalent to the **lord of the year**.
- **Sanguine**. See **Humor**.

- **Scorched**. See **Burned up**.
- **Secondary motion**. The counter-clockwise motion of planets forward in the zodiac.
- **Sect**. A division of charts, planets, and signs into "diurnal/day" and "nocturnal/night." Charts are diurnal if the Sun is above the horizon, else they are nocturnal. Planets are divided into sects as shown in V.11. Masculine signs (Aries, Gemini, *etc.*) are diurnal, the feminine signs (Taurus, Cancer, *etc.*) are nocturnal.
- **Sector**. A division of the **deferent** circle or **epicycle** into four parts, used to determine the position, speed, visibility, and other features of a planet. See II.0-1.
- **Seeing, hearing, listening signs**. A way of associating signs similar to **commanding/obeying**. See Paul of Alexandria's version in the two figures attached to I.9.6.
- **Separation**. When planets have completed a **connection** by **assembly** or **aspect**, and move away from one another. See III.8.
- **Sextile**. An **aspect** either by **whole sign** or degree, in which the signs have a 60° relation to each other: for example, Aries and Gemini.
- **Shift** (Ar. *nawbah*). Equivalent to **Sect**, and refers not only to the alternation between day and night, but also to the period of night or day itself. The Sun is the lord of the diurnal shift or sect, and the Moon is the lord of the nocturnal shift or sect.
- **Sign**. One of the twelve 30° divisions of the **ecliptic**, named after the constellations which they used to be roughly congruent to. In tropical astrology, the signs start from the intersection of the ecliptic with the celestial equator (the position of the Sun at the equinoxes). In sidereal astrology, the signs begin from some other point identified according to other principles.
- **Significator**. Either (1) a planet or point in a chart which indicates or signifies something for a topic (either through its own character, or house position, or rulerships, *etc.*), or (2) the point which is **released** in primary **directions**.
- **Sinister**. "Left": see **Right/left**.
- **Slavery**. Equivalent to **fall**.
- **Sovereignty** (Lat. *regnum*). Equivalent to **Exaltation**.
- **Spearbearing**. Equivalent to **Bodyguarding**.

- **Square.** An **aspect** either by **whole sign** or degree, in which the signs have a 90° relation to each other: for example, Aries and Cancer.
- **Stake.** Equivalent to **Angle**.
- **Sublunar world.** The world of the four **elements** below the sphere of the Moon, in classical cosmology.
- **Succeedent.** See **Angle**.
- **Sun's rays** (or Sun's beams). In earlier astrology, equivalent to a regularized distance of 15° away from the Sun, so that a planet under the rays is not visible at dawn or dusk. But a later distinction was made between being **burned up** (about 1° - 7.5° away from the Sun) and merely being under the rays (about 7.5° - 15° away).
- **Superior.** The planets higher than the Sun: Saturn, Jupiter, Mars.
- **Supremacy** (Lat. *regnum*). Hugo's word for **Exaltation**, sometimes used in translations by Dykes instead of the slightly more accurate **Sovereignty**.
- **Synastry.** The comparison of two or more charts to determine compatibility, usually in romantic relationships or friendships. See *BA* Appendix C for a discussion and references for friendship, and *BA* III.7.11 and III.12.7.
- *Tasyīr* (Ar. "dispatching, sending out"). Equivalent to primary **directions**.
- **Temperament.** The particular mixture (sometimes, "complexion") of **elements** or **humors** which determines a person's or planet's typical behavior, outlook, and energy level.
- **Testimony.** From Arabic astrology onwards, a little-defined term which can mean (1) the planets which have **dignity** in a place or degree, or (2) the number of dignities a planet has in its own place (or as compared with other planets), or (3) a planet's **assembly** or **aspect** to a place of interest, or (4) generally *any* way in which planets may make themselves relevant to the inquiry at hand. For example, a planet which is the **exalted** lord of the **Ascendant** but also **aspects** it, maby be said to present two testimonies supporting its relevance to an inquiry about the Ascendant.
- **Tetragon.** Equivalent to **Square**.
- **Thought-interpretation.** The practice of identifying a theme or topic in a **querent's** mind, often using a **victor**, before answering the specific **question**. See *Search*.
- **Time lord.** A planet ruling over some period of time according to one of the classical predictive techniques. For example, the **lord of the year** is the time lord over a **profection**.

- **Transfer**. When one planet **separates** from one planet, and **connects** to another. See III.11.
- **Transit**. The passing of one planet across another planet or point (by body or **aspect** by exact degree), or through a particular sign (even in a **whole-sign** relation to some point of interest). In traditional astrology, not every transit is significant; for example, transits of **time lords** or of planets in the **whole-sign angles** of a **profection** might be preferred to others. See VIII.2.4 and *PN3*.
- **Translation**. Equivalent to **Transfer**.
- **Traverse** (Lat. *discurro*). Hugo's synonym for a planet being in or **transiting** through a **sign**.
- **Trigon**. Equivalent to **Trine**.
- **Trine**. An **aspect** either by **whole sign** or degree, in which the signs have a 120° relation to each other: for example, Aries and Leo.
- **Turn** (Ar. *dawr*). A predictive term in which responsibilities for being a **time lord** rotates between different planets. See VIII.2.3 for one use of the turn.
- **Turned away**. Equivalent to **Aversion**.
- **Turning signs**. For Hugo of Santalla, equivalent to the movable signs: see **Quadruplicity**. But *tropicus* more specifically refers to the tropical signs Cancer and Capricorn, in which the Sun turns back from its most extreme declinations.
- **Twelfth-parts**. Signs of the zodiac defined by 2.5° divisions of other signs. For example, the twelfth-part of 4° Gemini is Cancer. See IV.6.
- **Two-parted signs**. Equivalent to the double-bodied or common signs: see **Quadruplicity**.
- **Under rays**. When a planet is between approximately 7.5° and 15° from the Sun, and not visible either when rising before the Sun or setting after him. Some astrologers distinguish the distances for individual planets (which is more astronomically accurate). See II.10.
- **Unfortunate**. Normally, when a planet's condition is made more difficult through one of the **bearings** in IV.
- **Unlucky**. See **Benefic/malefic**.
- *Via combusta*. See **Burnt path**.
- **Victor** (Ar. *mubtazz*). A planet identified as being the most authoritative either for a particular topic or **house** (I.18), or for a chart as a whole (VIII.1.4). See also *Search*.

- **Void in course.** Equivalent to **Emptiness of the course.**
- **Well.** A degree in which a planet is said to be more obscure in its operation. See VII.9.
- **Western.** See **Eastern/western.**
- **Whole signs.** The oldest system of assigning house topics and **aspects**. The entire sign on the horizon (the **Ascendant**) is the first house, the entire second sign is the second house, and so on. Likewise, aspects are considered first of all according to signs: planets in Aries aspect or regard Gemini as a whole, even if aspects by exact degree are more intense. See I.12, III.6, and the Introduction §6.
- **Wildness.** When a planet is not **aspected** by any other planet, for as long as it is in its current sign. See III.10.
- **Withdrawal.** Equivalent to **separation**.

APPENDIX A: SAHL'S *THE FIFTY JUDGMENTS*

The complete version of *Judges* contained Sahl's *The Fifty Judgments* as §A.123. Following is my translation, newly edited from the 2007 version in *WSM*. It is a handy set of guidelines for interpreting planets and their configurations. For a more complete set of considerations like these, see Tr. 5 of Bonatti's *BOA*, now published separately as *Bonatti's 146 Considerations*.[1]

The first, on the reception of disposition through the Moon

Know that the significatrix (that is, the Moon), whose circle is closer to the earth than the circles of all the planets, is similar to the things of the world, more so than all the planets. Do you not see that a man begins being small, then he grows until he is finished? The Moon does likewise. Therefore, consider the Moon as the significatrix of all matters: because her soundness is the soundness of every matter, and her detriment is the detriment of every matter. And she pushes (that is, "commits") her own disposition[2] likewise to the one [to] whom she projects her own rays, and to whom, of the planets, she is joined; and she changes her own being to that planet (and this planet[3] is called the "receiver of the disposition" because it receives what had been committed to it). Therefore the Moon herself is these planets' bearer of information,[4] and she reconciles them, and bears off [the light] from certain ones of them, to others.

Judgment 2: What the bad or good planets would signify

The bad planets signify detriment and evil on account of the excessiveness or overflowing of the power of cold and heat conquering and impeding in them.[5] But if a good planet were in the house of a bad one (or in its exaltation), [the bad one] receives [the good one] and restrains its own malice

---

[1] Considerations 9-60 and 74-77 contain Bonatti's rendition of, and commentary on, Sahl's *Fifty Judgments*.
[2] This is pushing "management": see *ITA* III.18.
[3] Reading *ipse* for *ipsa*.
[4] Lat. *delatrix*.
[5] *Cf. Tet.* I.5.

from it; or if there were an aspect of the bad ones by a trine or sextile aspect, it would even be restrained by that, because it would be an aspect of friendship without any enmity. But the good ones, because they are of a temperate nature and equal complexion (that is, because they are temperate in their mixture of heat and cold), always profit and perform, were they to receive or not—but reception with them is more useful and better.

Judgment 3: On the impediment of the planets—three judgments

[1] There are two kinds of stars, namely the good and the bad: therefore, wherever you saw bad planets, say evil; and wherever you saw a fortune, say good.

Judgment 4[6]

[2] And a planet is called "impeded" while a bad one is projecting rays over its light according to the quantity which I told you concerning their orbs.[7]

And if it transited a bound of the bad ones it is called "looking at the bad one," and [the bad one] would not be able to impede.[8]

And if a bad one transited a planet[9] by a complete degree, it sends in fear without the impediment of the body, and the bad one planet would not be able to act because it is separated from it. Likewise if a fortune transited a planet and were separated from it by a full degree,[10] he has hope, but the matter is not perfected.

And every impeding [planet], if it were cadent from the Ascendant, sends fear and does not impede. Likewise if the fortunes were cadent from the Ascendant: it is hoped for, but the matter is not perfected.

---

[6] Continuing the judgments of impediment from *Judgments* 3.
[7] For standard medieval orbs, see my introduction.
[8] I am not sure what this means. It probably only means that a planet has separated from a malefic by more than a few degrees—see a somewhat similar passage by Abū Ma'shar in *ITA* III.8.
[9] Reading *planetam* for *planeta*, in parallel with the following sentence.
[10] *Per gradum integrum. Integer* suggests that the degree itself is counted as a whole: so if the malefic were transiting a planet at 25° 57', it would be separated by a full degree as soon as it enters 26°, only 3' away.

Judgment 5[11]

[3] If a planet were in the angles of the bad ones (that is, if it were with one, or in the fourth from it, or in the seventh or in the tenth [from it]), it will be like one who fights on his own behalf[12] against the tribulation and evil which descends upon him. And if [the bad one] transited it, and it were separated from it by a full degree (as I said to you before), he has already escaped the impediment of that bad one, and the bad one would be able to do nothing besides sending in fear. Therefore, observe these chapters: because they are of the secrets of questions.

Judgment 6: On the void course of the Moon[13]

If the Moon were void in course—that is, joined to none of the planets—it signifies futility and annulment, and turning back from that same purpose,[14] and the impediment of that same purpose.

Judgment 7: On the conjunction of the Moon with the planets[15]

The conjunction of the Moon signifies what is going to be, and what is hoped for concerning matters, according to the quantity of the nature of the planet who receives the Moon's disposition[16] (that is, if it were a fortune, good; if it were a bad one, evil).

Judgment 8: On the separation of the Moon from the planets[17]

The separation of the Moon from a planet signifies what is past and what has already gone away, according to the quantity of the nature of that planet from whom the Moon is being separated.

---

[11] Continuing the judgments of impediment from *Judgments* 3.
[12] *Pro semetipso.*
[13] See *ITA* III.9.
[14] *Causa*, here and in the next clause.
[15] See *Carmen* V.28.
[16] That is, the one to which she applies.
[17] See *Carmen* V.28.

Judgment 9: On a planet in its own descension

If a planet were in its own descension, it signifies sorrow and prison and distress.

Judgment 10: On a retrograde planet

A retrograde planet signifies disobedience, and contradiction, and turning back and taking back, and diversity or discord.

Judgment 11: On a stationary planet

A planet in its own station[18] signifies evil and what has already gone inactive.

Judgment 12: On the bad planets

The bad ones signify difficulty, and pressure, and haste in work.

Judgment 13: On a planet slow in course

If a planet were slow (that is if it walks slowly), it postpones its own number[19] or its own promise. That is, it makes a delay in number or its own promise, both in the good and the bad. It does likewise if it were in the houses of Saturn or Jupiter. And in the houses of the light planets, it hastens.

Judgment 14: On the conjunction of the Moon with planets in one minute

If the Moon were conjoined to some planet and she perfected her own conjunction (that is, if she were with it in one minute), look to see what is going to be concerning that question, from the planet with whom the Moon is joined after this.

---

[18] This must be when it is stationing and about to be retrograde. Cf. Judgment 48 below.
[19] *Numerum*. This probably refers to planets which are decreasing or subtracting in number. In other words, planets which are slow and retrograde (technically defined through their epicycles).

Judgment 15: On a planet's being at the end of a sign

If a planet were in the last degree of a sign, its strength has already receded from that sign, and its strength will be in the next sign: like a man who put his foot upon the threshold of the gate, wanting to go out—which if the house then fell, it would not impede him. Indeed if a planet were in the twenty-ninth degree,[20] the strength of the planet will be in the same sign. Because there are three degrees of every planet in which its virtue is spread out—namely, the degree in which it is, and the degree which is behind it, and the degree which is in front of it.[21]

Judgment 16: On a planet which seeks and does not bring about a conjunction[22]

Sometimes a planet seeks a conjunction, but it does not bring it about in its own sign while it is accompanying [that] planet through its own hastening.[23] And if [the first, applying planet] caught up with [the second planet, being applied to] in the next sign, and [the second planet] was not joined to another, the purpose is perfected. And if [the second planet] were joined to another when it is changed [into the next sign], were it joined to it afterwards, the purpose will not be perfected (because it has already been commingled to the light of another planet).[24]

Judgment 17[25]

[Suppose] a planet [is] wishing to be joined to a planet in one sign, but it cannot catch up with it in that same sign until it goes out to the next sign. And if it catches up with it in the next sign, then the purpose is perfected

---

[20] That is, from 28°00'—28° 59'.
[21] This seems to be related to Sahl's allowing of out-of-sign conjunctions (*Introduct.*, end of §5.3; likewise 'Umar in §A.131 above).
[22] This and the next Judgment have to do with "escape" (*ITA* III.22, and §A.131 above).
[23] Reading *dum comitetur ipsum planetam* for *donec imitetur ipsum planeta*.
[24] For example, let Mercury be applying to Venus near the end of a sign. Before Mercury can complete the connection, Venus moves into the following sign. If Mercury can cross into that sign and connect with her *before* Venus does so with a third planet, the purpose is perfected. But if Venus had already been connected (or perhaps was in the process of being connected) to another before Mercury could connect with her, then the purpose will not be perfected.
[25] This is largely a repetition of the previous Judgment, except that information about aspects versus assemblies by body is added.

(unless it would then be joined to another); but if it were joined with another by aspect, this does not hinder it, on account of what I have told you: because a conjunction which comes to be through an aspect does not annul a conjunction which comes to be by body in one sign. And a conjunction of this kind[26] annuls the one which comes to be by aspect. And an aspect does not cut off an aspect, but it blocks the purpose; but a bodily conjunction cuts off an aspect.[27]

Judgment 18: On a bad planet well disposed

If a bad planet were eastern (that is, if it appeared in the east in the morning), in its own house or in its own exaltation, and it was not joined to a bad one who would impede it, it is better and more worthy than a retrograde and impeded fortune.

Judgment 19: On bad planets appearing as the lords of purposes

If bad ones were the lords of purposes,[28] and the lord of the Ascendant or the Moon were joined to them from a square aspect or the opposition (that is, from the fourth sign or from the seventh one [from it]),[29] they make the purpose but destroy it in the end. And if the bad ones were those who are joined to good ones (that is, if the bad ones would push and be joined to them), it will be better than if they were the ones receiving the disposition.[30]

Judgment 20: On bad planets in the Ascendant

If a bad one were in the Ascendant, in its own house or in the exaltation, it is restrained from evil; if however it is retrograde in the Ascendant, its evil is strengthened and its diversity and variation is multiplied.

---

[26] I.e., a bodily conjunction.
[27] See *Introduct.* §5.7, "the third way"; also Māshā'allāh in §A.132 above.
[28] That is, they rule the houses of the quaesited or the topic of an election.
[29] Again, this also includes the tenth sign from it.
[30] That is, it is better for an application to go to benefics rather than to malefics.

Judgment 21: On a planet appearing in a sign similar to its own nature

If a planet were in, of the signs, its own character[31] and likeness, it will be agreeable for it: that is, if Saturn were in his own house or in the exaltation, or in a cold sign, and Mars were (just as I have told you before) in a hot sign, it will be good. Indeed if it were in the contrariety of its nature, it will be bad for it: just like water and oil, which are not commingled nor complected. And if it were in a sign similar to itself, they are commingled and complected just like water and milk.[32]

Judgment 22: On the fortunes aspecting the bad ones

When the fortunes aspect the bad ones, they decrease [the bad ones'] impediment.

Judgment 23: On the bad ones aspecting the fortunes

When the bad ones aspect the fortunes from a square aspect or from the opposition, they decrease [the good planets'] fortune.

Judgment 24: On fortunes cadent from the Ascendant

If the fortunes were cadent from the Ascendant,[33] or retrograde, they will be impeded [and be] like the bad ones.

Judgment 25: On planets when they are received

When planets are received, and they are fortunes, their good will be stronger; and if they were bad ones, their impediment will be less.

Judgment 26: On bad ones appearing in a peregrine (or not-peregrine) sign

If the bad planets were in a peregrine sign, and if they were not in their own houses (nor in the exaltation, nor in triplicity), they increase evil and

---

[31] *Habitu*, a difficult word meaning "condition, style, quality, manner," *etc*.
[32] Cf. Abū Ma'shar's different forms of mixtures and complexions in *Gr. Intr.* VII.4.670-694.
[33] That is, in aversion to the rising sign.

their impediment is made greater; and if they were in signs in which they have testimony, they are restrained from evil, and there will not entirely be an impediment.[34]

Judgment 27: On the bad ones, if they were the lords of matters and well-disposed

If the bad ones were in their own houses (or in the exaltations or in triplicities or in their own bounds), and in the angles or in the followers of the angles, and they were the lords of matters, their strength will be like the strength of the fortunes. Understand what I have said.

Judgment 28: On fortunes appearing peregrine or not-peregrine

If the fortunes were in a sign in which they do not have testimony, their fortune and good is decreased; and if they were in a sign in which there is testimony for them (that is, in their own houses or exaltations or triplicities or bounds), their fortune is made greater, and the matter is perfected, and good is increased.

Judgment 29: On planets appearing in a malign place or under the rays

If the fortunes and bad ones were in a malign place (that is, in one of the houses which I have said before), or they were under the rays, burned up, they signify small and despicable things, and the planets would not be able to signify good or evil on account of the weakness which is in them. Because if a planet were under the rays, burned up, or in the opposition of the Sun, it will be weak, since in this place there is no usefulness nor anything good for the good planets, nor anything evil for the bad ones: because the fortunes signify a modicum of the good if they were under the rays; and likewise if the bad ones were under the rays, their impediment will be less.

Judgment 30: On planets appearing in their own dignities

And every planet (a fortune or a bad one), if it were in its own house or in the exaltation or in its own triplicity, and so on—whatever evil is in them is

---

[34] That is, there will be an impediment, but not one as bad.

turned away into the good. Marvel therefore at what I have told you, and take your measure of judging from it.

Judgment 31: On bad ones appearing in the angles

If the bad ones were in the angles of the Ascendant, and they impeded from the square aspect or the opposition, the bad ones will be strong at harming, and their affliction will be greater, and especially and most particularly if they were stronger than the planet whom they oppress or impede (that is, if they were in a stronger place, that is, if they had some dignity); but if they aspected from a trine or from a sextile aspect, they are restrained from evil and their impediment is decreased.[35]

Judgment 32: On a consideration which must be had concerning the places of the planets[36]

Always, a fortune does not signify except for fortune, and a bad one always signifies nothing except for evil (on account of the overflowing of its nature and the malignity of its complexion). Therefore it is necessary to look at the places of the planets—that is, their places from the Ascendant, and the signs in which they are: because even though a planet may be a bad one, if it were in its own likeness,[37] or in its own light,[38] or in its own house or exaltation or triplicity, or in a good place from the Ascendant, it signifies good.

Judgment 33: On a fortune, if it were badly disposed[39]

If a fortune were not in its own light (that is, if it were of the planets of the night, and it were a significator in the day, or it were of the planets of the day and were a significator in the night), or were it peregrine from its own

---

[35] See the relation of good and bad aspects to benefic and malefic planets in *ITA* III.6.2.
[36] This Judgment must be read with the next one, but cf. also Judgments 2, 21, and 27.
[37] Probably referring to Judgment 21 above.
[38] See the next Judgment: this refers to being a member of the sect of the chart, but perhaps even being in its domain (i.e., in its appropriate relationship to the Sun by hemisphere: see *ITA* III.2).
[39] This Judgment must be read with the previous one.

sign,[40] or cadent from the Ascendant, or under the rays, it impedes and is not profitable.[41]

Judgment 34: On that which Jupiter and Venus can[42] change

If Jupiter aspected a bad one, he changes its nature into the good; and Venus cannot turn a great thing (that is, the evil of Saturn) unless [Saturn][43] would aspect Jupiter. For Jupiter loosens what Saturn binds up: that is, if Jupiter is joined to Saturn, he breaks [Saturn's] malice and changes it. And Venus loosens what Mars binds up.

Judgment 35: On that which the pushing of the planets to each other, signifies

If a bad one pushes (that is, it is joined) to a bad one, it is turned—that is, an evil is changed into another evil. And if a bad one is joined to a fortune, the evil is converted into good. Indeed if a fortune is joined to a bad one, he will find evil after the good. And commingle matters in this way.

Judgment 36: On that which the fortunes free from the evils of the infortunes

If the Moon (and the lord of the Ascendant) were impeded[44] by the conjunction or from the square aspect or the opposition of the bad ones, if then fortunes are joined to her from a square aspect, whatever would find a man in terms of destruction will be loosened by the fortunes, and he will be freed from them. Likewise, if they[45] were joined to bad ones from the square aspect, and fortunes aspected from a trine aspect, the man will escape what happens to him in terms of that destruction, and he will fall into another; or he will hardly escape what happens to him in terms of the destruction, and he will not fall into another.[46]

---

[40] Or simply, "peregrine."
[41] *Non proficit.*
[42] Reading *possunt.*
[43] Reading a singular verb for "they."
[44] Reading *impedita* (referring to the Moon) for *impeditus*, since the sentence begins with her. But the Latin translator clearly means it to refer to either one of them.
[45] That is, the Moon or the lord of the Ascendant.
[46] The rationale here seems to be related to whole-sign aspects, since a square from the benefics would place them in a position to oppose the evil itself. For instance, if the Moon were in the first, and a malefic were in the tenth, then a benefic in the fourth would

Judgment 37: On a planet outside its own dignities and cadent from the angles

If a planet were not in its own house or in the exaltation or triplicity, or in its own bound or joy, and it were cadent from the angles, this will be an evil signification without any usefulness: and there is nothing of the good in the planet's impediment.

Judgment 38: On a planet under the rays toward the west

If[47] a planet were under the rays, toward the west (that is, if it arises in the evening), its strength will be weak as was said concerning the superiors: for there will be no strength for it, nor for its light; and its impediment will be less if it were a bad one; and if it were retrograde, it will be slow in all matters.[48]

Judgment 39: On a planet under the rays within 12°

If planets were under the rays, they will be weak in all matters: that is, if there were less than 12° between them and the Sun (unless a planet is in the degree of the Sun, because then it will be strong).[49]

Judgment 40: On a planet with the Sun

If a planet were far from the Sun by 12° in the morning from the east,[50] it will be strong in every beginning and in every work. And if it were prolonged from him by 15°, then it will be stronger—that is, then it will be in the greatest strength that it could be in. And if a planet were in front of the Sun from the side of the west (that is, if it would arise in the evening in the west), and

---

be able to oppose the malefic; but if the benefic were sextile or trine the Moon in the third or fifth, it would be in aversion to the malefic and therefore be unable to deal with the evil directly.

[47] In this judgment, the western planets would either be headed toward being burned up (superiors) or retrograding toward it (inferiors), or going direct but about to come out of the rays (inferiors).

[48] This latter point would only be possible for the inferiors, if they were retrograde and moving toward the Sun.

[49] For being in the heart of the Sun, see *ITA* II.9.

[50] That is, being eastern, arising in the east from the Sun's rays. This judgment applies particularly to the superiors.

there were from 15° up to 7° between it and the Sun, then it begins to be weakened from 7° until it comes to be in the heart of the Sun: the planet comes to be weaker than it could [ever] become. And if it were in the heart of the Sun, it will be strong through the heart of the Sun (he wants to be understood thusly, like when it is with the Sun in one degree).

Judgment 41: On a peregrine planet

If a planet were on a foreign journey,[51] that is, if it were not in one of its own dignities (as is the exaltation, face, and so on), its mind and nature becomes cunning.[52] And if it were not in its own house or exaltation and it were direct, and in a good place from the Ascendant, or in the Midheaven or in the eleventh, it will be good.

Judgment 42: On the receiver of disposition

If the Moon is joined to some planet, the one to whom she is joined is said to be the receiver of the Moon's disposition, and thus reception proceeds up until Saturn (because above Saturn there is no other who would receive the disposition).[53] The receiver of disposition, if it were pertaining-to-sinking[54] by 12° and less in front of the Sun, it will be weak and crushed, and what it judges is not perfected; and if it were pertaining-to-arising,[55] it will be strong and skillful [and] excellent[56] in the judgment. Because an impeded planet is like a building: and if it fell, it is rebuilt, improved, and comes to be good.[57]

---

[51] That is, peregrine.
[52] *Callidus*. The idea behind this statement is that people around us who have no clear sense of belonging or commitment where they are (which would be analogous to being in a dignity or at least received), are often viewed with suspicion.
[53] This sentence originally appeared with the previous Judgment, but belongs here.
[54] *Occidentalis*. That is, in a later degree than the Sun and setting after him. This particularly pertains to the superiors.
[55] *Orientalis*. That is, in an earlier degree than the Sun and rising before him.
[56] *Perfectus*.
[57] The falling down/rebuilding metaphor clearly relates to entering the Sun's beams and then re-emerging on the other side.

Judgment 43: On a planet in the eighth house

If a planet were in the eighth from the Ascendant, and it were a fortune, it does not perform good nor evil; and if the bad ones were in the same place, their evil is made greater.

Judgment 44: On a planet in the beginning of a sign and in the beginning of the angles

If a planet were in the beginning of a sign, it will be weak until it is made firm in it, and walks through it by 6°.[58] And a planet does not fall from the angles except after 5°.[59] For example: if the angle were the tenth degree of Aries, every planet which is in less than 5° [of Aries] is cadent and is not thought to be in the angle.[60]

Judgment 45: When a planet after the angle is understood to be in the angle

And every planet which is after the angle by 15° will be just like one which is in the angle; and if the degree increased, it will have no strength. For example: If the angle were the tenth degree of the sign of Aries, then every planet which is from that same tenth degree up to 25° of the same Aries,[61] is thought to be in that same angle. Which if one added 15° on top [of that], it will not be in the angle. But Ptolemy says a planet will be in the angle up into 25° after the angle.[62]

---

[58] This could be based on the average size of a bound: 30°/5 bounds = 6° each.
[59] Here Sahl or his translator uses *post* ("after") an angle to indicate being in an "earlier degree" than the angle, having passed it by primary motion.
[60] Here the angle is being associated with quadrant houses; this notion clearly derives from *Tet.* III.11, where Ptolemy applies the so-called "five-degree rule" in the context of longevity determinations. See also Judgment 45.
[61] Omitting *vir* with BN.
[62] This is because, in his longevity procedure, Ptolemy seems to be using equal houses from the Ascendant, with a 5° offset rule for cusps.

Judgment 46: What the planets would signify in the signs, concerning the stability of a matter[63]

If planets were in fixed signs, they signify fixity—that is, firmness and the stability of matters concerning which the question comes to be. And if they were in common signs, they signify the loosenings of matters, and repetitions, and other things[64] will be attached to that matter (or some such other thing). And if they were in movable signs, they signify the speed of the conversions or changes of matters into good or evil.

Judgment 47: What the signs would signify in questions

A fixed sign signifies the fixity (that is, the firmness) of questions and of the matters concerning which the question comes to be, and every fixed and very firm and stable matter; and it is a good ally of the question. And the common signs signify matters which cannot come to be, and which are repeated a second time. And a movable sign signifies the speed of a matter's changing into something else.

Judgment 48: On a stationary planet

If a planet stood toward retrogradation (that is, if it were in its first station), it signifies the dissolution of a purpose, and disobedience; and if it stood toward direction (that is, if it were in its second station), it signifies forward direction after the slowness or duress of the matter. And every planet which is a significator and wished to go direct (that is, if it were in its second station) signifies the renewal of the actions of matters, and their action and strength or forward movement. And if it were in the first station, wishing to go retrograde, it signifies their destruction and slowness and dissolution.

---

[63] This Judgment must be read with the following one. The paragraphs are virtually identical, and must have been so in the Arabic, because Hugo lists each separately, and Bonatti (in his Consideration 60) combines the two to form a single paragraph.

[64] *Altera.* This word has to do with repetition or pairs. See *On Elect.* §§16a-17, and *ITA* I.10.5.

Judgment 49: On a question made when the Moon is impeded

Know that on a day in which the Moon is impeded, everything concerning which one asks on that day, will be impeded—unless the bad one impeding her is cadent from the Ascendant and weak, and the Moon did not then have a role[65] in the Ascendant: because if a bad one impedes the Moon, and it was cadent from the Ascendant, it introduces fear and worry; and if it were in the angles or in the followers of the angles,[66] it heaps fear onto the body.[67]

Judgment 50: On the planet to which the Moon is joined; and concerning the Moon herself (and the lord of the Ascendant) in the opposite of her own house

Know that the planet to which the Moon is joined, signifies what is going to be, and the producing of the matter. Which if she is joined to fortunes, it signifies a good producing; and if she is joined to a bad one, it signifies a bad producing.

And know that the lord of the Ascendant (or the Moon), if it were in the opposition of its own house (that is, in the seventh of its own house), the owner of the question[68] will dread the purpose concerning which he asked: for it will be severe for him. Know all of this.

---

[65] *Partem.* This tends to mean having a dignity in the degree of the Ascendant.
[66] That is, the succeedents.
[67] See Judgment 4.
[68] That is, the querent.

APPENDIX B: EXCERPT FROM BONATTI'S *THE BOOK OF ASTRONOMY* TR. 6: ON QUESTIONS[1]

[PART 1]

Chapter 1

If you intended to attain to the judgments of astrology, let it be your first concern to consider whether he who has come to you in order to pose a question, asks with a purpose, just as is said elsewhere.[2] Likewise it is said there *how* you can know whether he asks from an intention or not, in a more extensive way than can be touched upon here; [but] here are certain things which are not dealt with there: for if the lord of the Ascendant and the lord of the hour were of the same triplicity, or of the same complexion, or if the lord of the Ascendant and the hour were the same [planet], the question will be from an intention and is rooted. But if it is otherwise, it does not appear that it comes to be from an intention or is rooted, unless perhaps in a sudden case, you will assign the Ascendant to the querent.[3] And if it were necessary, yield to the person, and see the sign that signifies the quaesited matter, and the planet ruling that sign, and the aspect of the significators; also attend to the conjunction of the fortunes and the bad ones to the significators, both by body and by aspect.

And you should know that the bodily conjunction of the Sun, which is called "burning up,"[4] is harmful beyond all other impediments. Likewise you will consider whether the significator of the querent or of the quaesited matter is in its own house or in any house from it, and whether it is free from impediments or not, and that it is not in the burnt path;[5] likewise, whether the significators (among which the Moon is always to be counted) are in strong places or weak ones, or mediocre ones, and whether they are in the beginnings of the houses, the middle, or their ends. In the same way you will

---

[1] These excerpts present Bonatti's general approach to questions. I have slightly edited the text from its 2007 version.
[2] See e.g., Tr. 5, Considerations 1, 2, 7, 143.
[3] In other words, if it is an emergency, go ahead and take the chart regardless of whether or not the lord of the Ascendant and the lord of the hour fulfill the requirements listed.
[4] That is, "combustion."
[5] Otherwise known as the *via combusta*.

look for helpers or hinderers of any one of them, according to their being.[6] All these things having been diligently considered, you will be able to weigh your judgment of the question proposed to you: because the fortunes signify good, but the bad ones on the contrary will herald evil. If however you found the fortunes and bad ones to be equal, they portend a judgment in the middle. But if [you found only] benefics, they will prevail [in terms of] good fortune; and if the bad ones, you will judge the opposite.

You will even consider the people asking the questions, how and in what way it matters to them that they are asking whatever they are—whether the querent asks for himself, or through another and [or] for another, and by what houses the people asking are signified;[7] and likewise with the quaesited, and what is signified by whatever house, the significations of which you have from the chapter above on the things signified by the twelve houses.

Chapter 2: How one ought to reach a judgment

Since judging about future things is most difficult (and that this is true, is clear by the Considerations assigned to you above);[8] nor did Hippocrates pronounce on a vain and difficult judgment (because nothing in the world is more difficult than predicting the truth about future things), before [making] judgments is arrived at, I will tell you certain things which pertain to the business of judgments, without which it would be impossible for me to believe you are able to know how to judge according to the march of truth (even though I made some mention of these very things above).

Wherefore it is important to know first, before you presume to judge, what are the causes perfecting matters, and which of them disclose the truth, and which are those that block them so they are not perfected, and from what causes the effecting of matters will come, and from what will come

---

[6] *Esse.* This refers both to planetary natures, categories such as benefic and malefic, and planetary conditions.
[7] Bonatti is hinting that the houses are allocated differently, depending on who the client is and why he is there. He clarifies this in below in Part 2, 5th House, Ch. 4, when he says that if a man is asking for a woman (in this case, presumably his wife) who has given her consent and is aware he is consulting an astrologer, then she is the true querent and is given the 1st house; but if the man is there of his own accord, and she is unaware, then he is the querent and is given the 1st house (she is given the 7th). The issue, then, is whether the person actually facing or writing to the astrologer is the one with the question, or is a messenger on the true querent's behalf. See also Part 2, 6th House, Ch. 1.
[8] I.e., in Tr. 5.

their detriment; and what is signified by whatever perfecting [cause] or even by whatever destroying or blocking cause; and what would signify the time when they ought to be perfected, or when they ought to be destroyed or blocked. And [this] is a function that the highest creator of everything gave to the planets and signs, and even to the fixed stars. And Māshā'allāh and others[9] said that the effecting and detriment of matters in this world must come to be by three[10] principal ways.

Namely, the first way is when the lord of the Ascendant and the lord of the quaesited matter are joined, and the Moon at the same time.[11]

Second, when the aforesaid are not joined together, so that there is some planet which transfers the light between them, namely so that it is separated from one and is joined to the other.[12]

The third, when there comes to be a collection of light from some other planet which is heavier then they, and they themselves are both joined to it, and any one of them commits its own disposition to it;[13] because [the heavier planet] itself is the one which perfects the matter.[14]

And sometimes a matter is perfected wholly as the interrogator wills it, and sometimes it is perfected in part, and sometimes neither wholly nor in part. And I will set out all of this for you, so that you may understand it better and may comprehend how you can judge with respect to matters that are presented to you.

---

[9] See §A.132 (Māshā'allāh), §A.130 ('Umar), and Sahl in §1.1 (from *On Quest.* §§1.4 and 1.8).

[10] Later Bonatti will implicitly add two other ways: by location (of which there are a couple of kinds), and what I am calling "benefic reception." Location is also suggested in §A.130 above.

[11] That is, by a direct connection.

[12] By a transfer or reflection of light.

[13] Below, Bonatti assumes (or perhaps prefers) that this involves reception.

[14] By a collection of light.

On the exposition of the first way

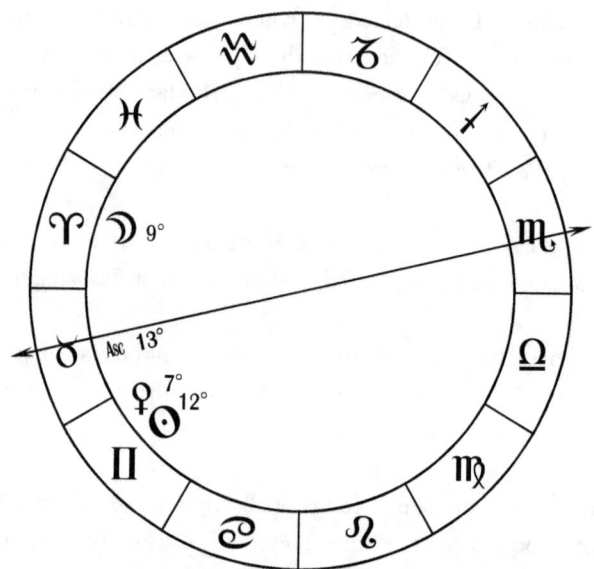

Figure 78: Perfection by a direct connection

The exposition of the first way by which matters are perfected, is when the lord of the Ascendant and the Moon are joined with the lord of the quaesited matter: for then the matter is perfected.

For example, a certain question was posed, whether a certain man was going to obtain a certain manor estate which he wanted to buy. And the Ascendant was Taurus, 13°; and Venus was in Gemini, 7°; and the Sun was in Gemini, 12°; and the Moon in Aries, 9°. And the lord of the Ascendant (namely Venus, who was going to a bodily conjunction of the Sun) and the Moon (who was going to his aspectual conjunction) signified that the matter ought to be perfected;[15] And it would be perfected if the one who had posed the question wanted to pursue it so that it would be perfected;[16] and especial-

---

[15] In this example, the querent is represented by Venus, who rules the Ascendant; the quaesited (the estate) is represented by the Sun, who rules the fourth. The Moon is a co-significator. All three are joined by a direct connection.

[16] The important point here is that something may be fated, but only if the agents who can make it happen, do act. In this sense, horary is something of a cross between elections and straightforward prediction (as with natal or mundane techniques), because it assumes

ly since the Sun, who was the significator of the quaesited, received the Moon from Aries by a sextile aspect.[17] And if not by sextile, the matter would perfect even by square or opposition, provided that reception intervened, even if it were with difficulty and anxiety and the greatest labor, and likewise obstacles and unfitness.

On the exposition of the second way

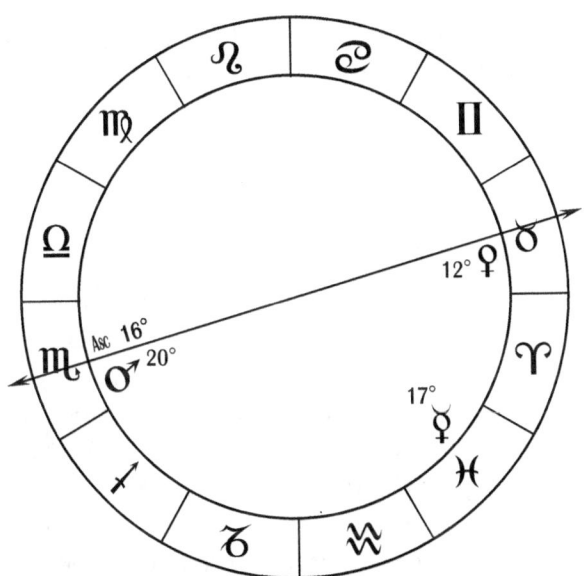

Figure 79: Perfection by a transfer of light[18]

The exposition of the second way is when one planet is separated from another, and is joined to [yet] another, and commits the disposition it had accepted from the first, to the one with which it itself is joined. For example, a question was put to me: a certain man asked whether he was about to have the goods of a certain uncle of his (who had no sons), the Ascendant of which was Scorpio, 16°; and Mars in it, 20°; and Venus in Taurus, 12°, going toward the opposition of Mars; and Mercury in Pisces, 17°. And Mercury was separated from Venus by a sextile aspect, by which he had been joined to

---

a degree of fate, but in many cases it must also assume that the agents take advantage of good timing.
[17] That is, he received her by exaltation, a case of "pushing nature" (*ITA* III.15).
[18] This chart is possibly from February-March 1243 AD JC, but the degrees are rather off.

her; [and] she received him from Pisces, which is her exaltation, and she committed her disposition to him. And Mercury carried it to Mars, and committed it to [Mars] by a trine aspect. And this signified that the man was going to possess his uncle's goods, on account of Venus, who was the significatrix of the goods of the querent's uncle, [and] who committed her disposition to Mercury, and Mercury carried it to Mars, who is the significator of the querent. For the 6th house is the significator of the uncle, namely the father's brother (just as was said above in the chapter on the houses), because the 6th is the 3rd from the 4th (which is the house of the father). And the 7th, which signifies the uncle's assets, is the 2nd from the 6th. And the transfer of light signified that the matter would come to be through the agency of legates,[19] who intervene in it; and it seemed that it ought to come to be through the agency of an ally of one of the querent's partners;[20] which if he did not have a partner, it would come to be through the agency of a certain ally of his enemy or his wife. If his wife did not live in the house with him, and if [such an] ally were not to be found, it will come to be through the agency of a certain servant of the querent's brother;[21] which if the brother did not have a servant, it would come to be through the agency of some stepson of the querent;[22] which if he did not have a stepson, it would come to be through the agency of a certain friend of his;[23] which if he did not have a friend, it would come to be through the agency of a certain soldier or ally of the king;[24] which if such people were not found, it would come to be through the agency of a certain person in whom his secret enemies trust.[25] And if such a person is not found, then it will come to be through the agency of one who is signified by the house in which the Moon is.

---

[19] Mercury is in the 5th, signifying legates.
[20] The word for "ally" here is *familiaris*, which can indicate a member of the household or a slave–basically, someone who personally attached to and beholden to the querent. In war charts the 2nd is the ally of the querent waging war, just as the 11th represents the ministers and advisors to the king (2nd from 10th). In this case, Mercury rules Gemini on the 8th house, which is the 2nd (ally) from the 7th (partners).
[21] The 8th (ruled by Mercury) is the 6th (servants) from the 3rd (siblings).
[22] Mercury rules the 11th, the other children (5th) of the spouse (7th).
[23] Mercury also rules Virgo on the 11th (friends).
[24] The 11th is the 2nd (allies) from the 10th (king).
[25] Perhaps people in the household of the enemy (the 8th is the 2nd from the 7th), unless the Midheaven is in Virgo, which would make Mercury also rule the 11th (friends) from the 12th (secret enemies).

On the exposition of the third way

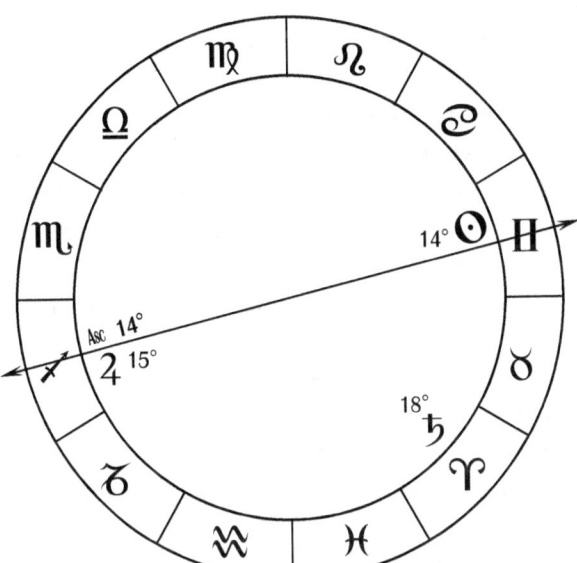

Figure 80: Perfection by a collection of light

The exposition of the third way is when one planet which is the significator of the quaesited matter is not joined to the lord of the Ascendant of the question, but they are both joined to another which is heavier than they, and they both commit their own virtue to it, and the heavier one perfects the quaesited matter. Just as for example, [when] a certain man asked whether he was about to obtain a certain church [position] for which he strove: the Ascendant was Sagittarius, 14°; and Jupiter in it, 15°; and the Sun (who was the significator of the church position) in Gemini, 14°; and Saturn in Aries, 18°. And each one was joined to Saturn, and [Saturn] himself collected the light of each;[26] indeed this collection of the light of Jupiter and the Sun that Sat-

---

[26] This example is unusual, because since the Sun is in an earlier degree than Jupiter, he should be able to perfect the matter at least somewhat by an opposition. But since their opposition lacks perfect reception, perhaps Bonatti is suggesting that it is easier for Saturn to perfect the matter by collection, than it would be for the Sun and Jupiter to do so by opposition without reception. On the other hand, there are two other problems with this chart. First, in this position Jupiter must be retrograde, which means he will not be applying to Saturn at all. Second, although the planets were in these signs in the spring of 1260 AD, the degrees do not match the chart even closely. Perhaps Bonatti wrote this passage

urn was making, signified that the matter would be perfected, and that he would obtain the church position inquired about. Because the Sun, who was the lord of the 9th house (which signified [the church position]), committed his own disposition to Saturn, because [the Sun] received [Saturn] from [the Sun's] exaltation; and Saturn entrusted and committed to Jupiter the quaesited matter which was being committed to him by the Sun,[27] and the matter would have been perfected all the more preferably if the querent had sought the quaesited matter for another than if he sought it for himself. Because even though [Jupiter] was joined to [Saturn] from a trine aspect, Saturn however did not receive him by perfect reception, because he did not receive him except by triplicity.[28] And it seemed that a brother of the querent would be the one by whose agency the matter was perfected;[29] which if he did not have a brother, it would have been the brother of someone who pretends to love him when he [really] does not.[30] And if there were no such person, it would have been a son of a friend of his;[31] and if such a person is not found, it would have been the slave of a magnate;[32] and if such a person were not found, it would have been a certain enemy of the church; and if such an enemy of the church were not found, it would have been an enemy of the querent's son; and if he did not have a son, or the son had no friend, it would have been a certain hidden enemy of the querent's father; which if the client did not have a father, or the father did not have such an enemy, it would

---

in 1260, knowing that the planets were at least in these signs, and simply assigned them values in order to create an example.

[27] Bonatti did not say that the collecting planet would have to commit the disposition he receives from one significator to the other in turn. This could be an elaboration of the definition, or else Bonatti is just pointing out that this in fact is what Saturn happens to be doing here.

[28] Bonatti seems to be saying that since there is no perfect reception, the disposition from the Sun (which was committed to Saturn) will not be able to be fully committed to Jupiter, because the reception is not perfect. Therefore, the matter will not be perfected in the best way for the *querent* (Jupiter), but since the dignity of triplicity is compared to having allies and helpers and friends (Tr. 2, Part 1, Ch. 19), it could perfect for a friend the querent is helping.

[29] Saturn rules the 3rd (siblings).

[30] Saturn rules the 2nd, which is the 3rd (siblings) from the 12th (secret enemies).

[31] The 3rd house is the 5th (children) from the 11th (friends).

[32] The 3rd is the 6th (servants, slaves) from the 10th (magnates, important people). I will omit explaining the rest of the examples Bonatti mentions.

have happened then through simony;³³ and this way of perfecting the matter is lasting.³⁴

On another way of perfecting matters

And there is another way of perfecting matters which can be said to be subordinate to the preceding one, which is neither lasting nor perfect, namely if two planets were joined to another one heavier than they, and they committed disposition and virtue to it (just as was said about Jupiter and the Sun, as to how they committed virtue to Saturn); and this heavier one which received the disposition were impeded (namely cadent or retrograde or burned up or joined to bad ones which impede it), or it was besieged by the bad ones.³⁵ I say that it can perfect the matter, and sometimes perfects it, but after the matter is arranged and perfected, it is destroyed and does not remain in its perfection. Whence you can make the judgment to the one who asks you, that it seems the matter will be perfected, but it will be destroyed after it is perfected.

On certain other accidents of matters which are perfected

Sometimes something happens in matters which are perfected, namely that certain ones of them come to be with difficulty and duress, and labor, and the greatest complications; others come to be with ease, others come to be with striving and inconvenience, certain ones come to be with striving and great inconvenience, certain ones come to be without striving and any difficulty—on the contrary, they come without any thought at all.

On those matters which come easily

Those which come easily and without striving or any difficulty, as unhindered things, are when the lord of the Ascendant or the significator of the querent and the significator of the quaesited matter are joined by a trine or sextile aspect, and with reception.

---

[33] Simony is the purchasing of ecclesiastical offices.
[34] This almost seems like a joke on Bonatti's part. He undoubtedly means that collection of light is lasting; but he could also be cynically noting that simony is a good way to get a lasting position.
[35] This is an example of collection of light, but where the collecting planet is afflicted.

On those matters which come to be shortly

Indeed those matters which come to be shortly and without striving (even if hope is not had, concerning them, that they will come to be) are when the lord of the Ascendant is joined with the lord of the quaesited by a trine aspect without reception, or by a sextile with reception.

On those matters which come to be with striving

Indeed, those which come to be with the querent's striving and effort, are when the lord of the Ascendant is joined with the significator of the quaesited matter, by a square aspect with reception, or a sextile aspect without reception.

On those matters which come to be with striving, effort, and labor

However, those which come to be with striving and effort and obstacles and labor, and great trouble, are when the significator of the querent is joined with the significator of the quaesited matter by opposition, or by a square aspect without reception.

On those matters which come to be with labor, yet are hardly perfected

Those things which come to be with the greatest labor, and obstacles, and striving and effort and distress, likewise sadness, and as though after the desperation of friends and blood relations, and yet hardly or never perfect (and if they were perfected their effect will be slow for a long time, and even then with expenses)—are those in which the lord of the Ascendant (or the Moon) and the lord of the quaesited matter, are joined by opposition without reception.

Aspect	Reception
Trine/sextile	Yes
Trine	No
Sextile	Yes
Square	Yes
Sextile	No
Opposition	Yes?
Square	No
Opposition	No

Figure 81: Ranking of effective connections (Bonatti)

When a matter someone wishes for, comes to be without reception

And there is another way that a matter (which someone intends to have) may be perfected, and it is easier than all other aforesaid ways: namely, when the significator of the quaesited matter is joined to the significator of the one desiring it, from a sextile aspect with reception, or from a trine without reception; or if the significator of the matter were in the Ascendant or in the house signifying the one for whom the matter is pursued. You should understand the same concerning the bodily conjunction as with aspects, for then the matter will come to be most easily.

When the matter which is sought is a magistracy or dignity

If perhaps the matter which is sought were a magistracy or lay dignity which is hoped for by someone, and the querent hoped to get it from the king or from some lord of his, and the significator of the aforesaid matter were in the Ascendant, or were joined to the lord of the Ascendant, or with the Moon from a trine or sextile aspect, or bodily and with reception, it signifies that the quaesited matter will perfect without his own striving, or by another on his behalf.

When some matter is hoped for from some magnate—how the matter will come to be

And if someone hopes for something from one who is lower [in status] than the king, or from some friend of his, or from a commoner of some land, or the like, the matter will come to be and will come by means of a fortuitous occurrence.[36]

When a conjunction or aspect does not intervene[37]

If however there were no conjunctional aspect between them, but there were a transfer of light, the matter will come to be through the agency of legates who introduce themselves into the situation so that it may be perfected. But for knowing who these legates are, you would look to the house whose lord is the significator of whichever of [the planets it is],[38] or to the house in which you found them, as has been sufficiently explained to you (for it would be tedious to explain it everywhere). And then look likewise at the Moon: because if she were then separated from the significator of the one desiring the matter (or even from the querent of [the matter]), and she were joined to the significator of the matter, it signifies that those who are running to and fro among them come from the side of the one desiring the matter, and with his knowledge and will. If however she were separated from the planet signifying the matter, and she were joined to the significator of the one desiring the matter, it signifies that they originate from the side of the thing or from those who can perfect it. And if the matter were perfected by legates, the legates themselves will be of the sort of persons signified by the houses of which they are lords: look, then, to see what persons are signified by those houses, and judge according to them, whether it is an ally, or brother or neighbor, or father, or child, or slave, or partner, or [the partner's] ally, or a religious figure, or a king or master, or friend or hidden enemy.

And[39] you must know that even though I told you that matters are perfected by trine or sextile aspects, you must however understand well: because if [1] the place from which the lord of the Ascendant (or the Moon) is as-

---

[36] I believe the only point of this paragraph is to note that 11th house matters, when they perfect, will do so in an 11th house way–with fortunate circumstances and fulfilled hopes.
[37] I.e., when the mode "by joining" does not apply–then we look for translation or collection of light.
[38] Bonatti means, "the house ruled by the planet making the transfer."
[39] For this paragraph, cf. Sahl in *Judges* §1.1 (*On Quest.* §1.6), and Sahl's *Introduct.* §5.9; also, al-Kindī's *Forty Chapters* Ch. 2.1.8. This is called "not-reception."

pected by the lord of the quaesited matter (namely by which the matter itself is signified), or [2] the place from which the lord or significator of the matter is aspected by the lord of the Ascendant (or the Moon) is the detriment of the one aspecting, the matter is not perfected, even if the aspect is a sextile or trine. Just as, for example, the Ascendant was Leo, and the question was about a marriage—whether it would take place or not—and the Sun is joined with Saturn or the Moon (which signifies women) from Aries, which is the detriment[40] of Saturn. Even if the aspect (however great in itself) is with reception, Saturn however will not perfect the matter, but rather impedes it so that it does not perfect—he not only impedes, but tries to destroy it if he can. And if [the Sun] were joined to [Saturn] from Cancer or Leo, he would do the same, because both of them are his fall.[41] Likewise if the significator of whatever matter (or the Moon) were joined to the Sun from Libra (which is his descension), or from Aquarius (which is his fall), because then the Sun would not receive any of them, and thus he would destroy the matter and not permit it to be perfected. Or if he were joined to Venus from Scorpio or Aries or Virgo, or to Jupiter from Capricorn or Gemini or Virgo. And you should know the detriment of whatever planet [you are dealing with]: nor does any aspect suffice (unless reception intervenes), that will break its malice.

And[42] you should understand the same if the significator or the Moon were joined to a planet which is in the detriment of that significator itself (or of the Moon): like if Mercury were the significator, and were joined to a planet which is in Sagittarius or Pisces, or the Moon were joined to a planet which is in Scorpio or Capricorn, or a planet were joined to any planet located in its own descension; or [if] the one which is in the descension of the other, is joined to the one whose descension it is,[43] it always tries to destroy the matter and annul it.

There[44] is even something else which introduces fear into matters, as when a planet which is the significator of the quaesited matter is an infortune, and it shows that the matter ought to be perfected by an aspect[45] or by

---

[40] Or rather, "fall." Note Bonatti's loose use of detriment and descension/fall.
[41] Or rather, "detriment."
[42] For this paragraph, see Sahl in *Judges* §1.1 (*On Quest.* §1.6).
[43] These last two clauses sound complicated, but are simple: if one is joined to the other, or the other to it.
[44] For this paragraph, cf. Sahl in *Judges* §1.1 (*On Quest.* §1.6) and Judgment 25 in Appendix A.
[45] Presumably by square, since Bonatti almost always pairs it with the opposition.

opposition, then the querent fears lest some trouble will come to him from it, whence he hopes more strongly that it will not perfect, than he does that it will perfect. But if the aspect were a trine or sextile with reception, it will be secured; if however without reception, it will not be evil in the way that he fears, even if it is not very secure in the way the querent wants.

Moreover,[46] if the significator of the querent and the significator of the quaesited matter were the same planet, just as often happens, nor were it received in the place in which it is, it signifies that the matter ought not to be perfected; indeed if it were received, it signifies that the matter ought to be perfected with a good perfection, unless the one which is receiving it were impeded by fall[47] or being burned up or retrogradation; because even if it comes to be, it is not perfected by a good perfection (as [it would be] when it is not impeded).[48]

And[49] there is another thing: when the planetary significators are aided to perfect the thing, namely when signs agree in nature with the planets, and help them, and some exhibit their testimonies by means of them.

And Sahl said[50] it is good that, if the Ascendant is a fixed or common sign, you understand that the Ascendant is made diverse according to the diversity of the persons, by beginning from the 1st house all the way to the 12th;[51] and the angles should not be wide, but of the proper size, that is, so that the 10th house is the tenth sign from the Ascendant, and the angle of the earth is the fourth sign from the Ascendant (indeed so that the 10th house is not the ninth sign from the Ascendant, nor the 4th house the third sign from the Ascendant).

---

[46] For this paragraph, see Sahl in *Judges* §1.1 (*On Quest.* §1.6).

[47] I take this to mean the essential weakness of "fall" (*casus*) and not being cadent (which also has connotations of falling); presumably it also includes detriment. But it could certainly also mean cadence.

[48] This paragraph suggests that a planet can still receive if in fall, retrograde, or burned up–but it will not be an *effective* reception.

[49] For this paragraph, cf. Sahl's Judgment 21 in Appendix A.

[50] See *Judges* §1.1 and *On Quest.* 1.7. Bonatti does not quite bring out what Sahl's point is. Sahl is saying that for matters to be effected more reliably, the Ascendant should be a fixed or common sign (since those are more stable than movable signs), and the degree of the Midheaven should be on the tenth sign—so that there is a good concordance between whole-sign houses and the meridian. Al-Kindī (*Judges* §4.13, *Forty Chapters* §477) echoes Sahl's statement here. This teaching represents a recognition that the ninth sign is still in some sense a cadent sign, even if the Midheaven is on it—that is, that the whole signs still have their own natural angularity apart from the quadrant-based house systems.

[51] This simply means that the houses are distributed through the signs to represent different topics or people. See also Part 2, Ch. 1 below.

By what significations it is known whether matters ought to be perfected[52]

Likewise, you ought to know the significations by means of which it is known whether matters ought to be perfected or not, of which the first is the lord of the Ascendant. The second is the Moon, because, as is said elsewhere, she herself participates in every matter. The third is the planet signifying the quaesited matter. Which, when they are all joined together, they signify the effecting of the whole matter in the houses signifying the matters. (And may you always be mindful to diversify the Ascendants just as I told you now).

But if two of them (namely the lord of the Ascendant and the lord of the [quaesited] matter, or the Moon and the lord of the quaesited) were joined together, it signifies that the matter will come to be by two thirds. But if only one of them were attested to, it signifies that the quaesited matter will be perfected for the querent by one-third. Understand this in matters which are susceptible to division, because if there were a matter which could not be divided, either it will come to be wholly, or it will not come to be wholly. If however in matters which are not divided, you had two of the aforesaid testimonies, declare the effect of the quaesited to be entire. If perhaps you had only one of them, it can hardly or never be perfected, but if it were perfected it would come to be with hardship and delays, and with the greatest labor besides, and complications, like a marriage which either comes to be entirely or does not come to be entirely, and the like: if a marriage, I say there would be a single one. For if there were multiple marriages at once, as sometimes happens when it is sought by multiple women and multiple men—as when someone were looking for himself, and for his father or brother or son or someone else—then certain ones of them could be perfected, and certain ones not, according to how you saw the significations and testimonies occurring in the question.

And these three testimonies or significations should be considered in any matter; which if all were strong, then without a doubt whatever the matter is, it will be wholly perfected for the querent. For the significators (namely the lord of the Ascendant, and the Moon, and the lord of the quaesited matter) are strong when they are free from being burned up, fall, retrogradation, the square aspect and opposition of the bad ones (and from their besiegement), and from the bodily conjunction of the same—which rarely happens. And if in addition to their being strong, they were received by the infortunes from

---

[52] For this whole passage, cf. Sahl in *Judges* §1.1 (*On Quest.* §1.8).

any aspect, the matter will be perfected, and for the good. Indeed, if they were received by the fortunes, again the good will be increased, as though the querent did not know how to strive better, nor believed that the matter he sought would come to be perfectly.

Nor should you dismiss these words, because they have proven accurate in each matter, and work for every question and every thing which someone intends to do. However, much is discovered by considering the helpful and harmful fixed stars which help or do harm (as they are accordingly discussed in the chapter on them).

PART 2: ON THE PARTICULAR JUDGMENTS OF THE STARS

Chapter 1: That which signifies the querent's person, and what happens to him in any question and any matter which he intends to undertake or begin, inasmuch as questioning or beginning pertains to him, and likewise on those things which naturally appear to pertain to this

In[53] this first chapter we must deal with those things which pertain to the 1st house (which is the rising sign, and signifies the querent), in accordance as the question pertains to [that]. And I will tell you certain things which you ought to know about these. For diverse questions can be made, and of diverse types, in accordance as their qualities diversify them. For questions can be made diverse according to their own nature, as when one is about one matter and another is different from it. They can even be diverse according to other diverse significations, for at one time someone asks when he asks for himself, at another time when he asks on another's behalf. And I will tell you in what way you ought to look in each case, and likewise at what house when someone asks. For it is not always necessary that you should look at the 1st house for the Ascendant of the thing signified[54] in every question.

But you might say, "Why didn't any of the sages write down what you're saying?" The reason for this is this: they themselves let it remain for the industry of the wise, because they did not then speak to those who had to be introduced, but for those who had been introduced, and for the overflowing and the wise, and the instructed.

For if someone asked about himself, you ought to look at the 1st. But if he asked about his own assets or other things signified by the 2nd house, you ought to look at the 2nd. If he asked about siblings or about other things signified by the 3rd house, you ought to look at the 3rd. If he asked about his father or about other things signified by the 4th house, you ought to look at the 4th. If he asked about children or about other things signified by the 5th house, you ought to look at the 5th. If he asked about slaves or about other things signified by the 6th house, you ought to look at the 6th. If he asked

---

[53] For the first two paragraphs, cf. Māshā'allāh in *Judges* §A.127, and Sahl in §1.1 (*On Quest.* §1.1).
[54] This may be a key to the business about diversifying topics and Ascendants (see above)–because Bonatti equivocally uses the term "Ascendant" here to refer to any cusp.

about a wife or about other things signified by the 7th house, you ought to look at the 7th. If he asked about death or about other things signified by the 8th house, you ought to look at the 8th. If he asked about religion or about other things signified by the 9th house, you ought to look at the 9th. And if he asked about a kingdom or about other things signified by the 10th house, you ought to look at the 10th. If he asked about friends or about other things signified by the 11th house, you ought to look at the 11th. If he asked about hidden enemies or about other things signified by the 12th house, you ought to look at the 12th. And may you always remember these things.

Chapter 2: How you ought to look at the shadow when questions are posed to you[55]

And when you are asked about some matter, concerning which the questioner wishes to pose a question to you, take the altitude of the Sun, if it is a diurnal question. If however it were a nocturnal one, take the altitude of whichever fixed star is inscribed on the astrolabe, or with another instrument suitable to this [purpose], as soon as you can, accurately, immediately, without any delay or any length of interval, once the words leave the mouth of the one asking about the matter.

And take care that you do not deviate in anything, lest some error take place in the matter about which the question was posed to you. And observe the method which I told you, in looking at the house which signifies the quaesited matter. And likewise, beware lest you mix diverse topics together with questions at diverse times. For if some question had been made to you (let us say about marriage), and you examine it, and a little while afterwards the same man (or perhaps another) poses another question to you, on whatever topic, do not mix it with the other, already-examined one.[56] For the Ascendant has already changed, and thus it is necessary that the judgment be changed; whence you could thereby be guilty of being deceived in your judgment. But you can take it up with the required altitude, and it will be another judgment than the first one. Nevertheless, however, you can accept more than one question under multiple headings under one Ascendant, if the

---

[55] Cf. Māshā'allāh in *Judges* §A.127, 'Umar in §A.128, and Sahl in §1.1 (*On Quest.* 1.1); also *OHT* §2.
[56] In other words, do not use the same chart as before. One must cast a new chart for every consultation, whether by the same person or another.

querent thinks of them; and he will have had it in his mind for one day, or a day and a night, so that the whole heaven has revolved at least once, provided that the questions are different, indeed so that one is not on the same topic as another. And likewise beware lest he who asks should come to you with the purpose of testing or deceiving you, as certain people tend to do, or that he does not have the question in his heart for a day and a night, just as was said elsewhere (if you remember it well).[57] For matters spring up according to the amount of worry, and hope, and trustworthiness of the querent. In fact, when someone asks about a matter, the house and places of the planets, and their disposition, signifies what will be so about the matter which he himself seeks, for the whole of the time of his life.[58] Likewise in nativities, even though nativities sometimes are altered by the revolution of years, sometimes according to increase and sometimes according to decrease.

And in general questions about fortune (namely whether someone's question [covers the whole course of life]), or a determinate [amount of time] (as for one or more years or months, or a week or a day, and the like): because whatever an agent intends the end of his acts to be, he acts according to his estimate of his intended ends, and according to the result which he foresees. And let this be known to you, because everyone who asks, does not ask except about this, and according to that which the planets and signs (and their disposition concerning any good or evil) prevail over, in the root of his nativity.

Chapter 3: What is the trunk and what are the branches of this tree[59]

For questions are the trunks of this tree, and the Considerations[60] which you must have about questions, are its branches. And thus by considering, you will see how the lord of the Ascendant of any question, and any nativity, and any beginning,[61] and any matter, is made fortunate; and how the Moon is made fortunate, and how the lord of the house signifying the topic (on which a question was) is made fortunate. For nobody asks about this except as I have told you now, and according to that (unless perhaps he asked knowing-

---

[57] Tr. 5 (2nd Consideration).
[58] Bonatti seems to mean that general questions about life will be valid just as a nativity generally is.
[59] Cf. Sahl in *Judges* §1.1 (*On Quest.* §1.1).
[60] I.e., the 146 Considerations from Tr. 5.
[61] That is, an election.

ly—for you ought not to look for him, just as is said elsewhere).[62] For no one is born or asks in a good hour, and under a good and fortunate Ascendant, unless he is fortunate and one whom goods and fortunes are supposed to surround. And no one is born or asks under an evil and unfortunate Ascendant, unless he is an unfortunate man whom evils and misfortunes are supposed to surround.[63] Thence it is that we see that certain people are fortunate, certain ones unfortunate.

Chapter 4: That the astrologer ought not to cast a chart for himself

It seemed to the ancient sages, and especially to Māshā'allāh,[64] that the astrologer ought not look for himself,[65] lest perchance he be deceived in his own matter; because it rarely happens but that he himself has some regret over the Ascendant; whence it is necessary that he ask someone else according to the aforesaid procedure. Indeed, after the other person understood his question, he would be able to look for himself and answer his own question, or he may give his own question to another (whether in writing or not)—naturally to such a person who is concerned about his matter.[66] And he may offer it on his own behalf after he has posed it, when he wishes. Or [else] he would put [it] in his mind, saying, "when such a sign will have occurred to me, let it be for the Ascendant of the question, which I intend to undertake on my own behalf, and it will be just as effective."

Whence if it were a question on a matter which ought to last or be stable, or which ought to be improved or made worse, or be concluded quickly, or changed, one must look then at the lord of the Ascendant, and see whether it itself is joined to the lord of the quaesited matter (or the lord of the quaesited matter is joined to it), and by what aspect. Because if they are joined by a trine or sextile, and in the angles or from the angles, or from succeedents, it signifies the effecting of the quaesited matter. It even signifies durability, and stability, and its improvement; and even better than this is if the aspect were

---

[62] Bonatti refers to people who try to deceive the astrologer, already knowing the answer to the question.
[63] Bonatti means that the condition of the chart will reflect the real-life situation of the querent, and so gives a clue as to what is going on in his life.
[64] *OR*, Ch. 2 (Appendix C below).
[65] That is, ask and answer his own question.
[66] That is, he can send someone to an astrologer on his own behalf.

with reception. Because then it signifies the whole goodness of the thing, without any decrease.

But if the aspect were a square, it reduces much of the querent's intention and the goodness and durability of that same matter, even if it were with reception. It even diminishes if it were a trine or sextile without reception, even if less so [than if it were a square]. If it were a square or opposition without reception, it signifies the destruction of the matter itself and that no good nor durability will be in it. But if the lord of the Ascendant and the lord of the quaesited matter are joined to some planet which is heavier than they,[67] and it receives their disposition, and it aspects the Ascendant or aspected some planet aspecting the Ascendant (and having some dignity in it [the Ascendant]),[68] nor is it impeded, it signifies goodness and the effecting and durability and stability of the matter. Indeed if the receiver of the disposition did not aspect the Ascendant, nor were it joined to a planet which aspected it from its own place, it will be evil, for it signifies annulling and malice and the destruction of the matter itself.

If however the lord of the Ascendant were heavier than the lord of the quaesited matter, and the lord of the quaesited matter were joined to it from a good aspect—or from any besides the opposition—with perfect reception, it signifies the goodness and the durability of the matter. Likewise, if the lord of the quaesited matter were heavier than the lord of the Ascendant, and the lord of the Ascendant were joined to it with perfect reception, it signifies the goodness and durability of the matter itself. You should understand the same thing about a conjunction with the lord of the quaesited matter, if the lord of the quaesited matter is not joined with the lord of the Ascendant. And you should always understand this: that the significators (as much the lord of the Ascendant as the lord of the quaesited matter, and the receiver of disposition, and the Moon) would be free from the bad ones and their impediments.

---

[67] That is, a collecting planet.
[68] This is like a reflection of light, where the collecting planet must aspect a key place. See *ITA* III.13.1, §A.132, and Sahl in *Judges* §10.1 (*On Quest.* §10.1).

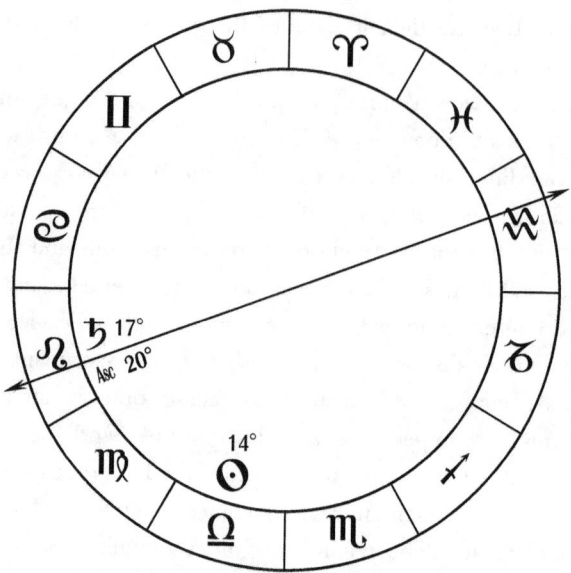

Figure 82: A question about marriage

For example, a certain question was posed about a marriage—whether it would be perfected or not—and the Ascendant of this question was Leo, 20°; Saturn in it, 17°; the Sun in Libra, 14°. It signified this, that the matter would come to be and be perfected freely, without contradiction, because each of the significators received the other; and that its perfection would be good and durable, and likewise peaceful and happy. You should say the same concerning other questions. If however the Sun were put in Libra at 20°, and Saturn in Aries at 25°, even though each of the significators receives the other, it signifies the impediment of the matter, whatever the topic of the question was; and the diminution of the good which was signified on account of the reception; and that it would hardly or never be perfected. And if it had been completely perfected, [it would be] with obstacles and the greatest labor and anxiety. Nor however will the perfection be good or durable, but rather it appears that it would be destroyed after its perfection; and if it were not destroyed by evil and unpeaceful means, it will endure; because their aspect is from the opposition, and each of the significators is impeded…[69]

---

[69] Both would be in their fall, and especially Saturn, who is getting the application. At this point, Bonatti inserts the chart and analysis from Sahl's *On Quest.* §1.8. I have omitted it here, because it appears in *Judges* §1.1 above.

Chapter 5: How to inspect planets that impede matters so they do not come to pass[70]

Even though it might have seemed more suitable to put this chapter somewhere else, still it seems to me that it should be put here, because if it is deferred until the Treatise on nativities, you could [still] need it in more than one place; for it has a place not only in nativities, but indeed even in all interrogations, in all journeys, and in all beginnings[71] of whatever things which we want or plan to undertake. And [the point of] this is that you look for the planet which impedes matters so that they do not come to pass, or are not perfected. And this planet can be called the strong "killing" or "blocking" or "destroying" one, or "cutter," because it is it itself which cuts off the life of a native, and destroys it, and does not permit the native to achieve a long life, namely to old age; and which corrupts a matter and destroys it after it has been thought to be arranged and seems that it must be perfected. And it is this which our ancients called the cutter or the one cutting, and which you ought to look at in nativities and in questions; and this, so that you know whether matters ought to be perfected or not and come to the required effect. And we take it from the planet with which the lord of the Ascendant or significator of the quaesited (or the Moon, if she herself participates with the lord of the Ascendant, or is the significator of the quaesited) is joined.

For you ought to consider the planet to which the significator of the querent, or the significator of the quaesited, or the Moon, is joined; and see how that planet is disposed, and the one to which *this* planet is conjoined. Because if the lord of the Ascendant, or the Moon, or the significator of the quaesited, is joined to a planet that is malefic and badly disposed, without reception—or if it is not badly disposed but joined to some bad one which is badly disposed, which does not receive it—it signifies the destruction of the quaesited matter.

I understand a "badly disposed" bad one to be peregrine, and retrograde, and burned up, and cadent from the Ascendant or from the house of the quaesited matter (so that it does not aspect it, or at least [the house's] lord—although an aspect to the house is stronger than an aspect to [the house's]

---

[70] For this chapter, cf. *On Quest.* §1.9. Sahl attributes the views about the cutter to Māshā'allāh. The natal cutter is most likely the malefic planet encountered by the direction of the longevity releaser.

[71] That is, elections.

lord in this)—or which is in its own fall or descension. Indeed that is the one which is called the cutter or destroyer.

Moreover, if the significator of the querent (or the quaesited matter, or the Moon, or a planet to which the Moon is joined, or if she herself were the significatrix or a partner with the lord of the Ascendant), were joined to some unfortunate planet (that is to say retrograde or burned up or cadent), you will see then if reception intervenes. Because even if by burdens and fatigue, the perfection of the quaesited matter is signified [in that case]. If however reception did not intervene, it signifies the corruption of the matter and the destruction of the same, and that the matter will not be perfected after it is thought to be arranged. If however [1] the one which receives the lord of the Ascendant or the Moon or the lord of the quaesited matter; or [2] a planet to which one of them is joined, were free, and neither the received[72] nor the receiving [planet] were made unfortunate, it signifies the perfection of the matter with ease.

And if the planet to which the lord of the Ascendant or the Moon or the lord of the quaesited matter is joined, were free from the bad ones, but were joined to some good planet which was joined to some bad one which is impeded, nor receives it[73]—and may you understand, by a planet among the seven planets[74]—the matter will not be perfected, nor come to a good end.

You should always understand this: if those conjunctions come to be without reception (because with reception it will be perfected, even if with weariness), this having been first considered and discerned, that if some planet cuts off the light of one of the aforesaid planets when it wishes to be conjoined to a bad one, that it takes away the harm, and it is not blocked without the matter being perfected. But if the cutting-off of light does not intervene,[75] the matter is blocked and does not perfect; and if it is perfected, it is destroyed. But you will consider this: if reception intervened—except do not let it be by the opposition or a square aspect; for if the planet were then

---

[72] Reading *receptus* for *receptor*.
[73] *Nec recipiat eum*. Based on the scenarios Bonatti considers below, he is speaking about the malefic receiving the other planet.
[74] I do not understand why Bonatti feels it necessary to emphasize the seven planets here–what else might we be talking about?
[75] This is a bit confusing. Bonatti means that if a significator is applying to a malefic that would normally destroy the matter, then the intervention of another planet (cutting off the threatening aspect) will prevent the matter from being destroyed. But if it did not intervene, then the upcoming aspect with the malefic would happen and destroy the matter. For more on cutting, see *ITA* III.23.

badly disposed, a reception which is by a square regard or by opposition will not profit, and especially if the receiver is impeded. But if the reception were by trine or sextile, it is strong and it is believed that the matter ought to perfect. Indeed if a planet which receives were then well disposed, by whatever aspect the reception was, it perfects the matter, and neither the square nor opposition will stand in the way. If however it were by trine or sextile, it perfects the matter because of the one which is well disposed, to which the significator is joined (whether with reception or without reception). However, [this is only so provided] that the aspect or conjunction is not yet complete [nor] that it begins to be separated in any way.

And if the significator is joined with an unimpeded fortune, the matter is perfected. And if one of the planets transferred light or virtue between the significator and some other, and the one to which it transfers is an infortune, and which is (as was said) impeded, the matter is corrupted unless the impeding or receiving bad one were received in turn. If indeed the significator of the querent (or the Moon) and the significator of the quaesited matter were joined to some planet which collected the light of both, and it were an infortune or made unfortunate, it destroys the matter and does not permit it to be perfected unless it itself receives both significators; [and] even if it receives [only] one of them, nevertheless the matter is destroyed.

You will even consider whether the significator of the querent is found in the house of the quaesited matter, or going toward a conjunction with its lord, because this signifies that the querent goes to the quaesited matter. If however the significator of the quaesited matter is found in the Ascendant, or going toward a conjunction with the significator of the querent, it signifies that the quaesited matter will go to the querent, however with the receptions and aspects and the Moon remaining in their own [current] state.[76]

---

[76] *Esse.*

APPENDIX C: SELECTING SIGNIFICATORS, FROM MĀSHĀ'ALLĀH'S *OR* CH. 2

Comment by Dykes. These instructions from *OR* Ch. 2 should be read along with 'Umar's version in §A.130. Note that when the text below uses "render" (*redditus*), it refers to the process of "reflecting" light: see my introduction and *ITA* III.13.2.

"And once the ascending sign and its degree were laid out for you, and the sign of the Midheaven and its degree, and you took note of the seven planetary dispositors (by the command of God) in their own degrees, and in the houses in which they were, and in their minutes, with a most precise and pure number, from which nothing shorter nor greater fell,[1] then look at the lord of the Ascendant and the Moon, and the one of them whom you found to be stronger, operate through that one, and the other will participate with it. That is, you will begin to look at the lord of the Ascendant: which if it aspected the ascending sign, this will be in accordance with[2] the strength of its testimony—therefore operate through it, and the Moon will participate with it, in whatever place she was. And if the lord of the Ascendant did not aspect the Ascendant, you should look to see whether it would be joined to a planet which aspects the ascending sign from *its* own place, and renders [the lord of the Ascendant's] light to the Ascendant itself; or [if the lord of the Ascendant] would be joined to a planet cadent from the Ascendant,[3] and that cadent planet would be joined to another one aspecting the ascending sign, which lifts it up[4] and renders its light to the ascending sign. Thus if the lord of the Ascendant is being joined to a planet aspecting the ascending sign, or that planet is being joined to another which renders its light to the ascending sign, it will lift up [the lord]. And if there were a conjunction from a planet to the seven planets, the work in these will be by means of a system,[5] namely

---

[1] That is, do not estimate the planetary positions, but calculate the positions exactly.
[2] *Ex.* It could also be translated as "of" or "from," but the idea is that the strength of his testimony (in the search for the querent's significator) goes along with, or is caused by, the aspect to the rising sign.
[3] I.e., not aspecting the rising sign.
[4] Remember that if a planet does not aspect the rising sign, then it is cadent or "falling from" (or "falling away from") the Ascendant—therefore if such a planet can somehow get its own light over to the Ascendant through a second planet, it is as though the second planet is "lifting" the first planet up from its falling away.
[5] *Ratione.*

where one renders and lifts up the light of one to another, until it arrives at the last of them. But as I said, if the lord of the Ascendant pushes its own light to the ascending sign, operate simply through it, and let the Moon participate with it.

"And if the lord of the ascending sign did not aspect the Ascendant, nor were it joined to a planet aspecting the Ascendant, and to one rendering his light to it, and pushing it (because the pushing is its aspect to the Ascendant), then its fall is there:[6] when it neither aspects the Ascendant, nor renders the light to an aspecting planet.

"Which if the lord of the Ascendant did not aspect the Ascendant, either through itself or through another to whom it renders its light, then it will be impeded and bad. Wherefore then, operate through the Moon in the same way you operated through the lord of the Ascendant: which if she aspected the Ascendant, or some one of the planets rendered her light to the Ascendant, operate through her, and the lord of the Ascendant will participate with her.[7] And know that, according to the quantity of the impediment which has entered in upon it (that is, upon the lord of the Ascendant), that same amount of impediment will enter in upon the matter about which it is asked.)

"Therefore, operate through the Moon if she aspected the ascending sign, and the lord of the Ascendant will participate with her—namely under the condition that the lord of the Ascendant did not aspect the Ascendant, nor were it joined to some planet which would render its own light to the Ascendant. Afterwards, see to which of the seven planets the Moon would be joined, and operate through her, even with the lord of the Ascendant adjoined.[8]

"And if [1] the Moon did not aspect the Ascendant, nor were she joined to some planet which would render her own light to the Ascendant—or even if she did aspect the Ascendant and she was not joined to any planet (which happens while she is void in course), and [2] likewise the lord of the Ascendant did not aspect the Ascendant, and it were void in course in the same way, then look to see which of them ought to go out more quickly from the sign in which it is, and which one would have fewer degrees for going out. After

---

[6] That is, since no planet will lift it up (by rendering its light to the rising sign), the lord of the Ascendant has fallen completely away from the rising sign and has little or no control over it.
[7] Obviously, though its participation will be weak, since it is now impeded.
[8] This probably means, "along with the lord of the Ascendant." Then we have three planets participating.

this, you will change the Moon to the following sign from her own place. After this, you will look to see to which of the planets she[9] would first be joined, and judge through that. And all of the planets are changed, but the lighter planet is more worthy in a change than a heavy one. In this way, Saturn, if he were void in course, will be worse than all the rest, because the emptying of the course of the planets (that is, when they are being joined to none) indicates the malice of the matter and its slowness. And every planet, with the emptying of its course, indicates a multitude of slowness. Also, the fewness of the degrees (or the multitude of them) of the planet which it ought to walk through in the sign in which it was, after the question, indicates the slowness or quickness of the effecting of the matter.

"Therefore the one which goes out more quickly from the sign in which it is, will be quicker in the matter; but a light one and heavy one, if they were void in course, indicate the slowness of matters, and their worthlessness.[10] Therefore, if you found the lord of the Ascendant and the Moon void in course, joining themselves to no one, foretell the slowness of the matter, and its prolonging, and that it ought to be postponed[11] according to what you saw.

"And see to whom the Moon is first being joined after her going out from the sign in which she is: judge the effecting of the matter according to [that planet], and the lord of the Ascendant will participate with it according to its [own] strength or weakness in the place in which it is. Also, a planet which was in the Ascendant will participate with them in the work, [and] moreover a planet which was in the house of the quaesited matter—which if it were concordant with the sign in which it is,[12] and it were received, it indicates the goodness of the matter, and its worthiness. And if were not concordant with the sign in which it is, nor were it received, it indicates the impediment of that same matter, and its worthlessness. But the effecting of the matter and

---

[9] The Latin could just as easily read "it," i.e., whichever the quicker planet was. But the instruction is ambiguous. In almost every case the Moon would be the one to leave her sign more quickly, which accounts for the instruction to change her specifically. But then the whole point seems moot, since the instruction also implies that one could use the lord of the Ascendant as well.

[10] So, even if we can change the planets into the next sign and look for perfection there, there will still be slowness and difficulty due to their hindrance in their *current* signs.

[11] This "ought" pertains to the planets, not to the querent. That is, it is not as though the *querent* ought to postpone things, but that the *planets will* postpone the matter because of *their* situation.

[12] This probably includes having a dignity there, or it being a sign of the same gender, or having similar elemental qualities, *etc.*

its being blocked does not come about from that one which is in the Ascendant, but it comes about from the direction[13] of the lord of the Ascendant or Moon, and from the stars to which they are being joined, and their conjunction and reception, and the rendering of their reception.

"And know that the Moon would always be the partner of the lord of the Ascendant, in whatever place she was, by the command of God. Therefore, if you found the lord of the Ascendant impeded, operate through the Moon just as you operate through the lord of the Ascendant.

---

[13] *Parte.*

APPENDIX D: APHORISMS ON QUESTIONS FROM AL-RIJĀL I.5.1

Following is a partial translation of al-Rijāl's *Book of the Skilled* I.5.1, in which he gives some general guidelines for looking at planets and houses.

Chapter I.5.1: On the main things (and others) which must be put up front

Heaven has good fortune and misfortune; likewise, the signs have fortune and misfortunes. The fortunes of heaven are the four angles and their succeedents; and their misfortune is remoteness from the angles—that is the cadent places. The fortune of the signs is when a sign is the house of some planet (or bound or face), or that [the planet] has a nature and strength in it. The misfortune of the signs is when a sign is the fall of some planet, or the obscuring of [its] face,[1] or that it is different from it in form and nature.

Now, colors are changed through the motion of heaven, and through the changing of the houses in the figure, just as the planets are changed through advancement or separation, or direct motion, or standing still, or its retrogradation.

The fortunate places of heaven agree with fortunes, and with planets which are bodily with others. The unfortunate places of heaven are those which agree with all unfortunate things, and planets [which are] light, solitary, and empty in course.

The Ascendant is the door and key of heaven, and is the house through which [the querent's significations and deeds are known],[2] and the other houses follow it and ascend [after it]: like the house of assets, brothers, fathers, children, and so on. Whichever one of them is firm, fortunate, strong, and well disposed, received in a good status, shows and signifies good and lucky success, and fortune in matters which are of the nature of that house, and of its significations. But whichever house of them is weak, shows condemnation and misfortune in the matters which are of that same house.

---

[1] I am not sure what this means.
[2] Reading for the strange *applicatur ad suas significations et facta*.

Every inquiry in which you found the Moon to be strong, firm, and fortunate, and the lord of her house were weak, unfortunate and bad, shows strength and luckiness in the beginning of that matter, and diminution, weakness, and hindrance at the end. And if the Moon were unfortunate, and the lord of the house of the Moon strong and fortunate, there will be roughness at the beginning of the matter, and tribulation, and its end [will be] good, complete, and smooth.

Which if the lord of the house of the question were fortunate, and it received the lord of the Ascendant, more will come to the owner of the question than what he sought, and in which he had trust, [as well as] usefulness, good and cheerfulness. But if the lord of the house of the question[3] were unfortunate and did not receive the lord of the Ascendant or the significator of the figure,[4] there will be labor, affliction, wavering, [and] loss in the proposed matter, until the inquirer abhors it, and regrets having proposed and undertaken it. But if reception would come to be from an unfortunate [planet], it shows a renewal, and the remainder of the proposed matter is going to be with tribulation, labor, and disturbance, because the nature of an unfortunate one is bad, harmful, and it gives nothing in which there is not disturbance [and] loss, through the power of God.

Likewise, when planets are in places appropriate to questions and their figures (like if the Sun is in the Midheaven, or Venus in the house of women, or Mars in the house of infirmities, or Jupiter in the house of assets), they help in prosperity and the demonstration of good and evil, according to their own strength and power in their places. But if they were contrary and divergent [from the meaning of the house], one destroys the other, and the signification and victory will belong to the stronger, more firm, and more fortunate.

The majority of the sages agree and say that if the Moon were in the Ascendant or Midheaven, or in the eleventh house, or fifth, received by the lord of her own house or by a fortunate planet which esteems her and is her friend,[5] and that planet had some strength in that figure, it signifies that the matter which is taken up is perfected and completed, nor would it be necessary to look back at the lord of the Ascendant, nor to its status, unless the lord of the fourth house were bad or unfortunate [or] retrograde, or [else] a

---

[3] Moving *quaestionis* from the end of the previous section, to match the beginning of the previous sentence.
[4] This is the significator of thought (see my introduction, and *Search*).
[5] See *ITA* III.27.

bad one in the house of the end[6] which harms it, disturbs [the matter] and impedes the things taken up, especially if there were an unfortunate [planet] in the opposite of the Ascendant, and hostile; or if the lord of the house of the matter set out were scorched or retrograde, or does not aspect the Ascendant: all of these indications demonstrate diminution, condemnation, hindrance, and the destruction of the proposed thing, even if the Moon would be in good conditions just as was enumerated.

When the degrees of the points of the houses[7] are fortunate or unfortunate, they demonstrate strength and weakness (by the command of God), according to the quantity of their misfortune or fortune: and the greater fortune of it, and the firmer one, is when a planet agreeing with that makes them fortunate; and the greater misfortune and what is of greater loss, is when a divergent planet (and one contrary to those degrees) weakens them. Jupiter sets the degree of the house of assets aright, and makes it fortunate, [but] Mars and the Sun harm and make it unlucky. Mercury sets the degree of the house of brothers aright and makes it fortunate, but Mars and Saturn harm and render it improsperous. The Sun and Saturn set the house of fathers aright, Mars harms and disturbs it. Venus[8] increases the degree of the house of children and makes it fortunate, Mars and Saturn harm and lessen it considerably. The Sun strengthens the degree of the house of travels and makes it fortunate, Mars and Saturn harm it. The Sun and Jupiter set the degree of the royal house right and make it fortunate, Mars and Saturn harm it. Jupiter arouses the degree of the house of children and makes it fortunate, Mars and Saturn harm it.

When a planet is unfortunate, it is like an infirm man. A retrograde planet proceeds in the likeness of a traitor. A scorched planet conveys the likeness of a captive. A planet cadent from its own good places,[9] has the likeness of a foreign traveler. One of the planets makes another fortunate, and one harms another: and they convey the example of men, who come to the aid of friends and fight for them, and throw enemies into confusion. The sage who can assimilate the higher things and apply them to lower things, will prove the truth of [these] statements, considerations, and works, from the power of God.

---

[6] That is, the fourth.
[7] That is, their "cusps."
[8] Venus is in her joy in the fifth. Normally, Jupiter is the planet whose natural signification indicates children.
[9] That is, peregrine.

When a planet is in the greatest latitude which it can occupy, it is proven true, whether it signifies good or evil, especially if the latitude were stretched towards the direction of the north; but if its latitude were in the southern direction, it is weaker, nor does it have the power of giving good fortune nor advantage, unless God wills.

APPENDIX E: QUESTIONS BY HOUSE

For easier reference, following is a table of the primary questions in *Judges* (arranged by house), with the sections corresponding to them.

Question	Sections in *Judges*
1st House	
Longevity	§§1.2-6
Success & failure in life	§2.15
2nd House	
Acquiring money	§§2.1-5
Source of money	§§2.6-10
Quantity of money	§§2.11-12
When acquired	§2.13
Collecting debts	§§2.13-14, 2.16
3rd House	
Status of siblings	§§3.1-3
An absent sibling	§3.4
4th House	
Buying & selling real estate	§§4.1, 4.3-10
Condition of real estate	§4.2
Leasing real estate	§§4.11-12
Building houses & cities	§4.13
Digging	§4.14
Buried treasure	§4.15-18
Outcomes	§§4.19-22
5th House	
Whether one will have a child	§§5.1-5
Whether a woman is pregnant	§§5.6-12
Time of conception	§§5.13-15
Miscarriage	§§5.16-20
Already given birth?	§§5.21, 7.35
Time of birth	§§5.22-25
Experience of labor	§5.26
Number of children	§§5.27-31, 5.37
Sex of child	§§5.32-38
Rumors: true or false?	§§5.39-40, 5.42-44, 5.47, 5.66, 5.68
Content of rumors/legations	§§5.41, 5.46
Outcomes of rumors	§5.45
Messengers & their return	§§5.48-59, 5.72
Letters, papers, & their arrival	§§5.60-73

APPENDIX E: TABLE OF QUESTIONS BY HOUSE

6th House	
Illness: outcome	§§6.1-8, 6.15-18
Nature of disease, where affected	§§6.9-14
Critical days	§§6.19-23
Whether he is infirm	§§6.24-26
Specific medical procedures	§§6.27-29
Would a captive be freed	§§6.30-34, 6.37-39, 6.66
How long the captivity is	§6.35
What happens afterwards	§6.36
When he will be freed	§§6.40-41
Die or suffer in captivity?	§§6.42-48, 6.68
Buying & selling captives & slaves	§§6.49-64
Whether he will be captured	§§6.65, 6.67
Prisoners & their freedom	§§9.17-19
7th House	
Whether a marriage will happen	§§7.1-6
When a marriage will happen	§7.7
Impediments to marriage	§§7.8-10
Marry the desired person?	§§7.11-12
Legal & sexual issues	§§7.13-14, 7.18-20, 7.34-36
Is the spouse beautiful?	§7.15
Background of spouse	§§7.16-17
Adultery	§7.21
Number of spouses	§§7.22-23
Relation between spouses, future	§§7.24-27
Which spouse dies first	§§7.28-29
Missing/runaway wives	§§7.30-33
Controversies: the opponents	§§7.37-41, 7.54
Who will win	§§7.42-47
The judge	§§7.48-51
Will there be peace?	§§7.37-41, 7.52, 7.55
Source of controversy	§7.53
Business deals and trades	§§7.56-59
Commodities & prices	§§7.60-71
Fugitives: be captured or return?	§§7.72-74, 7.77, 7.89, 7.91, 7.94, 7.99-100, 7.117, 7.119-21
Stolen goods: be recovered?	§§7.73, 7.76-78, 7.89-90, 7.92, 7.94-98, 7.101-04, 7.124
When recovered	§7.75
Where the goods are	§§7.79, 7.81-83, 7.87, 7.125-31
Where the fugitive is	§§7.80-82, 7.84-85, 7.122-23
Why it was lost	§7.86

Why/how the fugitive escaped	§7.87
Thief's background/nature/figure	§§7.88, 7.105-16, 7.118, 7.143
What was stolen	§§7.132-38
Name of thief	§§7.139-42, 7.144-45
Name/number of thief/goods	§7.146
Partnerships	§§7.147-51
Outcome of partnership	§§7.152-56
Find a specific person?	§§7.157-59
War: opponents & outcome	§§7.160-66, 7.171-72
Quality of war	§§7.167-69
Rebellions	§§7.170, 7.185-7
Peace and concord	§§7.173-76, 7.191
Origin & justice of war	§§7.177, 7.197
Who will win	§§7.178-80
Injuries of one going to war	§§7.181-82
Those sent to war	§§7.183-84
Besieged cities	§§7.188-90, 7.192-95, 7.198
Allies	§7.196
Hunting & fishing	§§7.199-203
8th House	
Death	§§8.1-5
Fear	§§8.6-7
9th House	
Travel: will it happen	§§9.1-8
Length of travel	§9.9
What will happen on the journey	§§9.10-12, 9.15-16
Should one travel	§§9.13-14
Ships: their cargo & condition	§§9.41-43
Absent persons: their status and return	§§5.49, 8.2, 9.20-35
Leaving one's current condition	§§10.25-26
Dream interpretation	§§9.36-37
Alchemy & other knowledge	§§9.38-40
10th House	
Attaining honors	§§10.1-10, 10.33, 10.36
Rulership & its course	§§10.11-16, 10.20-22, 10.34-35
Underofficials	§10.17
Predecessors & successors	§§10.18-19
The return of absent rulers	§§10.23-24
The life & death of kings	§§10.27-33
Others' relationship to the king	§§10.37-38
Trades	§10.39

11th House	
Attaining something hoped for	§§11.1-5
Friendships, loves & hates	§§11.6-12
12th House	
Horse racing	§§12.1-3
Revenge	§12.4b
Enemies	§§12.4a, 12.5-6
Corruption of matters	§Z.1
Z: Weather and disasters	
Predicting rains	§§Z.2-14
Disasters	§§Z.7, Z.9

APPENDIX F: TABLE OF 'UMAR PASSAGES

Most of the 138 chapters in 'Umar's *Book of Questions in the Judgments of the Stars* are represented in *Judges*. This table shows these sections in *Judges* as they correspond to the Arabic chapters, according to Charles Burnett. The use of *a, b, c*, indicates a part or half of the Arabic chapter. Some Arabic chapters are only in *Three Judges*, and some seem not to be represented in either book. At the end are sections for which Burnett does not indicate an Arabic source. As you can see, 'Umar's book seems to have no meaningful organization, ranging indifferently from children to absent people, from marriage to alchemy and the sciences. However, this list would enable someone to reconstruct almost the whole of it from *Judges* alone.

Arabic Chapter	*Judges* Section	Arabic Chapter	*Judges* Section
1a	§A128	70	§5.66
1b	§A129	71	§5.64
2a	*Three Judges*	72	§5.69
2b, 4	§A130	73	§2.2
2c	§A131	74	§2.13
3	*Three Judges*	75	§7.2
5	§4.19	76	§7.13
6a	§5.7	77a	§7.18
6b	§5.16	77b	§7.22
7	§5.33	78	§7.31
8	§5.28	79 and/or 133	§9.39
9	§5.14	80	§9.40
10	§5.22	81	§Z.2
11	§5.25	82	§Z.3
12	§9.2	83	§Z.4
13	§9.21	84	§Z.5
14	§9.30	85	§Z.6
15	§9.31	86	§7.60
16	§9.32	87	§7.61-62
17	§9.34	88	§7.63
18	§9.35	89a	§7.64
19	§7.91	89b	§7.65
20	§7.135	90	§10.27
21	§7.92	91	§10.28
22	§7.126	92	§10.31
23	§7.133	93	§10.32

Appendix F: Table of ʿUmar Passages

24	§7.102	94	§10.29
25	§7.130	95a	§10.30
26	§7.109	95b	§10.13
27	§7.110	96	§10.33
28	§7.113	97	§10.34
29	§7.106	98	§10.35
30	§7.139	99	§10.14
31	§7.140	100	§10.4
32	§7.141	101	§10.5
33	§7.142	102	§10.36
34	§7.143	103	§10.37
35	§7.144	104	§10.25
36	§7.145	105	*Neither Judges*
37	§7.73	106	*Three Judges*
38	§7.74	107	§7.168
39	*Three Judges*	108	§7.169
40	§7.80	109	§7.170
41	§7.75	110	§7.174
42	§7.38	111-12	*Unknown*
43	§7.49	113a	§6.32
44	§7.43	113b	§6.33
45	§7.52	114	§6.50
46	§7.55	115	§6.51
47	§7.54	116	§7.57
48	§7.53	117	§4.6
49	§§7.148, 11.7	118	§4.7
50	§7.153	119	*Three Judges*
51	§7.156	120	§7.183
52a	§6.2	121	§7.201
52b	§6.9	122	§7.203
53	§6.3	123	§11.3
54	§6.12	124	§8.6
55	§6.20	125	§4.20
56	§6.31	126	*Unknown*
57	§6.40	127	§9.36
58	§6.43	128	*Three Judges*
59	§6.42	129	*Unknown*
60	§6.45	130	§9.41
61	§6.47	131-32	*Unknown*
62	§6.48	133	= §9.39?
63	§6.65	134	§Z.1
64	§6.66	135-37	*Unknown*
65	*Unknown*	138	§Z.7

66	§4.15	Uncertain[1]	§2.7
67a	§5.40	Uncertain	§4.16
67b	§5.60	Uncertain	§4.21
68	§5.41	Uncertain	§7.161
69a	§5.55	Uncertain	§10.39
69b	§5.50		

---

[1] Probably a continuation of 'Umar's Ch. 73.

APPENDIX G: ALTERNATIVE WAYS OF EXTRACTING NAMES

In §§7.139-46, 'Umar and Jirjis offer instructions on how to identify the letters of a thief's name from planets and signs in the chart. In my comment to §7.139, I suggested that 'Umar's method was rather weak, since it relied on the Arabic spelling of the planets' and signs' names, rather than on some other method. Below, I have listed alternative associations using the Hebrew alphabet, which is common in traditional Qabalism. The column on the far left lists the planets, signs, and elements, and the next column gives the associations according to the Hermetic Order of the Golden Dawn. The letters for the planets have several schemes, as found in Kaplan's edition of the *Sefer Yetzirah*, one of the first and most famous Qabalistic works.

	Golden Dawn	*Sefer Yetzirah* ("Gra" Version)	*Sefer Yetzirah* ("Long" Version)
♄	ת [t]	ר [r]	ב [b, v]
♃	כ [k]	ת [t]	ג [g, j]
♂	פ [f, p]	ג [g, j]	ד [d]
☉	ר [r]	ד [d]	כ [k]
♀	ד [d]	כ [k]	פ [f, p]
☿	ב [b, v]	פ [f, p]	ר [r]
☽	ג [g, j]	ב [b, v]	ת [t]
♈	ה [h]		
♉	ו [v, w, ū]		
♊	ז [z]		
♋	ח [h, kh]		
♌	ט [t]		
♍	י [y, ī]		
♎	ל [l]		
♏	נ [n]		
♐	ס [s]		
♑	ע [ʿ, gh]		
♒	צ [tz, x]		
♓	ק [q]		

Fire	ש [s, sh]
Earth	ת [t, th][1]
Air	א [a]
Fire	מ [m]

---

[1] The Hebrew sources do not assign any letter to earth.

APPENDIX H: LOTS IN *JUDGES*

Following are the Lots described in *Judges*. For the most part, the authors here do not use any Lot except for the Lot of Fortune. 'Umar stands out as using many Lots (marked with a U), but he is also notable for using calculations that differ from most known versions of them, and in some cases gives nonsensical instructions. Below (and in the associated sections in the text) I provide my best understanding of his Lot calculations, as well as footnotes guiding the reader to alternative versions in *ITA*.

Lot	From (day)	To	Project from	Reverse?
Fortune	☉	☽	Asc	Yes
Money/assets[1]	Lord 2nd	2nd	Asc	No
Real estate (U)[2]	Lord 4th	♄	4th	Yes[3]
Outcomes (U)	Lord hour	Lord Asc	MC	?
Sect of birth (U)	Degree 5th	Lord 5th	Asc	?
Rumors	Lord hour	Lord 1st	☉	?
"Death-bearing"[4] (U)	Lord 8th	Lord Asc	8th	No
Death (U)[5]	8th	Lord 8th	Asc	No?
Infirmity (U)[6]	♄?	♂?	Asc?	?

---

[1] I have supplied the standard calculation for this from *ITA* VI.2.4.
[2] According to 'Umar, if Saturn rules the 4th, then one measures from the degree of the 4th to Saturn, but then projects from the 4th. This does not make sense, because then the Lot would be on Saturn himself. On the other hand, the Lot of real estate according to Abū Ma'shar (*ITA* VI.2.10) is measured from Saturn to the Moon by day or night, and projected from the Ascendant.
[3] According to 'Umar, by night one measures from Saturn to the 4th, but he does not specify where it should be projected from. He probably means that by night it should go from Saturn to the lord of the 4th, and projected from the 4th.
[4] 'Umar may have mixed up two other Lots. The Lot of death (*ITA* VI.2.27) is taken by day and night from the Moon to the eighth sign (or the eighth house), and projected from Saturn (though Rhetorius Ch. 77 projects from the Ascendant). The Lot of the killing planet (*ITA* VI.2.28) is taken from the lord of the Ascendant to the Moon, and projected from the Ascendant.
[5] Again, a common version (attributed to Hermes in *ITA* VI.2.27) is from the Moon to the eighth, and projected from Saturn.
[6] 'Umar does not give the calculation for this Lot, but it is probably the Lot of chronic illness (*ITA* VI.2.19), taken by day from Saturn to Mars (but by night from Mars to Saturn), and projected from the Ascendant.

Killing (U)[7]	☽	♂	8th	?
Torture (U)[8]	☽	♄	6th	?
Marriage (U)	7th	Lord 7th	Asc	?
War (U)[9]	♂	☽	Asc	No
Concord (U)[10]	☽	☿	Asc	?
Travel[11]	Lord 9th?	9th?	Asc?	No?
Royal (U)[12]	?	?	?	?
Attaining kingdom (U)	Stronger of ☉ & ♃	Weaker of ☉ & ♃	Mars	No
Office/king (U)[13]	♃	MC	Asc	No?
Office & carrying out orders (U)[14]	☉	♄	MC	?
Minister/resources of man in power (U)	Lord 11th	Lord 10th	Asc	No?
Rain (U)[15]	☿	Lord ☿	Asc	No?
Daily rains (U)	☉	♄	☽ at dawn	N/A

---

[7] I am not sure where 'Umar gets this Lot. The Lot of the killing planet (*ITA* VI.2.28) is taken by day from the lord of the Ascendant to the Moon (but by night the reverse), and is projected from the Ascendant.

[8] In §6.48, this Lot is identified with the Lot of death. Perhaps the calculation here should use the eighth and not the sixth.

[9] This Lot is probably the Lot of kingdom and authority (*ITA* VI.2.38), which is however reversed by night.

[10] This is the same as the Lot of friends according to al-Andarzaghar (*ITA* VI.2.45), and the Lot of peace between among soldiers (*ITA* VI.3.3). This should probably be reversed by night, as al-Qabīsī says that al-Andarzaghar reversed his Lot of friends.

[11] This Lot is mentioned by al-Kindī in *Judges* §9.3. I have supplied the calculation from *ITA* VI.2.31, since al-Kindī omits it.

[12] See for instance *ITA* VI.2.37-40.

[13] This Lot is probably the Lot of a job and authority according to Valens (*ITA* VI.2.42), which according to al-Qabīsī is taken from the Sun to the Midheaven. On the other hand, the Lot of the cause of a kingdom (*ITA* VI.2.43) is taken from the Sun to the Midheaven and projected from Jupiter, just as Hugo's 'Umar projects from Jupiter. I have followed al-Rijāl's version of this passage (§10.13).

[14] This seems to be another version of the natal Lot of power or kingdom or sovereignty (*ITA* VI.2.39), which is taken from the Sun to Saturn by day (but the reverse by night), and projected from the Ascendant (not the Midheaven).

[15] When Mercury is in his own house, 'Umar seems to say that we should measure from the beginning of his sign to his body, and project from the Ascendant (see §Z.2).

APPENDIX I: THE *ESSENTIAL MEDIEVAL ASTROLOGY* CYCLE

The *Essential Medieval Astrology* cycle is a projected series of books which will redefine the contours of traditional astrology. Comprised mainly of translations of works by Persian and Arabic-speaking medieval astrologers, it will cover all major areas of astrology, including philosophical treatments and magic. The cycle will be accompanied by compilations of introductory works and readings on the one hand, and independent monographs and encyclopedic works on the other (including late medieval and Renaissance works of the Latin West).

I. Introductions
- *Traditional Astrology for Today: An Introduction* (2011)
- *Introductions to Astrology: Abū Ma'shar & al-Qabīsī* (2010)
- Abū Ma'shar, *Great Introduction to the Knowledge of the Judgments of the Stars* (2013)
- *Basic Readings in Traditional Astrology* (2013)

II. Nativities
- *Persian Nativities I*: Māshā'allāh's *The Book of Aristotle*, Abū 'Alī al-Khayyāt's *On the Judgments of Nativities* (2009)
- *Persian Nativities II*: 'Umar al-Tabarī's *Three Books on Nativities*, Abū Bakr's *On Nativities* (2010)
- *Persian Nativities III: On Solar Revolutions* (2010)

III. Questions (Horary)
- Hermann of Carinthia, *The Search of the Heart* (2011)
- Al-Kindī, *The Forty Chapters* (2011)
- Various, *The Book of the Nine Judges* (2011)

IV. Elections
- *Traditional Electional Astrology: al-'Imrānī, Abū Ma'shar, and others* (2012)

V. Mundane Astrology
- *Astrology of the World* (multiple volumes): Abū Ma'shar's *On the Revolutions of the Years of the World*, *Book of Religions and Dynasties*, and *Flowers*, Sahl bin Bishr's *Prophetic Sayings*; lesser works on prices and weather (2012-13)

VI. Other Works
- Bonatti, Guido, *The Book of Astronomy* (2007)
- *Works of Sahl & Māshā'allāh* (2008)
- *A Course in Traditional Astrology* (TBA)
- Al-Rijāl, *The Book of the Skilled* (TBA)
- *Astrological Magic* (TBA)
- *The Latin Hermes* (TBA)
- Firmicus Maternus, *Mathesis* (TBA)

BIBLIOGRAPHY

Versions of *The Book of the Nine Judges* (*Liber Novem Iudicum*):
- Peter Liechtenstein: Venice, 1509
- Vienna National Library: *Codex Vindobonensis Palatinus* 2428 (12th Century)
- Spanish National Library: Madrid lat. 10,009 (13th Century)
- Biblioteca Apostolica Vaticana, Vat. Lat. 6766 (13th-14th Century)

Al-Bīrūnī, Muhammad ibn Ahmad, *The Book of Instruction in the Elements of the Art of Astrology*, trans. R. Ramsay Wright (London: Luzac & Co., 1934)

Allen, Richard Hinckley, *Star Names: Their Lore and Meaning* (New York: Dover Publications Inc., 1963)

Al-Rijāl, 'Ali, *De Iudiciis Astrorum* (Basel: Henrichus Petrus, 1551)

Al-Rijāl, 'Ali, *De Iudiciis Astrorum* (Venice: Erhard Ratdolt, 1485)

Bonatti, Guido, Benjamin Dykes trans. and ed., *The Book of Astronomy* (Golden Valley: The Cazimi Press, 2007)

Burnett, Charles, "A Group of Arabic-Latin Translators Working in Northern Spain in the mid-twelfth Century," *Journal of the Royal Asiatic Society*, 1977, pp. 62-108.

Burnett, Charles, "Al-Kindī on Judicial Astrology: 'The Forty Chapters,'" in *Arabic Sciences and Philosophy*, v. 3 (1993), pp. 77-117.

Burnett, Charles, "Al-Kindī on finding buried treasure," *Arabic Sciences and Philosophy* v.7, 1997, pp. 57-90.

Burnett, Charles and Gerrit Bos, *Scientific Weather Forecasting in the Middle Ages: The Writings of al-Kindi* (London and New York: Kegan Paul International, 2000)

Burnett, Charles, "The Establishment of Medieval Hermeticism," in Peter Linehan and Janet Nelson eds., *The Medieval World*, 2001.

Burnett, Charles, "A Hermetic Programme of Astrology and Divination in mid-Twelfth-Century Aragon: The Hidden Preface in the *Liber novem iudicum*," in Charles Burnett and W.F. Ryan, eds., *Magic and the Classical Tradition* (London: The Warburg Institute, 2006), pp. 99-105.

Burnett, Charles, *A complete list of the chapters of the* Liber novem iudicum (privately circulated, 2011)

Carmody, Francis, *Arabic Astronomical and Astrological Sciences in Latin Translation: A Critical Bibliography* (Berkeley and Los Angeles: University of California Press, 1956)

Deborah Houlding, *Key Principles of Horary Theory and Practice: STA Practitioner Level Course Text* (Nottingham, 2011)

Dorotheus of Sidon, *Carmen Astrologicum*, trans. David Pingree (Abingdon, MD: The Astrology Center of America, 2005)

Dykes, Benjamin trans. and ed., *Works of Sahl & Māshā'allāh* (Golden Valley: The Cazimi Press, 2008)

Dykes, Benjamin, *Traditional Astrology for Today: An Introduction* (Minneapolis, MN: The Cazimi Press, 2011)

Hermann of Carinthia, Benjamin Dykes trans. and ed., *The Search of the Heart* (Minneapolis, MN: The Cazimi Press, 2011)

Hermann of Carinthia, trans. Charles Burnett, *De Essentiis* [On Essences] (Leiden: E.J. Brill, 1982)

Jiménez, Aurelio Pérez, "*Dodecátropos, Zodíaco y Partes de la Nave en la Astrología Antigua*," MHNH vol. 7 (2007), pp. 217-36.

Jolivet, Jean and Roshdi Rashed, "al-Kindī," in *Dictionary of Scientific Biography* v. 15 suppl. 1 (New York: Scribner, 1978), pp. 261-67.

Kaplan, Aryeh, *Sefer Yetzirah: The Book of Creation In Theory and Practice* (York Beach, Maine: Samuel Weiser, Inc., 1997)

Lilly, William, *Christian Astrology*, vols. I-II, ed. David R. Roell (Abingdon, MD: Astrology Center of America, 2004)

Māshā'allāh, *Chapter on Rains in the Year*, in Benjamin Dykes ed., *Works of Sahl & Māshā'allāh* (Golden Valley: The Cazimi Press, 2008)

Māshā'allāh, *On Hidden Things*, in Benjamin Dykes ed., *Works of Sahl & Māshā'allāh* (Golden Valley: The Cazimi Press, 2008)

Niermeyer, J.F., *Mediae Latinitatis Lexicon Minus* (Leiden: E.J. Brill, 1993)

Pingree, David, *The Yavanajātaka of Sphujidhvaja* (Cambridge and London: Harvard University Press, 1978)

Ptolemy, Claudius, *Ptolemy's Almagest*, trans. and ed. G.J. Toomer (Princeton, NJ: Princeton University Press, 1998)

Ptolemy, Claudius, *Tetrabiblos* vols. 1, 2, 4, trans. Robert Schmidt, ed. Robert Hand (Berkeley Springs, WV: The Golden Hind Press, 1994-98)

Rhetorius of Egypt, *Astrological Compendium*, trans. and ed. James H. Holden (Tempe, AZ: American Federation of Astrologers, Inc., 2009)

Sahl bin Bishr, *On Elections*, in Benjamin Dykes ed., *Works of Sahl & Māshā'allāh* (Golden Valley: The Cazimi Press, 2008)

Sahl bin Bishr, *On Questions*, in Benjamin Dykes ed., *Works of Sahl & Māshā'allāh* (Golden Valley: The Cazimi Press, 2008)

Schmidt, Robert, *The Astrological Record of the Early Sages in Greek* (Berkeley Springs, WV: The Golden Hind Press, 1995)

Sezgin, Fuat, *Geschichte des Arabischen Schrifttums* vol. 7 (Leiden: E.J. Brill, 1979)

INDEX OF NAMES

In this volume I have elected not to create a comprehensive index of subjects, because the extensive Table of Contents, Appendices, and Glossary should serve well enough as reference guides to topics and techniques. Following is an index of key names, excluding most of the nine judges themselves.

Abū Ma'shar......... 4-5, 7-8, 16, 18, 27, 28, 30, 55, 346, 606, 645, 701

al-Qabīsī.... 4, 30, 77, 90, 346, 416, 549, 702

Burnett, Charles...... ...2-4, 6-9, 16, 18, 57, 70, 93, 116-17, 122-25, 133, 193, 342, 346, 353, 428, 473, 600, 603, 613-15, 696

Buzurjmihr 12

Hephaistio of Thebes 519, 521, 525

ibn Ezra, Abraham......... 47, 78, 93

Lilly, William 3, 9, 20, 34, 72, 303, 309, 354, 359-60, 362, 374, 516, 521

Ptolemy, Claudius......... 5, 7, 18, 93, 286, 314, 404, 435, 515, 521, 625, 630, 656

Raymond of Marseilles 7

Rhetorius 191, 521, 634, 701

Thābit bin Qurra 286

Valens, Vettius .. 12, 404, 549, 551, 573, 702

www.ingramcontent.com/pod-product-compliance
Lightning Source LLC
Chambersburg PA
CBHW060357230426
43663CB00008B/1297